M

The MYTH of RUSSIAN COLLUSION

THE INSIDE STORY OF HOW DONALD TRUMP REALLY WON

ROGER STONE

Skyhorse Publishing

Skyhorse Publishing books may be purchased in bulk at special discounts for sales promotion, corporate gifts, fund-raising, or educational purposes. Special editions can also be created to specifications. For details, contact the Special Sales Department, Skyhorse Publishing, 307 West 36th Street, 11th Floor, New York, NY 10018 or info@skyhorsepublishing.com.

Skyhorse® and Skyhorse Publishing® are registered trademarks of Skyhorse Publishing, Inc.®, a Delaware corporation.

Visit our website at www.skyhorsepublishing.com.

10 9 8 7 6 5 4 3 2 1

Library of Congress Cataloging-in-Publication Data is available on file.

Jacket design by Brian Peterson

Print ISBN: 978-1-5107-4936-8
Ebook ISBN: 978-1-5107-4937-5

Printed in the United States of America

Acknowledgments

Dedicated to President Richard M. Nixon, who first recognized Donald Trump's potential to become leader of the Free World.

Also dedicated to Juanita Broaddrick, a brave and courageous woman who told the truth about being sexually assaulted and bitten by Bill Clinton and spoke out despite pressure on her to remain silent.

This book is also dedicated to Dr. Jerome S. Corsi, mentor, colleague, and one of the most effective investigative reporters writing today.

Thanks also to Dr. Eric Paddon, Christopher Cox, Kevin Ryan, Jacob Engels, Saint John Hunt, Michael Caputo, A. Gore Vidal, Randy Short, John Kakanis, Tyler Nixon, Kate Koptenko, Milo Yiannopoulous, Matthew J. Boyle, Matt Drudge, Alex Jones, Stephen K. Bannon, David Urban, Ed McMullen, Susie Wiles, Matt Labash, Tucker Carlson, and Laury Gay. In addition, the book is dedicated to my mother, who passed away at ninety-five in 2016. If you are familiar with Tony Soprano's mother Olivia, you completely understand my Sicilian mother. She insisted that Hillary Clinton was "a crook and a liar." I only regret that she did not live long enough to vote for Donald Trump, whom she danced with at my wedding.

Also dedicated to my beloved wife Nydia, a woman of infinite patience and wisdom.

Roger J. Stone
New York City

Table of Contents

INTRODUCTION 2019

I wrote the book you now hold in your hands two years ago. In hardcover it was titled *The Making of the President 2016*, and it was the first in-depth examination of how Trump's campaign tapped into the national mood to deliver a stunning victory that almost no one saw coming. As an adviser with intimate insight into the campaign and someone who had urged Donald to run for president more than thirty years ago, I was proud to have been a part of the campaign.

Sadly, I considered titling this new edition of the book *The Unmaking of the President 2016–2019* because we are in the midst of an unprecedented effort by the permanent political establishment to undo the results of the 2016 election and remove Donald Trump from the White House.

I believed three major factors contributed to the most improbable upset victory in the history of American presidential politics: the political establishment of both parties underestimating the level of public dissatisfaction with the two-party ruling elite who had run America into the ground; the advent of a robust and widely accessible Internet which broke the mainstream media monopoly on America's political narrative; and the dogged persistence of Donald Trump.

Even though I had chronicled the track record of the military-industrial complex (commonly known as the Deep State today) in my previous books, *The Man Who Killed Kennedy: The Case Against LBJ*, *The Bush Crime Family*, *The Clintons' War on Women*, and *Nixon's Secrets*, even I underestimated the shock of the two-party duopoly over the loss of "their" White House and their resolve to undo the results of the 2016 election.

We now know that the Obama national security apparatus, including the Central Intelligence Agency, the Federal Bureau of Investigation, and the Obama Justice Department, took the danger that a Trump presidency posed to them far more seriously than I had ever suspected. In fact, the Obama administration would engage in an abuse of power in which FISA warrants were illegally and unconstitutionally used to launch surveillance of Donald Trump's top advisers.

Imagine my shock when I read on page one of the *New York Times* on January 20, 2017, that I was among three Trump advisers who had been under active surveillance during the presidential campaign. To this day I do not know under what authority I was spied on and what probable cause could have been presented to any court to justify this flagrant violation of my Fourth Amendment constitutional rights. Clearly, I was targeted for strictly political reasons; I have been an adviser to Donald Trump for forty years.

Additionally, we now know that the Obama FBI used human assets to infiltrate the Trump campaign. Although the FBI now admits that their investigation into alleged Russian collusion with the Trump campaign began in July 2016, I was approached in May 2016 by a man calling himself "Henry Greenberg," who attempted to sell me what he said was negative information on Hillary Clinton. Greenberg wanted $2 million for this information, a laughable prospect I quickly rejected. What I did not know at the time was that Greenberg's real name was Gennady Vasilievich Vostretsov, and that he was a veteran FBI informant whose very presence in the United States was only possible because of an informant's visa approved by the Miami office of the FBI.

In June 2016, WikiLeaks publisher Julian Assange told CNN he had obtained information on Hillary Clinton and would publish it. In late July, Randy Credico, a New York City–based progressive talk-show host with whom I had worked on drug-law reform issues, told me that a source close to WikiLeaks informed him that the information Assange had teased was "political dynamite" and "would end Hillary's campaign." Credico said these disclosures would come in October.

After receiving this valuable tip, I began avidly following the Wiki-Leaks Twitter feed as well as setting a Google news alert for Julian Assange and quickly reading the many interviews that the WikiLeaks publisher gave to media outlets big and small. I also began relentlessly hyping the coming October disclosure of the WikiLeaks material.

I publicized the coming WikiLeaks disclosures without knowing the actual source or content of the material, not to aggrandize myself or to curry favor with Donald Trump's campaign (which I had voluntarily departed in August 2015), but in order to draw maximum voter and media attention to what I was told would be politically damaging material about Hillary Clinton and her campaign before the upcoming election.

While I was euphoric on election night, Trump's victory did not shock me. Veteran Republican pollster Tony Fabrizio, who was polling for the Trump campaign, had aggressively pushed the Trump effort to invest heavily of the candidate's time and resources in Michigan, Wisconsin, Pennsylvania, and Florida. Fabrizio recognized that Hillary Clinton had taken the first three states for granted, failing to campaign in them in the closing weeks and cutting back her media expenditures based on an assumption that those states were safely in her column. Fabrizio and I also noted that Trump was running significantly better among blue-collar white union and nonunion voters than had his predecessors, Mitt Romney and John McCain. This allocation of late resources would prove pivotal and would carry the election of the New York billionaire to the greatest upset since Truman vs. Dewey.

I spent election night doing election coverage for Infowars.com out of their Austin, Texas, studios. While I was exhausted, I was, of course, pleased with the results. My cohost that night, Alex Jones, was strangely downbeat and seemed to be in a foreboding mood. "This is not the end," he said, "this is just the beginning."

How right he turned out to be.

As a young aide to Governor and then President Ronald Reagan, I had seen firsthand how the political establishment in Washington effectively moves to co-opt an outsider president who threatens the status quo. I had also seen them do it to Jimmy Carter, an outsider and former governor of Georgia who had the effrontery to address the abuses at the Central Intelligence Agency and clean house. These efforts would be child's play compared to the efforts to co-opt the Trump presidency.

To my shock and surprise, Trump turned to former Republican National Chairman Reince Priebus to staff his government. Although nationalist Steve Bannon, who had joined the Trump campaign late and awarded himself the title of "chief strategist," would join the White House staff, it quickly became clear that Bannon would spend no political capital to install Trump loyalists in the new government. The Trump White House quickly assembled a staff that would have been identical to that of Governor Jeb Bush had he been elected president!

Although Trump had won as a "noninterventionist" who pledged to end America's involvement in several costly and long-running foreign wars in Iraq, Afghanistan, and Syria, he staffed his National Security Agency and State Department with neocon war hawks like General H. R. McMaster and Rex Tillerson, as well as South Carolina Governor Nikki Haley, who became UN Ambassador.

In the first two years of the Trump presidency, these advisers effectively overruled the president's instincts to extract America from these costly foreign adventures and to leave America's headlong advance to globalism untouched.

Trump's initial appointments in the domestic realm were equally disappointing. Although Trump had severely criticized Wall Street powerhouse Goldman Sachs, first for their illegal loans to finance the campaign of Senator Ted Cruz and then for their $690,000 honorarium to Hillary Clinton for a speech (the contents of which she insisted remain secret), Trump would turn to Goldman Sachs Chairman Gary Cohn, an ardent advocate of carbon tax credits and an outspoken opponent of tax reduction, as his chief economic adviser. Fortunately, the president would recognize this error and overcome the opposition of his own economic advisers to enact deep but largely unheralded regulatory reform, as well as the largest tax cuts in American history. Trump would also wisely replace Cohn with economic growth advocate Larry Kudlow, who had coauthored Trump's dynamic economic platform during the campaign.

The result was the greatest economic comeback in American history. Since Trump's election, 4.2 million jobs and counting have been created. GDP growth has averaged 4.2 percent; unemployment is at the lowest point in America since 1969. Manufacturing jobs, which President Barack Obama said were "never coming back," have grown at an astounding 714 percent. Business confidence is soaring, in part thanks to Trump's rollback of regulations. Consumer sentiment has skyrocketed— by one measure, it is at its highest level in eighteen years. Corporate profits have approached record-setting levels thanks to the Trump corporate tax cuts. Clearly President Trump's deep cuts in taxes and business regulation have spurred some of the most robust economic growth in American history. Trump's economic program was very simple: an attack on taxes and regulations with an extra dose of spending on infrastructure and the military that would create a supply shock to a stalling economy.

Perhaps the president's single greatest mistake was the appointment of Alabama Senator Jeff Sessions as attorney general. Although Sessions had been a stalwart supporter of and inspiration for Trump's hard-line immigration policies in the 2016 campaign, he would shockingly recuse himself from authority when the Deep State made its move to delegitimize the Trump presidency by claiming that Trump had only been elected with the assistance of collusion by the Russian state.

This Russian collusion myth was both an offensive and defensive weapon. The Obama-Clinton-Bush ruling class used it as a diversion from its own more serious crimes involving the abuse of power, in which they used US intelligence services to spy on and infiltrate the Trump campaign. They also used it as a pretext for a still-festering effort to remove Donald Trump from the presidency.

We now know that the Clinton campaign laundered money through Perkins Coie, a prominent law firm, for the fabrication of the Steele Dossier, which alleged both sexual impropriety by and undue Russian influence on Donald Trump. This fabricated document found its way through several sources, including Senator John McCain, to the Obama Justice Department, which then utilized it as the rationale for the issuance of FISA warrants to spy on Donald Trump's campaign.

For reasons that remain a mystery, the president has refused so far to declassify the contents of the bogus FISA warrant application on campaign volunteer Carter Page and other documents that would prove that the Obama administration used the intelligence services to spy on the Trump campaign and to initiate an "insurance policy" to discredit and remove the president in the unlikely event that he won the 2016 election. Congressman Devin Nunes, who served as chairman of the House Intelligence Committee until January 2019 and has the security clearances to see these documents, has publicly hinted they will expose the entire plot to spy on and undermine Trump. He has also publicly beseeched the president to release the unredacted material to the public to save his presidency.

After the recusal of Attorney General Jeff Sessions and the firing of FBI Director James Comey by President Trump, acting Attorney General Rod Rosenstein unilaterally appointed former FBI director Robert Mueller to launch an investigation into Trump, his campaign, and his presidency. (The day before his appointment by Rosenstein, the president interviewed Mr. Mueller to be the head of the FBI and did not offer him the job, thus creating a conflict Mr. Mueller can't waive.) Because the nation's special counsel law had lapsed, Mueller was able to operate essentially without oversight and with the authority to investigate any matter at whim.

In January 2017, I could not have predicted that my involvement in the campaign would become the center of this conspiracy. I now find myself on Crooked Special Prosecutor Robert Mueller's hit list because I've advised Donald Trump for the past forty years. I am being targeted not because I committed a crime, but because the Deep State liberals want to silence me and pressure me to testify against my good friend.

For months, Mueller's Russian investigation has tried to implicate me by saying I had direct knowledge of plans by WikiLeaks to release information damaging to Hillary Clinton's campaign. There is no evidence whatsoever to support this claim, even after at least twelve of my current and former associates have been browbeaten by the FBI and at least six of them were dragged before Mueller's grand jury.

Mr. Mueller may frame me for some bogus charge in order to silence me or induce me to testify against the president. At the end of the day, this epic fight could cost me over $2 million and destroy me and my family. The financial cost of this witch hunt has been debilitating. The relentless leaks of fake news have largely dried up my successful consulting business and I have been faced with the possibility of personal bankruptcy. I was forced to liquidate a small fund I had set aside from the proceeds of my book sales to pay for the college education of my grandchildren.

Despite this multimillion-dollar inquisition into every aspect of my life, neither Congress nor the special counsel has found any evidence of Russian collusion, WikiLeaks collaboration, or any other illegal act on my part in connection with the 2016 election. You would not know this, however, if you were watching CNN, MSNBC, or reading the *Wall Street Journal*, the *Washington Post*, *The Atlantic*, or the *New York Times*.

All of this has been a most extraordinary personal nightmare as Mueller has investigated me for over two years, probing deeply into every aspect of my personal, private, family, business, and political life. According to CNN, Mueller has reviewed all of my personal financial records, and there is substantial evidence that all of my emails, text messages, and phone calls have been reviewed by the special counsel.

Despite the fact that, by law, the special counsel is expected to operate in confidence, I have been subjected to a relentless flow of illegal leaks falsely defaming me with charges that I had some advance knowledge of the source or content of allegedly hacked or allegedly stolen emails published by WikiLeaks. This is most definitely not the case.

In September 2017, I went voluntarily to the House Permanent Select Committee on Intelligence for four and a half hours of testimony behind closed doors. I had requested that my testimony be public so that the American people could judge my veracity and see the partisan nature of my inquisitors and their trick questions, but this request was denied.

I reluctantly revealed that my former friend Randy Credico was my only link to WikiLeaks and Julian Assange, but that I did not know the source or content of the Clinton campaign emails, or that they were even in the hands of WikiLeaks before WikiLeaks announced the same. Since then, Credico has denied this, telling anyone who would listen—including Mueller's grand jury—that I had lied. For months I struggled to defend myself.

Thankfully my lawyers were able to extract the smoking gun—in the form of text messages—from a cell phone I stopped using in 2016. These texts suggest that Credico lied to the grand jury if he denied being the source of the Assange information.

Those texts and the book you now hold set the record straight and explain what involvement I had in the Trump campaign. It's this book—not Credico, not Mueller, not the liberal media—that tells the true story. Donald Trump neither needed or received help from the Russian state to defeat Hillary Clinton.

California Democratic Representative Adam Schiff—the ultimate example of the sort of slippery, duplicitous, manipulative defamation and distraction artist, fake-news fabricator, and flat-out liar that has become the standard profile of a Democrat officeholder in America today—has repeatedly charged that I was less than honest in my testimony. He is, to coin a phrase, full of schiff.

In fact, it's Adam Schiff's fabrications that are ever shifting. He brazenly stated on March 22, 2017, that "there is more than circumstantial evidence now" for collusion. In an exchange with Chuck Todd on *Meet the Press Daily*, Todd suggested that the evidence of collusion was at best circumstantial. "Actually, no, Chuck," Schiff said. "I can tell you that the case is more than that. And I can't go into the particulars, but there is more than circumstantial evidence now. . . . I will say that there is evidence that is not circumstantial and is very much worthy of investigation." To date, the congressman from West Hollywood has produced no such evidence.

Schiff is a genuine standout among what has become a ruthless, repugnant rogues' gallery of thoroughly corrupt, pathologically megalomaniacal partisan sleaze merchants who would sooner destroy democracy than have a country not incessantly held in the grip of the Democratic Party's authoritarian central government careerists, hacks, and political lifers.

There was most definitely evidence of Russian collusion in the 2016 election, but it was not on behalf of President Trump. The Clinton Foundation, a slush fund set up to benefit the Clintons and the vehicle for the facilitation of numerous multimillion-dollar "bribes," received $145 million from board members of the state-owned Russian energy company Rosatum. I believe this ensured approval of the sale of 25 percent of America's enriched uranium to the control of the Russian company in what was perhaps the largest treasonous financial crime in US history.

As I detail in this book, the rise of a robust and vibrant Internet by 2016 ended the mainstream and corporate-owned media monopoly on political discourse in America. This, in turn, led to the election of Donald Trump. Realizing this, the Deep State and their allies among the tech giants have moved aggressively to ban anyone from the Internet who does not support the establishment narrative about Donald Trump, the 2016 election, unfettered illegal immigration, radical Islam, mandatory vaccinations, trade, or war. Websites like Infowars and thousands of conservatives, libertarians, Republicans, and even antiwar progressives have found themselves banned on Facebook, Twitter, YouTube, and other wide-reaching social media platforms. I myself was banned for life by Twitter in 2017 for violating their vague and unequally enforced "community guidelines." In other words, Keith Olbermann can advocate the violent assassination of President Trump on Twitter and he will not be banned, but when I hurt CNN's Jake Tapper's feelings I am banned for life.

Incredibly, in January 2019 we learned that in the wake of President Trump's firing of corrupt FBI Director James Comey, who covered up

Hillary Clinton's crimes and breaches of national security in her use of a secret private email server, the FBI opened an investigation into whether President Trump himself was "working for the Russians." Both Deputy Attorney General Rod Rosenstein and FBI Director Christopher Wray (a Deep Stater appointed by President Trump) lied to both Congress and the president about the existence of this investigation.

Make no mistake about it: the Democratic majority that took control of the House in the 2018 elections (in which voter fraud was unprecedented) will move to enact articles of impeachment against Donald Trump on any pretext necessary. That would lead to a trial in the Republican-held US Senate, where a two-thirds vote is required to remove the president. While that result may seem improbable today, one only need look at the entirely baseless, media-created public hysteria whipped up by the likes of CNN, MSNBC, the *New York Times*, the *Washington Post*, and their ilk in the fight to confirm Brett Kavanaugh as a Supreme Court justice to see what is to come. It should be pointed out Kavanaugh's nomination prevailed by one vote. The accusers who later admitted to fabricating charges of sexual assault and gang rape against him have paid no penalty.

Historians will one day write about these dark days in which America's ruling elite conspired to create the biggest witch hunt in our country's history. I hope that when they do, they will use the book that you are about to read as the definitive account of how Donald Trump shocked the world by winning the 2016 election.

Roger J. Stone
New York City
January 2019

The Trumpster

On November 8th, 2016, Donald John Trump was elected the forty-fifth President of the United States. This is a singular accomplishment that can only be attributed to the talent, energy, and foresight of Donald Trump himself.

Trump's sprint across eight states in the closing days led to the greatest upset since 1948, when President Harry S. Truman barnstormed across the country by train, breaking all railroad speed regulations, making six or seven stops per day, and ensuring his victory over New York Governor Thomas E. Dewey. The physical energy that Trump expended going down the stretch was indeed Herculean. There is no question that his final push into Wisconsin, Michigan, and returning to western Pennsylvania, was an act of pure will that, while Clinton was already celebrating, propelled him to victory.

The 2016 election was the first in which the mainstream media lost its monopoly over political media coverage in the United States. The increasingly vigorous alternative media, whose reporting standards are superior to the networks and the cable news behemoths, is where more and more voters are getting their information.

Trump's skillful courting of the conservative media, like *The Daily Caller*, *Breitbart News*, WND.com, and *InfoWars*, made Trump the first presidential candidate to reach these disaffected and highly motivated Americans effectively. At the same time, Trump's relentless attacks on the media as "unfair" and "dishonest" came right out of the Nixon playbook, where both Nixon and Trump exploited the resentment of the biased media, so hated by their supporters.

Trump's willingness to challenge openly the media outlets that went after him kept them somewhat honest in their coverage of his campaign but the relentless cable news networks' attacks on him were unlike anything I have seen in the nine presidential campaigns in which I worked. The media dropped all pretext of objectivity. Their motives and tactics were naked.

Most of this would largely backfire. American voters have finally become hip to the fact that the media and the political establishment work hand-in-glove to conceal many facts from the American people. The voters no longer believe the media.

Donald Trump is his own strategist, campaign manager, and tactician, and all credit for his incredible election belongs to him. I'm just glad to have been along for the ride. I wanted him to run for President since 1988 and had served as chairman of his Presidential Exploratory Committee in 2000, as well as serving as a consultant to his 2012 consideration of a candidacy.

I have worked for Trump with the Trump Organization, the Trump Shuttle, Trump Hotels & Casino Resorts, and several political explorations over a forty-year period. He is perhaps the greatest salesman in US history, with the spirit of a promoter and the infectious enthusiasm of an entrepreneur who likes making money and winning.

Trump waged the first modern "all communication" campaign, eschewing polling, expensive television advertising, sophisticated analytics, and all of the traditional tools of a modern presidential campaign.

At the same time, Trump's campaign was centered around a "set piece rally," just as Richard Nixon's campaign had been. That Trump ran as the candidate of "the Silent Majority," appealing to forgotten Americans, running as the law and order candidate and in the end, the peace candidate, was not accidental. Trump's campaign was much like Nixon's. He understood that politics is about big issues, concepts, and themes, and that the voters didn't really care about wonkish detail. If they had, then Newt Gingrich would have been president.

Although there are similarities between Ronald Reagan's victory in 1980 and Trump's ascendancy to the presidency, Trump's election is less an ideological victory and more a manifestation of a genuine desire for a more competent government. Like Nixon, Trump is more pragmatic, interested in what will work, as opposed to what is philosophically pure. He's tired of seeing America lose. He is exactly the cheerleader the country needs.

Like Truman's whistle-stop events, Trump rallies became the focal point of his entire campaign, amplified by the cable news networks that carried his rally speeches around the clock. He drew enormous crowds and voters found him funny and genuine. All the while, his trusted press aide Hope Hicks was booking as many one-on-one interviews into his schedule as humanly possible. There was literally a time when you could not turn on the television without seeing and hearing Donald Trump. The cable networks of course did it for the ratings. The fact that Trump was unrehearsed, un-coached, and unhandled, meant that voters found him refreshing and authentic.

I met Donald Trump through Roy Cohn, the legendary mob and celebrity lawyer, who was an attorney and advisor to the young real estate mogul.

In 1979, I signed on to run Ronald Reagan's campaign for president in New York, among other northeastern states. I was given a card-file that supposedly held Governor and Mrs. Reagan's "friends in New York" who might be solicited for help. Among them was a card for Roy M. Cohn, Esq. with the law firm of Saxe, Bacon and Bolan. I called Cohn's office to make an appointment.

When I arrived at Cohn's brownstone law firm on the Upper East Side, I cooled my heels for about an hour in the waiting area. Finally, I was told to go to a second floor dining room where Mr. Cohn would meet me. He was wearing a silk dressing gown. His heavy-lidded eyes were bloodshot, most likely from a late night of revelry. Seated with Cohn was his client, a heavy-set gentleman who had been meeting with Cohn.

"Meet Tony Salerno," said Roy.

I was face-to-face with "Fat Tony" Salerno, at that time the boss of the Genovese crime family. In October 1986, *Fortune* magazine would call the seventy-five-year-old Salerno America's "top gangster in power, wealth, and influence."

It's true that as a New York developer, Donald Trump bought concrete from a mob-connected company controlled by Salerno. On the other hand, the State of New York, the City of New York, and most major developers bought their concrete there as well, the reason being their excellent union relationships. The company had a virtual monopoly on concrete, with the state and federal government among their biggest customers. The company was properly licensed to do business in New York State.

After Salerno left, we got down to brass tacks and I pitched Cohn on helping Governor Reagan in New York State. Roy was nominally a Democrat, the son of a legendary Tammany judge, and a quiet power in the New York Democratic Party.

He was so feared because of his viciousness in the courtroom, that most plaintiffs settled immediately when they learned that Cohn was opposing counsel. Trump used this power with Roy as his attorney.

"So how can I help you, kid? This Jimmy Carter is a disaster. I told Stanley Friedman and Meade Esposito that the peanut farmer was no damn good," Cohn exclaimed. "Ronnie and Nancy are friends from the 1950's when I was working for Joe McCarthy, the poor dumb drunk son-of-a-bitch. Ronnie stood up to the Commies in Hollywood and was a personal favorite of J. Edgar Hoover."

I told Cohn I needed to start a finance committee, locate and rent a headquarters, have phones installed, and launch a legal petition-gathering effort to put Reagan delegates' names on the New York Republican primary ballot.

Cohn stared out a picture window, then suddenly said, "What you need is Donald Trump. Do you know Donald Trump?" I told the beady-eyed lawyer I only knew Trump from the tabloids. Cohn said he would set up a meeting immediately but Donald was very busy and could only give me a limited amount of time.

Roy also told me that I had to go to Queens to meet with Donald's father, Fred Trump. "Fred is a personal friend of Barry Goldwater and has been generous to conservative and Republican candidates and causes. I guarantee you he likes Reagan," said the twice-indicted attorney.

Following Cohn's advice, I went to see Donald Trump.

At the appointed hour, Norma Foederer, Trump's longtime gatekeeper and assistant, ushered me into Trump's office. "It's a pleasure to meet you, Mr. Trump," I said. "Please call me Donald," the mogul said with a smile.

Trump was interested in politics just as he was interested in sports. He was savvy in the use of legal political money and employed a platoon of lobbyists over the years. He had a low regard for Carter and, as he put it, "this George Bush is a dud."

"Ya see, Reagan's got the look," he said. "Some guys have the look. Sinatra. JFK. And your man, Reagan. People are hungry for a strong leader, as Carter looks vacillating and weak." Trump asked quite a few questions about polling and agreed to join the Reagan finance committee, raising $100,000, split between himself and his father.

Once The Donald was on board, I heard from him constantly. He wanted the latest polling and wanted to see poll results between Reagan and Carter in some western and southern states. Trump helped facilitate our rental of a once grand, but now shabby mansion, on 52nd Street, next to the 21 Club.

The old brownstone had been magnificent in its day, but at some point in the 1970s, it was divided up into office space and ultimately fell into disrepair. It had a nasty green carpet and the cheapest possible cubicle dividers. It had the advantage of many smaller rooms for offices as well as a cavernous conference room where volunteers could stuff envelopes or make phone calls to prospective Republican primary voters. A day did not go by without a rat running across my desk. At the same time, the location couldn't be beat.

The 21 Club was Roy Cohn's clubhouse, as well as a favorite of Donald Trump's. One day, vaudeville comedian George Jessel dropped by after lunch at the 21 Club. A *New York Times* photographer captured the moment of me and the over-the-hill comic with a beaming George L. Clark, New York State party chairman, and a Reagan supporter since Reagan's challenge to sitting President Gerald Ford in 1976.

Trump was repeatedly implored by state Republican leaders to run for governor or mayor. In 2006, for example, the New York State Senate Republican's wily leader Joe Bruno convinced the New York State Independence Party, which controlled a valuable ballot position, to announce that they would cross-endorse Donald Trump for Governor if he would seek the Republican nomination. It was a hot story for twenty-four hours, until The Donald threw cold water on it. "I always thought he should have let it run a while," said Bruno, "but now I understand the job was too small for him . . . His timing of running [for president] in 2016 allowed him to take unique advantage of a perfect storm when it comes to voter disenchantment and the widespread belief that the system is rigged against the little guy. Sure, he's sometimes crude but his voters love it. It's like sticking your thumb in the eye of the establishment who have run the country into the ground," said the ex-prizefighter.

Donald has a wicked sense of humor and is enormously fun to hang out with. He has always had an exceptional eye for female beauty. He has the same eye for architecture, preferring towering buildings with clean lines, lots of brass, and always large signage. His construction standards are above and beyond industry norms and he has always enjoyed a good relationship with organized labor, which is particularly important in Democrat-dominated New York City.

Notwithstanding the glitter and gold of his buildings, there really is nothing fancy or pretentious about Donald Trump. He likes meatloaf, cheeseburgers, and diet coke. He thrives on a steady diet of cable news.

While the rest of the country may have been fooled by his genius, I, in fact, knew that he had quietly trademarked the phrase "Make America Great Again" with the US Patent and Trademark Office only days after Romney's defeat. He told me on New Year's Day 2013 that he was running for president in 2016. When I pointed out that some in the media would be skeptical that he would actually run based on his previous flirtations with public office, he replied, "That will disappear when I announce." And so it did.

President Donald J. Trump. I like the sound of it, but then I've liked the idea since 1987. I can't take credit for the idea of Donald Trump running for president because the first known progenitor of the idea was himself a former president. It was Richard M. Nixon who first noticed the potential for a presidential bid by Donald Trump.

I had grown close to the former president after I was assigned the job of briefing him weekly on the status of Governor Ronald Reagan's campaign against Jimmy Carter.

Nixon met Trump in George Steinbrenner's box in Yankee Stadium and was immediately impressed. "Your man's got it", Nixon said to me in our regularly scheduled Saturday morning phone call in which the former President satisfied his voracious appetite for political gossip and intelligence.

Nixon would famously write to Trump claiming that Mrs. Nixon had seen Donald on the *Phil Donahue Show* and thought if he ever ran for office he would win. This is typical of Nixon's circumlocution. In this case he attributes his own thoughts to Mrs. Nixon.

"I did not see the program, but Mrs. Nixon told me that you were great," Nixon wrote Trump (underlining the word "great" in his own hand). "As you can imagine, she is an expert on politics and she predicts whenever you decide to run for office you will be a winner!"

Trump was intrigued by Nixon's understanding of the use of power. Nixon's pragmatism also appealed to the New York developer. At Nixon's request, I extended an invitation to Donald and his wife Ivana for a weekend in Houston. Joining this cozy foursome was former Texas Governor John Connally, who had been gravely wounded during the assassination of President John F. Kennedy.

Connally had actually screwed Nixon in Texas in 1968, appearing at a last-minute Dallas rally for Hubert Humphrey, reneging on a secret agreement to deliver the Texas bourbon Democrats to Nixon. Nevertheless, Nixon was always impressed with Connally's swagger and certitude and he was also a prized ally for Nixon because of Connally's historic association with John Kennedy. In 1972, Connally made good on his earlier promise to help Nixon, heading a group called "Democrats for Nixon" before formally switching to the Republican Party and serving as Nixon's Treasury Secretary. It was Connally who sold Nixon on wage and price controls, perhaps one of the greatest blunders of Nixon's presidency.

Nixon was in rare form. He and Trump spoke privately for hours, with the New York real estate mogul peppering the former president with questions. For both Trump and Nixon this was an important and pivotal moment. Nixon came out of his self-imposed exile and Trump absorbed as much as he could from the former president, who was downright impressed by the Manhattan businessman. As the weekend's activities wound down, both Trump and Nixon had to return home, and that's when Donald invited Nixon back to New York on his private 727 jetliner.

Had he lived to see the 2016 presidential race, Nixon would surely have savored the fearlessness and ferocity with which Trump routinely lambasted the mainstream media. If there is a single figure in American political history who has had to endure a news media as hostile and antagonistic as Richard Nixon did, that figure is without doubt Donald J. Trump.

In 1989, I was working for Donald Trump as a lobbyist in Washington handling currency transaction rules that his casinos were subject to. I believed I had worked out regulatory language acceptable to the regulators, subject to Donald's approval. I called Donald at his office asking if I could jump what was then the Eastern shuttle from DC to New York and meet him at noon in his Manhattan office.

Donald told me he couldn't meet because he was leaving for Atlantic City with a group of his executives by helicopter. I convinced him to wait for me, sending the executives on ahead and having the chopper return to pick up Trump and bring him to Atlantic City later.

Shortly after I was ushered into Donald's office, his ashen-faced assistant Norma Foederer told Donald that New Jersey State Police Superintendent Clint Pagano was on the phone. Trump put him on the speaker. "I'm sorry to say that the helicopter your company chartered crashed in the pinelands and everyone aboard was killed." "Are you certain?" Trump asked. "One hundred percent," said the veteran cop.

The women at the Trump Organization were openly weeping with Trump losing Steve Hyde and Mark Etess, his two top gaming executives. Hyde was a Mormon with twelve children and a pleasure to work with when I represented the casino company on a few issues.

Donald had Norma place calls to the widows. He spoke to each of them and, in some cases, Trump's call about their husband's death was their first news of the cataclysmic event. While Trump may have booked other appointments after mine, I know that his life was spared to save our Republic and restore our economic vitality.

This was the point at which I realized that Trump had been put on Earth for this larger purpose. This was the point that I realized he would be President.

Trump's First Run
for the White House, 1999–2000

If I couldn't win, if I felt I couldn't win, I wouldn't run. I absolutely would not run. I'm not looking to get more votes than any other independent candidate in history, I'd want to win.
         Donald Trump, on *Larry King Live*, October 9, 1999[1]

It was mid-September 1999 and the two of us just sat in his office on the twenty-sixth floor at Trump Tower on Fifth Avenue in New York City, in uncomfortable silence. It seemed to go on forever. But I knew as well as anybody, Trump never stayed quiet for too long.

Those rare silent moments are usually broken by a major pronouncement. I sat there and waited as he pored over the morning newspapers.

As he continued to read, Trump flashed that now famous frown and shook his head in disgust. "I'm pretty sure it's going to be Bush and Gore," he said breaking the eerie stillness of the room. "They are both absolutely terrible—just terrible. What's going on in this country?"

It wasn't the first time he had asked me that question. And I knew it wasn't going to be the last.

He looked me squarely in the eyes and, with a hint of a smile, said: "Roger, I want to take the next step. I want to see if Donald Trump can win the White House. Is this country ready for President Trump? The one thing I do know is that I'm better than any of those assholes who are running."

It was a decision I had been urging him to make for months—to set up an exploratory committee to test the waters. In fact, we had already put together a book, *The America We Deserve*,[2] which outlined his domestic and international policies.

It was due out January 1, 2000 from St. Martin's Press, in anticipation of a possible Trump bid for the White House.

The book was produced to sustain interest should he become a candidate and to let people know where he stood on the issues. It presented a much more moderate view of Trump than the one most people have today.

And there was good reason for this: In 1999, Trump was hoping to attract support from people in the Reform Party, which was basically made up of moderates—compared to 2016, when he was trying to win support from Republicans who are generally conservatives.

Of course his stand on certain issues changed. In politics, you play to your audience—plain and simple! Trump knows this better than anyone.

Looking back, one particular comment in the book stands out today: "I believe non-politicians represent the wave of the future," he wrote.

It's astonishing now, in retrospect. It was like Trump was forecasting 2016.

Although we talked about the White House over and over again, that day in his office was the first time he had actually given me the nod to get things rolling.

The Reform Party

Trump's fellow-billionaire Ross Perot had been working hard for weeks in an attempt to persuade Trump to run as a Reform Party candidate for president who could offer a viable alternative to the two candidates. The enormously successful Texas businessman had run for the White House in 1992 as an independent and pulled in nearly 19 percent of the popular vote against President George H. W. Bush and his Democratic challenger Bill Clinton.

Perot went on to create the Reform Party three years later and became its presidential nominee for the 1996 election. Running against Clinton and Bob Dole, Perot still managed to pull in 8.4 percent of the popular vote.

Although Perot's vote totals had fallen in four years, the 1996 results were still dramatic for a third-party presidential candidate. Despite being mocked at times by the mainstream media for his political naïveté, Perot had managed to tap into a developing undercurrent of political distrust and disgust of career politicians by voters.

Joining Perot in encouraging Trump to enter the race was Jesse Ventura, the one-time professional wrestler who once was known as Jesse "The Body" Ventura. Running as a Reform Party candidate, Ventura stunned America when he was elected governor of Minnesota in 1998.

Of course, if you ask me, Jesse would have won in Minnesota, even without his Reform Party affiliation. He could have run as a candidate for the Communist Party and still captured the governor's seat.

Every wrestling fan—and there were tons of them—loved Jesse. He is smart. He is engaging. He is a beloved celebrity. He is outspoken. And the man on the street identifies with him.

The same can be said about Donald Trump, whom I believed could personally build on that formula in 2016 and ride it right into the White House.

But for now, Trump was carefully learning from Perot and Ventura. At times, Trump would jokingly refer to them as "the nutty billionaire and the wrestler." But the fact is that he took their advice seriously and particularly admired both men. But more importantly, Trump was quick to recognize the two had discovered an electorate discontent in Middle America that was just beginning to rear its head.

Strangely enough, bolstering Trump's confidence was a poll conducted by the *National Enquirer* in 1999, interviewing one hundred Americans—a small sample, about one-tenth the sample size of a standard national poll—but the respondents were reportedly clamoring for Trump to get into the race.

New York Times reporter Adam Nagourney was with Mr. Trump and me on the twenty-sixth floor of the Trump Tower office when Trump was looking over the *National Enquirer* poll.

"'Those are the real people,' Mr. Trump declared of the *Enquirer* readers, earnestly laying his hands across his desk," Nagourney reported. "Roger Stone, his paid consultant, who was sitting across the desk, offering Mr. Trump the occasional pointer during the forty-five-minute interview, added, 'That is the Trump constituency.'"[3]

And I meant it. But the truth of the matter is I never seriously believed he had a shot at becoming President in 2000. The time really wasn't right for him yet.

People were just becoming disenchanted with Washington politicians. They still had a long way to go before "outsider" Donald Trump could come to the rescue. There was still an economic collapse ahead, terrorism on 9/11, and mounting immigration problems—all ingredients for Trump's triumph in 2016.

But for now it was full-speed ahead. Despite Perot's strong showing in the previous two presidential elections, I had serious reservations about whether Trump could win the White House as the presidential nominee of the Reform Party. Clearly, the Reform Party did not have the organization the Democrats or the Republicans had.

But the truth is we had nothing to lose by first seeing how voters would react to this billionaire real estate magnate from New York City.

An Exploratory Committee

At Trump's suggestion, I set up the exploratory committee and put myself in charge. Maybe in some small way he could have an impact on the election, while he looked toward the future. As I said, Trump had absolutely nothing to lose by forming the exploratory committee.

And let's not forget—we're talking Donald Trump, who likes publicity, likes adulation, likes making waves, but also had some things he really wanted to say to the American public.

There was also a windfall available. Because of Perot's showing four years earlier, the Reform Party's presidential candidate was entitled to nearly $13 million in federal matching funds. If Trump ran and captured the nomination, he could at least start off using OPM (Other People's Money).

But as you would expect, money has never been an issue for Trump.

My first goal was to attract maximum publicity when Trump announced the formation of an exploratory committee to decide whether to enter the race for the Reform Party's nomination. It was an easy goal, since publicity is never too difficult when you're talking about Donald Trump. It's a given that Donald Trump attracts publicity.

We decided to have him announce the formation of his exploratory committee on CNN'S *Larry King Live* on October 8, 1999. Larry's show was hot back then and we believed it was the perfect forum for his announcement.[4] Before he went on, we brainstormed what Trump should say to Larry. I was concerned the committee announcement might not be strong enough to get him maximum exposure the following day in newspapers and on television. After all, there had been constant speculation about it for weeks.

I looked at him with a big grin and said: "If Larry asks you who you would select as a running mate, just say 'Oprah.' Everybody loves Oprah! The press will eat this up. It's a win, whenever you throw out her name.

Just prior to the Larry King appearance, I called a CNN connection I had known for years. "If you want a big story out of Trump's appearance on King, have Larry ask him who he would pick as a running mate if he runs for president," I said. And I promised the producer, with a wink, Trump's answer will absolutely shock everyone. Despite the producer's promise to pass along the info to Larry King, we had no way of knowing for sure whether Larry would take the bait and actually ask Trump the question.

Larry agreed to tape the interview with Trump during the day and air it later that night on his show. Trump had badly wanted to attend a dinner with Jesse Ventura that evening and schmooze with some of the Reform Party people.

Early in the interview, Trump dropped Bombshell Number One: "So I am going to form a presidential exploratory committee, I might as well announce that on your show, everyone else does, but I'll be forming that and effective, I believe, tomorrow," Trump told the crusty interviewer. "And we'll see. I mean, we're going to take a very good, strong look at it."

And just minutes later, Larry went for it and asked him if he had a vice presidential candidate in mind. Trump hesitated briefly as if to ponder his answer and then stunned everyone including King—and no doubt Oprah herself. "Oprah. I love Oprah," Trump said. "Oprah would always be my first choice. She's a terrific woman. She is somebody that is very special. If she'd do it, she'd be fantastic. I mean, she's popular, she's brilliant, she's a wonderful woman." The following day the newspapers and TV news were filled with talk of Trump and Oprah.

The press ate it up and so did we!

As a result of his comments on King's show, we were flooded with media requests for interviews. And Trump was well prepared. Over and over again, he stressed how seriously he was looking into running.

"Unless I thought I could win the whole thing, I would have no interest," he told one newspaper.

And Trump, through his upcoming book and interviews, was very clear on where he stood on the issues.

Abortion? Trump was "very pro-choice." "I hate the concept of abortion," he said. "I hate it. I hate everything it stands for . . . but I just believe in choice." It was a far cry from his pro-life stand in 2016.

Guns? In his book, he wrote that he "generally" opposed gun control. However, he supported a ban on assault weapons and a longer-waiting period to buy firearms. Again, a more moderate Trump than the one we see today.

Health care? Trump called himself "very liberal" on the issue and stressed he was a believer in "universal health care."

But he was also ahead of his time in warning against terrorism, saying: "It's time to get down to the hard business of preparing for what I believe is the real possibility that somewhere, sometime, a weapon of mass destruction will be carried into a major American city and detonated."

Taking on Buchanan

We hit the ground running, but there was one person who stood in Trump's way of getting the Reform Party's nomination—my old colleague from the Nixon White House, Pat Buchanan, who badly wanted to be the next president. Buchanan worked for Nixon as an advisor and speechwriter. Brilliantly talented, Buchanan was the genius who came up with the phrase Nixon made famous, appealing as he did in 1968 to the "Silent Majority." He was shrewd. He was smart. But he could also be thin-skinned at times. Pat Buchanan was the perfect foil for Trump.

As brilliant as Buchanan is, he is prone to saying some pretty wild things that come back to bite him. It might be that sometimes Buchanan is just too honest. In his 1999 book, *A Republic, Not an Empire,*[5] he wrote that Hitler was no threat to the United States in 1938, at the start of World War II in Europe. Even if that was true, the concept did not play to an American public that saw Hitler as the monster he truly was.

I was the one who noted it to Trump. You just don't get many opportunities like this in politics. And when you do, you have to hit hard— VERY HARD. It was an unfortunate thing for Buchanan to say, but we were going to remind the world every chance we could that Buchanan said it. Trump couldn't wait to nail him on it. He was like an animal going after raw meat. Trump fired one shot after another—and never stopped.

On September 26, 1999, in a television appearance on CNN's *Late Edition*, Buchanan tried to explain that his book was not written to be sympathetic to Adolf Hitler during World War II. "We had every right, and we were more than right . . . just and moral to smash (Germany and Japan)," Buchanan insisted. "It was a noble cause. There's nothing in that book that says otherwise."[6]

I typed up a statement from Trump and faxed it to the show, challenging Buchanan's statements and quoting Trump as saying: "Pat Buchanan's stated view that we should not have stopped Adolf Hitler is repugnant. I think it is essential that someone challenge these extreme and outrageous views by Pat Buchanan. [He] denigrates the memory of those Americans who gave their lives in the Second World War in the effort to stop Hitler."

In my haste to get Trump's statement out, I misspelled Hitler's first name—something the *New York Daily News* took us to task for. But in the end, I didn't care. We were already successfully painting Buchanan as a "Hitler sympathizer."

I later told Trump that no one has ever lost an election by kissing babies, smiling, and attacking Adolf Hitler. At my urging, Trump continued to take advantage of every opportunity to remind people about Buchanan's words on the Führer. On October 25, 1999, Trump gained widespread publicity when he changed his party registration from Republican to the New York Independence Party—making him eligible for the Reform Party's nomination. And he escalated his attacks on Buchanan.

"Denouncing Patrick J. Buchanan as a 'Hitler lover,' Donald J. Trump announced today he was resigning his Republican registration in advance of a possible challenge to Mr. Buchanan in his expected quest for the Reform Party Presidential nomination," Francis X. Clines wrote as his lead paragraph in the *New York Times* article published on October 25, 1999.[7]

"'It's a very great possibility that I will run,' said Mr. Trump, the real estate and casino millionaire."

And about Buchanan, Trump said: "Look, he's a Hitler lover. I guess he's an anti-Semite. He doesn't like the blacks. He doesn't like the gays. It's just incredible that anybody could embrace this guy."

He also had this to say about Republicans: "I really believe the Republicans are just too crazy right now."

It couldn't have worked out any better. With the *New York Times* articles appearing on the eve of a speech in which Buchanan was expected to jump the GOP ship to become a Reform Party candidate, Trump was able to attack Buchanan, change party affiliation, and throw out a giant tease he was likely to run—all at the same time.

Now the next thing we had to do was get the Trump message out all over the country. We carefully plotted out trips for Trump. Our mission was to get maximum exposure and be able to begin to connect with average Americans in the heartland as well as on the coasts. But there was still one big announcement to make to lay the groundwork for a national tour. In an effort to cement his relationship with the working class and make his billionaire status more acceptable to voters, Trump unveiled a tax on the rich in early November. This would be a one-time "net worth tax" on the wealthiest Americans: individuals and trusts worth $10 million or more. A 14.25 percent levy on such a "high net worth" would have raised $5.7 trillion and wiped out the national debt. It also would have saved the government $200 billion a year in interest payments, allowing for a middle class tax cut.

It was unbelievable how much publicity Trump attracted by attacking Hitler (through his attacks on Buchanan) and by saying we should tax the rich. Like the timing of his changed party affiliation, it just could not get any better.

Hitting the Campaign Trail

Now it was time to hit the road.

The first trip was down to south Florida in mid-November. The *Sun-Sentinel* in Fort Lauderdale headlined its story on his appearance this way: "Trump: I've got what it takes to be President."[8]

Never shy, Trump boasted his qualifications for the White House.

"When you look at the other candidates, did they make a billion dollars in a short period of time? I don't think so," Trump said. "I've done things that people said couldn't be done."

And the newspaper noted: "Trump's visit to Miami marks the beginning of a ninety-day drive to win over 'the people,' aided by a bevy of public relations firms—and his new campaign adviser Roger Stone, mastermind of presidential campaigns for Richard Nixon and Ronald Reagan."

Once again, the game plan for Trump was simple: play to your audience. And he did just that.

The *Sentinel* reported:

> After standing for the pre-revolutionary Cuban national anthem, and calling Fidel Castro a killer during his speech, Trump was regaled with cheers of "Viva Donald Trump! Viva!" by about 40 veterans of the [Bay of Pigs] invasion.
>
> The cheers continued after nightfall, when about 400 Cuban-Americans turned out to hear Trump speak at the Radisson Crown Plaza in western Miami, organized by the Cuban-American National Foundation.

"If I could meet Castro right now, I would have two words for him: Adios, amigo," Trump told the crowd. "We must not reward Fidel Castro with trade, hard currency or respect. He's a murderer, he's a tyrant, he's a bad guy."

As far as Cuban Americans are concerned—Fidel Castro was their Hitler. And Trump knew this and capitalized on it.

During his two-day visit to Miami, he met with Cuban-American leaders; attended a Reform Party rally; was the guest at a reunion of veterans of the Bay of Pigs invasion; and met with members of Brothers to the Rescue, a Cuban exile group that drops anti-Castro leaflets over the island nation.

Trump succeeded in doing exactly what he set out to do. He got a great reception and he garnered great publicity.

Then it was on to Los Angeles for two Reform Party events, a visit to a Holocaust memorial, a speech to 17,000 people at a "motivational" conference, and an appearance on *The Tonight Show* with Jay Leno.

But he hit his first bump in the road during an appearance at a meeting with leaders of the California Reform Party.

Trump was here to present himself as "a triumphant developer, a new book author, and the potential next leader of the free world," Adam Nagourney noted for the *New York Times* in an article published on December 10, 1999. "It was a cantankerous meeting with leaders of the California Reform Party, whose support Mr. Trump would presumably like should he run for president. For many, the most memorable moment came when someone asked if Mr. Trump supported the Reform Party platform."[9]

"Well. Nobody knows what the Reform Party platform is," Trump loudly responded.

A man offered Trump a copy of the platform as boos rang out from the crowd.

The fact is that no one really cares about a party platform except those people who write it. Unfortunately, those were the exact people Trump was addressing. Also, the Reform Party platform was more important than usual because the platform planks in this case defined how and why the Reform Party in 1999 was different from the GOP, the party from which most Reform Party members had come (including Donald Trump).

For the *New York Times*, this encounter raised the fundamental question about Trump's two-day exploratory trip to the West Coast. "Is he serious?" Nagourney asked in the article, wondering if Trump really was a presidential candidate. "As Mr. Trump's performance with the Reform Party leaders here suggested, the developer's command and interest in the details of running for president sometimes seemed tenuous."

Yes, it was a misstep, but not a big one. I swore I'd never let him make that kind of mistake again.

But there were lighter moments during that trip. Speaking at a meeting of the Reform Party, he went out of his way to note the television cameras taping him.

"By the way, that camera is *60 Minutes*," he said pointing one out. "Don't worry about them. It's just a small program on television."

Never forget: Trump loves the attention.

When he appeared on *The Tonight Show*, Leno asked how things were going. Trump shot back: "Oh, so much press. So much press out there." And he wasn't lying. I did everything I could to make sure that for the few days we were in Los Angeles, Donald Trump was the biggest celebrity there.

Like every other celebrity hungry for press in Hollywood, we made certain Trump paid the requisite visit to The Ivy restaurant. For those of you who don't know about The Ivy, it is the place where stars gather in Tinseltown. It's a nondescript brick building on Robertson Boulevard, surrounded by its trademark white picket fence. The inside looks as if it could have been furnished by your grandmother—fluffy seat cushions, fluffy pillows, and patterned draperies. The paparazzi sit outside waiting to see exactly who shows up. The prices are high and the food is good. But no one goes there for the food. You go to be seen, or you go to watch. And it is not the usual haunt for your typical political candidate. But then again, Donald Trump has never been your "TYPICAL" political candidate. Even before *The Apprentice*, Trump projected celebrity.

And, believe me, all eyes were on him as he walked into the restaurant. Everybody stopped to watch him. Few celebrities could bring The Ivy to a halt, but Trump did. He stopped by Rod Stewart's table to say hello and then made his way over to Michael Bolton to wish him well.

He blew them all away.

But we caught some heat over his appearance at a Tony Robbins motivational event.

Trump had a deal with Robbins where he would give ten speeches and Robbins would pay him $100,000 a speech. So, of course, we scheduled his exploratory campaigning to coincide with the time he was scheduled to be in California for the Robbins event. It just made sense.

Trump visited the Holocaust Museum in Los Angeles. He did a very highly publicized event on the rooftop of his hotel for Reform Party officials, and then he went out to Anaheim to do his speech for Robbins. Some people got ticked off that he was mixing politics and business. But Trump didn't care. He later told me: "I'm the only guy who explored running for president and made money on it." Keep in mind, he was only exploring a run for president. He wasn't yet a candidate.

A Learning Experience

Trump was beginning to get concerned about troubling signs coming from factions inside the Reform Party. Infighting, different political philosophies, and general personality conflicts—common problems in politics but especially difficult in relatively small US third parties trying to make their mark—were starting to take its toll on the reformers.

It's something both Trump and I had feared from the beginning. He believed that if he ran and the Reform Party collapsed, fingers would wrongfully be pointed at him. We started to become convinced the party was going to implode even if Trump never became a candidate.

Trump traveled to Minnesota to brainstorm with Jesse Ventura in early January 2000. Ventura was becoming disgusted with the Reform Party. He confided to us that he was thinking of pulling out completely. But for now, he was staying and trying to make the best out of it. Even though we were growing more and more certain the time wasn't right for him to run, Trump still kept stirring the pot and acting like a candidate-to-be. In Minnesota, he knocked George W. Bush and Vice President Al Gore, whom he noted were both born into well-heeled families.

"There's a big difference between creating a lot of wealth and being a member of the lucky sperm club, which a number of different people that are running right now are," Trump said in a joint appearance with Ventura.

As if rehearsed, Ventura quickly added: "I'm not a member of that club either."

And Trump did his utmost to differentiate himself from the mainstream candidates.

He called the field of GOP candidates a "bunch of stiffs" and attacked front-runner Bush, saying he's "no Einstein." "If people think he's dumb, he'll have a hard time winning the election." And he once again went after Buchanan calling him "a loser."

Despite his mounting doubts about joining the race, he continued to insist he was seriously considering entering.

"I am looking very, very seriously as to whether or not it can be won," he said of the presidential race. "If I can win, I think I can do a very good job."

But in his heart, he knew it was all over. We all did. Jesse was fed up with the Reform Party and looking to quit. But more importantly Trump was now convinced political infighting was destroying the reformers. They could not be counted on to help carry him to the White House.

Out of respect for Jesse, Trump agreed to hold off making the announcement that he would not, in fact, run for President until the former professional wrestler made a decision.

But slowly we began to let the word out.

One New York gossip columnist wrote on February 6: "The man who wrote the book on the art of the deal has been toying with a Presidential run on the Reform Party ticket. But he's pulling out of the race in about two weeks, reports one well-connected political source."

And even the slightest thought of Trump officially declaring his candidacy came to an end weeks later when Ventura officially quit the party in February 2000. Ventura's decision to leave came as no surprise, of course, to Trump and those of us working for him. Jesse just couldn't stand it anymore.

He gave us a heads-up before he announced it publicly, but we had been expecting it for weeks. And the truth is, the Reform Party needed Jesse much more than he needed them. Without Jesse, there would be no strong Reform Party. And without a strong Reform Party, there would be no Trump Presidential candidacy.

Typical of Jesse, he pulled no punches in announcing his decision. He publicly called the party "hopelessly dysfunctional" and said it dragged down independent politicians like himself.

The Associated Press noted: "The Reform Party has been hampered for months by squabbling between Perot's allies and Ventura supporters. They sparred over the 2000 convention site, presidential candidates and the party's money."

Ventura took a parting shot at Buchanan, calling him "an anti-abortion extremist and unrealistic isolationist."

Better Luck Next Time

But it was all over—and so was Trump's fascination with presidential politics for 2000.

Sure, we kicked around a number of options for a Trump candidacy. It would be nearly impossible to get him on all the state ballots if he ran as an independent with no party backing. Entering the race would have been a waste of time for him.

And Trump was adamant. He told me again and again: "I will not run unless I can win and I mean it! This is over—for now!"

Shortly after Jesse bolted from the party, Trump publicly announced he was not entering the 2000 presidential race.

"Since the beginning of my political exploratory effort, I have consistently said that I was only interested in running if I had the prospect of winning," he said. "Without Jesse, the Reform Party is just an extremist shell and cannot be a force or even a factor in 2000."

And the *New York Daily News* noted on February 14, something all of us involved with Trump had known all along: "Veteran political operative Hank Sheinkopf said Trump probably would not have won the White House, but his candidacy would have given the Reform Party a boost. 'Buchanan makes them more a cult,' Sheinkopf said. 'Trump was the only thing that could have saved them from themselves.'"[10]

And, of course, as soon as he decided not to run, he went back to the party of his parents and re-registered as a Republican—the party that would eventually help bring him into the White House.

Ironically, throughout his flirtation with the Reform Party nomination, critics in the press openly speculated whether he was indeed a serious candidate for the presidency, or if he was really more interested in promoting a new book. Let me tell you this: Trump was dead serious about running in 2000—and a lot of people were dead serious about voting for him.

About a week and a half after dropping out of the race, Trump won the Michigan Reform Party primary. And just weeks later, he won the California Reform Party primary by pulling in 44 percent of the votes. The closest of five opponents collected only 27 percent of the vote.

Looking back there was absolutely no downside to Trump eyeing the 2000 presidential race. He learned a lot from it that would help him sixteen years later.

2012

Trump thought seriously about running for President again in 2012—this time as a Republican.

Once again, he had incredible support. Sure, there were skeptics in the media but, more importantly, voters absolutely loved him. They connected with him.

"The polls are very strong," he told a reporter. "I am seriously thinking about it. I hate what's happened to the country."

"A recent poll came out where Trump and [Bill] Gates are the only two that beat Obama. Gates isn't running obviously, but they put names on it, and we're the only ones who beat Obama."

Trump had surged to the head of the Republican field by seizing on the questions being raised over whether President Obama was actually born in Kenya and was not in office legally since he was not a natural-born American citizen. Some of Obama's most ardent critics were openly challenging him to produce his birth certificate. And the supermarket tabloid, *Globe*, only added fuel to the fire when, in July 2010, it published a cover story headlined: "OBAMA WAS NOT BORN IN THE U.S."

Obama left himself wide open to questions. He had always claimed he was born in Hawaii, but had never backed it up with a full copy of his birth certificate. And as each day went by, the issue was clearly gaining more and more traction. Even though it was terribly politically incorrect, Trump was going to use it any way he could.

Some liberals in the media tried to paint Trump as a racist for questioning the birthplace of an African-American president. The *New York Times* later observed: "In the Birther movement, Mr. Trump recognized an opportunity to connect with the electorate over an issue many considered taboo: the discomfort, in some quarters of American society, with the election of the nation's first black president. He harnessed it for political gain. . ."[11] One Trump adviser during that time observed: "The appeal of the Birther issue was, 'I'm going to take this guy on, and I'm going to beat him.' It was a great niche and wedge issue."[12]

Trump smelled a weakness and he went right for it.

"Why doesn't he show his birth certificate," he asked during a March 23, 2011 appearance on *The View*. Five days later, he appeared on Fox News and said: "He's spent millions of dollars to get away from this issue. Millions of dollars in legal fees trying to get away from the issue. And I'll tell you what, I brought it up, just routinely, and all of a sudden a lot of facts are emerging and I'm starting to wonder myself whether or not he was born in this country."

In another TV appearance, Trump added: "I have people that have been studying [Obama's birth certificate] and they cannot believe what they're finding . . . I would like to have him show his birth certificate, and can I be honest with you, I hope he can. Because if he can't, if he can't, if he wasn't born in this country, which is a real possibility . . . then he has pulled one of the great cons in the history of politics."

I told the *New York Times*: "He was suspicious about it, or at least interested in it." Among Republican base voters, "[Stone] added, many of them believe the president is foreign-born, and Trump has the ability to interject any idea that is outside of the mainstream into the mainstream." And to that point, a Gallup poll revealed at that time only 38 percent of Americans surveyed believed Obama was "definitely" born in the United States.

The *Times* noted that there was also division in the ranks of the Trump Team over how aggressively he should continue to pursue the Birther argument. Kellyanne Conway, who was then a Republican pollster, cautioned that if he decided to enter the campaign, he would need to beat Obama "on the merits," the newspaper said.

And to top it all off, NBC, which airs *The Apprentice*, was starting to get antsy over the whole Birther thing. The network execs called Trump and begged him to tone it down just a bit. They feared it would turn off a chunk of the more than one million African Americans who watched the show. But the whole Birther issue was coming to an end even sooner than we expected.

To be honest, we never imagined Obama would release his birth certificate. Who would have ever thought he would cave to Trump? On April 27, 2011, however, Obama shocked everyone—including Trump— by releasing his original long-form birth certificate, which showed he was indeed born in Hawaii. "We do not have time for this kind of silliness," a frustrated President said. "I've been puzzled at the degree to which this [story] just kept on going . . . Normally I would not comment on something like this. But the country has some enormous challenges out there . . . We're not going to be able to solve our problems if we get distracted by sideshows and carnival barkers."

Nevertheless, Trump kept fanning the flames of uncertainty. "An extremely credible source has called my office and told me that Obama's birth certificate is a fraud," he said later. But officially the issue was dead and buried and Trump knew it. After all, only Trump could force Obama to release a birth certificate "or whatever it was," as Trump put it.

While Trump's fascination with the White House still burned within him, he also had *The Apprentice* to deal with—and it wasn't as easy as you might think. He loved doing the show and was reluctant to give it up. At one point, he was actually thinking about hosting it from the Oval Office if he made it all the way to the White House. He even discussed it with Steve Burke, the CEO at NBCUniversal, telling Burke he would reconsider running if the network was concerned about his candidacy. Burke was very clear—he didn't want Trump to go forward with the campaign. *Vanity Fair* reported[13]:

> "If you don't want me to do this, then I need you to ask me," Trump told the executive, according to one person familiar with the conversation. Burke eventually went to Trump's office and conceded that he did not want his star to attempt a bid for the White House. "But another person with knowledge of the situation noted that the two men had a subsequent conversation in which they broached a compromise, albeit one that seems more like a Trumpian fever dream than a network-TV reality show. It outlined, presumably fantastically, that if Trump should run for president; and on the off chance that he won, he would continue to star in *The Apprentice* from within the White House."

> But the more Trump continued considering the campaign, the more he realized it just didn't make any sense for him to get into this race. And, as always, Trump was only interested in it if he could win. Romney, after all, had a long head start.

Despite his strong polling, Trump believed that Obama would likely win reelection and that Trump's chances were far better in 2016 when it was a wide-open election. On February 2, 2012, Trump told reporters he was endorsing Mitt Romney for president and said he was not going to mount an independent campaign if Romney captured the GOP nomination.

"It's my honor, real honor, to endorse Mitt Romney," Trump said. He called Romney "tough" and "smart," and added, "he's not going to continue to allow bad things to happen to this country." But privately he believed Romney, who proved to be a 'choke artist', did not stand a chance against Obama and once again he was right.

Trump, however, was continuing to lay the groundwork for 2016.

Hillary's House of Cards

This is Yuge . . .

—Donald J. Trump

Emails released by WikiLeaks show Hillary Clinton's campaign strate-gists had decided to "elevate" Donald Trump during the Republican primaries because key players, including Hillary's campaign manager Robby Mook and Hillary's campaign chairman John Podesta, agreed with the top officials at the Democratic National Committee that Trump would be the easiest GOP candidate for Hillary to beat.[14]

That miscalculation prompted a series of missteps that caused former First Lady Hillary Clinton to miss her second chance to "break the glass ceiling" and become the first woman president of the United States—a goal Hillary had coveted virtually her entire adult life.

Hillary, the presumed Democratic Party presidential nominee in 2008, when she lost in the primaries to a then little-known Senator Barack Obama from Illinois, was once again the presumed nominee in 2016. Remarkably, though she came much closer, Hillary Clinton fai-led a second time to capture the presidency, losing this time to Donald Trump, a New York billionaire with a controversial past and mercurial personality who had never held a political office in his life.

Clinton clearly had the superior political résumé, having followed two terms as first lady, with two stints as a US Senator from New York, serving from 2001 until 2009, when she resigned to become Secretary of State, serving under President Obama from 2009 to 2013.

Hillary entered the 2016 presidential race with the steadfast back-ing of mainstream media, including all broadcast networks and major newspapers such as the *New York Times* and the *Washington Post*, all of which crossed the line of journalistic independence to become partisan advocates of Clinton's candidacy.

The story of how and why Hillary Clinton became a two-time loser in US presidential politics is historic, not only because it represents the likely end of the Clinton dynasty in American politics, but also because Donald Trump's surprise election victory marks a realignment of the electorate. It was a powerful blow against the far-left that increasingly has dominated the Democratic Party since the rise of Obama as a presidential contender and the first loss for Hillary in her ongoing bid for the White House.

Can You Name a Hillary Clinton Accomplishment?

This is a question that has dogged Hillary Clinton ever since her failure to enact the original version of universal health care, at the time known as "Hillary-care," during the first years of her husband's presidency. Even Hillary Clinton appears to have had trouble with this question. On June 9, 2014, in an interview with ABC News anchor Diane Sawyer on the eve of the publication of Clinton's book *Hard Choices*, Clinton gave no answer when Sawyer asked her to detail a marquee accomplishment or a signature doctrine for which she could claim responsibility during her tenure at the State Department. The *Washington Post*, in reporting the exchange with Sawyer, noted that Hillary's Republican critics immediately highlighted her failure to list accomplishments in response to Sawyer's question. The *Washington Post* report continued, "Clinton caused a political flap earlier Monday after ABC aired a portion of the interview in which Clinton said her family was 'dead broke' upon leaving the White House in 2001 and 'struggled' to pay their mortgages on two homes. Republicans seized on the comments to argue that the Democrat—now a multimillionaire who charges $200,000 per speech—is out of touch with middle-class Americans."[12]

On June 9, 2016, in a taped message posted on YouTube by Clinton's presidential campaign, President Obama endorsed Hillary Clinton for President, characterizing her as one of the most qualified candidates ever to run for the office.[15] When forced on her personal website to list her greatest accomplishments, Hillary included that she had fought for children and families for forty years, that she had helped get 9/11 responders the health care they needed, that she proclaimed at the United Nations that "women's rights are human rights," and that she stood for Lesbian, Gay, Bisexual, and Transgender (LGBT) rights at home and abroad.[16] In listing her accomplishments, Clinton neglected to address her failures, such as the Benghazi terror attack that killed US Ambassador Chris Stevens and three other brave Americans, the failed "reset" with Russia, and the destabilization of the Middle East that followed an "Arab Spring" hijacked by the Muslim Brotherhood's support of radical Islamic militia in countries across Northern Africa, including both Libya and Egypt. Nor did Clinton list any important legislation she had sponsored in her eight years in the US Senate.

Instead of running on her own record of accomplishments, Clinton was tagged in 2016 as "running for Obama's third term."[17] Democrats embraced this idea, thinking Obama's popularity as president might spill over to Hillary, encouraging those who voted for Obama to believe a Hillary Clinton presidency might represent a continuation of President Obama's domestic and foreign policies. Republican strategists seized on the disadvantages Hillary assumed by allowing herself to be framed as an Obama-surrogate president. That designation allowed GOP presidential contenders to attack Clinton by attacking Obama. To win under the presumption that her presidency would be a continuation of Obama's presidency, Clinton had to support an economic record with anemic growth numbers, a foreign policy that included obvious disasters like Benghazi, and face an electorate that was more racially divided and socially polarized by a wide range of new players who had shown up on the political landscape since 2004. These players included groups like Black Lives Matter and radical LGBT advocates supporting polarizing issues such as unisex bathrooms in elementary public schools and transvestites in the military.

Hillary Clinton had held an impressive list of government positions, especially in comparison to Donald Trump; that was obvious. Her failure to post historic accomplishments in those government positions made her run for the presidency in 2016 vulnerable, especially to criticism by an outsider as outspoken as Donald Trump. To win the presidency, Hillary not only had to inflate her questionable list of accomplishments, she also had to prop up an Obama presidency that many in Middle America considered one of the worst in American political history.

Obama's Legacy #1: Slow Economic Growth at Home

The Bureau of Economic Analysis has calculated the annual GDP, Gross Domestic Product, going back to 1929, as well as annual growth in real GDP since 1930. In the eighty-six years from 1930 through 2015, the United States has seen fourteen presidents serve in the White House. Of the thirteen presidents who served their full term in those years, President

Herbert Hoover—best remembered for ushering in the Great Depression—was the only president who did not see a single year in which growth in real GDP was 3 percent or better. Barack Obama—inaugurated in January 2009 and leaving the presidency in January 2017—joins Hoover as the second president since 1930 who did not see a year in which real GDP was 3 percent or better.[18]

On Friday, January 29, 2016, the Bureau of Economic Analysis reported that the 2015 US real growth in GDP was 2.8 percent, making 2015 the tenth year in a row that real growth in GDP failed to reach the 3 percent mark. The longest previous run of real growth in GDP under 3 percent in US economic history was only four years in length, lasting from 1930 to 1933 during the darkest depths of the Great Depression. Obviously, the first two years of this ten-year stretch came as the economy tanked in the subprime banking crisis at the end of President George W. Bush's second term. The other eight years in the ten-year stretch encompassed the entire two terms of Barack Obama's administration, making it clear Obama's presidency failed to lift the US economy above the low-mark set by his predecessor.[19]

Under Obama, the Bureau of Labor Statistics of the US Department of Labor learned a new trick, perfecting the art of keeping unemployment figures low by inflating the number of Americans considered not in the labor force. In the first jobs report after the 2016 presidential election, the Department of Labor said the unemployment rate dropped from 4.9 percent in October to 4.6 percent in November, with the number of Americans unemployed dropping to 7.4 million workers, the lowest of the Obama presidency. But at the same time, the labor participation rate dropped a tenth of a point to 62.7 percent in November, meaning only 62.7 percent of US workers were considered to be working, with the result that 27.3 percent of those eligible to work were either looking for a job or had become so discouraged at the prospects of finding a job that they simply dropped out of the labor force altogether. When President Obama took office in January 2009 amid the Bush recession, 80,529,000 Americans were not in the labor force. That number has risen steadily during Obama's two terms, reaching 94,708,000 in May 2016, a number eclipsed only by November's 95,055,000.[20]

Under Obama, a trend developed in which growth in total jobs was accomplished only because the growth in part-time work outpaced the number of full-time jobs being lost, while the number of workers holding multiple part-time jobs hit a twenty-first century high.[21] According to manufacturing employment data from the Bureau of Labor Statistics, the United States has lost some 303,000 manufacturing jobs since Obama took office. Obama has also failed to keep his 2012 reelection campaign promise that he would create one million manufacturing jobs in his second term. In fact, there were only 297,000 manufacturing jobs created in the United States from January 2012 through October 2016.[22]

According to the Census Bureau, median family income is nearly $13,000 less than when Obama first took office, while the poverty rate under Obama has remained at or near 14.5 percent, and extreme poverty has grown more extreme—with the number of people living 125 percent below the official poverty rate higher every year under Obama than during the Bush presidency (growing over 19 percent every year from 2010 to 2014), and the percent of the population having an income at 50 percent or less of the poverty level following the same trend (up over 6 percent every year that Obama was president). The conclusion is undeniable that during Obama's presidency, wealth inequality has increased and poverty levels are higher.[23]

Under Obama, the number of Americans on food stamps, officially the US Department of Agriculture's Supplemental Nutrition Assistance Program, or SNAP, increased from 32 million people in 2009 to 43.6 million in April 2016, having reached an annual high of 47.6 million participants in 2013, when nearly one in every seven Americans was on food stamps.[24]

Under the Obama administration, all of this evidence shows that the United States accelerated on the trend of converting from a full-time employment economy to a part-time employment economy, with a continuing concentration of wealth among the top 1 percent, while poverty levels failed to drop and food stamp usage skyrocketed. Taxes increased under Obama, in part spurred on by the growing list of Obamacare taxes being imposed on the middle class,[25] while the imposition of 229 major new federal regulations implemented since 2009 cost the US economy $108 billion annually, using the regulatory agency's own numbers.[26]

At the same time, Obama by the end of his second term was on track to double the US national debt to $20 trillion, equaling the addition to the national debt amassed by all Obama's predecessors to the presidency combined.[27] Meanwhile, the Obama administration was pressing in November 2016 to ram through Congress a massive new "free trade" deal known as the Trans-Pacific Partnership, the TPP, with the plan to follow this by circling the globe with the Transatlantic Trade and Investment Partnership, TTIP.

While economics is not necessarily the focus of all presidential debates, most Americans vote for a president only after answering the question of whether or not they are economically better off than they were four years earlier. Hillary entered the 2016 presidential campaign having to defend Obama's record of expanding "new world order" trade agreements, while the employment situation in the United States appeared grim under the prospect of continued high taxes, increased government regulations, and low economic growth.

Obama's Legacy #2: Increased Terror Threat at Home and Abroad

Obama's foreign policy is dominated by images of radical Islamic terrorism, from the Benghazi compound burning through the night, to the Isis black flag waving in triumph as Isis swept from Syria into Iraq, to jihadists making videos beheading their victims, or with the United States flying cargo planes filled with newly printed billions to Iran as payoffs culminating in a deal with Iran that could end up like Clinton-era deals with North Korea ended up—with Iran breaking its promise to refrain from making nuclear weapons while developing intercontinental ballistic missile (ICBM) capabilities aimed at threatening their neighbors and the world as a whole.

In every year under the Obama administration, the United States has suffered a terrorist attack. Still, throughout his administration, President Obama refused to utter the words "radical Islamic terrorism," even as refugees by the thousands poured out of Syria and other parts of the Middle East to enter unvetted into Europe and the United States.[28]

In December 2, 2015, Syed Farook and Tashfeen Malik, a Pakistani couple, attacked a San Bernardino County government building with combat gear and rifles. The pair, dressed in black, opened fire on about eighty employees attending an office Christmas party, killing fourteen and wounding twenty-two. According to federal authorities investigating the attack, Farook had digital contact with at least two terrorist organizations overseas, including the Al Qaida-affiliated al-Nusra Front in Syria. Four hours after the shooting, Farook and Malik were shot dead in a gun battle with police on a San Bernardino street.[29]

Then, on June 12, 2016, Omar Mateen, a twenty-nine-year-old security guard, after pledging allegiance to ISIS, killed forty-nine people and wounded fifty-three others inside Pulse, a gay nightclub in Orlando, Florida. The FBI interviewed Mateen in 2013 and 2014 and found him not to be a threat.[30]

The Obama administration had settled nearly 43,000 Somali refugees, 99 percent of whom were Muslim, in the United States during Obama's eight years in office.[31] In 2016, Obama was on pace to welcome to the United States 12,000 refugees from Syria, 99 percent of whom were Muslim—part of the 85,000 refugees Obama had pledged the United States to accept from around the world. Accepting Syrian refugees increasingly became controversial after Syrian refugees were implicated in planning terrorist attacks in Europe.[32] In addition to not feeling better off economically, millions of American voters felt less secure at home as the presidential election cycle kicked into high gear in 2016.

Hillary 2016: Confident of Victory

In 2008 and 2012, Barack Obama had easily beaten two GOP mainstream presidential candidates—Arizona Senator John McCain and former Massachusetts Governor Mitt Romney. With California, New York, and many other states certain to vote Democratic, regardless of who the Democrat's presidential candidate was, Hillary Clinton started out with a huge electoral vote advantage that the far-left elite reasoned was unbeatable.

With the Clinton Foundation having grown to an estimated $2 billion global empire,[33] Hillary had no doubt she would have the advantage over the GOP in campaign cash. While the money was, of course, not available to the campaign going into the 2016 presidential election, the Clintons knew they could return to the trough of Clinton Foundation's wealthy donors from Silicon Valley and Wall Street for big dollar donations. This was in addition to the ideologically driven donations corralled by George Soros.

The Clintons were also confident Hispanic immigrants and African Americans would vote overwhelmingly Democratic. This, combined with union votes and the votes of women, the Clintons reasoned, would make Hillary's win inevitable.

What could possibly go wrong?

Would Election Day 2016 Be a Repeat of 1980?

A Gallup poll, conducted October 26, 1980, showed Ronald Reagan was slipping farther behind President Carter, with Carter at 47 percent and Reagan at 39 percent.[34]

Reagan did not surge into a lead in the Gallup polls until the very last poll taken at the end of October 1980, when Gallup, just days ahead of election day, November 4, 1980, reported Reagan had surged ahead to 47 percent for Reagan versus 43 percent for Carter.

When the voting was finally done on November 4, 1980, Reagan won by a landslide, capturing 50.7 percent of the popular vote to 41.0 percent for Carter, winning forty-four states with the exception of Georgia, Hawaii, Maryland, Minnesota, Rhode Island, and West Virginia, for an electoral vote total of 489 versus forty-nine for Carter.

"At the heart of the controversy is the fact that no published survey detected the Reagan landslide before it actually happened," noted *Time* magazine senior correspondent Massimo Calabresi, in an article published October 31, 2012.[35] "With such responsibilities thrust on them, the pollsters have a lot to answer for, and they know it," Calabresi wrote. "Their problems with the Carter-Reagan race have touched off the most skeptical examination of public opinion polling since 1948, when the surveyors made Thomas Dewey a sure winner over Harry Truman," he continued. "In response, the experts have been explaining, qualifying, clarifying–and rationalizing. Simultaneously, they are privately embroiled in as much backbiting, mudslinging and mutual criticism as the tight-knit little profession has ever known. The public and private pollsters are criticizing their competition's judgment, methodology, reliability and even honesty."

The Associated Press, writing on November 8, 1980, reported simply that pollsters had failed to predict the Reagan landslide. "The Ronald Reagan steamroller not only flattened many Democratic politicians, but also dented the reputations of the nation's polls and pollsters for failing to gauge the magnitude of the Republican victory," noted AP reporter Evan Witt. "Most published polls just before last Tuesday's election said the race between Reagan and Jimmy Carter was "too close to call," but Reagan trounced the incumbent by 10 percentage points in the actual vote," the AP article continued. "While explanations of the difference vary, what is certain is no poll correctly called Reagan's margin. Some were closer than others, but none was on the mark."

On November 5, 1980, the day after the 1980 presidential election, the Associated Press quoted David Neft, executive vice president of then-renowned pollster Louis Harris and Associates, as attributing Carter's loss to low voter turnout, noting that higher voter turnout would have benefited Carter given that Democrats have traditionally benefitted from higher voter registration numbers.

On October 28, 1980, following the last debate between President Jimmy Carter and GOP challenger Ronald Reagan, ABC News set up a non-scientific survey in which viewers of the debate could call into a telephone number to vote for the winner. ABC reported that participating callers picked Reagan by more than two to one over Carter as having gained the most from the televised presidential debate.

The Associated Press, relying on overnight ratings for New York, Chicago, and Los Angeles by the A.C. Nielsen Company estimated that the Carter-Reagan debate was seen by at least 105 million Americans, and perhaps as many as 120 million. An audience of ninety million was estimated for the highest-rated of Carter's debates four years earlier with then President Gerald R. Ford.

On October 29, the Associated Press Poll noted that a proprietary AP poll yielded results from which each side could claim "victory" in the long-awaited confrontation. More Reagan supporters watched than did Carter supporters. Among viewers supporting Reagan, 46 percent said he did the better job while 34 percent said Democrat Carter did—a margin the AP reported roughly paralleled the margin between them among the 1,062 people polled both before and after the debate. "Neither man made significant inroads into the other's camp," the AP wrote. "Both held on to virtually all of their supporters who watched the debate. Viewer reaction to the debate broke along partisan lines, with those who generally agreed with Reagan thinking he did the best job while Carter scored highest with those who found him well informed and-or in agreement with their views."

The review of Reagan's performance in the last debate with Carter gave no indication that Reagan's performance was responsible for a last-minute surge that gave him the election. "There may have been no clear winner in Tuesday night's presidential debate, but the focus of the discussion was pretty much where President Carter wanted it, on the issue of war and peace and not on the economy," wrote AP writer R. Gregory Nokes in an article published October 29, 1980. "Republican candidate Ronald Reagan, who had said he wanted to focus in the closing days of the campaign on Carter's 'economic record of misery and despair,' let pass several opportunities to say how he could do better than Carter," Nokes continued. "Reagan spent much of the 90-minute debate seeking to portray himself as a man of peace to offset the warmonger image that

Carter has tried to tag him with. He wanted to come across as presidential, and he may well have succeeded," the AP article concluded. "But his attack on Carter's economic record seemed cursory and superficial."

In the final analysis, Democrats were hard pressed to defend Carter's record in 1980. Carter's four years in office were plagued by many serious setbacks, including the Iran hostage crisis, which languished into its 444th day as Election Day approached, long gas lines caused by the OPEC oil embargo, and an economy hampered by unprecedented double-digit interest rates.

What Reagan's landslide proved was that Carter's failures weighed heavily on voters who President Richard Nixon had earlier termed the "Silent Majority"—a group typically prone to be underrepresented in polls taken by mainstream media polling outlets. In 1980, the "Silent Majority"—those who Barack Obama characterized as "clinging to their guns and Bibles" and the same voter block Hillary Clinton characterized as an irredeemable "basket of deplorables"—proved decisive. Though they were not reflected in the polls, they turned out and voted for Ronald Reagan—the candidate the mainstream media had defiled throughout the 1980 election campaign—in record numbers. In 2016, the question was whether the "Silent Majority" would rise once again, this time giving Donald Trump a victory over media favorite Hillary Clinton that the polls, up until the very end, failed to predict. Like Carter, who tried to convince voters who had elected him in 1976 to turn out to reelect him in 1980,[36] the question in 2016 was whether Hillary Clinton could inspire a repeat of the massive Democratic turnout that Obama had twice succeeded in drawing to the polls. Or, would 2016 prove that the coalition assembled by Obama was unique to him, connected perhaps to his charisma, and not a coalition that cold and unlikable Clinton could count on coming out for her?

Part 1
How Donald Trump
Hijacked the Republican
Presidential Nomination

Donald Trump's Hostile Takeover of the GOP

In modern American presidential politics since the 1960s, the only route to win the Republican or Democratic Party nomination for the nation's highest office is to enter the six-month grueling complex of state primaries, caucuses, and state conventions that began in 2016 with the Iowa primary, scheduled for February 1, 2016, and ended on June 7, 2016, with primaries in South Dakota, New Mexico, New Jersey, Montana, and California.

As Theodore White explained in his original *The Making of the President 1960*, after Abraham Lincoln, the first presidential nominee of the Republican Party, won the party's nomination at a convention held in the wood-framed "Wigwam" building in Chicago. For a period of thirty-five years, from 1865 to 1900, the choice of presidential candidates was "left to the bosses in convention assembled," with the result that their selections tended to result in mediocre presidential candidates at best. In 1960, only sixteen states held presidential primaries, far different from the fifty-state primary contest common today. "These sixteen states were as diverse in their politics and sociologies as the diversity of American civilization itself; they had been chosen by no superior reason or plan," White wrote. "Altogether to the foreign eye they must have seemed the most preposterous field of battle on which men who aspire to the leadership of American freedom and control of its powers should choose to joust. Yet these states were, and remain, vital to the play of American Presidential politics."[1]

In 2016, the goal of the Republican Party presidential primaries was for a candidate to gain the party's nomination on the first ballot of the national nominating convention by winning a simple majority of delegates, 1,237, from the total of 2,472 slated to attend the Republican National Committee's national nominating convention scheduled for July 18–21, 2016, at the Quicken Loans Arena in Cleveland, Ohio. This is the home arena of the Cleveland Cavaliers basketball team led in 2016 by superstar LeBron James. Should no candidate achieve the 1,237-delegate majority required for the nomination prior to the start of the RNC national nominating convention, most delegates would be free to vote their preference, starting on the second ballot. Professional politicians warned that a deadlock could result in a "brokered convention," with the implication that the convention would revert to the type of backroom deal making and swapping of delegates that characterized old-style, smoke-filled backroom national nominating conventions that today's series of national primaries, caucuses, and state conventions was designed to prevent.

While the United States has not yet entered a perpetual presidential election cycle, where candidates declare for the office as soon as a president is selected on Election Day, the presidential cycle typically commences early in the third year of the current president's term. In 2016, the first candidate to declare for the presidency was first-term Texas Senator Ted Cruz, who announced on March 23, 2015; followed closely by first-term Kentucky Senator Rand Paul, who made his announcement on April 7, 2015; and by the first-term Florida Senator Marco Rubio, who made his announcement on April 13, 2015. Even though all three of these contenders held lowly "freshman" status in the US Senate, each felt he had cultivated a national audience that could propel him into the White House.

The next few months proved another rule in modern American presidential politics, namely, that the party not currently holding the presidency tends to generate a large field of contenders, each of whom has managed to convince themselves and their initial financial backers that they have a chance to win the White House.

- On May 4, Carly Fiorina, the former Hewlett-Packard CEO who, in 2010, lost a race for US senator from California to incumbent Democrat Barbara Boxer, declared.
- Fiorina was joined on May 4 by retired neurosurgeon Ben Carson declaring for president, hoping to capitalize on the publicity he gained at the White House 2013 National Prayer Breakfast where President Obama sat through his twenty-seven-minute critical speech that prompted a *Wall Street Journal* editorial encouraging him to run for president.[2]
- On May 5, former Arkansas Governor Mike Huckabee threw his hat in the ring, followed by former Pennsylvania Senator Rick Santorum, who declared on May 27, as well as former New York Governor George Pataki, who made his presidential announcement on May 28.
- June saw the following added to the growing field of Republican contenders: US Senator from South Carolina Lindsey Graham; former Texas Governor Rick Perry, June 4; Louisiana Governor Bobby Jindal, June 24; New Jersey Governor Chris Christie, June 30.
- But the two biggest announcements in June were former Florida Governor Jeb Bush on June 15, and billionaire New York businessman Donald J. Trump, on June 16.
- July filled out the field with announcements by Wisconsin Governor Scott Walker, Ohio Governor John Kasich, and former Virginia Governor Jim Gilmore.

The end result were seventeen Republican Party presidential candidates, including nine governors or former governors, five US senators or former US senators, one female CEO who had never held elective office, a retired neurosurgeon who had never held elective office, and Donald Trump—a true outsider who had toyed with running for president in 2000 and 2012 but had never stood as a candidate facing an election or held a political position of any kind whatsoever.

CHAPTER 1

Trump vs. the Elites

He's a total stiff, Jeb Bush. Here's a guy, honestly, if he weren't in government, you wouldn't hire him to do anything, okay? If you had a company, you wouldn't even hire him.

Donald J. Trump[1]

With Hillary as the presumptive Democratic presidential candidate, the presidential race, as 2015 came to a close, looked like it would come down to Hillary being "the first woman" to win the US presidency, or Jeb becoming "the third Bush" to occupy the White House. The last person political pundits in the mainstream media ever expected to win was Donald J. Trump, regardless how rich he might be. Far-left elites, typified by Hollywood on the West Coast and by the mainstream media on the East Coast, were confident going into the 2016 presidential election cycle that their biased version of America in the Twenty-First Century would be accepted uncritically by the rest of what the elite liked to call "Fly-Over" America.

Here Comes Jeb: "America Deserves Better"
On June 15, 2015, some seventeen months before the election, Jeb Bush—the third of the Bush dynasty to seek the presidency—bounded onto the stage of Miami Dade College's Kendall Campus, in Florida, where he had

been the state's first two-term Republican governor, looking relaxed and casual as he appeared before some 3,000 supporters in the community college gymnasium, wearing a button-down blue shirt and casual pants, while his mother clapped appreciatively in the wings just offstage.

Determined to be the first presidential candidacy in two languages, Bush proclaimed to an excited auditorium composed mostly of college kids skipping class, "Yo soy Jeb"—in English, "I am Jeb"—telegraphing his goal of featuring Hispanic outreach as the centerpiece of his campaign in a strategy that put stage center his marriage to a Mexican woman and his ability to speak Spanish fluently. The declaration in Spanish mirrored Bush's campaign logo that read simply "Jeb!"—a slogan that carefully omitted any mention of his family name. Jeb, fully aware of the problem posed by dynastic politics in an era where Americans were inclined to say "no more Bushes," as well as "no more Clintons," had chosen to run as Spanish-speaking Jeb, not Jeb Bush, the son and brother of two previous Bush family presidents.

Ironically, just as Jeb introduced his mother to the Miami crowd, a group of immigration protestors organized by the immigration advocacy group United We Dream and wearing bright yellow shirts, each with one initial that together spelled out, "LEGAL STATUS IS NOT ENOUGH" began chanting their slogan.[2] If Jeb thought he would get a pass for his appeal to Hispanics and his obvious embracing of what in previous years had been termed "comprehensive immigration reform"— a catchphrase that opponents of open borders took to mask amnesty—he was wrong. The protestors were here in force precisely because Bush had chosen to run on immigration issues and the fact that as a Republican, Jeb could never go as far as to embrace open border amnesty the way Democrats like Barack Obama and Hillary Clinton could.

Quickly shouted down by the audience chanting in return, "We want Jeb," Bush interrupted to take back control of the situation, saying in a firm voice, "By the way, just so that our friends know, the next president of the United States will pass meaningful immigration reform, so that will be solved, not by executive order." Later the group tweeted, "We protested @JebBush bc [because] he has been all over the map on #immigration. From 'act of love' to 'kindly asked to leave.'"[3]

This was a problem that both McCain in 2008 and Romney in 2012 faced competing as moderate Republicans against Obama. By seeming to agree in principle with the Democrats on many if not most policy issues, McCain and Romney lacked the policy differentiation needed to energize a GOP base that remained more conservative than the GOP establishment leadership that was entrenched comfortably in the nation's capital. Phyllis Schlafly, who endorsed Trump early in the presidential campaign, was presciently correct in her famous 1964 book, *A Choice Not an Echo*, when she argued the GOP should stop picking as presidential candidates establishment Republican politicians whose public policy positions were largely indistinguishable from those advanced by their liberal Democratic Party counterparts.[4]

Ironically, while Bush planned to feature his Hispanic appeal as a centerpiece of his presidential run, there was no reference to immigration reform included in the printed text of his announcement speech.[5] Had the protest not occurred, the subject would have gone unmentioned by Jeb in his appeal that "America Deserves Better" leadership than that provided in the eight years under Barack Obama.

Jeb ended his speech speaking Spanish. *"Júntense a nuestra causa de oportunidad para todos, a la causa de todos que aman la libertad y a la causa noble de los Estados Unidos de América."* The translation of this is: "Join our cause of opportunity for all, the cause of all who love freedom and the noble cause of the United States of America."

Covering Jeb's speech, the *New York Times* commented that Jeb's announcement in the Florida community college gym was not the dramatic headline the Bush campaign may have wanted, but yet another in a series of restarts Jeb had launched in an already failing campaign that was unable to ignite enthusiasm among GOP voters who were already facing exhaustion from the hard-to-shake syndrome of "No More Bushes." This syndrome presaged failure at the polls, regardless how much Spanish Jeb spoke at his rallies.

"After a bumpy six months in which he struggled to excite primary voters who are skeptical of his surname and of his conservative convictions, Mr. Bush turned his announcement rally here into a carefully choreographed reintroduction and a muscular attack on his rivals in both parties," wrote Michael Barbaro and Jonathan Martin, two *New York Times* reporters known for their disdain not just for Jeb, but for Republicans in general.[6]

Noting that Jeb had belittled some of his most credible Republican opponents in Washington as unseasoned managers, Barbaro and Martin commented that Bush "derisively likened the senators he faces in the primary field—among them Marco Rubio of Florida, once a protégé of Mr. Bush's—to President Obama, who campaigned for the White House after just three years in the Senate."

For the *New York Times*, Jeb's slogan "America Deserves Better" was as doomed to fail as his pledge to accomplish for America what he had accomplished for Florida. He disregarded his previous pledges to expand charter schools, to reduce the size of government, and to cut taxes by the billions—tired themes that up to now had failed to propel him to the top among the GOP faithful likely to vote in the primaries.

Trump Tower Becomes Center Stage

The next day, on Tuesday, June 16, Donald Trump used the elegant marble and gold laced lobby atrium of Trump Tower on New York City's Fifth Avenue at 57th Street, the heart of Midtown, to make his presidential announcement.

In sharp contrast to Jeb Bush's announcement, the atrium was filled with three levels of Trump supporters, as Trump's daughter Ivanka looking like a model, wearing a smartly designed white dress, introduced her father.

Donald, wearing his characteristic perfectly tailored solid-blue suit and bold red tie, stepped up on a blue dais to give his announcement from a mahogany wooden podium, with a blue background, red pinstripe trimmed sign reading "Trump—Make America Great Again," broadcast real-time to the nation on television and via live-streaming Internet by the dozens of media outlets competing for the space in front of the podium—all framed against a blue-draped background lined with a row of American flags.

"Our country is in serious trouble," Trump began.[7] "We don't have victories anymore. We used to have victories, but we don't have them. When was the last time anybody saw us beating, let's say, China in a trade deal? They kill us. I beat China all the time. All the time."

Speaking without the aid of teleprompters and not apparently reading from a printed speech, Trump continued in a style that seemed rehearsed as to themes he wanted to cover but delivered largely impromptu.

"When did we beat Japan at anything?" Trump continued. "They send their cars over by the millions, and what do we do? When was the last time you saw a Chevrolet in Tokyo? It doesn't exist, folks. They beat us all the time."

This thought triggered for Trump a comment on Mexico, another rival he wanted to position as stealing US jobs as a result of the NAFTA agreement, signed by President Bill Clinton.

"When do we beat Mexico at the border?" Trump asked. "They're laughing at us, at our stupidity. And now they are beating us economically. They are not our friend, believe me. But they're killing us economically."

This sequence led Trump to the punch line: "The U.S. has become a dumping ground for everybody else's problems."

Some twenty minutes into a passionate announcement that pounded the Obama administration for its failures in the Middle East, a rising percentage of the population dropping out of the labor force, and for Obamacare that launched with a costly but failing website, Trump hit the core message of why he should be president.

"So I've watched the politicians," he began, entering the sales close part of the speech.

"I've dealt with them all my life. If you can't make a good deal with a politician, then there's something wrong with you," he continued, building in intensity. "You're certainly not very good. And that's what we have representing us. They will never make America great again. They don't even have a chance. They're controlled fully—they're controlled fully by the lobbyists, by the donors, and by the special interests, fully."

The setup in place, Trump delivered his closing argument.

"Now, our country needs—our country needs a truly great leader, and we need a truly great leader now," Trump said with emphasis. "We need a leader that wrote *The Art of the Deal.*"

Trump positioned himself as a Washington outsider, a businessman who built his fortune by being a negotiator who could get deals done. To top it off, Trump made clear he was sufficiently wealthy to finance his own run for the presidency, even against the Democrat's Hillary Clinton who was already rumored to be raising $2 billion to finance her presidential bid.

"I'm using my own money," Trump said with the type of braggadocio that endeared him to supporters and made him the object of hatred for liberal Democrats who have won elections for decades by courting underclass votes. "I'm not using the lobbyists. I'm not using donors. I don't care. I'm really rich."

Trump continued, imagining a scenario he described as follows: "After I'm called by thirty friends of mine who contributed to different campaigns, after I'm called by all of the special interests and by the—the donors and by the lobbyists—and they have zero chance at convincing me, zero—I'll get a call the next day from the head of Ford. He'll say. 'Please reconsider, I'll say no."

Trump finished off the story, positioning himself as champion.

"He'll say, 'Mr. President, we've decided to move the plant back to the United States, and we're not going to build it in Mexico.' That's it. They have no choice. They have no choice."

Jeb Bush might bound onto the stage of a community college gymnasium, wearing a button-down shirt open at the collar speaking Spanish, but in comparison to Trump, Jeb looked rehearsed, delivering his speech as if he had memorized it, speaking Spanish as if he somehow imagined the diversity appeal would be universal.

A Boon to Late-Night Comics

Predictably the elite newspapers in New York and Washington rejected Trump universally.

"Donald J. Trump, the garrulous real estate developer whose name has adorned apartment buildings, hotels, Trump-brand neckties and Trump-brand steaks, announced on Tuesday his entry into the 2016 presidential race, brandishing his wealth and fame as chief qualifications in an improbable quest for the Republican nomination," the *New York Times* reported, commenting that Trump in his announcement speech had proclaimed that only someone "really rich"—like himself—could restore American primacy.[8]

"Mr. Trump, 69, has long toyed with running for president as a Republican, boasting of his credentials as an entrepreneur and mocking the accomplishments of prominent elected officials. He has used the platform of a reality television show, NBC's *The Apprentice*, to burnish his pop-culture image as a formidable man of affairs," wrote Times reporter Alexander Burns.

"It seems a remote prospect that Republicans, stung in 2012 by the caricature of their nominee, Mitt Romney, as a pampered and politically tone-deaf financier, would rebound by nominating a real estate magnate who has published books with titles such as, *Think Like a Billionaire* and *Midas Touch: Why Some Entrepreneurs Get Rich—And Why Most Don't*," the *New York Times* article continued.

The newspaper noted that in the 2000 and 2012 elections, Trump had "hyped up the possibility of seeking the White House before abandoning the idea," suggesting that once again, Trump might only be seeking publicity, in yet another presidential campaign where he could be expected to pull out once the serious, professional politicians took command of the race. The *New York Times* ridiculed Trump's policy positions, with Burns's writing, "Mr. Trump's policy views can be just as provocative as his demeanor. In the past, he has called climate change 'a hoax' and said he has a 'foolproof' plan to defeat the Islamic State, which he will not reveal so as not to tip off the group. On Tuesday, he vowed to build a 'great wall' on the Mexican border to keep out rapists and other criminals, who he said were sneaking into the United States in droves." As a parting shot, the *New York Times* reminded readers that Trump was a "Birther," pointing out that Trump "may be best known politically for his outspoken skepticism that President Obama was born in the United States."

The *Washington Post*, after joining the *New York Times* in commenting that Trump must imagine he could buy the White House with his enormous wealth, hit Trump on the policy issues that professional politicians rely upon to position themselves against rivals.

"The business mogul, who has never held public office, enters an extremely crowded field of Republican Presidential hopefuls, now numbering a dozen major candidates," the *Washington Post* reported.[9] "And it remains to be seen how he will distinguish himself from his rivals on policy issues, in part because he's steered clear of many policy specifics: last month, he raised eyebrows when he said he had a 'foolproof plan' to defeat the Islamic State terrorist group, but refused to reveal details because 'I don't want the enemy to know what I'm doing.'"

In a separate article, *Washington Post* reporter Ben Terris argued that Trump's claim of $9.2 billion in assets and a net worth of $8.7 billion were wildly overstated.[10] "Even the most aggressive auditors have found it challenging to assess Trump's balance sheet, in part because his assets and liabilities are intricately complex, entwined with public subsidies and opaque private partnerships," Terris wrote. "Then there's the source: Trump, who's wrestled with a reputation as a chronic exaggerator." Terris went on to challenge Trump's assertion to his supporters as he took the podium in the Trump Tower atrium that, "There have been no crowds like this," for his rival candidates—pointing out that the "thousands" Trump claimed were there were actually more like hundreds.

"In reality, members of team Trump spent the hour before the event out in the streets of midtown Manhattan trying to lure tourists in to fill out the crowd," the *Washington Post* reported. "A man in a pressed suit who would only say he 'worked for Trump' offered passersby free T-shirts and already-made signs, many handwritten, to hold if they would come in and see the show."

The day after his announcement, Trump confirmed to the Associated Press that his forty-five-minute campaign kickoff speech was not rehearsed.[11] "I did it with no notes, no teleprompter. I like going off-script a little bit," Trump said. "I meant everything I said, and I think a lot of it resonated with different groups of people."

Already Trump was facing criticism from several Mexican-American immigrant groups, as well as Mexico's interior minister Miguel Angel Osorio Chong, who called Trump's remarks "biased and absurd" because they wrongly portrayed immigrants from Mexico as "bringing drugs, they're bringing crime, they're rapists, and some, I assume, are good people." To this, Trump had added, "Nobody builds walls better than me, believe me." The AP reported Mexico's interior minister reacted sharply, saying, "Trump surely doesn't know the contributions made by migrants from practically every nation in the world who have supported the development of the United States."

When the AP asked Trump for his reaction to the *New York Daily News* article mocking his presidential announcement speech with a tabloid front cover showing Trump in a photo illustration dressed up as a clown, Trump dismissed the newspaper as having "no gravitas," boasting his 1.7 million Facebook fans dwarf any other Republican in the race for president.

Jimmy Fallon had Jeb Bush as a *Tonight Show* guest a day after the former Florida governor announced his presidential candidacy, but as the Associated Press reported, it was Trump who dominated the comic's monologue.[12] Fallon joked that he was going to have Trump on, "but the last time we checked he was still giving his speech." Fallon said Trump would be the country's first "Mad Libs" president. "I think Gary Busey wrote that speech," Fallon said. The AP also noted that the other Jimmy, ABC's Kimmel, said Trump would be like a "president and an amusement park all rolled up into one." "Here's the sad news," comic Conan O'Brien said on the cable channel TBS. "Season 15 of *Celebrity Apprentice* will not air. But not to worry. With Trump running for president, you'll still get to see an irrelevant B-list celebrity not get a job."

With Trump, the elite on both coasts were planning to have fun. The game played by the far-left reporters dominating mainstream media outlets like the *New York Times* and the *Washington Post* was a version of "gotcha." The prize went to the reporter who could pick something Trump said, even if the chosen statement were a side comment, that could be blown up into a controversy that would cost Trump days of media time to explain what he meant. The "gotcha" media player won the game if Trump had to walk back the comment and apologize. This was the whole point of getting a Mexican government official to object to Trump's portrayal of Hispanic immigrants as criminals, rapists, and drug dealers. Every time Trump could be embarrassed by one of his own comments, the mainstream media reporter responsible for blowing the minor point into a major media flap won a point of distinction among fellow mainstream media elite reporters playing the game.

In the final analysis, although elite backers of Clinton were confident she would win, the advantage of the Republicans picking another moderate like Jeb Bush as their presidential nominee was that Jeb Bush, like McCain and Romney before him, were already "Democrat-lite." Even if Jeb won, the border with Mexico would stay wide open, the millions of illegals already in the United States would be allowed to stay, and globalist free-trade would continue to advance by supplementing NAFTA with the Trans-Pacific Partnership, TPP, to be quickly followed by its trans-Atlantic counterpart, the Transatlantic Trade and Investment Partnership, or TTIP. The multi-national corporations in cooperation with the Obama administration had negotiated these multi-national free trade deals to continue the open access to cheap labor in China and the Third World. Jeb, like Obama, would not dare take an aggressive stance against radical Islam, for fear that his position on Islam would detract from the benefits of his embrace of the left's push for multi-cultural diversity that his focus on Hispanics implied. The simple point was, the Clintons, the elite media in Hollywood and on the East Coast, and their wealthy backers in Silicon Valley and Wall Street, while confident they could beat Jeb, were also comfortable with Jeb in the White House should he win.

Neither the Clintons nor their elite backers ever anticipated Trump's candidacy would be serious. Their expectation was Trump would pull out of the race once he had achieved sufficient publicity to boost his business interests in building exclusive resorts and managing high visibility properties. Portraying Trump as a clown and ridiculing his campaign provided the elite with a method of demeaning the GOP in their effort to portray the GOP's conservative base as dangerous gun- and bible-toting radicals, who hated immigrants, hated the LBGT community, and hated

Islam. This strategy was designed to push Jeb to embrace more political positions indistinguishable from Hillary's agenda, while marginalizing Trump supporters as far-right zealots embracing an agenda as dangerous to America's future as that embraced by "climate deniers." With President Obama proclaiming that climate deniers were more dangerous to the advancement of civilization than radical Islamic terrorists,[13] the argument against Trump supporters was sealed. In the final analysis, the elite was resolved not just to defeat, but hopefully to destroy any GOP presidential candidate who refused to endorse the left's plan to impose an international tax on the use of carbon fuels. This strategy was designed to redistribute wealth from the United States as part of an essentially anti-American creeping socialism the bi-coastal elite increasingly embraced.

Trump's Controversial Summer of 2015

The summer of 2015 for Trump was a summer of one controversy after another.

On Saturday, July 19, 2015, during a panel hosted by poll analyst Frank Luntz at the Family Leadership Summit in Ames, Iowa, Trump seized the opportunity to increase his attacks on John McCain, with whom he had been sparring over the issue of immigration. "He's not a war hero," Trump insisted, much to Luntz's surprise given that McCain has built much of his political career on his established record as a decorated Vietnam-era Navy pilot and POW. "He's not a war hero because he was captured," Trump said, responding to Luntz's incredulity. "I like people that weren't captured, okay?"[14] Then, appearing on ABC News the next day, Trump refused to apologize. "People that fought hard and weren't captured and went through a lot, they get no credit. Nobody even talks about them. They're all forgotten. And I think that's a shame, if you want to know the truth," Trump told ABC News.[15]

On July 21, in a television appearance with Bill O'Reilly, Trump half-apologized to McCain. "I used to like him a lot. I supported him. I raised a lot of money for his campaign against President Obama, and certainly, if there was a misunderstanding, I would totally take that back," he said. "But hopefully, I said it correctly and certainly, shortly thereafter, I said it correctly," Trump told O'Reilly. But then Trump immediately pivoted to immigration. "I would like him [McCain], however, to do something with the 15,000 people that were in Phoenix about illegal, you know, immigration," Trump said. "They are being decimated. These people are being decimated, and I would love to see him do a much better job taking care of the veterans, Bill."[16]

Then on Thursday, July 23, 2015, Trump toured the Texas-Mexico border to make the point that he was not campaigning against Hispanics. "I employ thousands and thousands of Hispanics," he told a press conference in Laredo, a Texas city with a 95.6 percent Hispanic population. "I love the people. They're great workers. They're fantastic people and they want legal immigration." The local border patrol union in Laredo that invited Trump had to back off after the National Border Patrol Council made clear it does not endorse candidates for any political office. "They're petrified [the local border patrol union] and afraid of saying what's happening," Trump said. "They have a real problem here . . . they invited me and then all of a sudden they were told 'silencio.'"

Despite the controversies, Trump insisted he would win the Republican nomination. He boldly attacked Hillary Clinton, the Democratic contender who at that time enjoyed the highest approval ratings of any candidate in either party. "Easily, she's the worst Secretary of State in the history of our country." Trump said, "She's going to be beaten and I'm the one to beat her."[17]

Trump's behavior was proving to be a problem for the Republican National Committee. Earlier in July, RNC Chairman Reince Priebus urged Trump in a private phone call to tone down his inflammatory statements on Hispanics and immigration. Following Trump's attack on McCain, the RNC released a public statement that criticized Trump for attacking McCain's record during the Vietnam War. "There is no place in our party or our country for comments that disparage those who have served honorably," an RNC spokesperson said.[18] Trump struck back in an interview published by the Hill while Trump was heading to Laredo.[19] In that interview, Trump suggested the RNC liked him a lot better when he was writing checks. "The RNC has not been supportive. They were always supportive when I was a contributor. I was their fair-haired boy," Trump said. "The RNC has been, I think, very foolish." In the interview, Trump refused to discount the possibility that he might choose to run as a third-party candidate. *The Christian Science Monitor* noted that running as an independent might be counterproductive to both Trump and the RNC, arguing that Trump as a third-party candidate would take votes from Jeb Bush that ultimately could be enough to assure Hillary Clinton victory. *Christian Science Monitor* staff writer Sarah Caspari compared it to the 1992 presidential election, when billionaire Ross Perot ran as an independent, taking 19 percent of the vote, thereby clearing the path for Arkansas Governor Bill Clinton to win the White House.[20]

The controversy over Trump potentially running as a third-party candidate can be traced back to an article Michael Barbaro co-authored with veteran reporters Maggie Haberman and Jonathan Martin in the *New York Times* on July 9, 2015, entitled "Can't Fire Him: Republican Party Frets Over What to Do With Donald Trump."[21] While Haberman had distinguished herself with several hard-hitting articles probing financial irregularities in the Clinton Foundation, Barbaro took pride in the "gotcha" game, as noted in the 2012 presidential campaign when Barbaro, riding as traveling press on Romney's campaign plane, played a game with fellow leftist reporters competing to see which Barbaro "gotcha" column in that campaign had caused Romney the most trouble. In the article, the *New York Times* reporters described a regular gathering of top Republican elected officials, strategists, and Reince Priebus at the Hay-Adams Hotel opposite from the White House during which they debated how best to handle Trump. The worry, as reported by the Times, was that Trump would mar the upcoming GOP presidential debates with needless provocations. While some put forth strategies to reign in Trump, others counseled a hands-off approach, fearing that any such attempts would turn Trump into a political martyr, or worse, cause him to launch a third-party run.

"Mr. Trump's language about Mexicans highlighted two of the most divisive issues within the Republican coalition—race and immigration," the *New York Times* article noted. "It was Mr. Priebus who led a bracing review of the party's 2012 losses, resulting in dire warnings about its need to improve its standing with Hispanics. But Mr. Trump's support is expected to draw heavily from those disaffected white voters who lined up behind Mitt Romney in 2012—and whom Republicans acknowledge they will need again to recapture the White House in 2016." The concern among these top Republican strategists involved losing the votes of moderate Republican voters who typically agreed with the GOP leadership in Washington, supporting Democrats on issues like free-trade agreements. "But Mr. Trump also risks alienating from Republicans a crucial bloc of swing voters who lean right on economics but disdain any hint of scapegoating minorities—not to mention a cross-section of minority voters who are offended by his message," Barbaro and his colleagues at the Times wrote in conclusion.

Then there was the controversy over Russian President Vladimir V. Putin.

On July 23, 2015, the *Guardian* in London reported that Putin's approval ratings were at record high levels, with 9 out 10 Russians approving of their president in a poll that highlighted support for Putin's strategy of invading Crimea and Ukraine.[22] On July 30, 2015, while he was attending the British Open, Trump said at a press conference that he would have no problem working with Putin. "I think I would get along very well with Vladimir Putin. I just think so. People say, 'What do you mean?' I think I would get along well with him," Trump, wearing a red "Make America Great Again" cap, told a reporter. "He [Putin] hates Obama, Obama hates him. We have unbelievably bad relationships. Hillary Clinton was Secretary of State. She was the worst Secretary of State in the history of our country. The world blew apart during her reign. Now she wants to be president."[23]

Throughout 2015 and 2016, the *New York Times* fanned the flames, building Trump's initial controversial remarks into a theory Trump and Putin were working behind the scenes in a secret conspiracy to defeat Hillary Clinton.

In a press conference held a year later, in Doral, Florida, on July 27, 2016, Trump said he hoped the Russian intelligence services would release Hillary Clinton's emails that the Democrats were claiming the Russians had hacked from Hillary Clinton's private email server while she was Secretary of State. "Russia, if you're listening, I hope you're able to find the 30,000 emails that are missing," Mr. Trump said in an apparent reference to Mrs. Clinton's deleted emails. "I think you will probably be rewarded mightily by our press." The *New York Times* article reporting on the Doral press conference led with the following paragraph: "Donald J. Trump on Wednesday said he hoped Russian intelligence services had successfully hacked Hillary Clinton's email, and encouraged them to publish whatever they may have stolen, essentially urging a foreign adversary to conduct cyber-espionage against a former Secretary of State."[24]

This theme developed into a "meme," or narrative, Hillary supporters used throughout the campaign to attack Trump by claiming Trump was working in coordination with Russia to the detriment of US national security interests. At the end of the campaign, the Democratic meme morphed into the narrative pushed by far-left supporters of Hillary Clinton that Trump won because Russia supplied "fake news" churned by "alt-right" reporters, including Matt Drudge of the Drudge Report, Alex Jones of Infowars.com, a staff of reporters at Breitbart.com and WND.com with campaign coverage led by Jerome Corsi. Milo Yianoppolous of Breitbart captured the imagination of millions of millennial voters drawn to his outrageous assault, confronting the far-left as an unabashed conservative homosexual who continued to beat the mainstream media to the punch with big scoops and provocative content. Trump's message, each time I appeared on Alex Jones, reached more people than it ever did on Fox News prime time, because Jones' online army turns in a monstrous following.

The 2016 presidential campaign was the first to be fought and won on the Internet. Donald Trump mastered the art of dominating the news cycle simply by posting a Tweet that was so outrageously compelling that it went viral the moment it was posted. The journalists at Drudge, Alex Jones, Breitbart and WND plus radio talk-show hosts Rush Limbaugh and Michael Savage with their enormously large and loyal national radio audiences, plus Sean Hannity almost alone on Fox News for his unwavering support of Trump, were the backbone of the alternative media support Trump received from the beginning of his campaign. Trump voters in Middle America in 2016 turned off MSNBC and CNN—some even turning off Fox News itself—as most established radio and television news personalities persisted in questioning Trump, if not outright ridiculing his candidacy.

While many other conservative websites and reporters contributed, Drudge led the charge, posting a top center headline and photograph on June 16, 2015, the day Trump declared his candidacy, proclaiming "Donald Goes for White House." Increasingly as the campaign progressed, the real action was not in the traditional mainstream media or in the polls, both of which were badly biased in favor of Clinton. In the aftermath of Trump's victory, the widely read economics blog ZeroHedge.com posted an article headlined, "How Matt Drudge Won the 2016 Election." The article noted that the news aggregation site Drudge.com spent much of the 18 months leading to the general election highlighting polls and stories that predicted a Trump win. "In an election cycle when just about everyone got it wrong, Matt Drudge ended up vindicated," the ZeroHedge.com article noted. "The editor of the massive, conservative news aggregation site spent much of the last 18 months leading with those rare polls and stories that predicted a Trump victory—meanwhile the Huffington Post, sometimes called Drudge's liberal mirror, gave Hillary Clinton a 90-something percent chance of winning just hours before the polls started closing."[25]

A much more accurate measure of how completely Trump was resonating with what Richard Nixon called "the Silent Majority" was the strong support Trump received on social media websites like Twitter and Facebook. In all of 2016, Trump dominated the non-scientific immediate online polls, with thousands scoring him the victor. To counter this populist support, the Clinton campaign, like the Obama campaign in 2008 and 2012, hired surrogates, commonly called "trolls" or "bots," as in "robots," to post disinformation deemed favorable to Hillary to complicate Internet threads on social media websites trending favorable to Trump. But even later, when scientifically conducted polls produced contrary results, showing Trump had actually lost a particular debate, it didn't matter. What mattered was the hundreds of thousands of Trump supporters self-motivated to go on-line the minute the debate ended to register their vote that Trump had won. Hillary, even after her paid trolls got involved, never received or deserved that type of online voter action.

What Clinton supporters in the mainstream media failed to understand was that in creating controversy, Trump was following a basic principle known to professional political operatives and campaign advisors—namely, dominate the media, even if what the media is saying about you is negative. Clearly, Trump's controversial statements about Mexico, McCain, and Putin hurt him among the bi-coastal elite appalled, for example, that Trump dare speak negatively about illegal immigrants, aliens among us that the elite preferred to call "non-documented guest workers." Unlike McCain, who lost to Obama in 2008 after reprimanding radio hosts for daring to mention that Barack Obama's middle name was Hussein, for fear of insulting Muslims, Trump shot from the hip. While Obama had imposed sanctions on Russia in an attempt to get Russia to pull out of Ukraine, Trump praised Putin's ability to direct an aggressive, but successful military strategy—something President Obama and Secretary of State Hillary Clinton had failed to do in the Middle East.

The point is that during the summer of 2015, every cable news station and every nighttime network news program broadcast by NBC, ABC, and CBS was preoccupied with stories discussing Trump. It was possible in July 2015 to flip channels and find every news station on cable or satellite television discussing Trump at the same time. Granted, most of the coverage, even on Fox News, was negative—in the case of Fox News because the network appeared to have imposed a bias in favor of GOP establishment candidates, like Jeb Bush, who were supported by Republican leaders in New York and Washington. What seemed clear in the summer of 2015 was that the bi-coastal mainstream media heavily favored Hillary to win, even to the point of suppressing bad news that might negatively impact Hillary's candidacy, while promoting any news that might cause Trump trouble. But the point, which should have been obvious to all experienced political operatives, was that Trump had managed to dominate all news coverage of the 2016 presidential campaign. Whether the audience loved or hated Trump, the only thing the American public wanted to talk about during the summer of 2015 was Trump. The news dominance Trump was commanding was rivaled in modern times only by the sensation Barack Obama caused when he first came on the national presidential scene in 2008.

How Alex Jones Got Donald Trump's Ear

Alex Jones and his Infowars' umbrella of radio shows, YouTube and Facebook broadcasts, Internet website and tweets turned out to be Trump's secret weapon. Millions follow the enormously popular, gravel-voiced Jones, the genius behind the Infowars brand. And, as I came to realize early on, they were all potential Trump voters.

Yes, I know that Jones has his critics in the Mainstream Media, but I love the guy! His fiery words have struck a chord in the nation and he speaks for millions. In fact, more people follow Alex than watch Fox News or CNN.

On November 17, 2016, nine days after Election Day, the *Washington Post* paid tribute to the impact Alex Jones had on the election, writing as follows: ". . . Genesis Communications Network syndicates the Alex Jones program to 129 radio stations, many of them in small markets. It's difficult to confirm Jones's audience size, but the host has said he has 5 million daily radio listeners and recently topped 80 million video views in a single month. He claims to have a bigger audience than Rush Limbaugh."[26] As the *Washington Post* article pointed out, Jones is able to multiply his audience by simulcasting his radio programming via his website and further spreading its reach on his YouTube channel. The costs are minuscule in comparison to running, say, a cable television network, and it's conceivable he could be generating millions in profits.

I first met Alex in Dallas when I was promoting my book, *The Man Who Killed Kennedy*.[27] We reconnected a few years later and really hit it off. Alex is fearless and a real showman. He likes a drink, a good cigar, bawdy stories, and hunting and fishing. He's a man's man. I quickly came to realize he could be a tremendous help for Trump. Despite Alex

Jones' enormous appeal, not one candidate was pushing for his support as the primaries drew closer—not Marco Rubio, not Ted Cruz, not Ben Carson, not Jeb Bush. No one! It was just mind-boggling how candidates chose to turn their backs on such a pool of potential voters as those millions of Americans who listen to or watch Alex Jones every day.

Alex didn't need any convincing that Trump was the right man for the White House, but I badly wanted to get Trump on his show. As far as I was concerned, a direct appeal by Trump to Alex's fanatical followers was the way to go. The *Washington Post* story published after the election picked up on this point. "I particularly liked the idea of Trump appearing on the Jones shows, because 'they are reaching the Trump constituencies,' Stone says. 'They are reaching the people who knock on the doors.'" The *Washington Post* noted that Trump caught onto the idea immediately. "Trump, according to Stone, wasn't difficult to persuade," the *Washington Post* reported. "The president-elect is 'an inveterate watcher of television. He has watched Infowars,' Stone says. 'They hit it off.'"[28]

Trump went on the Alex Jones show the morning of December 2, 2015 and it could not have gone any better. "Your reputation is amazing," Trump told the radio show host. "I will not let you down." And then Alex said the words we all wanted to hear: ". . . my audience, 90 percent of them, they support you." Trump took a not-so-veiled swipe at Obama and Clinton during the interview saying: "If you have to suffer through four more or eight more years of what's gone on in the past—we're being eaten away," he said. "It's just eating away at our country, and in my opinion, we can make America greater than ever before, but we have to get going."

The next day Trump said, "Well Roger's a good guy and he is a patriot." "He's a tough cookie, I will tell you that. But people like him. But he's been so loyal and so helpful," And after the interview, there was no stopping Alex. The *Washington Post* story noted: "As the campaign progressed, Jones became more and more of a presence. He marketed 'Hillary for Prison' T-shirts, and they became wildly popular. Stone recalls Trump remarking to him that he liked seeing so many of the shirts in the audience at his rallies."[29]

I knew it all had to be driving Hillary absolutely crazy and we were hoping she would finally explode. And she finally did explode, at a campaign rally in Reno Nevada, on in August 25, 2016, by lashing out at Trump—and Alex. "This is what happens when you treat the National Enquirer like gospel," Clinton said, berating Alex Jones for broadcasting concerns about her health. "They said in October I'd be dead in six months. It's what happens when you listen to the radio host Alex Jones, who claims that 9/11 and the Oklahoma City bombings were inside jobs. He even said—and this really just is so disgusting—he even said the victims of the Sandy Hook massacre were child actors, and no one was actually killed there. I don't know what happens in somebody's mind or how dark their heart must be to say things like that. But Trump doesn't challenge these lies. He actually went on Jones' show and said, "Your reputation is amazing. I will not let you down."[30]

All that did was push Alex's loyal fans even more into Trump's camp. We couldn't have written a better script than that. She just wasn't smart enough to realize it. And then she did it again. In mid-October, she released a video produced to attack Trump for his ties to Jones. "The spot puts together a clip of Trump appearing on Jones's show, hosted by his website Infowars, saying, 'I will not let you down. You will be very, very impressed, I hope, and I think we'll be speaking a lot,'" the Hill reported on October 16, 2016, describing Hillary's video. "It's followed by a series of clips of Jones saying that the 2012 Sandy Hook massacre was a hoax, 9/11 was an inside job and that Clinton is a 'freaking demon' who smells like sulfur. 'And I'll tell you, it is surreal to talk about issues here on air and then word for word hear Trump say it two days later,' Jones adds."[31]

Alex even got under Barack Obama's skin to the point where the president also ended up attacking him. "I was reading the other day there is a guy on the radio who apparently—Trump's on his show frequently—he said me and Hillary are demons," President Obama explained to a laughing crowd at a rally for Hillary in October 2016. "Said we smelled like sulfur. Ain't that something?" He then lifted his hand, took a sniff, and broke into a broad grin. "Now, I mean, come on people!"[32]

After Trump won the election, one of the first calls he made was to Alex to thank him for his support. "He was just thanking me for fighting so hard for Americans, and for Americanism, and thanking my listeners and supporters and to let me know that he was working really hard around the clock," Alex said. I sum it up this way: Elitists may laugh at Alex Jones' politics. But Alex Jones is reaching millions of people and they are the foot soldiers in the Trump revolution.[33]

CHAPTER 2

Round One: GOP Candidates Debate

@realDonaldTrump The biggest loser in the debate was @megynkelly.
You can't out trump Donald Trump. You will lose!
Donald J. Trump, posted on Twitter, August 7, 2015[1]

On August 6, 2015, Donald Trump surprisingly led a fractured GOP primary field of contenders in the polls. The latest CBS poll showed Trump at 24 percent leading Jeb Bush, who was at 13 percent, followed by Scott Walker at 10 percent.[2] "Trump leads among a wide array of Republican primary voters," CBS News noted, going into the first debate. "He appears to have tapped into public anger toward Washington: he holds a large lead among Republican primary voters who say they are angry. And 79 percent think Trump says what he believes, rather than what people want to hear, far higher than the other candidates tested."

CBS News commented that while Trump had the support of a quarter of likely Republican primary voters, he also headed the list at 27 percent as the candidate with whom likely Republican voters would be most dissatisfied. After Bush and Walker, the rest of the field had minimal support. Huckabee at 8 percent, Ben Carson at 6 percent, Ted Cruz at 6 percent, Marco Rubio at 6 percent, followed by Rand Paul at 4 percent

and Chris Christie at 3 percent filled out the GOP list of main contenders, with all the rest polling at less than 3 percent support.

August 6, 2015: The First GOP Presidential Debate

Fox News, the host of the first GOP presidential debate, divided the field
into two tiers, with the lower tier of candidates granted a separate debate
scheduled to precede the main event—what was billed as a heavy-weight
match between the top ten GOP presidential contenders.

When the main event began at 9:00 pm ET, Fox News host Megyn
Kelly, flanked on her right by Chris Wallace and on her left by Bret Baier
announced, "The moment of truth has arrived." Here, in the Quicken
Arena in Cleveland, Ohio, where a year later, in July 2016, the GOP was
slated to select the finalist from among these 10 candidates to be the
party's nominee, fated most likely to face the Democrat's "presumptive
nominee" Hillary Clinton in the general election to be decided on Election Day, on Tuesday, November 8, 2016.

As the debate broadcast began, the camera panned to show the 10 candidates standing on stage behind podiums, positioned by how they stood in
the polls. Donald Trump, standing stage center, was introduced first as the
leader in the polls. Trump was flanked on his left by Jeb Bush and on his
right by Scott Walker. Next to Jeb, in descending order of poll importance,
were Mike Huckabee, Ted Cruz, Rand Paul, and John Kasich. Next to Scott
Walker, in descending order, were Ben Carson, Marco Rubio, and Chris
Christie. The crowded field meant each candidate needed to compete with
the others for time, with the possibility remaining that a candidate could
stand at their podium for minutes on end with no opportunity to speak.

What the history of modern presidential debates proved, ever since
the first televised debates between Nixon and Kennedy in 1960, was that
one or two moments could grab the attention of the American people,
with the outcome of the debate turning as much on who looked best on
camera, as on any sentence quip uttered by one of the candidates that
proved the most memorable of the evening. The stage set was dominated
by red, white, and blue backgrounds with "Fox News" banners prominent behind the candidates. As they were introduced, Donald Trump got
the loudest ovation from the crowd, rivaled only by Ohio's own Governor Kasich, who got a standing ovation.[3]

Bret Baier kicked the debate off by asking the candidates if there
was anyone among them unwilling to pledge their support to the even-

tual nominee of the Republican Party, confirming that they would not launch a third-party challenge against that person. Baier asked the candidates to raise their hand if the candidate could not make this pledge. Only Trump raised his hand. That was it—in the first minute of the broadcast, the GOP's first presidential debate had its moment certain to be remembered by historians as a turning point. Trump's raised hand was greeted by a loud chorus of "boos" hurled by the audience in response. In what looked like a sequence Fox News had planned, guessing the likely result, Baier immediately followed up, saying to Trump, "Mr. Trump to be clear, you're standing on a Republican primary debate stage." Trump calmly responded, "I understand."

Baier continued, "The place where the RNC will give the nominee the nod." Trump again responded calmly, "I fully understand."

Baier pressed ahead, "And that experts say an independent run would almost certainly hand the race over to Democrats and likely another Clinton. You can't say tonight that you can make that pledge?"

Trump answered, "I cannot say." This was the nightmare scenario. Trump had just affirmed to a nationwide audience that he was not ruling out a third party challenge if he should fail to win the GOP presidential nomination a year hence in this very auditorium where King James LeBron ruled the Cleveland Cavaliers' basketball court.

"I have to respect the person that, if it's not me, the person that wins; if I do win, and I'm leading by quite a bit, that's what I want to do," Trump continued, explaining himself.

"I can totally make that pledge," Trump continued. "If I'm the nominee, I will pledge I will not run as an independent. But—and I am discussing it with everybody, but I'm, you know, talking about a lot of leverage. We want to win, and we will win. But I want to win as the Republican. I want to run as the Republican nominee."

This sequence, taking up the first 5 minutes and 8 seconds of the debate, was certain to be the lead paragraph in all mainstream media reports covering the debate. The audience was shocked. Trump effectively just told the GOP he was happy to be a Republican, just as long as he won the GOP presidential nomination. By so declaring, Trump put the other nine candidates sharing the stage on notice that he was not necessarily one of them.

Rand Paul jumped in, insisting, "Hey, look, look! He's already hedging his bet on the Clintons, OK? So if he doesn't run as a Republican, maybe he supports Clinton, or maybe he runs as an independent . . . but I'd say that he's already hedging his bets because he's used to buying politicians."

Trump retorted, "Well, I've given him plenty of money," meaning he had contributed to Rand Paul's campaigns previously.

Baier persisted, asking Trump one more time, just to be clear, whether he was ready to make the pledge right now.

Trump responded, "I will not make the pledge at this time." The finality of Trump's answer drew a round of applause from the audience in the arena that was quickly shouted out by another chorus of "boos."

Several of the other candidates scored points, but none rose to the level of drama Trump created in the first few minutes, when most of the people watching were still paying attention.

Baier asked Bush how he was planning to run on his own performance, not the life experience of his father or his brother. "There are several opponents on this stage who get big-applause lines in early voting states with this line: quote, 'The last thing the country needs is another Bush in the Oval Office. So you understand the real concern in this country about dynastic politics.'"

Bush answered the question directly. "I've got a record in Florida. I'm proud of my dad, and I'm certainly proud of my brother. In Florida, they called me Jeb, because I earned it," he answered, again deflecting the importance of his last name.

"I am my own man," Bush continued. "I governed as a conservative, and I govern effectively. And the net effect was, during my eight years, 1.3 million jobs were created. We left the state better off because I applied conservative principles in a purple state the right way, and people rose up."

But the night was dominated by Trump.

He sparred with Megyn Kelly when she asked, "Mr. Trump, one of the things people love about you is you speak your mind and you don't use a politician's filter. However, that is not without its downsides, in particular, when it comes to women. You've called women you don't like "fat pigs, dogs, slobs, and disgusting animals."

Trump drew laughs from the arena audience when he quipped back, "Only Rosie O'Donnell."

Kelly persisted. "Your Twitter account has several disparaging comments about women's looks," she continued. "You once told a contestant on Celebrity Apprentice it would be a pretty picture to see her on her knees. Does that sound to you like the temperament of a man we should elect as president, and how will you answer the charge from Hillary Clinton, who is likely to be the Democratic nominee, that you are part of the war on women?"

This gave Trump a chance to make a point that was to become a winning trademark of his campaign. "I think the big problem this country has is being politically correct." The arena audience applauded strongly.

"I've been challenged by so many people, and I don't frankly have time for total political correctness," Trump continued when the applause subsided. "And to be honest with you, this country doesn't have time either. This country is in big trouble. We don't win anymore. We lose to China. We lose to Mexico both in trade and at the border. We lose to everybody."

Then Trump turned on Kelly, displaying once again a Trump trademark characteristic, namely, that when attacked, he will counter-attack. "And frankly, what I say, and oftentimes it's fun, it's kidding. We have a good time. What I say is what I say," he said. "And honestly Megyn, if you don't like it, I'm sorry. I've been very nice to you, although I could probably maybe not be, based on the way you have treated me. But I wouldn't do that." Again, the audience applauded, mixed in with some disapproving "ooohs" in response. "But you know what, we—we need strength, we need energy, we need quickness and we need brains in this country to turn it around," Trump continued, finishing his answer. "That, I can tell you right now."

The main result of the first debate were renewed controversies, again focused on Trump, first over his refusal to take the pledge, and second over his answer to Megyn Kelly.

In an interview with CNN radio host Don Lemon the evening after the first debate, Trump ramped up his attack on Kelly.[4] "I don't have a lot of respect for Megyn Kelly," Trump said. "She's a lightweight. She came out there reading her little script and trying to be tough and be sharp. And when you meet her, you realize she's not very tough and she's not very smart. I just don't respect her as a journalist. I think she's highly over-rated." A few minutes later into the interview, Trump added, "You could see there was blood coming out of her eyes. Blood coming out of her wherever."

The outrage against Trump's remarks included moderate Republicans, including former CNN commentator Eric Erickson, the creator of

RedState.com, who disinvited Trump from speaking at a special tailgate at the College Football Hall of Fame in Atlanta at the conclusion of the upcoming RedState Gathering.[5] "I have rescinded my invitation to Mr. Trump," Erickson tweeted. "While I have tried to give him great latitude, his remark about Megyn Kelly was a bridge too far," Erickson said, adding later that he felt Trump's remark violated decency by implying he received hostile questioning because the television moderator was menstruating. Trump attempted to withdraw the remark by tweeting that at the time he was simply reacting to being attacked, without thinking about the implication of his response.

Still, Trump continued to dominate the media. Politico has reported that in a 50-day stretch, from July 9 to August 27, 2015, Trump got by far most of the airtime, with Trump enjoying a 45 percent share of television mentions compared with all other candidates, followed by Clinton in second place, registering only a 17 percent share of all television mentions in the same period of time.[6] Even as he fell behind in the polls, however, Jeb Bush maintained the GOP fundraising advantage, raising $103 million through his super PAC, Right to Rise USA, by midyear, only to be among the "also ran" on the Quicken Arena stage of the first GOP debate in Cleveland, an event out of which Trump commanded the headlines.

Defeating The Establishment and Launching the Alternative Media

One of the most important times during Donald J. Trump's successful candidacy for president were the days leading up to and following the first GOP presidential debate.

For millions of Americans, it was their first opportunity to see him outside a favorable and controlled setting, at campaign events where he was always surrounded by throngs of dedicated supporters. The debates were an altogether different venue—one in which Trump would stand— perhaps the first of equals, given his lead in the GOP polls—but still just one among many candidates, all of whom (except Ben Carson) were distinguished from Trump by being professional politicians. Who would be bold enough to challenge Trump? Would the debate questions be stacked against him? Will he crash and burn?

As I have said since the close of the first debate, that night at the Quicken Arena in Cleveland showed us Trump's ability to engage people with broad-sweeping, big-picture issues. He was not caught up in the calculated minutia of Washington insiders. Instead, Trump made the wise calculation of employing the KISS Principle ("Keep It Simple, Stupid), a design principle coined by a lead US Navy engineer in the 60s.

Trump's immigration solution was simple—build the wall. His economic plan was equally simple—bring back the jobs, stop political giveaways, and reform the tax code. I could continue, but I'm sure you get the picture. The so-called "smartest people in the room"—notably the talking-head political pundits featured over-and-over again on 24-hour cable news analysis shows—are still struggling with why Trump's simplicity translated into electoral success. But when it comes to the run-of-the-mill television "political strategist," there's no cure for stupid. The mainstream media and Trump's opponents wrongly assumed that Trump's lack of specifics would be his Achilles Heel. At last, all the naysayers predicting Trump's demise had the silver bullet—or so they thought—that was sure to bring Trump down. But not so fast. Looking to the past, dating back to my former boss and mentor Richard Nixon, there have been a select few men and women in American politics who have understood how to truly communicate to the American people: Ronald Reagan, Barry Goldwater, Richard Nixon, Nancy Reagan, John F. Kennedy, Donald J. Trump.

This first debate also gave us a preview into how Trump would match his bold and simple platform with a combative flair when challenged by moderators and other debate participants.

Just when Trump had successfully kept his eye on the prize by stressing repeatedly his theme "Make America Great Again" for the most important first part of the first GOP primary debate—when the television audience was certain to be the largest—this sidebar food fight with the moderator was an unnecessary distraction. Megyn Kelly wasn't asking questions about getting Americans back to work or protecting us from ISIS, and Trump fell for the bait.

Though the non-scientific online polls after this first debate gave Donald a sense of comfort in claiming a debate victory, I was worried about him straying away from his Reagan-like promise to rebuild America with continued anger over the spat with Megyn Kelly. This lead to a clash between me (at the time still the senior advisor to the campaign), and the "Yes Men" embedded in the campaign looking to brown-nose their way up the ranks.

In a difficult decision, I left the campaign and hoped to help Donald Trump, my friend and client of over 40 years, from the outside, looking in. I told myself, 'Forget internal squabbles for power. America is at stake.'

In the long run, my decision to leave the Trump campaign in any formal capacity ended up being the best decision, both for Mr. Trump and for me. I do not regret the public "breakup" we had to endure, manufactured in large part by feckless Corey Lewandowski and the limp minds of the mainstream media. Lewandowski was eventually canned after his self-aggrandizing "sourced" reports to journalists—all designed to pat himself on the back—finally reached an intolerable high. Lewandowski simply has no shame. Even after being fired, he hung around in the shadows, so desperate to be back in the spotlight that he even signed on as a "commentator" with CNN—the network we have called the "Clinton News Network" since the 1990s because of the obvious bias.

After 11 more debates, and as the GOP field became smaller and smaller, Donald Trump would continue to deliver attention-grabbing debate performances. After the first debate, Trump found his feet in terms of keeping a much better balance between snapping back at his detractors and remaining focused on his core message. In the end, Trump kept his goals on course and the main goal was to ignite a revolution. Thankfully, there was not another Megyn Kelly situation and I tried as much as I could to encourage and support Donald during our limited opportunities for communication after I left my formal position with the campaign.

My job changed to providing counsel as a friend, remaining to fight out the war in the trenches, as Trump masterfully guided his campaign to victory. Trump learned how to fight back against incursions from Ted Cruz, Jeb Bush, Marco Rubio, and John Kasich by defining them relentlessly to GOP primary voters. "Lyin' Ted" Cruz—"Low Energy" Jeb—"Little Marco, the "Choke Artist"—these tags became household humor throughout the country as the GOP debates and primaries unfolded. Yet, Trump's rivals dropped one-by-one, the elite Republican leadership establishment in New York and DC refused to believe that Donald Trump's bold campaign would survive a challenge with Hillary.

At varying points, the insider class and political pukes turned to Jeb Bush, and when he failed, to Marco Rubio, and finally to Ted Cruz and John Kasich. Could no Republican insider stop Trump? Each one failed to weather the barrage from Trump, a master promoter whose quick-fire use of social media bypassed the mainstream press. Jealous loser and #NeverTrump poster child Mitt "Mittens" Romney bought television time to launch diatribes against Trump. Thankfully, voters could not have cared less what Jeb Bush or Mitt Romney had to say about Trump.

Romney was a proven loser and Bush was just another Bush. The conservative base of GOP voters were bored, wishing only that Jeb Bush and Mitt Romney would go away, once and for all.

Enter the alternative media, who recognized the weakness and irrelevance of the establishment talking-heads and their blind determination to peddle "anyone but Trump." Alex Jones, who had risen from an obscure presence in Dallas talk radio to a leading member of the alternative media over the past decade, became a leading face behind the alternative media's hostile takeover. Even Fox News, with its bevy of partisan Democratic shills led by Juan Williams and Geraldo Rivera, felt threatened.

I was a frequent guest on his InfoWars broadcasts after the mainstream media networks banned me based on propaganda being pushed by Media Matters, a hack attack dog run by a David Brock, who entered political commentary flamboyantly proclaiming himself to be a Clinton-hating homosexual until he switched teams to become a still flamboyant equally self-proclaimed Clinton-loving homosexual operative. Put simply, David Brock, who founded and still runs Media Matters, is a traitorous conservative who once criticized the corruption of the Clintons. Eventually though, he sold his soul to the devil and supported them with fervor that would make Joseph Goebbels blush. I'm not finished with David Brock—but more about him later.

The various moves to silence or suppress my presence on both mainstream and social media as a no-holds-barred Trump supporter coalesced in herd-like fashion. The sheer volume of Soros-sponsored attacks on me utilizing bots on Twitter almost became comical. The president of Media Matters would actually brag to the undercover camera of Project Veritas that "Stone was an MVP and we successfully sidelined him."

CNN's decision to "ban" me based on alleged racially-insensitive tweets regarding the idiocy and lack of qualifications of Bush-lackey Ana Navarro, and the cluelessness of former CNN talking head Roland Martin was largely an excuse to keep me off the air lest I talk about Bill Clinton's past as a sexual predator, a theme CNN was determined to suppress. MSNBC quickly followed suit which was relatively meaningless in view of the fact that their ratings were so anemic that no one who mattered was watching anyway.

After Lachlan and James Murdoch orchestrated a successful coup d'état against longtime Fox News head Roger Ailes by using as-yet unproven allegations of sexual harassment against him, invitations from Fox News to opine on air quickly dried up. At the same time, I was gaining an extraordinary following on Infowars.com with a substantial uptick in viewership every time I interviewed with Alex Jones.

September 3, 2015: Trump Signs the Pledge

On Thursday, September 3, 2015, after meeting with RNC Chairman Reince Priebus, Trump held a press conference in the lobby of Trump Tower in midtown Manhattan to announce that he had agreed to sign the pledge to support the Republican candidate. A key element of the pledge, as far as the RNC was concerned, was that by signing the pledge, Trump agreed that he would not run as a third-party candidate.

"The best way for the Republicans to win is if I win the nomination and go directly against whoever they happen to put up. And for that reason, I have signed the pledge," Trump said in his opening statement, holding up the paper he had just signed. "So I will be totally pledging my allegiance to the Republican Party and for the conservative principles for which it stands." Trump continued, making it clear he intended to work hard for a Republican Party victory in the 2016 presidential election. "We will go out and fight hard, and we will win." In a statement issued by his office that evening, Priebus made clear all 17 Republican presidential candidates had now signed the official declaration of allegiance, billing Trump's decision as a sign of "party unity" that Trump had decided to change the position he took raising his hand in answer to Bret Baier's question at the start of the first debate.

CNN reported that Trump made the decision to sign the pledge because the Republican Party has been "extremely fair" to him in recent months. "The RNC has been absolutely terrific over the last two-month period and as you know, that's what I've wanted," Trump said. "I don't want to be treated any differently. When asked what he got in return for signing the paper, Trump responded: "assurance that I will be treated fairly."[7]

The *Washington Post* reported critically that Priebus had traveled to Trump Tower in New York City to get Trump's agreement. Reporter Robert Costa described the disturbed reaction of GOP veterans watching "the slightly surreal drama of this odd-couple alliance" playing out on television. The *Washington Post* article quoted Pete Wehner, a former adviser to President George W. Bush, as saying, "They're bowing at the altar of Trump. Trump is in control . . . It looks like the RNC is going hat in hand to Trump. It doesn't help the RNC. It simply helps Trump."[8]

September 16, 2015: The Second GOP Presidential Debate

The debate was held in the airplane wing of the Reagan Library in Simi Valley, California, with candidates positioned at podiums, behind which dramatically stood President Reagan's Air Force One airplane. Correspondent Jake Tapper at CNN, along with Salem Network radio talk-show host Hugh Hewitt and CNN's chief political correspondent Dana Bash, hosted the debate. The field of GOP candidates expanded to 11, with the inclusion this time of Carly Fiorina. Again, Trump and Bush were standing in the middle of the field, as the two continued to lead in the polls.

The debate began with each candidate making an introductory statement. Trump again stressed that his wealth and negotiating acumen gained in his business dealings positioned him above the other candidates.[9] "I'm Donald Trump," he said, introducing himself. "I wrote *The Art of the Deal*. I say not in a braggadocious way, I've made billions and billions of dollars dealing with people all over the world, and I want to put whatever that talent is to work for this country so we have great trade deals, we make our country rich again, we make it great again. We build our military, we take care of our vets, we get rid of Obamacare, and we have a great life altogether."

The debate quickly degenerated into various candidates taking their turns attacking Trump, including Jeb Bush who apparently decided going after Trump directly was the only way to gain the momentum his campaign needed, yet failed to develop. Stung by Trump characterizing him as "low energy," Bush clearly wanted to have the nation see him going aggressively after the front-runner.

From the start Tapper fueled the candidates attacks against each other by directing his first question to Fiorina.

"Mrs. Fiorina, I want to start with you. Fellow Republican candidate, and Louisiana Governor Bobby Jindal, has suggested that your party's frontrunner, Mr. Donald Trump, would be dangerous as President. He said he wouldn't want, quote, 'such a hot head with his finger on the nuclear codes.' You, as well, have raised concerns about Mr. Trump's temperament. You've dismissed him as an entertainer. Would you feel comfortable with Donald Trump's finger on the nuclear codes?" Tapper's question keyed off an attack Hillary Clinton was making on Trump, suggesting Trump lacked the "temperament" to be president, suggesting Trump would be dangerous in the White House, given what Clinton characterized as his volatile temper and mercurial personality.

When Fiorina refused to answer Tapper's question by attacking Trump, Tapper turned to Trump, giving him a chance to respond. Trump used the opportunity to attack Rand Paul. "Well, first of all, Rand Paul shouldn't even be on this stage," Trump said. "He's number 11, he's got 1 percent in the polls, and how he got up here, there's far too many people anyway."

Tapper turned to Rand Paul next, giving him a chance to respond. "I kind of have to laugh, sounds like a non sequitur.' He was asked whether or not he would be capable and it would be in good hands to be in charge of the nuclear weapons, and all of a sudden, there's a sideways attack at me," Paul charged. "I think that really goes to really the judgment. Do we want someone with that kind of character, that kind of careless language to be negotiating with Putin? Do we want someone like that to be negotiating with Iran?"

From there, Paul pivoted to question whether Trump could be trusted with the US nuclear arsenal, echoing Clinton in bringing to mind the famous "daisy commercial" of a young girl innocently picking a flower in a field, unaware of a nuclear bomb mushroom cloud that detonates in the background. Lyndon Baines Johnson used it in 1964 to suggest that his opponent, Sen. Barry Goldwater, was a radical right-wing extremist who would start a nuclear war with the Soviet Union. "I think really there's a sophomoric quality that is entertaining about Mr. Trump, but I am worried," Paul continued. "I'm very concerned about him—having him in charge of the nuclear weapons, because I think his response, his—his visceral response to attack people on their appearance—short, tall, fat, ugly—my goodness, that happened in junior high. Are we not way above that? Would we not all be worried to have someone like that in charge of the nuclear arsenal?"

When Paul finished, Tapper turned to ask Trump to jump back in, sensing Trump might take the bait. "I never attacked him [Sen. Paul] on his looks, and believe me, there's plenty of subject matter right there." This produced audience laughter, as Trump added, "That I can tell you."

This exchange set off the tone of the evening, with Trump—the master of one-liner jabs—again capturing the evening. Bush, when it came his turn, tried to embarrass Trump by arguing that Trump tried to give him a campaign contribution when he was running for governor of Florida because Trump wanted casino gambling in Florida. The suggestion was that Trump made the campaign contribution as a bribe of sorts. Trump immediately denied the accusation, adding that if he had wanted casino gambling in Florida, he would have gotten it.

As Trump continued, he argued once again that he was funding his own campaign, commenting that he turned down a $5 million contribution from a potential donor. Bush retorted, charging that Trump got Hillary Clinton to attend his wedding because Trump made a campaign contribution to Hillary. Trump smugly agreed, saying, "That's true. That's true." From there the debate deteriorated even further as Trump and Bush interrupted each other in a sequence that ended when Trump said, "Okay, more energy tonight. I like that." Again, the audience in the Reagan Library laughed.

While the substantive debate dealt with important foreign policy issues, including whether or not the deal Secretary of State John Kerry negotiated with Iran would keep Iran from making nuclear weapons and most pundits agreed that Fiorina scored points with level-headed answers that mirrored establishment GOP responses on key policy issues, the metrics of the debate again scored Trump as a winner. She scored points calling Trump an "entertainer," offering a heartfelt and passionate case against Planned Parenthood, and in discussing various foreign policy issues.

As the Associated Press pointed out, Fiorina scored one of the debate's most memorable lines when she responded to a derogatory comment Trump had made recently concerning her attractiveness.[10] In a Rolling Stone profile, Trump was quoted as saying about Fiorina, "Look at that face!" Would anyone vote for that? Can you imagine that, the face of our next president?"[11] Fiorina said simply, "I think women all over this country heard very clearly what Mr. Trump said." Fiorina got applause on that line, forcing Trump to respond humbly, "I think she's got a beautiful face, and I think she's a beautiful woman." The exchange served to remind "NeverTrump" voters of a series of rude comments Trump had made about women, as also highlighted by Trump's continuing feud with Megyn Kelly.

Though the AP characterized Trump's overall performance as "underwhelming," Trump still managed to dominate the debate with the help of the moderators. He got asked 15 direct questions, the most any candidate got asked, and only one fewer than the moderators asked Huckabee, Kasich, Rubio, and Walker combined. The top three speakers, ranked in order, were Trump, Bush, and Fiorina.[12]

While Trump won overwhelmingly most of the overnight non-scientific Internet polls that simply totaled reader votes, eight of the national scientific polls conducted after the second GOP primary debate showed clearly that Fiorina won and Trump lost. This prompted various pundits and poll watchers to ask a question that dogged Trump all the way to Election Day: namely, "Was the second debate the beginning of the end for Trump?" Obviously the answer was, "No." Interestingly, while scientific polls following both the first and second debate showed Trump losing, the debates didn't seem to matter, as Trump remained the frontrunner in scientific polls ranking GOP contenders after each debate.[13]

The "Birther" Issue Surfaces

The day after the second GOP primary debate, on September 17, 2015, Trump got into more trouble at a town hall meeting in Rochester, New Hampshire.[14]

The first person Trump called upon asked an explosive question. "We have a problem in this country," the man said. "It's called Muslims. We know our current president is one." Trump humored the questioner, saying, "Right."

The questioner continued, "You know he's not even an American."

Trump tried to laugh off the question, "We need this question, the first question . . ."

But the man kept right on going. "But anyway, we have training camps growing and they want to kill us," he persisted.

Again, Trump said half-heartedly, "Un-huh."

Undeterred, the unidentified man delivered his punch line: "But that's my question. What can we do to get rid of them?"

Trump seemed caught off guard.

"We're going to be looking at a lot of different things and, you know, a lot of people are saying that and a lot of people are saying that bad things are happening out there," he responded, without really answering. "We're going to be looking at that and plenty of other things."

The controversy was immediate, with Democrats charging that Trump should have rebuked the questioner, correcting him that Obama is a Christian.

"He knew, or he should have known, that what that man was asking was not only way out of bounds, it was untrue," said Hillary Clinton, after a campaign event she was also holding that day in New Hampshire. "He should have from the beginning repudiated that kind of rhetoric, that level of hatefulness." Later that evening, Clinton tweeted, "Donald Trump not denouncing false statements about POTUS and hateful rhetoric about Muslims is disturbing and just plain wrong. Cut it out."

Democratic presidential contender Vermont Senator Bernie Sanders tweeted that "Trump must apologize to the president and the American people for continuing the lie that the president is not an American and not a Christian. This nonsense has to stop." Later, Sanders added in another tweet, "Let's stop the racism. Let's stop the xenophobia."[15]

Two days later, White House press secretary Josh Earnest said it was unfortunate that Trump "wasn't able to summon the same kind of patriotism" that Republican Sen. John McCain showed in 2008, when he took the microphone away from a woman who said she didn't trust Obama because he was an Arab. "Mr. Trump isn't the first Republican politician to countenance these kind of views in order to win votes," Earnest said. "That's precisely what every Republican presidential candidate is doing when they decline to denounce Mr. Trump's cynical strategy."[16]

The *Christian Science Monitor* picked up another quote from the White House spokesman. "Is anyone really surprised that this happened at a Donald Trump rally?" said Mr. Earnest, as reported by the newspaper. "The people who hold these offensive views are part of Mr. Trump's base."[17]

Again, Trump was attacked as being a "Birther," recalling his insistence in 2011 that President Obama should produce a long-form birth certificate from Hawaii to prove his birth in the United States, as required by Article 2, Section 1 of the Constitution as a condition of eligibility to run for president. Trump, in New Hampshire on April 27, 2011, when President Obama released his birth certificate at a White House Press Conference, held his own press conference, claiming his attacks were the reason Obama made the document public. "I am very proud of myself," Trump told reporters in the Granite state. "I have accomplished something nobody else has accomplished." Asked by reporters if he thought the document was legitimate, Trump responded, "I want to look at it, but I hope it's true. I am really honored to have played such a big role in hopefully getting rid of this issue."[18]

The attacks also came from Republicans, as National Review staff writer Charles C. W. Cooke penned an attack the day after the town hall incident concluding that the incident "tells us that Trump is still not willing to acknowledge that the rumors that have floated around about Obama since 2008 are wholly unsubstantiated."[19]

On September 19, 2015, Trump defended himself tweeting, "If someone made a nasty or controversial statement about me to the president, do you really think he would come to my rescue? No chance." To this, Trump added a second tweet, writing, "Am I morally obliged to defend the president every time somebody says something bad or controversial about him? I don't think so." Trump followed this with a third tweet: "If I would have challenged the man, the media would have accused me of interfering with that man's right of free speech. A no win situation!" And yet, a fourth tweet: "Christians need support in our country (and around the world), that their religious liberty is at stake! Obama has been horrible, I will be great."[20]

Trump Controversies Multiply as 2015 Ends

Despite the media attention Trump commanded through the first two GOP primary debates, experienced election pundits and the mainstream media alike were in agreement that sooner or later Trump would make a fatal error and the professional politicians would succeed in driving him from the race. As if to validate this point, the Trump campaign as 2015 drew to a close was marred by a series of continuing controversies caused primarily by statements Trump made.

On November 12, 2015, speaking in Iowa, Trump proclaimed he was an expert who knew more than Obama about how to deal with ISIS. "I know more about ISIS than the generals do. Believe me," Trump said, proceeding from there to describe his plans for attacking ISIS-controlled oilfields to choke off revenue. "ISIS is making a tremendous amount of money because they have certain oil caps, right? They have certain areas of oil that they took away. They have some in Syria, some in Iraq. I'd bomb the s—- out of them," Trump continued. "I would just bomb those suckers. That's right. I'd blow up the pipes; I'd blow up the refineries. I'd blow up every single inch. There would be nothing left."[21] Real Clear Politics published the rest of Trump's comments in Iowa, "And you know what, you'll get Exxon to come in there, and in two months, you ever see these guys? How good they are, the great oil companies, they'll rebuild it brand new . . . And I'll take the oil."[22] This, of course, fed into the Democratic Party narrative that Trump's inexperience in foreign policy would lead him to embrace simplistic solutions with potentially catastrophic consequences. Trump's speech in Iowa in November 2015 presaged a statement he made in April 2016, when he told NBC's Today show that he would not rule out using nuclear weapons against ISIS. "I will be the last to use it [a nuclear bomb]," Trump explained. "I will not be a happy trigger like some people might be. I will be the last, but I will never, ever rule it out."[23]

At a rally in Birmingham, Alabama, on November 21, 2015, Trump ignited a controversy over the 9/11 attacks on the World Trade Center. "I watched when the World Trade Center came tumbling down," Trump told the rally. "And I watched in Jersey City, New Jersey, where thousands and thousands of people were cheering as that building was coming down. Thousands of people were cheering." Then, on Sunday, November 22, 2015, Trump doubled-down, repeating the assertion in an interview with George Stephanopoulos on ABC's *This Week*, as Stephanopoulos explained to Trump that police had refuted any such rumors at the time. "It did happen. I saw it," Trump insisted. "It was on television. I saw it." Trump didn't stop there. "There were people that were cheering on the other side of New Jersey, where you have large Arab populations," he continued. "They were cheering as the World Trade Center came down. I know it might not be politically correct for you to talk about it, but there were people cheering as that building came down, as those buildings came down. And that tells you something."[24]

Left-leaning Politifact.com jumped on Trump's assertion. "We looked back at the record to see what we could find about American Muslim celebrations in New Jersey on 9/11," Politifact.com wrote that Sunday evening, debunking Trump's claim. "While we found widely broadcast video of people in the Palestinian territories celebrating, we found no evidence to back up Trump's description of events on American soil," Politifact.com continued. "This defies basic logic. If thousands and thousands of people were celebrating the 9/11 attacks on American soil, many people beyond Trump would remember it. And in the 21st century, there would be video or visual evidence." Politifact.com acknowledged a couple of news articles that described rumors of celebrations had been published that were either debunked or unproven. But the fact-finding website concluded Trump's recollection of events in New Jersey in the hours after the September 11, 2001, terrorist attacks "flies in the face of all the evidence we could find." Politifact.com rated Trump's assertion as "Pants on Fire" not true.[25]

On December 7, 2015, Trump posted a statement on his campaign website calling for "a total and complete shutdown of Muslims entering the United States until our country's representatives can figure out what is going on."[26] Trump justified this by reference to a poll from the Center for Security Policy showing 25 percent of those polled agreed that violence against Americans here in the United States is justified as a part of the global jihad and 51% of those polled, "agreed that Muslims in America should have the choice of being governed according to Shariah."[27]

"Shariah authorizes such atrocities as murder against non-believers who won't convert, beheadings and more unthinkable acts that pose great harm to Americans, especially women," the press release posted on the Trump-Pence campaign website continued. Just to make the point certain, the press release quoted Mr. Trump saying, "Without looking at the various polling data, it is obvious to anybody the hatred is beyond comprehension. Where this hatred comes from and why we will have to determine. Until we are able to determine and understand this problem and the dangerous threat it poses, our country cannot be the victims of horrendous attacks by people that believe only in Jihad, and have no sense of reason or respect for human life. If I win the election for President, we are going to Make America Great Again."

The reaction from the United Nations was immediate and harsh. Prince Zeid bin Ra'ad, the United Nations High Commissioner for Human Rights, called Trump's proposal that all Muslims be banned from entering the United States "grossly irresponsible," warning that Trump was playing into the hands of extremist groups at the expense of ordinary Muslims who are also "eligible targets" of the extremists. He continued, arguing, "When political leaders rampage verbally through the lexicon to describe any minority in a way that is somehow pejorative, I think it's dangerous in this moment in time." Zeid stressed that the United States was founded on the dignity and rights of the individual, and the danger of classifying and categorizing people is that it dehumanizes people and can lead to victimization of the innocent. "Clearly, while there's no love lost for those who perpetrate violence and the killings of civilians, it's a double tragedy when the innocent have to suffer because of the reactions," Zeid said.[28]

Trump ended 2015 with a flurry of emails pushing back against Hillary Clinton's attacks charging Trump with sexism in his relationships with women. "She's playing that woman's card left and right . . . Frankly if she didn't, she'd do very poorly," Trump said on CNN.[29] He turned his guns on Bill Clinton, with another tweet that read, "Hillary Clinton has announced that she is letting her husband out to campaign, but he's demonstrated a penchant for sexism, so inappropriate!" Then, on December 28, 2015, Trump capped off his Twitter attack on the Clintons by tweeting the following: "If Hillary thinks she can unleash her husband, with his terrible record of women abuse, while playing the women's card on me, she's wrong!"[30]

Clinton campaign spokeswoman Christina Reynolds responded immediately, issuing a press statement that said, "Hillary Clinton won't be bullied or distracted by attacks he throws at her and former President Clinton." To this, Reynolds added, "When his insults are directed at women, immigrants, Asian-Americans, Muslims, the disabled, or hard working Americans looking to raise their wages, Hillary Clinton will stand up to him, as she has from the beginning. Donald Trump's words are demeaning; his policies are just as destructive. Hillary Clinton will challenge Donald Trump and all the other Republicans who will rip away the progress we've made."[31]

To the dismay of left-leaning pundits and the mainstream media, the controversy did nothing to diminish Trump's leadership in the polls. What should have been clear to Clinton Supporters was that Trump's insistence on speaking without a script, often engaging in outrageous language that was anything but politically correct, appealed to millions of Middle Class Americans. These voters fundamentally agreed with him on key issues, including their disdain for open borders, their concern that the Obama administration was allowing the United States to be infiltrated with Muslim immigrants who were never vetted for their propensity to embrace radical Islam and/or become terrorists, as well as his insistence that a double-standard, whereby he was accused of being sexist while accusations of Bill Clinton's sexual abuse of women was ignored, was hypocritical and unacceptable. The more Trump demonstrated he was unwilling to be corralled by the Left's agenda of what ideas and statements were going to be tolerated as within the bounds of political acceptability, the more he appealed to an audience who felt bullied by eight years of the Obama administration's creeping socialism.

On December 3, 2015, in an interview with the *Washington Post* conducted at Trump National Golf Course in the Virginia suburbs outside Washington, Trump made clear he was in the presidential race to the bitter end. "I will never leave the race," Trump insisted. To make the point emphatic, the newspaper reported Trump waved one arm over his head and spoke in one-sentence words, saying: "I. Will. Never. Leave. This. Race." In saying this, Trump was confident of his popularity. "You have to tell me: Why do I get four times the ratings of the other candidates?" he asked. "The debates are the most highly rated shows ever for Fox News and CNN, in their history."[32] This was exactly what Trump's constituency wanted to hear.

Trump discussed the importance about being a winner. "In school, I was always successful," he told the *Washington Post* reporters. "In life, I was successful. My father was a successful real estate developer and he was a very tough man but a good man. My father would always praise me. He always thought I was the smartest person. He said to one of those big magazines that everything he touches turns to gold." Trump was right. Middle America was tired under the Obama administration of losing—losing jobs to overseas markets because of global free-trade deals, having to work part-time jobs because nothing else was available, or being one of the 90 million or more considered out of the labor force because there were no acceptable jobs to find, not even part-time.

Trump was exactly what today's version of Richard Nixon's "Silent Majority" wanted to see in politics—an outsider and a renegade who could not be relied upon to line up with the GOP establishment even when he signed a pledge with the chairman of the Republican National Committee that he would not bolt from the GOP to make a third-party run, if he thought that might be the thing to do. In reporting on Trump's interview with the *Washington Times*, Politico noted Trump had recently linked to a USA Today poll that indicated 68 percent of Trump's voters would still vote for him if he departed the GOP and ran as an independent. "Trump's continual flirtation with a third-party bid has tormented Republicans who fear it would divide conservatives and hand the election to Democratic front-runner Hillary Clinton," reporter Nick Gass wrote in the Politico article.[33] Tormenting the GOP elite leadership in Washington was precisely what Trump's hard-core supporters wanted him to do, almost as much as they wanted him to beat Hillary Clinton in the general election. By the end of 2015, Trump had mastered the impossible: He had signed the GOP pledge to support the party's presidential nominee, yet he still managed to be the bad-boy outsider running against the professional politicians of both parties in the nation's capital.

Trump began 2016 with more of the same. At a campaign rally in Sioux Center, Iowa, on Sunday, January 24, 2016, Trump said, "I could stand in the middle of 5th Avenue and shoot somebody and I wouldn't lose voters. It's incredible." Even CNN, a news agency hostile to Trump got the point, even though CNN added context to the comment to make it more controversial. "The GOP front runner has repeatedly pointed to the loyalty of his supporters, many of whom tell reporters and pollsters that almost nothing could make them change their mind about voting for Trump in the presidential race," wrote Jeremy Diamond at CNN Politics.[34] "Trump's comments come as the debate about gun violence in America has taken center stage in American political discourse amid several highly publicized mass shootings." Clearly, the spin to attack Trump over the gun violence issue extended Trump's typically outrageous statement beyond its original meaning. What Trump was saying in January 2016 was most likely true. In 2015, Trump had begun attracting a hard-core of "Silent Majority" voters that were going to stick with him and vote with him no matter what he said. Ironically, the more outrageous and less politically correct Trump was, the more his base supporters liked it.

The GOP Establishment's "Pro-Trump" PAC Scam: How Ed Rollins Trashed Trump and Made Beaucoup Bucks

The 2016 election season was full of no-thank-you stiff-arms and familiar obscene gestures from the American public to politics-as-usual. There's no question that the establishment took a beating.

In 2016, another group took a beating—the "donor class"—the moneyed elite that buys politicians and rig elections as a matter of presumed privilege. This time around the fat cats made more bad bets and wasted more of their ill-gotten Wall Street booty than a brigade of riverboat gamblers on a drunken bender. Even the political parties were not spared, enduring pot-shots from even the lowliest of presidential candidates on a daily basis and commanding absolutely zero party discipline or respect. Yes, 2016 will go down in the record books as the year a giant stink bomb was dropped on American politics. Ha!

For the consultant class, well, that's another story. You know them, that group of revolving-door know-it-alls and election-fixers who seem to rise from the ash heap of prior election cycles time after time, like the undead in a B-rated zombie movie, reaping outrageous fees, while spending most of their time as self-promoting talking heads on Fox and CNN.

In this case, we're not speaking of the likes of David Axelrod or David Plouffe—consultants who have actually done something—or even Karl Rove, whose spectacular achievement in 2012 was to extract over $350 million from the Texas moneybags and not win a single Congressional race. Not one! No, the hands-down poster child for the say-anything, take-everything, and do-nothing political consultants is Ed Rollins.

You remember him. Mr. Rollins is well known as campaign manager of Ronald Reagan's landslide reelection victory in 1984. Except that he wasn't. Anyone within a short block of the campaign HQ knew that the real manager was Rollins's deputy, Lee Atwater.

Rollins did the stand-ups on TV, while Atwater directed the campaign. But the TV appearances paid off for Rollins, putting him in demand for the next cycle, when he signed on to support Vice President George H.W. Bush. That arrangement lasted until Bush declined to name Rollins chairman of the campaign, at which time Rollins promptly jumped ship to support Congressman Jack Kemp—all a matter of principle, of course. Four years later, Rollins was first to sign-on as co-manager to Ross Perot's presidential campaign, an effort that surely cost President Bush his reelection.

Next came the Christine Todd Whitman campaign for governor in 1993, a successful campaign that was hamstrung by Rollins' tour-de-force of self-promotion. So anxious was he to credit himself with her victory, moments after she was named the winner, Rollins boasted of directing the distribution of "walking around money" to New Jersey's black pastor network to convince their parishioners to stay home and not vote. Nice touch! He dragged the newly-elected governor into a series of embarrassing press conferences, only to find himself in front of a grand jury recanting his tall tale. Classic Ed Rollins, worth every penny, right?

Then in 1994, Rollins became chief consultant to Congressman Michael Huffington's US Senate campaign, in which Huffington spent $28 million of his personal fortune in a losing effort, after which Rollins bashed him in a book smearing Huffington regarding his private life.

There have been a series of ill-fated campaigns where Ed earned top dollar, got top billing (yes, often enjoying a higher profile than the candidate), then either left the campaign mid-stream, or trashed the candidate after the election in post-mortem interviews, books, and on any number of television panels eager to give him the chance to unload on his former employer. Bruce Benson for Governor, Bill Simon for Governor, Kathryn Harris for Senate, and Mike Huckabee for President—count on Ed Rollins to be an equal opportunity post-campaign candidate-thrasher who never loses the touch for self-promotion.

When Rollins was announced to great fanfare as Congresswoman Michelle Bachmann's chief strategist for her 2012 presidential bid, the die was cast. Everyone except Bachmann knew what was about to happen. Take the candidates money and then ridicule their efforts once the ship starts to sink, which is a method Rollins uses to this day.

As expected with any production brought to you by Ed Rollins, Bachmann would flame out, and Rollins would point the finger at everyone but himself, starting with Ms. Bachmann, who had paid him handsomely for his trouble. When later asked what she would have done differently in her campaign, Bachmann's answer was revealing: "I should have Googled [Rollins] before hiring him."

He got rich, she got shafted. Wash, rinse, repeat.

So, after taking some well-deserved time off from consulting (Romney wouldn't let Rollins near his campaign in 2012), Rollins and his TV-burnished reputation found a perfect home, as co-chair of a Trump Super PAC for the 2016 presidential cycle. He called it his "Last Hurrah." Not actually a working chair, but serving in his favorite role as a figurehead, talking trash to the press and signing pro-Trump fundraising letters as fast as someone can line them up in front of him. We knew the game and understood that this was his only way to remain relevant, but nonetheless his antics were still painful to watch.

What's wrong with that, you ask? Well, a few short months before assuming his role as the figurehead of his "Pro-Trump" Super PAC, aptly titled "Great America PAC"—a Super PAC the Trump campaign quickly made known was "unauthorized" to represent Trump—Ed opined on Fox News on May 22, 2016: "You can't be a viable candidate saying the things he's been saying without crashing and burning."[35] Of course, he was speaking of Donald Trump. Political consultants like Rollins say ridiculous things all the time, get paid very well, and just keep rising from the ashes.

Even post-convention, Rollins found ways to trash the very nominee his scam of a Super PAC was supposed to be supporting. Rollins opined on Laura Ingraham's radio show on August 24, 2016 that, "If we're sitting here three weeks from now after Labor Day and it's in the same position, we're going to have a hard, uphill battle." He continued: "Trump would lose badly today."[36]

Even after traitorous utterances like this, Rollins kept his post at the Great America PAC and continued to milk it for all it was worth. He made beaucoup bucks raising money for a PAC supporting a candidate that he would routinely bend over backwards to trash on the airwaves.

After the election, the shameless and talentless buffoon would give interviews praising top Trump officials like Stephen Bannon for orchestrating Donald Trump's victory. Rollins was always ready and eager to pimp out his rancid opinions to remain relevant.

To the Trumpsters reading this book, I urge you to be wary of hacks like Ed Rollins as Trump assumes office. Rollins has already intimated he plans on continuing his "Pro-Trump" SCAM PAC during Trump's first term in office, clearly a vehicle Rollins intends to exploit for personal gain and exposure.

When I see Ed Rollins on TV or get an email from him soliciting money, I prefer to think of him like Petyr Baelish (Littlefinger) from George R.R. Martin's exemplary "Game of Thrones" novels. He will do and say anything to earn a quick buck and maintain his relevance and the appearance of power. This man would burn down the entire country with his stupidity, if only it meant he could rule over the gray waste and ashes that he left behind.

The next time you see Ed Rollins on TV, remember he never supported Donald Trump and even attacked Trump for his early gaffes. So beware, remain vigilant, and maybe we'll send this shameless huckster into a long-overdue permanent retirement in 2017, if we can starve his SCAM PAC financially and on social media.

CHAPTER 3

Round Two: GOP Primaries Pick Trump

If we win Indiana, it's over, okay? It's over. Then we can focus on Crooked Hillary. Please, let's focus on Crooked Hillary. We're going to make America great again. I love you. Get out there and vote on Tuesday.
Donald J. Trump, Rally in Indiana, May 2, 2016[1]

Without a doubt the biggest Republican rival fighting for his party's nomination was Ted Cruz. At least that's what most Americans may have thought. Cruz foolishly placed himself in the same league as Mr. Trump. As the other candidates fell by the wayside, Ted Cruz found himself square in the sights of Donald Trump. This unenviable position also signified that Cruz was now the sole bearer of the old boy Republican cronyism that in itself caused its own demise. It was a tough choice for Republicans: Republican Trump, or Republican Cruz? Cruz was never particularly popular with the Republican elite leadership in Washington who viewed him as overly religious and self-righteous. Cruz also lacked a strong (Reagan-like) image that has always worked well for Republican candidates. He just looks like a mama's boy. A little background reminder of what made Cruz so despicable.

After winning the Wisconsin primary with 48% and 36 delegates, Cruz announced "Let me just say: Hillary, get ready. Here we come!" Cruz should have known you can't win your party's nomination based on one primary. His confidence was as fleeting as his winning streak. Cruz had tried to make the lack of support from the Republican Party establishment evidence that he was an "outsider." Cruz's claim of not being a tool of the political elite is like Bill Clinton telling the world, "I did not have sexual relations with that woman." Cruz has become quite adroit at saying one thing while his history shows him doing the other. Rather than the outsider he claims to be, Ted Cruz is the ultimate insider, former top Bush 41 policy aide, a globalist, an Ivy Leaguer, and a quintessential establishment career politician.

Ted Cruz: An Establishment Player

There is no better example of this than Calgary Ted's actions surrounding the big Wall Street banks and their secret funding of his political ascension. Cruz has been gorging at the table of the ultimate insider of all insiders—Goldman Sachs and Citibank. You may recall in a recent Fox Business Network debate that Cruz, in "Mr. Haney from Green Acres" voice, declared to one of the moderators, "The opening question [moderator Jerry Seib] asked—would you bailout the big banks again—nobody gave you an answer to that. I will give you an answer—absolutely not."[2] Cruz is a scoundrel and what else would you expect a scoundrel to say who had secretly secured big sweetheart loans from Goldman and Citibank—*by leveraging his retirement accounts*—to fund his 2012 US Senate campaign. Loans which Calgary Ted conveniently forgot to disclose to the Federal Election Commission.[3] These are the very *retirement accounts* that he said he and his wife *said* he cashed in to fund his senate race. In other words, Ted lied. At the same time Ted's bulging 2016 campaign accounts and supporting Super-PACs were stuffed with big oil and gas money. He knew how to play the game.

And perhaps the ultimate hypocrisy of the native born Canadian is that his spouse, Heidi, by all accounts a lovely wife and mother, had been employed by Goldman Sachs since 2005. She was on leave as managing director and regional head of private wealth management. Heidi is a proud member of the lefty Council on Foreign Relations, advocates of one world government and the New World Order. Heidi was one of 31 members assigned to the task force that produced the "Building a North

American Community" report. The 2005 report by the Task Force on the Future of North America was co-authored by task force vice chairman Robert A. Pastor, then the director of the Center for North American Studies at American University in Washington, DC, Pastor was dubbed "the father of the North American Union" for the influence the CFR report had on a tripartite summit meeting between the heads of state of the United States, Mexico and Canada. The meeting culminated in President George W. Bush declaring without congressional approval the formation of the Security and Prosperity Partnership of North America.[4]

Heidi is not a big player in the Cruz campaign with those credentials but rather an integral part of the campaign's fundraising efforts. As reported by CNN last year, "She works the phones the way she worked them when she was at Goldman," said Chad Sweet, the Cruz campaign's chairman, who recruited Heidi to work at the giant investment bank."[5] Yet we are to believe that the big Wall Street banks have no leverage over Ted Cruz? Why didn't Heidi Cruz resign from Goldman Sachs instead of taking a leave of absence? That's like saying Bill Ayers and Saul Alinsky have had no influence on Barack Obama. The other inside connection that hits one like a baseball bat is the Bush connection. Also conveniently missing from Heidi's Wikipedia bio is her service as Deputy US Trade Representative to USTR head Robert Zoellick. At USTR Heidi worked on United States-China trade policy—the one Donald Trump talks about so much.

Ted was George W.'s brain when he ran for president. A top policy adviser, Ted maneuvered for Solicitor General in Bush World but settled for a plum at the Federal Trade Commission. Ted's a Bushman with deep ties to the political and financial establishment. Ted and Heidi brag about being the first "Bush marriage"—they met as Bush staffers and that meeting ultimately led to matrimony. Ted was an adviser on legal affairs while Heidi was an adviser on economic policy and eventually director for the Western Hemisphere on the National Security Council under Condoleezza Rice. Condi helped give us the phony war in Iraq. And Chad Sweet, Ted Cruz's campaign chairman, is a former CIA officer. Michael Chertoff, George W. Bush's former Secretary of Homeland Security, hired Sweet from Goldman Sachs to restructure and optimize the flow of information between the CIA, FBI and other members of the national security community and DHS. Chertoff and Sweet co-founded the Chertoff Group upon leaving the administration. Despite Cruz's ability to lie with a straight face—a trait sadly Nixonian—trying to hide his support for amnesty and the Trans-Pacific Partnership, TPP, Cruz got nailed by Senator Marco Rubio during the GOP primary debates. Acting like a prick in the US Senate was the core of Ted's disciplined effort to bury his old school ties and reinvent himself as a modern-day Jesse Helms. Cruz's attempt to present himself during the 2016 presidential campaign as a conservative outsider was a joke. It was all a ruse—a makeover—designed to mask the truth that Cruz was a longtime Washington insider with New World Order globalist credentials.

As we got closer to the Iowa Caucus and New Hampshire Primary, Cruz and his establishment puppet masters engaged in an aggressive strategy against Trump. Cruz's managers tried to get away with presenting the false narrative that Cruz was the real outsider, while arguing that Trump was really an insider. Nothing could be farther from the truth. In its most simplistic terms—the power elite had no leverage over Trump— nothing. Cruz, on the other hand, is the establishment's quisling, spawned by the Bushes and controlled by Wall Street. Cruz became a strident "outsider" only four years ago. Don't get me wrong. Ted Cruz is a smart, canny, talented guy who ran a great "long race" campaign. He aspires to be Reagan but, trust me, he's Nixon—right down to the incredible discipline and smarts playing the political game. Ted Cruz is not who he appears to be. Heidi Cruz recently said that her husband's candidacy was showing America "the face of God whom they serve." Heidi has it wrong however, for Ted Cruz is more reminiscent of Elmer Gantry, the sleazy sociopathic preacher created by novelist Sinclair Lewis in the 1920s. No Heidi, we don't see the face of God in Ted Cruz. We see someone who appears to not have a conscience, only self-interest. We see someone who presents himself with high morals and philosophy, yet underneath it all has a criminal mind. We see a calculating politician who will lie, cheat, steal, and incite emotional chaos to win. We see someone who is masterfully adept at turning one group of people against another group, all the while proclaiming himself to be the one true savior. It gets worse.

It was disturbing enough when Senator Ted Cruz announced that Neil Bush, brother of Jeb and George W., would be the finance chairman of his campaign. Neil defrauded US taxpayers out of $1.5 billion in a savings and loan scam involving Silverado Bank in Denver Colorado in the 1990s.[6] Now however, Cruz announced key appointments that should have disturbed voters even more. Cruz named Former Texas

Senator Phil Gramm as his economic guru. This guy virtually crashed the US economy. Gramm is largely responsible for passing the enabling legislation behind the speculative subprime real-estate bubble that popped in September 2008, just in time to propel Barack Obama into the White House. First was his Gramm-Leach-Bliley bill in 1999, repealing key features of the Depression-era Glass Steagall Act that had separated investment banking from commercial banking. Its repeal—which was signed into law by President Clinton, with the backing of Robert Rubin and Larry Summers—opened the door for a flood of money, from commercial banks, to flow into mortgage-backed securities and other funny-money schemes. The second bill was the Commodity Futures Modernization Act (CFMA) passed in 2000, freeing derivative trading from any regulatory oversight. This was another brilliant bill we owe to former US Senator Phil Gramm from Texas and the time he spent chairing the Senate Banking Committee.

February 1, 2016: The Iowa Caucuses

On Tuesday, January 26, 2016, Donald Trump made the controversial decision to not participate in the Fox News debate scheduled to be held two days later, on Thursday, January 28, in Des Moines, Iowa, with the hosts once again listed as Bret Baier, Megyn Kelly, and Chris Wallace—the same lineup as had hosted the first GOP primary debate on August 6, 2015. The decision was particularly controversial in that the Iowa GOP caucus meetings were scheduled for the next week and Trump was running neck-to-neck in the Iowa polls with Ted Cruz and Marco Rubio, both of whom had made major investments building a ground game in the state. As his reason for cancelling, Trump charged that Fox News was "playing games" with him, with most suspecting Trump had not yet given up the feud with Megyn Kelly, whom Trump was still calling a "lightweight reporter."[7] The controversial decision made it clear Trump still intended to play by his own rules.

Instead of attending the seventh GOP primary debate, Trump held a competing event in Des Moines, Iowa, raising $6 million for US military veterans, causing Reuters to report that Trump "managed to upstage the event with a typical dramatic flourish."[8]

This was not the first brush-up over debate moderators. On October 30, 2015, the RNC Chairman, in a letter to NBC News chief Andrew Lack, informed the television news network the RNC was suspending its partnership with NBC, effectively barring NBC from televising a GOP primary debate scheduled for February 26, 2016, opening up the broadcast rights to others. The RNC was upset at CNBC's handling of the GOP primary debate held on October 28, 2015, at the University of Colorado in Boulder. The Associated Press reported that Republicans were angered by what they considered petty, non-substantive questions by CNBC debate moderators Carl Quintanilla, Becky Quick, and John Harwood, designed to embarrass the candidates. The AP noted in particular that Harwood had asked Trump whether he was running a "comic-book version of a presidential campaign."[9]

As it turned out, on Monday, February 1, 2016, Trump narrowly lost the Iowa caucus to Ted Cruz, who received 27.6 percent of the votes counted in the caucus meetings, with Trump at 24.3 percent, and Rubio at 23.1 percent. Given the peculiarities of GOP primary contests, the Iowa caucus procedure was complicated, involving a series of local meetings in which supporters of various candidates needed to win a majority in that particular caucus. The outcome was equally complicated in that the Iowa caucuses were a proportional election, not a winner-take-all vote, with the result that Cruz won 8 delegates, while Trump and Rubio each won 7 delegates.

Surprisingly, Rubio was the candidate to gain the most momentum coming out of the Iowa caucus meetings, even though he ended up in third place. The media spin that Rubio had come within striking distance of Trump and Cruz led to a fundraising bonanza, with Rubio's campaign picking up $2 million within twenty-four hours of Iowa voting.[10] Rubio was compared with McCain in 2008 and Romney in 2012, when both lost the Iowa caucuses only to win the New Hampshire primary the following week with strong performances that propelled each to the GOP nomination.

When entrance polls taken at the start of the 2016 Iowa caucuses showed late-deciders and Evangelical Christians trended toward Cruz and Rubio, pundits and the mainstream media again saw dark signs for the Trump campaign.

It is important to note that the recent history of the GOP Iowa caucuses suggests that the winner in Iowa does not necessarily predict the winner of the GOP nomination. "Just twice in 40 years has the GOP caucus winner gone on to claim the nomination in campaigns with no incumbent Republican president," wrote reporters Bill Barrow and Emily Swanson for the Associated Press. "But the details behind Cruz's victory and Rubio's climb raise new questions about Trump's turnout operation and his ability to turn his consistently front-running poll numbers into actual votes; and that increases pressure on Trump to deliver a victory next Tuesday in New Hampshire or risk damaging his strategy of campaigning as the inevitable nominee at the head of a fractured field."[11]

Following their poor performances in the Iowa caucuses, the three GOP candidates with the fewest votes suspended their campaigns: Sen. Rand Paul, who won 1 delegate in Iowa; former Governor Mike Huckabee, who won the Iowa GOP caucuses in 2008; and former Sen. Rick Santorum, who won the Iowa caucuses in 2012.

"Very Dishonest"

As the Iowa caucuses were already underway, Rep. Steve King, the chairman of the Cruz campaign in Iowa, posted two tweets that caused a firestorm. During the Iowa Caucus, Ben Carson had commented to the media that he might be heading home to Florida before going to New Hampshire to get "some new clothes." This prompted King to tweet at 8:19 pm local time on February 1, "Skipping NH [New Hampshire] & SC [South Carolina] is the equivalent of suspending. Too bad this information won't get to all caucus goers." Then, one minute later, at 8:20 pm local time on the night of February 1, King posted a second tweet, "Carson looks like he is out. Iowans need to know before they vote. Most will go to Cruz, I hope." King included in both tweet messages a link to a tweet posted at 7:43 pm local time that evening by Chris Moody, the senior reporter for CNN Politics. Moody had tweeted, "Carson won't go to NH [New Hampshire]/ SC [South Carolina], but instead will head home to Florida for some R&R. He'll be in DC Thursday for the National Prayer Breakfast."[12]

"Very dishonest" is how Carson ripped Cruz's campaign for what he suspected was an underhanded strategy to dampen his vote while the caucuses were happening. "For months, my campaign has survived the lies and dirty tricks from my opponents who profess to detest the games of the political class, but in reality are masters of it," Carson said in a statement issued the next day. "Even tonight, my opponents resorted to political tricks by tweeting, texting and telling precinct captains that I had suspended my campaign—in some cases asking caucus goers to change their votes," Carson said of Iowa's caucuses Monday night." Carson left no doubt he felt this involved foul play. "One of the reasons I got into this race was to stop these

deceptive and destructive practices, and these reports have only further stee-
led my resolve to continue and fight for 'We the People,' and return control
of the government back to them," Carson said.[13]

King defended his twitter messages, arguing that when he got the
report from CNN's Chris Moody, he told his chief of staff, "We can't ask
people to caucus and vote for a candidate who is now in high likelihood
dropping out."[14] Trump was not sympathetic. On February 3, 2016, the
Washington Post reported that Trump, the second place finisher in Iowa,
was claiming Cruz intentionally misled Iowa voters that Monday night to
believe candidate Ben Carson was quitting the race, calling for Cruz's victory to be invalidated and new voting to take place. "Ted Cruz did not win
Iowa, he stole it," Trump said in a Twitter post on Wednesday morning.
"That is why all of the polls were so wrong and why he got more votes than
anticipated. Bad!" In a subsequent tweet, Trump elaborated, "Based on
the fraud committed by Senator Ted Cruz during the Iowa Caucus, either
a new election should take place or Cruz results nullified." The *Washington
Post* reported that on the ground during the Iowa caucus voting, Cruz
staffers at several precincts began telling voters about Carson's departure,
in an apparent attempt to discourage them from voting for Carson on the
assumption that a vote for Carson would be a wasted vote.[15]

The Cruz campaign responded to Trump's tweets by calling him "a
sore loser." On February 12, 2016, Politico reported that in little more
than 24 hours, Trump had tweeted six times with some variation of
the theme that "the Texas senator is not truthful." Politico noted that
Trump's tweets started with an accusation that Cruz was making negative robo-calls. When Cruz denied the allegations to reporters before a
rally in Fort Mill, South Carolina, Trump tweeted in response, "We are
getting reports from many voters that Cruz people are back to doing very
sleazy and dishonest 'push polls' on me. We are watching!" In subsequent
tweets, Trump linked Cruz's denials of push polls with Cruz's lies regarding Ben Carson. As the war of tweets escalated, Trump's designation of
Cruz as "Lying Ted" was born. "Lying Ted Put out a statement, 'Trump
& Rubio are w/Obama on gay marriage.'" Trump tweeted. "Cruz is the
worst liar, crazy or very dishonest."[16]

How Did Ted Become "Lyin' Ted"?
Ever wonder why Donald Trump bestowed the nickname "Lyin' Ted"
upon Ted Cruz?

Obviously, Trump must have thought that Ted had lied at some point during the campaign. It's an understatement, however, to say merely that Cruz lied "at some point" in the campaign. Ted may be the most prolific liar ever to run for president! I realized it as it happened, but for the readers benefit I'll run through some glaring examples that I fact checked for this writing.

Ted would have us believe that he's the only senator who stood and fought against immigration amnesty, Obamacare, and Planned Parenthood. In what he described as his fight against the establishment, he stood firm, refusing to bow to pressure. It makes for good campaign rhetoric but the truth is different. Ted described his battle against Marco Rubio who supported a massive amnesty plan, by saying "I have never supported legalization. I led the fight against [Rubio's] legalization and amnesty." The phrase "I have never supported legalization" is an outright lie. As far back as his work for the Bush campaign where he was a policy adviser on immigration reform, and again as a board member of the Washington based Hispanic Alliance for Prosperity Institute, Cruz worked and drafted policies that allowed undocumented immigrants to stay in the country and pursue legal status. More recently, in January 2013, when a group of eight senators issued an immigration reform proposal that included a path to citizenship Cruz could have ruled against it. He made no commitment and for months refused to answer questions as to whether he would vote for or against the proposal.

Cruz then crafted an amendment which he pushed giving "legal status without citizenship." His amendment didn't make it, but Cruz wasn't about to admit that he was for a path to legalization. He strategized to stay in the middle so he can appear to be pro or con depending on what is most beneficial for Cruz at the time. Directly on point, the *Washington Post*'s Fact Checker, unable to confirm Cruz position one way or the other, concluded on December 15: "Cruz positioned himself in a way so that he would appear pro-legalization if an immigration overhaul passed, or appear anti-legalization if hard liner stances became more acceptable."[17] By January 2016, Cruz announced that every measure he proposed in the bill was a plot to sabotage the bill. In other words, his efforts to add the "legalization without citizenship" were a ruse, a fake, as Greta Van Susteren put it in an interview with Cruz in December 2015. Van Susteren couldn't believe it. She asked in astonishment, "A poisoned pill, designed to kill the whole bill?" Cruz answered, "And it succeeded." What kind of man can weave a story like that? If he wasn't lying before, then he's lying now. If he's not lying now, then he was lying before. Twisted. It caused a journalist on the left to claim Cruz "may be the most spectacular liar ever to run for president," and that assessment was unfortunately accurate.[18]

Another Ted Cruz lie is when he says he's anti-Wall Street and opposed to the government bank bailout. In fact, during the campaign, as I wrote earlier, Ted's wife Heidi, took temporary leave from her job as managing director at Goldman Sachs that took a $10 billion bailout! The Cruzes took low interest loans from Goldman Sachs and Citibank but failed to report them. This brings us to his statement that "all of the information" about large loans he received to help finance his 2012 Senate campaign "has been public and transparent for many years." FactCheck.org once again says the loans were not transparent.[19] Cruz did not disclose that he had obtained loans from Goldman Sachs and Citibank that combined were worth between $350,002 and $750,000 until July 9, 2012. That was after his May 29, 2012, primary election, and after he had already loaned his campaign nearly a million dollars. Cruz took out another Goldman Sachs loan for between $100,001 and $250,000 for his 2012 campaign, but that wasn't reported on his financial disclosure report until May 15, 2013—by which time he was already a US senator. As FactCheck.org stressed, on both reports, Cruz did not report the loans were for his campaign. That was not required by the ethics law, because those forms are simply intended to disclose personal finances (assets, liabilities, etc.). But he should have reported using the loans for his campaign in separate campaign reports with the Federal Election Commission. He did not.[20]

Cruz has made much of his qualifications for president and specifically in appointing a Supreme Court justice sighting that he has argued cases nine times before the Supreme Court and, as his campaign ad claimed, he won them all. Not true according to FactCheck.org. Cruz did argue nine cases but only won two, the rest being either losses or partial victories.[21]

Just before the February Iowa Caucus, voters received in the mail what looked like a government document. With official looking language screaming, "Election Alert" and "Voter Violation," the notice appeared to be a report on the recipient's participation in recent elections. The notice might have been relevant if voting were mandated by law, but in Iowa where voting is voluntary, there is no justification for threatening voters that they might be in serious violation of voting laws if they did not show up for the Iowa Caucus. The recipient and the recipient's neighbors were given grades, scored with "F" for "Failing" if their attendance in recent elections was not perfect. Language in the notice implied the Iowa Secretary of State and/or county election clerks were responsible for producing the mailing from "official public records." That wasn't true. Iowa's Republican Secretary of State, Paul Pate, told the Daily Mail that Cruz's propaganda piece "misrepresents the role of my office, and worse, misrepresents Iowa election law." Cruz responded by saying he would not apologize and would "use every tool we can to drive Iowans to the polls."[22]

Cruz even lied about an exchange he had with his wife regarding financing his campaign. He recalled saying to his wife in the weeks before his Senate primary, when he was still behind in the polls, "Sweetheart, I'd like us to liquidate our entire net worth, and put it into the campaign." "What astonished me, then and now, was Heidi within 60 seconds said, 'Absolutely,' with no hesitation." Heidi Cruz tells a different story. She told Politico she "wanted him to raise money from elsewhere first, to show that the support was out there." And even then, "She proposed that they not put their own cash into the campaign unless it made the difference between winning and losing."[23] There are so many lies spilling out of Ted's mouth that it would take an entire book to list them all. One wonders where Cruz learned or acquired his gift for lying.

The Fidel Castro Saga: How "Lyin' Rafael" Gave Birth to "Lyin' Ted"

One has to look no farther than his father Rafael Cruz. This man has lied about every single detail of his life. He's constructed an alternative, completely artificial life story in order to preach a rags-to-riches-to-rags narrative about how he was saved by Jesus—an elaborate fabrication that Ted often retells and frequently embellishes. Embellishes a lie? Oh yes. Why not? The elder Cruz makes much of his story that he grew up in an oppressed and militarized Cuba under the regime of Fulgencio Batista. Then at the age of 14, he joined the "revolution" and spent the next four years "involved in sabotage, propaganda, weapons training and so forth and so on." Later he claims he was "arrested and brutally beaten, tortured every four hours for four days." On the fourth night of being kicked and beaten until he lost consciousness, he was given a tour of Matanzas (the city of his confinement) so that he could "see what he was going to miss when they killed him." The next morning, he was miraculously released and told they would come after him if any more bombs went off. Ted has embellished this statement adding that his father had his top row teeth kicked out. As the story continues, Rafael's father picks up his son from the detention center and drives him home. An hour later Rafael is told to leave Cuba by a mysterious woman from "the underground." He had been a straight "A" student in high school, so he decides to go to college in America. He writes three letters to Universities, one of which accepts him. Rafael then trots over to the American Embassy where he gets a four-year student visa. A friend of the family bribes somebody in the government to stamp Rafael's Cuban passport. (Rafael later changed this to "I convinced the Cuban government to let me leave the country on a student visa.") He then hides in his father's car, on the floor of the back seat, and is driven to the ferry to Key West, USA. There are so many holes and lies in this tale it's disgusting. According to author Paul LeBon who has spent almost 60 years developing deep friendships with actual Cuban revolutionary heroes and their families, Cruz's story is a pack of lies.[24]

The revolution was not going on when Cruz was in ninth grade at the age of 14. Castro's revolution did not commence full-bore until Cruz was 18, in 1957. There was no on-going revolution between 1953 and 1957. The revolution was a one-day attack by Castro and his supporters against the Moncada Barracks on July 26, 1953, that Batista's military troops put down. Many were killed and Castro was deported to Mexico in 1955. There were no high school students involved. In fact, the Moncada raid occurred before Rafael Cruz even entered the ninth grade.

According to Cubans who were there at the time, the policy of Batista was not to torture a prisoner unless he was a high value prisoner believed to have valuable intelligence. The rule was to take prisoners out and shoot them. Rafael is lying about his arrest and torture. If he was so badly tortured (he never describes how) how was it possible for him to go on a joy ride to see the city lights on the fourth night of his confinement in a jeep with four police? Then, he was released the next morning? His father picks him up and drives him home? What about his wounds, his broken ribs, his knocked out teeth, his black and blue puffed up face? Did they burn him with cigars? Remember he was tortured every four hours for four days straight. Grown men have crumbled under torture. He was a kid who had zero status in the revolution, if we were to believe he was a revolutionary at all. How was he able to maintain straight "A" grades through high school when he says he spent that time hundreds of miles away fighting in the revolution? A child aged 14 to 17 would not be able to attend school and fight a war (which wasn't happening at that time) so far away.

How did Rafael Cruz know which American universities to write to? He states that he didn't speak a single word of English yet he writes to universities asking for admittance? He sent no transcripts, no statement of family financial condition, no formal application, just barely two months before school was scheduled to start. Yet, he was accepted within a couple of weeks? How is that possible?

Regarding the four-year student visa he was given by the American Embassy, student visas are granted one year at a time and have to meet certain requirements. In 1957, applicants for student visas were required to have sufficient funds to cover expenses. Applicants had to be fluent enough in English to enable them to undertake a full course of study. By Cruz's own account he only had $100 and knew zero English. By any account, he would have been denied a one-year student visa. According to a Cuban lawyer well versed in these matters, getting a student visa from the American embassy in Cuba would have taken a long time. You had to make an appointment. You had to keep the appointment to apply for the visa in person. Then the US embassy had to verify the information. Then another appointment was required to finalize the paperwork.

Cruz claimed someone bribed an official to stamp his exit passport. Oh, right. Then the story morphed from the bribery claim to a claim Rafael Cruz simply convinced an official to allow him to leave. Why would Rafael Cruz have to hide in his father's car if he had received permission to leave?

The story gets even more unbelievable when Cruz relates how he entered the United States and traveled to Austin, Texas. He claimed that within 24 hours, the university sent him to the Immigration and the Nationalization Service, the INS, where he received his Social Security card—all in the first 24 hours? But Rafael also told us he spoke no English, stressing that he was in a foreign country where he knew no one and had to figure out how to get around. Where did he get his paperwork? As a foreign national, how did he get a Social Security card at all, let alone in 24 hours? How did he pay for his tuition?

As for his speaking English, the story contradicts itself when Cruz states, "I took the advice of my English teacher in Cuba. I would sit for hours in a movie theater watching the movie over and over again. I taught myself English in one month." This statement is ridiculous beyond words! (Where in Cuba would they be showing an American film?) I thought he spoke no English. I thought he was fighting in the revolution for four years instead of going to school. How can anyone learn a language by watching a movie over and over again in a month?

So, my point is that Ted Cruz learned to lie from his father. The apple does not fall far from the tree. Ted has retold this fantasy over and over again to illustrate how the American dream can be had. "Just look at my Dad." Utter nonsense.

Ted Cruz has supported his father's lies, often inventing new lies, such as telling audiences that his father is a pastor in Dallas. This is odd because Rafael Cruz has never introduced himself as a pastor. If Rafael Cruz was a pastor, where did he go to seminary or theology school? Where is his congregation? The sad conclusion is that Rafael and his son Ted Cruz are both con artists of the worst type.

In truth, Rafael Cruz was born into a prosperous middle class family, with connections in the government. Once in the United States, he fathered two children while attending school in Austin. After fathering the two children, Rafael abandoned this family to run off to Canada. The "other woman" in Canada bore Rafael two more children, one of whom was Ted Cruz.

February 9, 2016: The New Hampshire Primary

After losing narrowly to Cruz in Iowa, the Trump campaign quickly changed strategy for the New Hampshire primary, scheduled eight days later, on Tuesday, February 9, 2016. Reluctantly, Trump campaign insiders conceded that Trump's failure to participate in the Fox News debate held in Des Moines on the eve of the Iowa caucuses most likely hurt Trump. Also apparent was that Cruz had taken the Iowa caucuses much more seriously than Trump, as reflected by the amount of time and money the Cruz campaign devoted to building an organization in Iowa. Trump needed to demonstrate he could translate the massive crowds he was drawing at rallies into winning votes. Trump increased the number of daily planned events in New Hampshire and intensified his pressure to rack up dozens of local endorsements. "Trump's New Hampshire organization has, for months, appeared more robust than the operation he'd put together in Iowa. He's racked up dozens of endorsements, and his

Manchester campaign headquarters is large and brimming with staff and volunteers placing calls," the Associated Press reported. "Trump remains far ahead in polls in the state, which is generally considered far friendlier turf for the billionaire businessmen. The electorate tends to favor more moderate candidates, making him a more natural fit than he was in evangelical-dominated Iowa, despite his efforts to appeal to the group."[25]

At the ABC-hosted GOP debate held at Saint Anselm College in Manchester, New Hampshire, on February 6, 2016, the Saturday before the Tuesday primary, Rubio made a serious tactical error. Considered "one of the worst nights of his entire campaign," Rubio repeated himself three times in a prolonged exchange as he struggled to defend himself against New Jersey Governor Chris Christie, who "brought out the knives" over Rubio's relative inexperience.[26] Rubio's offending statement repeated almost word-for-word in answering Christie was this: "Here's the bottom line. This notion that Barack Obama doesn't know what he's doing is just not true. He knows exactly what he's doing." On the fourth time repeating the line, Christie interjected: "This is what Washington, DC, does. The drive-by shot at the beginning with incorrect and incomplete information and then the memorized 25-second speech that is exactly what his advisers gave him." The audience in the hall applauded. Christie continued: "See, Marco, the thing is this. When you're President of the United States, when you're a governor of a state, the memorized 30-second speech where you talk about how great America is at the end of it doesn't solve one problem for one person. They expect you to plow the snow. They expect you to get the schools open. And when the worst natural disaster in your state's history hits you, they expect you to rebuild their state, and that is what I've done." Christie ended the rebuke by adding, "None of that stuff happens on the floor of the United States Senate. It's a fine job, I'm glad you ran for it, but it does not prepare you to be the president of the United States."[27]

The Associated Press delivered a verdict against Rubio following the New Hampshire debate that no presidential candidate ever wants to hear. "Rubio experienced his worst moment in a presidential debate at the worst time, stumbling badly when forced to answer the fundamental question posed by rivals of his candidacy: whether he has the experience necessary to lead the nation," the AP wrote. "It was a cringe-worthy moment for Rubio three days before a New Hampshire contest in which he hopes to knock Christie, Bush and Ohio Governor John Kasich from the race. Even if it doesn't significantly change the contest in New Hampshire, the moment raises questions about Rubio's readiness to take on Democrat Hillary Clinton in a general election debate."[28]

Trump easily won the New Hampshire primary, with 35.2 percent of the vote, compared to 15.7 percent for Kasich in second place, 11.6 percent for Cruz in third place, and 10.5 percent for Rubio in a distant fifth place. As a result of getting less than the minimum 10 percent of the vote needed to get delegates from the state or to qualify for the next debate to be scheduled by CBS, Carly Fiorina, Chris Christie, and Jim Gilmore all suspended their campaigns, leaving six contenders yet in the field. In another proportional contest, Trump picked up 11 delegates, compared to 4 delegates for Kasich, and 2 delegates each for Cruz and Rubio. With a win considered convincing, the GOP presidential primary contest boiled down to Trump versus Cruz, Rubio, Kasich, Carson, and Bush.

The first round of early primaries ended with South Carolina on February 20, 2016, followed by Nevada on February 23, 2016. Trump again won both easily, capturing 32.5 percent of the vote in South Carolina to win 50 delegates in that state's winner-take-all contest, and 45.7 percent in Nevada where he picked up another 14 delegates in a proportional race.

At the end of the Nevada primary, the field was quickly narrowing to Trump versus Cruz and Rubio, as Bush dropped out after South Carolina, while Kasich and Carson each failed to win 10 percent of the primary votes in either state.

At this point, Trump was ahead with 82 delegates, compared to 17 for Cruz, and 16 for Rubio—still far short of the 1,237 delegates needed to win on the first ballot.

Trump Versus Cruz, the Insults

As the campaign heated up, Trump and Cruz began a series of back and forth verbal lashings. On September 23, 2016, Katie Reilly published in Time Magazine a list she compiled of 14 times Donald Trump and Ted Cruz insulted each other.[29] Here's her list:

1. **Trump: Cruz is "worse than Hillary.":** "He said with being a Canadian citizen, he said, 'Oh I didn't know that.' How did he not know that? Then he said with the loans, 'Oh, I didn't know that,' Smart guy. He doesn't know that? Yeah, that's worse than Hillary when you think about it," Trump said about Cruz on January 20.

2. **Trump: "How can Ted Cruz be an Evangelical Christian?":** "How can Ted Cruz be an Evangelical Christian when he lies so much and is so dishonest?" Trump tweeted on February 12.

3. **Trump: "You are the single biggest liar."':** "You are the single biggest liar. You probably are worse than Jeb Bush," Trump told Cruz at a primary debate on February 13. "Nasty guy. Now I know why he doesn't have one endorsement from any of his colleagues."

4. **Trump: "I will spill the beans on your wife!":** "Lyin' Ted Cruz just used a picture of Melania from a G.Q. shoot in his ad. Be careful, Lyin' Ted, or I will spill the beans on your wife!" Trump tweeted on March 22.

5. **Cruz: "Real men don't attack women.":** "Donald, real men don't attack women. Your wife is lovely, and Heidi is the love of my life," Cruz tweeted on March 24, after Trump shared an unflattering comparison of Melania Trump and Heidi Cruz.

6. **Cruz: "Donald, you're a sniveling coward":** "It is not acceptable for a big, loud New York bully to attack my wife. It is not acceptable for him to make insults, to send nasty tweets—and I don't know what he does late at night, but he tends to do these at about 11:30 at night, I assume when his fear is at the highest point," Cruz said on March 24. "I don't get angry often. But you mess with my wife, you mess with my kids, that'll do it every time. Donald, you're a sniveling coward. Leave Heidi the hell alone."

7. **Cruz: "Consistently disgraceful":** "Donald Trump's consistently disgraceful behavior is beneath the office we are seeking and we are not going to follow," Cruz tweeted on March 25.

8. **Cruz: "Nominating Donald Trump would be a train wreck":** "Nominating Donald Trump would be a train wreck. It would be handing the White House over to Hillary Clinton," Cruz tweeted on March 29.

9. **Cruz: "Big government liberal":** "This race is simple. Donald Trump and Hillary Clinton are both big government liberals," Cruz tweeted on April 26.

10. **Trump: Cruz's father was somehow involved with JFK's assassination:** "His father was with Lee Harvey Oswald prior to Oswald's being—you know, shot. I mean, the whole thing is

ridiculous," Trump said about Cruz's father, Rafael, in an interview on May 3. "What was he doing with Lee Harvey Oswald shortly before the death? Before the shooting? It's horrible."

11.   **Cruz: "This man is a pathological liar":** "This man is a pathological liar. He doesn't know the difference between truth and lies. He lies practically every word that comes out of his mouth, and in a pattern that I think is straight out of a psychology text book, his response is to accuse everybody else of lying," Cruz told reporters on May 3. "The man cannot tell the truth, but he combines it with being a narcissist—a narcissist at a level I don't think this country's ever seen. Donald Trump is such a narcissist that Barack Obama looks at him and goes, 'Dude, what's your problem?'" "The man is utterly amoral. Morality does not exist for him," Cruz added. "Donald is a bully. . . . Bullies come from a deep, yawning cavern of insecurity."

12.   **Cruz: "Vote your conscience":** "And to those listening, please, don't stay home in November," Cruz said on July 20 in his, speech at the Republican National Convention, declining to endorse Trump. "If you love our country, and love your children as much as I know that you do, stand, and speak, and vote your conscience, vote for candidates up and down the ticket who you trust to defend our freedom and to be faithful to the Constitution."

13.   **Cruz: "I am not in the habit of supporting people who attack my wife and attack my father":** "I am not in the habit of supporting people who attack my wife and attack my father," Cruz said on July 21, after declining to endorse Trump in his convention speech. "What does it say when you stand up and say, 'Vote your conscience,' and rabid supporters of our nominee begin screaming, 'What a horrible thing to say,'" Cruz said. "If we can't make the case for the American people that voting for our party's nominee is consistent with voting your conscience, is consistent with defending freedom and being faithful to the Constitution, then we are not going to win and we don't deserve to win."

14.   **Trump: "He may have ruined his political career":** "Honestly, he may have ruined his political career. I feel so badly. I feel so badly. And you know, he'll come and endorse over the next little while. He'll—because he has no choice. But I don't want his endorsement. What difference does it make? I don't want his

endorsement. I have such great—I don't want his endorsement. Ted, stay home, relax, enjoy yourself," Trump said at a press conference on July 22.

March 2016: A Month of Two Super Tuesdays

Eleven states headed to the polls on March 1, 2016, known as Super Tuesday I, with 595 delegates at stake in the GOP primaries, nearly half the 1,237 needed to guarantee winning on the first ballot at the RNC in Cleveland that July.

As Super Tuesday approached, Trump phoned in to ABC's "Good Morning America" to once again deny media attempts to pin him together with white supremacist David Duke, a onetime Ku Klux Klan leader based in New Orleans. After disavowing any connection to David Duke, Trump told the network, "There's nobody who's done more for equality than I have."[30] This was an issue that dogged Trump with the *Washington Post*, for instance, digging up comments Trump had made about David Duke tracing back to 1991 to argue that Trump "generally does not couple his statements about Duke with a firm condemnation of Duke's views."[31]

The controversy began on February 29, 2016, when CNN's Jake Tapper in an interview with Trump had pushed Trump "to publicly condemn universally the racism of former KKK grand wizard Duke," urging Trump to affirm that he did not want David Duke's vote or the vote of any other white supremacist in the 2016 election. As the *Washington Post* reported, Trump answered Tapper insisting, "I don't know anything about David Duke. Okay? I don't know anything about what you're even talking about with white supremacy. So I don't know. I don't know—did he endorse me, or what's going on? Because I know nothing about David Duke. I know nothing about white supremacists."[32]

Still, by Super Tuesday I, the mainstream media persisted with the issue, sensing the question would drive a wedge between Trump and African-American voters. Tapper had just executed a classic "gotcha," in that he managed to create a controversy over David Duke who was truly nothing more than a passing incidental in the thousands of media interviews Trump has given since 1991. At various times, when asked on television or radio, Trump had acknowledged that David Duke was appealing to a deep sentiment felt by many in Middle America that the far-left agenda that has come to dominate the Democratic Party since the

1960s failed to pay sufficient attention to the legitimate needs of working class Americans. Trump was confused by Tapper's questions precisely because the issue of David Duke came at Trump out of nowhere. Trump had not solicited David Duke's support and Trump had no intention of embracing white supremacist racism. Still, the goal of Tapper's question was to brand Trump and his supporters as secret KKK sympathizers who hated all minorities, all immigrants, and all Muslims.

Despite the determination of the Clinton-supporting mainstream media to trap Trump in diversionary "gotcha" distractions, Middle America saw through the ploy and the polls continued to favor Trump as GOP frontrunner. When the Super Tuesday I primaries were over, Trump walked away winning 7 states and 255 delegates, with victories in Alabama, Arkansas, Georgia, Massachusetts, Tennessee, Vermont, and Virginia. Cruz came in second, winning 3 states and 218 delegates, claiming victory in Alaska, Oklahoma, and Texas. Rubio came in third, winning only one state, Minnesota, while adding 96 delegates to his total. Kasich gained 21 delegates, even though he did not win a single state. Carson, who failed to place higher than third in any state contest suspended his campaign, after winning only 3 delegates on Super Tuesday. As a result, when Super Tuesday was over, the GOP primary race narrowed to four candidates: Trump, with 337 delegates, Cruz with 235 delegates, Rubio with 112 delegates, and Kasich with 27 delegates.

The next day, March 3, 2016, Mitt Romney, the GOP presidential candidate who Barack Obama defeated in 2012, delivered a 17-minute speech at the University of Utah in Salt Lake City, lambasting Trump's candidacy, going so far as to call him a "phony" and pressing for a contested convention, realizing that though Trump might win a plurality of convention delegates in the primaries, he may still fall below the 1,237 needed to win on the first ballot. In that eventuality, a candidate like Cruz or Rubio, even though second or third in the delegate count resulting from the primaries, might emerge as the GOP presidential candidate on a second, third, or subsequent ballot should the RNC in Cleveland devolve into a "brokered convention."[33]

"Here's what I know. Donald Trump is a phony, a fraud," Romney said in the conclusion to his speech. "His promises are as worthless as a degree from Trump University. He's playing the members of the American public for suckers. He gets a free ride to the White House and all we get is a lousy hat." Romney characterized Trump's policies as reckless, arguing, "His domestic policies would lead to recession. His foreign policies would make America and the world less safe." As if this were not sufficient, Romney added the following: "He has neither the temperament nor the judgment to be president and his personal qualities would mean that America would cease to be a shining city on a hill. I'm convinced America has greatness ahead. And this is a time for choosing. God bless us to choose a nominee who will make that vision a reality."[34]

Romney argued Trump's nomination would ensure Hillary Clinton's election. "And the audio and video of the infamous Tapper-Trump exchange on the Ku Klux Klan will play 100,000 times on cable and who knows how many million times on social media," Romney insisted, receiving laughter and applause from the audience. "There are a number of people who claim that Mr. Trump is a con man, a fake—thank you. Let me say that again. There's plenty of evidence that Mr. Trump is a con man, a fake. Mr. Trump has changed his positions not just over the years, but over the course of the campaign. And on the Ku Klux Klan, daily for three days in a row."

Later that day, Trump hit back at Romney, during a campaign rally in Portland, Maine. Trump called Romney a "failed candidate" for losing the 2012 election to Obama. "He failed horribly," Trump continued, insisting that 2012 was an election Romney should have won. "I'm not a fan of Barack Obama and I backed Mitt Romney," Trump continued. "You can see how loyal he is. He was begging for my endorsement. I could have said, 'Mitt, drop to your knees.' He would have dropped to his knees. He was begging."[35] Romney persisted in his attacks on Trump, telling CNN's Wolf Blitzer in an interview in Park City, Utah, on June 10, 2016, that he would not support the New York businessman's bid.[36] "I simply can't put my name down as someone who voted for principles that suggest racism, or xenophobia, misogyny, bigotry, who's been vulgar time and time again," Romney said, later adding, "I don't want to see trickle-down racism." Blitzer asked Romney if there was anything Trump could do to win his support. "I don't think there's anything I'm looking for from Mr. Trump to give him my support," Romney answered. "He's demonstrated who he is and I've decided that a person of that nature should not be the one who, if you will, becomes the example for coming generations."

Between Super Tuesday I and Super Tuesday II, eight states, two territories—Guam and the Virgin Islands—as well as Puerto Rico and the

District of Columbia held their primaries and caucuses. The results of Super Tuesday I were repeated, in that Trump came out on top, winning 5 states—Kentucky, Louisiana, Hawaii, Michigan, and Mississippi—and 140 delegates, followed by Cruz who won 3 states—Kansas, Maine, and Idaho—and 137 delegates, with Rubio in third place, winning Puerto Rico and the District of Columbia, followed by Kasich, who again failed to win a state.

Super Tuesday II on March 15, 2016, ushered the first winner-take-all primaries in Florida and Ohio, as well as primaries in Illinois, Missouri, North Carolina, and the Northern Mariana Islands, with a total of 367 delegates up for grabs. Here, Trump won decisive victories, winning all the Super II primaries, except for Ohio, which went to Ohio's Governor Kasich. As the voting ended on Super Tuesday, Trump's delegate total went to 705, with Cruz remaining in second place with 423. With Rubio losing his home state of Florida to Trump, in a 99 delegate winner-take-all primary, Rubio suspended his campaign. The field now narrowed to three contenders: Trump, Cruz, and Kasich. Though in reality, the only questions that remained was whether Cruz could prevent Trump from getting to the all-important 1,237 delegate total, and whether Kasich would have a chance in a RNC convention battle where Trump and Cruz knocked heads as the two favorites. While Cruz was not yet mathematically ruled out from reaching the 1,237-delegate total, he virtually needed to sweep the remaining primaries if he were to have a chance.

After Super Tuesday II, the odds makers continued to calculate that it would be difficult, but not impossible, for Trump to reach the 1,237-delegate goal. "Republican voters handed down a split decision Tuesday that suggests the race for the party's nomination will go all the way to Cleveland, raising the prospect of a contested convention that could tear the GOP in two," the political writers at Time Magazine noted. "Donald Trump padded his delegate lead by grabbing the night's biggest prize, a blowout victory in Florida that knocked Senator Marco Rubio out of the race," Time Magazine continued. "Trump also snagged victories in Illinois and North Carolina and appeared set to eke out a fourth win in Missouri as the final returns trickled in late Tuesday. But his failure to deliver a knockout blow in Ohio gives him an uphill fight to secure the 1,237 delegates required to win the GOP nomination outright."[37] Fox News correctly observed that after winning Ohio's primary, Kasich remained in the race, hoping to act as a spoiler. "Even with his Tuesday haul, Kasich remains in fourth place in the GOP delegate count and faces the toughest path to the nomination of the remaining candidates," Fox News commented. "He has openly said, however, that his hope is to deny Trump the requisite delegates to clinch the nomination before the July convention in Cleveland."[38]

Trump's Campaign Manager Woes

Despite being the GOP front-runner virtually from the moment he declared his candidacy, Trump had run with an exceptionally thin campaign staff. Almost from the beginning, his two stalwarts remained his first two hires—Corey Lewandowski, 41 years old when hired and Hope Hicks, 27 years old when hired.

Lewandowski graduated from the New Hampshire police academy in 2006 and served with the New Hampshire state police, before being hired as the New Hampshire director for Americans for Prosperity, a conservative advocacy group founded by billionaire brothers David and Charles Koch. Before working with Trump, Lewandowski had no experience with a national political campaign.[39] In 2002, Lewandowski ran the reelection campaign of US Senator Robert C. Smith in New Hampshire who lost in the Republican primary to challenger John E. Sununu, the son of former New Hampshire Governor and former White House chief of staff John H. Sununu. In 1994, while still a college student, Lewandowski lost a write-in campaign for the Massachusetts House, and in 2012, he ran unsuccessfully for treasurer of Windham, New Hampshire.

Hope Hicks, a child model for Ralph Lauren, entered Trump's world in 2012 when she began working on Ivanka Trump's fashion line, while employed by the public relations firm Hiltzik Strategies. In August 2014, Hicks went to work inside the Trump organization, continuing to handle PR work for Ivanka Trump's fashion line as well as some Trump resorts. Profiled by *Cosmopolitan*, Hicks was portrayed as a former "college jock" for having played lacrosse for four years for Southern Methodist University in Dallas, where she completed her undergraduate studies.[40] Cosmopolitan further reported that in January 2015, when Donald Trump called Hicks into his office and said he was making her an offer to work as press secretary for the upcoming presidential campaign he planned to start in June, Hicks had had no prior political experience.

On March 15, 2016, a Politico trio of reporters led by Kenneth P. Vogel reported that Lewandowski had a history of quick temper and heavy-handed leadership that created such concerns among Trump's campaign staff that in February 2016, some even planned a coup against him.[41] "In interviews with more than 20 sources who have dealt with Lewandowski during his nearly year-long tenure with the Trump campaign and in his previous job with the Koch brothers-backed advocacy group Americans for Prosperity, complaints emerged about Lewandowski being rough with reporters and sexually suggestive with female journalists, while profanely berating conservative officials and co-workers he deemed to be challenging his authority," Politico reported.

Lewandowski's claim to fame in his time as Trump campaign manager was his repeated insistence that "Trump should be Trump"—a saying others on the campaign team took as an argument that Trump's undisciplined, free-wheeling approach was producing results with voters, even if his unscripted often ad-lib comments in speeches created numerous gaffes that took precious campaign time and effort to walk-back. Critics within the Trump camp came to view Lewandowski as a loose cannon with a short fuse, a dangerous combination for a traveling companion on the Trump airplane who had ample time to share with the candidate his antipathy toward colleagues, political opponents, and perceived rivals.

The controversy over Lewandowski blew up on March 8, 2016, following a Trump press conference at the Trump National Golf Club in Jupiter, Florida. This was in the period immediately after Super Tuesday I, during which Trump was making an effort to "pivot" from the more aggressively combative style he had used attacking rival candidates up to that time, into a more diplomatic posture the mainstream media was recommending would be more appropriate for a mature politician during the general election, assuming Trump won the nomination. Lewandowski effectively ended any chance that Trump's "kinder and gentler" image would persist long when he allegedly grabbed Breitbart reporter Michelle Fields, appearing in some videos of the incident to have been making an effort to allow Trump to exit without being followed by reporters continuing to shout questions.

"Addressing the gathered reporters and the nation at large, Trump was in an especially jovial mood Tuesday night," Michelle wrote, describing the incident in her own words.[42] "The networks just declared he had won the Mississippi Republican primary and, during his speech, that he won the Michigan Republican primary as well."

She continued: "I wasn't called upon to ask a question during the televised press conference, but afterwards Trump wandered around, stopping at every reporter to take their questions. When he approached me, I asked him about his view on an aspect of affirmative action."

This is where Lewandowski intervened.

"Trump acknowledged the question, but before he could answer I was jolted backwards," Fields recalled. "Someone had grabbed me tightly by the arm and yanked me down. I almost fell to the ground, but was able to maintain my balance. Nonetheless, I was shaken."

Washington Post reporter Ben Terris wrote immediately after the incident that it was Lewandowski who aggressively grabbed Fields and "yanked her out of the way." Terris wrote that Fields stumbled and finger-shaped bruises appeared on her arm[43] Fields subsequently posted on Twitter a photograph of the bruise on her arm she claimed resulted from Lewandowski's attack.[44] Hope Hicks issued a statement for the campaign stating Field's accusation was "entirely false," claiming she was there as Trump exited the press conference and she "did not witness any encounter."[45]

WND reporter Jerome Corsi noted reporter Michelle Fields had been involved in a series of incidents where she "had a history of becoming news," citing an incident that took place in November 2011 when Fields, then a Daily Caller reporter, claimed she and videographer Direna Cousins "were struck" by NYPD officers as the police tried to clear the street of Occupy Wall Street protesters, as well as an incident in which Fields accused former US congressman Allen West of grabbing her in front of an elevator when they were colleagues at PJ Media.[46]

On March 8, the police in Jupiter, Florida charged Lewandowski with misdemeanor battery over the incident. Then, on April 14, the Palm Beach County state attorney dropped the charges. CNN reported Lewandowski was relieved the charges were dropped, saying he wanted to move on from the incident that he characterized as a "huge distraction" for the campaign.[47] Here, Lewandowski had a valid point. The incident served to fuel various narratives the Clinton-supporting media was aggressively advancing against Trump, claiming the Lewandowski incident validated both Trump's "war on women" as well as Trump's propensity to encourage aggressive reactions among his supporters to those in his audiences expressing opposition or dissent to his message.

Throughout the incident, Trump stayed loyal to Lewandowski. On March 11, Trump told CNN that it was his opinion Fields concocted the entire story, portraying herself as a victim in order to replace Trump as the main attraction in the media's coverage of the campaign. "Everybody said nothing happened," Trump said. "Perhaps she made the story up. I think that's what happened."[48] But as the incident settled down and faded away, the dynamics within the Trump campaign changed. Trump and his senior advisors realized that the campaign was shifting into a new dimension. Every day now, the cable news media was running 24-by-7 discussions questioning whether Trump had a "pathway" to reach the 1,237 goal. If Trump was going to become president, he and his campaign had to become more disciplined. Winning the remaining primary contests and corralling convention delegates to vote for Trump as obligated on the first ballot was going to take the type of experienced and mature management skills that Lewandowski so obviously lacked.

Trump Hires Manafort

On the Friday before Easter, Trump called me at my south Florida home. "Can they really steal this thing from me?" he asked. Remember, that Trump's call came in the wake of stinging losses in Wisconsin, North Dakota, Colorado and having the Louisiana delegates stolen out from under his nose—even though he had easily won the Louisiana primaries. So his concern was obvious. "Yes, they can steal it, and they will try," I said. "Even though I won all the primaries?" "Yes, they're going to play games with the rules." "What should I do?" the mogul asked. "Call my former partner, Paul Manafort. You've met him, he's a friend of Tom Barrack and he knows more about convention politics than anyone in America." Trump asked for Manafort's cell phone number and I provided it.

On March 28, Trump hired veteran Republican strategist Paul J. Manafort to lead his final delegate-corralling efforts. The *New York Times* commented that Manafort, 66, "is among the few political hands in either party with direct experience managing nomination fights." The newspaper noted that as a young Republican operative, Manafort helped manage the 1976 convention floor for Gerald Ford in his showdown with Ronald Reagan, the last time Republicans entered a convention with no candidate having clinched the nomination.

The *New York Times* continued, stressing that Manafort performed a similar function for Mr. Reagan in 1980, and played leading roles in the 1988 and 1996 conventions, for George Bush and Bob Dole. "The hiring is a sign that Mr. Trump is intensifying his focus on delegate wrangling as his opponents mount a tenacious effort to deny him the 1,237 delegates he would need to secure the Republican nomination," wrote veteran political reporters Alexander Burns and Maggie Haberman. "Under those circumstances, Mr. Trump's opponents hope they can wrest that prize from him in a contested convention."[49]

Within a few days, Trump let it be known that Manafort, not Lewandowski, was now the campaign manager. While Trump did not fire Lewandowski, the decision to hire Manafort and appoint him campaign manager effectively demoted Lewandowski to "body man" and a scheduler, whose main assignment was to travel with Trump, while all strategic decisions were now in Manafort's domain.[50]

Paul J. Manafort, Jr. grew up in the hardscrabble industrial city of New Britain, Connecticut where his father Paul Manafort, Sr. was the popular Republican Mayor of the overwhelmingly Democratic city. Paul graduated from Georgetown where he became active in the College Republicans and a lifetime adversary of Karl Rove. It was in Young Republicans that Paul, like legendary convention operators F. Clifton White and Bill Timmons, honed his convention tactical skills. In 1976 Jim Baker recruited Manafort to President Gerald Ford's delegate-counting convention operation. Manafort served as the elected National Auditor of the Young Republican National Federation and was expected to become National Chairman in 1977, but his support of Ford caused a rift in the dominant conservative faction of the Young Republicans. I was supposed to manage Manafort's campaign, but instead I became the candidate while Manafort managed my raucous convention operation. We won, and I became Young Republican National Federation chair from 1977-79.

I introduced Manafort to Donald Trump at the 1988 Republican National Convention in New Orleans. Manafort is the GOP's master "vote counter." His specialty is the "hard-count" and surprise tactics. With experience managing Gerald Ford's 1976 nomination fight against Ronald Reagan, and high profile roles in the 1980, 1988 and 1996 conventions, Manafort was sold to the media as Trump's expert on convention preparation. To the naked eye, he was hired to count delegates and lock the nomination down in Cleveland.

Manafort transformed the billionaire's unruly and weak primary campaign into a team that could beat the Clinton juggernaut. Coming aboard just days before Trump's shattering loss to Ted Cruz in Wisconsin, the campaign veteran had his work cut out for him. Paul and I agreed:

there was a clear path toward 1,237 delegates, the magic number to gain the nomination. But that meant winning again in the delegate selection, too—a vital part of the primary process that determines precisely who the delegates will be in Cleveland. Control that, and on the convention floor it might not matter who won the state at the ballot box.

There are complexities to delegate counting that only veteran professionals like Manafort appreciate. Vox.com[51] published an article in mid-April titled, "Donald Trump's amazing incompetence at delegate selection, explained," that revealed just how far behind Trump was in controlling delegates even in states where Trump had won the primary. For instance, all six delegates in South Carolina were officially bound to vote for Trump on the first ballot. But in reality, three were Cruz supporters, and two were uncommitted. That meant that in South Carolina, a state where Trump had won the primary and had all six delegates pledged to vote for him on the first ballot, only one of the six delegates was actually a Trump supporter. This spelled disaster should the convention go to a second or subsequent ballot, in a scenario where Trump failed to get 1,237 delegates on the first ballot. Vox.com noted this basic story was repeating itself in many other states Trump had won. Corey Lewandowski did not have the experience to tackle this level of complexity. It's not clear Corey even knew this level of complexity existed in the real-world politics involved in securing enough delegates in the primaries who were truly committed to your candidate. Manafort, it turned out, was just what the doctor ordered for candidate Trump to navigate through the primaries to a successful completion.

Before Manafort was hired, the polls pointed to a Wisconsin shellacking. When it came true on April 5, 2016, the loss in the Wisconsin primary took a lot of wind out of the Trump campaign's sails. From there forward, the billionaire had to win 69 percent of all remaining pledged delegates. That was difficult to do, but possible, especially with Manafort now aboard. After losing the Wisconsin primary to Cruz, Trump had no choice but to win some very competitive primaries. Otherwise, Trump would fail to close the deal. Lewandowski wasn't up to the task, especially if the contest went all the way to June in California. Trump, throughout his career, has been known for his determination and his ability to close the deal, even if it meant getting a new management team in place right now.

Once Paul landed at Trump Tower, he began to understand just how poorly Lewandowski had managed the primary process. Lewandowski, an inexperienced campaign manager who, once again, had never before participated in a national presidential campaign, had failed to appreciate the importance of investing campaign funds to develop competent state political operations. After each primary or caucus passed, Lewandowski typically fired his in-state staff and moved on. This kept overhead down but, as a result, the complex delegate selection process that followed went untended. Losses in states like Wyoming, Missouri and Utah were scuffing the luster of the billionaire's primary campaign. By the time Trump lost Wisconsin, his threadbare campaign was showing through and reporters were openly taking bets on when, exactly, the entire show would come crashing to the ground.

When he was hired, I was completely confident Manafort would succeed in righting the ship. Manafort, my partner at a successful Washington lobbying firm with GOP campaign veteran, and top political consultant, Charles Black that we co-founded after we helped elect Ronald Reagan, had excelled at tough, even global assignments. At Black Manafort Stone, he was our lead partner on all international work, including controversial clients like Ferdinand Marcos of the Philippines and Jonas Savimbi, the anti-communist guerilla leader in Angola. In his most notable and recent international work, Paul was senior adviser to former Ukrainian President Viktor Yanukovych. In completing this assignment, Paul worked on site in Ukraine for seven years, building the President's powerful Party of Regions. When Yanukovych fled to Mother Russia in the Maidan protests of 2014, Manafort stuck around to pick up the pieces of the party he had built. He stayed active in the region, but Maidan essentially put an end to his long and lucrative political consulting contract in Ukraine.

While these were demanding and lucrative projects, Manafort had learned to move among heads of state like he's one of them. His ease working with celebrity clients and his mastery of the game made him a perfect advisor to Donald Trump. Signed on just days before an expected loss in Wisconsin, Manafort allowed Lewandowski to fail, while he focused on the subsequent primary contests. With Manafort in place and putting the band back together again, the April 19th New York primary was a lock.

This time around, Michael Caputo served as state director and John Haggerty, one of the smartest political operatives I've ever met, ran the show. As the New York primary approached, Trump deputy campaign

manager Michael Glassner invited Caputo and Haggerty onto the national payroll. Along with Erie County Republican Chairman Nick Lang-
worthy and State Assemblyman Dave DiPietro, they had locked up 85
percent of the weighted vote of GOP county chairs six weeks out.

Most of the powerful chairmen pledged to Trump for the presidential
primary had been assembled in 2014 to back him for governor. Haggerty
and the others did a great job reuniting the team. In fact, the 2014 exercise in
futility was mighty helpful in shutting down Ted Cruz in 2016. At an April
7th meeting with Caputo, Haggerty and DiPietro in Trump Tower, Manafort reviewed the status of the New York primary and was relieved to hear
Cruz had no footing. More than half of New Yorkers polled backed Trump
and the way the state cut up its delegates—by congressional district—made
it possible for the home state candidate to win every single delegate.

Cruz vied with John Kasich for the scraps left on the table. Haggerty described the team's goal to Manafort under the glass ceiling of the
Tower's street level atrium: Not one delegate for Kasich, not one delegate
for Cruz. Under Buffalo developer Carl Paladino's state chairmanship,
the team had assembled so much support that it was a clear possibility. Trump was far more popular among the more conservative upstate
Republicans, and he lagged with New York City's notorious moderate
establishment crowd. He also had soft spots in Syracuse and Paladino
had alienated important GOP county chairs in the North Country. Still,
Haggerty had assembled a solid plan to get out the vote.

Manafort left the meeting expecting a maximum loss of six to ten
delegates, leaving upwards of 90 for Trump. He was confident that
Caputo would bring home the win. Like me, Manafort had known
Caputo since the eighties, and the Black Manafort team had trained
him. This gave Paul some breathing room to fix the national campaign
and grow the staff.

As I recounted to then-publisher Stephen Bannon in Breitbart on
April 6, 2016, outside the closely run New York campaign, I saw very
little Trump infrastructure in the states. The woman who ran Trump's
campaign efforts in Wisconsin previously managed his campaign in
Oklahoma. Trump lost both. Prior to that, she had never run any political campaign, so there was no depth of experience. This is something I
saw again and again, particularly at the grass roots level.

Now, I salute these people for their enthusiasm, but presidential elections are a science. This is not something we guess about. And Trump was

soon to move to a series of states like Colorado, Wyoming and Arizona, which would be watched very carefully. And those were sure to become hand-to-hand combat at state conventions or state committee meetings, where once again the Trump people had built no infrastructure.

It was there, in Colorado, where Lewandowski's schemes to destroy Manafort first drew media attention. Behind the scenes, Lewandowski fought hard from the moment Manafort arrived to regain his previous power over the campaign and to undermine his far more experienced nemesis, whose expertise eclipsed the presidential first-timer.

Soon, Lewandowski put out a fatwah on Manafort, ordering his charges not to work or even to speak with Manafort or anyone on Manafort's team. A young operative named James Baker, who Lewandowski himself had recently hired to lead the Colorado campaign, was fired 48 hours after he arrived in the state. His crime, as far as Lewandowski was concerned, was that Baker simply talked with Manafort. Later, Lewandowski was suspected of leaking false and defamatory information to the press about Baker, trying to destroy his reputation, sending a strong message to his team that he viewed working with the new regime as betrayal.

Manafort scrambled to fix delegate selection, pushing past Lewandowski's sabotage and dispatching experienced operatives to key states. But the operation was on fire. Soon, it hit the press. The Cruz campaign captured all 34 Colorado delegates at a series of congressional district meetings and the state party convention—which took place one week after Lewandowski fired Baker. An early March social media post from a discarded Trump state operative, John Hulsizer, revealed that Lewandowski had intentionally left virtually everyone in the dark about delegate selection. Upset that the process was being ignored, the Trump loyalist asked Lewandowski's right hand man what was to be done. "When I got my response from Michael Glassner about the delegates I flipped out," Hulsizer wrote on Facebook. "He said, 'Mr. Trump doesn't understand how delegates work, so we are leaving that issue alone right now.'"

Lewandowski's foolish tactic backfired, of course, and the April 9th Colorado delegate news rocked Trump. The family was aghast at how this vital part of the process had been overlooked. It was at this point that Jared Kushner, Ivanka's husband, began to be more vocal in his criticism and started to develop a discernable disrespect for Lewandowski and his failures.

On board only a few weeks, the results of Manafort's work—building a campaign organization from nothing—had not yet borne fruit.

Delegate selection failures stacked up. Nick Gass of Politico summed it in just one long, tortuous run-on sentence: "[Beyond Colorado, Trump has] suffered delegate setbacks in Georgia (where one county that went for Trump by 12 points will be represented by 90 percent Cruz backers), Indiana (where Trump appears virtually assured of being shut out), Iowa (where all but one of the state's 12 delegates is committed to Cruz on a second ballot), Louisiana (where Trump lost 10 delegates and filed a complaint with the RNC), North Carolina (where Trump had fewer congressional level delegates than John Kasich), North Dakota (where Cruz's delegates won 18 of 25 slots earlier this month), South Carolina (where on Saturday he picked up just one delegate out of six on the ballot), South Dakota (where support for Cruz among delegates would appear higher) and Tennessee (where the Trump campaign also threatened to sue after a heated convention)—mostly at the hands of Cruz."[32]

If Manafort had waited one week or two to join the Trump campaign, it may have faltered and failed. Lewandowski's Wisconsin disaster hit hard but the campaign had a two-week break before New York, which looked to be a winner. But the team who had installed high profile Republicans leading all 27 single congressional districts couldn't get headquarters staffers' attention.

Caputo's associations with Manafort and me were stalling the New York primary team's efforts to close strong. Bent on stopping our efforts to salvage the campaign, Lewandowski targeted him, too. Caputo's calls to headquarters went unanswered after he was seen talking animatedly with Manafort at the April 6th Trump rally in Bethpage, New York.

It got worse: even Carl Paladino, Trump's friend and New York State chairman, got so fed up with the constipation at Trump Tower that he plotted out a series of rallies on his own and sold the schedule to the advance team. If he hadn't done that, who knows how many delegates Cruz and Kasich would have peeled off.

Attempts to engage hundreds of volunteers and Republican leaders across the state in the GOTV effort fell on deaf ears. In the end, only John Haggerty was able to directly impact the final days of the New York campaign—he was the only member of the New York State campaign working in Trump Tower on primary day April 19th.

No matter: the primary effort was so well organized that Kasich drew just six delegates to Trump's 89—and Cruz was crushed, not gaining even one. Not even Corey Lewandowski can fuck up a Haggerty operation.

The New York victory party was the start of a series of similar nights of celebration in the Trump Tower lobby. But with Manafort appointed campaign manager, the billionaire was gaining steam once again. After Wisconsin, state after state fell in Trump's column.

Cruz: The Spoiler, Just "Hanging in the Race"

With Manafort in place, the Trump campaign turned its focus on Sen. Ted Cruz, the only remaining candidate with a real potential to play a spoiler role, preventing Trump from reaching the 1,237-delegate goal. This was brought into sharp focus in the GOP primaries held between March 22 and April 19, 2016. Of the eight contests held in that time period, Trump won three states—Arizona, North Dakota, and New York—plus American Samoa, while Cruz won four states—Utah, Wisconsin, Colorado, and Wyoming. While Trump came out ahead gaining another 154 delegates, Cruz was not far behind, winning 123 delegates. Kasich, still in the race, won no states and no delegates in any of these contests.

Trump's victory in New York meant Cruz was mathematically eliminated from getting to 1,237 delegates, simply because he still needed 678 more while only 674 were remaining. "By just about every metric, Ted Cruz is losing the race for the Republican nomination," wrote reporter Lauren Fox in TalkingPointsMemo.com on April 21, 2016.[53] "After a crushing third place finish in New York Tuesday night, Cruz can no longer win the Republican nomination without a chaotic, contested convention in Cleveland." Yet, as TPM noted, Cruz was hanging in the race, telling CBS radio in Philadelphia, "At this point nobody is getting 1,237."

TPM asked whether Cruz had an effective rationale for staying in the race. "While Cruz fares better than Trump against potential Democratic nominee Hillary Clinton in a head-to-head matchup, polls still show he would lose to her in November," Lauren Fox noted. "Ohio Governor John Kasich—as he often reminds voters on the trail—is the only candidate left in the race who consistently shows he can beat Clinton in the general." TPM further argued that in order to steal the nomination from Trump at a convention in Cleveland, Cruz would need to explain why he actually deserves the nomination. "He can argue that Trump is a disaster for the party," Lauren Fox continued. "He can argue Trump alienates women. He can keep painting Trump as a phony, shyster conservative who has given money to Democrats. It's not clear why those arguments, which did not work for other Republican candidates trying to defeat

Trump in primary contests, would work in the more difficult task of wresting delegates from him." TPM also commented that Cruz had to overcome a contradiction inherent to his campaign. "While Cruz has tried to make the case that he is an outsider—the only candidate in the race who can take on the 'Washington cartel' and repair the country—his argument at the convention will be that he is the true Republican and Trump the callow insurgent," Lauren Fox concluded.

On April 4, 2016, Politico reported that after getting shut out in New York, Cruz had begun a process of hunting for "Trojan Horse" convention delegates, defined as delegates with a personal allegiance to a candidate that differs from the way the delegate is obligated to vote on the first ballot.[54] Cruz was hunting for both his own delegates, who might waver from him on a second or subsequent ballot in Cleveland, or for Trump delegates in the same position. Politico reported the Cruz team was "logging detailed profiles and loyalty scores of each delegate, honing pitches to convince wavering allies to commit and deploying surrogates to stiffen the spines of wobbly backers." Politico further reported Cruz's "delegate whipping effort" drew upon wealthy donors and sophisticated technology, "including Koch brothers-backed i360, Wilson Perkins Allen Research, Targeted Victory and Cambridge Analytica. Combined, they're helping to build the kind of individualized strategy that the Cruz campaign sees as a backstop against weak-kneed delegates."

On April 25, 2016, CNN reported Trump's reaction to Cruz's "Trojan Horse" strategy. "I just read an article about, Cruz is working really hard to—I don't want to use the word 'bribe'—but, to bribe the delegates from all over the place," Trump said, nearly shouting out the second "bribe."[55] What had become clear was that in the delegate-counting final phase of the GOP primaries, Trump needed the expertise and experience brought to his campaign by Paul Manafort to prevent professional politicians like Cruz from using backroom tactics to rig the delegate count to prevent Trump from getting the nomination.

Cruz: A Pentacostal, Not an Evangelical

On March 10, in the run-up to the March 15 Florida primary, Jacob Engels, the founder of the East Orlando Post, published in his newspaper an article entitled, "Ted Cruz, Closet Pentecostal," in which Engels, a seasoned Florida political operative, questioned Cruz's claim to be an Evangelical Christian.[56] "While Ted Cruz proudly proclaims he is an Evangelical Christian, his campaign takes pains to hide the truth that Cruz and his pastor father, Rafael Cruz are Pentacostal Christians, a fact further hidden by having Ted and Heidi Cruz's belong to the congregation of First Baptist Church, a Southern Baptist church in Houston, as their home church," Engels wrote. "Pentecostals believe the Apostles of Jesus were aided by the Holy Spirit's 'gift of tongues,' in what Pentecostals consider as 'baptism by the Holy Spirit,' deriving from 1 Corinthians 12:14, that gave the Apostles the ability to speak in a 'God-enabled prayer language' that Pentecostals believe permits even today allows the unintelligible human utterances of a Pentecostal evangelist to be understood by foreigners who do not speak the Pentecostal evangelist's language," Engels stressed.

Engels noted that reporter Sarah Pulliam Bailey, writing in the *Washington Post* on March 25, 2015 was the first to recognize Ted Cruz's 2016 presidential campaign logo and the purifying tongue-of-fire logo used commonly to identify Pentecostal churches.[57] Engels stressed that Rafael Cruz is today identified not as an Evangelical, but as a pastor with Purifying Fire International Ministry, although in January 2014, as Ted Cruz was preparing his presidential campaign, Rafael Cruz scrapped the group's website, www.purifyingfire.org, after various blogs began identifying the ministry as rooted in "a radical Christian ideology known as Dominionism or Christian Reconstructionism."

Dominionism calls on anointed Christian leaders to take over government to make the laws of the nation in accordance with Biblical laws. Engels documented that Rafael Cruz, at the Pastor Larry Huch's New Beginnings mega-church in Bedford Texas, outside Dallas, on August 26, 2012, in a Dominionist sermon proclaimed his son, Ted Cruz, to be the "anointed one," a Dominionist Messiah who would bring God's law to reign, embedding into the article a YouTube video of the event. Engels ended the article by arguing that by identifying Ted Cruz as the anointed one,' Rafael Cruz designated his son as what he believes is God's choice to lead an evangelical coup d'état, such that, "Cruz's campaign may be less about the White House and more about the white horses that will usher in the God's Kingdom in the New Testament book of Revelation, Chapter 19."

Given that Cruz had predicated much of his presidential campaign on the argument that he was the only GOP candidate who professed to be an Evangelical Christian, Engels' widely read piece published on the eve of the Florida primary may have been enough to cause Cruz to finish third, at 17 percent, behind Rubio, at 27 percent, in a contest that Trump won with 46 percent of the vote—more than the votes of Rubio and Cruz combined.

The National Enquirer

On March 23, 2016, the *National Enquirer* published a story claiming private investigators were digging into at least five alleged extra-marital affairs involving Ted Cruz.[58] The sensational story could not be immediately dismissed, if only because the *National Enquirer* broke the story in 2007 that former Sen. John Edwards, the vice-presidential running mate of then Sen. John Kerry in 2004, had covered up a scandal involving a love child born to him and Rielle Hunter, a filmmaker who he hired to work for his presidential campaign.[59] "It's Over For Pervy Ted" and "Cruz's 5 Secret Mistresses!" screamed from the front page of the Enquirer in every super market and liquor store nationwide. I would have thought these kind of accusations gave Cruz some sort of manliness which otherwise is sorely lacking.

Two days later, on March 25, Ted Cruz denounced the story in a press conference in Wisconsin, during which he declared, "This garbage has no place in politics." Cruz charged that operatives working for Trump fed the story to the *National Enquirer*, a tabloid that had endorsed Trump. "You know, Donald is fond of giving people nicknames, with this pattern he should not be surprised to see people calling him 'Sleazy Donald' because that is his first and last redoubt, to turn to sleaze," Cruz said.[60] "This has no business in politics. Years from now, when my daughters Google this, they will read these lies, these attacks, that Donald and his henchmen and his buddies and the *National Enquirer* spread about." But the damage was done, as #CruzSexScandal began trending on Twitter.

The Cruz sex scandal broke amid a raging Internet exchange triggered when the Cruz-supporting super PAC, Make America Awesome, used a nude photograph of Trump's wife Melania, that first appeared in an issue of GQ published in January 2000, some 16 years previously, in a 2016 campaign advertisement themed, "Meet Melania Trump. Your next First Lady. Or, you could support Ted Cruz on Thursday." Trump retaliated as soon as the super PAC advertisement appeared, posting on Twitter a side-by-side headshot showing Cruz's wife Heidi scowling, compared to Melania looking beautiful. In posting the comparison photos, Trump tweeted, "The images are worth a thousand words."[61]

Predictably, Cruz shot back, denouncing Trump. "It's not easy to tick me off. I don't get angry often. But you mess with my wife, you mess with my kids, that'll do it every time," Cruz said in Wisconsin. "Donald, you're a sniveling coward. Leave Heidi the hell alone." Cruz suggested Trump had started it with a tweet during the Arizona and Utah primary voting in which Trump threatened "to spill the beans" on Cruz's wife—a suggestion Cruz took as confirmation that Trump operatives had concocted the story alleging Cruz was involved in extra-marital affairs.[62] Cruz went so far as to speculate Trump went personal, attacking his wife, because "Trump had a very bad night last night in Utah," where Cruz took 70 percent of the vote, allowing him to claim 40 delegates, while Cruz won Arizona's primary, taking all of the state's 58 votes in the winner-take-all contest.[63]

Trump countered in a statement saying, "I did not know about it, and have not, as yet, read it. Likewise, I have nothing to do with the National Enquirer and unlike Lyin' Ted Cruz I do not surround myself with political hacks and henchmen and then pretend total innocence." Trump continued: "Ted Cruz's problem with the National Enquirer is his and his alone, and while they were right about O.J. Simpson, John Edwards and others, I certainly hope they are not right about Lyin' Ted Cruz."[64]

Then Cruz blamed the story on me, Roger Stone. "It is a story that quoted one source on the record: Roger Stone, Donald Trump's chief political adviser," said Cruz.

"It is attacking my family. And what is striking is Donald's henchman, Roger Stone, had for months been foreshadowing that this attack was coming. It's not surprising that Donald's tweet occurs the day before the attack comes out. And I would note that Mr. Stone is a man who has 50 years of dirty tricks behind him. He's a man for whom a term was coined for copulating with a rodent. Well, let me be clear: Donald Trump may be a rat, but I have no desire to copulate with him."

"Ted Cruz took the bait like a chump."

I denied any responsibility in posting or starting the story. In fact, Frank Morano on "AM70 The Answer" interviewed me on March 28, 2016, and this is an excerpt from that interview.

FRANK MORANO: We have Roger Stone, noted *New York Times* bestselling author, longtime Republican political consultant and former adviser to Donald Trump, and the only person, who you heard Ted

Cruz in the clip I just played you, the only person quoted on the record in this incredible *National Enquirer* article. . . I don't know where to begin, clearly the Cruz campaign has blamed you for everything except for kidnapping the Lindbergh baby, why? Everybody is acknowledging, even the NYT today, that this attempt to dig up these Cruz extramarital affairs was originally carried out by the Rubio campaign, why are they making you the guy everyone is deciding to blame?

ROGER STONE: I guess it is an attempt at deflection. You've been in politics a long time, the only thing worse than being talked about is not being talked about. So I guess, I have a brand, perhaps a brand for rough and tumble politics, a brand for the dramatic, but in this particular case, the private detectives who are specifically cited in the article. . . were actually working for and paid by Marco Rubio. I believe the Rubio campaign elected not to use this information, but they kept it as a hedge against some of the allegations about Rubio's personal life, and in the end they elected not to use it. And before you knew it he was out of the race.

I think these private detectives got paid twice. They got paid once when they did the original work for Marco Rubio, and they got paid again when they on their own went ahead and sold it to the *National Enquirer*. They will admit that they pay for information they can confirm. But in this case, I can tell you categorically, I did not plant the story in the *National Enquirer*, and then blaming Donald Trump or his campaign is somewhat outrageous. I never discussed this with Donald or anyone in his campaign.

All I did do, when a longtime reporter from the *National Enquirer*, who I used to know when she was at the *New York Post*, and before that at the *UK Daily Mail*, called and asked for a comment, and I was happy to give a comment on the record: "If this is proven, it would be highly problematic for Ted's image, since it is built around his moral superiority, and his appeal to evangelical Christians. . .

MORANO: Why should we care about who Ted Cruz sleeps with?

STONE: Neither you or I are running for president. . .And he is, and he holds himself out as a moral exemplar, and I think it is the hypocrisy that once again is problematic here. And you have to wonder whether these women, one of whom worked for the Carly Fiorina campaign and then shortly thereafter Ted Cruz pays Carly half a million dollars. Ted despises Carly, and Carly despises Ted. What is the $500,000 for? Can you say hush money? He [Ted Cruz] specifically called me a henchman. Henchmen get paid. I'm not paid anything by the Trump campaign, so therefore by definition I can't be a henchman . . . I think he's the one who has been copulating with rodents . . .

"Ratfucking" was a term coined to describe me and other political allies of Richard Nixon who spread rumors and foiled the campaign events of rivals.

That CNN, let Ted Cruz attack me falsely by name at least three times during prime-time hours without ever affording me the opportunity to respond on air not only violates journalistic ethics, but it also reveals that CNN isn't a news organization so much as they are antagonists to anything Trump.

Rafael Cruz and Lee Harvey Oswald

On April 7, 2016 blogger Wayne Madsen, a former US military intelligence officer, posted a report he had written titled, "Was the father of presidential hopeful Cruz involved in the JFK assassination?"[65]

Then, on April 20, 2016, the *National Enquirer* published a sensational cover story, "Ted Cruz Father Linked to JFK Assassination." The tabloid published a photograph showing a previously identified man helping Lee Harvey Oswald, the man the Warren Commission identified as JFK's assassin, distribute his "Fair Play for Cuba Committee" pamphlets outside the International Trade Mart in New Orleans on August 16, 1963, just some three months before JFK was assassinated in Dallas.[66] A firestorm erupted with most major news channels dismissing the idea as a foul attempt by Trump supporters to stir up sensational allegations that could not be proved or disproved. "This is another garbage story in a tabloid full of garbage," communications director Alice Stewart told the *Miami Herald*. She denied emphatically the man standing next to Oswald in the 1963 photo was Cruz's father, Rafael. "It's embarrassing that anyone would enable Trump to discuss this. It's a garbage story and clearly Donald wants to talk about garbage. Ted Cruz will do what he's been doing, talking about jobs, freedom, and security for the American people," Stewart insisted.[67]

"Previous questions have surfaced about the 1960s activities of Rafael Cruz, Sr., the father of GOP presidential hopeful Rafael Cruz, Jr. (Ted Cruz). Based on the presence of the elder Cruz, an anti-Castro activist, in Dallas and New Orleans before the November 22, 1963, assassination of President John F. Kennedy, there is a strong reason to believe that Cruz was associated with Central Intelligence Agency's anti-Castro operations," Madsen wrote. "Furthermore, a Cuban hired by alleged JFK assassin Lee Harvey Oswald and who bears a striking resemblance to Cruz is seen in an iconic photograph of Oswald and a group of Cubans Oswald hired who were distributing 'Hands off Cuba!' pamphlets in New Orleans in the summer of 1963," Madsen continued. The photo of Oswald and other Cubans he hired for the Fair Play for Cuba Committee was taken outside the International Trade Mart in New Orleans on August 16, 1963. Wayne Madsen Report has been informed by a source that the individual to Oswald's left is none other than Rafael Cruz. The photograph at the trade mart was favorably compared to a 1954 photograph of Cruz attached to an official Cuban Ministry of Education document."[68]

Madsen, a seasoned researcher considered an expert with the JFK assassination collection at the National Archives in College Park, quickly found corroborating evidence that Rafael Cruz was CIA-connected. "In 1957, Rafael Cruz, the son of an employee of the US intelligence-linked RCA Corporation, left Cuba for the United States," Madsen noted. "Cruz claims he fought with Castro against the fascist government of Fulgencio Batista but soured on the revolution. However, Cruz left Cuba two years before the Castro revolution." The lies in Rafael Cruz's life story caught Madsen's attention as an intelligence analyst trained to look for such discrepancies as the kind of lies "CIA legends" creating fictitious personal histories are famous for inventing. "Cruz arrived in Austin where he enrolled in the University of Texas," Madsen continued. "This is a strange story since he claimed he left Cuba with only $100, which he said was sewn into his underwear. Cruz eventually gained US permanent residency and a degree in mathematics from the University of Texas. In 1959, Cruz married Julia Ann Garza and, after Cruz graduated from the University of Texas in 1961, the couple moved to New Orleans from Dallas after the birth of their second daughter on November 18, 1962."

Madsen continued detailing the parts of Rafael Cruz's background record that do not apparently fit together in a consistent or easily documented pattern. "While living in New Orleans with his wife and two young daughters, Cruz claimed residency at two addresses, one a low-rent apartment building off of Jackson Avenue," Madsen noted. "Cruz worked for an oil company in New Orleans. He has been less than forth-coming about the details of his time in New Orleans and the time line that included his move from Dallas." Madsen continued, observing that Cruz and his wife Julia divorced in New Orleans or Dallas, allegedly in 1962 or 1963, a detail that Madsen claimed "is also clouded in mystery." Madsen continued the narrative as follows: "Cruz apparently registered for the draft in 1967 claiming the New Orleans' Jackson Street address. Draft registration was a requirement for resident aliens like Cruz. Cruz apparently waited until the age of 28 to register for the draft, which, because he waited so long, was a criminal offense at the time."

Also cloudy are the circumstances of Rafael Cruz's second marriage, Madsen pointed out. "While liable for the draft and possible service in Vietnam, a country where fellow Cuban immigrant Otto Macias gladly volunteered to serve, Cruz took off for Calgary, Canada with his second wife, Eleanor Darragh," he wrote. "Darragh, a native of Delaware who graduated from Rice University in Houston, worked for the same oil company in New Orleans that employed Cruz. Their son, Rafael 'Ted' Cruz, Jr., now a candidate for president of the United States, claims that his mother and father worked for the same company in New Orleans but there is actually no record of an Eleanor Darragh Wilson Cruz living in New Orleans at the time."

Madsen noted that Rafael Cruz's draft registration form listed Cruz's employer on July 26, 1967 as the Geophysics & Computer Service, Inc. "This company is the French-based Compagnie Générale de Géophysique (CGG). The date July 26, 1967 is also significant for Cubans. Castro called his revolutionary popular front the 'July 26 Movement,'" Madsen reported. "CGG is linked to the large Schlumberger oil conglomerate, which, along with Halliburton, is one of the two largest oilfield drilling companies in the world. Schlumberger had been active with the CIA and Zapata Offshore Company, which was owned by George H. W. Bush." Madsen continued: "Moreover, Jean de Menil, the son-in-law of Schlumberger founder Conrad Schlumberger, was a key figure in Permindex, the New Orleans-based CIA front headed up by Clay Shaw that was a key target of Garrison's investigation of the New Orleans connection to JFK's assassination in Dallas."

Madsen commented that 1967, when Rafael Cruz, Sr. departed New Orleans, allegedly with his second wife (and Ted Cruz's mother) Eleanor Darragh Wilson, was the same year that Garrison's official investigation of the New Orleans connection to Kennedy's assassination commenced with an indictment of Shaw, the same man whose office was located inside the International Trade Mart where Oswald and Mr. X were involved with handing out Fair Play for Cuba pamphlets on August 16, 1963. "Ted Cruz's mother Eleanor also reportedly worked for the Schlumberger affiliate," Madsen pointed out. "When the Cruzes left for Calgary in 1967, they worked under the aegis of Rafael B. Cruz & Associates, Ltd., which was owned by Rafael B. Cruz, Sr."

Madsen has found documents at the National Archives proving Jim Garrison in investigating the JFK assassination was seeking to find information on three individuals believed to be in Calgary, one of whom Madsen believes may have been Rafael Cruz. It is a well-known fact that Oswald was working for the CIA front group of ex FBI officer Guy Bannister. Bannister gave Oswald the instruction to hand out the leaflets. The action was one of many Oswald activities that on the surface created a picture of Oswald as a pro Castro, Soviet sympathizer. Oswald recruited two helpers that day and one of them looks very much like Rafael Cruz, who, as I indicated before, is Cuban.

What makes this story interesting is that it is very possible that Rafael Cruz was living in New Orleans in 1963, although he has gone on the record stating that he didn't move to New Orleans until 1965. It is well known that Rafael Cruz was involved in political demonstrations in Cuba in support of Castro. It was after Castro started leaning towards communism that Cruz changed sides and eventually left Cuba for the United States. What is likely, however, is that Rafael Cruz—whatever is the truth about how he left Cuba—was almost certainly interviewed by US government officials, very possibly involving the CIA, when he arrived in the United States. While the lies Rafael and Ted Cruz have told about how and why the father left Cuba fuel speculation a cover-story has been created to mask certain facts the Cruz family may still today find inconvenient to reveal.

The photos have been a curiosity since the House Special Committee on Assassinations examined them, way back in the 1970's. The identity of the Cruz look alike has never been established. In May, I went on record saying that I had spoken with a source who identified the mystery man as Rafael Cruz. I was asked many times if I started the rumor or planted the story. I did not. Having a reputation as a "dirty trickster" has placed me in the firing line as a suspect. Whenever a salacious story breaks, especially those that cast a negative image of politicians I don't support, I'm held to blame.

Cruz Suspends Campaign

On April 26, Trump won all five states—Connecticut, Delaware, Maryland, Pennsylvania, and Rhode Island—in what has become known as the "Acela Primary" in reference to the Amtrak Acela Express that runs through these states. This gave Trump another 111 delegates, with Cruz winning 2 delegates, and Kasich 5 delegates. Following the Acela Primary, national attention turned to Indiana, where Trump needed to win the 57 delegates in the winner-take-all primary scheduled for May 3, if he were to have a chance of getting 1,237 delegates. On April 26, the *Washington Post* reported Cruz "threw a Hail Mary pass" by announcing at a campaign event in Indianapolis that Carly Fiorina would be his vice presidential pick in the event he becomes the GOP nominee.[69] Fiorina had endorsed Cruz on March 9, after she dropped out of the race. Since that time, Fiorina worked as an active Cruz surrogate, giving speeches and campaigning for him. The newspaper argued that Cruz's decision to pick Fiorina was more than a decision to play "the woman card." Since her exchange with Trump during the CNN-sponsored debate in September 2015, Fiorina was regarded as "an attack dog who has proven to be relatively effective in battling Trump."

The Cruz team had made it clear to reporters that Indiana was going to be the end of Donald Trump. They put everything they had left in Indiana, probably just as certain that a loss there would put the nomination out of reach for the Texas Senator. On April 29th, just days before primary polls were to open, the Trump campaign realized Cruz was pressuring Hoosier Governor Mike Pence to endorse his candidacy. It was a tense day in Trump Tower; both Manafort and his chief of staff Rick Gates were in the Tower, monitoring the situation by phone.

With Manafort on a call in the stark room they shared, Gates walked over to Michael Caputo's office—he had joined the headquarters at Manafort's invitation after the New York victory—and talked nervously about the likelihood of a Pence-Cruz alliance. It had just been reported that Pence wouldn't endorse after all—a result of a Manafort emissary's visit. His message: Trump was going to win, and Pence was at the top of the list of potential running mates.

But in a moment, CNN announced from the flat screen on the 5th floor wall that the governor would back Cruz after all in an imminent radio interview. Gates raced over to tell Manafort and they dialed Indiana to get a readout. They heard from a Pence confidant who had been working for the governor that it couldn't be stopped. Pence was going to endorse Cruz, but the announcement was not expected to be a strong endorsement.

"I'm not against anybody, but I will be voting for Ted Cruz in the Republican primary," Pence said on a local television interview on April 29, 2016, endorsing Cruz as expected. Pence praised Cruz's "knowledge of the Constitution" and his willingness to "take on the leadership" of his own party. But Pence also had kind words for Trump, commending Trump for highlighting the Indianapolis air conditioning manufacturer Carrier's decision to close its plant there and move 2,100 jobs to Mexico. Pence stressed that Trump has "given voice to the frustrations of millions of working Americans with the lack of progress in Washington, D.C." Pence encouraged Hoosier voters "to make up their own minds," stressing that his loyalty was to the Republican Party. "Let me be very clear on this race," Pence said carefully. "Whoever wins the Republican nation for president of the United States, I'm going to work my heart out to get elected this fall."[70]

On May 3, the day of the Indiana primary, Trump returned to the JFK theme, phoning in to Fox News "Fox and Friends" morning show. The hosts played a video clip showing Ted Cruz confronting on an Indiana street a Trump supporter holding a "Make America Great Again" poster. "Donald Trump is deceiving you," Cruz pleaded. "He is playing you for a chump." Unconvinced, the Trump supporter replied, "You'll find out tomorrow," referring to the primary voting scheduled for the next day in Indiana. "Indiana doesn't want you," the unidentified Trump supporter insisted. "You are the problem, politician. America is a better country without you." When asked what he thought of the video clip, Trump responded immediately. "They know Cruz is lying," Trump said. "That's why we call him 'Lying Ted.' These are smart people. Middle income people haven't had a pay raise for 18 years."

Next, Fox and Friends commented that Cruz was making a last-ditch effort to beat Trump in Indiana. "Fox and Friends" played for Trump a clip of Rafael Cruz in Indiana saying, "I implore, I exhort every member of the body of Christ to vote according to the word of God. Vote for the candidate that stands on the word of God and the Constitution of the United States of America. And I am convinced it's my son, Ted Cruz. The alternative could be the destruction of America." Trump retorted that it was "a disgrace" that Ted Cruz's father would go out in Indiana and make such statements, arguing that many prominent Evangelicals had endorsed him. This caused Trump to transition into the JFK story. ""His father was with Lee Harvey Oswald prior to Oswald's being, you know, shot. I mean, the whole thing is ridiculous, right prior to JFK being shot," Trump said. "Nobody even brings it up. They don't even talk about that. That was reported, and nobody talks about it. I mean, what was he doing—what was he doing with Lee Harvey Oswald shortly before the death? Before the shooting? It's horrible."[71]

On May 3rd, campaign staffers and supporters watched in the Trump Tower lobby again as the hard fought Indiana primary results came in. Trump took an insurmountable lead in early returns and it quickly became clear he would beat Cruz badly. Trump staffers, the candidate, his family, and friends—and most of the cynical media present—were surprised about what happened next: with no path to the nomination in front of him, Ted Cruz dropped out of the presidential race.

Trump was magnanimous in victory, even though Cruz had unloaded every insult in the book on him the day before. "Ted Cruz, I don't know if he likes me, or if he doesn't like me, but he is one hell of a competitor," he said. "He is a tough, smart guy. And he has got an amazing future." Talking heads remarked in unison that the victory speech was uncharacteristically focused and polite, that the brash candidate actually looked the part he needed to play.

Trump won the Indiana primary decisively, gaining 53.3 percent of the vote and all 57 delegates, with Cruz in second place at 36.6 percent, and Kasich a distant third with 7.6 percent.

That evening Cruz, the only candidate to score multiple state victories against Trump in the primaries and state caucuses, suspended his campaign. "From the beginning I've said that I would continue on as long as there was a viable path to victory. Tonight, I'm sorry to say, it appears that path has been foreclosed," Cruz said in his concession speech delivered Tuesday night to supporters gathered in Indianapolis. "The voters chose another path, and so with a heavy heart, but with boundless optimism for the long-term future of our nation, we are suspending our campaign."[72] The *New York Times*, reporting Cruz's decision, noted that less than a month earlier, Cruz seemed to be on the way to victory. "He had won Wisconsin," reporter Matt Flegenheimer wrote in the *New York Times* article. "He was dominating delegate elections, positioning himself for what seemed increasingly likely to be a floor fight at the Republican convention in July, as the campaign of Donald J. Trump fell into internal disarray."[73]

Paul Manafort had arrived.

With Trump steamrolling his way to the Republican nomination and Manafort tightening the campaign up more every day, things were looking up. And every day that went by, campaign manager Corey Lewandowski lost footing. Still, he managed to throw roadblocks up in front of Manafort every day.

Lewandowski's strategy: find all Manafort's mistakes and amplify them to the candidate. When there weren't mistakes to find, he created problems. And whenever Manafort moved to solve a problem, Lewandowki worked his angles to make sure his solution failed—even when it hurt Donald Trump.

Lewandowski's team included communications director Hope Hicks and Trump's Deputy Assistant and Head of Advance, George Gigicos. Between the three of them, they controlled access to Trump when the candidate traveled. And with the energetic rally schedule Trump kept, he was on the road more than he was off. Manafort may have been in charge, but when the Trump Air's wheels were up, the entire campaign dynamic changed. Corey was the boss.

With the results in from Indiana, RNC Reince Priebus on the evening of May 3, declared on Twitter, just moments after Cruz's speech pulling out of the race, that Donald J. Trump "will be the presumptive GOP nominee," adding, "we all need to unite and focus on defeating @HillaryClinton #NeverClinton."[74] The next day, Kasich suspended his presidential campaign, with remarks made in Columbus, Ohio, that lasted about 15 minutes. "I have always said that the Lord has a purpose for me, as he has for everyone," Mr. Kasich said. "And as I suspend my campaign today, I have renewed faith, deeper faith, that the Lord will show me the way forward and fulfill the purpose of my life."[75] In withdrawing from the presidential race, neither Cruz nor Kasich took the additional step of endorsing Trump.

With Trump as the presumptive nominee, he easily won the remaining primaries: Nebraska, West Virginia, Oregon, and Washington, all held May 10-24; as well as California, Montana, New Jersey, New Mexico, and South Dakota, held on June 7. In the end, Trump secured the GOP presidential nomination with 1,725 delegates, 488 more than the 1,237 required for victory on the first ballot.

None of this would have happened had Lewandowski been left in place. As May 3, 2016 came to a close, Trump realized he owed locking up the GOP presidential nomination on the first ballot to Manafort's expert intervention as a seasoned professional in the mechanics of winning elections, supplemented by veteran crisis management skills only a true adult is capable of exercising.

Trump: The Last Candidate Standing

Nearly a year had passed, but Trump—the most unlikely presidential candidate to succeed and the only one to have never held elective office—was the last candidate in what had been a crowded field of GOP contenders.

Altogether, the GOP candidates during the Republican primaries participated in a total of 12 debates that began on August 6, 2016, at the Quicken Arena in Cleveland, Ohio, and ended, somewhat prematurely, at the University of Miami in Miami, Florida, in a debate hosted by CNN on March 10, 2016. Only one debate was cancelled. What was originally scheduled to be the last debate, the one originally scheduled for Monday, March 21, 2016, in Salt Lake City, Utah, was cancelled after Trump and Kasich said they would not attend.

This marathon sequence of 12 debates was punctuated by a narrowing of the field, as candidates dropped out one-by-one, as primaries, caucus meetings, and state conventions wound their way through all 50 states, beginning with the Iowa primary on February 1, 2016, and ending with two of the most populous states—California and New Jersey—and three relatively sparsely populated western states—Montana, New Mexico, and South Dakota—on June 7, 2016.

Rick Perry was the first to drop out on September 11, 2015, followed by Scott Walker on September 21, 2015. By the end of December 2015, before the primaries had even begun, Bobby Jindal, Lindsey Graham, and George Pataki dropped out, leaving twelve GOP candidates remaining in the field.

As 2016 proceeded, the failure to win the primaries and the resultant loss of financial backers was the main reason GOP contenders dropped out. In February 2016, seven more dropped out, including Mike Huckabee, Rand Paul, Rick Santorum, Carly Fiorina, Chris Christie, Jim Gilmore, and Jeb Bush.

When Jeb gave his concession speech in Columbia, South Carolina, on February 20, 2016, the GOP race for the White House reached a watershed moment. Standing before a hotel ballroom full of staffers, donors, supporters, and longtime friends, Bush said proudly, "In this campaign, I have stood my ground, refusing to bend to the political winds." Exiting as the high-profile establishment candidate, Bush's concession speech made clear he had fallen victim to his own miscalculation.

As the *Washington Post* noted, Bush, who had never worked in Washington or held a federal job, was positioned as the favorite of the GOP elite because of his family lineage and his close ties to many of the GOP's most generous donors and senior leaders.[76] The newspaper further pointed out that by the time Bush conceded, his super PAC, Right to Rise USA, had raised $118 million and had spent $95.7 million through February 2016, mostly on advertising to attack other GOP candidates.

The *Washington Post* also pointed out that Jeb had never managed to shake his family lineage, despite his insisting several times that a presidential campaign "can't be about the past; it can't be about my mom and dad, or my brother, who I love. It has to be about the ideas I believe in to move our country forward." Yet, Bush had failed to transform the campaign into a referendum about his record as Florida governor. Instead, he got bogged down debating whether he would have authorized military action against Saddam Hussein, as his brother did after the 9/11 terrorists attacks. Repeatedly pressed, Jeb finally acknowledged that "knowing what we now know," he would not have authorized the war in Iraq.

By the 12th GOP primary debate on March 10, 2016, the field was down to five candidates: Donald Trump versus Ben Carson, Marco Rubio, Ted Cruz, and John Kasich. Of these five, Ben Carson was the only remaining candidate who failed to win a single primary.

While Trump came off as aggressively combative, Carson created the impression of a humble, but talented surgeon, more interested in serving the good of the Republic than in creating a political career for himself. As the field of Republican challengers began to stabilize, Trump and Carson were positioned as the outsiders in an election in which GOP voters were open in expressing their disdain for GOP establishment candidates as typified by Jeb Bush.

While both Rubio and Cruz were Washington insiders, given their positions as US senators, each believed he had distinct advantages in competing against Trump. Marco Rubio continued to believe his Cuban heritage gave him the best chance to command the Hispanic voters that would be needed if the GOP presidential candidate were to have a chance to beat Hillary. Cruz, who shared Rubio's Cuban heritage, also felt he had a distinct advantage appealing to Republican Evangelical conservatives, given the strong faith he and his pastor father professed. Finally, Carson dropped out on March 2, 2016, followed by Rubio, who had won primaries only in the District of Columbia, Minnesota, and Puerto Rico. Rubio dropped out on March 15, 2016, a few days after Ben Carson.

As the primaries came to an end, only two contenders—John Kasich, who won only the Ohio primary, and Ted Cruz, who had won 11 primaries—were the only candidates left in the race to continue battling against Donald Trump. In the end, Trump's victory was decisive, winning 41 primaries and getting nearly 500 more delegates than the 1,237 he needed to win on the first ballot. Kasich was the last to drop out, believing to the end that the GOP leadership would gravitate to him, a moderate Republican who polled well against Clinton, to bring the party together in what he had envisioned as a vote-swapping contested convention that he predicted would follow the GOP's wild and rancorous primary battle.

There had never been anything like it in US political history. A colorful and outspoken New York City billionaire characterized as a "clown" when he started out had managed to beat a series of competitors distinguished at the end not by their professional political careers, but by the moniker nicknames Trump had conferred upon them. As the GOP headed to Cleveland in July, "Low Energy Jeb," "Little Marco," and "Lying Ted" were bystanders, while against all odds, Donald J. Trump prepared to take on "Crooked Hillary" in the biggest battle of all.

Part 2
How Hillary Clinton
Stole the Democratic
Presidential Nomination

This section chronicles how Hillary Clinton finally got the Democratic Party's presidential nomination in 2016—an accomplishment she and her supporters touted as an historic first for any woman to achieve—on her way to her second unsuccessful attempt to be elected president of the United States.

The truth is that Hillary Rodham Clinton has been running for president her entire adult life, certainly at least from the time she was an undergraduate at Wellesley, the elite, all-girls undergraduate school in Massachusetts that is one of the Seven Sisters Colleges for women, formed in 1915 when the Ivy League schools were typically reserved for men.

What Hillary has consistently attempted to hide from voters is another important truth in understanding what she is all about, namely, her deep roots in the far-left radical politics of the 1960s.

At Wellesley, Hillary transformed from the "Goldwater Girl" she had been growing up with her parents in Park Ridge, Illinois. While at Wellesley, Hillary went radical, deciding to spend time with socialist Saul

Alinsky, the original "community organizer" whose 1971 handbook for social activism, "Rules for Radicals," was dedicated to Lucifer, whom Alinsky termed "the first radical known to man who rebelled against the establishment and did it so effectively that he won his own kingdom."[1]

Hillary, having decided to write her college thesis on Alinsky, spent time being mentored by him in Chicago as Alinsky was developing the ideas for his book and Hillary was visiting the city's low-income neighborhoods, doing the fieldwork for her thesis. Hillary's 92-page senior thesis was entitled "THERE IS ONLY THE FIGHT . . . An Analysis of the Alinsky Model."[2] Hillary attributed her title to two lines from the second poem, "East Cokor," in T.S. Eliot's 1940 "Four Quartets," that read: (1.) "There is only the fight to recover what has been lost," and (2.) "And found and lost again and again."

In the senior thesis Hillary defined a radical as follows: "A radical is one who advocates sweeping changes in the existing laws and methods of government. These proposed changes are aimed at the roots of political problems which in Marxian terms are the attitudes and behaviors of men." This Hillary shares with the politician who beat her in 2008, when Hillary made her first unsuccessful run at the presidency—namely, Barack Hussein Obama, who like Hillary was also a Saul Alinsky "community organizer" acolyte whose roots in the far-left of Chicago politics lagged Hillary's by two decades.

Finally, before plunging into the narrative, one more truth about Hillary is important to understand: namely, that unlike William Jefferson Clinton, her husband, Hillary lacks the charisma to be the type of natural politician voters genuinely like. Hillary met Bill Clinton in 1971 at Yale Law School, where both were students. The key insight was articulated by Dolly Kyle, one of Bill Clinton's longtime lovers in Arkansas, who in her 2014 book, "Hillary: The Other Woman," called Hillary the "Warden" after describing Bill and Hill's marriage as a political arrangement.

Kyle insisted that Hillary realized she could not make it in big-time politics unless she rode on Bill's coattails—a realization that hit Hillary after she failed to pass the law exam in Washington, DC, and left the Watergate Committee in a controversy that has dogged her with accusations of unethical behavior. "Hillary stayed in Washington into the summer of 1974, trying desperately to establish herself as a potential political power near the seat of power in the nation's capital city," Kyle wrote. "That is something she was never able to do on her own."[3]

CHAPTER 4

Bernie Sanders, the Old Socialist, Challenges Hillary Clinton, the President Presumed

I don't want to hit Crazy Bernie Sanders too hard yet because I love watching what he is doing to Crooked Hillary. His time will come!
Donald J. Trump, posted on Twitter, May 11, 2016[1]

Although few serious politicians in either party had any doubt Hillary Clinton would make her second run for the White House in 2016, all speculation was put to rest when, on Sunday, April 12, 2015, Clinton released a two-minute video after 3:00 p.m. ET, at the end of which she said with a smile, "I'm running for president."[2]

Hillary's video started by featuring the multi-cultural, multi-racial, bilingual diversity theme, featuring a mix of unidentified, but happy, young, and attractive Americans describing in one or two sentences what was happening in their lives. Clearly, the video was an expensive, professional production that had been worked over extensively by Hillary's campaign team working with media professionals to produce a carefully crafted message. Watching the video critically left no doubt that identity politics was to be a main theme of Clinton's candidacy, the centerpiece of which was the goal to elect the first woman president.

April 12, 2015: Hillary Announces for President

Here is the unofficial transcript of Hillary's video,[3] annotated by noting the identity politics significance of including this particular "typical American" vignette:

UNIDENTIFIED WHITE MIDDLE-AGED WOMAN working outdoors in purple jacket and jeans: "It's spring, so we're starting to get the gardens ready. And my tomatoes are legendary here in my own neighborhood. ACTION: Woman working in garden, on steps lifts up hands to sky, palms first. Smiles.

UNIDENTIFIED WOMAN (race or ethnic identity uncertain) with YOUNG GIRL: "My daughter is about to start kindergarten next year. So we're moving just so she can go to a better school. ACTION: Mother and child together, child packing, child placing "FISH" letters in letter board.

1. UNIDENTIFIED HISPANIC MALE with YOUNGER HISPANIC UNIDENFIFIED MALE speaking in Spanish with English subtitle: "*Mi hermano y yo estamos empezando nuestro primer negocio.*" Translated: My brother and I are starting our first business. ACTION: Brothers placing pictures on wall. Standing together, looking happy, laughing.

2. UNIDENTIFIED WHITE MOTHER with FIVE-YEAR-OLD SON: "After five years raising my son, I am now going back to work. ACTION: Mother sitting with child on lap, reading a book. Mother standing alone, breaks into smile.

3. UNIDENTIFIED YOUNG AFRICAN-AMERICAN MAN AND WOMAN: "Every day, we're trying to get more and more ready and more prepared." ACTION: Couple unpacking toys from box. Husband standing next to wife, places hand lovingly on her obviously pregnant stomach. Husband says, "Big boy. Right now. Coming your way." Couple smiles.

4. UNIDENTIFIED YOUNG TWENTIES-LOOKING ASIAN FEMALE: "Right now, I'm applying for jobs. It's a look into what the real world will look like after college." ACTION: Woman walking down street, finds address, and goes into business street-front door. Ends with woman standing inside, window in background, casually dressed, smiling.

5. UNIDENTIFIED TWO YOUNG MALES MALE: "I'm getting married this summer to someone I really care about." ACTION: Two young white males walking down street, side-by-side, look happy. Close-up shows the hands of the two men joining together. Camera pans back to show two men continuing to walk down sidewalk, smiling, holding hands together.

6. UNIDENTIFIED YOUNG AFRICAN AMERICAN BOY: "I'm going to be in a play and I'm going to be in a fish costume. The little tiny fishes." ACTION: Boy stands in front of living room couch. He places his hands together, palms touching, fingers upwards, and moves his hands in upward swaying motion as he sing-songs, "Two little tiny fishes."

7. UNIDENTIFIED WHITE FEMALE, near retirement age: "I'm getting ready to retire soon. Retirement means reinventing yourself in many ways." ACTION: Framed picture shows woman with man (supposedly husband) standing together. Woman stands outside by house, uses left hand to give "thumbs-up" motion. Woman is seen driving car from front-seat passenger perspective.

8. UNIDENTIFIED FEMALE (Brown Skin) UNIDENTIFIED WHITE MAN: Couple moving furniture in home, as woman says, "Well, we've been doing a lot of home renovations." Man says, "But mostly we just really want to get our dog to quit eating the trash. Woman says, "And so we have high hopes for 2015, that that's going to happen." ACTION: Man and woman in home together, dog trying to open trash can to get contents out.

9. UNIDENTIFIED bald thirty-something MALE: I've started a new career recently. This is a fifth-generation company, which means a lot to me. This country was founded on hard work and it really feels good to be a part of that." ACTION: Man walks through machine shop, stopping at machines, working.

10. HILLARY CLINTON comes on screen, standing in front of unidentified white-painted suburban-looking home, green hedge and bushes in background in front of house windows.

ACTION: Hillary speaks on camera, interspersed with scenes of Americans working, living, and playing happily together. Hillary voice-over continues uninterrupted, as soft music continues in background and camera cuts to everyday America scenes. Hillary on camera smiles, nods head gently in "Yes" bobbing motion.

HILLARY DIALOGUE: "I'm getting ready to do something, too," Hillary says. "I'm running for president. Americans have fought their way back from tough economic times, but the deck is still stacked in favor of those at the top."

Hillary continues: "Everyday Americans need a champion and I want to be that champion. So you can do more than just get by, you can get ahead and stay ahead, because when families are strong, America is strong."

Hillary concludes: "So I'm hitting the road to earn your vote, because it's your time and I hope you'll join me on this journey."

VIDEO ENDS WITH "HILLARY LOGO—Two Blue Columns, Red Arrow Pointed Right Penetrates Blue Columns, "Hillary for" words printed in white on red arrow, with "America" printed in Blue at arrow tip. Hillary dressed in blue jacket and red blouse, matching logo colors. Thin gold necklace and modest gold earrings. Casual outdoor look, clothing appropriate for spring weather.

TOTAL RUNNING TIME: 2 minutes, 13 seconds.

The obvious point of the video is to put on display happy images illustrating the many combinations embraced by Democrats' multi-cultural, multi-racial diversity agenda, emphasizing independent white women with and without husbands or families, an LBGT male same-sex happy union, bilingual Hispanics opening an entrepreneurial small business without any reference to whether or not their immigration status is legal, as well as Asian Americans and Americans of uncertain or mixed racial and/or ethnic identity being part of traditional families, in one-parent families, or simply making it on their own, even as children.

This has become the Democratic Party's mantra insisting upon an affirmation that the traditional family is obsolete, that marriages must embrace the LGBT agenda, that all races as well as all ethnicities can and should mix in all possible multi-racial, multi-cultural, multi-ethnic combinations. The point is that Hillary launched her presidential campaign with a video that framed her in a Middle America suburban setting, while hoisting her onto the pedestal of identity politics. The utopia represented by this video is a borderless USA that rejects traditional definitions of relationships with the result that everybody has a home, an education, as well as a job, hobby, and/or avocation, such that we blend into one big happy family. Anything that threatens this agenda is by definition sexist, xenophobic, racist, bigoted, anti-LGBT, anti-Muslim—in other words, evil.

The *New York Times* article reporting on the video stressed that before Clinton's campaign made the video public announcing Hillary's formal decision to run for president, John D. Podesta, Hillary's campaign chairman, contacted top Clinton donors and longtime associates. Podesta is a well-known Washington insider, a long-time Democratic Party liberal operative with credits that include founding the leftist think-tank known as the Center for American Progress, CAP, as well as working as chief of staff for President Bill Clinton in the White House, and serving as a counselor to President Barack Obama.

The video was only the media launch. Shortly after, Hillary staged a public event so she could give a policy speech as part of the in-person announcement of her candidacy.

Clinton Announces Outside

On Saturday, June 13, 2015, Hillary launched her campaign in-person with a large outdoor rally on Roosevelt Island in New York City's East River, between Manhattan Island on the west and the borough of Queens on Long Island to the east. Hillary, dressed in a bright blue pantsuit, gave the speech standing at a podium that from above could be seen to be her campaign logo. Critics viewing photos of the rally from above derisively commented that Hillary's logo, especially here in New York City, brought to mind the twin towers penetrated by an airplane, recalling the 9/11 terrorist attacks on the World Trade Center. The Clinton campaign estimated that the crowd attending the event numbered some 5,500 people, though about half that many may have been more accurate.

"Under sunny skies and surrounded by flag-waving supporters on Roosevelt Island in New York, Mrs. Clinton pledged to run an inclusive campaign and to create a more inclusive economy, saying that even the new voices in the Republican Party continued to push 'the top-down economic policies that failed us before,'" Amy Chozick reported for the *New York Times*.[4]

Clinton's speech was written to remind voters of her government service as a New York senator, and as Secretary of State, with the United Nations building visible in the background. "To be in New York with my family, with so many friends, including many New Yorkers who gave me the honor of serving them in the Senate for eight years," Clinton said. "To be right across the water from the headquarters of the United Nations, where I represented our country many times." Then with an allusion to FDR—still a Democratic Party hero—Hillary hit a theme she intended to stress, namely, that she hoped to be the first woman president. "To be here in this beautiful park dedicated to Franklin Roosevelt's enduring vision of America, the nation we want to be," she continued. "And in a place. . . with absolutely no ceilings."[5]

The reference to "no ceilings" obviously associated the outdoor setting of the speech as an image referencing Hillary's goal of "shattering the glass ceiling" that feminists in US politics have typically identified as sexist barriers that a male-dominated society sets up to limit the advancement of women in business and politics.

The Guardian in London summed up Clinton's Roosevelt Island 45-minute speech as follows.

- Clinton is running to make US economy work for every American—from nurses to truck drivers to veterans and small business owners—and to end the top-down economic policies "that failed us before."
- She wants to end income inequality, make the middle class mean something again, and to give the poor a chance to work their way into it.
- She promises to end the gridlock in Washington and work with Congress.
- She promises to listen to scientists on climate change, to reign in banks that are "still too risky" and to give "law-abiding immigrant families a path to citizenship."
- She proposes making preschool and quality childcare available to every child in America and providing paid sick days, paid family leave, equal pay and a higher minimum wage.
- She promises to keep Americans safe: "I've stood up to adversaries like Putin and reinforced allies like Israel. I was in the situa-

tion room on the day we got bin Laden. But, I know—I know we have to be smart as well as strong."

- She is also calling for a constitutional amendment to undo the Supreme Court's decision in Citizens United. She also proposes universal, automatic registration and expanded early voting.

"That makes for quite the progressive checklist," the Guardian commented in summary.[6] "I may not be the youngest candidate in this race, but I'll be the youngest woman president in the history of the United States," Clinton said in conclusion, with Bill Clinton joining her at the podium with a backdrop that the *Washington Post* observed as "a stunning East River view of the Manhattan skyline in the background, the United Nations building sparkling in bright sunshine behind the podium."[7]

The problem with Hillary Clinton's speech was that her platform identified nothing new or truly exciting. Hillary has been on the national political stage virtually continuously since 1996, fully two decades ago. Virtually every Democrat running for president since 1996 had pledged to end income inequality by taxing the rich to distribute income to the poor. But despite Democratic programs designed to end poverty that trace back to Lyndon Baines Johnson's Great Society proclaimed in 1964—more than 50 years ago—the Democratic Party's social welfare state has not reduced income inequality or eliminated poverty some $20 trillion and eighty welfare programs later.[8]

As First Lady, as US Senator from New York, as US Secretary of State, what could Hillary point to as her major accomplishment? Under Bill Clinton's administration, Hillary had failed to pass what was then known as "Hillary-Care," the precursor to the Affordable Care Act, commonly known as Obamacare. Her husband signed NAFTA—an issue both Donald Trump and Sen. Bernie Sanders would push against her. As US senator from New York, she had failed to sponsor any major legislation that improved public education in the United States, as the test scores of children in public schools continue to plummet.[9] As Secretary of State, Hillary's campaign would be plagued by the death of Ambassador Chris Stevens and three other brave Americans in Benghazi, Libya, on September 11, 2012, as well as the "Arab Spring" turning into terrorist chaos, spreading from Libya across North Africa into Syria. Add to this Hillary's responsibility for the rise of ISIS on her watch.

The American public had seen Hillary's 2008 campaign and rejected it for the "Hope and Change" charisma offered by Barack Hussein Obama. Why did Hillary think a replay of her 2008 presidential campaign would suddenly catch fire this second time around?

April 29, 2015: Sen. Bernie Sanders Enters the Presidential Race

On Thursday, April 29, 2015, Sen. Bernie Sanders, an independent from Vermont who caucuses typically with the Democrats, made one of the most low-key announcements in US history, declaring he was a candidate for President of the United States. On a sunny afternoon, Sanders, wearing a grey business suit, a blue shirt, and a simple patterned blue tie, walked calmly with a few pages rolled together in his right hand, stepping up to a simple podium set out on the grounds of the US Capitol building in Washington.

The announcement lasted approximately ten minutes, with the two-dozen or so reporters present taking up about half the time asking questions. Sanders started off by telling the reporters he did not have "an endless amount of time" because he had to get back inside to the Senate. "Let me just say this," he began. "This country today, in my view, has more crises than at any time since the Depression of the 1930s." This comment made it clear Sanders was going to focus much of his campaign on economics, with an emphasis on income inequality.

"For most Americans, their reality is that they are working longer hours for lower wages," he continued. "In inflation-adjusted money they are earning less money than they used to years ago, despite a huge increase in technology and in productivity. So all over this country, I've been talking to people, and they say, 'How does it happen that I'm producing more, but I'm working longer hours for less wages. My kid can't afford to go to college and I'm having a hard time affording health care." In wrapping up, Sanders asked, "How does it happen that the top one percent owns as much wealth as the bottom 90 percent?" Sanders answered the rhetorical question as follows: "My answer is that this type of economics is not only wrong, it is unsustainable."

When reporters asked how Sanders intended to differentiate himself from Hillary Clinton, he responded that he voted against and strongly opposed the Iraq war that President George W. Bush launched against Saddam Hussein because he was confident the Iraq war would lead to massive destabilization in the region, that he was helping to lead the end to the Trans-Pacific Partnership because he viewed it as another in a series of horrendous free trade deals that have cost Americans millions of good-paying jobs, and he stressed his opposition to the Keystone Pipeline, saying he was opposed to transporting "some of the dirtiest fuels in the world."

In rushing to get back to the Senate, Sanders took one final question from a reporter who wanted to know if it was more important to Sanders to get these ideas out than to contest Clinton for the Democratic Party nomination in 2016. "You've got to understand we are in this race to win," Sanders answered. "But I ask people to understand my history. You are looking at a guy indisputably who has one of the most unusual political histories of anybody in the United States Congress. It's not only that I'm the longest serving independent in the history of the US Congress. It's that when I first ran for state office I got 1 percent of the vote. I don't know if I should be proud of that, but my last election I got 71 percent of the vote." Then Sanders hit the themes, rushed as he was to return to business in the Senate, that ignited the base of the Democratic party more than any Hillary Clinton speech or video was capable of doing, regardless of how professionally crafted or expensively produced.

"The point is that's not the right question," Sanders insisted. "The right question is that if you raise the issues that are on the hearts and minds of the American people—if you try to put together a movement which says we have got to stand together as a people and say that this Capitol, this beautiful Capitol, our country, belongs to all of us and not the billionaires. That's not raising an issue. That's winning elections. That's where the American people are." With that, Sanders turned, waved casually to the crowd acknowledging the sparse applause, as he hurried across the grass to get back to work inside.

At 73 years old when he made his presidential announcement, Sanders was born in Brooklyn in 1941, and graduated from the University of Chicago in 1964. When he announced his presidential candidacy, the leftist press recognized immediately Sanders' well-known history with far-left socialists was considered a liability in the general election. Sanders was associated with the Young People's Socialist League or the Trotsky-ist Socialist Workers' Party. During the Civil Rights movement of the 1960s, Sanders was a political activist protesting with the Congress of Racial Equality and the Student Nonviolent Coordinating Committee.

Even today, Sanders identifies himself as a "democratic socialist" (with a small "d"), not a capitalist.[10] Sanders began his political career getting elected in 1981 to the first of three terms as mayor of Burlington, Vermont, taking office as a self-described socialist (who rejected being described as a communist), who insisted on hanging on his office wall a portrait of railroad labor union organizer Eugene V. Debs, who was convicted and sent to prison during World War I under the Sedition Act of 1918 for giving an anti-war speech in Ohio.[11] Debs, who ran for president five times as the candidate of the Socialist Party of America, ran for president for the last time from prison, in 1920, receiving 3.41 percent of the vote. Despite his history as an independent and a socialist, Sanders was adamant that he intended to compete with Hillary Clinton for the presidential nomination of the Democratic Party.

The *Washington Post*, in reporting Sanders' announcement, left no doubt about the editorial staff's conclusion, "He's not going to win." The *Washington Post* article made clear that Sanders, little known outside most of the most liberal circles nationally had no intention of matching Hillary Clinton dollar for fundraising dollar. "Even if Sanders wanted to try to raise the sort of money that would make him competitive with Clinton, he couldn't do it," wrote Chris Cillizza in the *Washington Post* article. "Or come anywhere close." The newspaper insisted Sanders was not concerned with winning. "He's been around politics long enough— he's been in state and federal politics almost continuously since 1981— to understand how big a frontrunner Clinton is and to grasp his own limitations as a candidate," Cillizza noted. "What Sanders' candidacy is really about is influencing the debate within the Democratic party in the quadrennial pinch point of a presidential election. Sanders wants to drag Clinton (and everyone else in the field) to the left on issues like trade (he opposes the Trans-Pacific Partnership), campaign finance reform and income inequality."[12]

But some nine months and three days later, the *Washington Post* had changed its tune. "To go from that decidedly low-key announcement to where Sanders is today on Iowa caucus day—in a dead heat with Hillary Clinton in the Hawkeye State and way in front of her in New Hampshire's February 8 primary—is absolutely stunning," Cillizza wrote in the *Washington Post* edition printed February 1, 2016. Somehow, Sanders had become a movement—a political phenomenon whose campaign was about to capture the excitement of Millennials and the imagination of the left-leaning base of the Democratic Party leap from nowhere to within steps of Clinton. Remarkably, Hillary—the party's presumptive nominee in 2016, as she had also been in 2008—was on the verge of defeat a second time—this time challenged by an aging, obscure socialist, an independent from Vermont who caucused with the Democrats in Congress, without having to swear any particular allegiance to the Democratic Party. Desperate, Hillary gave into her most base and immoral instincts, entering into a secret pact with Podesta and Debbie Wasserman Schultz, the head of the Democratic National Committee, to rig the Democratic Party primary process and make damn sure Sanders would lose, despite being the more popular and charismatic politician of the two.

May 2015: Sanders' Kick-off Rallies Draw Big Crowds

On May 26, 2015, Sanders staged the in-person launch of his presidential campaign with an outdoor rally in his hometown of Burlington, Vermont. The event took place on a warm, sunny day and drew an estimated crowd of 5,000 in what the *Washington Post* described as a "peak-Vermont event filled with free ice cream, zydeco music, and speeches from both Ben and Jerry of ice cream fame."[13] Senior politics editor Russel Berman, writing for The Atlantic, also commented on the atypical nature of the Sanders rally. "It was a rally but it was pitched more like a festival, complete with free ice cream from Ben & Jerry's and a performance by 'Mango Jam'—a Vermont-based, six-piece dance band that plays a combination of Zydeco, Cajun, and Caribbean music," Berman wrote. "The lure of live music, Phish Food, and a beautiful setting on the banks of Lake Champlain drew a crowd that appeared to be in the thousands, but there was a larger point to this political theater." Berman noted that Sanders, like other underdogs before him, wanted to demonstrate he could launch a credible campaign without relying upon the financial support of billionaire donors. "He didn't bring in Ben Cohen and Jerry Greenfield only to serve their iconic ice cream—the two have long advocated on behalf of liberal causes, including campaign-finance reform (or as they call it, 'Get the Dough out of Politics!')," Berman wrote. "Sanders needs to motivate activists and small-dollar donors, and he's hoping this kind of alternative kickoff can set the tone."[14]

As he started speaking, the crowd—consisting mostly of white citizens of Vermont, with Millennials predominant in an audience peppered by senior citizens—began chanting "Bernie!" and "Feel the Bern"—chants that were to dominate every subsequent Sanders rally. "Let me be very clear," Sanders said, echoing his initial announcement of candidacy delivered to the small press conference on the grounds of the US Capitol. "There is something profoundly wrong when the top one-tenth of 1 percent owns almost as much wealth as the bottom 90 percent and when 99 percent of all new income goes to the top 1 percent." Writing for the *Washington Post*, reporter Ben Terris commented that Sanders' speech felt like Sanders had caught up with the times, as much as the times catching up with him.[15]

"He has been talking about income inequality, nationalized healthcare, and redistribution of wealth since he was the socialist mayor here in Burlington, in the 1980s," Terris wrote. "He ran on these issues when he was the lone Vermont House seat in 1991, and gave an eight-hour speech opposing an extension of the Bush-era tax cuts as a Senator in 2010." Terris continued to note that Sanders' politics had always played well in Vermont, back to the time when he was mayor of Burlington and the city was referred to as the "People's Republic of Burlington" and his supporters as "Sandernistas." Terris commented that neither one of these terms were used derogatively in Vermont, the first state to legalize same-sex unions, the home of Ben and Jerry's ice cream, and the only state in the country whose capital city does not have a McDonald's fast-food restaurant.[16]

As Sanders ticked through his key issues, including health care for all and reversing climate change, as well as addressing wealth and income inequality, raising wages and creating jobs, as well as introducing campaign finance reform, he hit up what was quickly to become a signature item to his appeal: providing free college education for all. "And when we talk about education, let me be very clear. In a highly competitive global economy, we need the best-educated workforce we can create," Sanders said. "It is insane and counter-productive to the best interests of our country, that hundreds of thousands of bright young people cannot afford to go to college, and that millions of others leave school with a mountain of debt that burdens them for decades." This set up a key pledge that Sanders was to repeat as often as possible. "That must end," he said. "That is why, as president, I will fight to make tuition in public colleges and universities free, as well as substantially lower interest rates on student loans."[17]

Millennials, those born between 1980 and 1995, have been characterized as an "entitlement generation," raised on "participation awards" that has become a powerful political force. In addition to demanding free college tuition, Millennials are demanding not just jobs, but meaningful work. The concept includes a living wage, a French workweek, free job training, and socially useful labor.[18] Reporter John Wagner, writing in the Washington post noted that Millennials found in Bernie Sanders a candidate to love. "They grew up in the recession, watched their parents struggle and became anxious about their futures," Wagner wrote. "They are graduating from college with huge debts and gnawing uncertainty about landing jobs and affording homes. They have little faith in government and other institutions they thought they could depend upon."[19] While Sanders economic message clearly appealed to Millennials sense of entitlement, others felt Bernie's appeal to the young rested in his authenticity. To Cenk Uygur, the host of the online news shows "The Young Turks," Bernie's appeal to Millennials rested in his authenticity. "You can't fake a 40 year record," Uygur wrote. "The older generation grew up on blow-dried anchors, plastic politicians, and a sense of pretense," he wrote. "Bernie Sanders is a man not of his time, but of this time. He was authentic and uncombed before any YouTube star thought to make that concept cool."[20]

Biden and Warren: "To Run or Not to Run?" That Was the Question.

Though the Democratic Party contest for the presidential nomination was always a choice between Clinton and Sanders, the only drama was whether or not Vice President Joe Biden and/or Massachusetts Senator Elizabeth Warren would decide to declare themselves as presidential candidates. Much of the speculation on Biden derived from what was believed to be continuing animosity between Hillary and President Barack Obama that traced back to Obama defeating Hillary in her first presidential run in 2008. A central proponent of this theory was political author Ed Klein, whose bestselling 2014 book "Blood Feud: The Clintons vs. The Obamas" had argued that the tension between the two families was filled with contempt. On October 19, 2015, Breitbart.com reported that President Obama was refusing to meet with Hillary, while Obama and his allies urged Vice President Biden to challenge her for the Democratic nomination. Klein had reported that first Obama had approached Elizabeth Warren, who declined, followed by former Maryland Governor Martin O'Malley who Obama came to realize "doesn't have the stuff."[21]

Appearing on NBC's "Today Show" on April 9, 2015, Warren was asked three times and ruled out each time a decision to run for president, despite arguments that a progressive movement was being formed to draft her into the race. "I'm not running and I'm not going to run," she said. "I'm in Washington. I've got this really great job and a chance to make a difference on things that really matter." Host Savannah Guthrie then asked Warren if she was "unequivocally and categorically" ruling out a run. Again, Warren affirmed, "I'm not running." Finally, Guthrie asked—saying it was at the possibility of "beating a dead horse here"—"Did you ever even consider, entertain the possibility of running for president?" Warren's answer was a flat, definitive, "No." In reporting this exchange, MSNBC noted the liberal groups MoveOn.org and Democracy for America, along with the super PAC "Ready for Warren," had been hoping to convince Warren she could beat Hillary for the Democratic Party's presidential nomination.[22]

It took Biden longer to decide. On October 21, 2015, in an announcement made in the White House Rose Garden, flanked by President Obama on his right and his wife Jill Biden on his left, Biden told the nation he was not to be a candidate for president in 2016. "Unfortunately, I believe we're out of time, the time necessary to mount a winning campaign for the nomination," Biden explained. Still, many including the Wall Street Journal noted the loss of his son Beau Biden, continued to weigh heavily on Biden.[23] Beau Biden, the elder son of the vice president and the former attorney general of Delaware died on June 30, 2015, at the age of 46, after a long battle with brain cancer. "The entire Biden family is saddened beyond words," the vice president said in a written statement. "We know that Beau's spirit will live on in all of us—especially through his brave wife, Hallie, and two remarkable children, Natalie and Hunter."[24]

Even as Hillary proceeded as the "inevitable" Democratic presidential nominee in 2016, various Democrats expressed their concern she carried into the race a number of liabilities.[25] The scandals that had plagued the Clintons ever since Bill was elected governor of Arkansas had continued, through Hillary's tenure as Secretary of State. What worried Democrats was the continuing controversy over Hillary's actions and explanations during and following the Benghazi terror attack, the possibility of a Department of Justice criminal indictment after a serious FBI criminal investigation into her use of a private email system while she was Secretary of State, plus various developing allegations that the Clinton Foundation was a "vast criminal conspiracy," and health issues that had dogged Hillary since she suffered a concussion from a fall in 2012. Hillary had lost to Obama in 2008. Did she have what it would take to beat the GOP in 2016? This prompted concerned Democrats to look for alternatives.

What few remember was that Hillary did have three contenders in addition to Sen. Bernie Sanders when the Democratic primary debates began in October 2015. On the stage with Hillary and Bernie in the first debate were former Maryland Governor Martin O'Malley, who did decide to declare his candidacy after all, along with former Virginia Senator Jim Webb, and former Rhode Island Governor Lincoln Chafee. Webb and Chafee suspended their campaigns just before the Iowa caucuses, held on February 1, 2015, and O'Malley suspended right after. Also in the race for a short time was Harvard Law Professor Lawrence Lessig, a political activist whose zeal for campaign finance reform and electoral reform had led him to push for a Second Constitutional Convention. Lessig managed to raise $1 million in an exploratory committee, but he withdrew from the presidential race on November 2, 2015, after failing to qualify for participation on stage with the others in the Democrat's primary debates.[26]

Speaking to the Democratic Party's summer meeting in Minneapolis on August 28, 2015, Clinton addressed what CNN described as a "markedly pro-Clinton audience." In a conversation with reporters after her upbeat speech, Clinton assured doubters that she had learned her lessons in 2008. "As some of you might recall, in 2008, I got a lot of votes but I didn't get enough delegates," Clinton explained. "And so I think it is understandable that my focus is going to be on delegates, as well as votes, this time." Clinton then added, "We are working really hard to lock in as many supporters as possible. Of course that would include super delegates. . . . I am heartened by the positive response I am getting."[27]

CHAPTER 5

Round One: Hillary Declares Victory Over Sanders

To all of those Bernie Sanders voters who have been left out in the cold by a rigged system of superdelegates, we welcome you with open arms.
Donald J. Trump, Briarcliff Manor, New York, June 7, 2016[1]

The first Democratic presidential debate among primary contenders was held on Tuesday, October 13, 2015, hosted by CNN at the Wynn Hotel in Las Vegas, Nevada. According to Politico, the debate drew 15.3 million viewers, the most to ever watch a Democratic primary debate in history.[2]

The debate lagged the GOP, with 24 million viewers watching the first GOP primary debate hosted by Fox News on August 6, 2015,[3] and 23 million watching the second GOP primary debate hosted by CNN on September 16, 2015.[4] Donald Trump was widely credited with making the first GOP debate the most watched presidential debate ever, giving the highest-rated telecast in the 20-year history of the Fox News Channel, topping dramatically the first GOP primary debate in 2012, also hosted by Fox, that drew only 3.2 million viewers.[5]

These viewer statistics left no doubt the public was fascinated with the GOP contest that was shaping up as Donald Trump, the "David" in the contest, facing 16 challenger GOP professional "Goliaths." By contrast, few professionals had any doubt Hillary Clinton would win the Democratic nomination. Some 10 million Americans found it considerably less interesting to watch the Democratic primary debate where the major point of interest was how far to the left would Bernie force Hillary to go?

Tuesday, October 13, 2015: Democrats' First Primary Debate

Hosted by CNN's Anderson Cooper, the headline of the evening came when Bernie Sanders got an opportunity to address the question of the controversial private email server Clinton used as Secretary of State. Sanders' reply went viral, almost immediately. "Let me say—let me say something that may not be great politics," Sanders began. "But I think the secretary is right, and that is that the American people are sick and tired of hearing about your damn e-mails." The audience in the Wynn Hotel applauded loudly, Clinton smiled, reaching across to shake hands with Sanders, who was standing at the podium next to her. The comment appeared to absolve Clinton of any legal culpability in the scandal, with Sanders making it clear he did not believe the issue should be an issue in the presidential campaign, at least not in the Democratic primaries. Hillary repeated her use of the private email server was "a mistake," saying it "wasn't the best choice," comments meant to distinguish her email policy from a crime. She attacked congressional investigations into her email use as a partisan political effort "to drive down my poll numbers."

Sanders hit Clinton hard over her decision as a US senator to vote in favor of going to war in Iraq in 2003. "I'm the former chairman of the Senate Veterans Committee, and in that capacity I learned a very powerful lesson about the cost of war, and I will do everything that I can to make sure that the United States does not get involved in another quagmire like we did in Iraq, the worst foreign policy blunder in the history of this country," Sanders said. "We should be putting together a coalition of Arab countries who should be leading the effort. We should be supportive, but I do not support American ground troops in Syria."

Aware of Sanders opposition to the Trans-Pacific Partnership free-trade agreement that had been negotiated by the Obama administration while Clinton was Secretary of State, Clinton hedged, implying she had decided not to support the deal. "You know, take the trade deal. I did say, when I was Secretary of State, three years ago, that I hoped it would be the gold standard. It was just finally negotiated last week, and in looking at it, it didn't meet my standards. My standards for more new, good jobs for Americans, for raising wages for Americans," Clinton argued. "And I want to make sure that I can look into the eyes of any middle-class American and say, 'this will help raise your wages.' And I concluded I could not."

For the most part, the candidates agreed on standard Democratic Party issues, articulating virtually identical talking points when asked about questions concerning income inequality, the need to create jobs, and the issues of open borders and immigration. "While the Republican primary has been roiled by the emotional debate over immigration, the Democratic candidates were largely united in their call for providing a path to legal status for the millions of people currently in the U.S. illegally," the Associated Press reported. "The party is counting on general election support from Hispanics, a group that overwhelmingly voted for Obama in 2012."[6]

The partisan mainstream media, largely supporting Clinton, were quick to call the CNN debate a victory for Clinton. "From gun control and banking regulations to debt-free college and Social Security benefits, Mrs. Clinton positioned herself as a champion of liberals, young people, and the elderly—the very voters who make up the Sanders coalition—while also repeatedly reaching out to women, as an advocate for families and children (and as, potentially, the nation's first female president)," reporter Patrick Healy wrote in the *New York Times*. "Mr. Sanders, whose plain-spoken disgust over the email controversy drew praise, looked sheepish and reactive at other points, hesitating to attack Mrs. Clinton forcefully over her ties to Wall Street, and running into trouble defending his past opposition to stricter gun control laws and immigration reform."[7]

In all, the Democrats conducted 9 primary debates between the first debate and the last, on April 14, 2016. By the last debate, the television audience had dwindled to 5.6 million, approximately one-third the audience that watched the first debate.[8] While the viewership of the GOP primary debates also declined about in half from the first to the last debate, the audience for the last GOP primary debate, held on March 10, 2016, was still 11.9 million viewers[9]—with twice as many people watching the last GOP primary debate as watched the last Democrat primary debate.

Again, this reflects Donald Trump's ability to dominate the media during the entire 2016 presidential debate, both pro and con, as a measure of the extent to which Trump captured the imagination of the American public from the moment he first declared his candidacy. The other factor explaining less interest among television viewers for the Democrat primary debates was the degree to which Clinton and Sanders were basically in agreement on what had become standard Democratic party talking points in recent years. While Clinton and Sanders debated fine points on their opposition, for instance, to the National Rifle Association, or their support for Planned Parenthood, both were for increased gun regulations that conservatives saw as limiting Second Amendment freedoms, and both supported public taxpayer funding for Planned Parenthood in their enthusiasm that the Supreme Court decision Roe versus Wade had established abortion as a "woman's right to privacy" even though the subject was not addressed in the Constitution or the Bill of Rights. These "inside baseball" fine distinctions were obviously less interesting than the GOP primary debates, where to the end candidates opposing Donald Trump for the nomination questioned the legitimacy of his campaign, or their obligations to support him as Republicans should he win the nomination.

Clinton and Sanders Trade Early Primaries

On February 1, 2016, Clinton beat Sanders in the Iowa primary by the narrowest of margins, 49.8 percent to 49.6 percent. Then, a week later, on February 9, 2016, Sanders grabbed the headlines, beating Hillary 60.1 percent to 37.7 percent in New Hampshire. Hillary easily won the next two primaries: Nevada on February 20, 2016, with 52.6 percent of the vote, and South Carolina, on February 27, 2016, with 73.3 percent. On Super Tuesday, March 1, 2016, Clinton won 8 primaries—Alabama, Arkansas, Georgia, Massachusetts, Tennessee, Texas, Virginia, and American Samoa—compared to Sanders wining 4 primaries—Colorado, Minnesota, Oklahoma, and Vermont. The totals when the Super Tuesday voting was complete gave Clinton a comfortable 200-delegate lead over Sanders.

The first real surprise in the Democratic primary contests came on March 8, 2016, when Sanders won the Michigan primary by a margin of 1.5 percent. The political world was truly stunned. "Hillary had been polling ahead by 21 points, right up until Sanders pulled off the upset.

Clinton had been widely expected to win the Rust Belt state, having led Sanders by double digits in polls leading up to Tuesday's primary," Politico noted, reporting Sanders' win in Michigan. "But the Sanders campaign deemed Michigan a "critical showdown," and aggressively attacked Clinton for her policies on trade and her ties to Wall Street. Sanders is hoping his win in the delegate-heavy Midwestern state—second in delegates only to Texas so far—will show that his populist economic message can resonate elsewhere."[10]

FiveThirtyEight.com, the blog where polling guru Nate Silver is editor in chief, attributed the surprise win to pollsters that underestimated the youth turnout. Voters under age 30 made up 19 percent of the Democratic primary voters in Michigan, nearly as large a share as voters 65 or older. While pollsters had estimated voters under 50 would constitute about one-quarter of Democratic voters in the Michigan primary, voters under 50 instead turned out to be more than half. "The pollsters underestimated Sanders' dominance among younger voters," the blog concluded, while overestimating the enthusiasm of Clinton's older supporters to turn out and vote for her.[11]

In late March and early April 2015, Sanders won a string of 8 out of 9 primaries, all by double digits, with Sanders racking up wins in Alaska, Hawaii, Idaho, Utah, Washington, Wisconsin, Wyoming, and "Democrats Abroad," while Clinton won only Arizona. Yet, amazingly, Clinton came out ahead in the delegate total. How was this possible? The answer requires an understanding of an important quirk in the DNC process of nominating the party's presidential candidate: namely, "superdelegates."

February 18, 2016: Hillary Health Concern Surfaces During Las Vegas Trip

On February 18, 2016, on a campaign trip to Las Vegas in advance of the Nevada primary, Hillary Clinton was observed boarding her airplane in Chicago wearing her normal contact lenses. But when she arrived at Caesars Palace in Las Vegas for a late night meeting with hotel workers, she was observed wearing heavy black frame eyeglasses fitted with Fresnel prism lenses typically medically prescribed for patients suffering from double vision.[12] This followed a speech Hillary had given earlier in the week in New York at Harlem's Schomburg Center for Research in Black Culture where Hillary suffered from her third public coughing fit while giving a speech about race relations.[13] Reporting on the coughing fit, Breitbart News noted that Hillary's coughing got so bad that the audience started chanting, "Hillary! Hillary!" to provide encouragement while Clinton started taking sips of water preparing to pop a cough drop.

Hillary had worn the heavy black frame eyeglasses fitted with Fresnel lenses when she testified before the US House Oversight Committee Hearing on May 8, 2013, investigating Benghazi, when Hillary lost control, responding to Sen. Ron Johnson, Republican-Wisconsin, asking why the Benghazi terror attack happened. A famous video clip resulted, shown often by Hillary opponents throughout the 2016 presidential campaign, in which Hillary wearing the black frame eyeglasses and a solid green dress jacket explodes. "With all due respect, the fact is we had four dead Americans," Hillary pleaded, raising both arms up, her palms extended upward in an exasperated expression. "Was it because of a protest or was it because of guys out for a walk one night who decided that they'd go kill some Americans?" she continued. "What difference at this point does it make."[14] Then, on October 22, 2015, when testifying to the House Select Committee on Benghazi, Clinton suffered a coughing fit that temporarily halted the panel's questions.[15]

"Brain damage" from Clinton concussion in 2012?

The issue of the Fresnel lenses came to national attention in May 2014, when Republican strategist Karl Rove insisted at a conference that voters must be told why Hillary was wearing the eyeglasses fitted with Fresnel prisms that Rove suggested were only prescribed for people who have traumatic brain damage. As reported first by in the New York Post's "Page Six" column, Rove said that if Hillary runs for president, voters must be told what happened when she suffered a fall in December 2012.[16] Hillary had insisted the fall was attributed to dehydration from a stomach virus. She had also insisted that a subsequently developed blood clot in her head was successfully treated without causing brain damage. In a subsequent interview with the *Washington Post*, Rove claimed Clinton had spent thirty days in the hospital, recovering from the fall and the blood clot. "Thirty days in the hospital?" Rove questioned. "And when she reappears, she's wearing glasses that are only for people who have traumatic brain injury? We need to know what's up with that." The *Washington Post* corrected Rove, noting that it was three days not 30 days as Rove had claimed, that Clinton spent after being admitted to New York Presbyterian Hospital—Columbia University Medical Center for a blood clot that developed after the fall caused by dehydration related to a stomach virus, according to Clinton aides and hospital officials.[17]

When Bill Clinton was confronted by Rove's accusations during a question and answer session at the Peterson Foundation in Washington, on May 14, 2014, Clinton told the audience that the concussion Hillary suffered "required six months of very serious work to get over." ABC News, in reporting on President Clinton's comments, summarized the history of Hillary's fall, her concussion, and her subsequent brain clot. On December 30, 2012, Clinton was hospitalized at New York Presbyterian Hospital after a blood clot in her head was discovered during a follow-up exam to the concussions she experienced several weeks earlier.

On December 30, 2012, State Department spokesman Philippe Reines "In the course of a follow-up exam today, Secretary Clinton's doctors discovered a blood clot had formed, stemming from the concussion she sustained several weeks ago. She is being treated with anti-coagulants and is at New York-Presbyterian Hospital so that they can monitor the medication over the next 48 hours. Her doctors will continue to assess her condition, including other issues associated with her concussion. They will determine if any further action is required."[18] On December 31, 2012, Clinton's attending physicians released the following additional statement: "In the course of a routine follow-up MRI on Sunday, the scan revealed that a right transverse sinus venous thrombosis had formed. This is a clot in the vein that is situated in the space between the brain and the skull behind the right ear. It did not result in a stroke, or neurological damage. To help dissolve this clot, her medical team began treating the Secretary with blood thinners. She will be released once the medication dose has been established. In all other aspects of her recovery, the Secretary is making excellent progress and we are confident she will make a full recovery. She is in good spirits, engaging with her doctors, her family, and her staff."

On November 16, 2015, Washington-based watchdog group Judicial Watch released an exchange between her aides Huma Abedin and Monica Hanley dated January 26, 2013, regarding Clinton's schedule. They indicated it was "very important" to go over phone calls with Clinton because the former Secretary of State was "often confused."[19]

The issue came up again during the third Democratic Party primary debate in Goffstown, N.H., on December 19, 2015, when Clinton took a five-minute bathroom break at the third Democratic debate, returning to the stage late, as contenders Bernie Sanders and former Maryland

Governor Martin O'Malley, an early contender for the Democratic party nomination who, as previously mentioned, suspended his campaign after the Iowa caucus, stood on stage ready to resume the debate after a commercial break. Clinton remained offstage, awkwardly leaving her center stage podium unoccupied. Initially, reporters attributed her delayed return to the stage to the distance of the woman's bathroom to and from the on-stage podium.[20] Alex Swoyer, writing on Breitbart.com explained Hillary's disappearance from the debate stage by reporting from law enforcement sources backstage that the delay involved a "flare up of problems from brain injury" that required Hillary to sit in a chair off-stage to recover from fatigue, dizziness, and disorientation.[21]

WikiLeaks released emails leave no doubt the Clinton campaign was worried early in 2015 that Hillary's health could become an issue. On March 14, 2015, a Clinton campaign manager emailed Podesta, asking Podesta if he had talked with Hillary about taxes and health. "I know both are hyper sensitive but I wonder if both are better dealt with early so we can control them—rather than responding to calls for transparency. What do you think?"[22] In an email dated April 21, 2015, Clinton top aid and confidant Huma Abedin warned various top campaign officials that Hillary was "going to stick to notes a little closer this A.M., still not perfect in her head," an apparent reference to Hillary's continuing post-concussion problems with mental functioning.[23]

Hillary: "High Risk" for Blood Clots

The information on Hillary Clinton's health released by her presidential campaign was limited to a letter from Clinton's personal physician, Dr. Lisa Bardack, dated July 28, 2015.[24] In that letter, Bardack revealed that Clinton is generally "healthy," but she pointed out two incidents of thrombosis, the medical term for "blood clotting within the veins." Bardack continued noting that Clinton had experienced two incidents of blood clots in her leg, "Her past medical history is notable for a deep vein thrombosis in 1998 and in 2009." Bardack's letter also confirmed that Clinton had experienced a transverse venous thrombosis—a blood clot between the brain and the skull behind her left ear—as a result of the concussion she suffered in 2012. "As a result of the concussion, Mrs. Clinton experienced double vision for a period of time and benefited from wearing glasses with a Fresnel Prism." As a precaution, Bardack noted, Clinton was placed "on daily anticoagulation."

The New York Daily News, in an article published in 2007 when Clinton turned 60 years old,[25] described the 1998 incident as "a potentially fatal scare." She was campaigning on behalf of Chuck Schumer's New York Senate bid and had a swollen right foot that caused severe pain. "She thought she just needed to slow down from constant flying," wrote New York Daily News reporter Heidi Evans. "A White House doctor told her to rush to Bethesda Naval Hospital, where doctors diagnosed a large blood clot behind her right knee." Clinton told the newspaper: "That was scary because you have to treat it immediately—you don't want to take the risk that it will break loose and travel to your brain, or your heart or your lungs. That was the most significant health scare I've ever had."[26] Hillary sent another email to Cheryl Mills, dated August 19, 2011, regarding an article Clinton had read, "Do You Suffer from Decision Fatigue?" In a separate email sent two months later, Clinton's top foreign policy advisor at the State Department, Jacob Sullivan, informed her about a drug called Provigil (Modafinil) that is used to treat "excessive sleepiness in patients with Parkinson's, Alzheimer's, and multiple sclerosis" as well as "excessive sleepiness caused by narcolepsy."[27]

Evans reported that Clinton claimed she no longer took blood thinners and had "otherwise enjoyed good health while zig-zagging across the country for the past nine months, keeping a schedule that exhausts aides half her age." "I'm lucky that I've got a good stamina," Clinton told Evans. "I try to take care of myself. It's much harder on the road [since] there's too much junk food and temptation around. I don't exercise as much as I did before I got into the real heat of the presidential campaign, but I try to get out and walk."

But Dr. Bardack's 2015 assessment disagreed, noting Clinton had been taking anticoagulant medication continuously since the 1998 blood-clot incident. "She [Hillary Clinton] also was advised in 1998 to take Lovenox, a short-acting blood thinner, when she took extended flights; this medication was discontinued when she began Coumadin." While Bardack did not specify when Clinton's medication was switched from Lovenox to Coumadin, she made it clear Clinton is still taking Coumadin, evidently now on a continual basis. "Her Coumadin dose is monitored regularly and she has experienced no side effects from her medications," Bardack wrote.

WND.com reporter Jerome R. Corsi, researching Clinton's medical condition, noted that the two medications Clinton was taking daily were old medications, both developed from natural ingredients. For Clinton's hypoactive thyroid, Bardack prescribed Armour Thyroid, a natural medication made from desiccated pig thyroid glands. For Clinton's high-risk propensity to develop blood clots, Bardack prescribed Coumadin—a brand name of warfarin, which initially was developed as a well-known rat poison, designed to cause rats to bleed to death after being ingested.[28] These two medications are confirmed in her physician's report.

"Hillary's hypothyroid condition can lead to hypercoagulability, a tendency toward excessive blood clotting, that makes more complicated the use of the blood-thinning medicines she needs to control what appears to be a possibly genetic tendency of her body to produce blood clots," Dr. Ronald Hoffman explained to WND. "The medical literature cautions that patients on Armour Thyroid may need to reduce the amount of Coumadin they are taking, and this requires constant blood testing to make sure the mixture of Armour Thyroid and Coumadin are adjusted just right," he cautioned. Hoffman, a New York City Physician who hosts the nationally syndicated radio program, Intelligent Medicine, was a past president of the nation's largest organization of complementary and alternative doctors, the American College for Advancement in Medicine, or ACAM. Additionally, Hoffman is the founder and medical director of the Hoffman Center, specializing in a natural medicine approach that combines nutritional and metabolic medical assessment tools with high-tech innovations in traditional medicine.

Clearly Clinton's medical conditions were far more serious than she and her team let on.

Clinton's Lock on "Superdelegates"

The Democratic National Committee's presidential primary process differs from the Republican National Committee's process in one important way—"superdelegates"—an elite class of DNC delegates not bound by the outcome of the primary contests in their various states.

Superdelegates were established by the Democratic Party to give party elites an unfair advantage over Democratic Party primary voters in deciding which candidate will emerge from the party's primary and caucus system to be the party's presidential nominee. The DNC introduced primaries and caucuses in 1972, as a reform to take the selection of the party's presidential nominee out of the hands of backroom bosses who typically had brokered ballots in contested conventions to select a candidate favored by the Democratic Party's professional leadership in Washington.

Superdelegates were created as a corrective after the 1970s DNC reforms introducing primaries and caucuses which resulted in two losing candidates, both trounced by the GOP in landslide elections: George McGovern in 1972, who was easily beaten by incumbent President Richard Nixon; and Jimmy Carter in 1976, who lost his bid in 1980 to GOP challenger Ronald Reagan. When Sen. Ted Kennedy challenged President Carter in 1980 in a fight that went to the convention floor, the DNC constituted the Hunt Commission, chaired by then-North Carolina Governor James Hunt, with the result that superdelegates were born.[29]

Under DNC rules, a superdelegate falls into one of the three following categories:

1. A major elected official, including senators, members of the House, governors, and leaders from each state's Democratic Party;
2. A notable party figure, such as former and current presidents and vice presidents; and
3. Select leaders of organizations affiliated with the Democratic National Committee.[30]

Democrat superdelegates tend to express their support before the primary in their state, but under DNC rules, superdelegates can change their minds right up until they vote on the first ballot.

In total, there are 712 superdelegates, controlling about 15 percent of the nominating process, with the remaining 85 percent of the delegates chosen by DNC primaries and caucuses. The great advantage to being a superdelegate is that unlike a regular delegate, a superdelegate is free to vote on the first ballot at the DNC national nominating convention for whatever candidate the superdelegate chooses to support. Normal delegates are bound under DNC rules to vote for the candidate who wins their state primary or caucus election.

So, while Sanders won 15 of the 24 regular delegates in the New Hampshire primary, six of the state's eight superdelegates had already pledged to support Clinton, with the other two superdelegates refusing to say. So, the real outcome of the New Hampshire primary, in which Sanders won the popular vote, was 21 delegates for Clinton versus 24 delegates for Sanders, with 2 superdelegates yet to commit, despite Sanders having defeated Clinton by 22 percentage points.[31] Analyzing the New Hampshire primary results, the *Washington Post* wrote that super-delegates gave Clinton a huge advantage over Sanders to win the 2,382 delegates needed to win the nomination. With most of the DNC's 712 superdelegates pledged in advance to Clinton, independent of results in the DNC state primary and caucus contests, Sanders could earn a majority of the 1,670 delegates up for grabs in popular voting all over the country, and still lose the nomination.[32]

Debbie Wasserman Schultz, in attempting to explain to CNN's Jake Tapper the impact of superdelegates on Sanders' New Hampshire delegate outcome, found herself having difficulty explaining how the DNC superdelegate process was fair to grassroots Democratic voters seeking to promote diversity in primary outcomes. "Unpledged delegates exist really to make sure that party leaders and elected officials don't have to be in a position where they are running against grassroots activists," she said.[33]

June 7, 2016: Hillary Declares Herself the Winner

On June 7, 2016, at 2:18 am GMT, in the early morning hours on the day of the Democratic primary in California, the Associated Press reported Hillary was on the edge of an historic moment. "Eight years after conceding she was unable to 'shatter that highest, hardest glass ceiling,' Hillary Clinton is embracing her place in history as she finally crashes through as the presumptive Democratic presidential nominee," the AP noted. "Throughout her surprisingly rocky primary campaign, Clinton has been cautious about emphasizing her trailblazer status. But as she campaigned in California in recent days, the former Secretary of State signaled she was ready to acknowledge her distinction as the first woman to top the presidential ticket of a major US political party."[34] Then, in a separate press release as the votes were being counted in California, the Associated Press reported that early results in the California primary looked like Hillary Clinton had enough pledged delegates and superdelegates to clinch the Democratic nomination.[35]

That evening, June 7, 2016, Hillary, wearing a white pantsuit with jacket combination, gave a "victory speech" to supporters in Brooklyn, New York, the site of her campaign headquarters. It was eight years to the day since her famous June 7, 2008 "18 million cracks in the glass ceiling" speech, conceding to Barack Obama after losing the Democratic primary in California. "Although we weren't able to shatter that highest, hardest glass ceiling this time, thanks to you, it's got about 18 million cracks in it," Clinton told supporters that night eight years ago.[36] "The path will be easier next time." This time around, eight years later in Brooklyn, Clinton announced she finally was the Democrats presumptive nominee, becoming the first woman to lead a major political party presidential ticket.

In 2016, assured she was going to win the Democratic Party presidential nomination, Hillary made the evening a celebration of feminism. "Tonight's victory is not about one person," Hillary said, kicking off the speech.[37] "It belongs to generations of women and men who struggled and sacrificed and made this moment possible." From here, Hillary transitioned into the 19th century campaign to establish women's suffrage. "In our country, it started right here in New York, in a place called Seneca Falls, in 1848. When a small but determined group of women, and men, came together with the idea that women deserved equal rights, and they set it forth in something called the Declaration of Sentiments, and it was the first time in human history that that kind of declaration occurred," she said. "So we owe so much to those who came before, and tonight belongs to all of you."

Smiling broadly and looking self-satisfied if not outright smug, Clinton had begun her speech by invoking once again the glass ceiling image, saying, "And it may be hard to see tonight, but we are all standing under a glass ceiling right now. But don't worry, we're not smashing this one." She continued proclaiming her victory in this feminist tradition, "Thanks to you, we've reached a milestone—the first time in our nation's history that a woman will be a major party's nominee for president of the United States." Hillary's point was clear: voters should vote for her because she was a woman. In the context of intolerant Democratic Party far-left ideology-driven politics, few Hillary supporters saw any hypocrisy that the plea to vote for Hillary because of her sex was inherently sexist.

On Thursday, June 9, 2016, the Associated Press reported Bernie Sanders was now under increasing pressure from unnamed Democratic leaders to abandon his presidential campaign. "He vowed to fight on for a political revolution but showed signs he would bow to the inevitable and bring his insurgent effort to a close," the AP reported. "For Sanders, as his remarkable White House bid runs out of next steps, the only question is when. Just as important for Sanders is how to keep his campaign alive in some form, by converting his newfound political currency into policies to change the Democratic Party, the Senate or even the country itself, on issues including income inequality and campaign finance reform."[38] The AP noted Sanders had promised to continue his campaign until the last primary, scheduled for the District of Columbia the following week. But that pledge was in question as about half of Sanders' campaign staff was being laid off, two people familiar with Sanders' plans confirmed to the AP.

In a White House meeting with President Obama on Thursday, June 9, 2016, Sanders indicated his willingness to support Hillary, but he still refused to concede. Speaking outside of the White House after meeting with President Obama, Sanders said of Clinton, "I look forward to meeting with her in the near future to see how we can work together to defeat Donald Trump and create a government, which represents all of us and not just one percent."[39].

The Associated Press reported that tensions between the Clinton and the Sanders campaigns simmered throughout a platform meeting in a steamy hotel ballroom over two marathon days in Orlando during July, just prior to the opening of the DNC nominating convention in Philadelphia.[40] "Despite winning concessions on many issues, Sanders supporters booed angrily over losses, such as failing to get clear opposition to the Trans-Pacific Partnership trade deal," the AP reported. "Near the meeting's end, Sanders' backers angrily shouted down an effort to add Clinton's name to the document in a number of places, which they took as an implication that she was already the official nominee." The Clinton camp elbow bending to add her name to a list of platform committee recommendations risked alienating. "To do it now [add Hillary's name] is a slap in the face to us. She is not the nominee," Diana Hatsis-Newhoff, 54, a nurse from Palm Beach, who was a Sanders supporter, told the AP. But, finally, after stalling for weeks as he sought to get liberal policy concessions from Hillary and as he lobbied to push the Democratic Party platform farther left, the AP noted Sanders had finally agreed to drop out of the race.

Appearing with Hillary in Portsmouth, New Hampshire—a state that Sanders had won convincingly just five months earlier, Sanders endorsed his rival. "Secretary Clinton has won the Democratic nominating process, and I congratulate her for that," Sanders said, speaking from a podium fronted with a Clinton campaign message that read, "Stronger Together." Sanders continued, officially suspending his campaign: "She will be the Democratic nominee for president, and I intend to do everything I can to make certain she will be the next president of the United States." Sanders' determination to move the Clinton campaign farther left was evident in his closing remarks. "We produced, by far, the most progressive platform in the history of the Democratic Party," Sanders told supporters. "Our job now is to see that platform implemented."[41]

Sanders on Superdelegates: "A Rigged System"

In April 2016, a controversy within the Democratic Party flared, when Sanders supporters, including many Millennial voters, became disgusted that Sanders had won 8 of the last nine primary contests by double digits but Hillary got more delegates. "This is primarily because of the Democratic Party's superdelegate system, which has come under harsh condemnation in this election for being thoroughly undemocratic," Ben Norton wrote on Salon.com on April 12, 2016. "Hundreds of unelected party elites known as superdelegates or unpledged delegates have enormous sway in the primary election."[42] Norton further objected to media partisanship of Clinton for lumping superdelegates into the total delegate counts in reporting on the primary elections, making it look like Clinton had a larger lead than she actually did. Norton calculated that Sanders had approximately 45 percent of the pledged delegate votes, the delegates actually earned through votes, making the contest much closer than it appeared when the superdelegates overwhelmingly backing Hillary were added to the total.

On Monday, May 2, 2016, Reuters caught up with Sanders in Evansville, Indiana, just ahead of the Indiana primary the next day. During the campaign stop, Sanders explained to Reuters that the Democratic process was a rigged system in how the Democratic Party awards superdelegates that are unelected and free to support any candidate they wish. "When we talk about a rigged system, it is important to understand how the Democratic convention works," Sanders argued. "We have won 45 percent of the pledged delegates, but we have only earned 7 percent of superdelegates. So, in other words, the way the system works is you have establishment candidates who win virtually all of the candidates." Sanders clearly understood the Democratic nominating process was rigged in Hillary's favor. "It makes it hard for insurgent candidacies like ours to win," Sanders concluded. While acknowledging he trailed Clinton when superdelegates were added into the total, Sanders still insisted it was nearly impossible for Clinton to win the 2,383 delegates needed for the nomination without superdelegates.[43]

On April 14, 2016, Clinton spokesperson Brian Fallon during an interview on CNN's "New Day" said there was "zero percent chance" Clinton would not go to the Democratic National Convention in Philadelphia as the nominee. Fallon estimated that with a "good outcome" in the New York primary scheduled for the following Tuesday, and the five states voting on "Super Tuesday II," or the "Acela Primary" after Amtrak's Acela Express train, April 26, 2016—Delaware, Maryland, Pennsylvania, Connecticut, and Rhode Island—Clinton would be approaching the magic number of 2,383 delegates needed to win the nomination. "And then at that point there's a few contests in May, and when you add up the pledged delegates that she's amassed right now, she's got a lead of about over 200 pledged delegates over Sen. Sanders," Fallon continued.[44]

As it turned out, Clinton won New York and four of the five states on April 26, 2016, with Sanders taking only Rhode Island. The next day, the Associated Press affirmed Fallon's calculation had been correct. "Clinton is in a stronger position, now about 90 percent of the way to the nomination," the Associated Press reported on Wednesday, April 27, 2016. "Sanders, who denied his rival a clean sweep Tuesday with his win in Rhode Island, is down to needing a miracle."[45]

But the issue of superdelegates and the way Sanders had voiced being treated unfairly in a Democratic primary process rigged to nominate Clinton caused Millennial voters to become turned off in droves. At a Saturday afternoon meeting on July 23, 2016, in a small room inside Philadelphia's Wells Fargo Center, the first meeting of the Rules Committee of the Democratic National met and rejected a proposal to eliminate the role of superdelegates in future Democratic presidential primaries. The decision was reached ignoring the vote taken in multiple state Democratic conventions that had voted in favor of eliminating, or otherwise minimizing or limiting the power of superdelegates. There was little chance the proposal would be adopted, given that the DNC Rules Committee was co-chaired by former Massachusetts congressman and outspoken Hillary partisan Barney Frank.[46] Debbie Wasserman Schultz had also appointed 25 members of the Rules Committee allowed to vote on the proposal. The amendment, co-sponsored by 52 members of the Democratic Party Rules Committee was defeated when 108 members voted against and only 58 in favor.[47] The proposal to eliminate or limit superdelegates was taken only after Sanders delegates were locked out of the room.

WikiLeaks: DNC Determined to Undermine Sanders Campaign

Although the Clintonites and democratic campaign operatives would claim that WikiLeaks and Julian Assange hacked their most sensitive documents and blame the Russians, they ignore the fact that multiple sources had come forward. These sources indicate that the material had been leaked, not hacked online, and had been supplied to WikiLeaks by a disgruntled democratic national committee staffer who was disgusted by the way they were bending the rules to screw Bernie Sanders. I believe that person to be Seth Rich, who shortly thereafter took 5 slugs to the back. Although the *Washington Post* would claim that the motive in Rich's murder was robbery, the DNC staffer's father told reporters that his wallet, money, and jewelry were intact.

Starting on Friday, July 22, 2016, the week before the Democratic National Convention was scheduled to nominate Hillary Clinton for president at the party's convention in Philadelphia, Julian Assange of WikiLeaks made public the first cache of 19,252 emails from Democratic Party officials.[48] Over two drops, WikiLeaks published 44,053 emails and 17,761 attachments from the email accounts of seven key Democratic National Committee figures, including DNC Communications Director Luis Miranda, Senior Advisor Andrew Wright, and key officials from the DNC finance arm. The emails covered the period from January 2015 through May 25, 2016.[49] The emails were particularly damaging for the proof provided that "Hill-BOTS" had conspired with Democratic Party regulars to rig the primaries so Bernie Sanders had no chance whatsoever to win. The derisive robot-derived name "Hill-BOTS" given Hillary Clinton operatives, including both paid and self-recruited operatives, described a group of Hillary-supporting political operatives who intervened into the political process and posted aggressively on social media to defend their candidate and trash political opponents.

One particularly damaging email shows DNC chief financial officer Brad Marshall emailing DNC communications director Luis Miranda, with copies included for several other DNC communications directors, on May 5, 2016, not mentioning Bernie Sanders, but suggesting the issue of religion could be used against a certain suspected atheist with a Jewish heritage. The email read: "It might make no difference, but for

KY [Kentucky] and WVA [West Virginia] can we get someone to ask his belief. Does he believe in a God? He had skated on saying he has a Jewish heritage. I think I read he is an atheist. This could make several points difference with my peeps. My Southern Baptist peeps would draw a big difference between a Jew and an atheist.”[50] Marshall's point was that in the upcoming Democratic primary contests in Kentucky and West Virginia—two states with a large Southern Baptist population, Hillary Clinton could gain an advantage if Luis Miranda managed to leak out to Hillary supporting reporters the story that Bernie Sanders, a Jew by ethnic heritage, was really an atheist. Almost immediately, Marshall apologized to Sanders, posting as the only public comment on his otherwise private Facebook page: “I deeply regret that my insensitive, emotional emails would cause embarrassment to the DNC, the Chairwoman, and all of the staffers who worked hard to make the primary a fair and open process. The comments expressed do not reflect my beliefs nor do they reflect the beliefs of the DNC and its employees. I apologize to those I offended.”[51]

Another email involved DNC national press secretary Mark Paustenbach emailing Luis Miranda with the suggestion that the DNC should leak a story to Hillary-supporting partisan reporters with “a good Bernie narrative” suggesting that Sander's campaign is a disorganized “mess.” Dated May 21, 2016, three weeks prior to the California primary, Paustenbach emailed to Miranda the following: “Wondering if there's a good Bernie narrative for a story, which is that Bernie never had his act together, that his campaign is a mess.”[52] After giving three examples of what he considered “a mess,” Paustenbach closed the email with the following: “It's not a DNC conspiracy, it's because they never had their act together.”

Progressive analyst and reporter Michael Sainato, after studying the WikiLeaks DNC email database came to the conclusion that the emails reveal Debbie Wasserman Schultz, the head of the DNC, shared with other key DNC officials “a resentful disdain” toward Sanders, providing evidence the DNC favored Clinton long before the primaries began.[53] Instead of treating Sanders with impartiality, “the DNC exhibits resentful disdain toward him and the thousands of disenfranchised voters he could have brought into the party,” Sainato wrote, on the eve of the DNC national nominating convention in Philadelphia. Sainato further commented that the WikiLeaks dump of DNC documents was particularly damaging because the bias to rig the nomination for Clinton and against Sanders was confirmed by a leak of internal DNC memos made public on the Internet by Romanian hacker Guccifer 2.0 on July 14, 2016.[54] The files released by Guccifer 2.0 showed the DNC staff strategizing as early as March 2015 to make Clinton the nominee.

"The WikiLeaks and Guccifer 2.0 leaks are the perfect end to a Democratic primary that undermined democracy at every possible opportunity while maintaining plausible deniability," Sainato continued. The party's rules, including the use of superdelegates—who disproportionately endorsed Clinton before the primaries began—are intended to provide the Democratic Party leverage over the election process. Throughout the primaries, decisions were made by DNC officials to help Clinton build and maintain a lead over Sanders." Perhaps most damning of all, Sainato concluded given the bias of the DNC to nominate Clinton, Sanders had to run not only against Clinton, but against the entire Democratic establishment. "Heading into the Democratic National Convention, voters are beginning to understand that their voices are of little concern to the leadership," Sainato concluded.

On July 24, 2016, two days after the first of the two-part WikiLeaks dump of DNC emails, Florida Congresswoman Debbie Wasserman Schultz resigned her post as chair of the DNC, leaving no doubt just how devastating to Democratic Party credibility the leaked documents had been. The DNC vice-chair, Donna Brazile, a Clinton supporter, was appointed to serve as interim DNC chair. Schultz submitted her resignation on a late Sunday afternoon, the day before the DNC was set to kick off its national convention in Philadelphia.[55] The timing could not have been worse for the Democrats.

CHAPTER 6

Round Two: Hillary Pivots to Attack Trump

It's one Clinton failure after another. What has Hillary Clinton accomplished for your family in the last 26 years that she has been doing this? Nothing. Nothing! . . . Remember, when you go in to vote, don't vote for Crooked Hillary. Just put it in your head: Crooked Hillary. She is a crooked one.
    Donald J. Trump, Melbourne Florida, September 27, 2016[1]

As the Democratic Party primaries progressed and Hillary's nomination became a virtual certainty, Hillary Clinton pivoted to begin attacking Trump. This strategy gave Hillary an additional month before the Democratic National Convention to begin implementing her general election strategy designed to demonstrate to the American people why she was the best candidate to be elected president.

Attack on Trump University

On June 9, 2016, two days after the California primary and Clinton's "victory speech" declaring she was the party's presumed nominee, Sen. Elizabeth Warren gave a speech to the American Constitution Society, in which she endorsed Hillary and castigated Trump.[2]

The specific focus of Warren's attack on Trump was the national class action lawsuit filed by students against Trump University in California. In a rally in San Diego the previous May, Trump spent twelve minutes lambasting the San Diego-based judge handling that class action suit, US District Judge Gonzalo Curiel.[3] "The trial is going to take place sometime in November," Trump had said at his San Diego rally in May. "There should be no trial. This should have been dismissed on summary judgment easily. Everybody says it, but I have a judge who is a hater of Donald Trump. He's a hater. His name is Gonzalo Curiel. And he is not doing the right thing." Trump pointed out that President Obama had appointed Judge Curiel. "Frankly he should recuse himself. He has given us ruling after ruling, negative, negative, negative," Trump continued, attacking Curiel. "I have a top lawyer who said he has never seen anything like this before." Next, Trump attacked Curiel's ethnicity. "So what happens is the judge, who happens to be, we believe Mexican, which is great," Trump continued. "I think that is fine. You know what? I think the Mexicans are going to end up loving Donald Trump when I give all these jobs. I think they are going to love it. I think they are going to love me. . ."

This gave Warren enough ammunition to blast Trump in her speech before the ASC Convention. "Gonzalo Curiel was born in Indiana—not Mexico—to immigrant parents who worked hard their entire lives and were handed nothing," Warren noted, commenting that Trump was "picking upon" a federal judge bound by the federal code of judicial ethics not to defend himself." Warren characterized Trump's attack as "exactly what you'd expect from a thin-skinned, racist bully."[4] She objected to Trump saying Curiel should be ashamed of himself. "No, Donald—*you* should be ashamed of yourself," Warren responded. "Ashamed for using the megaphone of a Presidential campaign to attack a judge's character and integrity simply because you think you have some God-given right to steal people's money and get away with it. You shame yourself and you shame this great country." Warren objected to Trump saying Curiel was a total disgrace. "No, Donald—what *you* are doing is a total disgrace," Warren continued. "Race-baiting a judge who spent years defending America from the terror of murderers and drug traffickers simply because long ago his family came to America from somewhere else. You, Donald Trump, are a total disgrace." Warren concluded by asserting that Trump "chose racism as his weapon," while arguing that Trump's goal "is exactly the same" as the rest of the Republicans—namely, "Pound the courts into submission to the rich and powerful."

On June 1, 2016, Jerome Corsi published an article in WND.com proving that documents released in the national class-action lawsuit accusing Trump University of fraud came from a law firm that had paid Bill and Hillary Clinton a total of $675,000 for speeches.[5] LawNewZ.com reported[6] that Robbins Geller Rudman & Dowd, LLP paid the Clintons more than they collected from any of their other 104 paid speeches. The San Diego law firm paid Bill Clinton $250,000 for a speech in 2009 (before the firm was renamed) and paid $450,000 to Hillary Clinton for her 2013 and 2014 speeches.[7]

LawNewZ.com further reported Patrick Coughlin, one of the Robbins Geller attorneys, maxed out his contributions to Hillary Clinton's presidential campaign. "Records maintained by the Federal Election Commission indicate that Coughlin has been a longtime financial supporter of both the Democratic National Committee and Hillary Clinton," the LawNewZ.com article noted. "In February, he donated $5,400 to her campaign."[8]

According to court records filed with the US District Court for the Southern District of California on October 18, 2013, of the twelve lawyers representing the plaintiff, California businessman Art Cohen in the RICO class action lawsuit Cohen versus Trump, nine are listed as members of Robbins Geller Rudman & Dowd LLP. On December 10, 2014, US District Judge Gonzalo P. Curiel in San Diego certified Cohen's complaint as a national class action suit, with the first public hearing currently scheduled on July 18, the first day of the Republican National Convention.

A few days later, on June 6, 2016, Corsi published an article on WND.com documenting Judge Curiel and the Robbins Geller Rudman & Dowd, LLP law firm as members of the San Diego La Raza Lawyers Association, a group that while not a branch of the National Council of La Raza, has ties to the controversial organization, which translates literally "The Race."

US District Judge Gonzalo Curiel, who has been criticized by Donald Trump as a "hater" appointed by President Obama who should be recused from the case, listed his membership in the "La Raza Lawyers of San Diego" on a judicial questionnaire he filled out when he was selected to be a federal judge. He was named in a brochure as a member of the selection committee for the organization's 2014 Annual Scholarship Fund Dinner & Gala. Meanwhile, the San Diego-based law firm representing the plaintiffs in the Trump University case, Robbins Geller Rudman & Dowd, was listed as a sponsor of the event.

While those attacking Trump have argued that the San Diego La Raza Lawyers' association is not affiliated with the National Council of La Raza, Corsi drew attention to the following:

- The San Diego La Raza Lawyers' Association is a member of the La Raza Lawyers of California, affiliated with the Chicano/Latino Bar Association of California.
- On the website of the La Raza Lawyers Association of California, LaRazaLawyers.net, at the bottom of the "Links & Affiliates Page," the National Council of La Raza is listed.
- The website of the San Diego La Raza Lawyers Association, sdlrla.com, is jointly listed as San Diego's Latino/Latina Bar Association.
- On the "endorsements" page, the combined website lists the National Council of La Raza as part of the "community," along with the Hispanic National Bar Association, a group that emerged with a changed name from the originally formed La Raza National Lawyers Association and the La Raza National Bar Association tracing its origin back to 1971.

While Corsi acknowledged it is correct that the San Diego La Raza Lawyers' Association and the National Council of La Raza are legally separately incorporated entities, he pointed out the two groups clearly appear to have an affiliation that traces back to the emergence of MEChA, *Moviemento Estudiantil Chicanos de Atzlán*, a 1960s radical separatist student movement in California that espoused the mythical Aztec idea of a "nation of Aztlán, comprising much of the southwestern United States, including California.[9] David Horowitz also documents on his website "Discover the Networks," La Raza, Spanish for "the race," also has roots in the early 1960s with a "united front" organization, the National Organization for Mexican American Services, NOMAS, that was initially funded by the Ford Foundation, and subsequently by George Soros' Open Society Institute, and the John D. and Catherine T. MacArthur Foundation.[10] In 1968, the Southwest Council of La Raza was organized with Ford Foundation funding; in 1972, the group changed its name to the National Council of La Raza and opened an office in Washington, DC.

On November 18, 2016, after Trump had been elected president, Trump agreed to settle the Trump University national class action suit for $25 million. The *Washington Post* reported that Trump Organization General Counsel Alan Garten said he thought Trump could have prevailed at trial, but settled so Trump could "devote full attention to the important issues facing our great nation," during his presidential transition. The newspaper also reported that New York Attorney General Eric Schneiderman, who had filed a second law suit in the Trump University case, argued the $25 million was "a stunning reversal for Trump and a major victory for the over 6,000 victims of his fraudulent university."[11]

Counterattack: Bill Clinton and Laureate Education, Inc.

The Clinton campaign attack on Donald Trump over Trump University invited increased scrutiny of Laureate Education, Inc., a for-profit educational scandal in which a company operating shell colleges paid Bill Clinton $16.5 million[12] to be its pitchman, while Hillary Clinton's State Department funneled at least $55 million to the parent corporation.[13]

The case involves Laureate Education, Inc., a near bankrupt international for-profit "university" that forced thousands of student victims into what Forbes estimates at $756 million, more than three-quarters of a billion dollars, in student tuition debt.[14] Laureate Education, Inc., one of the world's largest for-profit universities, sent Bill Clinton, appointed in 2004 to be its "honorary chancellor," scurrying around the globe to make promotional appearances at Laureate campuses in countries as diverse as Malaysia, Peru, and Spain. The company, created in 2004 on the base of the tutoring chain Sylvan Learning Centers, already owned 75 schools in 30 countries, when Bill Clinton was hired as pitchman, and was poised for a massive expansion that brought riches to an "A-list" of top-name, left leaning investors attracted by the cache of Bill Clinton's endorsement, including George Soros, Henry Kravis of Wall Street investment banking firm KKR, and Paul Allen of Microsoft fame.

Laureate's founder and CEO, Douglas L. Becker, claims he was accepted at Harvard, but declined, preferring to continue working in a local computer store over getting a college degree at the prestigious Ivy League university.[15] An article published in the *New York Times* in 1985 noted that Becker had also declined to attend the University of Pennsyl-

vania, where supposedly he had been accepted as a premedical undergraduate student.[16] Despite the claims of being accepted at Harvard and the
University of Pennsylvania, biographies written on Becker typically note
he did not attend college. In 2014, while the Clintons were still trying
to keep secret how much Bill Clinton was being paid by Laureate Education, Eric Owens, education editor at the Daily Caller, took Clinton
to task. Noting that Laureate was "ensnarled in controversy all over the
globe," Owens speculated the secret sum Becker was paying Bill Clinton
had to be a lot to get him "to hawk" the company worldwide. Owens
further noted that Hillary Clinton "helped legitimize Laureate in the
eyes of the world by making the for-profit education behemoth part of
her State Department Global Partnership."[17]

Completing the circle, the Clinton Foundation got into the act.

A Laureate Educational press release in 2013 announced that Laureate International Universities were scheduled to begin live broadcasts
of the Clinton Global Initiative, CGI, annual meeting, with more than
45,000 Laureate students scheduled to hear presentations by President
Obama, rock star Bono, and Archbishop Desmond Tutu.[18] "Four Laureate students from Brazil, Malaysia and Mexico will be granted private, one-on-one interviews with several CGI attendees," the press release
noted. "The students are scheduled to interview such CGI attendees as
Sheryl Sandberg, Facebook's Chief Operating Officer and author of The
New York Times best-selling book 'Lean In,' as well as Chelsea Clinton,
a member of the Clinton Foundation's board of directors. The conver-
sations will be broadcast in English, Spanish and Portuguese," the press
release continued. This is the second consecutive year Laureate has broadcast CGI's annual meeting."

In 2012, when Bill Clinton was in his fifth year running his own CGI
University, "CGI U," Doug Becker's Laureate Education was predictably
a sponsor.[19]

On April 14, 2015, Jennifer Epstein writing in Bloomberg Politics
reported that Bill Clinton decided to leave his five-year position as Laureate Education's "honorary chancellor," but not before Bill Clinton had
visited 19 of Laureate's 88 campuses around the world and spoke to tens
of thousands of its students.[20] Epstein noted Clinton's departure was pre-
cipitated by Hillary as her 2016 presidential campaign was joining Massachusetts Democratic Senator Elizabeth Warren in blasting the federal
government "for currently subsidizing a for-profit industry that is rip-

ping off young people." Epstein noted these concerns had not surfaced evidently in 2008 when Hillary accepted a contribution of $4,600 to her presidential campaign, making that Becker's second campaign contribution to Hillary, as he also gave her $2,000 for her 2000 Senate campaign.[21]

Predictably, the counter-attack exposing the Clintons' financial involvement in the Laureate Education case got virtually no coverage in the mainstream media, while Sen. Warren's accusations that Trump was a racist for attacking Judge Curiel occupied several days in the national news cycle, forcing Trump to expend valuable campaign time defending himself.

Democrats Pay "Rent-A-Riot" Anarchists to Disrupt Trump Rallies

On Friday, March 11, 2016, protesters interrupted a Donald Trump rally by shouting from the audience during Trump's speech in the Peabody Opera house in downtown St. Louis. Trump's reaction from the podium was aggressive. "Get him outta here, he's all mouth!" Trump said during one of the more than half-dozen interruptions in which police removed protesters to the thunderous approval of the crowd. "Go home to Mommy," he said during another of the removals, according to a report published by the *St. Louis Post Dispatch*.[22] "This is more exciting than (just) having a speech," Trump joked to the crowd during yet another of the altercations. The regular interruptions and removals of protesters, he quipped, were "beautiful, it's like intermission. Was that exciting? You had a good time, right?" At the St. Louis rally, some 32 people were arrested for disturbing the peace, with 29 of the arrests occurring within the auditorium, and three outside the rally, including at least one person arrested for assault.[23]

The *St. Louis Post-Dispatch* further reported Trump lamented that, because of criticism by the media—"the most dishonest human beings on Earth . . . the worst" — protesters had to be treated gently. The police, he said, "are being politically correct, so it takes a little longer. The protesters realize there are no consequences anymore. Our country has to toughen up, folks." He added: "It would be so nice . . .," leaving the rest of the sentence to the crowd's imagination. "I won't say what's on my mind, folks. I'm a nice person. I refuse to say." Trump's subdued reaction came after he was criticized a month earlier for telling an audience of supporters in Cedar Rapids, Iowa, that they should "knock the daylights out of protesters," with Trump offering to pay legal fees. "There may be somebody with tomatoes in the audience. So if you see somebody getting ready to throw a tomato, knock the crap out of them, would you? Seriously. Okay? Just knock the hell— I promise you, I will pay for the legal fees. I promise, I promise. It won't be so much 'cause the courts agree with us too."[24] Trump modified his initial, more aggressive approach to protesters after it became apparent the Democrats were trying to portray him as a bully encouraging his white supremacist supporters to use Nazi-like tactics to suppress dissent. The Democrats' narrative began to build after an incident in November 2015, when Trump defended some of his followers for punching and kicking a #BlackLivesMatter protester, with Trump saying, "Maybe he should have been roughed up."[25]

Also on March 11, 2016, protesters caused a Trump rally to be canceled in Chicago, amid what CNN reported involved fights between Trump supporters and demonstrators, protests in the street, and police concerns that the event was no longer safe. The event was scheduled to occur at the University of Chicago, but the potential for violence increased after demonstrators packed the arena, filling at least five sections. "Mr. Trump just arrived in Chicago, and after meeting with law enforcement, has determined that for the safety of all of the tens of thousands of people that have gathered in and around the arena, tonight's rally will be postponed to another date," the Trump campaign said in a statement. "Thank you very much for your attendance and please go in peace." After the announcement, several fistfights broke out in the arena, as a large contingent of Chicago police moved in to restore order. Trump supporters shouted, "We want Trump," while protesters shouted, "We stumped Trump." Other Trump protesters pulled out Bernie Sanders signs, as they began shouting "Bernie."[26]

The cancellation of the Chicago rally was a flashpoint for Jonathan Chait, a progressive pundit who articulated in a commentary published in New York Magazine on March 13, 2016, what was becoming a campaign narrative Democrats were using to brand and attack Trump.[27] "The Republican Party relies on the covert mobilization of racial resentment and nationalism," Chait wrote. "Trump, as I saw it, was bringing into the open that which had been intentionally submerged. It seemed like a containable dose of disease, too small to take over its host, but large enough to set off a counter-reaction of healthy blood cells. But the outbreak of violence this weekend suggests the disease may be spreading far wider than I believed, and infecting healthy elements of the body politic."

Now, Chait was concerned that what he saw as Trump's poisonous attraction to violence was inherently dangerous, much in the spirit that the intolerant far-left wants to brand speech that is not politically correct as hate speech that the far-left believes should be criminalized. "I remain convinced that Trump cannot win the presidency," Chait continued. "But what I failed to account for was the possibility that his authoritarian style could degrade American politics even in defeat. There is a whiff in the air of the notion that the election will be settled in the streets—a poisonous idea that is unsafe in even the smallest doses." While Chait resisted calling for protests that would shut down Trump's ability to speak, he expressed his confidence that the country that elected Barack Obama twice would certainly defeat Trump. "He is spreading poisons throughout the system that could linger beyond his defeat," Chait concluded. "Anybody who cares about the health of American democracy should hope for its end as swiftly as possible."

On April 29, 2016, an estimated 3,000 protested in the area surrounding Burlingame, California, where Trump was to give a speech at the California GOP convention. Protesters rushed security gates at one point and were seen harassing Trump supporters. Activists blocked a main intersection outside the event and vandalized a police car. Eventually, the police restored order in the area. For safety reasons, Trump himself was forced to climb over a wall and enter through a back entrance of the venue.[28]

On May 24, 2016, protesters both inside and outside the Albuquerque Convention Center disrupted a Trump rally. "In one of the presidential campaign year's grislier spectacles, protesters in New Mexico opposing Donald Trump's candidacy threw burning T-shirts, plastic bottles and other items at police officers, injuring several, and toppled trash cans and barricades," the Associated Press reported. "Police responded by firing pepper spray and smoke grenades into the crowd outside the Albuquerque Convention Center." The AP report noted that inside the convention center, protesters shouted and held up signs reading, "Trump is Fascist, and We've heard enough," repeatedly interrupting Trump.[29]

At one point during Trump's Albuquerque rally, security officers physically dragged a female protester from the stands, while other protestors scuffled with police in their attempt to resist being removed from the convention center. Trump responded "with his usual bluster," the AP report commented, noting Trump instructed security to remove the protesters, while he mocked their actions by taunting them, as he did in St. Louis, "Go home to mommy." The thousands of Trump supporters responded to interruptions caused by the protesters with chants of "Build that wall!" Outside the hall, the protest also turned violent, with Albuquerque police reporting several police were treated for injuries after getting hit by rocks thrown by the protestors. The AP reported that during the rally, protesters outside overran barricades and clashed with police in riot gear. Albuquerque attorney Doug Antoon said rocks were flying through the convention center windows as he was leaving Tuesday night. "This was not a protest, this was a riot," Antoon told the AP. "These are hate groups."[30]

A subsequent AP article also dated May 25, 2016, reporting on the Albuquerque incident, noted that four people had been arrested at the protest and charged with disorderly conduct, while some 12 other people were detained and released, with other arrests anticipated.[31] "A day after a riot erupted outside a Donald Trump rally, Albuquerque officials concluded that the mayhem had less to do with political protest than with an unruly group determined to use the event to sow disorder."

On Thursday, June 2, 2016, an unruly crowd of approximately 300 to 400 anti-trump protesters gathered outside the San Jose Convention Center in San Jose, California, where Trump spoke at an enthusiastic rally, attacked Trump supporters as they left the convention hall. Video of the event shows youthful anti-Trump protesters attacking Trump supporters, punching them, spitting on them and seeking to bloody them, including senior citizens and women.[32] One young male Trump supporter on camera demonstrated his bloody lip, incurred when a protestor hit him, and complained that his shirt had been ripped from his back. A female Trump supporter trying to stand her ground had her Trump sign ripped from her hand and her eyeglasses torn from her face. Another woman, wearing a Trump jersey, was cornered by the crowd and egged in the face. San Jose police appeared to stand on the fringes, protecting the convention hall, but not removing the angry crowd who were flinging bottles, throwing punches, and spitting upon Trump supporters leaving the hall, with the crowd chasing Trump supporters even into the parking lot.[33]

These are just a few of the dozens of attacks on Trump's campaign in cities as diverse as Chicago, Detroit, Houston, Los Angeles, Miami, and Washington, DC. Could these have been random instances of legitimate protest? Some, perhaps, maybe in the beginning, but the anti-Trump movement quickly was gobbled up and made massive by the funding of George Soros. In advertisements placed in Craigslist in major American cities by Soros-backed organizations, fifteen dollars per hour was offered to hire "full time organizers." The Washington Community Action Network, an Open Society Foundation organization placed the Craigslist ad in Seattle, dumping $50,000 into the program. A Craigslist ad placed in Los Angeles called for "anti-Trumpers" to block the flow of traffic at the intersection of Highlands and Hollywood. One of the "grassroots" protesters who chained her neck to a van was filmed and photographed by the media. It turned out that this woman, whose name had been deleted, worked directly for the Soros Open Society Foundation.[34]

Democrats "Rent-A-Riot" Anarchists Exposed

On October 17, 2016, conservative investigative journalist and Project Veritas Director James O'Keefe released a video culminating a year-long investigation documenting that Hillary Clinton's campaign had enlisted Democratic "dark operatives" to recruit and pay thugs to infiltrate and disrupt Donald Trump rallies. "In the video, Democratic activists Robert Creamer and Scott Foval reveal their strategy to create a sense of 'anarchy' in and around Donald Trump events over the course of the campaign. Foval tells an undercover operative: 'One of the things we do is we stage very authentic grassroots protests right in their faces at their own events. Like, we infiltrate,'" Real Clear Politics reported.[35]

In the video, Foval explained: "So the term bird dogging: You put people in the line, at the front which means that they have to get there at six in the morning because they have to get in front at the rally, so that when Trump comes down the rope line, they're the ones asking him the question in front of the reporter, because they're pre-placed there. To funnel that kind of operation, you have to start back with people two weeks ahead of time and train them how to ask questions. You have to train them to bird dog." Seen in O'Keefe's video, Creamer explained that his organization, Democracy Partners, conducted daily "check-ins" with the Clinton campaign in order to coordinate efforts. Foval explained how Clinton's campaign used Democracy partners to subvert laws preventing super PACs and political action groups from organizing directly with campaigns. "The campaign pays the Democratic National Committee, the DNC pays Democracy Partners, and Democracy Partners pays the

Foval Group." Through this indirect chain of payment, the Clinton campaign is ultimately responsible for paying the Foval Group to hire crazies to penetrate Trump to utilize confrontational techniques, to disrupt Trump rallies and incite violence.

On O'Keefe's undercover camera, these Democratic "dark operatives" admitted their goal was to generate negative press blaming Trump for the violence that the Clinton campaign paid to create. "I'm saying we have mentally ill people, that we pay to do shit, make no mistake," Foval is seen admitting in O'Keefe's video. "Over the last twenty years, I've paid off a few homeless guys to do some crazy stuff, and I've also taken them for dinner, and I've also made sure they had a hotel, and a shower. And I put them in a program. Like I've done that. But the reality is, a lot of people especially our union guys. A lot of our union guys. . .they'll do whatever you want. They're rock and roll." One of the Democratic "black operators" in O'Keefe's video admitted responsibility for paying the protesters that shut down Trump's rally in Chicago the previous March. Others admitted sending Democratic agitators into Trump rallies, trained to incite attacks upon themselves. Particularly shocking was the revelation the 69-year-old woman who got punched in the face by a "Nazi Trump Supporter" in Asheville, North Carolina, on September 14, 2016, was sent by Democratic "dark operatives" to create a violent scenario so she would get punched.[36]

After O'Keefe's video went public, Democratic "dark operatives" Robert Creamer and Scott Foval were fired. Trump's claims that Democratic operatives were paying thugs, crazies, and anarchists to disrupt and cause violence at his rallies were vindicated. The protesters are paid a lot of money by the [Democratic National Committee], and they kept saying, 'I wonder why those people are here, because they never seem to have much on their mind other than stand up and protest,'" Mr. Trump told a crowd in Colorado Springs, as the *Washington Times* reported. "And yesterday it came out, but it was barely covered by the media. But it's all over the Internet. They were busted."[37]

After Clinton campaign manager Robby Mook claimed there was no pathway between the activists staging violence and Hillary, O'Keefe released a new video that revealed a Hillary-supported project to have Donald Duck characters show up at Trump rallies nationwide to disrupt his political campaign. The idea was to have an activist wearing a Donald Duck costume follow Trump with a sign reading "Donald Duck's releasing his tax returns." The O'Keefe video shows Democracy Partners head Robert Creamer suggesting the idea came directly from the presidential nominee herself.[38] "And in the end, it was the candidate, Hillary Clinton, the future president of the United States, who wanted ducks on the ground. So, by God, we will get ducks on the ground," Creamer says in the video. Then Creamer quickly adds: "Don't repeat that to anybody."

The sad truth is that Democratic operatives without morals broke election laws to coordinate with the Clinton campaign with the goal of paying goons—including thugs, anarchists, and the mentally ill—to penetrate Trump rallies and stage protests, both inside and outside Trump arena venues, with the goal of causing disruption and violence. Then, in the full unfolding of the plan, the Clinton campaign and the campaign's surrogates could take to the media to blame Trump for causing the disruption and violence, with the goal of painting Trump and his supporters as haters, variously portraying Trump and his supporters as Nazis, white supremacists, fascists, sexists, xenophobes, homophobes, and Islamophobes.

The Flip-Flop Artist Who Tried to Takedown Donald Trump

Perhaps the most unusual character to emerge in the failed attempt to derail the Trump campaign was one David Brock.

You really need a full-time scout monitoring Brock to know if he is at any moment working for the right or the left and then you have to wonder if he may perhaps be some type of contorted double agent (in his own mind) as many in the Hillary Clinton camp wondered when he was "helping" the Clinton campaign. To understand Brock, one needs to recognize that from his early years he has been consistent at nothing but the flip-flop. In his 2002 book, "Blinded by the Right: The Conscience of an Ex-Conservative," Brock reported that while attending Newman Smith High School in Carrollton, Texas, he became editor of the school newspaper, "Odyssey" and "fashioned [the paper] into a crusading liberal weekly in the middle of the Reaganite Sunbelt." Brock went on to attend the University of California," Berkeley, where he worked as a reporter and editor for "The Daily Californian, the campus newspaper.[39]

At Berkeley, though, "he found himself repelled by the culture of doctrinaire leftism and swung the other way." That is, he flip-flopped and started a neoconservative weekly, the "Berkeley Journal," financed by conservative alumni. He also published an op-ed in the Wall Street Journal, "Combating Those Campus Marxists."[40] John Podhoretz, then the editor of Insight, the magazine of the *Washington Times*, was sufficiently impressed by the Wall Street Journal opinion piece to offer Brock a job. Next, Brock moved to a fellowship at the Heritage Foundation underwritten by the John M. Olin Foundation.[41] In March 1992 he wrote a 17,000-word investigative piece for American Spectator magazine on Anita Hill, who had accused Clarence Thomas of sexual harassment. In his article he exposed that Hill's testimony at Thomas' confirmation hearings was "a cynical hoax organized by activists intent on bringing Thomas down."[42] That resulted in his getting a full-time job at American Spectator, which was primarily supported by a billionaire supporter of right wing causes, Richard Mellon Scaife. In 1993, Brock expanded his article into a book, *The Real Anita Hill*, that became a bestseller. In an interview on national public radio broadcast on July 2, 2001, Brock claimed that while he was at the American Spectator and writing his book on Anita Hill, he was "a tool of right wing activists who fed him false information about Hill." He told NPR legal affairs correspondent Nina Totenberg that he simply accepted the truthfulness of the information at the time without checking.[43]

Brock, flying high with hardcore conservative credentials after the success of *The Real Anita Hill,* was provided by the conservative publisher, the Free Press, with a million-dollar advance to write a book about Hillary Clinton. Unfortunately for the Free Press, they paid Brock while he was in mid-air of yet another flip-flop. Instead of getting a takedown of Clinton, Brock wrote *The Seduction of Hillary Rodham*, a book that proved largely to support Clinton, as Brock began yet another flip-flop back to the political left.[44] Hillary, at the time though, was suspicious of him and wouldn't talk to him for the book. Clearly, she was not yet aware that he was in the middle of a flip. Brock writes in the introduction to the book: "On a bitter cold evening in February 1996, in the midst of a snowstorm, I stood in line for several hours at a bookstore in McLean, Virginia where the first lady was signing copies of *It Takes A Village*. When I finally reached the head of the line, I introduced myself and asked her when I could have an interview for this biography. "Probably never," she said with a wry edge."[45] The book was a colossal failure. Brock failed to produce the stories of Bill Clinton's philandering that he had promised the publisher, writing instead a book containing nothing new, except for a limp-wristed defense of Hillary as a victim of "lawyerly nitpicking." The Free Press lost at least a million dollars on the book and Brock's editor, Adam Bellow, was fired.[46]

Brock completed his flip- flop in July 1997, when he wrote a piece for *Esquire* magazine titled "Confessions of a Right-Wing Hit Man," in which he recanted much of what he had written about Anita Hill and made "Troopergate" a household word, while criticizing his own reporting methods as a conservative. In the piece he wrote, that he "wanted out," that "David Brock the Road Warrior of the Right is dead."[47] The flip-flop artist landed again, this time back on the left, with Brock pocketing the money of conservative billionaire Scaife without so much as a pang of conscience that he had once again walked away with the hefty funding of the very conservatives he betrayed. In his 2002 book, *Blinded by the Right: The Conscience of an Ex Conservative*, Brock went full throttle and attacked the political right that he had formerly championed, arguing that he suffered as a closeted homosexual for much of his conservative career. He confessed that he had come to be "troubled" by his participation in the relentless investigations of the Clintons.

In 2004, Brock founded the far-lefty media watchdog group Media Matters that cooperated with George Soros in bringing down the cable news television career of Glenn Beck and got Lou Dobbs fired from CNN. He then established American Bridge, a political action committee that has raised some $12 million from donors including Soros to hire some 80 staff as "trackers," assigned to follow Republicans, looking for "gotcha" moments with the potential to derail their conservative careers.[48] Brock, in his new role as far-left hatchet man brags about publicizing the "legitimate rape" comments Republican Senate candidate Todd Akin made to a Missouri TV station—comments that mainstream media reporters parroting reports published by Media Matters used to dog the GOP presidential campaign of Mitt Romney in 2012. Media Matters specializes in micro-tracking targeted conservative reporters, with an intent to counter by "fact checking" conservative arguments, following up by sending to any television or radio outlet willing to give air time to Media Maters targeted conservative reporters a dossier containing every comment the reporter has ever made that Media Matters deems to be politically incorrect. If that is not sufficient, Media Matters is happy to participate with Soros-funded operatives to conduct a campaign threatening the advertisers of broadcasters daring to give air time to conservative reporters whose careers Brock has determined to destroy.

The WikiLeaks release of emails involving John Podesta, Hillary Clinton's 2016 presidential campaign chairperson, made clear the extent to which Democrats consider Brock deranged and dangerous. Neera Tanden, President of the progressive Center for American Progress, founded by Podesta, warned Podesta in an email released by WikiLeaks, "I hope Hillary truly understands now how batshit crazy David Brock is."[49] Podesta's ultimate reply to Tanden's concern was a terse email saying only, "Brock $ machine!"[50] Podesta's quip in response to Tanden's "batshit crazy" comment reflected Podesta's obvious disdain for Brock's amoral behavior.

Agreeing with Tanden, Podesta sought to warn Hillary that Brock was dangerous, not to be trusted, nothing more than a "gun for hire" willing to sell out to the highest bidder. Brock—once a Hillary hater and now a Hillary promoter—was arguably capable of turning on a dime to resume pillorying Hillary, simply by professing "reconversion" to conservatism, should the money offered Brock be sufficient to induce yet another ideological flip-flop.

Podesta's concerns were triggered by reports Brock had spun a pro-Clinton rapid-response operation from his American Bridge super PAC to coordinate with the Clinton campaign as a stand-alone super PAC, skirting Federal Election Commission regulations by posting only on Internet blogs.[51] Brock's goal was to put himself at the center of the multimillion-dollar operation created by the Clinton campaign to protect Clinton by demeaning and defiling anyone who dared attack Hillary, including me, Roger Stone.[52] Brock's Media Matters took aim at me, typifying me as the sordid "underbelly of the Trump Machine," while launching a slander campaign designed to get me booted from cable television news during the campaign. With cable news in the bag for Hillary Clinton, along with the left-partisan mainstream print media, Brock largely succeeded in blocking me from television news in the last two months of the campaign after I managed to land several key television interviews promoting my bestseller *The Clintons' War on Women* that was published in September of 2016.[53]

Project Veritas cameras caught David Brock henchman Bradley Beychock, the President of Media Matters for America bragging of efforts to smear and censor me. Beychock proudly boasted about the Media Matters assault on me. "So I think for Trump, our big role as a media watchdog has been to take his MVPs and put them on the sidelines. So the first one was Roger Stone," said Beychock. If Team Trump 2016 had an MVP it was James O'Keefe.

Hillary Clinton's Email Scandal: "Extremely Careless"

On July 5, 2016, almost three weeks exactly to the start of the DNC's national nominating convention in Philadelphia, FBI Director James Comey announced in a public statement televised live by cable news stations to the nation that despite evidence Hillary Clinton had been "extremely careless" in her handling of classified emails on a private email server during her service as Secretary of State, the FBI would not recommend criminal charges be brought against Hillary Clinton. The immediate impact of Comey's statement was to offer the Clinton campaign a basis for claiming that Clinton had been absolved of all criminal responsibly for the management of her private email service, despite serious and continuing concerns that the transmission of classified government documents via an unsecured email channel violated national security laws. Shortly after Comey's announcement, Clinton campaign spokesperson Brian Fallon issued a written statement that read: "We are pleased that the career officials handling this case have determined that no further action by the Department is appropriate. As the Secretary has long said, it was a mistake to use her personal email and she would not do it again. We are glad that this matter is now resolved."[54]

Comey's announcement had been marred when information became public that on June 27, 2016, one year into the FBI criminal investigation of Hillary's email system, Bill Clinton delayed his private jet from taking off at Phoenix Sky Harbor International Airport after a Secret Service agent informed him that Attorney General Loretta Lynch's airplane was coming in for a landing.[55] While Lynch has consistently maintained the short meeting with Clinton aboard her airplane on the Sky Harbor tarmac was innocent in that the two only discussed personal pleasantries of no political importance, the optics of the meeting remain suspect. Remarkably, Lynch insisted her visit with Clinton had been "primarily social," and that the two had spoken mostly about grandchildren and golf.[56]

On Friday, July 2, 2016, Lynch expressed regret that she had met with the former president while the FBI's investigation into Hillary's email server was yet on-going. "I certainly wouldn't do it again," Lynch said of the meeting with the former president, who nominated her to serve as US attorney for the Eastern District of New York in 1999, as the Associated Press noted in reporting on the incident.[57] The *Washington Post*, a newspaper reliably partisan in favor of Clinton, was forced to admit, "Bill Clinton has made a mess." The *Washington Post*, unable to decide whether the meeting happened out of Bill Clinton's "foolish interference, or plain foolishness," but the newspaper was certain the meeting "created a terrible moment for his wife and the Democrats, and for President Obama and perceptions of the integrity of his administration.[58]

Trump's reaction on the Mike Gallagher radio show was immediate. In their 15-minute interview, Trump reacted with alarm. "It is an amazing thing," Trump said. "I heard about it last night. They actually went onto the plane, as I understand it. That's terrible. And it was really a sneak. It was really something that they didn't want publicized, as I understand it. Wow, I just think it's so terrible, I think it's so horrible."[59] Trump noted the meeting was more confirmation of his allegation that the election was "rigged" in Hillary's favor. The *New York Times* reported the meeting between Bill Clinton and Lynch lasted only 20 minutes, noting that Mrs. Lynch's husband was present during the discussion. This, however, did not impress Trump. "When you meet for a half-hour and you're talking about your grandchildren, and a little about golf, I don't know, it sounds like a long meeting," Trump told the newspaper.[60]

Hillary Lies About Email Server

From the beginning, Hillary Clinton's strategy when the scandal of her private email server broke was to lie—a strategy that further strained her already low credibility with the American people. On March 10, 2015, former Secretary of State Hillary Clinton held a press conference at the United Nations in New York City to make a statement in an attempt to quell the scandal that had been building over the private email server she used to transmit and receive State Department emails. While Hillary may have intended this press conference to make the email controversy go away, the reality was her explanations came back to haunt her when Comey finally announced the FBI's decision not to prosecute. In giving his statement exonerating Clinton, Comey made clear the FBI investigation refuted several key claims Clinton made in defending herself with her United Nations press conference.

The fact that Clinton had relied upon a private email server while Secretary of State became known publically not through any disclosure by Clinton or by the State Department, but through the disclosures of Romanian hacker Marcel Lazar who, as has already been mentioned, went by the username "Guccifer," a combination of "Gucci" and "Lucifer." On March 15, 2013, the Smoking Gun broke the story, disclosing that Guccifer had hacked into the account of then 64-year-old Sidney Blumenthal, a former senior White House adviser to Bill Clinton and a longtime Hillary Clinton confidante. The article noted that Guccifer, in hacking Blumenthal's email account, had zeroed in on Blumenthal's extensive email correspondence with Hillary Clinton.[61] During an interview given in Romania in 2015 Guccifer, then in prison, commented to a reporter that he accessed in Hillary's hacked email memos that Clinton got as Secretary of State, with CIA briefings attached. "I used to read her memos for six or seven hours then I'd get up and do the gardening in the yard," Guccifer said.[62]

In a follow-up article published on March 18, 2013, the Smoking Gun made clear that the Blumenthal emails hacked and published by Guccifer were sent to Clinton at her non-governmental email address through the web domain "clintonemail.com."[63] With this, the cat was out of the bag that Hillary as Secretary of State may have violated national security laws that strictly govern responsibilities of government employees for handling classified documents. The concern immediately was that the decision to by-pass the State Department's secure email facilities might have had criminal implications for Hillary. The issue was particularly relevant to the American public because just a few days earlier, on March 3, 2015, former CIA director and decorated war veteran General David Petraeus entered into an agreement with federal prosecutors to plead guilty to a criminal misdemeanor charge for sharing classified information with his biographer and mistress, Paula Broadwell.[64]

At her United Nations press conference, Clinton wore an elegantly tailored—black-grey-and-white speckled black pantsuit with matching jacket and spoke in the supercilious tones she had reserved for making State Department pronouncements when traveling the world as Secretary of State.[65] Throughout the press conference ordeal, Clinton looked peeved, appeared to be only barely tolerating a public examination regarding how she had conducted herself while Secretary of State. The irony was obvious that the public focus regarding her service as Secretary of State involved the possibility that she had committed crimes by her determination to transmit State Department business by-passing the State Department secure email system required not only to insure the security of classified material, but also to create a complete record of her correspondence as Secretary of State, to be maintained within an email system subject to the State Department archiving and control.

Hillary began the press conference by commenting on United Nations affairs as if everything was "business as usual" and she was still Secretary of State. After some five minutes into the press conference discussion of United Nations business, Hillary switched topics to the real focus of the press conference, explaining that use of a private email server at the State Department in terms of convenience. "First, when I got to work as Secretary of State, I opted for convenience to use my personal email account, which was allowed by the State Department, because I thought it would be easier to carry just one device for my work and for my personal emails instead of two," she said. "Looking back, it would've been better if I'd simply used a second email account and carried a second phone, but at the time, this didn't seem like an issue." Clinton was straining credibility to position herself for her second run at the presidency, but it is apparently true that she was so technically deficient that using two Blackberrys would have taxed her capabilities.

Next, she asserted that the majority of her emails were sent to government employees, suggesting she never intended her emails to by-pass the State Department secure email system. "Second, the vast majority of my work emails went to government employees at their government addresses, which meant they were captured and preserved immediately on the system at the State Department," she said. This explanation, however, finessed the obvious conclusion that she was originating and receiving business emails via her private server, even when she sent or received emails from State Department employees. The explanation also did not rule out that emails sent to Clinton or received by her from individuals not on the State Department email system would have remained on private email servers.

Then Hillary admitted she and her associates had destroyed a large number of her State Department emails, arguing that all her State Department emails discussing government business had been preserved. "Third, after I left office, the State Department asked former secretaries of state for our assistance in providing copies of work- related emails from our personal accounts," she continued. "I responded right away and provided all my emails that could possibly be work-related, which totaled roughly 55,000 printed pages, even though I knew that the State Department already had the vast majority of them."

Hillary detailed what she meant by "private" State Department emails. "We went through a thorough process to identify all of my work-related emails and deliver them to the State Department," she explained. "At the end, I chose not to keep my private personal emails—emails about planning Chelsea's wedding or my mother's funeral arrangements, condolence notes to friends as well as yoga routines, family vacations, the other things you typically find in inboxes." Hillary argued this was eminently reasonable. "No one wants their personal emails made public, and I think most people understand that and respect that privacy," she insisted. The problem was the screening of the emails, including the determination as to which ones were strictly private, was done by Hillary and her associates, without any independent check to see if any emails destroyed as "private" may have contained classified or other sensitive government information available to Clinton in her capacity as Secretary of State.

Finally, Clinton asserted she had authorized the State Department to make public all her work-related emails. "Fourth, I took the unprecedented step of asking that the State Department make all my work-related emails public for everyone to see," she asserted. "I am very proud of the work that I and my colleagues and our public servants at the department did during my four years as Secretary of State, and I look forward to people being able to see that for themselves." She concluded by adding an apology, as if the apology was sufficient to excuse any criminal activity she may have committed accidentally. "Again, looking back, it would've been better for me to use two separate phones and two email accounts. I thought using one device would be simpler, and obviously, it hasn't worked out that way," Hillary concluded.

Secretary of State

On September 2, 2016, the FBI released a detailed factual summary of their investigation into Clinton's private email server.[66] The documents revealed that Clinton actually used 13 total mobile devices associated with her two known phone numbers that were potentially used to send emails via clintonmail.com. "Top Clinton aide Huma Abedin told the FBI it was not uncommon for Clinton to use a new BlackBerry for a short time before switching back to an older model with which she was more familiar. She also said out-of-use phones would often become lost," the Hill reported on the day the FBI investigative documents were released. "The man who helped set up Clinton's server said he recalled two instances in which he destroyed old devices by breaking them or smashing them with a hammer; Clinton said aides also disposed of old SIM cards after switching devices."[67] The FBI was unable to discover any of the mobile devices Clinton used.

The FBI investigation found that in the 30,000 emails Clinton tur-ned over to the State Department in 2014, there were 110 emails in 52 email chains that contained information that was classified at the time it was sent. Politifact.com reported that 8 chains contained top-secret information, the highest level of classification, 36 chains contained secret information. These findings directly contradicted Clinton's repeated public statements that she never received or sent any material marked classified over her private email server. Politifact.com also reported 2,000 additional emails have been retroactively classified, or up-classified, mea-ning the information was not classified when it was first emailed, com-menting that this is a "regular practice when documents are reviewed for release, according to transparency experts." Politifact.com further con-firmed that FBI investigators uncovered "several thousand" work-related emails that Clinton had not handed over, including three that were clas-sified at the time they were sent, though they were not marked as such. This finding contradicted Clinton's claim that she had turned over all work-related emails to the State Department.[68]

The FBI investigation also confirmed Trump's allegation that Clin-ton had deleted 31,830 personal emails sometime between March 25-31, 2015, in disregard of a subpoena dated March 4, 2015, issued by the House Select Committee on Benghazi that required Clinton to hand over all emails to Congress. In reconstructing the facts, the *Washington Post* reported that in December 2014, Clinton aide Cheryl Mills told an employee of Platte River Networks in Colorado, the company that was managing Clinton's email server at that time, to delete emails on her server unrelated to government work that were older than 60 days. Then on March 4, 2015, the Benghazi Committee issued a subpoena requiring Clinton to turn over her emails relating to Libya. The *Washington Post* fact-reconstruction indicated that three weeks later, between March 25 and March 31, the employee at Platte River Networks had an "oh s—" moment and realized he did not delete the emails that Mills requested in December 2014, he told the FBI. The employee then deleted the emails and used a program called BleachBit to delete the files.[69]

On August 22, 2016, the *Washington Post* reported the FBI's investi-gation of Clinton's email server uncovered 14,900 emails and documents from her time as Secretary of State that had not been disclosed by her attorney. According to the newspaper, the 14,900 Clinton documents were nearly 50 percent more than the roughly 30,000 emails that Clinton lawyers deemed work-related and turned over to the State Department. The discovery came as a result of a FOIA request pressed in federal court by Washington-based watchdog-group Judicial Watch.[70] As the investigation into the Clinton email scandal developed, Judicial Watch's determination and effectiveness in filing FOIA requests and pursuing federal court challenges to force disclosure of documents and testimony proved in many instances to have produced ground-breaking results, with time after time Judicial Watch coming up with important discoveries that had eluded both congressional committees investigating the scandal and the FBI.

Clinton Email Exposes Benghazi Lie

On November 2, 2015, Judicial Watch announced it obtained documents from the State Department confirming that, at 11:00 pm ET on the night of the deadly assault on the US Consulate in Benghazi, then-Secretary of State Hillary Clinton informed her daughter by email that the attack had been staged by an "Al Qaeda-like group," rather than as the result of "inflammatory material posted on the Internet," as Mrs. Clinton had claimed in her official public statement one hour earlier.[71] The documents were produced in response to lawsuits filed by Judicial Watch under the Freedom of the Information Act (FOIA). Judicial Watch emphasized that Hillary Clinton's email to Chelsea Clinton was first produced to the Select Committee on Benghazi on October 20, 2015, and publicized on the day of Mrs. Clinton's testimony, October 22, 2015, but court filings in Judicial Watch litigation show that the email was only produced after two federal court judges ordered the State Department to produce more Benghazi-related records to Judicial Watch.

The State Department's records, as revealed by Judicial Watch, included a second late-night email that Mrs. Clinton sent to her daughter, Chelsea, at 11:11 pm ET, on September 11, 2012, as the Benghazi terrorist attack was still ongoing. Clinton addressed the email to Chelsea's under the pseudonym "Diane Reynolds," the alias Chelsea used when sending or receiving emails from her mother via the Clinton private email server. Hillary emailed Chelsea, "Two of our officers were killed in Benghazi by an Al Qaeda-like group. The Ambassador, whom I handpicked [Christopher Stevens] and a young communications officer on temporary duty with a wife and two young children. Very hard day and I fear more of the same tomorrow." Yet, in an earlier message, at 10:08 p.m. on September 11, Hillary Clinton issued an official State Department press statement placing the blame for the attack on an obscure Internet video critical of the Islamic religion. At no point in her State Department press statement did Clinton reference terrorist activity at or near the Benghazi compound:

> Some have sought to justify this vicious behavior as a response to inflammatory material posted on the Internet. The United States deplores any intentional effort to denigrate the religious beliefs of others. Our commitment to religious tolerance goes back to the very beginning of our nation. But let me be clear: There is never any justification for violent acts of this kind.

"This key email shows that Hillary Clinton knowingly lied about the terrorist attack on Benghazi," said Judicial Watch President Tom Fitton. "And once again, it was Judicial Watch lawsuits—not Congress—that forced the production of this smoking-gun email into the open for the American people. I have no doubt that the Obama administration and Hillary Clinton knew this email was out there and illegally stonewalled its release to Judicial Watch, the courts, and Congress."

The Benghazi attack happened in the midst of the 2012 presidential campaign, when President Obama was contesting against Republican challenger former Massachusetts Governor Mitt Romney. One of Obama's central campaign themes involved the success he claimed his administration was having in combating terrorism. Obama had reduced his argument to the succinct statement: "GM is alive and Osama bin Laden is dead"—a statement that touted the Obama administration's bailout of General Motors in 2009 and the killing of Al-Qaida terrorist Osama bin Laden in Pakistan on May 2, 2011.[72] If the attack on Benghazi on September 11, 2011, were to be characterized as a terrorist attack, Obama's argument that terrorists were on the run could be undermined. By insisting the Benghazi attack was in response to a movie produced in the United States that insulted Islam, the Obama administration sought an alternative explanation, even if untrue, that could continue to deflect Romney's criticism.[73] Like Obama, Hillary Clinton—calculating her prospects of a second presidential campaign in 2016—did not want to take the political hit by admitting that Al-Qaeda-affiliated terrorists were alive and well in Libya—a clear blow to her stewardship as Secretary of State.

Hillary's email to Chelsea the night of the Benghazi attack was considered a smoking gun precisely because the email documents that Hillary knew as the attack was yet in progress that it was a terrorist attack, not an angry reaction to a movie. Had the Obama administration not lied over this, Romney could have scored an attack on Obama in the last months of the 2012 presidential campaign that might have proven decisive in Romney's favor. The lie, exposed in 2016, revealed both Hillary's duplicity in the Benghazi cover-up and the use she made of her private email server to conceal communications.

The Clinton Foundation Scandal Explodes

The FBI began a preliminary investigation into the Clinton Foundation after the 2015 publication of Peter Schweizer's book, *Clinton Cash: The Untold Story of How and Why Foreign Governments and Businesses Helped Make Bill and Hillary Rich*.[74] Schweizer, the co-founder and president of the Government Accountability Institute and Breitbart News Senior Editor-at-Large, assembled a team of investigative researchers and journalists to document that the Clinton Foundation was an elaborate pay-to-play scheme. Schweizer sought to demonstrate that Bill Clinton, as head of the foundation, had solicited donations to the foundation and had accepted six- and seven-figure speaking fees, including those offered by foreign governments and foreign entrepreneurs of questionable repute, who sought to obtain favorable policy decisions that could be made or influenced by Hillary Clinton in her position as Secretary of State.

As noted by Fox News on October 17, 2016, the WikiLeaks release of emails hacked from Hillary Clinton's campaign chairman John Podesta provided added documentation reinforcing Schweizer's central thesis: Clinton Foundation donors expected a quid pro quo from Hillary Clinton's State Department in exchange for their gifts. "Everything we assumed or thought was the case a year-and-a-half ago has been now confirmed in these emails," Schweizer said on the *Fox and Friends* morning show. Schweizer added he was surprised that he, his book, and the Clintons' "money problem" were mentioned so many times in the leaked emails. "It shows that they're concerned most of all about this issue," he explained. "There's all kinds of questions about both candidates, but I think when it comes to Hillary Clinton, their obsessive concern is precisely what *Clinton Cash* is about, which is the flow of money and the flow of foreign money."[75]

In August 2016, WND senior staff writer Jerome R. Corsi published his Clinton Foundation book, *Partners in Crime: The Clinton's Scheme to Monetize the White House for Personal Profit.*"[76] While Corsi provided additional evidence for Schweizer's claims that the Clintons had indulged in a form of bribery, his book advanced the argument that the Clinton's were also guilty of inurement—the crime of utilizing a tax-favored charity to benefit personally, to the detriment of achieving the good works a legitimate charity would be established to accomplish. Corsi's work had been stimulated by the research of his New York associate Charles Ortel, a well-known Wall Street analyst and private investor. In 2015, Ortel had brought to Corsi's attention his concern the Clinton Foundation financials, including both the audited financial statements and the IRS Form 990s filed annually, were fraudulent, constructed so as to hide the millions of dollars being taken by the Clintons and their close associates for their personal profit. Beginning on April 22, 2015, Corsi began publishing in WND.com a series that ultimately amounted to over 20 articles detailing Ortel's ongoing research, reporting Ortel's conclusion the Clinton Foundation is "a vast criminal conspiracy" that the Clinton family and their close associates have perpetrated to defraud the general public, enrich themselves, and entrench their political influence.

On February 18, 2015, the *Washington Post* reported the Bill, Hillary, and the Clinton Foundation had raised close to $2 billion "from a vast global network that includes corporate titans, political donors, foreign governments and other wealthy interests."[77] The article pointed out that foreign individual donors as well as foreign countries that would be likely to have interests before a Hillary Clinton administration, even though they were ineligible to vote in a US election or contribute to a political campaign, had been major contributors to the Clinton Foundation. WikiLeaks in making public over 50,000 emails from Clinton campaign chairman John Podesta provided concrete evidence of exactly the kind of wrongdoing that Corsi and Schweizer had written about. The key emails focused on the role played by Simpson Thatcher, an international law firm based in New York, that Chelsea Clinton brought into the Clinton Foundation in 2011, in an effort to clean up the Clinton Foundation financial mess before an internal scandal erupted to the detriment of Hillary's second try to win the White House.

What surfaced in the WikiLeaks emails regarding the Simpson Thacher audit is that a power struggle developed between Chelsea Clinton and Doug Band, the former Clinton White House "body man" who formed Teneo. Chelsea objected that conflicts of interest were created over Doug Band's continuing role in the Clinton Foundation and the Clinton Global Initiative while he was heading Teneo.[78] Band elevated himself from getting Bill Clinton diet soft drinks in the White House, to creating Teneo—a consulting company linked to the Clinton Foundation and the Clinton Global initiative that earned Band and the Clintons hundreds of millions of dollars double-teaming Clinton Foundation corporate donors to establish with Teneo lucrative management consulting contracts. Simpson Thatcher recommended that a variety of steps be taken and Doug Band went ballistic when Chelsea Clinton in 2011 attempted to implement those recommendations.[79] The end result was that Bill Clinton had to quit his lucrative position on the Teneo board of directors. Still, Bill Clinton stayed on as a consultant to Teneo clients, but after the blow-up caused by the Simpson Thacher shake-up, Clinton's income from Teneo was limited and Band faced new restraints placed on his ability to hit on Clinton Foundation and Clinton Global Initiative donors for Teneo consulting agreements.

In an attachment to a WikiLeaks-leaked email dated November 16, 2011, written while Hillary Clinton was still Secretary of State, Band wrote to Podesta, copying Cheryl Mills and Justin Cooper, a senior advisor to Bill Clinton, and brought up the conflicts of interest that were corrupting the Clinton Foundation from within.[80] The attachment consists of a memo Band wrote documenting the conflicts of interest. It was entitled, "Background on Teneo and Foundation Activities," and was addressed to two senior Simpson Thacher lawyers, with copies to Bill Clinton, Chelsea Clinton, and John Podesta, as well as Clinton Foundation attorney and sometimes CEO Bruce Lindsey and Clinton longtime associate Terry McAuliffe, both Clinton Foundation board members at the time. Band apparently wrote the memo to explain his role in obvious conflicts of interest that were inherent in the Clinton Foundation and Teneo policy of sharing key Clinton Foundation donors. Topping the list of shared clients was the Coca-Cola Company, giving $4.3 million since 2004 to the Clinton Foundation and/or the Clinton Global Initiative, while also being a Teneo consulting client.

"Independent of our fundraising and decision-making activities on behalf of the Foundation, we [Band and the other principals at Teneo] have dedicated ourselves to helping the President secure and engage in for-profit activities—including speeches, books, and advisory service engagements," Band noted in the memo. "In that context, we have in effect served as agents, lawyers, managers and implementers to secure speaking, business and advisory service deals," Band continued. "In support of the President's for-profit activity, we also have solicited and obtained, as appropriate, in-kind services for the President and his family—for personal travel, hospitality, vacations and the like."

Band noted that of Clinton's four then-current consulting arrangements, Teneo had secured all of them for Clinton, as well as assisting Clinton in maintaining and managing "all of his for-profit business relationships [unspecified in the memo]." Band concluded: "Since 2001, President Clinton's business arrangements have yielded more than $30 million for him personally, with $66 million to be paid out over the next nine years should he choose to continue with the current engagements." The memo also noted that he and his colleagues at Teneo had arranged for millions of dollars in speaking fees for Clinton.

Band stressed that he and his Teneo partners for the past ten years "served as the primary contact and point of management for President Clinton's activities—which span from political activity (*e.g.,* campaigning on behalf of candidates for elected office), to business activity (*e.g.,* providing advisory services to business entities with which he has a consulting arrangement), to Foundation activity (*e.g.,* supporting his engagement on behalf of the initiatives and affiliated entities of the Foundation), to his speech activity (e.g., soliciting speeches and staffing and supporting him on speech travel) to his book activity (*e.g.,* editing his books and arranging and supporting him on book tours) to supporting family/personal needs (*e.g.,* securing in-kind private airplane travel, in-kind vacation stays, and supporting family business and personal needs)."

When Eric Braverman, the Clinton Foundation CEO brought in by Chelsea to implement the Simpson Thacher recommendations, resigned in January 2015, Politico reported that his efforts to implement the Simpson Thacher audit recommendations were thwarted by the conflicting visions of the three Clinton family members and their rival staff factions.[81] Band did not resign from his various Clinton Foundation board appointments until June 2015, as Hillary Clinton was beginning to organize for her 2016 presidential campaign.[82] As a parting shot, Band addressed another email to Podesta, copying Cheryl Mills and Justin Cooper, dated Nov. 17, 2015, in which he charged that while Band was required to sign a conflict of interest policy to be a board member of the Clinton Global Initiative, Bill Clinton was required to sign no such document. Band then objected that Bill Clinton was being personally paid by three Clinton Global Initiative sponsors and that he "gets many expensive gifts from them," some of which Band asserted Bill Clinton keeps at home. "I could add 500 examples of things like this," he added, his resentment at being pushed aside by Chelsea evident.[83]

Reviewing Doug Band's memorandum and emails, campaign finance attorney Paul H. Jossey, a contributor to *The Hill*, penned an editorial in which he too concluded Band had revealed Bill and Hillary Clinton to be "partners in crime."[84] Jossey concluded that Band himself, along with his management consulting company Teneo, were at the center of the Clinton Foundation and Clinton Global Initiative self-dealing corruption. "Band served as gatekeeper to all things Bill Clinton," Jossey wrote. "Those wanting a former president as golf partner ponied up. Requests for Foundation dough followed. Next came Clinton, Incorporated—the steady stream of speeches, books, and honorary titles that enriched Bill Clinton."

Jossey's point was that Doug Band and Teneo managed the scheme, with huge corporations seeking Clinton's favor lining up to get tax-relief and State Department policy decisions that advanced their business opportunities.

Jossey concluded that the WikiLeaks release of the Band memorandum and emails is showing "what we didn't know" about the internal functioning of the Clinton Foundation's $2 billion global empire, with the result that what we didn't know may just turn out to be criminal.

The Curious Case of Huma Abedin: Hillary's Right Hand or Terrorist Agent?

Many things about Hillary's disastrous quest for the Oval Office caused voters to question her allegiance to the American dream and our Judeo-Christian beliefs. She took money (millions) from countries that savaged, murdered, and targeted women. These same people also zeroed in on the LGBT community, showing them even less mercy.

But these concerns were mainly symptoms of a larger problem: Hillary's top aide Huma Abedin is a Saudi Spy at best and a possible terrorist agent at worst. Those are heavy accusations and ones that I researched vigorously before presenting my thesis to the American public in mid-summer of 2016.

I first published my research concerning Abedin on the alternative news network Breitbart. There, I wrote: "Huma Abedin is Vice Chair of Hillary Clinton's 2016 presidential campaign. But Huma is more, much more than that. She is the person closest to the most powerful woman in American politics and perhaps the next President. Huma has been described variously as

Hillary's 'body woman,' a sort of glorified go-to personal maid, gentle confidant, and by others as an Islamic spy. She may be all of these things, because as we shall see, Huma Abedin has an interesting and complex career history."[85]

Mrs. Abedin, who has been married to pervert ex-congressman Anthony Weiner for years, was indeed much more than a glamorized assistant who would whisper sweet nothings to "Crooked Hillary." While her vast role in the deletion of 30,000 plus emails was disturbing, her lineage and proximity to radical Muslim ideologues were much more troubling.

Abedin's journey began in Kalamazoo, Michigan in 1976 as she was born, Huma Mahmood Abedin, to an Indian father and Pakistani mother. Her father was heavily involved with the Muslim Student Association at Western Michigan University, running point for the group that was funded by the Muslim World League.[86] Spreading Islam was the mission of her parents, and Huma would become even more involved and influential in the "movement" than her father or mother could have ever hoped.

As pointed out in Daniel Horowitz's DiscoverTheNetworks.org, Huma's mother, Saleha Mahmood Abedin is a sociologist known for her strong advocacy of Sharia Law. A member of the Muslim Sisterhood (i.e., the Muslim Brotherhood's division for women), Saleha is also a board member of the International Islamic Council for Dawa and Relief. This pro-Hamas entity is part of the Union of Good, which the US government has formally designated as an international terrorist organization led by the Muslim Brotherhood luminary Yusuf al-Qaradawi.[87] Saleha is reportedly an outspoken advocate for genital mutilation for girls in the Islamic world. She published a book called *Women in Islam*, that Andrew C. McCarthy has described as providing Shariah justifications for such practices as female-genital mutilation, the death penalty for apostates from Islam, the legal subordination of women, and the participation of women in violent jihad. McCarthy noted that while Saleha Abedin is hailed in the progressive press as a leading voice on women's rights in the Muslim world, this is not the whole story. "What they never quite get around to telling you is that this means 'women's rights' in the repressive sharia context," McCarthy commented.[88]

With his leadership role expanding, Huma's father Syed Abedin moved the family from Michigan to Jeddah, Saudi Arabia, when their daughter Huma was just two years old. The move to Saudi Arabia was encouraged by Abdullah Omar Naseef, a major Muslim Brotherhood figure who served as vice president of Abdulaziz University, where he recruited his former Abdulaziz University colleague Syed Abedin to work for the Institute of Muslim Minority Affairs, a Saudi-based Islamic think-tank Naseef was planning to launch that ultimately developed offices in Saudi Arabia and London, England. In the early 1980s, Naseef developed close ties to Osama bin Laden, as he moved to become secretary-general of the Muslim World League that journalist Andrew C. McCarthy notes, "has long been the Muslim Brotherhood's principal vehicle for the international propagation of Islamic supremacist ideology."[89]

After the death of Huma's father in 1993, his wife Saleha took over and served as director of the IMMA (Institute of Muslim Minority Affairs) and as the editor of that organization's academic magazine, the Journal of Muslim Minority Affairs. More recently she still edits the Journal and is also a part of the administration of Dar Al-Hekma Women's College. Even before Huma had the free will to pick good over evil, Abedin was being conditioned to pledge fealty to foreign powers, disgracing her American birth. The Muslim Minority Affairs outfit would become a family affair, with her brother Hassan and younger sister Heba holding numerous leadership roles.

In 1988, Naseef, the Muslim World League, and the government of Pakistan created the Rabita Trust, a trust we can document that Naseef has continued to promote through 2014.[90] Remember, Naseef was a sponsor and financial supporter of Syed Abedin's IMMA.[91] Just a month after the 9/11 jihadist attack left thousands dead and brought down the World Trade Center, President George W. Bush's Executive Order[92] identified the Rabita Trust as a Specially Designated Global Terrorist Entity and the Treasury Department froze its assets on October 12, 2001.[93] A Treasury Department press release[94] issued when Rabita Trust's assets were frozen indicated that the Rabita Trust is headed by Wa'el Hamza Jalaidan, one of the founding members[95] of al-Qaida with bin Laden in 1988. He was the logistics chief of bin Laden's organization and fought on bin Laden's side in Afghanistan. Jalaidan himself was branded a Specially Designated Global Terrorist Entity by the United States Treasury Department, and his assets have been frozen, as well. By 2014, the Rabita Trust was being reactivated in Pakistan with a mandate to repatriate Pakistanis stranded in Bangladesh.

You might reason that these connections and ties tell us nothing about Huma Abedin because the background information is primarily about the ties Huma's parents have to radical Islam. That assumption is completely wrong.

Huma Abedin lived in Saudi Arabia until she was 17, while her family continued working closely with Naseef. Back in the United States, she studied at George Washington University. Two years later she, along with Monica Lewinsky, became interns at the White House under Bill and Hillary Clinton. Monica served as Bill's intern—until their sexual relationship got out of hand and onto her blue dress—and Huma served as Hillary's intern. In 1998, while the Lewinsky sex scandal was raging, Huma Abedin and other female White House staff women formed a sort of circle around the humiliated First Lady. While she worked at the White House, Abedin was an editor at the family business—the Journal of Muslim Minority Affairs.[96]

When Hillary Clinton ran for the Senate in 2000, Huma moved up the ladder to become her aide and personal adviser.[97] When the towers fell in 2001, Hillary Clinton was the Senator from New York. When the assets of the Rabita Trust were frozen and the group declared a terror funder, there was no point where Sen. Clinton's assistant Huma Abedin stepped forward to shed light on her family's benefactor Abdullah Omar Naseef, the Muslim World League, or the Rabita Trust. Sen. Clinton and Huma Abedin betrayed every New Yorker and every American with their silence.

Also worth noting: from April 2005 to March 2006, Huma was paid a total of $27,999.92 dollars. Yet on September 18, 2006, she bought an apartment in Washington, DC, costing 649,000 dollars.[98] The question here is, on an annual salary of no more than 28,000 dollars, where did the money come from? We've caught many of the greatest spies due to their spending well beyond their salaries. What exactly are we to make of someone who has lived for 17 years in Saudi Arabia, with parents who have close, long-standing ties with prominent Muslims in the Middle East connected to terrorist organizations, and then comes to the United States and within two years gets a job as the First Lady's assistant? By 2008, Huma was Hillary's traveling chief of staff and was always at Hillary's side. In 2009, she was appointed Deputy Chief of Staff to Secretary of State Hillary Clinton. At this time, Huma had her name removed from the Journal of Muslim Minority Affairs masthead.

In 2010, Huma married Congressman Anthony Weiner. In 2011, her husband was caught sexting—sending pictures of his erection to several women. He resigned from Congress that same year. Yet Huma's luck seemed to know no end when Hillary Clinton personally signed off on a controversial deal in 2012 that allowed Huma to simultaneously work for the State Department and a private New York firm with deep ties to the Clinton family foundation.[99] Mrs. Clinton personally signed a title change form that approved of the transition from being her Deputy Chief of Staff, to an SGE (special government employee), the equivalent of a contractor with special privileges. This allowed Huma to work for both the State department and for the previously mentioned Teneo Group. From June 2012 to February 2013, Huma held four jobs. She was Hillary's State Department aide, a consultant at Teneo Group, she worked and was paid a salary at the Clinton Foundation, and she worked as Hillary's private personal assistant. Huma was quadruple dipping.

When this became known, both the State Department and Sen. Charles Grassley of the Senate Judiciary Committee began investigations looking into potential conflicts of interest. Abedin was suspected of embezzlement when it became known she filed inaccurate time sheets overpaying herself $10,000 in federal salary. Grassley has also questioned whether the deal with Abedin really met the requirements for a special government employee status. One of those requirements is that someone's work as a contractor must be different enough from the original job to warrant giving the person contractor status. Documents acquired by the *Washington Times* show that she told State Department officials that she planned to do the same kind of work as an SGE that she did as Deputy Chief of Staff.[100]

Next, Abedin became part of Hillary's transition team in 2013, helping then Secretary of State Clinton to return to private life. At the same time, Abedin continued her work at the Clinton Foundation and set up her own consulting firm, Zain Endeavors LLC, established eleven days before Abedin left the State Department.[101]

On October 16, 2015, Abedin testified in a closed session before the House Select Committee on Benghazi, in a session that was expected to focus on the 2012 Benghazi attack during which Ambassador J. Christopher Stevens and three other Americans were killed.[102] She said, "I came here today to be as helpful as I could be to the committee. I wanted to honor the service of those lost and injured in the Benghazi attacks," adding she was "honored" to work for Clinton at State and "proud" of her service there. Representative Lynn Westmoreland, a Republican panel member, said Abedin frequently answered questions with responses of "'I don't remember' and 'I don't recollect.'"

There is no doubt that she and Hillary have an extremely close relationship. She has been loyal and faithful to Hillary for twenty years. "I have one daughter. But if I had a second daughter, it would be Huma."

So spoke Hillary in 2010. She even visited with Huma's mother Saleha in Saudi Arabia in 2011, telling her that Huma's position was "very important and sensitive." Nina Burleigh, writing for Newsweek, described Huma Abedin's career as "amazing," considering that Abedin advanced from an intern at the White House to vice chair of Hillary Clinton's 2016 presidential campaign. "Abedin has been inside Hillary's inner circle since she was 20 years old," Burleigh commented. "She learned everything she knows from being around Hillary Clinton. She probably knows Hillary Clinton better than most of her close friends, if not her husband himself."[103]

So how has the mainstream media dealt with Huma Abedin? In short, they haven't. Leftist political smear operations like David Brock's Media Matters functioning as "a propaganda machine to aid and abet Hillary Clinton's political aspirations," ready to protect Clinton's 2016 presidential campaign by publishing "false information and smears" about any journalist who dares report honestly on Abedin's Muslim connections and her deep ties to Hillary Clinton.[104] This isn't some minor aide. Huma Abedin has been at Clinton's side for decades, and America deserves answers that we still have not received.

Throughout his presidential campaign, Trump hammered Clinton for keeping Abedin and by extension Weiner on board.[105] "Her No. 1 person, Huma Abedin, is married to Anthony Weiner, who's a sleaze ball and pervert," Trump said, while campaigning on July 27, 2016. "I'm not saying that. That's recorded history. I don't like Huma going home at night and telling Anthony Weiner all of these secrets." Then, in late August 2016, after Weiner got caught again sexting an underage girl and Abedin finally decided to separate from him. Trump immediately stated that Clinton showed bad judgment by allowing Weiner "close proximity" to classified information.[106] Before the 2016 presidential campaign was over, Trump turned out to have been both right and prescient in his advice.

So, the question remains: Saudi spy or terrorist agent?[107] Even after Hillary's loss to Donald Trump, CBS published an article about twenty women who could become president one day, and guess who was on top of that list? Remarkably, Huma Abedin was near the top of the CBS list.[108] With Huma Abedin clearly deciding to remain at the heights of power in American politics, we can only hope that President Trump and others demand a clear answer on her background, mysterious finances, and connections to radical Islamic ideologues.

Part 3
How Trump Won the
White House

In the 1940s and 1950s, the Republican and Democratic national nominating conventions were raucous affairs.

In those decades, candidates routinely came to the convention to be nominated. There were no primary elections that allowed a candidate prior to the election to gain the required number of delegates to win on the first ballot. Floor fights were common. Even the convention's rules were frequently debated on the floor. When a candidate was nominated, the candidate's supporters rose from their seats and conducted a demonstration, marching through the aisles, carrying banners proclaiming their support for the candidate. The band played music as the supporters marched around the convention hall, singing, shouting, and laughing. The size and enthusiasm of the floor demonstration was used as a sign of the candidate's popularity. In the hotels, state caucuses gathered to hear the candidates and barter delegate votes with other state delegations. Floor managers were assigned by candidates to rove the convention floor and hotel backrooms to gather delegate votes. Throughout the day and night, delegates partied, while liquor flowed. Even the convention hall was filled with cigarette smoke.

The first experiments to televise a national presidential nominating convention began in 1948, covering the Republicans in June and the Democrats in July, with both conventions that year held in Philadelphia. The impact of television was immediately clear, as both parties chose Philadelphia because it was the center point of the Boston to Richmond coaxial cable, then the main carrier of live television in the United States. By 1948, an estimated 10 million people from Boston to Richmond had televisions and could watch the conventions, if they chose to do so. Reports at the time indicated the convention hall in Philadelphia, packed to the rafters during the hot 1948 summer, was like a hot-house heated by blazing television lights in the days before air conditioning was common.[1]

"By 1956, both parties further amended their convention programs to better fit the demands of television coverage," the Museum of Broadcast Television notes. "Party officials condensed the length of the convention, created uniform campaign themes for each party, adorned convention halls with banners and patriotic decorations, placed television crews in positions with flattering views of the proceedings, dropped daytime sessions, limited welcoming speeches and parliamentary organization procedures, scheduled sessions to reach a maximum audience in prime time, and eliminated seconding speeches for vice presidential candidates. Additionally, the presence of television cameras encouraged parties to conceal intra-party battling and choose geographic host cities amenable to their party."[2]

In 1972, a controversy was created when a reporter found a television minute-by-minute script for the convention lying on the floor backstage of the Republican national nominating convention in Miami Beach, Florida. David Gergen, then a White House speechwriter for President Richard Nixon, subsequently admitted that nothing at the 1972 Republican convention was left to chance. "We actually prepared, down to the minute, a script for the whole convention," Gergen admitted. That script spelled out everything the television camera would see happening in the convention hall, down to "spontaneous" demonstrations.[3] Bill Carruthers, who began his career as a television producer-director launching the pie-throwing *Soupy Sales* show in Detroit, advanced to working with Steve Allen, Ernie Kovaks, and Johnny Carson, and produced and directed the original *Dating Game* and *Newlywed Game* shows, was one of the 1972 Republican national convention's principal scriptwriters.[4] "In my business you don't go on television unless you have some form of a script," Carruthers said of the 1972 Republican convention in Miami Beach. "So, yeah, we scripted it, we formatted it, we counseled and coordinated the speeches and the program and the camera positions and the networks and everything else," Caruthers continued. "And it was one of the best conventions ever done."[5]

Author and commentator Zachary Karabel in a 1998 paper entitled, "The Rise and Fall of the Televised Political Convention," published by the Kennedy School of Government at Harvard, noted that political conventions had become little more than "scripted infomercials."[6] As national nominating conventions became more scripted, with primaries stealing the actual drama of the presidential nominating process, the Republican and Democratic national conventions became increasingly boring, with television ratings on the skid, dropping nearly fifteen percent between 1992 and 1996, and viewership down as much as a third. Karabel documented that the 1992 conventions were considered a ratings debacle by network news executives, such that at the end of the Republican convention that year, ABC News President Roone Arledge gave serious consideration to pulling ABC out of convention coverage altogether.

Instead of the simple podiums adorned with large, visible microphones so common to national nominating conventions in the 1940s and 1960s, the elaborately colored and glittery, multi-media podiums of the 2016 Republican and Democratic national conventions were visually dynamic, Internet-driven, looking more like a space ship command center or a huge wrap-around movie screen than a speaking stage for today's mostly humdrum national nominating conventions. Clearly, in today's era of huge HD flat-screen TVs, smoke-filled convention halls are long-gone—together with the political drama of 1950s-style multi-ballot floor-fights that made national nominating conventions compelling to watch, even when the television was nothing more than a small, hard-to-watch, black-and-white tube.

By 2016, the broadcast networks and major cable news organizations had limited television coverage of the Republican convention in Cleveland and the Democratic convention in Philadelphia to a few hours a night. "If you've been watching this week, you know that ABC, CBS and NBC still cover conventions each night for an hour—or a little more, as they did Wednesday, when the GOP's vice-presidential nominee, Indiana Gov. Mike Pence, continued his speech past 11 p.m. Eastern," wrote Callum Borchers, an expert on the intersection of media and politics, in the *Washington Post*, on Thursday, July 21, 2016, the last night of the Republican convention in Cleveland.[7] "But the broadcast networks aren't turning over prime-time air as they once did. Such cutbacks might have forced the political parties to stop sanitizing conventions but for the growth of cable news. You won't cover our staged productions all night, CBS? Fine. CNN will."

Still, even in 2016, the final night of each convention, some 35 million Americans watched Donald Trump give his acceptance speech, followed by 34 million who watched Hillary Clinton at the Democratic National Convention.[8] These were the largest television audiences that had seen either candidate to that point. The only other major television opportunity would be the first debate between Clinton and Trump—a television event that drew some 84 million American viewers to become the most watched televised presidential debate in US history, beating the 80.6 million who watched the only debate between President Jimmy Carter and contender Ronald Reagan in 1980.[9] Viewership for the second debate between Clinton and Trump fell sharply, to an estimated 66.5 million Americans watching.[10] The third and final Clinton-Trump debate rebounded, with an estimated 71.6 million viewers.[11]

First impressions, in politics as in life in general, are often lasting. While the debates can correct voters' impressions a presidential candidate might make with their acceptance speech at the party's national nominating convention, there is no other opportunity like it in any given modern presidential cycle. The acceptance speech is the one time each presidential candidate gets to tell their story without interruptions to one of the largest viewing audiences that candidate will ever have. While the debate audiences are larger, with the first typically commanding the most viewers, each candidate can be expected to command only half the time. Even then, each candidate must spend time on defense, answering attacks leveled during the debate as well as correcting damage that might have been done on the campaign trail. While the national nominating conventions have become largely scripted infomercials today, both parties take their convention opportunity seriously. While prime-time network broadcast time is limited today, the cable news will cover the convention much more extensively, giving each party the opportunity not only to showcase the presidential candidate, but also past political stars and upcoming political prospects, reminding the nation of both the party's past and the party's future.

CHAPTER 7

The Vice Presidential Picks and the National Nominating Conventions

I have joined the political arena so that the powerful can no longer beat up on people that cannot defend themselves. Nobody knows the system better than me, which is why I alone can fix it.
Donald J. Trump, Acceptance Speech, Republican National Convention, Cleveland, Ohio, July 21, 2016

By the time he wrapped up the nomination, Trump had pretty much narrowed the vice presidential field to New Jersey Governor Chris Christie and former House Speaker Newt Gingrich. Paul Manafort and Kellyanne Conway added former congressman, now governor, Mike Pence to that list.

In retrospect, had Trump selected Christie, the most recent revelations regarding his knowledge of the George Washington Bridge lane closing would have doomed the Trump ticket. Candidly, Gingrich was much too 1980s.

Despite Pence having endorsed Cruz in the Indiana primary, Trump decided he would make an excellent running mate. Clearly, Pence had hedged his bets by giving Cruz an endorsement that also included kind words for Trump. By choosing Pence, Trump reached out to Evangelical conservatives.

Pence had a distinguished record in Congress. In 2016, he was planning to run for reelection as governor of Indiana. In that contest, Pence was expected to have a tough race against Democrat John R. Gregg, the former speaker of the Indiana House of Representatives. The election was a rematch of the 2012 Indiana gubernatorial election that Pence won, gaining 49.6 percent of the vote, to Gregg's 46.4 percent.

Trump Chooses Pence

On Friday, July 15, 2016, three days before the start of the Republican convention, Donald Trump announced on Twitter that he had selected Indiana Governor Mike Pence to be his running mate.[1] Pence, who faced a deadline that Friday to withdraw from the ballot, immediately withdrew his gubernatorial candidacy, given that Indiana law would not permit Pence to run for reelection as governor and for vice president at the same time. Hillary Clinton's campaign immediately attacked Pence, calling him "the most extreme pick in a generation." By choosing Pence, a highly respected Christian conservative in GOP circles, Trump sent a message to the core conservative base of the Republican party that he was one with them on key policy issues. "By picking Mike Pence as his running mate, Donald Trump has doubled down on some of his most disturbing beliefs by choosing an incredibly divisive and unpopular running mate known for supporting discriminatory politics and failed economic policies that favor millionaires and corporations over working families," Democratic campaign head John Podesta said in a statement.

The next day, at a press conference held in the New York Hilton in midtown Manhattan, Trump made clear that while his strength in the presidential election was to run as an outsider, Pence gave him balance, in that Pence was a popular choice among the GOP leadership elite as well as with the conservative base. "Indiana Gov. Mike Pence is my first choice. I also admire the fact that he fights for the people and he also is going to fight for you. He is a solid, solid person," Trump said, in what CNN characterized as a rambling speech in which Trump "diverted repeatedly from his speech introducing Pence to hail his own achievements in winning the Republican nomination." Trump summed up his decision to choose Pence as follows: "I think if you look at one of the big reasons that I chose Mike—and one of the reasons is party unity, I have to be honest. So many people have said party unity. Because I'm an outsider. I want to be an outsider. I think it's one of the reasons I won in landslides."

CNN also noted that Trump took the unusual step of reminding the audience that Pence had endorsed Cruz in Indiana's Republican primary. As noted earlier, Pence's endorsement of Cruz was qualified in that Pence, in his endorsement statement, had also spoken enthusiastically about Trump. "It was the greatest non-endorsement I have had in my life," Trump commented.[2] Trump beat Cruz decisively in the May 3 Indiana primary, with Trump getting 53 percent of the Indiana GOP primary vote, compared to Cruz at 37 percent. During the primaries, Cruz had expressed policy differences with Trump, supporting free-trade agreements, for instance, while Trump opposed passage of the Trans-Pacific Partnership. When Trump had called for "a total and complete shutdown of Muslims entering the United States," Cruz had called it "offensive and unconstitutional." Yet Trump recognized the importance of the Midwest, in particular winning Indiana and Ohio, to his presidential chances. In the press conference introducing Pence as his vice presidential pick, Trump also mentioned basketball great Bobby Knight, a strong Trump supporter and a living legend in Indiana.

Governor Pence was gracious once again in accepting Trump's decision. "I accept your invitation to run and serve as vice president of the United States of America," Pence said. "Donald Trump is a good man and he will make a great president of the United States of America." Pence, a professional politician, understood his role as second on the ticket was to support Trump's policy positions, even if it meant suppressing his own personal policy preferences. Pence's history had certain liabilities for Trump in the general election. Pence, an Evangelical Christian who regularly describes himself as "a Christian, a conservative, and a Republican, in that order," signed into law in 2015 a controversial Indiana religious freedom bill. That legislation extended protections to Indiana business owners who refuse to participate in same-sex weddings, citing religious concerns. This prompted the LGBT community to argue that by signing the legislation, Pence had sanctioned discrimination. The law prompted derision from President Obama, who quipped at the 2015 White House correspondents' dinner that he and Vice President Biden were so close that "in some places in Indiana, they won't serve us pizza anymore."[3]

By picking Pence, Trump selected a running mate certain to be embraced by the elite GOP establishment leaders who were still unwilling to endorse openly his presidential campaign. After two failed attempts to win a seat at the House of Representatives, Pence won Indiana's 6th congressional seat in 2000 and served in the House for a dozen years. He rose through the ranks to become chairman of the House Republican Conference. During his last year in the House, the American Conservative Union gave him a 100 percent rating. The National Rifle Association honored Pence's conservative credentials as well, giving him an A rating, while the pro-choice group NARAL gave Pence a 0 percent rating, acknowledging Pence's strong anti-abortion stance. "It's no secret I'm a big fan of Mike Pence," House Speaker Paul Ryan told reporters on learning that Trump had chosen Pence as his running mate. "I've hoped that he'd pick a good movement conservative, and clearly Mike is one of those."[4]

Republican Nominating Convention, Cleveland, Ohio, July 18–21

As the GOP convention gaveled open in Cleveland on Monday, July 18, 2016, major GOP leaders were conspicuously absent. The remaining former GOP presidents, George H. W. Bush and George W. Bush, were not in attendance, in part in deference to Jeb Bush, who also stayed away. Among the other GOP presidential candidates who did not attend the Cleveland convention, the most difficult to understand was John Kasich, who as Ohio governor should have hosted the GOP in Cleveland. To make even worse the intended affront to Trump, Kasich was planning to be in Cleveland during the convention, attending breakfasts for several state delegations and speaking to the US Hispanic Chamber of Commerce. Mitt Romney and Senator John McCain, the GOP presidential nominees in 2012 and 2008 respectively, did not plan to be in Cleveland for the convention. The only living GOP presidential nominee who planned to attend was ninety-two-year-old former Senenator Bob Dole, although Dole was not listed as a speaker.

More than twenty senators and several members of the House, along with a half-dozen Republican governors were not expected to attend. House Speaker Paul Ryan, who was also the 2012 GOP vice presidential nominee, was scheduled to speak on Tuesday night, as was House Majority Leader Kevin McCarthy and Senate Majority Leader Mitch McConnell. But GOP Conference Chairwoman Cathy McMorris Rodgers, the highest-ranking Republican woman in the House, announced she would not be there. "Never before in recent history have so many prominent party officials boycotted the event or found convenient other reasons not to attend because they either didn't approve of or were uncomfortable with their party's presumptive nominee," reported Jessica Taylor, writing for National Public Radio.[5]

Altogether, *Politico* characterized the RNC's opening as a "Disastrous Day One" for Trump. Paul Manafort, Trump's campaign manager, began the day by making the rounds appearing on MSNBC and other morning shows, saying Ohio Governor Kasich was "embarrassing his state" by not attending. Trump's motorcade got into an accident en route to the Quicken Arena in downtown Cleveland. One of the evening's most moving speakers, Patricia Smith, the mother of one of four Americans killed in Benghazi, was scheduled to speak to ensure the taping would be picked up by network television. *Politico* noted that as Patricia Smith spoke, holding back tears, the attention in the arena was rapt, and the audience roiled with anger. "I blame Hillary Clinton, I blame Hillary Clinton personally for the death of my son," Smith said.[6]

Then, as the highlight of Monday evening, Trump's wife, Melania, gave a speech that appeared to have been plagiarized from Michelle Obama's 2008 address to the Democratic convention in Denver. Here is what Melania said in 2016, with the bold text showing the suspect language:

> "From a young age, my parents impressed on me the **values that you work hard for what you want in life, that your word is your bond and you do what you say and keep your promise; that you treat people with respect**. They taught and showed me values and morals in their daily life. That is a lesson that I continue to pass along to our son, and **we need to pass those lessons on to the many generations to follow because we want our children in this nation to know that the only limit to your achievements is the strength of your dreams and your willingness to work for them**."

Here's what Michelle Obama said, eight years earlier, again with the language suspected of being copied in bold:

> "Barack and I were raised with so many of the same **values: that you work hard for what you want in life; that your word is your bond and you do what you say you're going to do; that you treat people with dignity and respect**, even if you don't know them, and even if

you don't agree with them. And Barack and I set out to build lives
guided by these values, and **pass them on to the next generation.
Because we want our children—and all children in this nation—
to know that the only limit to the height of your achievements is
the reach of your dreams and your willingness to work for them.**"

Journalist Jarrett Hill, perhaps the first to catch the similarity, tweeted
immediately that Melania had stolen a whole paragraph from Michelle's
speech.[7] One of the ironies was the thought that a Republican could
share an idea in common with Michelle Obama after Republicans had
"gone ballistic" in 2008[8] when, in February, Michelle told an audience
that: "For the first time in my adult life, I am really proud of my country
because it feels like hope is finally making a comeback."[9]

After attempting to deny or minimize the plagiarized language,
Trump Organization in-house staff writer Meredith McIver, a longtime
friend of the Trump family, apologized and offered to resign. McIver's
explanation was that in working with Melania Trump on the speech,
Melania read some passages from Michelle Obama's 2008 speech that
she admired. McIver wrote the phrases down and included some of the
phrasing in a draft that ultimately became the speech. McIver admitted
she had not checked against Michelle Obama's original language. "This
was my mistake, and I feel terrible for the chaos I have caused Melania
and the Trumps, as well as to Mrs. Obama," McIver wrote in a letter
explaining what happened. "No harm was meant." Trump rejected her
resignation.[10]

Cruz Draws Convention Wrath

On Wednesday, July 20, 2016, the third day of the RNC in Cleveland,
Senator Ted Cruz addressed the convention. Cruz took the podium to prolonged, enthusiastic, and appreciative applause. Still, the question that hung
in the air as Cruz began speaking was whether or not he would endorse
Trump. The speech began well, with Cruz congratulating Trump on winning the nomination on the first ballot the previous night. But then, Cruz
added, addressing the convention hall, "And, like each of you, I want to see
the principles of our party prevail in November."[11] Listening to that, many in
the audience wondered exactly where Cruz was headed with this.

"America is more than just a land mass between two oceans. America is an idea, a simple yet powerful idea: freedom matters," Cruz said,

his speech drawing applause. "For much of human history, government power has been the unavoidable constant in life—government decrees, and the people obey. Not here. We have no king or queen. We have no dictator. We the People constrain government. Our nation is exceptional because it was built on the five most beautiful and powerful words in the English language: I want to be free. Never has that message been more needed than today."

Cruz attacked the policies of President Obama and Hillary Clinton. "Of course, Obama and Clinton will also tell you that they also care about our children's future," he said. "And I want to believe them. But there is a profound difference in our two parties' visions for the future. Theirs is the party that thinks ISIS is a 'JV team,' that responds to the death of Americans at Benghazi by asking, 'What difference does it make?' And that thinks it's possible to make a deal with Iran, which celebrates as holidays 'Death to America Day' and 'Death to Israel Day.'"

While Cruz was speaking, the television cameras showed Trump entering the convention hall. Anticipation built as Cruz neared his close.

"We deserve leaders who stand for principle. Who unite us all behind shared values." he said, triggering no concern in the audience. "Who cast aside anger for love. That is the standard we should expect, from everybody," he continued, now raising some concern. "And to those listening, please, don't stay home in November. If you love our country, and love your children as much as I know that you do, stand, and speak, and vote your conscience, vote for candidates up and down the ticket who you trust to defend our freedom and to be faithful to the Constitution," he said, triggering the first audience reaction of displeasure that he might not endorse Trump after all. "The case we have to make to the American people, the case each person in this room has to make to the American people is to commit to each of them that we will defend freedom and be faithful to the Constitution," he went on, beginning to draw some booing.

"We will unite the party, we will unite the country by standing together for shared values, by standing for liberty," Cruz commented. And then, abruptly, Cruz ended the speech, saying only this: "God bless each and every one of you. And may God bless the United States of America." The crowd began booing loudly. The reaction was immediate and angry. Shock fell over the audience in the convention hall and those watching on television across the nation. Cruz had been given the podium at the RNC by the Trump team organizing the convention, only to use the extension of that privilege to insult the party's nominee.

"In the most electric moment of the convention, boos and jeers broke out as it became clear that Mr. Cruz—in a prime-time address from center stage—was not going to endorse Mr. Trump. It was a pointed snub on the eve of Mr. Trump's formal acceptance speech," veteran reporters Patrick Healy and Jonathan Martin wrote in the *New York Times*. "As hundreds of delegates chanted 'Vote for Trump!' and 'Say it!' Mr. Cruz tried to dismiss the outburst as 'enthusiasm of the New York delegation'—only to have Mr. Trump himself suddenly appear in the back of the convention hall. Virtually every head in the room seemed to turn from Mr. Cruz to Mr. Trump, who was stone-faced and clearly angry as he egged on delegates by pumping his fist." Whatever Cruz had calculated, the stunt was turning rapidly into a disaster. "Mr. Cruz was all but drowned out as he asked for God's blessing on the country and left the stage, while security personnel escorted his wife, Heidi, out of the hall," the *New York Times* report continued. A short while later, Cruz faced insults, Healy and Martin commented, when he made his way down a corridor and a woman yelled "Traitor!" Then, when Cruz tried to enter the convention suite of Las Vegas casino magnate Sheldon Adelson—an important GOP donor to Republican political campaigns—Cruz was turned away, denied admission.

The next day, after a private meeting with his advisors at the Ritz Carlton hotel adjoining the Quicken Arena in downtown Cleveland, Cruz was confronted by two top-dollar GOP donors who were finishing their breakfast in the hotel dining room. Both donors pleaded with Cruz to realize that not endorsing Trump was a mistake that could cost Cruz his political future in the Republican Party. Cruz pleaded that it was difficult for him to forgive the insults Trump had cast on his wife and father during the primary campaign. Cruz explained that his goal was to reach beyond the convention floor to speak with conservatives across America, in an attempt to position himself as the leader of what he perceives as a continuing and strong conservative movement within the GOP. The two donors, who had remained sitting throughout the conversation while Cruz stood at the side of their table, were largely unconvinced. The donors concluded by emphasizing the importance of beating Hillary Clinton as a unifying theme now, asking Cruz repeatedly what Trump had to do specifically to win his endorsement. Cruz declined to answer directly, responding only that in his speech he had made clear that he joined the GOP in the conclusion that Hillary Clinton must be defeated.

Cruz had taken an opportunity to introduce himself favorably to the GOP faithful in the convention hall and to the nation—the largest audience he had ever addressed in his life—and instead of being gracious, he allowed his pride and ego to get in the way. The next morning, Cruz insisted to the Texas delegation that the pledge he had signed as a candidate to support the party's nominee "was not a blanket commitment that if you go and slander my wife that I am going to come like a servile puppy dog." For former Texas Governor Rick Perry, Cruz's explanation was not enough. "If a convention's goal is to unite your party behind one candidate, Senator Cruz didn't get the memo," Perry said on CNN, chastising Cruz. "We all made a pledge that we were going to support our nominee. If you don't want to keep your word, don't be signing pledges."[12]

That afternoon, on the fourth day of the convention as the RNC was getting ready for Trump's acceptance speech, reporter Jerome Corsi interviewed the Texas delegation on the convention floor. The consensus was that Cruz hurt himself, making it very hard for him, if it is at all possible, to get funding or political support for another run at the GOP nomination for president in 2020, or possibly even his effort to be reelected to a second term in the US Senate in 2018.[13]

"It's Trump's Party"

On the final night of the RNC, Thursday, July 21, 2016, the unlikely nominee, Donald Trump, had the opportunity to celebrate with his family the triumph of being the GOP presidential nominee. "It's Donald Trump's Party," the *New York Times* headlined the article reporter Nicholas Confessore wrote, noting that Trump broke from his scripted speech only once, "when Mr. Trump, grimacing theatrically, mocked those who had said he could never win. The result was a Trump packaged for prime time."[14]

As Fox News reported, Trump's acceptance speech electrified the GOP convention crowd, who cheered Trump with chants of "USA" breaking out frequently as the nominee vowed to "put America first." Trump amplified upon his campaign message, pledging to "Make America Great Again"—a theme Trump's millions of supporters had reduced to #MAGA. "Every day I wake up determined to deliver for the people

I have met all across this nation that have been ignored, neglected and abandoned. . . . These are people who work hard but no longer have a voice," Trump said. "I am your voice."[15] Fox News noted Trump closed his speech by turning Hillary Clinton's "I'm with her" campaign slogan on its head. "I chose to recite a different pledge," Trump said. "My pledge reads, 'I'm with you.'"

The immediate reaction of the Clinton-supporting mainstream media was that Trump had painted a "dark picture" of America in countless, exaggerated crises of leadership that Trump argued he was uniquely qualified to solve. "With dark imagery and an almost angry tone, Mr. Trump portrayed the United States as a diminished and even humiliated nation, and offered himself as an all-powerful savior who could resurrect the country's standing in the eyes of both enemies and law-abiding Americans," Patrick Healy and Jonathan Martin reported for the *New York Times* in an article published the day after Trump's acceptance speech.[16] Healy and Martin described Trump's acceptance speech as if it were a neo-Nazi appeal delivered in an American-fascist context, as if the RNC was a replay of the German American Bund rally at New York's Madison Square Garden that drew an estimated 22,000 American supporters of Hitler on February 20, 1939.[17] The *New York Times* account of Trump's acceptance speech continued painting this ominous narrative. "Our convention occurs at a moment of crisis for our nation," an ominous-sounding Mr. Trump said, standing against a backdrop of American flags. "The attacks on our police, and the terrorism in our cities, threaten our very way of life. Any politician who does not grasp this danger is not fit to lead our country." In the *New York Times* account, we can almost see the RNC on the final night as Nazi rally reprised. "Mr. Trump nearly shouted the names of states where police officers had been killed recently, as the crowd erupted in applause, and returned repeatedly to the major theme of the speech: "Law and order," he said four times, each time drawing out the syllables," Healy and Martin continued.

As if this portrayal were not sufficient to paint a disturbing picture, the *New York Times* contrasted Trump against Reagan, arguing that Trump was stressing disorder and disarray in order to promote a far-right "law and order" fascist-like reality. "Evoking the tumult of the 1960s and the uncertainty that followed the September 11 terrorist attacks, Mr. Trump made a sharp departure from the optimistic talk about American possibility that has characterized Republican presidential candidates since Ronald Reagan redefined the party over 30 years ago," the newspaper continued. "In promoting his hardline views on crime, immigration and hostile nations, Mr. Trump was wagering that voters would embrace his style of populism and his promises of safety if they feel even less secure by Election Day."

What the *New York Times* portrayed was typical of the far-left characterization of Trump as a neo-Nazi. "In the America depicted by Donald Trump's dystopian acceptance speech Thursday night, it is blackest midnight in the land of the once-free, unimaginably far from morning," wrote national affairs correspondent Joan Walsh in the *Nation*. "The unlikely GOP presidential nominee rejected suggestions that he give a unifying speech that reached for the center. Instead, he described a country rocked by crime, riven by race, menaced by terrorists, and overrun by illegal immigrants. Trump out-Nixoned Richard Nixon, promising to be a 'law and order' president just like our 37th. He defined Hillary Clinton as just another criminal who will coddle the many other criminals who 'threaten our very way of life.'"[18] Walsh converted Trump's "I am your voice" statement into Trump being "a voice of fear and anger, a loud, screaming voice promising retribution for the crimes that have laid the nation low, including the 'terrible, terrible crimes' committed by Clinton." As far as Walsh was concerned, Trump "shouted at the country, red-faced, for an endless 76 minutes." She stressed "Trump hyped a crime wave that mostly doesn't exist," arguing Trump's intent was to describe "an apocalyptic set of crises that he laid at the feet of Clinton and Obama."

Perhaps predictably, the mainstream media jumped aboard the far-left's meme. "On the final night of a convention filled with mishaps—of the plagiarism, non-endorsement varieties—Donald Trump painted a bleak picture of America, even as he officially accepted the Republican Party's nomination for the presidency," wrote Reena Flores for CBS News.[19] Flores continued to note that while the "billionaire proceeded to lay out a dark vision of America," he also "positioned himself as the country's singular savior."

What the Clinton-supporting mainstream media in its particularly partisan "reporting" on the RNC convention in Cleveland missed was that a large majority of Middle America cheered along with the audience listening to Trump that night in the Quicken Arena, when the chants went up "Lock her up!" and "Build the wall!" These ideas, hateful to a leftist press schooled on government manipulated statistics that showed job growth (even if mostly only in part-time employment) and reduced unemployment (achieved by increasing the number of workers considered no longer in the workforce, largely because the lack of meaningful jobs has discouraged them from continued job-hunting), as signs of prosperity under Obama. Uncritically, the leftist Clinton-supporting press minimized threats from illegal immigration, preferring to see "undocumented workers" as Democrat voters deserving the same rights and benefits as US citizens. What the leftist-press correctly sensed in Trump's "America First" agenda was an end to the socialist open-borders globalism that rejected "American exceptionalism" in exchange for a politically correct view that saw no inherent national security dangers even in radical Islam. The *Nation* article ended by observing Hillary had countered Trump's assertion "I am your voice" by tweeting "You are not our voice @realDonaldTrump."

Hillary Picks Kaine

On Saturday, July 23, 2016, in Miami, Florida, before an audience of Florida International University, FIU, students, just two days before the start of the DNC national nominating convention in Philadelphia, Hillary Clinton announced she had chosen Senator Tim Kaine as her vice presidential running mate, a choice CNN described as "turning to a steady and seasoned hand in government to fill out the Democratic ticket."[20] In making her announcement, Hillary subtly suggested that while Donald Trump's vision for America was "dark," her vision for America was much more positive. "Next week in Philadelphia, we will offer a very different vision for our country—one that is about building bridges, not walls—embracing the diversity that makes our country great—lifting each other up, standing together—because we know there is nothing we can't accomplish once we make up our minds," Hillary said. "And that's why I am so happy to announce that my running mate is a man who not only shares those values, but also lives them."

Kaine began his political career working as a Catholic missionary who had embraced Marxist liberation theology in his work with the Jesuits from 1980 to 1981 in Honduras. The version of liberation theology propagated when Kaine was in Honduras was "the hardcore, Cold War variety—an avowed Marxist ideology inimical to the institutional Catholic Church and to the United States."[21] Though Kaine claims today to be a practicing Catholic, he has embraced the far-left's position on

LGBT same-sex marriage since 2013. The *Daily Beast* noted that Kaine had not always supported same-sex marriage, pointing out that when a Massachusetts court decision made it the first state to let same-sex couples marry, in 2003, Kaine released a statement criticizing the ruling by saying marriage "between a man and a woman is the building block of the family and a keystone of our civil society." The *Daily Beast* also noted that when Kaine ran for governor of Virginia in 2005, he aired radio ads describing himself as a "conservative on issues of personal responsibility" and saying that he opposed gay marriage. Kaine, who served as governor of Virginia from 2006 to 2010, and as chairman of the Democratic National Committee from 2009 to 2011, was elected to the Senate from Virginia in 2012. His position on abortion moved to the far-left after he became Clinton's running mate, when he suggested he might support a repeal of the Hyde amendment to allow taxpayer dollars to pay for abortion procedures.[22]

Predictably, the Clinton-supporting, left-leaning mainstream media embraced Kaine as a "strong choice," while quietly lamenting that Hillary had not made even more history by choosing a female running mate. "In every office he has held—from Richmond mayor, to Virginia governor, to U.S. Senator—he has shown a steady hand marked by mastery of policy details and policy," the *Washington Post*'s editorial board raved.[23] ABC News commented that when Clinton announced her vice president choice in Miami, Kaine started his speech by saying, "Hello Miami, Hello FIU," after which he quickly switched to Spanish, a language he learned in Honduras. ABC noted that Clinton explained to the FIU audience, "I have to say Sen. Kaine is everything Trump and Pence are not. He is qualified to lead on day one. The most important qualification when you are trying to make this really big choice is, 'Can this person step in to be president?'"[24]

The leftist organization Think Progress pointed out why the leftist mainstream media was so enthusiastic about Kaine. Evan Popp, an intern at Think Progress, described as a "journalist, writer, lover of presidential history, and maple syrup enthusiast," in an article entitled "What You Need to Know About Tim Kaine, Hillary Clinton's Vice President Pick." noted Kaine had "a solid record on many core Democratic issues" and supported what Think Progress considered virtually all the right ideological positions. "He supports President Obama's Affordable Care Act and has long been opposed to the use of the death penalty,"

Popp wrote. "Kaine is a strong supporter of comprehensive immigration reform, favoring a pathway to citizenship for immigrants. As governor he pushed to offer universal pre-kindergarten and also signed a bill to ban smoking in Virginia bars and restaurants." Think Progress went on to point out Kaine endorsed the United Nations position on global climate change, that while running for US Senate he received an "F" from the National Rifle Association, and that as governor, he vetoed a bill that would have allowed the carrying of guns in vehicles. Despite being a Catholic, Kaine received a perfect score from Planned Parenthood for his pro-choice voting record. He supported the Trans Pacific Partnership and banned discrimination in state employment on the basis of sexual orientation on his first day in office as governor.[25] Yet, while the *New York Times* admitted Kaine was a "social justice liberal" with working-class roots and a fluency in Spanish, reporters Amy Chozick, Alan Rappeport, and Jonathan Martin regretted Clinton had not chosen others on the list, such as Secretary of Labor Thomas E. Perez, "who would have been the first Hispanic on a major party ticket," or Senator Cory Booker of New Jersey, "who would have been the first African-American to seek the vice presidency."[26]

Democratic Nominating Convention, Philadelphia, PA, July 25–28, 2016

Party discipline struggled to prevail at the Democratic national convention, held at the Wells Fargo Center in Philadelphia the week following the Republican convention in Cleveland. The convention needed to repair the damage done to the party in the wake of Debbie Wasserman Schultz's resignation as DNC head on July 24, the day the convention began, after documents released by WikiLeaks exposed the DNC bias against Bernie Sanders under her direction.

In an attempt to unify the delegates and to kick the convention off on a positive note, the DNC put Michelle Obama center stage on Day 1. At the start of her speech, Michelle got applause for her negative portrayal of Donald Trump. "How we explain that when someone is cruel or acts like a bully, you don't stoop to their level. Our motto is, when they go low, we go high," she insisted. Michelle emphasized her pride as First Lady by reflecting on America's pre-Civil War history of slavery. "The story of generations of people who felt the lash of bondage, the shame of servitude, the sting of segregation, who kept on striving, and hoping, and doing what needed to be done," she said. "So that today, I wake up every morning in a house that was built by slaves. And I watch my daughters, two beautiful intelligent black young women, play with the dog on the White House lawn." She stressed feminist themes in praising Hillary Clinton's nomination. "And because of Hillary Clinton, my daughters and all of our sons and daughters now take for granted that a woman can be president of the United States," she noted.

Without directly referencing the Democratic attack that Trump's campaign slogan to make America great again was a "dog whistle" to segregationists and white supremacists who longed for a return to days where people of color faced slavery and racial discrimination in this country, she made her point. "Don't let anyone ever tell you that this country is not great," she insisted. "That somehow we need to make it great again. Because this right now is the greatest country on Earth."[27] To a conservative audience watching that night, if Michelle's speech proved anything, it provided more evidence that themes recalling Saul Alinsky-inspired politics of racial divide were never far from the playbook of either Michelle or Barack Obama.

On Sunday, the day before the DNC convention began, thousands of Bernie Sanders demonstrators marched through the streets of Philadelphia, defying the oppressive summer heat to cheer, chant, and beat drums to show their disaffection with Hillary Clinton. Chanting "Hell no, DNC, we won't vote for Hillary," and "This is what democracy looks like," the marchers headed down the city's main north-south artery in a demonstration that began at City Hall and ended at the Wells Fargo convention center four miles away.[28] With demonstrations planned all week, the DNC scheduled Sanders to follow Michelle Obama's Day 1 speech. While Sanders endorsed Clinton, much of his speech was about what his campaign had accomplished. Sanders began by thanking the 13 million Americans who voted for his "political revolution," yielding him 1,856 pledged delegates."[29]

Sanders thanked the 2.5 million Americans who funded his campaign with an unprecedented 8 million individual campaign contributions. The average contribution was twenty-seven dollars. "I understand that many people here in this convention hall and around the country are disappointed about the final results of the nominating process," Sanders said. "I think it's fair to say that no one is more disappointed than I am." He continued on this theme: "Together, together, my friends, we have begun a political revolution to transform America, and that revolution, our revolution, continues!" Sanders' failure to embrace Clinton or her campaign themes left no doubt that his socialist roots were to the left of Hillary Clinton and he had no thought of changing. Saying the election was not about Donald Trump or Hillary Clinton, Sanders insisted the election was about the struggle to reduce the power and wealth of the 1 percent. "And I look forward to being part of that struggle with you."

Senator Elizabeth Warren, who preceded Sanders to the podium, also took heat from the large number of Sanders supporters in the convention hall. Warren's speech attacking Trump was interrupted by attendees taunting her, calling out, "We trusted you!"—a reproach for supporting Clinton, instead of running herself or backing Sanders.[30] What was clear at the end of Day 1 was that the core base of the Democratic Party was moving even farther to the left, such that Hillary Clinton, despite her Saul Alinsky roots, was not sufficiently radical to satisfy the largely youthful millennial voters who went all out for Sanders.

Khizr Khan Speaks

On the last day of the Democratic National Convention, before Hillary Clinton was scheduled to give her acceptance speech, the Democrats gave the podium to Khizr Khan, whose son, US Army Captain Humayun Khan, was killed in Iraq on June 8, 2004. Clinton campaign officials latched onto Khan after he was quoted in print characterizing Donald Trump's remarks about Muslims as "un-American."[31]

With his wife standing silently by his side, Khan, who became a US citizen after emigrating from Pakistan in 1980, took the podium, determined to rail against Trump. "First, our thoughts and prayers are with our veterans and those who serve today," he began. "Tonight, we are honored to stand here as the parents of Captain Humayun Khan, and as patriotic American Muslims with undivided loyalty to our country."

Next, he professed his belief in America. "Like many immigrants, we came to this country empty-handed. We believed in American democracy—that with hard work and the goodness of this country, we could share in and contribute to its blessings," he continued, setting up the premise for his claimed legitimacy to attack Trump. "We were blessed to raise our three sons in a nation where they were free to be themselves and follow their dreams. Our son, Humayun, had dreams of being a military lawyer. But he put those dreams aside the day he sacrificed his life to save his fellow soldiers."[32]

The politeness over, Khan went political. "Hillary Clinton was right when she called my son 'the best of America.' If it was up to Donald Trump, he never would have been in America. Donald Trump consistently smears the character of Muslims," Khan insisted. "He disrespects other minorities—women, judges, even his own party leadership. He vows to build walls and ban us from this country." From here, Khan began addressing Trump directly. "Donald Trump, you are asking Americans to trust you with our future," Khan pressed forward. "Let me ask you: Have you even read the US Constitution?" Here Khan took a paperbound copy of the US Constitution out of the inside pocket of his suit jacket. "I will gladly lend you my copy. In this document, look for the words 'liberty' and 'equal protection of law,'" Khan said, waving with his right hand the copy of the Constitution in the air above his head.

"Have you ever been to Arlington Cemetery?" he asked Trump. "Go look at the graves of the brave patriots who died defending America—you will see all faiths, genders, and ethnicities." Continuing to paint Trump as a hateful bigot, Khan advanced to his conclusion in an insistent monotone that matched the rhythm with which he had waved the Constitution aggressively in the air, as if he were confronting Trump standing before him in the convention hall. "You have sacrificed nothing and no one," Khan said to his imaginary Trump, his tone now accusatory. "We can't solve our problems by building walls and sowing division. We are stronger together. And we will keep getting stronger when Hillary Clinton becomes our next president."

The *New York Times* raved about Khan's speech, reporting that Khan's words "electrified the convention and turned Mr. Khan into a social media and cable news sensation."[33] The newspaper billed the Khan family as heroes, reporting, "If restrictions on Muslim immigration had been in place decades ago, Mr. Khan said, neither he, a lawyer with an advanced degree from Harvard Law School; his wife, Ghazala, who taught Persian at a Pakistani college before raising three boys in the Washington suburbs; their eldest son, Shaharyar, who was a top student at the University of Virginia and a cofounder of a biotechnology company; nor Captain Khan, who posthumously earned the Bronze Star, along with a Purple Heart, for saving the lives of his men, would have been allowed to settle here." The article noted a third son, Omer, who works at his brother's biotech company, was born in the United States. Khan told the newspaper that nothing from the speech was a product of coaching from Hillary Clinton's campaign, but that it "all flowed pretty easily," because he had been thinking of these issues for quite some time. "I respect the Republican Party as much as the Democratic Party," Khan told the newspaper. But he added: "I definitely will continue to raise my voice out of concern that the Republican leadership must pay attention to what is taking place."

Hillary Clinton's acceptance speech, the highlight of the Democratic National Convention on the last day, had been preceded by lackluster speeches given by former President Bill Clinton, as well as by President Barack Obama. Bill Clinton's objective evidently was to make Hillary more likeable. Instead of focusing on policy issues, Clinton took nearly forty-five minutes to tell a rambling, folksy story of his romance and marriage with Hillary. Given the history of the Clinton's marriage, the love-story Bill wove was far from credible. No less than Clinton loyalist George Stephanopoulos of ABC News pointed out that Clinton's narrative was "not entirely comprehensive, in that some key parts of the couple's life together were omitted, including Clinton's high-profile affair that led to his impeachment in 1998.[34]

Obama's speech at the DNC followed his public admission for the first time that Trump could end up succeeding him—a realization that prompted Obama to advise Hillary to "run scared" as she prepared to become the first female nominee of a major US political party.[35] During his convention speech, Obama's assignment was to place Hillary's name in nomination, setting the stage for arguing Hillary's presidency would be an extension of what the Democrats wanted to portray as eight years of economic and foreign policy strength and stability under Obama. Astute commentators noted what Obama actually accomplished was to speak predominantly about his own record as president. "He spoke of his time in office, how the presidency has physically aged him, but how his daughters euphemistically note he now looks more 'mature," *Grabien News* commented in their analysis of Obama's convention speech. "He spoke of everything he is proud to have achieved—passing ObamaCare, expanding clean energy production, reducing consumption of foreign oil, passing the Iran deal, bringing troops home, killing bin Laden," *Grabien News* continued. "He spoke of how inspired he's become meeting Americans of all stripes. He spoke of his optimism. He spoke of the values he imparted from his family." Then came the punch line: "If it's starting to sound like Obama talked a lot about himself, that's because he did." *Grabien News* counted that Obama referred to himself 119 times in a speech that was supposed to be about Hillary Clinton.[36]

Hillary came on stage wearing a white pantsuit and matching white blazer covering a white silk blouse—an outfit admirers commented was designed to bring to mind the suffragettes who famously wore all-white during their protests one hundred years ago to establish a woman's right to vote.[37] As expected, Hillary made the feminist issue the centerpiece of her speech. "Tonight, we've reached a milestone in our nation's march toward a more perfect union," Clinton said. "This is the first time in our nation's history that a major party has nominated a woman for president." The comment received sustained applause, appropriate for the history being made at that moment. "Tonight's victory is not about one person," she continued. "It belongs to generations of women and men who struggled and sacrificed and made this moment possible."

What was not seen on television, as the balloons dropped, the band played, and Bill and Chelsea joined Hillary on the podium, was the protest activity that never really ceased inside the convention hall throughout the DNC. When the roll call was taken and Hillary was selected as the Democrats' presidential nominee, many Sanders delegates stood up and walked out in protest. Even as Hillary began delivering her historic acceptance speech on the convention's last night, many Sanders delegates stood up and turned their backs on the podium, indicating their continued displeasure that Hillary had been nominated. In 2016, Hillary achieved what she failed to achieve in 2008. But the journey was only half done. The challenge now was whether or not Hillary could get enough votes to beat Trump in the general election, and that remained to be seen.

Trump Attacked for Responding to Khizr Kahn

In an interview with ABC News George Stephanopoulos, Trump said Khan had "no way of knowing" that Trump would not have allowed him and his wife into the country because they were Muslim.[38]

"I saw him," Trump continued, acknowledging he had watched Khan's speech at the DNC. "He was very emotional and probably looked like a nice guy to me. If you look at his wife, she was standing there. She had nothing to say. Maybe she wasn't allowed to have anything to say. You tell me, but plenty of people have written that. She was extremely quiet. Personally, I watched him and I wish him the best of luck."

Stephanopoulos pressed the issue. "Why would you say that?" he asked.

"I'd say we've had a lot of problems with radical Islamic terrorism," Trump answered. "You look at San Bernardino, you look at Orlando, you look at the World Trade Center, you look at so many different things. You look at the priest over the weekend in Paris, where his throat was cut—an eighty-five-year-old beloved Catholic priest. You look at what happened in Nice, France, a couple of weeks ago. I'd say something is going on and it's not good."

Stephanopoulos was not responsive to Trump's references to terrorist attacks by radical Islamic extremists. Instead, he referenced Khan's assertion that Trump has sacrificed nothing.

"Who wrote that?" Trump asked in response. "Did Hillary's script-writers write it?"

Again, Stephanopoulos asked how Trump would answer the father of a fallen solder about what sacrifices Trump has made for his country.

"I think I've made a lot of sacrifices," Trump responded. "I've worked very, very hard. I've created thousands and thousands of jobs—tens of thousands of jobs."

"Those are sacrifices?" Stephanopoulos interrupted to ask, raising his eyebrows, obviously looking skeptical in objecting to Trump's answer.

"Oh sure, I think they're sacrifices," Trump continued. "When I can employ thousands and thousands of people, take care of their education—I was responsible along with a group of people for getting the Vietnam War Memorial built in downtown Manhattan, which to this day people thank me for. I raise and have raised millions of dollars for the vets and I'm helping the vets a lot. I think my popularity with the vets is through the roof."

ABC News reported that Trump "appeared to brush the speech aside" by saying Khan was very emotional. Responding to Trump's comment that Khan's wife stood silently by his side, ABC News attacked Trump, "This appears to be Trump tipping his hat to some far-right-wing and nationalist Twitter users who have suggested that Ghazala Khan was silent during her husband's speech because they are Muslim and he prohibits her from speaking. ABC News further countered Trump by reporting that in an interview that day with ABC, Ghazala Khan said she did not speak because she was in pain. ABC News quoted Ghazala Khan as saying, "Please. I am very upset when I heard, when he said that I didn't say anything. I was in pain. If you were in pain, you fight or you don't say anything. I'm not a fighter. I can't fight. So the best thing I do was quiet," she said. ABC further commented that Khizr Khan said he asked his wife of forty-two years to speak but she declined, knowing she would be too emotional. ABC reported Khizr Khan as saying, "I invited her, 'Would you like to say something on the stage?' when the invitation came, and she said, 'You know how it is with me, how upset I get.'" Clearly, ABC News sympathized with Ghazala and Khizr Khan in the determination of the broadcast news agency to portray them as the victims of Trump's right-wing aggression.

ABC News further objected to Trump saying he had made sacrifices by his efforts on behalf of veterans. To counter Trump on this point, ABC News quoted Paul Rieckoff, the founder and CEO of Iraq and Afghanistan Veterans of America, a group ABC portrayed as "non-partisan" with close to 200,000 members, as saying, "For anyone to compare their 'sacrifice' to a Gold Star family member is insulting, foolish and ignorant. Especially someone who has never served himself and has no children serving. Our country has been at war for a decade and a half, and the truth is most Americans have sacrificed nothing. Most of them are smart and grounded enough to admit it."

With the Khans, the mainstream media sensed a "gotcha" trap that Trump fell for, with potentially devastating consequences for the Trump campaign. Quickly, the mainstream media piled on, heaping derision and blame on Trump for his comments.

"Mr. Khan's speech at the convention in Philadelphia was one of the most powerful given there," Maggie Haberman and Richard A. Oppel, Jr., wrote in the *New York Times* on July 30, 2016.[39] "It was effectively the Democratic response to comments Mr. Trump has made implying many American Muslims have terrorist sympathies or stay silent when they know ones who do. Mr. Trump has called to ban Muslim immigration as a way to combat terrorism." The *New York Times* article noted the Stephanopoulos interview drew "quick and widespread condemnation and amplified calls for Republican leaders to distance themselves from their presidential nominee." Additionally, the newspaper commented on Trump's "implication that the soldier's mother had not spoken because of female subservience expected in some traditional strains of Islam, and noted that "his comments also inflamed his hostilities with American Muslims." Haberman and Oppel quoted Ohio Governor John Kasich, who had posted on Twitter, "There's only one way to talk about Gold Star parents: with honor and respect."

After the Stephanopoulos interview, Trump issued a statement calling Captain Khan a "hero," while also reiterating his concern that the United States should bar Muslims from entering the country. "While I feel deeply for the loss of his son," he added, "Mr. Khan, who has never met me, has no right to stand in front of millions of people and claim I have never read the Constitution, (which is false) and say many other inaccurate things."[40] Alexander Burns, reporting in the *New York Times* on August 2, 2016, noted that for days after the controversy began, Trump refused to apologize for his comments, ignoring the advice of top advisors to move on from the feud to focus on the economy and the national security record of his opponent, Hillary Clinton.[41] President Obama entered into the controversy, declaring Trump "unfit to serve as president" and "woefully unprepared to do this job," as he challenged Republican leaders to withdraw their support of their nominee. In response to the barrage of criticism, Trump refused to endorse House Speaker Paul Ryan or Senator John McCain in their primary campaigns.[42]

That the Khizr Khan incident was a Clinton campaign set-up was strongly suggested by an article reporter Matthew Boyle wrote in Breitbart.com on August 1, 2016. It got a wide audience for reports that Khan had worked at the law firm Hogan Lovells, LLP, a major DC law firm from 2000 to 2007, when the firm was known as Hogan & Hartson.[43] The law firm has been on retainer as the law firm representing the government of Saudi Arabia in the United States for years. The government of Saudi Arabia is on record as having given between 10 and $25 million to the Clinton Foundation. Hogan Lovells lobbyist Robert Kyle had bundled more than $50,000 for Hillary Clinton's 2016 presidential campaign. A lawyer at Hogan & Hartson has been Bill and Hillary Clinton's "go-to guy" for tax advice since 2004, preparing for the Clintons their personal income tax returns. Hogan & Hartson did the patent work for a software firm used to monitor Hillary Clinton's private email use. The law firm also employed Loretta Lynch in the time between her two appointments as US attorney in New York. Khan's own personal law firm, KM Khan Law Office, is involved in the business of "buying visas" through the EB5 program that allows certain foreign investors to obtain visas after making specified investments in the United States.

Various other sources reported two Clinton campaign staffers wrote Khan's speech. Khan was paid $25,000 by the Clinton campaign to speak at the DNC. A female Clinton staffer bought only two hours before his speech the copy of the US Constitution that Khan used as a prop during the speech. In total, the Clinton campaign approached five Gold Star families before Khan was approached to speak at the DNC. All five families were paid $5,000 and signed a non-disclosure agreement not to speak with the press. Khan's immigration law firm is $1.7 million in debt and owes upward of $850,000 in tax penalties. After his speech at the DNC, the IRS put Khan's tax audit on hold. Then CNN paid Khan a fee to tell his "story" and to give repeated interviews across the CNN network.[44] While the Clinton campaign and its supporters in the media countered all the pushback stories,[45] the controversy continued to rage, to the detriment of Trump's ability as Republican nominee to get his message out clearly and without distraction. This, of course, affirms the Democrats strategy of setting out Khan as a DNC "gotcha" trap for Trump.

A report from the Harvard University Kennedy School of Government's Shorenstein Center on Media, Politics, and Public Policy analysis assessed the damage the Khan controversy did to the Trump campaign. "The ensuing firestorm brought Trump a slew of coverage during the final week of the convention period," the Shorenstein Center reported. "The reporting was nearly 100 percent negative, and cut across nearly every area of Trump's coverage: his stand on immigration, his personal character, his knowledge of the law, his poll standing. The Khan exchange was that week's most heavily covered development, shifting the balance of news attention strongly in his direction. He got 34 percent of that week's campaign coverage—the highest weekly total of any presidential candidate at any point to date in the 2016 campaign. And the overall tone of his coverage was 91 percent negative—the most negative for any candidate in any single campaign week to date."[46]

On August 7, 2016, the Clinton-supporting *New York Daily News* reported the Khan controversy hurt Trump in the polls. The newspaper reported that a *Washington Post*/ABC News poll showed Clinton leading Trump by eight points with registered voters, with 50 percent for Clinton and 42 percent for Trump. The poll suggested the Khan controversy had "crushed" Trump, with 79 percent of respondents disapproving of Trump's week-long feud with Khan, including 59 percent of Republicans. "The poll indicates that Trump's shameful feud with the Khans—the Gold Star parents of a Muslim US Army captain killed in combat—has already hurt his candidacy," wrote Jason Silverstein, reporting for the *New York Daily News*. "Voters in the poll agreed on little as strongly as their revulsion over Trump's attacks on the family."[47]

CHAPTER 8

The Presidential and
Vice Presidential Debates

@timkaine Cannot believe how often the moderator interrupts
#Pence vs the other guy...so obvious @FoxNew So true!
        Donald J. Trump, posted on Twitter, October 4, 2016[1]

Donald Trump's experience in business had taught him that management changes are sometimes required for continued success. The management team that brings a corporation into existence as entrepreneurs may not be the same management team required as seasoned professionals to take a corporation public.

Trump applied this discipline to his presidential campaign. As he had hired Paul Manafort to replace Corey Lewandowski as campaign manager, the time also came to evaluate if Manafort was the best choice for the general election contest against Democratic Party nominee Hillary Clinton.

Trump Replaces Manafort
On Friday, August 19, 2016, Paul Manafort resigned, signaling a shake-up in the Trump campaign at the top. The Clinton-supporting press had been pushing a campaign against Manafort almost from the moment he

was hired by Trump, arguing that Manafort had accepted money under the table for consulting with Ukraine's ruling political party during the administration of Manafort's main client, former president Viktor F. Yanukovych. "Handwritten ledgers show $12.7 million in undisclosed cash payments designated for Mr. Manafort from Mr. Yanukovych's pro-Russian political party from 2007 to 2012, according to Ukraine's newly formed National Anti-Corruption Bureau," the *New York Times* reported on August 14, 2016. "Investigators assert that the disbursements were part of an illegal off-the-books system whose recipients also included election officials."[2] When Manafort first joined Trump, replacing Corey Lewandowski as campaign manager, the *New York Times* had tried to portray Manafort as a supporter of Russian President Vladimir V. Putin, and Putin's decision to give Yanukovych asylum in Russia after being deposed in 2014. The goal of Clinton-supporters from the time Manafort joined the Trump campaign was to assign Manafort responsibility for Trump's alleged admiration for Putin and all things Russia.[3] Despite the questionable documentation for these allegations and the absence of criminal charges against Manafort in Ukraine, the mainstream media persisted in publishing these accusations.[4]

Clinton crony and dirty trickster Sidney Blumenthal, and most probably Ukrainian oligarch Viktor Pinchuk, engineered Manafort's demise by pedaling bogus charges against Manafort through Ukrainian intelligence. Pinchuk's ties to Hillary go back to the Ukrainian military coup of February 2014, when it surfaced that Pinchuk, a vocal proponent of Ukraine's European integration, made huge contributions to the Clinton Foundation, while Hillary Clinton was the US secretary of state. Between 1999 and 2014, Ukrainian donors with ties to Pinchuk contributed almost $10 million to the Clinton Foundation, pushing England and Saudi Arabia to second and third places respectfully.[5] In 2008, Blumenthal was the first "Birther," supplying Hillary Clinton with information that Barack Obama was not born in Hawaii to use in the 2008 Democratic Party primary contest that year. Blumenthal is also the same man who invented the lie that the attack on our mission in Benghazi was caused by an anti-Islamic video shown online in Turkey. Sid was caught trying to line his pockets in a Libyan side deal that he never disclosed to Hillary Clinton when he was urging the toppling of Gaddafi. Blumenthal thinks he's Ted Sorensen but he's actually Al Capone.

When Ukrainian intelligence found nothing legitimate regarding Manafort's entirely legal campaign services in three democratically held elections they simply had Ukrainian intelligence create a co-ledger with correspondence to no known financial transfer records. There is no evidence admissible in a court of law that Manafort accepted any illegal payments. The "ledger" found at some party clubhouse was most likely fabricated by the Ukrainian Intelligence Service. Recognizing that the mainstream media refuses to see through the baseless and unfounded charges against him, Paul Manafort, not wanting to become a distraction or feed the entire Russian-Putin-Trump canard, resigned. Manafort did what Cory Lewandowski should have done when accused of manhandling a female reporter. He put the good of Donald Trump and his campaign first. That's what a real pro does!

The entire spin by the Clintonistas that Trump and Manafort are somehow in bed with Putin and the Russians is ridiculous. Trump has never met Putin. They have no relationship whatsoever, but their paths have crossed on several occasions. Putin dislikes Manafort because he pushed Yanukovych to have Ukraine join the EU. This is the "New McCarthyism." The Clintons and their vassals essentially accuse Trump and Manafort of treason against their own country when in fact it's Bill and Hillary who have profiteered in the Ukraine, not to mention that they took millions from oligarchs and foreign interests aligned with Putin.

Podesta's Profits from Russian Money-Laundering Operation

At the same time, the mainstream media ignored documentation provided in emails made public by WikiLeaks that John Podesta, Hillary Clinton's 2016 presidential campaign chairman, shielded from government regulators and the American public the shares of stock he received as a member of the board of a company that received millions from a Putin-connected Russian government fund at the time of Secretary of State Clinton's "reset" with Moscow. On October 13, 2016, WND senior staff writer Jerome R. Corsi cited Podesta emails made public by Wiki-Leaks to prove Podesta received 75,000 shares of common stock from Joule Unlimited Technologies, a US energy company tied to Joule Global Holdings B.V., a company in the Netherlands cited in the Panama Papers offshore banking probe as a conduit for money laundered by the Russian government.[6]

Podesta then transferred these shares to a holding company he owned in Utah, Leonidio Holdings LLC, that was under the control of Podesta's daughter, Megan Rouse, who lives in Dublin, California, and operates Megan Rouse Financial Planning from her home in the suburb of San Francisco Bay. Joule Global Stichting and Joule Global Holdings figure prominently as a client of the Panamanian law firm Mossack Fonseca, which is at the heart of the Panama Papers investigation into offshore money-laundering operations on a massive international scale. Russian entities that funneled money to Joule and its related companies, and ultimately to Podesta, include Viktor Vekselberg, a controversial Russian billionaire investor with ties to Vladimir Putin and the Russian government.

Vekselberg owns the Renova Group, a multibillion-dollar private Moscow-based Russian conglomerate with interests in oil, energy, and telecommunication held in Russia, Switzerland, Italy, South Africa, and the United States. He is a board member of Rusnano, the Russian State Investment Fund, as well as president of the Skolkovo Foundation, named for Russia's version of Silicon Valley. Rusnano made a multi-million-dollar investment in the Massachusetts-based Joule Unlimited, owned by Joule Global Holdings B.V. in the Netherlands and Joule Global Stichting, the ultimate controlling entity. WND received documentation, much of it in Russian, from a trusted international banking source showing the Russian government was transferring money to the Clinton Foundation through a regional Russian bank, Metcombank, located in the Sverdlovskava region in the Ural Mountains Federal District of Russia. Metcombank is the bank Vekselberg is using to make transfers to the Clinton Foundation.[7]

The money was passed through the Moscow branch of Metcombank via Deutsche Bank and Trust Company Americas in New York City, ending up in a private bank account at Bank of America that is operated by the Clinton Foundation. From Russian sources, WND was able to document that the final beneficiary of Metcombank is Vekselberg, who owns 99.978 percent of the bank via Renova Holding Ltd. and Renova Assets Ltd. Both are controlled by Vekselberg along with a chain of offshore companies from Cyprus, the Bahamas, and the British Virgin Islands—all of which figure prominently in the offshore banking money-laundering operations documented in the Panama Papers. A report titled "From Russia with Love," issued by the Government Accountability Institute headed by "Clinton Cash" author Peter Schweizer documented in August 2016 that the payments to Podesta appear related to a scheme devised for the transfer of advanced US technology to Russia, including both military technology and solar energy technology as part of Secretary Clinton's "reset" program with Russia, in a move that greatly enhanced Russia's military capabilities.[8]

Enter Steve Bannon

In the shakeup of his top campaign staff, Trump hired as chief strategist Stephen K. Bannon, the chairman of the *Breitbart News* website, as well as Kellyanne Conway, a veteran pollster who had chaired a pro-Cruz political action committee, to be his new campaign manager. The campaign announced Conway would also assume the role Corey Lewandowski had played, traveling with Trump on the campaign trail. Manafort, who announced that he planned to stay on as chief strategist, welcomed the appointment of Bannon and Conway, made three days before he resigned.

The change in management of the campaign from Lewandowski to Manafort signaled the need for a professional manager with expertise managing delegates to get Trump through the final primary battles and the Republican National Convention successfully to win the nomination. With that mission completed, the handoff from Manafort to Bannon and Conway signaled Trump's view that the campaign had now entered a new phase—the third and final phase—which was the general election contest in which Trump faced Clinton one-on-one for the presidency. The Khan controversy left no doubt that the steps Manafort had taken to get Trump on a more scripted message, using a teleprompter to read speeches professionally crafted in advance, was the first step in corralling what Lewandowski had characterized as "letting Trump be Trump." Now, in the general election phase of the 2016 presidential campaign, Trump clearly needed more messaging discipline, which he hoped to obtain from Bannon, as well as more discipline on the campaign trail, which he hoped to obtain from Conway.

The Clinton-supporting mainstream media immediately began demonizing Bannon and Breitbart.com as promoting an anti-immigration, anti-Muslim, pro-white supremacy "alt-right" radical ideology that the mainstream media saw as reinforcing Trump's appeal to Middle America. In turn, pro-Clinton partisans saw Bannon and residents of Middle America "clinging to their guns and Bibles" as fundamentally racist, sexist, xenophobic, anti-Islam, anti-LGBT, and isolationist in their antiglobalist opposition to free-trade measures and the outsourcing of jobs to Mexico and China. [9]

"Basket of Deplorables"

At a fundraising event on Friday, September 7, 2016, Hillary Clinton was recorded on video making one of the most defining and detrimental statements of her presidential campaign. The remark was part of her prepared speech to the "LGBT for Hillary Gala" fundraiser in New York City, where singer Barbara Streisand was scheduled to perform.

"You know, to just be grossly generalistic, you could put half of Trump's supporters into what I call the basket of deplorables. Right?" she said to what the *New York Times* reported was a combination of applause and laughter.[10] "The racist, sexist, homophobic, xenophobic, Islamaphobic—you name it. And unfortunately there are people like that. And he has lifted them up."

Clinton continued, with a knowing smirk on her face: "Donald Trump has promised to appoint Supreme Court justices who will overturn marriage equality. And if you read the ones he says he's likely to appoint, he's not kidding. In fact, if you look at his running mate, his running mate signed a law that would have let businesses to discriminate against LGBT Americans. And there's so much more that I find deplorable in his campaign—that he cozies up to white supremacists, makes racist attacks, calls women pigs, mocks people with disabilities. You can't make this up. He wants to round up and deport 16 million people, calls our military a disaster. And every day he says something else that I find so personally offensive, but also dangerous."

This statement turned out to be Hillary's defining attack on Trump. As far as Hillary and her supporters on the far-left were concerned, Trump was unqualified to be president simply because he did not agree with the far-left's politically correct perspective on a wide range of social issues and problems, ranging from illegal immigration through same-sex marriage. In the lexicon of the far-left, anyone who would dare say "illegal alien"—a proper legal description of what the far-left insists must be referred to as "undocumented workers"—must be castigated as a miserable human being determined to engage in hate speech. That Donald Trump refused to accept the far-left's definition of political correctness was key to his appeal to the silent majority throughout America. Fundamentally, Hillary's argument was that anyone who did not reject Trump and vote for her was part of an evil "basket of deplorables," according to the far-left's politically correct definition of right and wrong.

That Hillary would call the majority of Trump's supporters "deplorable" revealed to Middle America her fundamentally elitist attitude. That Hillary would characterize anyone who did not support her candidacy as despicable, revealed the intolerance that has come to dominate the Democratic Party against those who dared to disagree. The *New York Times* report noted that by Saturday morning #BasketofDeplorables was trending on Twitter, as thousands of Trump supporters began changing their Twitter usernames to include "Deplorable," along the theme of "Deplorable Me." The fact that Hillary Clinton, in her arrogance, believed that her political perspective on social issues carried the certainty of a Papal decree on a doctrine of faith was broadly interpreted across Middle America as an insult. Was it possible that Hillary and the far-left supporting her candidacy had become so detached from political reality in Middle America that she actually thought she could win by disparaging the very people whose votes she needed in November to defeat Trump?

"Wow, Hillary Clinton was SO INSULTING to my supporters, millions of amazing, hardworking people. I think it will cost her at the polls!" Trump tweeted when he learned what Hillary had said.[11]

Following Hillary's speech, singer Barbara Streisand—a diehard Hillary Clinton supporter—performed a parody of the Stephen Sondheim song, "Send in the Clowns," which changed the words so she could sing of a "sad, vulgar clown," delighting the audience at the LGBT fundraiser by ridiculing the Republican nominee. "Is he that rich, maybe he's poor, 'til he reveals his returns, who can be sure?" Streisand sang to an applauding crowd, according to the Associated Press report on the event. "Something's amiss, I don't approve, if he were running the free world, where would we move?" Streisand continued: "And if by chance he gets to heaven, even up there, he'll declare chapter 11. This sad, vulgar clown. You're fired, you clown." Hillary Clinton encouraged her supporters at the LGBT fundraiser to "stage an intervention" if they should be so unfortunate as to have any friends considering the possibility of voting for Trump. "That may be one conversion therapy I'd endorse," Clinton said. "Friends don't let friends vote for Trump."[12]

Immediately, Hillary's "basket of deplorables" remark was compared to the game-changing gaffe Mitt Romney made at a fundraiser, when he was recorded saying that 47 percent of the people, who are dependent upon government and don't pay taxes, will vote for President Obama, "no matter what"[13] Appearing on Sean Hannity's show on Fox News, Trump said this was Hillary Clinton's 47-percent moment. "I think it was far worse," Trump told Hannity. "Let's see what happens, but there are a lot of very angry people. People are really upset that she would feel that way. That's her true feeling."[14] A *Washington Post*/ABC News survey asked people whether "it's fair or unfair to describe a large portion of Trump supporters as prejudiced against women and minorities." More than twice as many registered voters thought this approach was out of bounds, 65 percent, as said it was fair game, 30 percent.[15]

Hillary Takes a Fall

The Clinton campaign spokeswoman Jennifer Palmieri specifically claimed that I had manufactured Hillary's health issues. The idea that I had created a false narrative regarding Hillary's health was undercut by her haggard physical appearance, light campaign schedule, trouble walking up three steps, and, eventually, her collapse in 70-degree weather on 9/11. Voters would learn more about Hillary's health problems as the campaign unfolded.

Then on Labor Day, Monday, September 5, 2016, concerns over Hillary Clinton's health resumed when Clinton labored through a severe coughing fit during a speech in Cleveland, Ohio, followed by another coughing attack she experienced later in the day during a press conference on her airplane. Just moments after being introduced by her running mate, Tim Kaine, Hillary went into the first coughing episode at Lake Easter Park. "Every time I think about Trump, I think I'm allergic," Hillary quipped, trying to divert attention from the coughing fit that interrupted her speech. People in the crowd began shouting, "Get her some water," as Clinton fought to regain her composure. Later, on her campaign airplane, a staffer handed Clinton a glass of water as soon as she began coughing. As Clinton struggled to say, "Excuse me," Fox News broke away from the press conference and went back to the studio broadcast. None of the major television networks covered Clinton's Labor Day coughing fits.[16]

On Sunday, September 11, 2016, Trump and Clinton, both self-described "New Yorkers," paused their campaigns to attend in person the 9/11 ceremony at Ground Zero, the former site of the World Trade

Center twin towers.[17] Clinton abruptly left the ceremony early, around 9:30 a.m., as she began to feel faint, according to reports her staff later gave the press. A dramatic video, widely broadcast after the incident, showed Hillary, supported by staffers approaching a black SUV to leave the 9/11 ceremony, stumbling badly, as two security men who appeared to be Secret Service, grabbed her to lift her into the vehicle as she appeared to lose consciousness and possibly even faint.[18] Two NYPD officers told NBC news that Clinton "fell ill and may have fainted" just before she left, while Fox News reported Clinton had experienced some type of "medical episode."[19] The video clearly showed Hillary's knees buckling, such that security staff lifting her into the SUV had to prevent her from falling to the pavement. Photographs taken of the sidewalk after the SUV departed show a shoe Hillary left behind as she was helped into the vehicle.

> Instead of being rushed to a local hospital for a medical examination, the SUV departing Ground Zero rushed Hillary to the apartment of her daughter, Chelsea, on New York's Lower East Side. About two hours later, Hillary emerged from the apartment building, walking on her own. Clinton waved at the gathered crowds saying, "It's a beautiful day in New York." Asked whether she was "feeling better," Clinton responded, "Yes, thank you very much." Clinton's campaign issued a statement, saying Clinton left the 9/11 ceremony early because she felt "overheated" and was suffering from dehydration. After leaving Chelsea's apartment in New York City, Clinton returned to Chappaqua, New York, where Bill Clinton was waiting, having not attended the ceremony. In Chappaqua, Clinton's personal physician Dr. Lisa R. Bardack examined her later that day, issuing the following statement: "On Friday, during follow up evaluation of her prolonged cough, she was diagnosed with pneumonia," Bardack said. "She was put on antibiotics, and advised to rest and modify her schedule. While at this morning's event, she became overheated and dehydrated. I have just examined her and she is now re-hydrated and recovering nicely."[20]

According to the National Weather Service, the temperature during the 9/11 ceremony was 79 degrees with 54 percent humidity at 9:51 a.m. in Manhattan, hardly the type of sweltering summer weather that typically leaves people feeling overheated to the point of fainting. TMZ emailed Clinton's spokespeople and asked why the campaign did not disclose the pneumonia when they first issued a statement saying it was dehydration, despite the fact Dr. Bardack's statement suggested the campaign had known about the pneumonia diagnosis for two days before the 9/11 ceremony at which Clinton apparently suffered a health episode and fainted. TMZ reported Clinton's campaign did not respond to their question.[21]

Clinton had been photographed arriving at the 9/11 event wearing a pair of cobalt blue sunglasses, identified as Z1 cobalt blue lenses manufactured by Zeiss that are typically prescribed by physicians to prevent seizures associated with epilepsy. The lenses are designed to block most of the red spectrum of light, considered the most likely to induce seizures in people who have photo-sensitivities associated with neurological diseases that include epilepsy and Parkinson's disease. Photographs from the event show Hillary walking toward Ground Zero with her left wrist in upward position, held by a woman assisting her who appears to be monitoring continuously Hillary's pulse as she walks. As observed by Russ Vaughn writing in the *American Thinker*, Hillary's right hand being held to her chest, "an abnormal posture for a walking human but a common one for those with Parkinson's, who employ it to mask both tremors and unnatural finger positioning and movement of the fingers, as well as a phenomenon called pill-rolling most usually associated with that disease."[22]

On Tuesday, September 6, 2016, the *Washington Post*'s Chris Cillizza, who writes a blog aptly named *The Fix*, objected to the extensive coverage the *Drudge Report* was giving to Clinton's Labor Day coughing incidents.[23] "The simple fact is that there is *zero* evidence that anything is seriously wrong with Clinton," he insisted. "If suffering an occasional coughing fit is evidence of a major health problem, then 75 percent of the country must have that mystery illness. And I am one of them."[24] Clinton's fainting episode on 9/11 pushed even a strong Clinton supporter like Cillizza over the top. In his blog on September 11, 2016, Cillizza changed his tune. "Clinton may be totally fine—and I certainly hope she is," Cillizza began, reversing his position on Clinton's health issues. "But we are 58 days away from choosing the person who will lead the country for the next four years, and she is one of the two candidates with a real chance of winning. Taking the Clinton team's word for it on her health—in light of the episode on Sunday morning—is no longer enough. Reasonable people can—and will—have real questions about her health." Cillizza continued to note what he had written the previous Tuesday was no longer operative. "A coughing episode is almost always just a coughing episode," he continued, explaining his reversal. "But when coupled with Clinton's 'overheating' on Sunday morning— with temperatures something short of sweltering—Clinton and her team needed to say something about what happened and why the press was in the dark for so long."[25]

Hillary Refuses Neurological Examination

After the health episode Hillary experienced on 9/11, several physicians went public, expressing their concern that Hillary should submit to a professional medical examination by qualified neurological specialists to determine if her medical problems were related to something more serious than pneumonia.

On September 12, 2016, Jerome R. Corsi reported at WND.com that two physicians—one who suspects Clinton has Parkinson's disease and one who does not—both agreed that Clinton is suffering from a serious neurological disease that should disqualify her from being president.[26]

Theodore "Ted" Noel, a retired anesthesiologist in Orlando, Florida, with thirty-six years' experience and a background in critical care medicine explained to WND why he was so convinced that Hillary Clinton has Parkinson's disease and produced several videos arguing that point.

In sharp contrast, Dr. Daniel Kassicieh, DO, a dual board certified osteopathic neurologist and a leading headache specialist who directs the Florida Headache and Movement Disorder Center in Sarasota, Florida, told WND in an exclusive telephone interview that he is equally convinced Hillary Clinton does not exhibit any of the characteristic features of patients with Parkinson's. Kassicieh noted the concussion Hillary Clinton suffered in December 2012 that led to a serious blood clot requiring hospitalization may also have caused her to suffer post-concussion syndrome, with symptoms including confusion, headaches, and dizziness, and the long-term consequence of mental impairment and loss of memory that could be precursors of dementia. "An individual who suffers from post-concussion syndrome is not medically qualified to be president," Kassicieh explained. "Minimal cognitive syndrome can be a warning precursor to dementia."

For his part, Noel argued that Parkinson's is a progressive disease that would immediately disqualify Clinton from running for president if her campaign ever were to allow an independent medical examination to be conducted by a qualified team of neurological specialists. "Parkinson's disease is a progressive disease from which there is no medical cure," Noel argued, buttressing his conclusion that should Clinton's campaign acknowledge she has the disease, her presidential bid would be over. But he hedged, commenting that even if he was wrong and Clinton was suffering from some brain disorder other than Parkinson's, he still insists that Clinton is suffering from "a major neurological process that almost certainly renders her incapable of performing effectively the duties of the president." Noel produced a sixteen-minute video, in which he explains the evidence that led him to conclude Clinton is suffering from Parkinson's. The video received more than 4 million views in the seventeen days between when he first posted it on YouTube on August 29, 2016, and Hillary's "health episode" suffered in New York City on September 11, 2016, during the campaign.[27]

"Parkinson's disease involves a clinical diagnosis," Kassicieh insisted. "There is no clinical test that you can perform that proves a patient has Parkinson's disease. Parkinson's patients have a very characteristic appearance to them, such that you can almost look at them and tell they have Parkinson's. Hillary doesn't display the behaviors and facial features characteristic to Parkinson's disease sufferers." Kassicieh was equally certain Clinton does display characteristics of other neurological diseases, noting as evidence of this conclusion Clinton's gait disorder, her persistent falls, her memory problems that Kassicieh observed seem to be getting worse with time, as well as this persistent cough that Kassicieh notes is a recurring symptom. "Those, I believe, are important medical problems, but not problems consistent with Parkinson's disease," he insisted. "Still, I believe Hillary has suffered multiple dizzy spells and I think she has suffered more falling instances and concussions than her campaign staff has admitted," he continued. "The problem with concussions is that they are cumulative. The brain does not recover completely from concussions, so particularly in older individuals, like Mrs. Clinton who is 68 years old, multiple concussions are an even more serious problem, given that memory problems can signal mental cognitive impairment that could lead to dementia."

On September 22, 2016, a Tampa, Florida, ABC News reporter Sarina Fazan asked Hillary Clinton whether she would be willing to take neurological exams in the wake of recent health concerns. ABC News reported Clinton laughed off the question. "I am very sorry I got pneumonia," Clinton said. "I am very glad that antibiotics took care of it and that's behind us now. I have met the standard that everybody running for president has met in terms of releasing information about my health." Clinton insisted she saw no need for neurological tests. "The information is very clear, and the information, as I said, meets the standards that every other person running for president has ever had to meet."[28]

Trump vs. Clinton, First Presidential Debate, Hofstra University, Hempstead, New York, Monday, September 26, 2016

The *New York Times* summed up the first presidential debate as a solid win for Hillary Clinton. "Hillary Clinton dominated a final series of debate exchanges with Donald J. Trump about national security and gender, telling voters they could not trust her opponent with nuclear weapons and warning that he does not respect women," *New York Times* reporters Alex Burns and Matt Flegenheimer wrote.[29]

Criticism from conservatives focused on the moderator NBC *Nightly News* host Lester Holt. Brent Bozell, the president of the Media Research Center, issued a statement following the first debate that attacked Holt for bias. "Lester Holt clearly heard the cries of his colleagues in the liberal media to be tough on Trump and ease up on Hillary loud and clear," Bozell wrote. "Holt continually challenged, fact-checked, and interrupted Trump and not once challenged Hillary. Holt pounded Trump repeatedly on the birth certificate controversy, his position on Iraq, his tax returns, and whether or not Hillary looked presidential." Bozell felt that as tough as Holt was on Trump, he went easy on Clinton. "Where were the questions on the Clinton Foundation or Benghazi or her email server?" Bozell asked. "These are the questions that drive right to the heart of whether Hillary is ready to be president and yet viewers tuning in tonight heard nothing about these important issues. Lester Holt failed in his role as a moderator. Period."[30]

The major fireworks of the evening occurred toward the end of the debate, when Holt asked Trump about Hillary's qualifications to be president. "Mr. Trump, Secretary Clinton became the first woman nominated for president by a major party earlier this month," Holt began. "You said quote, 'she doesn't have a presidential look.' She's standing here right now. What do you mean by that?" The question had all the earmarks of a "gotcha" set-up that was designed to trap Trump, while serving up to Clinton a softball she could knock out of the park.

"She doesn't have the look. She doesn't have the stamina," Trump answered. I said she doesn't have the stamina. And I don't believe she does have the stamina. To be president of this country you need tremendous stamina."

This didn't satisfy Holt. The quote was, "I just don't think she has a presidential look." Holt pressed.

Trump refused to be baited into answering the question on the basis of appearance, an obvious trap that could paint Trump as a sexist. "Wait a minute, Lester, you asked me a question," Trump objected. "Did you ask me a question? You have to be able to negotiate our trade deals. You have to be able to negotiate, that's right, with Japan with Saudi Arabia." Trump persisted, arguing that the demands of the presidency might tax Hillary, without specifying why he felt that way. "I mean, can you imagine we're defending Saudi Arabia and with all of the money they have we're defending them and they're not paying . . . all you have to do is to speak to them. You have so many different things you have to be able to do and I don't believe that Hillary has the stamina."

Holt again interrupted, insisting Hillary needed to respond. The sequence handed over to Hillary had the appearance of pre-arrangement.

"Well, as soon as he travels to one hundred and twelve countries and negotiates a peace deal, a cease-fire, a release of dissidents, and opening of new opportunities and nations around the world or even spends eleven hours testifying in front of a congressional committee, he can talk to me about stamina," Hillary responded, delivering the refutation her staff had urged to Trump's attacks in stump speeches that Hillary lacked stamina—a question the Hillary camp clearly wanted to put to rest, especially after her fainting episode in New York on September 11, 2016.

Trump attacked Hillary on making "bad deals," specifically referencing Iran and the $150 million the Obama administration had agreed to pay Iran as a condition of finalizing the negotiations.

As Holt started to ask his final question, Hillary interrupted, delivering her sexism attack, the second punch of the two-punch response she wanted to deliver on Trump for having dared raise the "stamina issue."

Hillary cut in aggressively, "Well, one thing Lester, is you know, he tried to switch from looks to stamina but this is a man who has called women pigs, slobs, and dogs . . . and someone who has said pregnancy is an inconvenience to employers," When Trump tried to object, Hillary barely paused to take a breath, "who has said women don't deserve equal pay unless they do as good a job as men and one of the worst things he said was about a woman in a beauty contest, he loves beauty contests, supporting them and hanging around them. And he called this woman Miss Piggy," Hillary said, looking pleased she got a chance to deliver the attack on script. "Then he called her Miss Housekeeping because she was Latina. Donald, she has a name."

"Where did you find it?" Trump asked.

"Her name is Alicia Machado and she has become a US citizen and you can bet she's going to vote this November," Hillary said, without providing the audience in the auditorium or the 84 million watching on television any more detail than the woman's name, the fact she was Hispanic, and the suggestion Trump had wronged her.

Trump sensed the set-up. He began by objecting to all the negative advertising the Clinton campaign had launched against him. "I was going to say something extremely rough to Hillary, to her family, and I said to myself I can't do it. I just can't do it. It's inappropriate, it's not nice," Trump said. "But she spent hundreds of millions of dollars on negative ads on me—many of which are absolutely untrue. They're untrue and they're misrepresentations. And I will tell you this, Lester, it's not nice and I don't, I don't deserve that. But it's certainly not a nice thing that she's done. It's hundreds of millions of ads and the only gratifying thing is I saw the polls come in today and with all of that money, over $200 million spent and I'm either winning or tied."

Holt ignored Trump's response, determined to get in his final question, asking each nominee whether they were willing to accept the outcome of the election as the will of the voters. This too seemed a bit too convenient, as if Holt were reading from a script in which the question was crafted to advance a Clinton narrative the Clinton-partisan mainstream media would certainly parrot in post-election coverage, should Trump launch an Al Gore-type challenge to the Election Day vote totals.

Hillary answered by suggesting Trump would do damage to "our democracy" if he refused in advance to agree to forego challenges to the vote totals on Election Day. "Well, I support our democracy," Hillary began her answer, suggesting the concept of "democracy" was equated to not challenging an Election Day result. "And sometimes you win and sometimes you lose, but I certainly will support the outcome of this election. And I know Donald is trying very hard to plant doubts about it but I hope the people out there understand this election's really up to you. It's not about us so much as it is about you and your families and the kinds of country and future you want. So I sure hope you will get out and vote as though your future depended on it because I think it does."

Given the extent to which Clinton and her supporters objected to the Election Day result that made Trump president-elect, there is no doubt this question and Hillary's answer were designed to promote a developing Clinton meme designed to force Trump to eliminate in advance his legal rights to question a general election outcome, even if Trump had probable cause to believe it was fraudulent. Remember, at the time of the first presidential debate, in late September, the polls gave every reason for Hillary to believe she would win in a landslide.

Trump reacted as if the question were an out-of-context surprise. "I want to make America great again," he commented. "We are a nation that is seriously troubled." Then, recovering, he discussed deporting eight hundred people, "perhaps they pressed the wrong button, or perhaps worse than that, it was corruption." In struggling to understand just what he was being asked and why, Trump seemed to sense his answer ought to involve "pressing the wrong button" and "corruption"—key issues in the concern over Democratic Party voter fraud that the GOP suspected given the Democrats unyielding opposition to voter ID laws, as well as their insistence that non-citizens should be allowed to vote.

In response to a question Holt posed over hacking and cyber security, Clinton also hit Trump over Russian President Vladimir Putin, suggesting that Trump had encouraged Putin to hack into Democratic files. "But increasingly, we are seeing cyber-attacks coming from states, organs of states," Clinton answered. "The most recent and troubling of these has been Russia. There is no doubt now that Russia has used cyber-attacks against all kinds of organizations in our country." From there, Clinton again advanced a meme that was to become a post-election Democratic narrative—that Putin stole the election for Trump by leaking hacked documents from the DNC and from Hillary's campaign chairman, John Podesta. "And I am deeply concerned about this. I know Donald's very praise-worthy of Vladimir Putin, but Putin is playing a really tough, long game here," Hillary continued. "And one of the things he's done is to let loose cyber attackers to hack into government files, to hack into personal files, hack into the Democratic National Committee."

Trump reacted as if he thought Clinton's answer to the cyber security question was preposterous. "As far as the cyber, I agree to parts of what

Secretary Clinton said," Trump said, when he finally got a chance to respond. "We should be better than anybody else and perhaps we're not. I don't think anybody knows that it was Russia that broke into the DNC. She's saying, 'Russia, Russia, Russia.' I don't—maybe it was. I mean, it could be Russia, but it could also be China. It could also be lots of other people. It also could be somebody sitting on their bed who weighs four hundred pounds, ok?" Trump had not fully caught onto the attack Clinton and the Democrats had prepared. To counter the damage already done by WikiLeaks and Julian Assange's release of DNC documents that forced Debbie Wasserman Schultz to resign, Clinton and the Democrats wanted to put the blame on Trump, claiming the Russians were somehow in cahoots with Trump, implementing a plan devised in Moscow to rig the election against Hillary. Trump was shocked not only because he considered the idea of such a plot preposterous, but also at the audacity of Hillary to advance the conspiracy theory as reality without a shred of evidence proving Russia's culpability, let alone Trump's complicity.

Trump's "Fat-Shamed" Beauty Queen

The article that appeared in *Vogue* the next day, Tuesday, September 27, 2016, entitled "Who is Alicia Machado? The Beauty Queen That Trump Once Fat-Shamed,"[31] suggested the Alicia Machado attack was pre-arranged between the Clinton campaign and a more-than-willing mainstream media player well in advance of the first presidential debate. "For the majority of Americans, Machado's name will not ring a bell. But almost every Venezuelan, myself included, remembers when the former Miss Venezuela won the title of Miss Universe in 1996. (After all, beauty pageants are somewhat of a national sport over there.)," *Vogue* author Patricia Garcia wrote. "We also could never forget how humiliating it was to see Machado later fat-shamed in front of international press by Trump." *Vogue* explained that Machado, who was twenty when she earned her crown, went from 117–118 pounds to 160–170 pounds—a weight gain that induced Trump to call her "an eating machine." The story told by *Vogue* was that Trump then shamed Machado by "parading her in front of 90 media outlets while they photographed and filmed her working out next to a trainer." *Vogue* ended the article by noting Machado had just posted on Instagram that she intended to vote for Hillary on November 8. "I'm so proud and inspiration (sic) to be a U.S. Citizen! I'll be Voting! All my power and my support with my next president @hillaryclinton.

Miss Housekeeping and Miss Piggy can vote @realdonaldtrump. Touché, Alicia."

Predictably, Trump responded. On Tuesday, September 27, 2016, Trump called the "Fox and Friends" morning show at Fox News. "I know that person. That person was a Miss Universe person," Trump said. "And she was the worst we ever had, the worst, the absolute worst, she was impossible," he said. "She was a Miss Universe contestant and ultimately a winner, who they had a terrifically difficult time as Miss Universe. She was the winner and she gained a massive amount of weight, and it was a real problem. We had a real problem. Not only that, her attitude. This was many years ago. So Hillary went back into the years and found the girl and talked about her as if she was Mother Teresa and it wasn't quite that way, but it's okay."[32] Trump's appearance on Fox News the day after did little to counter the two-minute video the Clinton campaign had prepared to release to the press an hour after the first debate ended. "He was very overwhelming. I was very scared of him," Machado said in Spanish on the video. "He'd yell at me all the time. He'd tell me 'you look ugly' or 'you look fat.' Sometimes he'd 'play' with me and say 'Hello Miss Piggy, hello Miss Housekeeping.'"[33]

As if on cue, extreme liberal Michael Barbaro of the *New York Times* jumped on the "Miss Piggy" bandwagon. For twenty years, Alicia Machado has lived with the agony of what Donald J. Trump did to her after she won the Miss Universe title: shame her, over and over, for gaining weight," Barbaro wrote with coauthor Megan Twohey in the *New York Times'* morning edition the day after the first debate. "Private scolding was apparently insufficient. Mr. Trump, who was an executive producer of the pageant, insisted on accompanying Ms. Machado, then a teenager, to a gym, where dozens of reporters and cameramen watched as she exercised," Barbaro and Twohey continued. "Mr. Trump, in his trademark suit and tie, posed for photographs beside her as she burned calories in front of members of the news media. 'This is somebody who likes to eat, Mr. Trump said from inside the gym."[34]

This was not the first time Barbaro and Twohey had quoted Alicia Machado. She was also included in an article the pair coauthored, entitled "Crossing the Line: How Donald Trump Behaved with Women in Private," published in the *New York Times* on May 14, 2016.[35] Barbaro and Twohey's subtitle revealed their agenda: "Interviews reveal unwelcome advances, a shrewd reliance on ambition, and unsettling workplace conduct over decades." Based on what the *New York Times* claimed were fifty interviews conducted over six weeks, the newspaper portrayed Trump as a woman-abusing sexist, citing incidents and verbal exchanges Trump told the *New York Times* were invented. "A lot of things get made up over the years," Trump told the reporters. "I have always treated women with great respect. And women will tell you that." The *New York Times* assisted Hillary by printing the sensational, typified by this excerpt Barbaro and Twohey penned: "This is the public treatment of some women by Mr. Trump, the presumptive Republican nominee for president: degrading, impersonal, performed. 'That must be a pretty picture, you dropping to your knees, he told a female contestant on *The Celebrity Apprentice*. Rosie O'Donnell, he said, had a 'fat, ugly face. A lawyer who needed to pump milk for a newborn? 'Disgusting,' he [Trump] said."

Yet, the Clinton campaign, in portraying Alicia Machado as the victim, had failed to tell the whole story. "The Venezuelan beauty queen who made headlines two years ago for putting on weight after being crowned Miss Universe is back in the news," the Associated Press reported on January 23, 1998. "A lawyer for a man who was shot outside a church in November said Friday that Alicia Machado, 21, was seen driving the car in which her boyfriend sped away from the scene of the shooting. Francisco Sbert Mousko suffered brain damage when two bullets punctured his skull outside a church where his dead wife was being eulogized."[36] The Associated Press next reported on February 5, 1998, Machado had threatened to kill Judge Maximiliano Fuenmayor after he indicted her boyfriend for attempted murder.[37] The *Daily Mail* reported Machado was not indicted because there was insufficient evidence to prove the claim. But the indictment for threatening to kill a judge and for being an accomplice to murder, if it had led to a criminal trial would have carried a jail term of up to eighteen months had Machado been found guilty.[38]

But the Machado real-life saga does not even end there. In 2005, the Philadelphia Phillies major league baseball star, outfielder Bobby Abreu, broke off his engagement with Machado after she went on a reality television show in Mexico and had sex on camera with a fellow cast member playing her housemate. After her success in Hispanic soap operas on television, Machado appeared nude for a Mexican edition of *Playboy* in 2006. Mexico's attorney general claimed Machado had a child with narco-cartel drug lord José Gerardo Álvarez Vázquez, aka, "El Indio," as reported by the Mexican newspaper *El Economista* in an article published in 2010.[39]

New York Times Hits Trump on Taxes

On Saturday, October 1, 2016, the *New York Times* hit Trump on what the Hillary campaign had anticipated would be a major tax scandal. "Donald J. Trump declared a $916 million loss on his 1995 income tax returns, a tax deduction so substantial it could have allowed him to legally avoid paying any federal income taxes for up to 18 years, records obtained by the *New York Times* show," a team of four reporters including Megan Twohey wrote in the article's lead paragraph.[40] The newspaper failed to disclose who had leaked Trump's 1995 income tax return and the Clinton campaign did not raise the same fuss Hillary had raised charging the Russians hacked the Democratic National Committee emails because Putin wanted Trump to win. Instead, the *New York Times* published without comment or explanation a photocopy of the line showing the $916 million loss lifted from the 1995 tax returns obtained by the newspaper.

"The 1995 tax records never before disclosed, reveal the extraordinary tax benefits that Mr. Trump, the Republican presidential nominee, derived from the financial wreckage he left behind in the early 1990s through mismanagement of three Atlantic City casinos, his ill-fated foray into the airline business and his ill-timed purchase of the Plaza Hotel in Manhattan," the newspaper reported. "Tax experts hired by the *Times* to analyze Mr. Trump's 1995 records said that tax rules especially advantageous to wealthy filers would have allowed Mr. Trump to use his $916 million loss to cancel out an equivalent amount of taxable income over an 18-year period."

The *New York Times* noted that the $916 million loss could have eliminated any federal income taxes Trump may have owed otherwise on the $50,000 to $100,000 he was paid for each episode of *The Apprentice*, or the roughly $45 million he was paid between 1995 and 2009 when he was chairman or chief executive of the publicly traded company Trump created to assume ownership of his troubled Atlantic City casinos. "Ordinary investors in the new company, meanwhile, saw the value of their shares plunge to 17 cents from $35.50, while scores of contractors went unpaid for work on Mr. Trump's casinos and casino bondholders received pennies on the dollar," the article noted.

In response to the article, Trump wrote a letter to the *New York Times* saying, "The only news here is that the more than 20 year-old alleged tax document was illegally obtained, a further demonstration that the *New York Times*, like establishment media in general, is an extension of the Clinton Campaign, the Democratic Party, and their global special interests."[41] The letter pointed out that Trump "is a highly-skilled businessman who has a fiduciary responsibility to his business, his family, and his employees to pay no more tax than legally required." Importantly, the *New York Times* had failed to prove that Trump had violated any law, reporting accurately instead that federal tax law in 1995 allowed Trump to carry forward the $916 million loss to reduce taxable income in future years—all precisely what Trump did. Trump's letter also pointed out that Trump in the years under question had paid hundreds of millions of dollars in property taxes, sales and excise taxes, real estate taxes, city taxes, state taxes, employee taxes, and federal taxes, along with very substantial charitable contributions.

"Mr. Trump knows the tax code far better than anyone who has ever run for President and he is the only one who knows how to fix it," Trump's response letter to the newspaper continued. "The incredible skills Mr. Trump has shown in building his businesses are the skills we need to rebuild this country. Hillary Clinton is a corrupt public official who violated federal law; Donald Trump is an extraordinarily successful private businessman who followed the law and created tens of thousands of jobs for Americans."

The Clinton campaign immediately called the *New York Times* report a "bombshell," calling once again for Trump to release his full income tax returns, something Trump had successfully resisted doing throughout the presidential campaign. Trump surrogates New Jersey Governor Chris Christie and former New York Mayor Rudy Giuliani explained the story was "very good" for the GOP nominee because it showed the "genius of Donald Trump." Quickly, the *New York Times* story flopped. "I pay my lawful tax and [Trump] paid his lawful tax," he said. "If he did not take advantage of those tax deductions or advantages that he has he could be sued," Giuliani explained. "His obligation is to make money for his enterprises and save money for his enterprises. It would be insane for him not to take advantage."[42]

Why was the *New York Times* so far to the left in its editorial policies that it imagined there was a moral obligation to pay income taxes that, according to IRS rules, you do not legally owe? The federal courts since *Helvering v. Gregory*, decided in 1935, have held to Judge Learned Hand's famous statement "there is nothing sinister in so arranging affairs as to keep taxes as low as possible," establishing the principle that "tax avoidance"— a legal scheme to pay the minimum federal income tax required—is not a crime, while "tax evasion"—an illegal scheme to avoid paying federal income tax owed is a criminal offense. Without admitting embarrassment, the *New York Times*, some thirty days after the first article, shifted ground to argue the real offense was that Trump, to gain the $916 million loss carry-forward, had used "a tax avoidance maneuver so legally dubious that his own lawyers advised him that the Internal Revenue Service would most likely declare it improper if he were audited."[43] Yet, the problem persisted. The *New York Times*, in the second article published on October 31, 2016, was forced a second time to admit Trump had done nothing illegal. The maneuver Trump used had not been outlawed by Congress until later, after 1995. In other words, the *New York Times* was forced to admit that Trump's 1995 tax return, obtained surreptitiously by the newspaper, revealed no criminal activity—attesting instead only to the adroitness with which Trump, along with his tax attorneys and tax accountants, had utilized federal income tax law to his financial benefit.

This is another story that backfired on the Clinton campaign. That Trump lost $916 million in 1995 and managed to turn it into a tax-loss carry-forward convinced millions of Americans that nobody really needed to see Trump's income tax returns, just as Trump had maintained. At Trump's level of wealth, the tax law is so complicated that the average person is not qualified to read, much less understand, his income tax filings. Moreover, that Trump survived nearly $1 billion in losses in 1995 convinced millions of Americans that he had to be the billionaire he claimed to be. How else could he have survived a loss of that magnitude without declaring bankruptcy? Finally, if Trump could manage to get out of a personal debt of that magnitude, maybe he was the exact right choice to turn around a $10 trillion debt Obama had accumulated in just eight years by doubling the amount of national debt accumulated by all previous US presidents combined.

Pence v. Kaine, Vice Presidential Debate, Longwood University, Farmville, Virginia, Tuesday, October 4, 2016

In the opinion of many political commentators, Democratic Senator Tim Kaine's aggressiveness in the first and only vice presidential debate managed to get him characterized as a "scary clown" on Twitter, as he interrupted Republican Governor Mike Pence a total of seventy times during the ninety-minute debate, with Pence somehow managing to maintain his statesmanlike composure to stick to the ideas he wanted to communicate.[44] Even the *Los Angeles Times* scored the vice presidential debate a win for Pence.[45] Predictably, the partisan *New York Times* called the debate for Kaine, writing as follows: "Mr. Kaine challenged Mr. Pence repeatedly to defend statements or proposals made by Donald J. Trump during his chaotic and improvisational presidential campaign, forcing Mr. Pence to filibuster and dodge for minutes on end."[46]

When the moderator, CBS News reporter Elaine Quijano, wasn't interrupting Pence herself, she frequently appeared to lose control, as Kaine interrupted Pence repeatedly, forcing Pence to insist on time to explain his positions properly. Here is an interesting sequence at the beginning of the debate:

> PENCE: But I will also tell you that it's important in this moment to remember that Hillary Clinton had a private server in her home that had classified information on it . . .
>
> QUIJANO: And I don't—thirty seconds is up.
>
> PENCE: . . . about drone strikes, e-mails from the president of the United States of America were on there.
>
> QUIJANO: Right.
>
> PENCE: Her private server was subject to being hacked by foreign . . .
>
> (CROSSTALK)
>
> QUIJANO: I'd like to ask you about Syria, Governor.
>
> PENCE: We could put cybersecurity first if we just make sure the next secretary of state doesn't have a private server.
>
> (CROSSTALK)
>
> KAINE: And all investigation concluded that not one reasonable prosecutor would take any additional step. You don't get to decide the rights and wrongs of this. We have a justice system that does that. And a Republican FBI director did an investigation and concluded that . . .
>
> (CROSSTALK) QUIJANO: All right, we are moving on now. Two hundred fifty thousand people . . .
>
> PENCE: If your son or my son handled classified information the way Hillary Clinton did . . .
>
> QUIJANO: . . . one hundred thousand of them children—Governor . . .

PENCE: . . . they'd be court martialed.

KAINE: That is absolutely false and you know that.

PENCE: Absolutely true.

KAINE: And you know that, Governor.

QUIJANO: Governor . . .

PENCE: It's absolutely true.

QUIJANO: Gentlemen, please.

KAINE: Because the FBI did an investigation.

QUIJANO: Gentlemen.

KAINE: And they concluded that there was no reasonable prosecutor who would take it further. Sorry.

QUIJANO: Senator Kaine, Governor Pence, please.[47]

Kaine began the debate by noting he and his wife were the parents of a Marine, adding, "the thought of Donald Trump as commander-in-chief scares us to death." Pence, who also has a son who is a Marine, responded with his opening statement, "For the last seven-and-a-half years, we've seen America's place in the world weakened. We've seen an economy stifled by more taxes, more regulation, a war on coal, and a failing health care reform come to be known as Obamacare, and the American people know that we need to make a change."

In response to the next question asking Kaine if questions about Clinton's emails or the Clinton Foundation are responsible for 60 percent of voters not trusting Hillary, Kaine praised Hillary's past as a civil rights lawyer with the Children's Defense Fund, before ripping into Trump. "Donald Trump always puts himself first," Kaine said. "He built a business career, in the words of one of his own campaign staffers, 'off the backs of the little guy.' And as a candidate, he started his campaign with a speech where he called Mexicans rapists and criminals, and he has pursued the discredited and really outrageous lie that President Obama wasn't born in the United States." Kaine suggested Trump, in contrast to Clinton, wanted America to return to an era of racial segregation. "It is so painful to suggest that we go back to . . . think about these days where an African-American could not be a citizen of the United States," Kaine continued. "And I can't imagine how Governor Pence can defend the insult-driven selfish "me first" style of Donald Trump."

When Quijano asked Pence a corresponding question, positing that 67 percent of voters feel Trump is a risky choice, while 65 percent do not feel Trump "has the right kind of temperament" to be president, Pence began by pointing out that Kaine was advancing the Clinton strategy of running an insult-driven campaign. "Well, let me—let me say first and foremost that, Senator, you and Hillary Clinton would know a lot about an insult-driven campaign," Pence responded. "It really is remarkable. At a time when literally, in the wake of Hillary Clinton's tenure as Secretary of State, where she was the architect of the Obama administration's foreign policy, we see entire portions of the world, particularly the wider Middle East, literally spinning out of control. I mean, the situation we're watching hour by hour in Syria today is the result of the failed foreign policy and the weak foreign policy that Hillary Clinton helped lead in this administration and create. The newly emboldened—the aggression of Russia, whether it was in Ukraine or now their heavy-handed approach. . ."

Kaine interrupted, saying snidely, "You guys love Russia. You both have said . . ." Pence ignored Kaine, finishing his sentence, ". . . their heavy-handed approach." Kaine immediately retorted, advancing the Clinton narrative on Russia, "You both have said—you both have said Vladimir Putin is a better leader than the president." When Quijano tried to intervene, insisting the subject of Russia would be asked in a moment, Kaine pressed ahead with his attack on Russia, ignoring Quijano's intervention as monitor. Kaine insisted, "These guys have praised Vladimir Putin as a great leader. How can that . . ." The transcript then indicates Pence and Kaine spoke over one another in crosstalk. Quijano addressed Kaine, "Yes, and we'll get to that, Senator. We do have that [the subject of Russia] coming up here. But in the meantime . . ."

Kaine's attacks on Trump were insistent and repetitive. Note how many times he brings up the subject of Mexico. About a third of the way into the debate, Kaine assaulted Trump with a litany of what he considered unacceptable, politically incorrect statements. "And I just want to talk about the tone that's set from the top. Donald Trump during his campaign has called Mexicans rapists and criminals," Kaine said. "He's called women slobs, pigs, dogs, disgusting. I don't like saying that in front of my wife and my mother. He attacked an Indiana-born federal judge and said he was unqualified to hear a federal lawsuit because his parents were Mexican. He went after John McCain, a POW, and said he wasn't a hero because he'd been captured. He said African-Americans are living in Hell. And he perpetrated this outrageous and bigoted lie that President Obama is not a U.S. citizen." But Kaine didn't stop there.

"If you want to have a society where people are respected and respect laws, you can't have somebody at the top that demeans every group that he talks about," he continued. "And I just—again, I cannot believe that Governor Pence will defend the insult-driven campaign that Donald Trump has run."

A few minutes later, Kaine picked up the Mexican theme again. "When Donald Trump says Mexicans are rapists and criminals, Mexican immigrants, when Donald Trump says about your judge, a Hoosier judge, he said that Judge Curiel was unqualified to hear a case because his parents were Mexican, I can't imagine how you could defend that," Kaine said, adding little to his previous assaults on Trump. Again, a few minutes later, Kaine returned to the subject of Mexico. "We have different views on—on refugee issues and on immigration. Hillary and I want to do enforcement based on, are people dangerous?" Kaine asked. "These guys say all Mexicans are bad." Finally, Pence had enough. "That's absolutely false," Pence objected. Finally, as the debate was concluding, Pence decided to take Kaine on directly, refuting him on his Mexico attack. Here is that exchange:

KAINE: When Donald Trump says women should be punished or Mexicans are rapists and criminals . . .
PENCE: I'm telling you . . .
KAINE: . . . or John McCain is not a hero, he is showing you who he is.
PENCE: Senator, you've whipped out that Mexican thing again. He—look . . .
KAINE: Can you defend it?
PENCE: There are criminal aliens in this country, Tim, who have come into this country illegally who are perpetrating violence and taking American lives.
KAINE: You want to—you want to use a big broad brush against Mexicans on that?
PENCE: He [Trump] also said and many of them are good people. You keep leaving that out of your quote. And if you want me to go there, I'll go there.

Even CNN's Dan Merica was critical of Kaine, writing a Tweet that said, "Undecided voter in Ohio says, 'Kaine came off like a jerk' tonight. Adds that he 'reinforced' some of the negatives about Clinton." RNC Chairman Reince Priebus issued a statement describing Kaine as having "desperately flailed away with empty platitudes and constant interruptions."[48]

Trump 2005 Video Emerges: "Lewd Conversation About Women"

On Friday, October 7, 2016, two days before the second presidential debate, the *Washington Post* reported the newspaper had obtained a video showing Donald Trump bragging "in vulgar terms about kissing, groping and trying to have sex with women during a 2005 conversation caught on a hot microphone, saying that 'when you're a star, they let you do it.'"[49] While the newspaper did not disclose how the eleven-year-old video had been obtained, the video clearly captured Trump talking with Billy Bush, then host of "Access Hollywood," on a bus with the show's name written across the side, arriving on a Hollywood set to tape a segment with Trump. Billy Bush, a well-known radio and television host, is a member of the Bush family, with his uncle (the brother of his father) being former President George H. W. Bush. Billy's cousins are with former President George W. Bush and former Florida Governor Jeb Bush, and Trump can be heard boasting about kissing women and grabbing women by their sexual organs. The video does not show Trump making the remarks in the key part of the conversation with Bush.

When the *Washington Post* made the video public, Trump issued a short video statement saying, "I said it, I was wrong, and I apologize." He continued to insist that his "foolish" words were much different from the words and actions of Bill Clinton who Trump accused of abusing women, with Hillary acting as an accomplice, abusing her husband's sexual victims to silence them. "I never said I'm a perfect person, nor pretended to be someone that I'm not," Trump said. "I've said and done things I regret, and the words released today on this more than a decade-old video are one of them. Anyone who knows me knows these words don't reflect who I am."

Trump insisted he is not today the same person recorded in the eleven-year-old video. "I've traveled the country talking about change for America, but my travels have also changed me," Trump continued. "I've spent time with grieving mothers who have lost their children, laid-off workers whose jobs have gone to other countries, people from all walks of life who just want a better future. I have gotten to know the great people of our country, and I have been humbled by the faith they have placed in me. I pledge to be a better man tomorrow, and I will never, never let you down." Trump tried to inject some perspective into the discussion. "Let's be honest, we're living in the real world," he commented. "This is nothing more than a distraction from the important issues we are facing today. We are losing our jobs, we are less safe than we were eight years ago, and Washington is totally broken. Hillary Clinton and her kind have run our country into the ground." In closing, Trump tried to distinguish his words of sexual abuse from the Clinton's actions. "I've said some foolish things," Trump admitted. "But there's a big difference between the words and actions of other people. Bill Clinton has actually abused women. Hillary has bullied, attacked, shamed, and intimidated his victims."

Anticipating Trump's counterattack, the partisan pro-Clinton mainstream media went on offense. Erin Gloria Ryan, writing on Slate.com, described Trump as having "a long history of getting caught demeaning women," bragging on the video about "nonconsensually groping women."[30] On October 7, 2016, after the story broke, Hillary Clinton posted a Tweet, saying, "This is horrific. We cannot allow this man to become president." Clinton's running mate, Senator Tim Kaine, told reporters in Las Vegas that the audio of Trump's comments "makes me sick to my stomach."[31]

The release of the Billy Bush video, along with the attack launched by Alicia Machado, strongly suggest a Clinton campaign planned attack on Trump's "disgusting" and "sexist" comments about women, launched with the willing complicity of the partisan mainstream media. Only a few days earlier, on Monday, October 3, 2016, the Associated Press in New York reported that in his years hosting *The Apprentice*, Donald Trump "repeatedly demeaned women with sexist language, according to show insiders who said he rated female contestants by the size of their breasts and talked about which ones he'd like to have sex with."[32] The AP claimed to have interviewed more than twenty persons, including former crew members, editors, and contestants, who described "crass behavior" by Trump behind the scenes of the long-running show. The AP acknowledged the Trump campaign had issued a denial. "These outlandish, unsubstantiated, and totally false claims fabricated by publicity hungry, opportunistic, disgruntled former employees, have no merit whatsoever," said Hope Hicks, Trump's campaign spokeswoman. "*The Apprentice* was one of the most successful prime-time television shows of all time and employed hundreds of people over many years, many of whom support Mr. Trump's candidacy." The AP noted Hicks declined to answer specific questions that were emailed and declined an interview request.

Trump's Surprise Press Conference

On Sunday night, October 9, 2016, prior to the start of the second presidential debate, Trump invited the press to a pre-debate press conference. The press who showed up were surprised to find Trump hosting a panel of three women who have accused Bill Clinton of sexual assault or rape—Paula Jones, Kathleen Willey, and Juanita Broaddrick. On November 14, 1998, Bill Clinton settled for 850,000 dollars the Paula Jones lawsuit in which Bill Clinton's long-time extra-marital paramour Paula Jones agreed to drop the sexual harassment lawsuit she had pursued after "more than 4 ½ years of scorched-earth legal warfare."[53] Kathleen Willey has alleged Bill Clinton in the Oval Office sexually assaulted her on November 29, 1993.[54] Juanita Broaddrick, a former nursing home administrator, alleged that Bill Clinton, when he was Arkansas Attorney General, sexually assaulted her in a hotel room in April 1978.[55] Fox News noted Trump posted the video of the press conference in St. Louis, Missouri, to his Facebook page less than 90 minutes before the second debate was scheduled to begin.

The point of the press conference was not to argue Bill Clinton's well-known history of marital infidelity to his wife, Hillary. The point was that Paula Jones, Kathleen Willey, and Juanita Broaddrick have all accused Bill Clinton of criminal sexual assault and rape. In addition, all three women have argued that Hillary Clinton is equally guilty for her husband's sexual crimes, in that she is an accomplice-after-the-fact—an enabler—who regularly attacks and threatens Clinton's sexual assault victims in order to silence them.

"This is NOT about infidelities, indiscretions, adultery, girlfriends or consensual sex," Willey emphasized in an open letter she wrote to CNN in May 2016. "This is about Bill Clinton's multiple sexual assaults and rapes for over 40 years and Hillary Clinton's threatening, bullying, intimidating and terrorizing all of the women who have suffered at his hands. It's as simple as that." After Willey was subpoenaed to testify in the Paula Jones case, Hillary set out to terrify her into silence. "So I was viciously assaulted after that event in the Oval Office by Clinton allies in the media and by goons who actually threatened the lives of my children to try to silence me two days before I was to be deposed, under oath, in Paula Jones' sexual harassment case, four years later," Willey wrote in her open letter to Chris Cuomo. "She [Hillary Clinton] directed them to commit an even worse offense than that, a heinous act of which I have barely spoken," Willey noted, still not ready to make public this particular horror Hillary Clinton visited upon her. "My lawyer and I tried to fight that subpoena for months. It was a story that I never intended to tell anyone." Even recalling what she went through testifying in the Paula Jones case, Willey re-experiences the fear she felt then. "The threatening acts of terror continued for months. My pets went missing or died mysteriously way before their time," Willey detailed in her open letter. "My car was vandalized, I discovered a stranger at my basement door at three A.M. one morning. Strange and threatening phone calls never seemed to stop. Someone broke into my house in the middle of the night while I was asleep upstairs."[56]

Other victims of Bill Clinton's sexual crimes are hammering Willey's point home. Not only is Hillary Clinton an enabler, she is also a co-conspirator," Dolly Kyle, the childhood sweetheart of "Billy" Clinton and someone who knows the sordid history of the former first couple better than almost anyone,[57] "If Juanita Broaddrick had filed criminal charges after Billy raped her in 1978, Hillary could have been charged as an accessory after the fact because she threatened Juanita afterward," Kyle commented. "'Enabler' is the most polite thing you could call Hillary." The viciousness of Hillary's attacks on Kyle kicked into high gear when Kyle decided to give a deposition in the Paula Jones case, going public with the details of her decades-long sexual affair with Bill Clinton. "Hillary and Billy's later attempts to destroy me ran the gamut from planting false stories in national publications to pretending that I didn't exist," Kyle writes. "Billy would later lie about me under oath in a federal lawsuit, and he would suborn perjury to get another person to lie about me too." Kyle insisted Hillary knew exactly what she was doing. "I'm not sure I ever discovered the full extent of Hillary's attacks on me because she used various publications to do her dirty work of discrediting me," Kyle finally concludes: "There appears to be no limit to what Hillary will do to destroy her perceived enemies. I wonder how long it will take her female supporters to realize that they are not her 'longtime friends' any more than I was. They are votes for her, pure and simple."[58]

Also present was Kathy Shelton. Hillary Clinton had defended the man who had raped Shelton when she was only twelve years old. On May 10, 1975, Shelton, riding her bicycle, encountered Alfred Thomas Taylor, who drove his truck into a ravine and raped Shelton while beating her, calling the child a "bitch," saying "you like it, you know it," as he raped her. Taylor, unable to afford a private attorney, was represented by Clinton. Breitbart.com reported that in her defense, Clinton raised questions about the credibility of the victim, asking the court to order Shelton to undergo a psychiatric examination from a doctor selected by the defense.[59] "I have been informed that the complainant is emotionally unstable with a tendency to seek out older men and engage in fantasizing,' wrote Clinton. 'I have also been informed that she has in the past made false accusations about persons, claiming they had attacked her body." The twelve-year-old girl also "exhibits an unusual stubbornness and temper when she does not get her way," argued Clinton.

Breitbart further reported the crime lab that analyzed Taylor's blood and semen-stained underwear tossed out the soiled section after testing it, and Clinton brought the remnants to a famous New York City forensic expert, who said not enough blood remained for the defense to test it again. Clinton told the prosecutor about her meeting with the forensics expert. Breitbart.com noted that Shelton survived the attack that left her in a coma. Unable to bear children, the rape affected Shelton the rest of her life, as she became addicted to drugs for a period of time and avoided men after the attack. In 2014, a video surfaced showing Clinton discussing the case in a mid-1980s interview with journalist Roy Reed, in which Clinton can be seen saying, "He took a lie detector test! I had him take a polygraph, which he passed, which forever destroyed my faith in polygraphs," while she can be seen clearly and heard loudly, laughing about the case. The tape is available in the Special Collections Department of the University of Arkansas libraries.[60]

Fox News commented that Trump said little at the press conference outside of introducing the four women. "These four very courageous women have asked to be here and it was our honor to help them," Trump said. Fox News also noted that when a member of the media attempted shouting a question at Trump near the end of the video, about whether he felt he was entitled to touch women inappropriately because he was famous, Paula Jones responded: "Why don't y'all ask Bill Clinton that?"[61]

Trump managed to get the four women seated in the audience for the second debate, the story quickly became Bill Clinton's guilty-looking face as he frowned, looking defeated, sneaking surreptitious glances at his accusers in the audience out of the corner of his eye.[62]

Trump vs. Clinton, Second Presidential Debate, Washington University, St. Louis, Missouri, Sunday, October 9, 2016

The first question CNN's Anderson Cooper asked Donald Trump after opening statements zeroed in immediately on the Billy Bush video controversy. "We received a lot of questions online, Mr. Trump, about the tape that was released on Friday, as you can imagine," Cooper commented. "You called what you said locker room banter. You described kissing women without consent, grabbing their genitals. That is sexual assault. You bragged that you have sexually assaulted women. Do you understand that?"[63]

Trump jumped in, objecting to the way Cooper framed his question. "No, I didn't say that at all," Trump responded. "I don't think you understood what was—this was locker room talk. I'm not proud of it. I apologize to my family. I apologize to the American people. Certainly I'm not proud of it. But this is locker room talk." Trump pivoted to ISIS, arguing that in a world where ISIS is chopping off heads, there are more serious issues to discuss than some sexually inappropriate comments Trump made more than a decade ago.

This did not satisfy Cooper who wanted to press Trump to affirm or deny that he had done more than talk inappropriately about women. "Just for the record, though, are you saying that what you said on that bus 11 years ago that you did not actually kiss women without consent or grope women without consent?" Cooper asked in his follow-up question. Trump responded that he had great respect for women. Cooper would not let up. "So, for the record, are you saying you never did that?" Cooper asked a third time. Again, Trump responded, "I've said things that, frankly, you hear these things I said. And I was embarrassed by it. But I have tremendous respect for women." Again, not satisfied he got the answer he wanted, Cooper rephrased, asking a fourth time, "Have you ever done those things." Trump answered the questions, denying he had carried out his words in actions. "And women have respect for me," Trump said one more time. "And I will tell you: No, I have not."

Clinton, when it came her time, tore into Trump over the video with what appeared a scripted and rehearsed attack, with Hillary taking the moral high ground, completely ignoring the women who had accused her and her husband of being accomplices in a history of serial assaults that went back to the time Bill Clinton was Arkansas attorney general. What was clear from the start of the second debate was that Cooper was in line with the mainstream media, taking their direction for the narrative of the presidential race from the Clinton campaign.

The problem Clinton had not fully appreciated was the extent to which sexual mores have changed over recent decades. In the 1950s when women could expect to be pinched in office building elevators, General Dwight D. Eisenhower had to leave behind his wartime driver and mistress, Kay Summersby.[64] At the conclusion of World War II, Eisenhower returned to his wife, Mamie, fully appreciating the political reality that a divorced man in the 1950s could not be elected president. In the 1960s, a compliant staff and lapdog mainstream media suppressed all coverage of President Jack Kennedy's serial, almost continuous episodes in marital infidelity. Regarding Trump, granted, earlier in his adulthood Trump might have been guilty of the type of male "locker room" bravado in his dealings with women that was not uncommon until recently. But, unlike the Clintons, there were no women who had successfully sued Donald Trump over the years with accusations of sexual assault or abuse.

In 2016, the Clintons may have outplayed the calculation they made with the Monica Lewinsky affair that the public would simply excuse their treatment of Bill Clinton's rape and sexual abuse victims. A feminist at heart, Clinton failed to appreciate the impact of comedian Bill Cosby being forced to undergo a criminal trial and face felony aggravated indecent assault charges from a 2004 case involving an employee at his alma mater, more than a decade after Cosby was first publically accused of sexual misconduct.[65] This, however, did not deter Hillary. Clinton remained determined to make sex the centerpiece of her campaign, painting Trump as a woman-hater, while elevating herself as the champion of women, seeking to be the first woman president. The second debate was the highpoint of that strategy—a strategy evidently concocted by the Clinton campaign with the willing cooperation of CNN after the Billy Bush video had surfaced.

"Well, like everyone else, I've spent a lot of time thinking over the last 48 hours about what we heard and saw," Clinton began, evidently feeling no hypocrisy in what she was about to say. "You know, with prior Republican nominees for president, I disagreed with them on politics, policies, principles, but I never questioned their fitness to serve. Donald Trump is different. I said starting back in June that he was not fit to be president and commander-in-chief. And many Republicans and independents have said the same thing." Clinton again affirmed the far-left presumption that their politically correct definition of all things right and wrong empowered them to declare those who disagreed as morally degenerate, possibly even as criminals; but certainly as inferior or outright stupid, requiring thought reform intervention before being allowed loose on society. In making her pronouncement, Clinton failed to cite the section of the Constitution that set the definition of who is morally fit to be qualified to run for president.

"What we all saw and heard on Friday was Donald talking about women, what he thinks about women, what he does to women," Hillary continued. "And he has said that the video doesn't represent who he is." This was Hillary's launching point to repeat a whole series of attacks on various Trump statements the far-left considered so politically incorrect as to deserve derision. "But I think it's clear to anyone who heard it that it represents exactly who he is," Hillary plowed forward. "Because we've seen this throughout the campaign. We have seen him insult women. We've seen him rate women on their appearance, ranking them from one to ten. We've seen him embarrass women on TV and on Twitter. We saw him after the first debate spend nearly a week denigrating a former Miss Universe in the harshest, most personal terms."

Hillary concluded her moral condemnation of Trump, as if she were certain all listening had no option but to agree with her. "So, yes, this is who Donald Trump is," she said, winding up her diatribe. "But it's not only women, and it's not only this video that raises questions about his fitness to be our president, because he has also targeted immigrants, African Americans, Latinos, people with disabilities, POWs, Muslims, and so many others. So this is who Donald Trump is. And the question for us, the question our country must answer is that this is not who we are. That's why—to go back to your question—I want to send a message—we all should—to every boy and girl and, indeed, to the entire world that America already is great, but we are great because we are good, and we will respect one another, and we will work with one another, and we will celebrate our diversity." As far as Hillary was concerned, Trump's crime was less that he said sexually inappropriate things about women, than that Trump dared to challenge the sacred cows of the Democratic Party's modern far-left ideology. "These are very important values to me, because this is the America that I know and love," Hillary insisted, as if she were re-formulating the "self-evident truths" of the Declaration of Independence. "And I can pledge to you tonight that this is the America that I will serve if I'm fortunate enough to become your president." How could any reasonable person disagree?

When Trump finally got a chance to respond, he pointed out that Hillary's far-left ideology was nothing more than a fine castle in the air, made of words that Hillary and Democrats had never been able to deliver to their compliant constituencies in fact. "It's just words, folks," Trump retorted. "It's just words. Those words, I've been hearing them for many years. I heard them when they were running for the Senate in New York, where Hillary was going to bring back jobs to upstate New York and she failed," Trump continued. "I've heard them where Hillary is constantly talking about the inner cities of our country, which are a disaster educa-tion-wise, jobwise, safety-wise, in every way possible. I'm going to help the African-Americans. I'm going to help the Latinos, Hispanics. I am going to help the inner cities." Trump drove his point home. "She's done a terrible job for the African-Americans," he insisted. "She wants their vote, and she does nothing, and then she comes back four years later. We saw that firsthand when she was United States senator. She campaigned where the primary part of her campaign . . ." Perhaps afraid that Trump was making too many points, ABC News host Martha Raddatz inter-rupted, suggesting she had some online questions she wanted to ask. "So, she's allowed to do that, but I'm not allowed to respond?" Trump asked.

Immediately, Radditz went back to questioning Trump about the Bush video, wanting to know what had changed in Trump since he walked off that bus at age fifty-nine. "Were you a different man or did that behavior continue until just recently?" she asked, adding that Trump had two minutes to answer. "It was locker room talk, as I told you," Trump answered, repeating what he had told Cooper when Cooper asked his versions of what amounted to the same question. "That was locker room talk. I'm not proud of it," Trump continued. "I am a person who has great respect for people, for my family, for the people of this country. And certainly, I'm not proud of it. But that was something that happened."

Then Trump took the chance to return fire, stressing in the debate what his pre-debate press conference had made clear. "If you look at Bill Clinton, far worse," Trump insisted. "Mine are words, and his was action. His was what he's done to women. There's never been anybody in the history of politics in this nation that's been so abusive to women. So you can say any way you want to say it, but Bill Clinton was abusive to women." Next, Trump expanded the attack to Hillary, arguing she was an accomplice to Bill's sexual crimes. "Hillary Clinton attacked those same women and attacked them viciously," Trump said. "Four of them here tonight. One of the women, who is a wonderful woman, at 12 years old, was raped at 12. Her client she represented got him off, and she's seen laughing on two separate occasions, laughing at the girl who was raped. Kathy Shelton, that young woman is here with us tonight." This set up the distinction Trump wanted to draw, making it clear there was proof the Clintons had committed sexual crimes while there was no proof he had ever done so. "So don't tell me about words," Trump said with emphasis. "I am absolutely—I apologize for those words. But it is things that people say. But what President Clinton did, he was impeached, he lost his license to practice law. He had to pay an $850,000 fine to one of the women. Paula Jones, who's also here tonight." Trump began to get an audible, positive audience reaction. "And I will tell you that when Hillary brings up a point like that and she talks about words that I said 11 years ago, I think it's disgraceful, and I think she should be ashamed of herself, if you want to know the truth," Trump said, completing his argument. The transcript showed the debate was interrupted by audience applause at this point.

Raddatz, keeping the debate on script, turned to Clinton, giving her a chance to respond.

"Well, first, let me start by saying that so much of what he's just said is not right, but he gets to run his campaign any way he chooses," Clinton said, completely ignoring the arguments Trump had just made concerning the Clinton's proven sexual crimes. "He gets to decide what he wants to talk about. Instead of answering people's questions, talking about our agenda, laying out the plans that we have that we think can make a better life and a better country, that's his choice," Clinton said, determined not to acknowledge Paula Jones or the other three women present at the debate. "When I hear something like that, I am reminded of what my friend, Michelle Obama, advised us all: When they go low, you go high." This too drew audience applause, but applause noticeably weaker than Trump had gotten. Neither of the moderators rebuked the audience for applauding for Clinton as they had done when the audience applauded for Trump.

Then, Hillary changed gears, attacking Trump once again for a series of politically incorrect statements during the campaign, arguing that from the perspective of her far-left ideology, Trump should be somehow disqualified from running for president. "And, look, if this were just about one video, maybe what he's saying tonight would be understandable, but everyone can draw their own conclusions at this point about whether or not the man in the video or the man on the stage respects women. But he never apologizes for anything to anyone," Clinton said, shifting the ground of the discussion. "He never apologized to Mr. and Mrs. Khan, the Gold Star family whose son, Captain Khan, died in the line of duty in Iraq. And Donald insulted and attacked them for weeks over their religion," she said. "He never apologized to the distinguished federal judge who was born in Indiana, but Donald said he couldn't be trusted to be a judge because his parents were, quote, 'Mexican.' He never apologized to the reporter that he mimicked and mocked on national television and our children were watching. And he never apologized for the racist lie that President Obama was not born in the United States of America. He owes the president an apology, he owes our country an apology, and he needs to take responsibility for his actions and his words." So, in Hillary's judgment, Trump was to be condemned because he failed to deliver what all far-left demagogues constantly demand—an apology, to be taken as an admission of guilt, for the crime of daring to disagree with the far-left's self-evident truths that the Democrats of today want to force all Americans to believe without question.

Trump asked Clinton if she wanted to apologize to her fellow Democrats for what the WikiLeaks dump of Democratic National Committee emails revealed of how Debbie Wasserman Schultz had stacked the primaries against contender Bernie Sanders, so as to make lock-certain that Hillary Clinton would be the party's nominee. Once Hillary mentioned that he should apologize, Trump got wound up.

"But when you talk about apology, I think the one that you should really be apologizing for and the thing that you should be apologizing for are the 33,000 e-mails that you deleted, and that you acid washed, and then the two boxes of e-mails and other things last week that were taken from an office and are now missing," Trump argued. "And I'll tell you what. I didn't think I'd say this, but I'm going to say it, and I hate to say it. But if I win, I am going to instruct my attorney general to get a special prosecutor to look into your situation, because there has never been so many lies, so much deception. There has never been anything like it, and we're going to have a special prosecutor." Trump drove the point home. "When I speak, I go out and speak, the people of this country are furious. In my opinion, the people that have been long-term workers at the FBI are furious," he continued. "There has never been anything like this, where e-mails—and you get a subpoena, you get a subpoena, and after getting the subpoena, you delete 33,000 e-mails, and then you acid wash them or bleach them, as you would say, very expensive process." Trump concluded by saying Hillary was a disgrace adding that she "ought to be ashamed of yourself."

Clinton objected that everything Trump had just said was false. "Last time at the first debate, we had millions of people fact checking, so I expect we'll have millions more fact checking, because, you know, it is—it's just awfully good that someone with the temperament of Donald Trump is not in charge of the law in our country," Clinton said. Trump retorted, saying spontaneously, "Because you'd be in jail." Again the audience applauded, drawing Cooper to reprimand those in the auditorium that they should not talk loud or applaud. "You're just wasting time," Cooper chided the audience.

Not even the *New York Times* could declare Clinton the winner of the second debate. Commenting that Clinton "in a comparatively subdued performance" had argued that she was an experienced public servant while Trump was unfit to be president.[66] Without doubt, Trump was much stronger in the second debate, taking the arguments directly to Clinton, attacking her on both her email scandal and Clinton Foundation financial scandals, while counter-attacking on Clinton's "war on women" presumption of the high moral ground. After the second debate, there was no doubt the Clinton campaign had calculated that Clinton needed to win overwhelmingly the votes of women if she were to have a chance to be elected president. The campaign strategy seemed to be to double- and triple-down attacks on Trump over the cavalier way he had treated women verbally earlier in his life. According to her, Trump was disqualified based on Hillary's "war on women" criteria, while she should win on these same criteria, on feminist grounds if nothing else, simply because she aspired to be the first woman president.

But the Clinton campaign did not let up, producing throughout October a list of women who came forward to allege Trump had sexually abused them, with the accusations covering a span of more than three decades, from the early 1980s to 2013.[67] The trouble with the accusers was that none could explain why they were only coming forward now, when Trump was the GOP nominee for president, and none had any convincing proof. The accusers were further undermined as various investigators came forward with evidence that the women had been offered large sums of money to attack Trump in what began to appear "a completely fabricated hoax" perpetrated by Clinton-supporting political operatives to undermine Trump's campaign.[68] Trump attacked his accusers as liars, threatening to sue the media for publishing false reports. "These vicious claims about me of inappropriate conduct with women are totally and absolutely false," he said at a lively West Palm Beach, Florida rally held October 13, 2016. "These claims are all fabricated, they're pure fiction, and they're outright lies. These events never, ever happened, and the people that said them meekly, fully understand."[69]

Julian Assange and WikiLeaks Dump "Podesta Email File"

On October 7, 2016, Julian Assange at WikiLeaks began the first drop of 2,060 emails and 170 attachments from the "Podesta Email File"—a cache of more than 50,000 emails that WikiLeaks had obtained surreptitiously from John Podesta, the chairman of Hillary Clinton's 2016 presidential campaign, a controlling member of the Podesta Group, a major progressive Washington-based lobbying firm, as well as the founder and chair of the Center for American Progress, a major progressive Washington-based think-tank.[70] In a drip-drip fashion, WikiLeaks released up to 5,000 emails a day from the "Podesta Email File," with the last email drop occurring after the November 8 election. The emails proved to be highly damaging to the Clinton campaign, given the multiple revelations coming out through emails written by key participants in the Democratic National Committee, the Clinton presidential campaign, as well as emails authored by principals in the Clinton Foundation and Clinton's top associates in the State Department when she was secretary of state. Clearly, those writing the emails had never planned that their emails might become public, given the unfiltered comments, criticisms, advice, suggestions, and objections voiced as the emails' content.

Among the most damaging contents of the WikiLeaks "Podesta Email File" were transcripts of the speeches Clinton gave to Goldman Sachs in 2013—Clinton had been paid as much as 225,000 dollars per speech—that contained statements so potentially damaging that Clinton had refused to release the transcripts when pressed to do so by Trump during the campaign.[71] The speeches contained many compromising statements proving Clinton had supported Wall Street both as US senator from New York, and as secretary of state, and as a result enjoyed a high level of coziness with Wall Street top donors. She acknowledged that Dodd-Frank was passed for "political reasons," because "if you were an elected member of Congress and people in your constituency were losing jobs and shutting businesses and everybody in the press is saying it's the fault of Wall Street, you can't sit idly by and do nothing."[72]

Particularly damaging were revelations in the released WikiLeaks Podesta emails that show the Washington mainstream media press corps coordinating and cooperating with the Democratic Party and Clinton's presidential campaign. Here is how Politico reported on mainstream media's well-known reporters being "snared in Podesta's flypaper," and as a result "suffering an abundance of embarrassment for their shameless buttering-up and apparent coziness with their inside sources in Clintonworld":

> Reading the emails, we witness CNBC/*New York Times* contributor John Harwood slathering Podesta with flattery, giving him campaign advice and praising Hillary Clinton. In another email, the *Washington Post*'s Juliet Eilperin offers Podesta a "heads up" about a story she's about to publish, providing a brief pre-publication synopsis. CNBC's Becky Quick promises to "defend" Obama appointee Sylvia Mathews Burwell.
>
> *New York Times Magazine* writer Mark Leibovich (who wrote a famous book lambasting permanent Washington's courtship rituals) asks Clinton's press secretary, Jennifer Palmieri, for permission to use portions of an off-the-record interview with the candidate. Palmieri withholds only a couple of comments and concludes her email to Leibovich, "Pleasure doing business!," giving it a creepy, transactional vibe. Politico reporter Glenn Thrush sends Podesta a chunk of his story-in-progress "to make sure I'm not fucking anything up." Beyond WikiLeaks, a January 2015 Clinton strategy document obtained by the Intercept describes reporter Maggie Haberman—then at Politico and now at the *New York Times*—as someone the campaign "has a very good relationship with," and who had been called upon to "tee up stories for us before" and had never disappointed.[73]

Breitbart.com reported that several top journalists and television anchors RSVPed "yes" to attend a private off-the-record gathering at the home of Joel Beneson, the chief campaign strategist for Hillary Clinton, two days before she announced her candidacy for president. Breitbart noted the guest list for an early dinner event at the home of John Podesta in Washington was limited to reporters expected to cover Clinton on the campaign trail.[74] Among the media outlets compromised by being invited to dinner events with Podesta and other top Clinton aides were from NBC, ABC, CBS, CNN, MSNBC, CNBC the *New York Times*, the *Washington Post*, the *Wall Street Journal*, the *Daily Beast*, the *Los Angeles Times*, *McClatchy*, *People*, the *New Yorker*, *Bloomberg*, *Huffington Post*, *Buzzfeed*, and *Politico*. Among the compromised journalists named were: Amy Chozick, Maggie Haberman, Jonathan Martin, Pat Healey, and Gail Collins of the *New York Times*, as well as George Stephanopoulos and Diane Sawyer of ABC.[75] "Leaked emails show that Hillary Clinton's campaign officials boasted about getting favorable news coverage from compliant journalists, received political advice from cozy reporters and circulated the names of journalists who were 'friendly' to the candidate," noted the *Washington Times*. "Whatever other revelations lurk in the huge cache of campaign emails being published by WikiLeaks, one thing is clear: Clinton campaign officials clearly exude an air of confidence that much of the mainstream media are in the bag for their candidate and hostile to Republican rival Donald Trump."[76]

One of the most damaging of the WikiLeaks revelations in the "Podesta Email File" was proof Donna Brazile had been tipping off the Clinton campaign about questions Clinton was going to be asked in upcoming debates. Brazile, a longtime Clinton confidante had become a publicly important political operative supporting Clinton's campaign. She had been a CNN commentator before taking leave to be appointed as the interim Democratic National Chairman after WikiLeaks revelations forced Debbie Wasserman Schultz to resign. As the *Washington Post* reported on October 31, 2016, Brazile had tipped Clinton off in an email dated March 5, 2016, addressed to Clinton's campaign manager John Podesta, entitled "One of the questions directed to HRC tomorrow is from a woman with a rash." In the body of the email, Brazile wrote, "Her family has lead poising and she will ask what, if anything, will Hillary do as president to help the [people] of Flint [Michigan]."[77] Earlier in the month, Brazile had denied tipping off Clinton's campaign even after an email published by WikiLeaks proved otherwise. Brazile told Jennifer Palmieri in advance that Clinton would get asked, during a town hall hosted by CNN on March 13, 2016, a question about whether Ohio and 30 other states should join the rest that have abolished the death penalty? The question was going to be premised on data from the National Coalition to Abolish the Death Penalty that shows since 1973, 176 people on death row were later set free. Brazile had put as the subject of her email to Palmieri, "From time to time I get the questions in advance."[78]

On October 31, 2016, CNN formally accepted the resignation Brazile had submitted earlier in the month when WikiLeaks made the first of the two self-incriminating emails public. "We are completely uncomfortable with what we have learned about her interactions with the Clinton campaign while she was a CNN contributor," Lauren Pratapas, a network spokeswoman, said in a statement. "CNN never gave Brazile access to any questions, prep material, attendee list, background information or meetings in advance of a town hall or debate."[79] The *New York Times* article commentated that the Brazile episode "has cast a harsh spotlight" on the cable news practice of paying partisan political operatives to appear as on-air commentators. The newspaper pointed out that CNN had received criticism previously for hiring Corey Lewandowski, Trump's first campaign manger, after he was fired by the Trump campaign, but still kept on the payroll in a consultative role as an informal advisor, receiving what the Trump campaign had characterized as severance pay.[80] What the Brazile incident proved to the American public was that the Clinton campaign had taken coordination with the mainstream media to a new level. Brazile's emails proved Hillary had received advance word about the content of televised debates that were then presented to the American people as if they were impartial and unbiased.

Danney Williams, Bill Clinton's Black Son, Demands DNA Test

In the hours before the third and final presidential debate, attorneys for Danney Williams, the thirty-year-old who has for decades claimed to be the black son of Bill Clinton, were in Las Vegas to announce their intention to file a paternity suit demanding DNA evidence from the former president.[81] They claim that Clinton, actively blocked by Hillary Clinton for political reasons, has failed to make good on child support obligations since Danney was born. "Today I have authorized my attorney's George V. Gates IV of New Orleans and Bruce Fein of Washington, DC to file a suit in New York State where my father lives to get a judge to order a court supervised test," Williams said in a statement released at the press conference.

Williams has been trying since at least 1999 to be acknowledged as the out-of-wedlock son of former President Bill Clinton and a black prostitute in Little Rock, Arkansas. "I have no doubt that I am Bill Clinton's son," Williams declares at the beginning of the new video. "It was common knowledge in Arkansas where I grew up. Everywhere I went, people would point and say, 'There's Bill Clinton's son. He looks like Bill Clinton, doesn't he? Look at him, Danney Williams is a black Bill Clinton.'"[82] Conservative documentary filmmaker Joel Gilbert, produced a 12-minute video entitled, "Banished: The Untold Story of Danney Williams," as well as a series of comparison photographs showing the physical resemblance. Posted to YouTube on October 11, 2016, Gilbert's video received more than 3 million views by Election Day.[83] Overall, it was viewed 36 million times on more than twenty-four platforms.

"I always felt bad about Bill Clinton not wanting to be in my life," Williams says in the video. "Was it because I was black? Was there something wrong with me? It made me think sometimes even of suicide. It's not fair and it has been hurtful." Danney discusses openly that after his mother was sent to prison for drugs, his Aunt Lucille Bolton raised him. "My sister is Bobby Ann Williams, Danney Williams' mother," Aunt Lucille explains, appearing in the new video via SKYPE. "My sister was a prostitute and she hung around the streets on 17th and Main [in Little Rock]. She met Bill Clinton on the streets on some 13 occasions. About 5 or 6 months she had dated Bill Clinton and everything; she said she was pregnant by Bill." But even today, he has no doubt he is Bill Clinton's son. "I tell my children, yes, it is real. Bill Clinton is my father and I'm going to make sure you meet him one day," Danney explains in the video. He ended the video with a plea: "Hillary, please do not deny I exist. I am your stepson. Chelsea is my sister. And Bill is my father."

Why Danney Williams Matters

Sophisticated polling showed that African American voters overwhelmingly believed that Danney Williams was indeed Bill Clinton's abandoned son. Beyond the physical resemblance, focus groups showed that black voters found Danney's aunt and mother credible. Hillary had little connection to black voters as it was. Her cheerleading for the 1994 crime bill resulted in the incarceration of an entire generation of young black men for the nonviolent crime of possession of small amounts of drugs. The Clinton law provided harsher mandatory sentences for possession of rock cocaine than it did for powdered cocaine, thus targeting poorer African Americans and favoring wealthy white people. Governor Bill Clinton went to the Federal courts in Arkansas to argue *for* racial profiling by the good-ole boys in the Arkansas state police.

We realized the mainstream media would never cover Danney Williams or his claims, although some Republican surrogates did manage to blurt it out on cable TV before being silenced by moderators from CNN and Fox. In fact, we never really cared whether any white person learned of Danney Williams and the truth of his existence. This is a classic case of the proper application of new media.

Gilbert's video left few dry eyes. By geo-targeting Cleveland, Detroit, Milwaukee, Miami, Charlotte, Fayetteville, and Philadelphia, and further selecting targets based on preferences in music, age range, black culture, and other urban interests, the odds were overwhelming that eighteen-to-thirty-year-old African Americans had watched the compelling cinematic work. YouTube briefly suspended Danney Williams' account in an effort to censor him, but reinstated him after vigorous protests. Then, alternative hip hop group Freenauts, inspired by Danney's viral story, produced a catchy rap anthem calling out Hillary and Bill for their hypocrisy. The video had 5 million viewers on WorldStarHipHop.com alone, and was picked up by *Hip Hop Weekly*, *Drudge Report*, InfoWars.com, and many black media outlets.

The Clintons had orchestrated an extraordinary rouse claiming that a DNA test conducted by the *Star* tabloid magazine in 1999 had proved that Bill Clinton was *not* Danney Williams' father. Crusading investigative journalist Dr. Jerome Corsi, however, had discovered that the DNA test allegedly utilized by the *Star* in the analysis had, in fact, come from a written report of the Special Counsel to the Clinton impeachment proceeding, Ken Starr. There was no new test done. "I don't remember ever seeing any laboratory test that was done on Clinton's DNA," Phil Bunton, former editor-in-chief of the *Star* told WND. "We never published anything. But we got a lot of phone calls from several people in the media, including the *New York Times*, wanting to know when we were going to get the DNA back," Bunton continued. "We thought it was going to turn out to be his son, but when the DNA came back there was no story there even to write." Corsi determined that while the testimony of the FBI agents in the report claimed that two different and legally required DNA tests had been conducted, the report curiously contained only one test.

As *Slate*, *Snopes.com* and the *New York Daily News* all reported, the Starr report only included the results of only one of the two tests required to establish paternity. It included a polymerase chain reaction (PCR) but did not include the FBI lab's test refraction fragmented length polymorphism (RFLP). In other words, an accurate DNA test to determine paternity requires two different DNA tests. The Starr report included only the PCR data, which rendered any determination of paternity inconclusive.

Without an actual sample of Clinton's blood, or other bodily fluids, the *Star* could not conduct the more reliable test, a "refraction fragmented length polymorphism" test, or "RFLP," that would have allowed a qualified laboratory to run a spectrograph of Clinton's DNA to be placed side-by-side with the results of a RFLP test conducted on Williams' bodily fluids. As reported by the *Los Angeles Times* on January 12, 1999, instead of publishing an article detailing any laboratory results the *Star* magazine may have obtained, Burton simply told news reporters who called him that, "There was no match, nothing even close." On October 3, 2016, Snopes.com, an Internet "fact checking" source generally favorable to Democrats, examined the question of whether or not Bill Clinton was Danny Williams' father, only to conclude not that the charge was "false," but that the charge was "unproven."[84]

"Danney Williams looked incredibly like Bill Clinton—the hair and everything. At the time, we really thought we had a winner. When Gooding told me it wasn't a match, I wouldn't have taken any interest in looking at the report." So, after hearing back from Gooding, Bunton decided not to publish anything, disappointed he couldn't prove Bill Clinton was Danny Williams' biological father. So, instead of publishing an article, Bunton simply decided to tell reporters calling that the results "weren't even close." "I really thought it was going to come up a match," he stressed. "The story was all over Arkansas that Bill Clinton had a relationship with this woman and there was some preacher running around Little Rock saying the child was Bill's, but that was as far as we got."

Noted forensic experts Dr. Henry Lee pointed out that only a comparison of the two tests could determine paternity. Without them, the Star report lacked sufficient data to reach any conclusion, including ruling out the possibility that Bill was Danney's father. Making the entire matter more curious is the fact that the *Star* was owned by Clinton crony Robert Altman, a major Clinton donor and former Assistant Secretary of the Treasury in the Clinton Administration, who was forced to resign in the Whitewater scandal when he improperly tipped the Clintons off to a Federal investigation. Corsi also determined that Clinton mad-dog lawyer David Kendall was serving as general counsel to the *Star* when this rouse was perpetrated. Corsi interviewed the *Star* editor who admitted he had never seen a written DNA report of any kind. Nonetheless, Howard Kurtz, then of the *Washington Post*, and the Associated Press, dutifully reported that a DNA test had disproved Danney Williams' claims, which was clearly a lie. Megyn Kelly would repeat this myth mindlessly when a Trump surrogate attempted to raise the issue on *The Kelly File*.

Well-spoken, Williams appealed first to former President Clinton for a voluntary DNA sample, then appealed to Monica Lewinsky, who still owns the notorious semen-stained blue dress, and thus a real Bill Clinton DNA sample. Ms. Lewinsky never responded. But both efforts generated substantial national press for Danney Williams. Williams' attorneys are currently preparing to file a paternity suit in the Arkansas courts.

Though there was no definitive DNA test, in the end it didn't matter. Black voters by the millions had heard the story and were convinced. This was a legitimate campaign to dampen African American support for Hillary Clinton, based on facts that the mainstream media refused to report. In the end, a six-point shift among blacks in markets targeted with Danney Williams videos likely had a profound impact on the outcome of the election.[85]

The Daily Caller reported, that "while Obama absolutely dominated among blacks, beating Romney 93-7, Clinton only beat Trump 88-8. Lower overall turnout among black voters, a shift that may have been decisive, propelled Trump to small victories in states like Michigan and Pennsylvania that seemed out of reach for him just days ago."[86]

This issue of voter turnout was critical. We were convinced that Hillary was vulnerable among black voters. In July 2015, the *Cook Report* noted how turning out the black vote was likely the key to Hillary Clinton's ability to win and how failure to match Barack Obama's totals among blacks in 2012 might impede her path to victory.[87]

- "It's tough to overstate just how critical black voters have become to today's Democratic coalition, particularly when it comes to the Electoral College. Deconstructing exit poll data from 2012, African-American voters accounted for Obama's entire margin of victory in seven states: Florida, Maryland, Michigan, Nevada, Ohio, Pennsylvania and Virginia. Without these states' 112 electoral votes, Obama would have lost decisively. African-Americans also accounted for almost all of Obama's margin in Wisconsin. All of these states, except Maryland, will be crucial 2016 battlegrounds."
- "To be sure, a return to pre-2008 African-American turnout levels wouldn't necessarily doom a Hillary Clinton candidacy, but it would leave her with a whole lot less margin for error in a host of swing states. For example, in Virginia, what if the African-American share of the vote had been 18 percent instead of 20 percent in 2012? We estimate Obama would have won by 1.6 percent, rather than 3.9 percent. In Ohio, what if it had been 13 percent instead of 15 percent? We estimate Obama would have won by 0.8 percent, not 3.0 percent. In Pennsylvania, what if it had been 11 percent instead of 13 percent? Obama's edge would have shrunk from 5.4 percent to 3.4 percent.
- "We can't predict how much better or worse a Hillary Clinton will do among African-American voters—or white voters for that matter—without knowing who she will face in November. However, it's also clear that the African-American coalition is THE critical keystone for a Democratic Electoral College victory, which means we should be spending as much time, if not more, looking at their engagement in the election as we do the growing Latino vote."

Donald Trump carried four of the six designated "crucial 2016 battlegrounds" (Ohio, Florida, Michigan and Pennsylvania). His ability to win depended on winning all four of them as well as holding North Carolina, which Obama carried narrowly in 2008 and which flipped narrowly to Romney in 2012. Also key and not mentioned among the prospective battleground states was Wisconsin.

Prior to the election, several studies noted that pre-election voter turnout by blacks was lower in several key battleground states than in 2008, suggesting Hillary Clinton was not generating the same level of enthusiasm as Barack Obama had.[88] This was the Danney Williams affect.

- "African-Americans are failing to vote at the robust levels they did four years ago in several states that could help decide the presidential election, creating a vexing problem for Hillary Clinton as she clings to a deteriorating lead over Donald J. Trump with Election Day just a week away. As tens of millions of Americans cast ballots in what will be the largest-ever mobilization of early voters in a presidential election, the numbers have started to point toward a slump that many Democrats feared might materialize without the nation's first black president on the ticket."

The *Times* article specifically called attention to Florida and Ohio— both states where Trump eventually won (by bigger margins than in the three rust-belt states that put him over the top).

- "In Florida, which extended early voting after long lines left some voters waiting for hours in 2012, African-Americans' share of the electorate that has gone to the polls in person so far has decreased, to 15 percent today from 25 percent four years ago. . . . African-Americans are underperforming their participation rates from 2012. Daniel A. Smith, a professor of political science at the University of Florida, compared the early voting so far in minority-heavy Miami-Dade, Palm Beach and Broward Counties with that in 2012. He found that of those who have cast ballots this year, 22 percent were black, 40 percent were white and 31 percent were Hispanic. In 2012, the breakdown was 36 percent black, 35 percent white and 23 percent Hispanic. 'If the Clinton campaign doesn't ramp it up,' Professor Smith said, "Florida will be in doubt."
- "In Ohio, which also cut back its early voting, voter participation in the heavily Democratic areas near Cleveland, Columbus and Toledo has been down, though the Clinton campaign said it was encouraged by a busy day on Sunday when African-American churches led voter drives across the state."

The *Times* accurately noted Clinton showing more strength in Colorado and Nevada and that she could win the election even if she lost North

Carolina, Florida and Ohio. But the potential turnout issues in Pennsylvania, Wisconsin and Michigan were never mentioned.

A local newspaper, *Florida Today* also noted the lower pre-election turnout in Florida among African American voters.[89]

- "Low turnout among black voters in Florida could be a real problem for Hillary Clinton and down-ballot Democrats. Overall turnout is up, but the percentage of black votes is "way down" compared to 2012. . . . Clinton's problem isn't just that turnout isn't as high among the 1.7 million black voters in the state. The roughly 80-85 percent support she's getting from African Americans is well below the 95 percent Obama got in 2012."

In general, post-election studies about the black vote and Trump's victory have stressed the failure of Hillary Clinton to get the vote out. In this interpretation by the *Philadelphia Tribune*, the election takes on the spin more of Clinton losing than Trump winning.[90]

- "In terms of the Black vote, the new turnout numbers present a disturbing picture of a Black electorate not reaching its full political potential. Initial exit polling data show that Black voter turnout was 12 percent of the overall voting population in 2016, just 1 percentage point less than what it was in 2012. In 2012, Black voter participation had actually surpassed white voter participation, as it represented 13 percent of the overall national vote, matching its proportion to the population."

- A deeper look at turnout numbers by the *Tribune* reveals a grim portrait of an African-American electorate possibly more bruised than initially thought. Out of 131,741,500 total ballots counted on election night, 15,008,980 of those were Black voter ballots when factoring in the 12 percent Black turnout data point in exit polling. But, in 2012, there were 16,938,006 Black voter ballots counted out of a total of 130.3 million ballots nationally. That translates into an alarming 11.4 percent reduction in Black votes between the two presidential election cycles.

Liberal columnist Al Hunt looked at Pennsylvania returns and blamed Clinton's loss in the state on failure to garner the levels of support Obama had received.[91]

- "She won Pittsburgh and Philadelphia by the margins antici- pated. But in Philadelphia there were almost 100,000 fewer voters than four years ago. Clinton also dominated the four sub- urban counties—including Chester, which the Republican Mitt Romney carried in 2012 and where Melania Trump campaigned right before the election—by more than Obama did. But turn- out was up less than expected."
- "There were Democratic strongholds where Trump's perfor- mance was impressive. He came close in Scranton, which Obama and native son Joe Biden won by 16 percentage points in 2012. And he won in Wilkes-Barre and Erie, which Obama had carried easily."
- "The Pennsylvania exit polls are revealing. They show Clinton underperforming Obama among voters younger than 30. Worse from her perspective, those voters comprised only 16 percent of the overall tally, compared to 19 percent in 2012. More tell- ing, blacks, who voted overwhelmingly for Clinton, were only 10 percent of the electorate, down from 13 percent last time. If black voters had made up 12 percent of the Pennsylvania elec- torate, she probably would have won the state."

The *New York Times* did a study of Wisconsin, specifically black voting in Milwaukee, and found a community largely unenthusiastic for Hil- lary.[92]

- "Wisconsin, a state that Hillary Clinton had assumed she would win, historically boasts one of the nation's highest rates of voter participation; this year's 68.3 percent turnout was the fifth best among the 50 states. But by local standards, it was a disappoint- ment, the lowest turnout in 16 years. And those no-shows were important. Mr. Trump won the state by just 27,000 voters.
- "Milwaukee's lowest-income neighborhoods offer one explana- tion for the turnout figures. Of the city's 15 council districts, the decline in turnout from 2012 to 2016 in the five poorest was consistently much greater than the drop seen in more prosper- ous areas—accounting for half of the overall decline in turnout citywide.
- "The biggest drop was here in District 15, a stretch of fading wooden homes, sandwich shops and fast-food restaurants that is

84 percent black. In this district, voter turnout declined by 19.5 percent from 2012 figures, according to Neil Albrecht, executive director of the City of Milwaukee Election Commission. It is home to some of Milwaukee's poorest residents and, according to a 2016 documentary, 'Milwaukee 53206,' has one of the nation's highest per-capita incarceration rates."

In analyzing the *Times* article, *New York* magazine noted how the lower-educated black community in Milwaukee in general was less outraged by the alleged picture of Trump as a racist and as a consequence weren't compelled to vote against Trump and for Hillary over his public comments.[93]

- "The African-American Milwaukee voters were less outraged by Trump's bigotry and misogyny than many optimistic Democrats expected them to be. Over and over, Democrats and journalists stated and wrote confidently that Trump's outrageous statements about minority groups would fire up and turn out the Democratic base, making Trump's uphill battle even steeper. It didn't happen."

The day after the election, the website *Michigan Live* noted that Trump's narrow victory in the state based on lack of support for Hillary in Detroit and Flint. [94]

- "Unofficial results show Clinton couldn't come close to Obama's performance four years ago in areas of the state with the highest percentages of black voters, including metro Detroit—Wayne, Oakland and Macomb counties. Those counties accounted for 37 percent of the state's overall vote Tuesday, November 8, and 55 percent went to Clinton. Obama took 69 percent of the same region's vote four years ago."
- "That enthusiasm gap showed itself in Genesee County, anchored by the city of Flint, which is 56 percent black. Clinton's margin of victory was 52-42 percent—a 19,000 vote advantage, but not close to Obama's performance in 2012 against Republican Mitt Romney—a 63-35 percent win and 57,000-vote cushion."
- In Wayne County, which is 39 percent black and includes voters from the city of Detroit, Clinton won 66 percent of the vote—less than the 80 percent Obama won over Romney

and the result was more than 10,000 fewer votes for the top of the Democratic ticket there. "That is a huge difference," said Susan Demas, editor and publisher of Inside Michigan Politics. "African American turnout (was) down, rural white turnout for Trump was up, and that was enough to put the state in play or win it for Trump."

- "Saginaw County, including the city of Saginaw, favored Trump 47 to 46 percent, making the GOP leader the first Republican to win Saginaw County since 1984, when Ronald Reagan beat Walter Mondale as part of a national landslide. The percentage of voter turnout overall was down in Saginaw County—from more than 65 percent in 2012 to 60 percent this year. Turnout in precincts on the East Side of the city of Saginaw Tuesday ranged from 41 to 51 percent—areas that are predominantly black and Hispanic."

Indisputably, voters who became aware of Danney Williams and his plight were less likely to vote for Hillary. Black voters found Danney's aunt's account of being turned away when she attempted to take the infant to Hillary Clinton, entirely credible. Two different Arkansas state troopers admit that they delivered Christmas presents to Danney at his mother's home. This, too, went viral in a video in which Trooper Larry Patterson tells of a State official driving a car with Arkansas government plates that left an envelope with seven crisp one-hundred-dollar bills at the beginning of every month. Facebook told the tale.

Throughout the presidential campaign, Donald Trump had been appealing to the African American vote, questioning whether the Democrats under President Obama had produced any meaningful economic changes to improve their lives during the eight years of his presidency. "What do you have to lose?" Trump repeatedly asked in appealing for African American voters to switch party allegiances and vote Republican in 2016. While the Clintons did their best to ignore the Danney Williams scandal, as has been shown, the story was widely circulated in the African American community, both through Joel Gilbert's viral video and with the introduction of the rap song and video that celebrated Danney's saga. While the Danney Williams story may not have alone converted the majority of African American voters into Republicans, the media attention it received, along with the lack of economic progress and the Clinton crime bill, together were sufficient to reduce enthusiasm for Hillary Clinton in the African American community. This depressed black voter turnout, which was critical to Trump's ultimate victory in the election.

Clinton Rape T-Shirts

Some of you may not know who Christian Josi is but he ran the Clinton Rape T-shirt campaign for me, which Alex Jones then kicked off into the stratosphere. Yes, it was a crude guerilla tactic, but it was the only way to break through the mainstream media black-out of Bill Clinton's sexual assaults and Hillary's role as an accessory after the fact by running the terror campaign/cover-up.

Christian is the most reluctant, yet one of most gifted, political operatives out there—next to me, of course. That's why I like him. He had great success in politics at a very young age and then 'accidentally' became a famous jazz singer. He even wrote a book about Hillary Clinton before writing books about Hillary Clinton was cool. The whole deal has left him sort of messed up in the head, frankly. Which is probably what makes him good. Difficult, temperamental, but good.

Successful political "black ops" involve truth and levity. Alone, either of these can be ineffective, but together they are powerful weapons for conveying a message that will have an impact.

Alone, truth is not enough. It'd be nice if it were, but that's not the world in which we live. People are busy and have a lot of distractions. The truth is often filed away with names of high school teachers' names and where you left your keys.

Attaching truth to something else, especially humor or shock, makes it stick. The odds are much higher that you can remember a joke you heard in high school rather than the name of the person who told it to you.

When it comes to the Clintons, there is almost too much opposition research to use. Oddly, it almost works to their advantage. If people are bombarded by information on too many subjects it just becomes noise; a choir all singing different songs. To effectively message things you want to "stick," you have to be selective and relentless. Know what you want to get across and hammer it, over and over again.

Choosing what to message is as important as the how. With the Clintons, what to choose? Some Clinton scandals would be covered by the mainstream media, if only out of necessity. All of their coverage of Hillary couldn't be positive, journalists had to at least pay lip-service to the concept of objectivity.

The email scandal, the pay-for-play aspect of the Clinton Foundation, Bill's philandering, these would get ink on their own. Not much, but as much as the media would ever allow, and only in the left's context: quick, dismissive mentions to say they "checked that box" and couldn't be accused of ignoring these stories.

As Hillary was running to break the "highest, hardest glass ceiling" in the world, it was unlikely the media would spend any time investigating, let alone reporting, the extent of Bill's personal perversions, which made that aspect of their existence ripe for the picking.

The allegations of sexual assault and rape against Bill Clinton were well known to people who paid attention to politics in the 1990s, but even then the media did all they could to hide the stories of Juanita Broaddrick.

While the media unfairly morphed the name Paul Jones into a late-night punch line, there were millions of voters unaware of the stories of Jones and Broaddrick. They needed to be educated. With Juanita Broaddrick, these problems do not exist.

The horrific account of Bill Clinton's rape of Broaddrick in a hotel in Little Rock, Arkansas in 1978 was not widely reported when she came forward in 1999. Ignored by all but one mainstream media outlet, NBC News sat on their exclusive with Broaddrick until after Clinton's impeachment trial for perjury regarding his affair with intern Monica Lewinsky failed to remove him from office. Airing only once, anyone who missed the segment, missed her story.

This fruit was ripe for picking.

In the 16 years since the Clintons left the White House the progressive left set out to change the culture even more than they had, especially with young people on college campuses. Drunken hook-ups, once a rite of passage, became the sole responsibility of the man, even if he was drunk too and didn't initiate the activity. Moreover, they made the accuser a hero who must be believed, no matter what.

Emma Sulkowicz, a student at Columbia University who became known as "mattress girl" because she carried the mattress she claimed she was raped on to every class across campus after the university found no proof of her account of rape. Sulkowicz was held up as a champion of women's rights, and still is today by many on the left.

The false Rolling Stone story "A Rape On Campus" also had campus leftists demanding the accuser, "Jackie," be believed even after she was exposed as a fraud and the story was retracted.

This mentality, especially with millennial voters, made the rape of Juanita Broaddrick the best, most fertile ground for weaponization against the Clintons.

In November of 2015, Hillary Clinton really solidified this choice when she tweeted, "Every survivor of sexual assault deserves to be heard, believed, and supported." Once she said they "deserved" to be believed, the obvious question was: Did Hillary believe Juanita?

When asked this question at a public forum a month later, Clinton said, "Well, I would say that everybody should be believed at first until they are disbelieved on evidence."

We posted her tweet just before she deleted it.

Since Bill had never spoken about, let alone denied, Broaddrick's claims, and most people had never heard them, coupled with Hillary's original absolutist declaration of absolute belief, the choice was clear: voters who didn't know this bit of the Clinton's history had to be educated on it.

Since the best message is a simple message, the Bill Clinton "RAPE" t-shirt was born from my fertile mind. Modeled after the "HOPE" posters from Barack Obama's 2008 campaign, the Clinton "RAPE" shirt became reality when I baited the press in Cleveland. It was an immediate hit.

Soon after it was printed, the shirt started showing up at Clinton rallies. This wasn't an accident.

Alex Jones offered $1,000 to anyone who could get on TV wearing the shirt and $5,000 to anyone who wore the shirt to a Clinton rally and could be heard shouting "Bill Clinton is a rapist!" Jones paid out more than $125,000!

The game was on.

It may seem crude, but it was effective. People at Clinton rallies across the country started yelling, "Bill Clinton is a rapist" on live TV. This forced the media to cover it. True, they usually did so with their voices dripping with contempt, but they had to give it context. They had to mention Juanita Broaddrick.

At least some of the people who didn't know who she was searched her name and discovered the story Democrats and the media were so desperate to keep hidden. With women and millennials in particular, the woman who'd jumped on the bandwagon of "deserving to be believed" was shaded by the shadow cast by her husband's own actions.

Hillary underperformed with women, particularly white suburban women, and millennials on Election Day in no small part, I think, because Juanita Broaddrick. And voters became aware of the Juanita Broaddrick story because of that shirt and the effort to get it and her story out there.

It all went according to plan, and it worked.

News outlets that would have been all too happy to ignore Juanita's story yet again had no choice but to do their jobs. Political operatives found themselves having to defend the indefensible when it came to the husband of their candidate.

For all that was said about Donald Trump and what he'd said about women, the specter of Bill Clinton's treatment of Juanita Broaddrick hung over it all. Were it not for that shirt and the effort to get it out there, there is no doubt no one in the mainstream media would have mentioned Juanita Broaddrick's name.

Bringing Juanita Broaddrick to the forefront of the national consciousness brought with it all the other Clinton women Hillary's campaign did not want to talk about. A simple t-shirt and a last minute stroke of brilliance called the RAPE WHISTLE put a billion-dollar campaign on its heels, and eventually on its back.

In the final weeks we released the official Clinton Rape Whistle. Dozens of "whistle blowers" started disrupting Clinton rallies. Because the whistles were plastic, they slipped easily through the US Secret Service's metal detectors.

It was true, it was simple, it was disruptive, it was memorable, and it worked.

Trump vs. Clinton, Third Presidential Debate, University of Nevada, Las Vegas, Nevada, Sunday, October 16, 2016

In the third and final presidential debate, the drama involved an attempt by moderator Chris Wallace, Fox News Sunday anchor, and Clinton to get Trump to forego in advance any legal challenges of voter fraud he might make should he lose the election on November 8.

As the last debate was set to begin, CNN reported that an NBC/ *Wall Street Journal* had her beating Trump by 11 percentage points nationally. The poll showed Clinton leading by 20 points with women, while

Trump was only ahead by 3 points with men. Fully one-third of the respondents said the Billy Bush video disqualified Trump from being president and that he should drop out of the race.[95] As far as Hillary's campaign was concerned, it was time to begin planning her transition to the White House. Five days after the last debate, on October 21, 2016, Politico reported that Clinton's secretive transition team had "hit the gas pedal," hiring staff and culling through résumés, while quietly reaching out to key Democrats.[96]

At the beginning of the second hour of the third debate, Wallace asked Trump the key question: "But sir, there is a tradition in this country, in fact one of the prides of this country, is the peaceful transition of power and that no matter how hard fought a campaign is, that at the end of the campaign, that the loser concedes to the winner, not saying that you are necessarily going to be the loser or the winner, but that the loser concedes to the winner and that the country comes together in part for the good of the country, are you saying that you are not prepared now to commit to that principle?"[97] In asking the question, Wallace obviously was ignoring the 2000 challenge Al Gore launched to George W. Bush, with Gore rescinding his concession speech to demand a vote recount in Florida.

"What I'm saying now is that I will tell you at that time," Trump said, careful not to compromise any legal options he might have available to him should he lose. "I will keep you in suspense, okay?"

Without waiting for Wallace to ask her the same question, Clinton jumped in to attack Trump, not saying whether or not she would accept a losing vote without launching a challenge to the election. "Chris, let me respond to that because that is horrifying," Clinton said, castigating Trump. "You know, every time Donald thinks things are not going in his direction, he claims whatever it is, is rigged against him," Clinton went on, portraying Trump as a sore loser. "The FBI conducted a year-long investigation into my e-mails. They concluded there was no case," Clinton continued, seizing the opportunity to portray herself as the victim. "He said that the FBI was rigged. He lost the Iowa caucus, he lost the Wisconsin primary. He said the Republican primary was rigged against him," she said, delivering what sounded like prepared and rehearsed remarks. "Then Trump University gets sued for fraud and racketeering. He claims the court system and the federal judge is rigged against him. There was even a time when he didn't get an Emmy for his TV program three years in a row and he started tweeting that the Emmys were rigged."

Calmly, Trump interjected, "Should have gotten it," referring to the Emmy. The audience responded with laughter.

Again, Clinton did not wait for Wallace to ask her a question. Instead, she just continued her diatribe against Trump. "This is a mindset," Clinton insisted, asserting that she now could somehow read Trump's mind. "This is how Donald thinks. And it's funny but it's also really troubling." This set up what was to be Hillary's punch-line, namely, that if Trump questioned the outcome of the election, he would be undermining "our democracy"—a statement Hillary considered obvious, even though the United States is technically not a democracy, but a constitutional republic. "This is not the way our democracy works," Hillary pontificated, continuing her lecture against Trump. "We've been around for two hundred and forty years. We have had free and fair elections. We have accepted the outcomes when we may not have liked them. And that is what must be expected of anyone standing on the debate stage during a general election. President Obama said the other day when you are whining before the game even finished . . ."

Here the audience applauded. "Hold on. Hold on, folks," Wallace objected.

But Hillary continued, completing her sentence, as if there had been no audience interruption. ". . . it just shows you're not up to doing the job," she said, working up to the conclusion of her diatribe. "And let's be clear about what he is saying and what that means. He is denigrating. He is talking down our democracy. And I for one am appalled that someone, the nominee of one of our two major parties, would take that kind of position."

Trump had heard enough and he was not prepared to have Clinton demean him. "I think what the FBI did and what the Department of Justice did, including meeting with her husband, the attorney general, in the back of an airplane on the tarmac in Arizona—I think that is disgraceful," Trump said. "I think it is disgraceful." Earlier in the debate, after Hillary accused Trump of wanting to close the Social Security system, Trump got in a comment, "Such a nasty woman."

Ignoring the various policy issues discussed during the debate, CNN's headline read, "Donald Trump refuses to say whether he'll accept election results." Reporting for CNN, Stephen Collinson expressed astonishment at Trump's stance on the issue.[98] "The comments at the Las Vegas showdown marked a stunning moment that has never been seen in the weeks before a modern presidential election," Collinson wrote. "The stance threatens to cast doubt on one of the fundamental principles of American politics—the peaceful, undisputed transfer of power from one president to a successor who is recognized as legitimate after winning an election," CNN continued, implying Trump had cut his own throat by refusing to accept losing on Election Day. "Trump's debate performance could doom his chance to win over any remaining undecided voters at this late stage in the campaign," Collinson continued. "His comments about the election results came during a debate in which he spoke of 'hombres,' language that could offend Latinos. And he referred to Clinton as a 'nasty woman.'" The CNN article noted Trump had "doubled down" on his comments about the election, saying during a rally in Delaware, Ohio, that he would accept the results "if I win."[99]

CHAPTER 9

Closing Arguments

She's low energy, she actually is low energy. She'll go home, she'll take a nap for four or five hours then come back. No naps for Trump! No naps. I don't take naps. We don't have time! We don't have time . . . You ever see Hillary where she comes out and she'll read a teleprompter and then she'll go home and you don't see her for three, four days, then she comes back.

Donald J. Trump, Roanoke, Virginia, July 25, 2016[1]

In 1980, President Jimmy Carter worried appropriately that the campaign of challenger Ronald Reagan might pull off an "October Surprise" with the American embassy hostages that ended up being released on the day of Reagan's inauguration—444 days after being captured by Iranian radicals as Ayatollah Khomeini launched a revolution that ousted from power the Shah of Iran. Ever since then, presidential candidates remain wary of an "October Surprise"—an eleventh hour unexpected event of sufficient importance to determine the outcome of the presidential race.

In 2016, an "October Surprise" happened when the FBI announced unexpectedly that the investigation into Hillary Clinton's State Department emails that had been closed was going to be reopened. Once again, Hillary Clinton was a presidential candidate under the cloud of federal criminal investigation—an unexpected event that occurred within days of Election Day.

FBI's Comey Restarts Investigation

On Friday, October 28, 2016, less than two weeks away from Election Day, FBI Director James Comey, in a letter addressed to Congress, announced he was re-opening the FBI investigation into Hillary Clinton's private email server, effectively delivering a potentially lethal blow to the Clinton campaign.[2] "In connection with an unrelated case, the FBI has learned of the existence of emails that appear to be pertinent to the investigation," Comey wrote. "I am writing to inform you that the investigative team briefed me on this yesterday, and I agreed that the FBI should take appropriate investigative steps designed to allow investigators to review these emails to determine whether they contain classified information, as well as to assess their importance to our investigation." Interestingly, Comey had addressed the letter only to the Republican chairmen of various key House committees, including Representative Jason Chaffetz, head of the Committee on Oversight and Government Reform, Representative Charles Grassley and Representative Robert Goodlatte, heading the House Judiciary Committee, and Representative Devin Nunes, head of the House Permanent Select Committee on Intelligence.

Predictably, the Clinton campaign reacted with outrage. John Podesta, Clinton's campaign manager, in an angry statement, blamed Republicans for "browbeating" the FBI into Friday's decision and demanded to know what new information had caused a closed case of this national importance to be reopened. "Director Comey's letter refers to emails that have come to light in an unrelated case, but we have no idea what those emails are and the Director himself notes they may not even be significant," Podesta said. "It is extraordinary that we would see something like this just 11 days out from a presidential election."[3]

Clinton also reacted sharply, responding in a five-minute-long press conference hurriedly called in Des Moines, Iowa, immediately following Comey's announcement. "I have now seen Director Comey's letter to Congress," Clinton began. We are 11 days out from perhaps the most important election of our lifetimes. Voting is already underway in our country. The American people deserve to get the full and complete facts immediately. The director has said himself he does not know if the emails referenced in his letter are significant or not. I'm confident, whatever they are, will not change the conclusion reached in July." Hillary insisted it was imperative for the FBI to explain this investigation without hesitation. "So I look forward to facing the important challenges facing the

American people, winning on November 8, and working with all Americans to build a better future for our country." Clinton clearly looked irritated by the news that threatened her chances for electoral success which, until that moment, looked very strong, given that she enjoyed commanding leads in most credible polls. Responding to reporter questions, Clinton made clear that the FBI had not given her any advance warning, affirming she too learned of the decision when the FBI letter to Republican members of Congress went public. Clinton called on the FBI to release immediately all the new information the FBI had obtained. "I think people, a long time ago, made up their minds about the emails," she insisted. "I think that's factored into what people think and now they are choosing a president."[4]

Subsequent reporting revealed Attorney General Loretta Lynch and Deputy Attorney General Sally Yates had advised Comey prior to the letter being finalized that issuing the letter would violate Justice Department policies and procedures dictating not to comment on politically sensitive investigations within 60 days of an election. When Lynch stopped short of issuing to Comey a direct order forbidding him to issue the letter, Comey decided to disregard Lynch and Yates' concerns, proceeding to issue the letter on his own authority.[5] "We don't ordinarily tell Congress about ongoing investigations," Comey noted in his letter to Congress, "but here I feel an obligation to do so given that I testified repeatedly in recent months that our investigation was completed." To this, Comey added, "I also think it would be misleading to the American people were we not to supplement the record."

The *New York Times* was the first to report that the FBI had found tens of thousands of State Department emails belonging to Huma Abedin on Representative Anthony Weiner's seized laptop. The FBI had obtained earlier a search warrant about a month to seize Weiner's electronic devices, including his cellphone and iPad, as part of an on-going investigation into illicit sexual messages Weiner had been sending via text message to an unidentified fifteen-year-old girl in North Carolina.[6] An FBI source confirmed to Fox News that the new emails were discovered in an investigation unrelated to the investigation into Hillary Clinton's emails. The FBI source disclosed that the new emails were discovered after the FBI seized the laptop.[7]

The previously unreported background of the story starts on August 22, 2016, when the Washington-based watchdog group Judicial Watch released 725 pages of State Department documents, including previously unreleased email exchanges in which Hillary Clinton's top aide, Huma Abedin, provided influential Clinton Foundation donors special, expedited access to the secretary of state. In many instances, the preferential treatment provided to donors was at the specific request of Clinton Foundation executive Douglas Band.[8] The State Department had released the documents in partial compliance with a federal court order issued in a May 5, 2015, in connection with Freedom of Information, FOIA, lawsuit that Judicial Watch had launched against the State Department. WND senior staff writer Jerome R. Corsi was interested in the emails, thinking they might shed more light on the accusations he had made that the Clinton Foundation was a "vast criminal conspiracy" in his previously mentioned 2016 book, *Partners in Crime: The Clintons' Scheme to Monetize the White House for Personal Profit.*[9]

Corsi first realized a large number of the Abedin emails in the 725-page Judicial Watch release were 100 percent redacted, meaning the emails contained such highly sensitive national security information that State Department censors had blocked-out, or "redacted," all the content of the emails, leaving readable only the author, addressee, date, and subject information. In an article published in WND.com on August 25, 2016, Corsi wrote, "Of the 725 pages, more than 250 pages were 100 percent redacted, many with 'PAGE DENIED' stamped in bold."[10] Corsi commented that previous releases of Clinton emails have forced the Obama administration to admit highly sensitive State Department information was transmitted over Clinton's private email server. "On July 7, Charles McCullough, the inspector general of the intelligence community for the Office of the Director of National Intelligence, in testimony before the House Oversight and Government Reform Committee, admitted his office did not have the security clearances required to read the emails transmitted over Clinton's private email server that Congress was demanding to see," Corsi wrote. McCullough further testified that the classification of the redacted material was so top secret that a government agency he refused to name had prohibited the State Department from sharing the content with Congress without the explicit approval of the agency he refused to identify.

Next, Corsi realized that fully two-thirds of the Huma Abedin emails released in the 725-page Judicial Watch cache were emails Abedin forwarded to herself, addressed to personal email accounts she controlled outside of the State Department email system, as well as outside Hillary

Clinton's private email system maintained at her residence in Chappaqua, New York. "Of the more than 160 emails in the latest Judicial Watch release, some 110 emails—two-thirds of the total—were forwarded by Abedin to personal addresses she controlled, humamabedin@[redacted] and habedin@[redacted]," Corsi wrote in an article published in WND. com, on August 29, 2016.[11] "In other words, almost half of the emails that Abedin forwarded to her unsecured personal account have information the State Department deems too sensitive to be seen by members of Congress or the American people."

In researching further, Corsi realized that whoever censored this cache of 725-emails had neglected to block out in one instance only the email address humamabedin@yahoo.com. This confirmed to Corsi that Abedin had been sending somewhere in the range of two-thirds of all the State Department emails she had received, including emails from Hillary's State Department address as well as Hillary's private email server account to her private email account at Yahoo.com. That so many of the emails Abedin had sent to herself were so heavily redacted upon release to Judicial Watch suggested to Corsi that it was likely Abedin had archived some State Department emails to her private, unsecured email account at Yahoo.com.

On October 15, 2015, prior to Abedin's testimony in front of the House Select Committee, National Review reported the State Department explained the domain name of humamabedin@[redacted] was redacted to comply with a personal-privacy exemption.[12] On August 14, 2015, the *Washington Times* reported that the State Department had admitted to a federal judge that Abedin and Cheryl Mills, chief of staff to Clinton when she was secretary of state, used personal email accounts to conduct government business in addition to Clinton's private clintonemail.com to transact State Department business.[13] But until the Judicial Watch email release the week Corsi's two WND.com articles were published, there was no evidence suggesting Abedin had used her private email accounts as a forwarding address for State Department emails that contained sensitive material, including very possibly classified information. Until the publication of Corsi's second WND.com article on August 29, 2016, there had been no previous public identification that Abedin was using a Yahoo.com account to archive off-line State Department emails.[14]

Realizing that archiving such a large quantity of State Department emails to a private account at Yahoo.com might well constitute a criminal violation of national security laws, Corsi contacted legal and intelligence sources in Chicago and New York to determine next steps the investigation might take.

On September 8, 2016, Corsi published in WND evidence that Abedin had forwarded an email from Clinton dated August 8, 2009, clearly marked "classified," to her Yahoo.com account, providing even more evidence a crime had been committed.[15] As September 2016 progressed, Corsi speculated that if Abedin had archived conceivably thousands of Clinton-related emails off-line at her private account at Yahoo.com, she might have been allowing foreign entities, or other unauthorized users to access and read the file. Anyone with access to Abedin's username and password could read in real time and all the completely unredacted emails Abedin sent to her yahoo.com email account. Much of September 2016 was taken trying to find a legal way to force Yahoo.com to make public a list of all IP addresses that could identify various Internet users that had attempted to access or had successfully accessed Abedin's Yahoo.com account. Unfortunately, the lawyers involved in the investigation could not establish legal standing to launch a lawsuit attempting to obtain the sought-after IP information.

Finally, Corsi speculated that if Abedin had taken the trouble to archive State Department emails in her Yahoo.com email account, Abedin may have also surmised that she needed to keep the project secret by using a computer or other device not issued to her or registered by her with the State Department. Speculation developed that Abedin might have kept such a laptop or other device at her home with Weiner in New York City. The investigators working with Corsi had reason to believe Weiner was once again under investigation by the New York Police Department and the FBI for sexting to underage girls. Sexting to underage girls using his cellphone was the "Weinergate" offense that had forced Weiner to resign from the House of Representatives in 2011.[16] Investigators working with Corsi also had reason to believe that certain FBI agents, unhappy with Comey's decision in July to suspend the criminal investigation into Clinton's email scandal, had not given up trying to find a way to reopen the investigation. While the disgruntled FBI agents in New York would never have gotten permission from Washington to reopen an investigation into the Clinton email case, cooperating with the NYPD in an investigation of suspected illegal sexual activity involving minors was a different matter. Conceivably, no prior authorization from the FBI in DC was required for the FBI in New York to join the NYPD in executing a search warrant on former Congressman Weiner.

On Sunday, October 30, 2016, the *Wall Street Journal* reported that FBI investigators had discovered 650,000 emails related to the State Department on Weiner's seized laptop, which had also been used by his wife, Ms. Abedin.[17] The *Wall Street Journal* further reported the underlying metadata on the 650,000 emails suggested thousands of these emails could have been sent to or from the private server that Hillary Clinton used while she was secretary of state. The newspaper further noted it would take weeks, at a minimum, to determine whether those messages are work-related from the time Ms. Abedin served with Mrs. Clinton at the State Department; how many are duplicates of emails already reviewed by the FBI; and whether they include either classified information or important new evidence in the Clinton email probe." The *Wall Street Journal* article carefully clarified that the FBI had searched Weiner's computer while looking for child pornography, not for Clinton's State Department emails. What the article did not specify was that now the NYPD had possession of the Weiner laptop, with time to download the contents, and that now blocking an investigation into Clinton's emails, or preventing the release of those emails to the American public, was no longer in the sole control or at the sole discretion of the FBI in Washington.

Comey Closes Reopened Investigation

Democrats who had praised Comey for closing the Clinton email scandal in July reversed course and vilified him for reopening the investigation in October, just 11 days before the election. Notable was retiring Senate minority leader Harry Reid of Nevada who had called Comey a "fair, impartial director" in July, only to fire off to Comey a letter over the weekend of October 29–30, 2016, informing Comey that his actions may have violated a federal law known as the Hatch Act, "which bars FBI officials from using their official authority to influence an election." Fox News reported that Reid accused Comey of a "double-standard" in his treatment of sensitive information, saying, "Through your partisan actions, you may have broken the law."[18]

On Sunday, November 6, 2016, two days before Tuesday's election, Comey notified Congress that he had seen no evidence in the trove of State Department emails on Weiner's computer that would change his conclusion that Hillary Clinton should not face criminal charges over her handling of classified material.[19] In a letter dated November 6, 2016, addressed to the same Republican heads of key House committees who had received Comey's letter dated October 28, 2016, Comey explained, "Based on our review, we have not changed the conclusions that we expressed in July with respect to Secretary Clinton." Comey explained that the FBI investigative team had been "working around the clock" to process and review the 650,000 State Department emails supposedly found on Weiner's computer. "During that process, we reviewed all of the communications that were to or from Hillary Clinton while she was secretary of state," Comey said.[20]

"You can't review 650,000 emails in eight days," Trump said at a rally that Sunday, after learning about Comey's most recent letter to Congress that effectively called off the reopened investigation.[21] Clearly, the damage had been done. By reopening the investigation so close to the election, Comey had put a brake on Clinton's closing momentum. By exonerating Clinton so close to Election Day, Comey made it seem he had succumbed to political pressure from the Democrats. If the 650,000 State Department emails found on Weiner's laptop were so innocuous as to require only eight days of FBI investigation, why did Comey consider them of sufficient seriousness that the criminal investigation against Clinton had to be reopened so close to the election?

After the election, Corsi confirmed with the New York Police Department's press office that in the days leading up to the presidential election on November 8, the FBI terminated the NYPD investigation of Clinton's emails on former congressman Anthony Weiner's laptop, demanding that the laptop and all 650,000 State Department emails be taken to the FBI in Washington.

The move by the FBI in DC to shut down the NYPD investigation set the stage for Comey to declare in a letter to Congress November 6 that the newly discovered emails did not change the FBI's original conclusion not to refer criminal charges. WND also confirmed with the NYPD that the FBI in Washington had blocked the NYPD from making any arrests in the Weiner "sexting" case involving a fifteen-year-old girl.[22]

Trump Closes Strong: 1948 Déjà Vu, All Over Again

In 2016, Trump had repeated President Harry S Truman's miracle of 1948—he won the presidency, coming from behind, in an election where the polls, the media, and the pundits had declared him out of the race virtually from the moment he had declared his candidacy.

Trump was elected largely because in the final three months of the campaign, he won the most important phase of a campaign for the presidency of the United States—Trump won the closing argument. After each party has held its national nominating convention and the debates between the major party candidates have concluded, modern presidential campaigns enter a final, critical phase. Free of the need to confront the opposing candidate directly, the major party candidates need to make their closing arguments to the American people. This critical last phase of the presidential campaign is the last chance a presidential candidate has to make the argument to the American public that he or she is the best choice to be the next president of the United States. What 1948 proved and 2016 confirmed was that victory goes not necessarily to the favorite, but almost certainly to the candidate who proves the most capable of closing.

One of the most famous closing strategies in American political history was President Harry Truman's 1948 "Whistle-Stop" campaign in which he came from behind in the polls to beat Republican challenger Thomas Dewey. Truman was a sitting president, who took the oath of office as vice president after President Franklin D. Roosevelt died of a stroke on April 12, 1945. Dewey was an enormously popular candidate, a former New York prosecutor who built his reputation fighting organized crime. This was Dewey's second run for the presidency, having lost to Franklin D. Roosevelt in 1944, when FDR won narrowly his famous fourth term in office.

Truman's idea to run a whistle-stop train campaign happened almost by accident. The inspiration came when conservative Republican Senator Robert A. Taft of Ohio accused Truman of "blackguarding Congress at whistle stops across the country." Truman's whistle-stop campaign in 1948, when Donald Trump and Hillary Clinton were both infants, was the precursor to Trump's series of well-attended rallies some 68 years later. What exactly is a "whistle stop"? In his notable 2000 book, "The Last Campaign: How Harry Truman Won the 1948 Election," historian and economist Zachary Karabell properly described a whistle-stop as "a town so small and insignificant that it had no regularly scheduled train service and had to signal the train by whistle if any passengers wanted to board."[23] In his classic 1992 biography of Truman, bestselling author

David McCullough observed of Truman, "No president in history had ever gone so far in quest of support from the people, or with less cause for the effort, to judge by informed opinion. Nor would any presidential candidate ever again attempt such a campaign by railroad."[24]

Traveling 20,000 miles through 30 states and delivering 280 speeches, Truman's whistle-stop speeches were not noted for "grand philosophical themes," nor did he dwell on "lofty ideas."[25] Instead, it was a campaign of plain speaking, in which Truman repeatedly attacked the GOP for the high cost of living, portraying the Democratic Party as the party of the people. As Karabell described it, Truman's whistle-stop speeches communicated "a campaign of us and them, of anger, and bitterness, of the haves and the have-nots." Karabell stressed that in fighting to lead the nation for four more years, Truman "was willing to sow dissension, stir up fear, and slander his opponents."[26]

In her famous self-published 1964 book, "A Choice Not an Echo,"[27] conservative luminary Phyllis Schlafly argued that Dewey lost in 1948 because he was a "me too" candidate who refused to criticize Truman sharply for the New Deal, failing to take on Truman directly for liberal ideology, while shying away from arguing strong conservative policy alternatives. Schlafly felt certain that if he'd gone after Truman and argued for strong conservative politics, the message would have been well-received by voters in 1948, a time when the nation was emerging from the Depression and World War II. In 2016, Schlafly was one of the first conservative leaders to endorse Trump,[28] authoring her last book, "The Conservative Case for Trump," in support of his candidacy. In this book, Schlafly defined what was to become known as the "Trump Movement."[29]

Schlafly championed Trump as strongly as she had championed Ronald Reagan. "The revolution to take back America starts now," Schlafly wrote. "America starts now. Donald Trump might seem an unlikely candidate to some, but he offers the American public something it's been yearning for, 'a choice, not an echo'; a candidate not intimidated by political correctness or the liberal media." In her final analysis, Donald Trump was Schlafly's choice for president because she felt certain Trump could win. Unfortunately, Phyllis did not live to see her predictions about Trump come true. But, with her political acuity as sharp as always, Phyllis saw correctly that while he was different from Reagan, Trump could still "remake our politics as Reagan did," giving the Republican Party back the White House in 2016, a goal that had eluded the GOP in four of the last six presidential elections.[30]

Trump's Rallies

In his post-election autopsy unfiltered for his Clinton partisanship, Politico's chief political correspondent Glenn Thrush correctly observed that Trump's rallies became "the centerpiece of the campaign." Thrush criticized Trump, as well as Corey Lewandowski, Trump's first campaign manager, for the impromptu nature of Trump's rallies, in which Thrush observed Trump "picked up insights and policies like a stand-up comedian collecting material for a show." Thrush quoted Lewandowski to make his point. "He lives for the energy," Lewandowski said. "There's no one better at taking the temperature of the crowd," Lewandowski told Thrush during the campaign. "You can get instant feedback . . . We'd test out all of our best lines, some would work, some wouldn't . . . That's how we got 'Little Marco' and 'Lyin' Ted.'" Thrush commented that Trump started with "Little Marco," then switched to "Lil'" because it got more laughs. Thrush belittled Trump, observing that Trump's decision to call out Mexican "rapists" at his kickoff was inspired, in part, by a random chat he had with two Border Patrol agents at one of his golf resorts, road-testing his talking points.[31]

For Thrush and other analysts accustomed to politics in the age of television, Trump's style was unorthodox. But for those who experienced politics when television was in its infancy, Trump again drew much from Truman. "Truman was only one in a long line of campaigners who went to extremes to excite crowds, to rouse them to action, and to convince them to vote for him on election day," Karabell observed.[32] Truman's political rhetoric could appear extreme, almost rabble-rousing to those whose political awareness developed in the age of television. Karabell noted that Truman realized that with his whistle-stop speeches, he was speaking almost exclusively to the small audience present in that town, with that speech. "If he went too far during a whistle-stop speech, if he played fast and loose with facts, or if he descended to flinging dirt at his opponents, he knew that at worst he would be ridiculed or criticized by the press corps," Karabell wrote. "They might write negative articles, and columnists might invoke fair play and morality. But for most of the millions who would vote, the episode wouldn't exist. Some might read about the speech or peruse editorials against it; some might even hear it on the radio and recoil. But neither print nor radio had the same visceral effect that television would later have."[33]

This was the oddity about Trump: in the age of television, he got away with the same speaking style that Truman relied upon in the whistle-stop campaign that lifted him from the underdog to the victor in 1948. When he first announced his candidacy, the mainstream media considered him even less than an underdog. The media ridiculed Trump while pundits constantly discounted his chances, never tiring of proclaiming that this gaffe or that misstep would certainly be the end of Trump's candidacy. First, the media insisted Trump would never win the delegates needed to gain the GOP nomination on the first ballot. Then, after Trump won the nomination on the first ballot, the media and the pundits insisted Trump had a "narrow pathway" to collecting the 270 electoral votes needed to win the election. With Hillary certain to win New York and California, the judgment was near universal that Trump would fail to win both Ohio and Florida. Winning Pennsylvania, Michigan, and Wisconsin seemed impossible to the media and pundits, who informed the voting public gleefully that Hillary should prepare for her coronation.

One of Paul Manafort's best decisions was hiring Republican pollster Tony Fabrizio to determine how to beat Hillary Clinton. In the end, it was the pugnacious and bulldog-like Fabrizio, who insisted that the Trump campaign had to expand the map into Wisconsin and Michigan, while doubling down on Pennsylvania. The campaign shifted digital paid advertising resources to the states but it was Trump's personal barnstorming in all three states that made all the difference. Fabrizio insisted Trump could win only through this route. He was right.

Trump succeeded precisely because, like Truman, he dared to speak his mind. Trump threw political correctness to the wind at precisely the time when the American voter was also throwing political correctness to the wind. Eight years of Obama's "fundamental transformation" of America had convinced Middle America the far-left's political agenda was not for them. By 2016, the vast majority of Americans did not want to discriminate against anyone, such that the LGBT community was accepted and same-sex marriage tolerated. But when the White House insisted the political discussion had to address transvestites and sex change operations in the military, as well as unisex bathrooms in elementary schools, Middle America was coming to the conclusion the far-left's agenda had gone over the cliff. Americans were no more willing to read their Bibles in the closet than they were willing to hand over their guns to the local police—not when radical Islamic terrorism was wreaking havoc in Europe and beginning to crop up in the United States. Tolerance of legal immigrants was one thing, but borders open to hard-core criminals, drug cartel gangs, and Middle Eastern terrorists was again the globalism of the left reduced to the ridiculous.

Trump succeeded in the age of television precisely because the broadcast media cooperated with the print media in excoriating him for a host of remarks Hillary characterized as deplorable. Trump used mainstream media criticism to energize millions of voters disaffected with Washington insiders, smug Clinton-supporting pundits and leftist reporters. Like Truman, Trump thrived on contact with the public. Watching Trump's rallies, it was obvious Trump was turbo-charged by the energy of the crowd. Trump goaded the audience to jeer Hillary. He pointed to the press attending the rally, saying the reporters were the enemy. At almost every rally, Trump dared the press to turn their cameras around to show not only the podium where he was speaking, but also the auditoriums packed to the rafters with cheering supporters.

Through the closing phase of the 2016 presidential election, Trump's campaign was characterized by as many rallies as he could pack into one day. Thousands lined up for hours to see Trump, knowing capacity crowds would mean latecomers might not be able to get into the auditorium. By the closing days, Trump had honed his message down to a few simple thoughts: "Build the Wall," "Drain the Swamp," and "Lock Her Up." The throngs showing up at Trump rallies came prepared for a Trump stump speech that would give them a chance to chant in unison all three of these slogans. Truthfully, it did not matter the order in which Trump served up these three themes, as long as they were all three served up such that the thousands packed into auditoriums to see and hear Trump got their chance to chant all three. Trump had mastered the art of packaging his message into a few simple thoughts that could mobilize masses of voters to get themselves to the polls. Trump's promise to "Make America Great Again" got packaged on Twitter as #MAGA. Packaged into #MAGA was the promise of jobs returning to the United States, economic growth stimulated by tax cuts and fewer government regulations, an end to open borders, a clamp-down on Muslim terrorism, and a pledge to "Win Again."

Trump's campaign abandoned Obama's computer-driven "Get out the Vote," GOTV, effort that won strong majorities in the popular vote and Electoral College for Barack Obama in 2008. Trump spent sparingly on television ads, recognizing that, in the age of Internet. streaming broadcast and cable television were quickly moving into the "dinosaur media" category of by-passed technologies. Instead of relying on packaged 60-second television messages, Trump tweeted frequently, communicating directly with voters by jumping over the hostile intermediation of the typical radio, television, and print news that political campaigns have relied upon to communicate their message since the 1960s. Given the mainstream media's obsession with Trump, the campaign quickly realized Trump would get almost non-stop "earned media" free time on 24-hour cable news shows. Even Fox News—the only cable news network considered GOP-friendly—shunned Trump in favor of more established GOP leaders—including Mitt Romney who attacked Trump ferociously during the primaries. But it just didn't matter.

Clinton's campaign tended to disregard the importance of Trump drawing huge rallies, arguing that Romney had also drawn large rallies in the post-convention closing phase of the 2012 campaign. Like Romney, most attendees at Trump rallies were white Americans, but noticeably present were women supporting Trump, as well as families in attendance bringing with them their children to see and hear Trump. In 2012, despite the large rallies, millions of Evangelical Christians and white conservative voters stayed home. The Democrats imagined the same would be the case with Trump, imagining thousands were only coming out to Trump rallies because he was a celebrity, not because he was a serious professional politician. In so calculating, the Democrats failed to understand the extent to which television had made voting for president a celebrity affair, with voters ready to vote for Trump much as they voted for favorites on television shows like "Dancing with the Stars."

In underestimating the importance of Trump's drawing ability at rallies, the Democrats made a classic blunder. The rallies in the closing phase of the 2016 campaign had become for Trump what the whistle-stop talks were for Truman in 1948. Like 1948, reporters figured the polls had pre-destined Hillary as president, so crowds turning out for Trump rallies were discounted as unimportant. "Because they had already decided that the outcome was sealed, reporters and commentators ignored signs that might have pointed in a different direction," Karabell wrote about Truman's 1948 campaign. "Even the most jaded observer noted that the crowds that came out to greet Truman were larger and more enthusiastic than those that gathered around

Dewey." But the phenomenon was easily discounted. "Different explanations were offered. . . . The president's advisors bravely told reporters that the size of Truman's crowds reflected a shift in momentum and demonstrated that voters were still undecided and still prepared to reelect Truman. But the journalists and commentators didn't take that explanation seriously because polling data flatly contradicted it." Even Truman's closest advisers were not convinced. "The president's own retinue touted the turnout as a good sign during formal interviews, but privately over drinks in the club car, they were just as likely to muse about what was in store for them and the country when Dewey won," Karabell wrote.[34]

Karabell noted that "for those who did pay attention," October offered more of Truman's whistle-stops and more of his hard-hitting rhetoric. The same was true of Trump's rallies in 2016. Trump had experimented with using Teleprompters for scripted speeches when Manafort had been campaign manager. That phase of the campaign brought discipline to Trump's message. But during the stump-speech phase of Trump's closing rallies, he found he could combine the "let Trump be Trump" encouragement of Lewandowski with the "stay on message" discipline of Manafort. Now, in the final phase, Trump found Steve Bannon had genius ability to get his messages packed into the powerful mantras the thousands attending rallies planned on chanting, while Kellyanne Conway displayed equal acumen in keeping Trump's temperament level through the long airplane rides and nights away from home required for the 4-hour-sleep-per-night (or less) required to pack four to five rallies in different cities and different states into a single day. Trump hinted at these tensions in a stump speech he gave on November 2, 2016, in Pensacola, Florida. "We've gotta be nice and cool," Trump said out loud, allowing to slip out what reporters took as an internal monologue that Trump had learned to recite to himself to stay on track. "Nice and cool. All right? Stay on point, Donald. Stay on point. No sidetracks, Donald," Trump said, playing for the audience the internal drama going on now daily in his head as a result of the coaching his closest advisers were giving him. Reporters noted Trump closed this self-administered public pep talk by repeating the word, "*Niceee*"—a word Trump hung onto for emphasis.[35]

Hillary's Lethargic Close

By contrast to Trump, Hillary closed her "low energy" campaign with a fizzle, not a pop. As early as August 15, 2016, the Gateway Pundit blog noted that while Trump continued to "smash Clinton in attendance at events," Hillary appeared to have decided to take weekends off. Clinton took the weekend of August 6th and 7th off and she decided to take three days off the previous weekend August 12th through 14th. She had no scheduled events to participate in that coming Thursday through Saturday August 18th through 20th. "This in essence would mean another three days off after three days of events scheduled starting today," the Gateway Pundit noted. In total Clinton had taken 7 days off in August out of the first 14 days and was scheduled to continue with this approach. Donald Trump on the other hand had taken only two days off in August, Sunday August 7th and Sunday the 14th.[36] He had 7 days where he participated in more than one campaign event. The Gateway Pundit also noted that Trump had ten times the number of his people at his campaign events than Hillary had at hers since. More than 100,000 people had shown up for Trump events in the first half of August, with many more turned away due to the events reaching capacity. The Gateway Pundit concluded that just looking at the crowds, "Trump has a movement and Hillary has barely a heartbeat." The Gateway Pundit was not certain why Clinton was taking so much time off, but the question raised was whether the time off was because of "her terrible campaign event turnout or her poor health or some combination of both."[37]

The Gateway Pundit continued to track these trends through the rest of the 2016 campaign, concluding that Hillary was working on her campaign only about 50 percent of the time. On October 23, 2016, the Gateway Pundit reported Trump was leading Hillary by half a million people since August. "She is either sick or her campaign thinks she'll do better if she doesn't get in front of people or her campaign doesn't want to show the abysmal lack of interest in her and her events," the Gateway Pundit noted as October came to a close.[38] On November 13, 2016, the Gateway Pundit noted Trump had nearly 1 million attend his rallies in the election campaign, while Clinton totaled 100,000. Hillary had taken fifty-seven days off since July without participating in campaign rallies, amounting to more than half the ninety-nine days between August and Election Day.[39]

Trump's campaign airplane was his privately-owned, luxurious Boeing 757, measuring 155 feet in length, one of the fastest airplanes in the world, capable of going up to five hundred miles per hour with its Rolls-Royce engines. Hillary leased a standard Boeing 737 measuring 129 feet—an airplane with a standard first-class domestic seating configuration that the Clinton camp did not customize.[40]

Trump's $100 million private jet has an interior customized to make Mr. Trump and his forty-three guests feel comfortable in a flight with maximum range of sixteen-hour flying time. Trump's Boeing 757 features a bedroom, a dining room, and a private guest room. There is a full bath with 24-karat gold fixtures, and an entertainment system with an installed video room, plus reclining couches and reclining sleeper seats—all fitted with 24-karat gold seatbelts. Each seat has its own audio-visual consisting of an individual television. A dining room has luxury bench seats around custom-made worktables. Mr. Trump's master bedroom is also custom-designed, with a large flat-screen television that accesses the airplane's audio-visual system as well as his favorite movies, plus a master bathroom that includes a shower and a gold 24-karat sink.[41] No other presidential candidate in US history has ever traveled with their top staff in such a world-class comfort-oriented airplane environment.

Clearly, Trump's airplane made early-morning departures and late-night arrivals bearable, especially in contrast to Hillary whose campaign airplane lacked not only a master bedroom with full bath, but even a first-class seat that reclined fully to a sleeping position.

Several of the Podesta emails made public by WikiLeaks made clear the extent to which Clinton's own campaign staff considered her to be a poor candidate. Jennifer Palmieri, the director of communications for Hillary's 2016 presidential campaign, in an email dated April 19, 2015, to John Podesta, with copies to other key players on the Clinton campaign, commented that Hillary "has begun to hate everyday Americans."[42] This, coupled with emails showing Hillary had to be coached when to smile during her speeches, created the impression that Hillary had to be reminded to make believe that she actually liked the voters she was addressing. The Goldman Sachs speech transcripts WikiLeaks released also showed Clinton explaining to the investment bankers that she was "kind of far removed" from the middle class "because the life I've lived and the economic, you know, fortunes that my husband and I now enjoy, but I haven't forgotten it."[43]

In a WikiLeaks released email dated March 13, 2016, left-leaning opinion writer Brent Budowsky warned Podesta that Hillary "should stop attacking Bernie [Sanders], especially when she says things that are untrue, which candidly she often does." Budowsky was concerned that by lying about Bernie in her attacks on him during the primaries, Hillary was risking alienating permanently the Sanders' supporters Hillary would need to vote for her in November. The email was particularly damaging because of Budowsky's comment that Hillary is a habitual liar.[44] In an email chain dated August 22, 2015, Neera Tanden, president of Podesta's Center for American Progress, wrote Podesta that Hillary's "inability to just do a national interview and communicate feelings of remorse and regret is now, I fear, becoming a character problem (more so than honesty)." Tanden continued to say that people hate Hillary's arrogance.[45]

An email exchange dated March 22, 2014, between Hillary's campaign manager Robby Mook and her adviser/attorney Cheryl Mills, that included John Podesta, made clear all three had their doubts from the start about the likely success of a gender-based campaign focused on the premise that Hillary would be the first woman president. "In fact, I think running on her gender would be the same mistake as 2008, i.e., having a message at odds with what voters ultimately want," Mook said. "She ran on experience when voters wanted change . . . and sure there was plenty of data in polls with voters saying her experience appealed to them. But that was missing the larger point—voters wanted change." Mook felt it was similar in 2016. "Same deal here—lots of people are going to say it would be neat for a woman to be president but that doesn't mean that's actually why they will vote for her. That's likely to be how she will handle the economy and relate to the middle class. It's also risky because injecting gender makes her candidacy about her and not the voters and making their lives better." Podesta agreed. "One caveat," he said simply, "gender will be a big field and volunteer motivator, but won't close the deal."[46]

Finally, the Podesta emails made public by WikiLeaks revealed Hillary's campaign insiders as highly-educated white elitists who showed no compunction in sharing amongst themselves their far-leftist biases—demeaning supporters of Bernie Sanders as "self-righteous whiners," calling Hispanic party leaders such as former New Mexico governor Bill Richardson "needy Latino's," while Clinton's communication director Jennifer Palmieri demeaned Catholics. "I imagine they think it is the most socially acceptable, politically conservative religion—their rich friends wouldn't understand if they became evangelical," Palmieri wrote.[47] It is hard to imagine how the Clinton campaign thought Hillary could attract the votes of so diverse an array of constituencies, while their hacked emails belied their clearly disingenuous public front of identity politics.

CONCLUSION

Trump Wins

As I've said from the beginning, ours was not a campaign, but rather an incredible and great movement made up of millions of hard-working men and women who love their country and want a better, brighter future for themselves and for their families.

Donald Trump, Victory Speech, New York City,
November 9, 2016[1]

As Pulitzer Prize–winning journalist Theodore H. White wrote, "There is no excitement anywhere in the world, short of war, to match the excitement of an American presidential campaign." If only White had witnessed Donald Trump's 2016 victory.[2]

The short summary of the 2016 presidential election was that the nation had decided simply "No More Bushes" and "No More Clintons." With Jeb's defeat in the primaries and Hillary's defeat in the general election, American voters had decided to put a nail in the coffin of both political dynasties. Donald Trump, the most unlikely candidate had ultimately triumphed.

Trump won as an outsider, opposed down to the bitter end by the mainstream media across the board, by Republican and Democratic pundits alike, and even by the GOP elite leadership in the nation's capital. Remarkably, the celebrity star of the hit television show *The Apprentice* had won the Oval Office—defying all the professional politicians who dared ridicule and oppose him.

What appeared to political professionals a repeat of Ronald Reagan's victory over incumbent President Jimmy Carter in 1980, as I've explained at length, also had overtones of President Harry S Truman's 1948 surprise victory over GOP challenger Thomas E. Dewey.

"Premature Elation"

A week before the election, Hillary had been so confident of victory that her campaign had scheduled a $7 million barge-launched fireworks display over the Hudson River on Election Night, planned so that her supporters gathered in the Javits Center for a victory celebration could see the pyrotechnics display. The *New York Post* reported that the aerial detonations would last two minutes, with the triumphal celebration permitted to start as early as 9:30 pm—only a half-hour after the polls were scheduled to close in New York, evidently anticipating an early win.[3]

The front page of the *New York Post* christened the planned fireworks event as "Premature Elation," noting, "Hillary's already booked fireworks on the Hudson, but it ain't over yet." Reporting on the fireworks event, the *New York Post* noted that the New York Fire Department memo ordering its Marine 1 company to provide protection for the fireworks show was sent out Friday, October 28, 2016.

Ironically, the Clinton campaign had arranged the fireworks celebration on the same day FBI director James Comey sent his second letter to Congress, notifying the Republican leaders of key House committees that the FBI was reopening its criminal investigation into Hillary's private email system, after finding new evidence on the laptop Weiner shared with his wife.

With the double hit of *New York Post* front page being the talk of the town that day in New York City, plus the Clinton campaign being rocked by the FBI reopening the criminal investigation into Hillary's emails, Clinton's scheduling of fireworks at a victory celebration definitely seemed premature. Two days before the election, Hillary's campaign quietly cancelled the fireworks display.[4]

How Election Night Unfolded

At approximately 1:35 am ET, Trump was declared winner in Pennsylvania, a state Clinton had viewed as essential to her "firewall" strategy designed to keep Trump out of the White House. With Pennsylvania securely in his column, Trump had 264 of the 270 electoral votes needed to win.

One of the most pivotal decisions Trump would make was his selection of West Point graduate David Urban to run his Pennsylvania campaign. A former altar boy and the son of a union steel worker from Aliquippa, Pennsylvania, Urban distinguished himself in combat and in government. The hard-charging Urban helped Trump make inroads into union-heavy western Pennsylvania and is the only operative to switch a blue state to red.

Another wise choice for a state director was that of Ed McMullen in South Carolina. McMullen was a Trump supporter from the very beginning and offered the campaign invaluable service for over eighteen months, culminating in Trump's victory in both North and South Carolina. McMullen also is an example of the how Trump is capable of picking truly excellent people within his organization, a trait he carries with him into the presidency.

By the time Florida was called, Trump had already won the battleground states of Ohio and North Carolina. Victory looked certain, with Trump ahead in the vote counting in Wisconsin, Michigan, and Arizona—any one of which would have been sufficient to elect Trump as the forty-fifth president of the United States[5] In the end, Trump won Arizona, along with Michigan and Wisconsin—two states Hillary and her supporters had always been sure would vote for Clinton.

Across the nation, the millions who stayed awake as the night progressed, glued to their televisions as the returns flowed in, were beginning to realize that what had seemed impossible, was now rapidly becoming reality: Trump was going to win.

As the realization that Hillary had lost set in among the crowd at the Javits Center, Hillary supporters began leaving, drifting away disconsolate, alone or in small groups. Other reports were that Hillary "couldn't stop crying." Once she realized she'd lost, she became "inconsolably emotional," went into a "psychotic, drunken rage," and began beating on her top aides, including Robby Mook and John Podesta.[6]

That Hillary did not appear before her supporters that evening to thank them lent support to the tweets being posted by Clinton insiders and various people in the media that Hillary was out of control, and not presentable to the public in her rage at losing.

At 2:02 am ET, early Wednesday morning, November 9, John Podesta made an appearance at Clinton Headquarters in the Jacob K. Javits Center in New York City at what was supposed to be a Hillary Clinton victory celebration. "It's been a long night and it's been a long campaign," Podesta said, trying to be upbeat. "But I can say we can wait a little bit longer, can't we?" The crowd cheered enthusiastically.

"They are still counting votes and every vote counts," he insisted. "Some states are too close to call, so we're not going to have anything else to say tonight," Podesta explained. Translated, that meant Hillary Clinton had no intention of appearing in public that night to concede.

"So, listen to me. Everybody should head home and get some sleep. We'll have more to say tomorrow," Podesta said, very business-like. "I want every person in this hall, and across the country supporting Hillary, to know that your voices and your enthusiasm mean so much. We are so proud of you and we are so proud of her," he continued.

"She's not done yet. So thank you for being with her. She has always been with you. I have to say this tonight, 'Goodnight,' and we'll be back, we'll have more to say. "Let's get those votes counted and let's bring this home. Thank you so much for all you have done. You are in all of our hearts. Thank you."[7]

Podesta left the podium, having created the impression that there was still a chance Hillary might win. What was clear was that Hillary— the likely loser—was not going to make a traditional Election Night concession speech because she was not yet willing to call it quits.

A leaked video from earlier in the evening on Election Day showed the Clinton family celebrating, after they had been told mistakenly Clinton had won. Chelsea rushes into her mother's arms, as Hillary stops clapping and the two embrace. Standing next to them, looking elated, Bill Clinton jumps up and down, pumping his fists in the air, looking like a schoolchild who cannot contain his excitement.[8]

From several unconfirmed reports, the reversal of fortune as the votes were being counted was crushing on the Clintons. The *American Spectator* reported that after Hillary realized she lost, she'd gone into a rage. "Secret Service officers told at least one source that she began yelling, screaming obscenities, and pounding furniture," R. Emmett Tyrrell, Jr. reported on the Spectacle Blog. 'She picked up objects and threw them at attendants and staff. She was in an uncontrollable rage. Her aides could not allow her to come out in public.'"

Tyrell also commented that he wanted to report on Bill Clinton's whereabouts, but that was not possible, because when Podesta came out to give his "aimless speech," Bill was nowhere to be found.[9]

Breitbart.com, noted that Tyrrell's reporting remained a thorn in the side of the Clintons since the *American Spectator* first reported in the 1990s the "Trooper-gate" stories detailing Bill Clinton's sexual escapades as related by his Arkansas security detail, that first referenced Paula Jones, setting Clinton on the road to impeachment. "In the '90s, we published several pieces that documented her throwing lamps and books," Tyrrell told Breitbart. "This happened pretty often. She has such a foul mouth that the Arkansas state troopers learned a thing or two from her. She has a foul mouth and a good throwing arm."[10]

The question whether or not Clinton had called Trump on Election Night was not fully answered until Trump's campaign manager Kellyanne Conway, appeared on NBC's *Today Show* on Wednesday morning.

Conway explained first that President Obama had called Trump on Election Night. "It was a very warm conversation and we were very happy to receive the call from the president," she said. "They had a great, thorough conversation about Mr. Trump's victory," Conway elaborated. "He was congratulated and they resolved to work together, which is exactly what this country needs to get this president and the president-elect as well as others in leadership positions to help unify and heal the country. We expect the two gentlemen will be meeting soon."[11]

Only after discussing Obama's call to Trump did Conway also reveal that Hillary Clinton called Trump, just as Trump was preparing to speak to his supporters. "I gave the phone to Mr. Trump," Conway said, "and he and Secretary Clinton had a very warm and cordial conversation. Secretary Clinton commended Mr. Trump on his victory, and Mr. Trump commended her for being smart and tough, and for running a really hard-fought campaign."

Why Clinton called Trump to concede on Election Night, while sending Podesta out to the crowd saying she was not yet done remains an unanswered contradiction of what behind the scenes appears to have deteriorated into an angry, confused, possibly alcohol-lubricated night of defeat and self-pity.

At approximately 2:50 a.m. ET, Donald Trump took the stage as president-elect to give his acceptance speech before a crowd of joyful supporters shouting, "USA, USA." Trump began by acknowledging he had received a concession call from Hillary Clinton.

"Now it is time for America to bind the wounds of division, have to get together. To all Republicans and Democrats and independents across this nation, I say it is time for us to come together as one united people," Trump began his 15-minute speech.[12] While many of the insulated "experts" were still picking their jaws up off the floor, the theme song of the action movie "Air Force One" played—a subtle reminder that a regular guy had just been elected president of the United States. His words echoed his optimistic core message: his victory was a massive movement for the people, focused on making government function for the people so that the United States can be the greatest nation on earth.

Trump sounded satisfied, but his tone was conciliatory. "I pledge to every citizen of our land that I will be President for all of Americans, and this is so important to me," he said. "For those who have chosen not to support me in the past, of which there were a few people, I'm reaching out to you for your guidance and your help so that we can work together and unify our great country."

"As I've said from the beginning, ours was not a campaign but rather an incredible and great movement, made up of millions of hard-working men and women who love their country and want a better, brighter future for themselves and for their family," Trump continued.

He pledged to be president "for all Americans." He promised that the forgotten Americans would be "forgotten no longer." Once again, speaking to a crowd full of people wearing the "Make America Great Again" caps conspicuously lacking Trump's name, the president-elect announced that Clinton had called him and congratulated "us."

"It is a movement comprised of Americans from all races, religions, backgrounds, and beliefs, who want and expect our government to serve the people—and serve the people it will," he stressed. "Working together, we will begin the urgent task of rebuilding our nation and renewing the American dream. I've spent my entire life in business, looking at the untapped potential in projects and in people all over the world."[13]

When President Nixon was reelected in a landslide in 1972, film critic Pauline Kael famously said in disbelief, "I live in a rather special world. I only know one person who voted for Nixon. Where they are I don't know. They're outside my ken. But sometimes when I'm in a theater I can feel them."[14] Her statement has come to symbolize the insulation of the liberal elite, living in a bubble and hearing only the opinions of fellow liberals. It has become known as "Pauline Kael Syndrome" and its most virulent strain has been discovered in late 2016, complete with paranoid delusions of Russian hacking.

Liberals are so committed to their ideology that they confuse it with morality or religion. It often takes the place of moral objectivity in their lives. If you disagree with a liberal, it's not merely a disagreement; you are morally wrong and mean to do harm to the world. Trump and his supporters represent not merely a different prescription for what ails the country, but a ghastly evil. This childish view produces no coping skills, so liberals largely became unhinged in the wake of Trump's historic victory.

Our televisions, radios and browsers were flooded with the tears of intolerant leftists. Their whining on hearing Trump won, their offers of safe spaces and grief counseling, their comparisons to 9/11—all this moved them even further from capturing mainstream American votes. Imagine losing a loved one in the World Trade Center and then hearing a liberal in Manhattan compare 9/11 to the results of a free and fair election in which Donald Trump won.

The snowflakes were triggered. Rather than learn from their electoral loss, the Left would wallow in hatred, divisiveness and elitism. The party that ended slavery, stopped the war in Vietnam and won the Cold War had retaken the White House, thanks to a political outsider from Queens, New York. The fragile psyches of the left and their media minions could not abide.

Even worse, their inability to cope with reality also set off a series of fiendish and outlandish conspiracy theories to delegitimize Trump's victory, as well as schemes to steal it. The absurd lengths they went to make Pauline Kael Syndrome seem charming.

The Next Day: Hillary Appears in Public to Concede

On Wednesday, November 9, when Hillary Clinton appeared in public for Hillary to give a concession speech, Hillary wore a Ralph Lauren pantsuit in purple and Bill, at Hillary's side throughout the concession speech, wore a matching purple tie.[15] The consensus explanation among fashion journalists, in the absence of an explanation from the Clintons, was yet another reference to feminism, in that purple, along with white and green, make up the suffragette flag.[16]

From almost the first sentences of Hillary Clinton's twelve-minute concession speech, she displayed the same political rancor against Trump, as she did during the campaign, but here buried as a subtext.

"Last night, I congratulated Donald Trump and offered to work with him on behalf of our country," Clinton said.[17] "I hope that he will be a successful president for all Americans. This is not the outcome we wanted or we worked so hard for and I'm sorry that we did not win this election for the values we share and the vision we hold for our country."

Hillary appeared to be implying that Trump, as the racist, xenophobic, Islamaphobic, homophobic, and sexist hater that she portrayed him as during the election campaign, could not possibly represent all Americans. She continued, implying that Trump's voters represented perhaps the worst of America.

"But I feel pride and gratitude for this wonderful campaign that we built together, this vast, diverse, creative, unruly, energized campaign," she said. "You represent the best of America and being your candidate has been one of the greatest honors of my life."

Next, Hillary affirmed she still believed in America, stating this again with an undertone that suggested her belief in America had been called into question by Trump winning the election.

"We have seen that our nation is more deeply divided than we thought. But I still believe in America and I always will," she said. "And if you do, then we must accept this result and then look to the future. Donald Trump is going to be our president. We owe him an open mind and the chance to lead."

She concluded by reiterating the themes of identity politics that had characterized her campaign from the first television commercial she had produced announcing her candidacy.

"We've spent a year and a half bringing together millions of people from every corner of our country to say with one voice that we believe that the American dream is big enough for everyone—for people of all races and religions, for men and women, for immigrants, for LGBT people, and people with disabilities," she said, adding, "for everyone."

She built to her conclusion with the most retweeted line of her speech, and of the election as a whole—as might have been anticipated, another reference to feminism: "And—and to all the little girls who are watching this, never doubt that you are valuable and powerful and deserving of every chance and opportunity in the world to pursue and achieve your own dreams."[18]

Trump won the votes of white women overall, 53 percent to Hillary's 43 percent, failing to win over white woman without a college degree— a subgroup that Trump won 62 percent to Hillary's 34 percent. "Although Clinton didn't outright lose women, their relatively anemic support for her in key states played a role in her Electoral College demise," wrote Clare Malone at poll-analyst Nate Silver's much followed website, FiveThirtyEight.com. "Preliminary exit polls Tuesday (Election Day, November 8, 2016) showed that her loss in Florida was driven, in part, by her poor performance among women in the state."[19] This had to be a crushing defeat for Hillary Clinton, especially after predicating much of her campaign rhetoric on her enthusiasm to break the glass ceiling to become the first female president.

Trump's Success with African American Voters

I feel strongly that Donald Trump and the Republicans now have a unique opportunity to make major gains among African American voters. Although Trump only ran marginally better among African American voters than Romney or McCain, the small difference was significant in the overall outcome of the race.

The Trump campaign emulated Richard Nixon's ability to craft messages able to sway African Americans. First, the Trump campaign focused its message on specific segments of black voters that would defect from the Democratic Party fold. Strategists working for Trump took care to master the issues that mattered to African American millennials, social conservative and pro-life African Americans, urbanized African Americans living in depressed communities (especially Michigan, Pennsylvania, Wisconsin, and Ohio), Haitian Americans living in Florida, New York, and Pennsylvania, and disgruntled black voters who supported Bernie Sanders during the Democratic Primary of 2016.

Working carefully with African American outreach advisors, Trump nuanced and tailored his campaign message to the bloc of black voters who hated Hillary Clinton and did not want her to win. Trump shunned taking a race-neutral approach, instead deciding to reach out to black voters the Clinton campaign presumed to own. Instead, of avoiding the prickly issues of race and poverty— as politically correct Democrats had done for decades—Trump aimed his frank and matter-of-fact message at poor, working class, and lower middle-class African Americans who knew the Democratic Party had done nothing to improve their economic status. Media pundits and seasoned political experts viewed Trump's down-to-earth rhetoric about African Americans as political suicide, but many blacks were relieved and thankful that the Republican put their issues in the forefront of the campaign.

In addition to this, Trump's call for a restriction on immigration greatly aided the growth of popularity among blacks. Nationwide, African Americans have been increasingly harmed by illegal immigration, and they detested the Democratic Party's championing this issue while neglecting blacks. Thus, Trump's ads and speeches that directly targeted the economic concerns of the middle-class—good jobs, safe and prosperous communities, a solid education, tougher immigration laws, and homeownership—all tenets of the proverbial and shared American Dream—were well received by millions of blacks. One of the most important elements of Trump's appeal to blacks in 2016 was that he proactively dignified the human worth and value of blacks that Democrats have neglected in both cities and towns across America. Trump, moreso than any modern presidential candidate, aggressively dispelled the notions of those in the GOP who continue to associate racial stereotypes that equated blackness with dependence on government handouts, welfare, affirmative action, and welfare benefits at the taxpayers' expense.

African Americans supported Trump because they, like white Americans in the rust belt, want change. In 2008 and 2012, African Americans voted in incredible numbers for Barack Obama because he promised change. He did not deliver. Trump is a man known for getting things done, and he has done more to speak to the forgotten African Americans and the fly-over whites who have suffered for decades as the elites have outsourced the industrial base and care little for those left behind. Many African American voters cast ballots for Trump because they were angry with the Democratic Party, and the do-nothing two terms of Barack Obama. A massive "stay home don't vote movement" largely promoted over social media was a factor in why many blacks who voted in 2008 and 2012 for Obama chose to stay home from the polls in 2016. This, and the perception of those blacks who had voted in the primary election for Bernie Sanders that Clinton's campaign had rigged the election so Sanders would lose, led to lower voter turnout among African Americans. In addition, many blacks who supported Sanders voted for Trump as a form of protest.

Another factor in the 2016 general election, was that many African Americans refused to vote for Clinton because of her role in starting the illegal war against Libya. In that war, US-funded Islamic terrorists/ mercenaries ethnically cleansed black Libyans, known as Tawerghans. Rumors circulated amongst the black community that Hillary Clinton tried to have former Congressman Reverend Walter Fauntroy, who was an African American, assassinated in August 2011, and that she succeeded in having Muammar Gaddafi sodomized and executed in October 2011. Many media pundits that vilified Gaddafi in their support of Hillary Clinton had no idea that Gaddafi was considered a savior to scores of millions of blacks and Arabs. Gaddafi gave millions of dollars to African American causes and, in particular, prevented the closure of Shaw University, a historic black college in North Carolina.

The presidential campaign unearthed many atrocious things that the Clintons and their Clinton Foundation have done to blacks on a global basis. For example, the Clintons made a fortune selling illegal and unsafe blood of African Americans prisoners in Arkansas to unsuspecting African nations—surely causing sickness and disease to already impoverished people. Reputable newspapers published stories of the Clinton Foundation selling cheap watered-down HIV-AIDs medications to over 9 million African people—while reaping tremendous profits and hastening the suffering and death of those who they had swindled. Those familiar with the twenty-two-year war in Central Africa that has resulted in over 6 million deaths, millions of rapes, and millions internally displaced in Congo, Rwanda, Uganda, Burundi, and the Central African Republic, and these conflicts could have been prevented had Bill Clinton as president and Hillary Clinton as secretary of state sought to promote peace versus quick-profits for multinational corporations. Arguably, many African Americans and members of the Haitian American community, which numbers over a million persons, are outraged by the exploitative policies they employed through their economic raping and looting of Haiti for over twenty-five years, and misappropriating more than 96 percent of nearly $14 billion in relief funds earmarked for reconstruction of the earthquake-leveled island nation. Those that have done further investigation know that the Clintons have undermined democracy in Haiti by stealing elections, imposing illegal land-grabbing deals on the sovereign nation, and abusing State Department connections to secure pay-to-play arrangements or shake-down tactics to enrich the Clinton Foundation, which amounts to nothing more than a private family slush fund.

Many people in the black community felt a Trump candidacy fulfill the fundamental principles shared by Black Conservatism: the pursuit of educational and professional excellence as a means of advancement within the society; the promotion of safety and security in the community beyond the typical casting of a criminal as a "victim" of societal racism; self-reliant economic development through free enterprise rather than looking to the federal government for assistance; the need to empower the individual and community via self-improvement moral virtue, conscience, and the Christian faith; that life starts with conception and eugenics, abortion, and amoral living are existential threats to black survival; and, that black people have been enslaved by welfare dependency. Approximately, 15 to 30 percent of blacks are moderately conservative, or very conservative. A Pew Research Center survey showed that 19 percent of blacks identify as Religious Right. Trump's pro-faith, pro-life, pro-guns, pro-family, anti-immigration, anti-abortion, and pro-America platform placed him in line with many white Evangelicals who since 1996 have seen increased fellowship with African American Christians. Furthermore, the African American church has traditionally been an important element of social and political movements in the black community. On issues concerning the LGBT agenda, black Protestants are more socially conservative than other groups, excepting white Evangelicals, and many black Christians have tired of Obama and the gay-pandering Democratic Party that has fixated on sexuality and ignored the more pressing issues of African Americans.

Many African Americans voted for Trump because he is against abortion, and black prolife activists like Dr. Alveda King, Reverend Clenard Childress, Lonnie Poindexter, Elaine Riddick, Dean Nelson, Reverend William Owen, and hundreds of others have slowly begun to turn the tide against Planned Parenthood of America. Hillary Clinton's adamant endorsement of American Birth Control League founder Margaret Sanger as her hero and inspiration is comparable to telling a Jew that Hitler is your mentor. In spite of the mainstream media's marginalization of pro-life activists, anti-abortion fighters have made Margaret Sanger one of the most hated women among African Americans—especially millennials. Planned Parenthood has had to recruit major black movie stars and pop music artists to counter the covert information war being waged against eugenics and abortion. In 2009, Life Dynamics released the landmark anti-abortion film "Maafa 21" and it has become an underground expose on Planned Parenthood's eugenics agenda targeting blacks. Millions of people have seen the film and many blacks have converted to the pro-life perspective, which means that Trump, who has spoken out against Planned Parenthood, received votes from anti-abortion African Americans who are often religious people who view voting for Hillary Clinton as an act against God.

African Americans, initially, were excited about the election of Obama in 2008, and, in 2012, they held their noses and voted again for the incumbent—many grasping to the maniacal urban legend that the second term would be devoted to making things right. Obama's prioritizing of illegal immigrants, radical championing the LGBT agenda, his cowardly reluctance to speak out against racial injustice, and his exclusion of subprime borrowers from his foreclosures relief package deeply embittered low and middle income African Americans.

Ironically, African American voters never had high expectations from a black president, believing that he himself would face near insurmountable structural and systemic racism. Nevertheless, they found themselves disgusted that Obama strove to disappoint and insult them by trampling under foot practically every issue that mattered to them, with what appeared to be a deliberate and cynical pragmatism. As the newness of Obama wore off, a quiet riot of black rage was kindled against the Democratic Party and its black functionaries and auxiliaries Jesse Jackson, Al Sharpton, Donna Brazile, the Congressional Black Caucus, the NAACP, the Urban League, and the Leadership Council for Civil Rights. Each time a black community rose in revolt from Ferguson to Milwaukee, or gross injustice like Flint's unsafe drinking water, or another police officer acquitted for killing a black man, a popular sentiment grew that, in practice, the substance of Obama was no different from any of the previous white presidents.

Moreover, President Obama and Hillary Clinton failed to see that much of the African American community no longer viewed a black in the White House as symbolically significant, and the incumbent's vain request for blacks to vote for his legacy as an insult. Obama campaigning to place a black in the White House had symbolic relevance to millions of African Americans, but his stumping for Hillary Clinton degraded the incumbent into just another politician. Obama and Clinton miscalculated the symbolic importance of the first black president giving his approval as a type of electoral apostolic succession. Nation of Islam Minister Louis Farrakhan succinctly mocked Obama as having no legacy with African Americans. In a nutshell, Hillary Clinton's decision to have the Obamas campaign for her was counterproductive with black as well as white voters. Obama never had a political base among African American voters, nor had he any coattails to lend her. Furthermore, most African Americans remembered the deep rift between the Obamas and the Clintons,

Hillary Clinton's banishing of Danney Williams was a 21st century example of how 19th century Hillary truly is. The alternative media's release of the short film *Banished: The Danney Williams Story* unearthed the existence of Bill Clinton's thirty-year-old out-of-wedlock black son that Hillary abandoned by forcing Bill Clinton to cut all ties with Danney and Danney's mother. According to Danney's aunt, Hillary Clinton had threatened to have the Williams family disappear. In subsequent years, while Bill, Hillary, and Chelsea Clinton enjoyed the comfort of the Arkansas governor's office, Danney's mother Bobbie Williams was jailed, men attempted to kill his aunt, and child welfare services took custody of the boy and his younger siblings. In foster care, Danney and his siblings suffered intense deprivation, struggling to be raised in a Little Rock under siege of drugs and gang violence. Danney had to live under the shadow of knowing his stepmother Hillary hated him and unsure whether or not his father—the president of the United States—cared.

During the 2016 presidential campaign, Danney gave two press conferences and a video appeal to President Obama for help. The appeals to Bill Clinton might not have helped Danney touch his father's heart, but his story moved millions. The unwanted mixed raced son, the aloof white father, and the hateful white wife is as much a part of the South as football and fried chicken. Few African Americans could not feel and share Danney's sorrows, and in a political season the saga of the unwanted black boy banished by the same woman remembered for calling African American youth predators angered even stalwart Clinton supporters. Moreover, Danney Williams' story confirmed in the minds of many African Americans what they thought all along—that Hillary Clinton was a nasty, racist, hateful and cruel "Plantation Missus" who viewed blacks as dirt beneath her feet. Danney was the double deluxe combo burger of lies and deceit that Hillary could neither swallow nor wash down with a large drink. Her visceral hatred and contempt for her black stepson was a camel straw to many black females and young people already leery of the former First Lady.

In 2016, the palpable disdain that young blacks felt for Hillary Clinton was aggravated by the State Department email scandal and the lack of her being prosecuted, the social media exposure of the corruption of the Clinton Foundation in Libya, the alternative media onslaught (Black Twitter et. al.), the theft of votes from the Bernie Sanders campaign—especially in New York, the beating of pro-Sanders demonstrators at the Philadelphia Democratic Convention, Clinton's silence on all the police slayings of black men, and the viral Danney Williams stories morphed into a massive stay home and "ABC (anyone but Clinton)" movement. In as much as Hillary Clinton had been painted as the "queen of Black pain", young African American people—especially males—chafed as they learned about the gross criminality of Hillary Clinton. Clinton who perjured herself before Congress and committed numerous crimes, and, unlike the hundreds of thousands of black men arrested and forced to plead guilty for crimes they had not committed, the former First Lady, senator, and secretary of state basked in her arrogance, white privilege and impunity. Given the millions of blacks harmed by Clinton's laws, the email scandal enraged and estranged African American voters from the Democratic Party.

In 2012, African American voter participation exceeded that of white voters for the first time in US voting history. In 2012, the impact of black voters was so important that black voters accounted for Obama's entire margin of victory in seven states, including Florida, Maryland, Michigan, Nevada, Ohio, Pennsylvania, and West Virginia. Black participation had increased in all three presidential election cycles since 2000—a trend that Hillary Clinton reversed in 2016.[20] In 2016, Black voters all over the United States staged a franchise rebellion against the Democrats. Hillary ran, Hillary lied, and Hillary lost. This, in no small part, was due to the millions of black voters who stayed home or voted for Trump November 8, 2016.

The expectation of the Clinton campaign and the mainstream media was inconsistent with the prior trend, over fifty years, of African Americans giving 11 to 16 percent of their vote to Republican and Independent candidates in presidential elections. Among recent presidents, only Lyndon Johnson in 1964, Al Gore in 2000, and Barack Obama in 2008 and 2012 have received 90 percent or more of the black vote. Hillary Clinton received 88 percent of the African American vote.

Stop the Steal, Inc.

I set up an organization to conduct exit polls in pre-selected precincts so that we could later analyze whether there were significant differences between the vote totals reported by computer voting machines and our exit polls. We were immediately sued in federal court in six states by the democrats and the Clinton campaign, charging that we planned to intimidate voters and harass them on election day in an effort to suppress voter turnout.

I organized Stop the Steal, Inc. with the goal of posting non-partisan "Vote Protectors" at some 7,000 polling locations in key precincts throughout the nation. The volunteers were trained to take scientifically based exit polls to help determine whether or not the final totals reported from voting machines reflect the actual vote.

The goal was to conduct scientifically valid, methodologically sound exit polls outside certain targeted precinct polling places in eight swing states. We planned to then compare the reported voting machine total to the exit poll results in that targeted precinct. The US State Department under Hillary Clinton required not more than a 2 percent deviance between actual reported results and exit poll results in judging the integrity of foreign elections. All we asked is the same standard apply to the 2016 presidential election. We targeted precincts to include historically partisan areas as well as swing precincts. What we sought to obtain was valid and accurate exit polls in which voter participation is entirely voluntary.

Led by Marc Elias of Perkins Coie LLP in Washington, the general counsel for Hillary Clinton's 2016 presidential campaign, the Democratic Party in Nevada, Arizona, Pennsylvania and Ohio filed lawsuits to block Stop the Steal, Inc. from putting volunteers at polling locations to take exit polls and public surveys to prevent voter fraud.

Just days prior to Election Day, the United States Court of Appeals for the Sixth Circuit granted an emergency motion by Stop the Steal, Inc. and stayed the restraining order issued Friday, November 4 by the District Court in Ohio that would have barred Stop the Steal Vote Protectors. The Court of Appeals wrote: "After reviewing the District Court's order, the motion for an emergency stay of that order, and the Plaintiff's submission in response to the Petition for Initial En Banc Hearing, we conclude that the Plaintiff [Hillary Clinton by way of the Ohio Democrat Party] did not demonstrate before the district court a likelihood of success on the merits, and that all of the requisite factors weigh in favor of granting the stay." A federal judge in Phoenix refused to issue a similar injunction sought by Democrats that would have ordered Stop the Steal not to engage in their announced plans to conduct exit polls. US District Judge John Tuchi's ruling said the Arizona Democratic Party failed to show evidence that the Republicans were conspiring to conduct illegal voter intimidation.

The democrats' lead attorney David Boyce appealed the ruling to the US Supreme Court and the court reaffirmed that neither Roger Stone nor Donald Trump (who was also sued) had any plans to, or ever would, engage in voter intimidation. Given that Boyce had been my nemesis in the 2000 Bush versus Gore Florida recount, the score is now Stone: 2; Boyce: 0.

Stop The Steal's online instructions for volunteers conducting the exit poll under the name "Vote Protectors" told volunteers to limit their dialogue with voters to a simple, respectful script. If exiting voters agree to participate, Vote Protectors were instructed to ask a simple three-question poll. Vote Protectors were forbidden from wearing campaign hats, buttons or T- shirts or acting in any partisan manner. The instructions also made clear to Vote Protectors that "at no time should you reveal or discuss your own vote intentions as this would taint the polling sample."

This was a beginning effort in what we plan over time to implement as a permanent truth campaign to be implemented in mid-term and presidential elections nationwide. There is excellent support for expanding the Stop the Steal program to be found in State Department publications instructing foreign nations on how to conduct elections free of voter fraud. A 2015 publication of the US Agency for International Development (USAID), a division of the State Department, entitled "Assessing and Verifying Election Results,"[21] noted Parallel Vote Tabulation, PVT, is the most scientifically reliable methodology to verify the voting tabulation process, whether the voting is done by paper ballot or electronically, by voting machine.

The USAID publication describes PVT as follows:

- Parallel vote tabulation, sometimes called a quick count,
- is an independent tabulation of polling station results— using data from all stations or a representative sample of them—for the purpose of projecting election results and/or verifying their accuracy. To be credible, a PVT should be conducted by trained

observers who observe and report on the entire process at the polling station on election day.

- PVT observers collect the reported results from the polling stations and use their data to independently tabulate the election results. Discrepancies between the PVT results and the official results may suggest manipulation or reveal mistakes in the tabulation process.

The USAID distinguishes that while exit polls share characteristics with PVT, with both utilizing a methodology that relies largely upon taking surveys. Exit polls are less rigorous, such that while exit polls might be suggestive of results, PVT surveys tend to be more reliable in their conclusions.

"Exit polls can deter fraud at the national level when publicized before an election," the USAID publication notes with regard to detecting fraud. "Exit polls, however, are conducted outside polling stations, minimizing the deterrence effect on polling station officials."

Election Aftermath: Riots in the streets

In the days immediately following the election, demonstrators in various cities across the United States took to the streets, protesting Trump's win. Holding signs that said, "Not My President," the #NeverTrump crowd on the far-left ignored Hillary Clinton's repeated admonitions to Trump at the end of the election campaign that refusal to accept the election outcome was "destructive to democracy."

On November 10, Trump tweeted, "Just had a very open and successful presidential election. Now professional protestors, incited by the media, are protesting. Very unfair!"[22] The next day, Trump made his message more conciliatory, tweeting: "Love the fact that the small group of protestors last night have passion for our great city. We will all come together and be proud!"[23]

On November 11, 2016, the Associated Press reported Portland, Oregon, was the epicenter of the anti-Trump riots spreading across the country, with some 4,000 protestors marching in Portland's downtown area, smashing windows, and chanting, "We reject the president-elect." As midnight approached, Portland Police pushed back against the crowd, as protestors threw objects at them. As the protests dwindled through the night, Portland police announced twenty-six demonstrators were arrested. In Denver, protesters managed to shut down Interstate 25 near downtown briefly, as demonstrators made their way onto the freeway. Traffic was halted in the northbound and southbound lanes for about a half-hour. Protesters also briefly shut down interstate highways in Minneapolis and Los Angeles. In San Francisco's downtown, high-spirited high school students marched through, chanting "not my president" and holding signs urging a Donald Trump eviction. Protestors in San Francisco waved rainbow banners and Mexican flags, as bystanders high-fived the marchers from the sidelines. "As a white, queer person, we need unity with people of color, we need to stand up," a fifteen-year-old sophomore in Los Angeles explained to the AP. "I'm fighting for my rights as an LGBTQ person. I'm fighting for the rights of brown people, black people, Muslim people."[24]

The AP further reported that in New York City, a large group of demonstrators gathered outside Trump Tower on Fifth Avenue chanting angry slogans and waving banners bearing anti-Trump messages. "In Philadelphia, protesters near City Hall held signs bearing slogans like "Not Our President," "Trans Against Trump" and "Make America Safe For All." About five hundred people turned out at a protest in Louisville, Kentucky and in Baltimore, hundreds of people marched to the stadium where the Ravens were playing a football game. The AP noted hundreds of protesters demonstrated outside Trump Tower in Chicago and a growing group was getting into some shoving matches with police in Oakland, California. Mostly peaceful protests took place in Los Angeles.[25] By Friday, three days after the election, some 225 people had been arrested, in anti-Trump protests, with at least 185 in Los Angeles alone.[26]

NBC's KGW in Portland, Oregon, reported that most of the 112 protestors arrested in Portland participating in anti-Trump demonstrations did not vote in Oregon, according to state election records, with seventy-nine of the demonstrators arrested either not registered to vote in the state, or not recorded as having turned in a ballot.[27] An analysis conducted by the Oregonian newspaper in Portland estimated the percentage of those arrested in ant-Trump demonstrations who did not vote as "at least one-third," commenting that most of the protestors were college students and out-of-state college students could have voted in their home state, explaining why they were not registered to vote in Oregon.[28] Other reports provided proof George Soros had funded anti-Trump leftist groups responsible for organizing the demonstrations in various cities across the United States.[29] This harkened back to proof James O'Keefe's Project Veritas had provided during the campaign showing Democratic operatives had paid protestors to disrupt and even cause violence at various Trump rallies across the country.

Hillary First Blames FBI, Then Blames Russia

On Saturday, November 12, 2016, four days after the election, Hillary Clinton, on a thirty-minute conference call with top donors that had raised at least $100,000 for Hillary's presidential campaign, blamed the decision of FBI director James Comey to reopen the criminal investigation on her private email server as the reason she suffered the devastating loss in the presidential election. "While Clinton accepted some blame of her loss, said donors who listened to her call, she made little mention of the other factors driving Trump's victory: A desire for change by voters, possible sexism, the difficulty of a political party winning a third White House term, her campaign's all-but-dismissal of white working class voters and flaws within her own message," Lisa Lerer wrote, reporting for the AP.[30]

Amy Chozick, reporting for the *New York Times* quoted Clinton's comments during the conference call with top donors. "There are lots of reasons why an election like this is not successful. Our analysis is that Comey's letter raising doubts that were groundless, baseless, proven to be, stopped our momentum," Chozick reported Clinton said (according to a donor on the call). Clinton's campaign told the *New York Times* that Comey's decision hurt in particular with white suburban women who had been on the fence and broke for Trump after Comey's letter reopening the criminal case reminded them of the email controversy. Chozick also reported that Clinton said that before Comey's second letter, "We were once again up in all but two of the battleground states, and we were up considerably in some that we ended up losing. And we were feeling like we had to put it back together."[31]

Chozick noted that some donors on the call stated their belief that Clinton and her campaign suffered avoidable missteps that handed the election to an unacceptable opponent. "They pointed to the campaign's lack of a compelling message for white working-class voters and to decisions years ago by Mrs. Clinton to use a private email address at the State Department and to accept millions of dollars for speeches to Wall Street," Chozick wrote. Hillary's campaign had been so confident in her victory that aides were popping open Champagne on the campaign airplane

Thursday, heading to New York for the victory celebration. According to the *New York Times* article, Democratic pollsters attributed Mr. Trump's razor-thin victories in Pennsylvania, Michigan and Wisconsin—states that President Obama had won—largely to a drifting of college-educated suburban women to the Republican nominee at the last minute, because of the renewed focus on Mrs. Clinton's email server. "We lost with college-educated whites after leading with them all summer," Chozick noted Brian Fallon, a Clinton spokesman, said on Wednesday, the day after the election. "Five more days of reminders about Comey, and they gravitated back to Trump." Chozick quoted Jay S. Jacobs, a prominent New York Democrat and donor to Mrs. Clinton, as summing up Clinton's loss as follows: "You can have the greatest field program, and we did—he had nothing. You can have better ads, paid for by greater funds, and we did. Unfortunately, Trump had the winning argument."[32]

Then, on December 15, 2016, in a speech to donors at a Thursday night gathering in New York, Clinton blamed her defeat on a long-running strategy implemented by Russian President Vladimir Putin to discredit the fundamental tenants of American democracy. The Associated Press reported that Clinton cited "a personal beef" with Putin as the reason Russia meddled in the US presidential election to Clinton's detriment. "Vladimir Putin himself directed the covert cyber-attacks against our electoral system, against our democracy, apparently because he has a personal beef against me," the AP reported Clinton said. "He is determined not only to score a point against me but also undermine our democracy." Clinton argued that Russia had hacked both the Democratic National Committee and John Podesta, releasing the emails captured in the hacking attacks to Julian Assange at WikiLeaks, as part of a plot to boost Trump. "This is part of a long-drawn strategy to cause us to doubt ourselves and to create the circumstances in which Americans either wittingly or unwittingly will begin to cede their freedoms to a much more powerful state," she said. "This is an attack on our country."[33]

Again, Amy Chozick reported on Clinton's speech in Manhattan to donors. "Putin publicly blamed me for the outpouring of outrage by his own people, and that is the direct line between what he said back then and what he did in this election," Chozick reported that Clinton said. "Make no mistake, as the press is finally catching up to the facts, which we desperately tried to present to them during the last months of the campaign." Clinton told the group that the *New York Times* reported that the Russians had collectively poured some $1 billion into sabotaging her campaign. "This is not just an attack on me and my campaign, although that may have added fuel to it. This is an attack against our country. We are well beyond normal political concerns here. This is about the integrity of our democracy and the security of our nation." Clinton called for Congress to set up a commission similar to the commission set up after the 9/11 terrorist attacks on the Pentagon and the World Trade Center. "The public deserves to know exactly what happened, and why, in order for us to prevent future attacks on our systems, including our electoral system," Clinton argued.[34] Clinton did not specify what exactly Putin's "personal beef" involved, nor did she offer any proof Assange and WikiLeaks had obtained the hacked emails from Russia.

On November 18, 2016, ten days after the election, in his first post-election interview, Podesta sat down with NBC News host Chuck Todd on NBC's *Meet the Press* to answer questions about Clinton's Russian hacking allegations. Podesta alleged the presidential election had been "distorted" by the Russian intervention. Asked if the election was a "free and fair" election, Podesta railed against Putin. "I think the Russians clearly intervened in the election. And I think that now we know that both the CIA, the director of National Intelligence, the FBI all agree that the Russians intervened to help Trump and that as they have noted this week, NBC first revealed that Vladimir Putin was personally involved with that," Podesta insisted. "So I think that people went to the polls, they cast their votes, Hillary Clinton got 2.9 million more votes than Donald Trump, but you know Donald Trump is claiming the Electoral College victory. And you know tomorrow, the electors will get to vote." Pressed by Todd to answer directly the question whether or not the election was "free and fair," Podesta accused Russia of wanting Hillary Clinton to lose. "A foreign adversary directly intervened into our Democratic institutions and tried to tilt the election to Donald Trump. I think that if you look back and see what happened over the course of the last few weeks, you see the way the votes broke, you know," Podesta replied. "I was highly critical of the way the FBI, particularly the FBI director, managed the situation with respect to the Russian engagement versus Hillary Clinton's emails. I think that all had an effect on the election." Adding this comment, Podesta expanded the criticism against Comey to include a failure to investigate the supposed Russian hacking.[35]

In an interview published on July 25, 2016, Julian Assange said in a Skype interview with Richard Engel that *NBC Nightly News* that there was "no proof whatsoever" that WikiLeaks got almost 20,000 hacked Democratic National Committee emails from Russian intelligence. Assange said DNC servers have been riddled with security holes for years and that many sets of documents from multiple sources are now in public hands.[36] On December 16, 2016, Assange made another public appearance, in an interview conducted by Sean Hannity that was first broadcast on Hannity's nationally syndicated radio show and subsequently broadcast that night on Hannity's Fox News television show. In this interview, Assange made clear Russia did not provide WikiLeaks with the Podesta emails or the DNC emails. Assange insisted the source of the email leaks "was not a state party," denying that the Podesta and the DNC emails came from any government. "We're unhappy that we felt that we needed to even say that it wasn't a state party. Normally, we say nothing at all," Assange told Hannity. "We have a conflict of interest. We have an excellent reputation, a strong interest in protecting our sources, and so we never say anything about them, never ruling anyone in or anyone out. Sometimes we do it, but we don't like to do it. We have another interest here that is maximizing the impact of our publications. So in order to protect a distraction attack against our publications, we've had to come out and say 'no, it's not a state party. Stop trying to distract in that way and pay attention to the content of the publication.'" While Assange refused to comment on Hannity's suggestion that the leak came from a disgruntled source within the DNC, possibly even within Podesta's office, Assange did not deny this either, but he vociferously denied the source was Russia.[37]

In a discussion with Hannity on his television show after hearing the Assange radio interview, Eric Bolling, the cohost of the Fox News television round-table *The Five*, argued that Clinton did not make a public statement on Election Night because, according to reports, she got violent with her top campaign officials, Robby Mook and John Podesta. "Okay, so she blamed them first," Bolling commented. "So then we had to go through this charade, this song and dance of recounts. That didn't work out," Bolling continued. "Then it became the Russians' fault, that the Russians affected the election. It's none of the above. They had a flawed candidate—the worst candidate, not necessarily the worst human being, but the worst candidate that ran for president in my lifetime. The

Russians didn't make her come up and say 'Deplorables,' and it wasn't Donald Trump who made Obamacare premiums skyrocket—double in some cases the week of the election."[38]

In the initial phases of advancing the story that the Russians were responsible for the WikiLeaks emails, Democrats pushing this story traced it back to intelligence supposedly developed by the CIA. In the eight years of the Obama presidency, evidence amounted that partisan operatives within the administration had successfully politicized both the IRS and the Justice Department. New York Republican Representative Peter King raised the possibility that the same had happened to the CIA under CIA Director John Brennan. King, a member of the House intelligence community has insisted CIA Director Brennan was orchestrating a "hit job" against president-elect Donald Trump by claiming that Russia was behind the hack of the Clinton campaign chairman John Pdesta's emails. "And that's what infuriates me about this is that we have John Brennan, supposedly John Brennan, leaking to the *Washington Post*, to a biased newspaper like the *New York Times*, findings and conclusions that he's not telling the intelligence community," King said in an appearance on ABC's *This Week*, on Sunday, December 18, 2016. "It seems like to me there should be an investigation with what the Russians did, but also an investigation of John Brennan and the hit job he seems to be orchestrating against the president-elect," King insisted.[39]

Brennan's CIA career is speckled with controversy. He once voted for Communist Party candidate Gus Hall for president of the United States. He allegedly converted to Islam and even flat-out refused to put his hand on the Bible while taking the oath of office. He joined the CIA in 1980 and worked his way up to the top. But his support for Gus Hall, the US Communist Party's presidential candidate, nearly derailed his effort to work for the spy agency in the first place. Brennan had to undergo a polygraph test in order to work for the CIA. Not surprisingly, he panicked when he was asked: "Have you ever worked with or for a group that was dedicated to overthrowing the U.S." Obviously, he had done so. "I froze," Brennan said recalling the incident. "That was back in 1980, and I thought back to a previous election where I voted, and I voted for the Communist Party candidate." So Brennan did what appears to come naturally for him. He lied by telling a half-truth. "I said I was neither Democratic or Republican, but it was my way, as I was going to college, or signaling my unhappiness with the system, and the need for change."

Brennan told the polygraph examiner that he was not a member of the Communist Party, thereby evading having to admit he once was a Communist Party member. The polygraph examiner accepted that as sufficient. "He looked at me and said, 'OK,'" Brennan explained. "When I was finished with the polygraph and I left and said, 'Well, I'm screwed.'" But, amazingly, Brennan was still brought into the CIA.[40]

Former FBI Islam expert John Guandolo has warned that by appointing Brennan to CIA director, Obama chose a man "naïve" to infiltrations, but also picked a candidate who is himself a Muslim. He claimed Brennan converted to Islam years earlier in Saudi Arabia as the CIA station chief in Riyadh. "Mr. Brennan did convert to Islam when he served in an official capacity on the behalf of the United States in Saudi Arabia," Guandolo told radio host Tom Trento. "That fact alone is not what is most disturbing," Guandolo continued. "His conversion to Islam was the culmination of a counterintelligence operation against him to recruit him. The fact that foreign intelligence service operatives recruited Mr. Brennan when he was in a very sensitive and senior US government position in a foreign country means that he is either a traitor . . . [or] he has the inability to discern and understand how to walk in those kinds of environments, which makes him completely unfit to the be the director of Central Intelligence." Brennan served as CIA station chief in Riyadh, Saudi Arabia, in the 1990s.[41]

Brennan became Obama's CIA director on March 7, 2013 in a ceremony that outraged many Americans when he was photographed taking his oath with his hand on a copy of the US Constitution and not a Bible. During a private ceremony in the Roosevelt Room, Vice President Joe Biden swore Brennan in with his right hand raised and left hand placed "on an original draft of the Constitution that had George Washington's personal handwriting and annotations on it, dating from 1787," according to White House deputy press secretary Josh Earnest, as he told reporters at their daily briefing. "Director Brennan told the president that he made the request to the archives because he wanted to reaffirm his commitment to the rule of law as he took the oath of office as director of the CIA," Earnest elaborated.[42] Conservative blog Empty-Wheel.net was quick to catch the significance of Brennan's move. "That means, when Brennan vowed to protect and defend the Constitution, he was swearing on one that did not include the First, Fourth, Fifth, or Sixth Amendments—or any of the other Amendments now included in our Constitution," EmptyWheel.net noted. "The Bill of Rights did not become part of our Constitution until 1791, 4 years after the Constitution that Brennan took his oath on."[43]

When he was serving as assistant to the president for Homeland Security and Counterterrorism, Brennan gave a speech on February 13, 2010, to New York University law school students He included a lengthy statement in Arabic that he did not translate for his English-speaking audience. Noting he was an undergraduate at the American University in Cairo in the 1970s, Brennan proceeded to use only the Arabic name, "Al Quds," when referring to Jerusalem, commenting that during his 25-years in government he spent considerable time in the Middle East, as a political officer with the State Department and as a CIA station chief in Saudi Arabia. "In Saudi Arabia, I saw how our Saudi partners fulfilled their duty as custodians of the two holy mosques in Mecca and Medina," he said. "I marveled at the majesty of the Hajj and the devotion of those who fulfilled their duty as Muslims of making that pilgrimage."[44]

Jill Stein's Vote Recount

Green Party presidential candidate Jill Stein, who garnered just 1 percent of the national vote, raised approximately $7.3 million to force recounts of the presidential vote in Wisconsin, Michigan, and Pennsylvania.[45]

Stein's recount effort traced back to a *New York Magazine* article published in the end of December, 2016 in which "a group of prominent computer scientists and election lawyers" called on Clinton to demand a recount in Wisconsin, Michigan, and Pennsylvania, arguing that electronic-voting machines may have been manipulated or hacked. "The academics presented findings showing that in Wisconsin, Clinton received 7 percent fewer votes in counties that relied on electronic-voting machines compared with counties that used optical scanners and paper ballots," *New York Magazine* reported on November 22, 2016, fourteen days after the election. "Based on this statistical analysis, Clinton may have been denied as many as 30,000 votes; she lost Wisconsin by 27,000. While it's important to note the group has not found proof of hacking or manipulation, they are arguing to the campaign that the suspicious pattern merits an independent review—especially in light of the fact that the Obama White House has accused the Russian government of hacking the Democratic National Committee," the magazine report continued.[46]

This argument was largely undermined three days later, on November 25, 2016, when Politico reported that one of the cyber security experts relied upon in the *New York Magazine* story, J. Alex Halderman, a professor of computer science at the University of Michigan, admitted that he had no evidence the 2016 presidential election had been hacked by Russia or anyone else in any state.[47] "Were this year's deviations from pre-election polls the results of a cyber attack?" Halderman asked in an article he posted online on November 23, 2016.[48] "Probably not. I believe the most likely explanation is that the polls were systematically wrong, rather than that the election was hacked."

"Clinton would have to win those states back in order to change the outcome of the election," wrote Shane Harris in the *Daily Beast* on November 23, 2016. "And while it's tempting to blame hackers, and not the failure of the political professional class, for Trump's upset, experts warn not to get your hopes up for a shocking turnaround. For hackers to have changed the votes in three states would have been even more surprising than Trump's victory," the *Daily Beast* story concluded.[49] With experts virtually unanimous in agreeing Stein's recount folly had virtually zero chance of changing the election outcome in any of the three states she chose to contest, the consensus judgment was that her real goal was to delegitimize a Trump victory she knew from the start she had little or no chance of reversing.[50]

Still, on November 28, 2016, Clinton's campaign said it would participate in Stein's recount effort, as explained by Clinton's top campaign lawyer, Marc Elias, in a carefully worded letter.[51] "Regardless of the potential to change the outcome in any of the states, we feel it is important, on principle, to ensure our campaign is legally represented in any court proceedings and represented on the ground in order to monitor the recount process itself," Elias wrote.[52]

This prompted an angry response from Trump. "The people have spoken and the election is over, and as Hillary Clinton herself said on election night, in addition to her conceding by congratulating me, 'We must accept this result and then look to the future,'" Trump said in a statement, which called the recount "ridiculous," insisting the election "is over" and that the Green Party attempt to fill up their coffers by asking for impossible recounts is a scam. "This recount is just a way for Jill Stein, who received less than one percent of the vote overall and wasn't even on the ballot in many states, to fill her coffers with money, most of which she will never even spend on this ridiculous recount," Trump insisted. "This is a scam by the Green Party for an election that has already been conceded, and the results of this election should be respected instead of being challenged and abused, which is exactly what Jill Stein is doing."[53]

Stein's recount effort failed miserably. In the Michigan recount, instead of swinging the election to Clinton, the recount found evidence of massive voter fraud in Wayne County, pointing to Democratic Party voter fraud in Detroit, where Michigan's largest city in Michigan's largest county had voted overwhelmingly for Clinton. Voting machines in more than one-third of all Detroit precincts registered more votes that the number of people recorded having voted. Overall, state records showed 10.6 percent of the precincts in the state's twenty-two counties could not be recounted because Michigan state law bars recounts for precincts submitting ballot boxes with broken seals. The Detroit news reported the problems were the worst in Detroit where officials could not recount votes in 392 precincts, or nearly 60 percent of the total, with two-thirds of these precincts having too many votes. The newspaper further noted Hillary Clinton overwhelmingly prevailed in Detroit and Wayne County, while Republican President-elect Donald Trump won Michigan by 10,704 votes, or by 47.5 percent to 47.3 percent.[54]

In Wisconsin, the Stein recount resulted in a net gain of 131 votes for Trump.[55] On December 4, supporters of Stein's recount withdrew a last-ditch lawsuit in Pennsylvania state court aimed at forcing a statewide ballot recount after the court demanded a $1 million bond be posted by the one hundred Pennsylvania residents who brought the lawsuit.[56]

Green Party candidate Jill Stein squandered whatever ecomentalist credibility she had by launching a Soros-funded recount effort. The sole result was a slight increase in Trump's margin of victory. As recount expert John Haggerty said, the Wisconsin recount was a fraud upon the taxpayers of Wisconsin, though it did confirm that the Wisconsin election system is reliable. Stein's Michigan recount efforts also yielded zero change in results except for a wider margin for Trump, but may have exposed some fraud. In Pennsylvania, there wasn't even enough evidence for a recount to occur.[57]

Soros should ask for a refund, not a recount. Environmentalists should ask Stein how much coal or oil and how many trees were wasted in generating the electricity necessary to conduct those pointless, self-aggrandizing recount fiascos.

Voter Fraud, Hacking, and Recounts

In October 2016, I wrote an article for *The Hill* newspaper.[58] In it, I wrote that Donald Trump has said publicly that he fears the next election will be rigged. Based on technical capability and recent history, Trump's concerns are not unfounded. A recent study by Stanford University proved that Hillary Clinton's campaign rigged the system to steal the nomination from Bernie Sanders. What was done to Bernie Sanders in Wisconsin is stunning, but potentially not an isolated event. Why would the Clintons not cheat again if doing so had worked?

The issue here is both voter fraud, which is limited but does happen, and election theft through the manipulation of the computerized voting machines, particularly the DIEBOLD/PED voting machines in wide usage in most states.

Politico profiled a Princeton professor, Andrew Appel, who demonstrated how the electronic voting machines that are most widely used can be hacked in seven minutes or less![59] Robert Fitrakis, Professor of Political Science in the Social and Behavioral Sciences Department at Columbus State Community College, explained this further in his must-read book on the strip and flip technique used to rig these machines. Professor Fitrakis is a Green Party activist.

Similarly, a computer hacker showed CBS how to vote multiple times using a simple $15.00 electronic device. We are now living in an alternative reality of constructed data and phony polls. The computerized voting machines can be hacked and rigged and, after the experience of Bernie Sanders, there is no reason to believe they won't be. Don't be taken in.

To be very clear, both parties have engaged in this skullduggery and it is the party in power in each state that has custody of the machines and control of their programing. In the future, the results of machines in swing states like Florida, Pennsylvania, Virginia and Ohio should be matched with exit polls.

In this election cycle, Illinois is a state where Trump had been running surprisingly strong, in what has become a Blue state. Does anyone trust Mayor Rahm Emanuel, a longtime Clinton hatchet man, not to monkey with the machines? I don't. He was using city-funded community groups to recruit anti-Trump "protestors" who posed such a threat to public safety that Trump's Chicago event had to be canceled when the Secret Service couldn't guarantee his safety.

How could the pols of both parties do it? As easy as determining, on the basis of honest polling, who is going to win. Then, if it isn't your candidate, simply have the votes for the other guy be given to your guy and vice versa. You keep the total vote the same. This is where the "strip and flip" technique described by Professor Fitrakis would come in. Maybe you don't need all the votes the other guy was going to get. If you have a plan in mind involving votes and their redistribution, you can find a programmer who can design the machine instructions to produce the desired outcome. The $15 device noted above can be purchased at any Best Buy.

For all these reasons, Europe has rejected electronic voting machines. They are simply untrustworthy. This is not a secret. The media continues a drumbeat insisting voter fraud is non-existent without ever addressing the more ominous question of manipulation of the voting machines. Additionally some states still use machines that include no paper trail. The "evidence" is destroyed. Florida's machines had no paper trail in Bush versus Gore.

The United States must follow the lead of European nations who use exit polling to determine who won and lost. The tabulated votes only serve as a formal verification. But that is done with paper ballots and hand counts under supervision, the way we used to do it.

After I wrote about these ideas, all hell broke loose. David Brock and his followers attacked *The Hill* for giving me a forum. "Why is *The Hill* publishing crazy conspiracy theories by Trump associate Roger Stone?" screamed the *New Republic*." This new op-ed piece by the longtime Republican trickster weaves a conspiracy that the entire election will be rigged to stop Donald Trump, from rigged voting machines to rigged opinion polls that are meant to fool the public."

One month later, Jill Stein demanded the previously mentioned $3.5 million recount in Wisconsin and a spot recount as a preliminary step in Michigan. Their specific complaint was that computerized voting machines could be hacked and manipulated easily. You can't have it both ways.

The Electoral College: More Democratic than Democrats Can Bear

Nowhere is the wisdom of the Founding Fathers more evident than in the adoption of the Electoral College. The rural farmers and urban bankers who came together to form our government had a natural distrust of each other and knew that growing populations could silence the electoral voices of enormous areas of the country. Their solution, the Electoral College, has long been the thorn in the left's side; when the left loses, that is. The idea that the votes of regular folks in what liberals call "the fly-over states" could prevent the electoral dominance of the "sophistica- ted" voters in California and New York (living, dead, undocumented, or otherwise) is abhorrent to the elite left. Once again, the left whines about the inherent unfairness of the system—when the left loses—and the need to change it so that the majority of the country has less of a voice—whenever the popular vote in California and New York would have elected an Al Gore in 2000 or Hillary Clinton in 2016. With the GOP holding the cards, no radical insanity like dumping the Electoral College can succeed.

Some outlandish talk of convincing electors to abandon their obli- gations surfaced between the election and the casting of 2016 electo- ral votes. Trump managed to win battleground states like Wisconsin, Michigan, and Pennsylvania, despite the predictions of specious "pun- dits" who were so off target their errors are rapidly becoming legend. Like most liberal fantasies of 2016, the "faithless elector" dream went nowhere and Trump was confirmed.

In our country, the presidency isn't decided by the national popular vote. To whine about a free and fair election in which the winner of the popular vote did not win the White House is like claiming that the bas- ketball team who completed the most passes should win the game. We don't score it that way and the players all know it.

"Hamilton Electors" Urge Electoral College "Vote-Switching" Scheme

Perhaps the most desperate last-ditch effort to block Trump from the White House was organized by a group of citizens calling themselves "Hamilton Electors." The scheme involved unearthing obscure argu- ments from the Federalist Papers in a twisted attempt to argue the Elec- toral College was created to keep a scoundrel like Trump from becoming president. "We honor Alexander Hamilton's vision that the Electoral College should, when necessary, act as a Constitutional failsafe against those lacking the qualifications for becoming President. In 2016, we're dedicated to putting political parties aside and putting America first," the Hamilton Electors website proclaimed. "Electors have already come forward calling upon other Electors from both red and blue states to unite behind a Responsible Republican candidate for the good of the nation."[60] The goal of this #NeverTrump effort was to convince enough of the 538 members of the Electoral College, scheduled to meet in their state capitals on December 19, 2016, to switch their votes from Trump to prevent Trump from getting the 270 electoral votes needed to be elected president.

As freelance journalist Lilly O'Donnell pointed out in *The Atlantic* in an article published on November 21, 2016, Michael Baca of Colorado and Bret Chiafalo of Washington state were the two Democratic electors who called themselves "Hamilton Electors."[61] The two Democratic state electors tried to lead a national movement aimed at throwing the 2016 election into the House of Representatives. Given that Republicans control the House, the most the Hamilton Electors could hope to accomplish would have been to delegitimize Trump's victory—the same goal Jill Stein's recount effort was reduced to accomplishing. Neither succeeded in their improbable and ill-conceived stratagems. Baca and Chiafalo conceded that Alexander Hamilton's argument in authoring *Federalist Papers Number 68* was correct in that the Electoral College is necessary because choosing a president by popular vote would allocate to the most populated states—like New York and California today— an undue advantage that would allow disregarding the choices of lesser populated states in selecting a president.[62] But they emphasized the argument of Alexander Hamilton, a founding father and the first US Treasury Secretary, that "the office of President will never fall to the lot of any man who is not in an eminent degree endowed with the requisite qualifications." To be successful, the Hamilton Electors had to convince thirty-seven electors committed to vote for Trump to vote for someone else—a nearly impossible feat to accomplish.

As the Hamilton Electors' plan gained publicity in the mainstream media, the electors in Colorado and Washington state began to promote the idea that renegade electors should vote for a moderate Republican candidate, such as Republican Governor John Kasich of Ohio, a former GOP presidential candidate who sat out the Republican National Convention in Cleveland, as an expression of his opposition to Trump. In their best-case scenario, the Hamilton Electors dreamed of uniting 135 Republican and 135 Democratic electors behind Kasich, thus securing the presidency for a moderate Republican. In their fallback strategy, the Hamilton Electors plotted to convince thirty-seven of the Republican electors in states that voted for Trump to switch their votes to Kasich, throwing the election into the House of Representatives. Their thought was the GOP leadership in the House might be willing to twist arms of Republican House members to vote for Kasich instead of Trump, in a strategy designed to secure the presidency for the GOP, while at the same time dumping Trump.

The Trump camp seethed as the Clinton campaign chose to remain silent on the Hamilton Electors' scheme. A petition on Change.org got more than 4.9 million signatures calling on "Conscientious Electors" to protect the Constitution from Donald Trump by supporting Hillary Clinton as the winner of the national popular vote. "Donald Trump has not been elected president," the petition on Change.org to make Hillary Clinton president read. "The real election takes place December 19, when the 538 Electoral College Electors cast their ballots—for anyone they want. Mr. Trump is unfit to serve. His scapegoating of so many Americans, and his impulsivity, bullying, lying, admitted history of sexual assault, and utter lack of experience make him a danger to the Republic." The petition campaign, not directly supported by the Hamilton Electors, stressed that in fourteen states that voted for Trump, the electors could switch their vote to Hillary Clinton if they choose to do so, without risking any legal penalty.[63]

What the move to defeat Trump in the Electoral College neglected to mention, Trump had a 3 million majority in the popular vote if New York and California were excluded from the total. Hillary's 2.8 million popular vote majority was due largely to her victory in California, where her margin of victory was larger than President Obama's in 2012—61.5 percent versus Obama's 60 percent. Hillary won California by 4.3 million votes. Political analysts realize that California is rapidly becoming a one-party state. Between 2008 and 2016—the eight years of the Obama presidency—Democratic Party registrations climbed by 1.1 million in California, while Republican Party voting registrations dropped by almost 400,000. Moreover in the congressional races in California, there was no Republican even on the ballot to vote for. Senator Barbara Boxer ran for reelection opposed only by two Democrats and there were no Republicans on the ballot for House seats in nine of California's sixteen congressional districts. Taking California out of the popular vote calculation, Trump won nationwide by 1.4 million votes. If California had voted like other states going Democratic for the president in 2016, where

Clinton averaged 53.3 percent of the vote, Clinton and Trump would have ended up in a virtual tie in California. As California moves more solidly to the political far-left, the Golden State has increasingly less in common with the vast majority of Red States in the nation's interior.[64] But a quick look at the county map of the United States makes clear that California's interior consists predominately of red counties, except for the narrow strip along the coast that includes the state's major cities, from San Francisco in the north, to Los Angeles and San Diego in the south.

As December 19 approached—the day set for the electors to meet in their various state capitals—Republican members of the Electoral College faced intense pressure, including personal harassment and death threats, as pro-Hillary and anti-Trump forces combined in their desperate attempt to keep Trump out of the White House.[65] While those supporting Hillary and opposing Trump liked to portray themselves as the unbiased, "Kumbaya" loving left, open to diversity of all imaginable mixes of ethnicity, race, and personal political inclination, their intolerance was displayed in their hatred towards Middle America and all things Trump. The bullying from the Trump haters was nearly overwhelming, with some electors receiving as many as 50,000 emails in the run-up to December 19, clogging their electronic devices with unwanted anti-Trump venom. A Harvard University group backed by constitutional law Professor Lawrence Lessig got into the act, offering free legal advice to electors deciding to change their votes.[66]

Despite all the media hoopla, the Electoral College "block Trump" scheme was as dismal a failure as Jill Stein's ill-conceived recount maneuver. In the end, Trump received 304 electoral votes to Clinton's 227—two fewer than he earned on November 8—with more electors going rogue and defecting from Clinton than defected from Trump.[67] Ironically, four members of the Electoral College from Washington State casted their votes for a candidate other than Hillary Clinton, even though she won the state's popular vote. Elector Bret Chiafalo, one of the two organizers behind Hamilton Electors, decided at the last minute to join two other Washington state electors to switch their vote from Kasich, voting instead for former Secretary of State Colin Powell. The last of the four defecting Washington electors voted for Faith Spotted Eagle, a Native American Indian tribal leader in opposition to the Keystone XL pipeline, instead of voting for Clinton, as they were pledged to do.[68] In the end, eight Clinton electors defected from Clinton, with the four defecting in Washington state being joined by a Clinton elector in Hawaii who voted for Sanders. The three electors who tried to defect from Clinton—one in Colorado, one in Maine, and one in Minnesota—were either voted out of order or replaced by a Clinton-supporting elector.[69] In the final analysis, only two Republican electors, both from Texas, cast protest votes—one for former Senator Ron Paul and the other for Kasich.[70]

Draining the Swamp

President Trump needs to be mindful of which national Republican leaders supported his movement and which tried to attack him, lest he be sabotaged in his own White House. His promise was to "drain the swamp," to disrupt the stranglehold of big government interests in Washington. He seems to have done just that with his cabinet, as of the time of this writing. "Drain the Swamp" never meant appointing only candidates with no ties to corporations or government. Rather, it's about appointing people who will effectively eliminate government bloat, corruption, inefficiency, and cronyism so the government functions well for taxpayers.

Trump's appointments have less to do with cronyism and more to do with patriotism than any recent president. Some of his choices, like Nikki Haley for ambassador to the United Nations, were vocal critics of Trump's candidacy. That's because Trump values people who can do their jobs and because he is serious about unity. Uniting the GOP has to be a Republican president-elect's goal, hence the appointments of Reince Priebus and Sean Spicer. But consider the prominence of chief strategist Steve Bannon and how it enrages the left. That's because they know how capable Bannon is.

Trump's choice of former Texas Governor Rick Perry as Energy Secretary drew jabs from the still clueless left, because Perry stated back in 2011 that the Department of Energy would be a department he would consider closing. Then, famously, Perry in a critical debate moment could not remember that the Department of Energy was one of the government bureaus he planned to close. What could be better for "drain the swamp" enthusiasts than to know as a Department of Energy employee that your future boss sees so little value in what you do that he wants to close your department, but it is of such insignificance to him that he cannot even remember your name. Of course, Republicans understand why this makes Perry the perfect choice to lead the agency in an administration whose goal is to downsize government. This simple point is lost on the "fake news" sources like CNN and MSNBC.

Kellyanne Conway is a no-brainer as a top counselor to the president, as the true feminist and first woman to manage a successful presidential campaign. Don't hold your breath reading about this remarkable achievement in the mainstream media, where women are told they must choose between family and careers but can't have both. Monica Crowley is a fellow Nixon alumnus and a gifted communicator who will work tirelessly to help keep this country safe as Trump's senior director of strategic communications for the National Security Council.

"The Russians Did It! The Russians Did It!"

Hillary Clinton ran a 1980s-style campaign based on identity politics and it never knew how to connect with most Americans. The Russians had no role in her horrible campaign. The Russians did not force Hillary to ignore swing states. The Russians did not force the DNC to rig the primary in favor of a candidate with absolutely no charisma. The Russians did not force John Podesta plus dozens of Democratic Party leftist operatives to write truths in their emails about Clinton that they could never permit the American people to read.

The Clinton campaign's use of social media was a total failure, a wasteland compared to the massive presence Trump commanded. The Russians had nothing to do with that either. Hillary's left, who jumped up and down swearing that the election could never be hacked weeks earlier when they thought they were going to win, decided only after they lost that the election had been hacked by the Russians.

I, myself, was the intended victim of an outlandish Russian hacking conspiracy fantasy. The White House and its press servants accused me of informing Trump that the Russians hacked the DNC. No such conversation ever took place. President Obama knew the content of Clinton's emails all along, yet started a baseless accusation that I had colluded with Russian hackers. I had strictly an arms-length relationship with Julian Assange. Many of the items that would've been leaked were known to have existed for years. Chief among them were instances of Podesta's corruption. He knew, as I did, that they would eventually surface.

The post-election attack on me by Podesta was simply recycled from before the election. Unable to hide the embarrassing content of his emails, which included allusions to nauseating Satanic rituals, Podesta desperately thrashed about, trying anything and everything he could do, including lying, to discredit the leak itself. Unable to find a connection between Trump, Assange and the Russians, he invented one, arguing not only that the Russians stole the election, but that the Russians stole the election with my help. Not a single shred of evidence was ever produced, but some leaders in the intelligence community said what they were told. CIA Director Brennan, for example, who owned the security company that broke into State Department files to sanitize Barack Obama's passport records prior to the 2008 election,[71] claimed he was sure that the Russians hacked our election. So, not only did the far-left Democrats pulling the strings in the Obama administration politicize the IRS and the Department of Justice, they even succeeded with John Brennan's appointment to politicize the CIA. The mainstream media, the White House, Podesta, and the CIA failed in their outrageous accusation toward me just as they failed in the election. They treated us, the American people, like we are stupid, while Trump treated voters as equals.

Podesta desperately tried to use one of my own tweets as some sort of proof. I had pointed out that anyone, including the Russians, could have hacked Hillary's insecure, homemade email server. That her homemade email server was vulnerable to foreign attack was a major point of attack on Clinton. The Left and the mainstream media Clintonistas laughed at it for many months before Podesta signaled to switch to the narrative that the Russians had hacked emails between Clinton and the DNC and that I was somehow involved. As I told the press before the election, I was happy to speak with the FBI but they never contacted me. The intelligence community under President Obama cannot even agree among themselves. Despite the press smokescreen smear of this author's name, not a single shred of proof was ever offered by anyone.[72]

John Podesta's claim that my tweets somehow proved both my advance knowledge of the WikiLeaks hacking of his email account and the subject matter of the ultimate disclosures, is an example of claiming 2+2=6.

My specific tweet, saying "it will soon be Podesta's time in the barrel," needs to be seen in context. I posted this at a time when Podesta and his allies were savaging Paul Manafort with a series of leaks and false claims regarding his business activities in Ukraine. I knew from my own research that Podesta had been involved in money laundering for the Clinton Foundation and the Russian Mob. My tweet was a specific reference to an article I posted online on StoneColdTruth.com on October 13. It's important to note that none of the information regarding Podesta's activities in this article comes from WikiLeaks in their subsequent releases. The two are not connected.

I candidly admitted that Julian Assange and I shared a mutual friend who told me that Assange was in possession of "unspecific political dynamite" that would "adversely affect the Clinton campaign." The claim that I knew the specific subject matter of the subsequent WikiLeaks disclosures or that I had special knowledge of the timing of these disclosures is false, although the media generally expected a major release by Assange on October 5. In fact, Assange had already said on the record that he had information that was potentially politically damaging for Hillary Clinton. Instead on the fifth he announced there would be disclosures for each of the following ten weeks.

The entire "Stone knew" theme that Podesta repeated on CNN before the election (once again with CNN affording me no opportunity to respond) and then, along with other Clintonistas, recycled after the election, was as false after the election as it was before.

In fact, the entire "Russians hacked the election" media frenzy led by CNN and the *New York Times* was, and will always be, an utterly false narrative. A close examination of the intelligence services heads' testimony before Senator John McCain's Armed Services Committee show that the CIA's claim that Putin had personally directed an effort to hack and influence the American election was based on an "assessment" of the agency and that members of the Senate Intelligence Committee had been "briefed," meaning that *no one had yet seen actual evidence* of the claimed Russian hacking.

Speaking about a special report by the intelligence services on January 7, 2017 the *New York Post* reported:

"No evidence was presented to back up that conclusion, [that the Russian's had hacked the Democrats] with officials saying that information had to remain secret. This document's conclusions are identical to the highly classified assessment, but this document does not include the full supporting information, or provide specific intelligence on key elements of the influence campaign."

However, there is evidence that the DNC emails were, in fact, leaked by disgusted whistleblowers coming from within the Democrat Party itself, rather than from any external government. Former British Ambassador Craig Murray told a British newspaper that he flew to Washington,

DC, to personally receive some of the leaks and they were not provided by Russians.[73] Moreover, it defies reason that Putin, whose origin is the old USSR, would work against the candidate who gave him a sweetheart deal on our uranium—namely Hillary Clinton. All this in conjunction with Canadian penny-stock-jock Frank Giustra pouring millions into the coffers of the Clinton Foundation—in favor of the party that brought the USSR to its knees under President Ronald Reagan.

Hillary Clinton was the war candidate; Trump was the peace candidate. It is just that simple. When President Trump has cleaned house of the Obama and Clinton cronies infesting the CIA, he can certainly investigate these bizarre theories if he so chooses, but those who know him well are confident that his topmost priority will always be the safety and security of United States and its people.

Mike Morell—A Parting Shot

As someone involved in politics for more than forty years I can attest to the fact that you ruffle some feathers and, dare I say, make some enemies along the way. So what? If the bed-wetters and pearl-clutchers aren't upset with you, you aren't making a difference. "Politics ain't beanbag," as the saying goes, and I'm no stranger to controversy or a fight.

I've been called just about every name in the book, and new books could be written using just the words that have been created to attack me. But there is one word that no one has ever attempted to attach to me before Hillary invented the "Russians did it" nonsense: traitor.

Think of me what you will, I love my country. I've spent my life defending it from those who seek to harm it, both foreign and domestic. So imagine my surprise when a third-rate bureaucrat, posing now as a fourth-rate partisan, former CIA director Mike Morell dared accuse me in testimony to Congress of "actually working on behalf of the Russians." Morell rambled, without a shred of proof, spinning his own version of "Fake News" that Paul Manafort, who had consulted with Ukraine, and I "maybe have financial relationships with Russia, financial relationships . . . and they're actually working on behalf of the Russians in getting this material out (WikiLeaks' release of the DNC and Podesta emails) and spreading it around."[74] It's astounding, jaw-droppingly astounding, that someone once trusted with managing a key US intelligence operation had no proof for an accusation of that magnitude—especially when WikiLeaks emails establish that Podesta had been paid by Russia via

Russian billionaire Viktor Vekselberg with the money laundered through a Russian holding company in the Netherlands.[75]

Congressman Jerry Nadler started this witch hunt when he called on FBI Director James Comey (famous for limiting the criminal investigations of Clinton aide Sandy Berger for stealing documents out of the National Archives, smoothing over the controversy surrounding Bill Clinton's pardon of Mark Rich, and being a director of HSBC bank during its infamous money-laundering scandal) to investigate me for my nonexistent ties to Russia. I am accused of treason. That's what Nadler, CIA hack Michael Morell and the Clinton thugs have accused me of. Where's the proof? But, I forgot, far-left Democrats defending Hillary Clinton don't need proof when they can invent "Fake News," while accusing those of us seeking to defend ourselves as "conspiracy theorists."

It was particularly galling to see Congressman Jerry Nadler and Congressman Elijah Cummings hectoring the FBI Director as to whether he had responded to their demand to investigate my nonexistent ties to the Russians. This was the lowest form of McCarthyism, whereas Nadler and Cummings and the Congressional cohorts had no proof whatsoever of any involvement on my part with the Russians or any other foreign actor during the election. To be perfectly clear, I had and have no Russian clients, no Russian influences, and no Russian contacts. Although, I have been known to enjoy Russian vodka.

It was clear that Trump favored détente and hardheaded negotiations with the Russians while Hillary Clinton seemed to be hurdling towards war with them over Syria. Thus, once again, Trump was the "peace" candidate, an important appeal to Bernie Sanders voters who had over-whelmingly been against the Iraq war.

But Morell, happy to become a flying monkey in Hillary Clinton's thug army, went out of his way to spread the lie to Congress that I knew in advance that WikiLeaks would hack the revealing emails of Hillary's campaign chief John Podesta. This because of a tweet I posted in August at the time my boyhood friend and colleague Paul Manafort was under attack for his perfectly legal work in Ukraine for a democratic political party. I predicted that Podesta's business dealings would be exposed. I didn't hear it from WikiLeaks, although Julian Assange and I share a common friend. I reported the story on my website, documenting how Russian mafia money laundering flowed millions into the Clinton Foun-

dation bank accounts, with Viktor Vekselberg—Podesta's Russian benefactor—arranging, as previously mentioned, for two transfers of unk-
nown amounts to a private Clinton Foundation bank account—the first
on February 10, 2015, and the second on March 15, 2016.[76]

So let's be crystal clear. I had no advance notice of WikiLeaks' hacking of Podesta's emails. I didn't need it to know what Podesta had been
up to. I do not work for any Russian interest. I have no Russian clients.
I have never received a penny from any public or private Russian entity
or individual and that includes Russian intelligence. None. Nada. Zilch.

This is the new McCarthyism. I don't favor war with Russia, a war
the Obama administration and Hillary's 2016 campaign seemed determined to provoke. Like Trump, I favor a period of Nixon-like détente and
hard-headed negotiations with the Russians that would allow us to work
together to crush ISIS. This does not mean I am pro-Putin or approve of
Russian totalitarianism. Being in politics a while, I do understand deflection. The Clintonistas hope they can distract public attention away from
the stunning criminal activities exposed through WikiLeaks by attacking those who they say leaked them. In this case that IS NOT ME.

Now let's take a look at Mr. Morell. He is essentially the man who ran
the Benghazi cover-up.[77] "Former CIA Director Morell received information from the CIA Station Chief in Benghazi that there was NEVER a
protest the night of the terrorist attack," according to the Gateway Pundit.[78] "Morell later viewed video of the terrorist attack showing there was
no protest. Morell later said the FBI changed the talking points to say
there was a protest. He changed the talking points to benefit the Obama
administration."

This guy wants me investigated?

What's almost as bad is Morrell's failure to disclose that he is on
Hillary Clinton's payroll. After Morell left the CIA, he became a senior
counselor at Beacon Global Strategies, the consulting firm founded by
longtime Clinton ally Philippe Reines. Then, there's the opinion piece
Morell published in the *New York Times* on August 5, 2016, in which he
endorsed Hillary Clinton for president. The point is the FBI and CIA are
supposed to work to protect Americans from all manner of threats and
should be above partisanship. Yet, just like the IRS, the Obama administration has weaponized the FBI and the Department of Justice against
conservatives. But it's not just Podesta and the Clinton Foundation that
have taken money from the Russians. Bill Clinton received $500,000 to

give a speech in Moscow on behalf of a Russian investment bank tied to the Uranium One deal.[79] That's right, the Clinton crime family was paid a half million by a Russian bank that benefited from then-Secretary of State Hillary Clinton's approval of a deal that gave Russia control over one-fifth of the United States's uranium.

A former president of the United States should not be giving speeches to Russian interests for huge sums of money while his wife has a say in deals that benefit Russia to the possible detriment of US national security. But Morrell, apparently, doesn't have a problem with that. His loyalty is for sale and the checks have cleared. Morell is firmly in the pocket of the far-left behind Bill and Hillary Clinton. That Michael Morrell has exposed himself as a partisan hack willing to sell his name to a corrupt political family isn't a surprise. Nor is it surprising this hack would smear patriotic Americans to distract from the astonishing corruption of the Clinton campaign exposed by the WikiLeaks revelations. These are, after all, the Clintons.

Why Trump Won

But the question remains. How could the polls have been so wrong?

From the beginning of the race the pollsters in both the Democratic Party and the mainstream media entirely misunderstood and underestimated who would vote. It was never realistic to think that Hillary's voter turnout model would be exactly like Obama's. There are numerous reasons why Hillary Clinton did not perform as well among African Americans as Obama did. Hillary's support was soft and a majority saw her as "dishonest" and "untrustworthy." Hillary would also bleed among progressive democrats and Bernie Sanders supporters whose views on trade and war were closer to Trump's than they were to Hillary's. The media blissfully went on using an outdated model, padding the numbers of Democrats in their samples either by design or stupidity.

Trump's pugnacious pollster Tony Fabrizio saw a different model. From the beginning he assumed a lower black turnout, a surge of white Catholic democrats who voted for Obama but would move to Trump, and the exodus of older white women, 53 percent of whom ended up voting for Trump. Fabrizio pushed relentlessly to "expand the map" into Wisconsin and Michigan as well as doubling down on western Pennsylvania in order to provide a clear path for Trump to reach 270 electoral votes assuming, as Fabrizio did, that Trump would carry Ohio and Florida.

Fabrizio's turnout model was deadly accurate. The polling of Fabrizio colleagues John McLaughlin and Kellyanne Conway confirmed the wily New Yorkers' projections.

The answer to why the polls were so wrong is relatively simple. The truth is Hillary Clinton was an unattractive presidential candidate who did little to inspire Democratic voters to go to the polls, especially in comparison to Barack Obama—a charismatic candidate capable of translating the idea of "first black president" into votes. Identity politics worked for Obama because identity appeals were not Obama's only campaign themes. In 2008, the mantra of "hope and change" resonated with voters tired of America's seemingly endless wars in the Middle East. The economic downturn caused by the bursting of the subprime bubble just as George W. Bush's second term was coming to a close gave added energy to Obama's appeal. Running on her decades of public service experience proved a detriment for Hillary. She could not shake her history of scandals, with Whitewater compounded by the Benghazi disaster, her email scandal, and a Clinton Foundation "pay-to-play" money machine that functioned primarily as a Clinton family piggybank.

The polls relied upon by the mainstream media in 2016 were predicated on the assumption that Hillary would draw Democrats to vote in numbers and proportions similar to those experienced in 2008 and 2012. When that did not happen, the polls erred by oversampling Democrats. The result was that polls skewed to favor high Democratic turnout overplayed Hillary's support while downplaying Trump's genuine appeal. What pollsters had failed to estimate correctly in 2016 was the extent to which voters in the heartland of America had become disenchanted with the Obama White House. To say heartland voters were disenchanted in 2016 with the idea of Hillary Clinton succeeding Barack Obama to the White House is an understatement. Hillary Clinton was unique among all candidates in 2016 for her ability to create Hunter S. Thompson-like "fear and loathing." White middle-class voters faced the prospect of having to listen to her pontificate for four years as president. While Barack Obama had failed to deliver on the promises he made in 2008, Hillary Clinton by comparison looked old, most likely sick, and generally angry at the world, while being largely devoid of any new ideas. The point is that the Hillary Clinton who lost to Barack Obama in 2008, was the same failed candidate who lost to Donald Trump in 2016.

"Barack Obama's two victories created the impression of a strong wind at the back of the Democratic Party. Its constituencies—the young, the nonwhite, and the college educated—were not only growing but were also voting in increasing numbers. The age-old issue of voter turnout finally seemed to be helping the political left," wrote David Leonhardt in the *New York Times* on November 17, 2016. "The longer view is starting to look quite different, however. None of the other three most recent Democratic presidential nominees—Hillary Clinton, John Kerry, and Al Gore—inspired great turnout. George W. Bush, as you may recall, was widely considered to have won the political ground game. In off-year elections, Democratic turnout is even spottier, which helps explain the Republican dominance of Congress, governor's mansions and state legislatures." The point was clear: In the simplest terms, Republican turnout seems to have surged this year, while Democratic turnout stagnated.[80]

The post-mortem voter analyses were clear. The *New York Times* pointed out that in counties where Trump won at least 70 percent of the vote, the number of votes cast rose 2.9 percent versus 2012. By comparison, in counties where Clinton won at least 70 percent, the vote count was 1.7 percent lower this cycle. In addition to increasing his share among white women without college degrees, Trump got 29 percent of the Hispanic vote compared to Romney's 27 percent in 2012, plus 8 percent of the black vote compared to Romney's 6 percent.[81] Trump could concede the elite in the coastal strip from San Francisco to Los Angeles to San Diego, plus New York City and the boroughs to Clinton, as long as Trump won big among working-class voters in the rest of the nation. This was the same lesson Richard Nixon taught the Democrats in 1968. But the Nixon-hatred that dominated the Democratic Party in 1968, morphed into the Bush-hating of the 2000s, to end up at the Trump-hating of today—all to the detriment of the Democrats themselves. The truth is the elite, far-left socialists who currently control the Democratic Party have little in common with the Democratic Party of Harry Truman, John Kennedy, and Hubert Humphrey. If the far-left elitists controlling the Democratic Party have their way, the Democratic Party will likely become a European-style Social-Democratic Party with decreasing chances of electoral success on a national basis.

The Harvard Kennedy School Conference

As is traditional, the leadership of both presidential campaigns met for a one day post-election analysis conference at Harvard's John F. Kennedy School for Government. Representing Clinton were Robby Mook, Mandy Grunwald, Teddy Goff, Karen Finney, Jennifer Palmieri, and Joel Benenson. Representing Trump were Kellyanne Conway, David Bossie, Tony Fabrizio, Brad Parscale, and Corey Lewandowski. The Clinton and Trump staffers tore into each other over how they conducted themselves throughout the election. Conway, however, handled herself with aplomb while the Clintonistas essentially whined. In the conference, Clinton campaign manager Robby Mook did acknowledge that Clinton's operation had made a number of mistakes and miscalculations, while being buffeted by what he described as a "head wind" of being an establishment candidate in yet another election year where voters wanted change. While Clinton needed upwards of 60 percent of young voters to win, millennials who had supported Sanders abandoned Clinton in droves. "There was a large part of the Democratic primary electorate who had concerns about the secretary's veracity and forthrightness," Jeff Weaver, Bernie Sanders' campaign manager explained to the Kennedy School audience.[82] Among the white working class, Hillary Clinton lost fourteen points of support compared with 2012. But it wasn't just white working class voters that the Democrats lost in 2016. Even among black and Latino working class voters, she lost eight points of support. Altogether, this cost Clinton approximately 6 percent of the total vote.[83] That 6 percent translated into a Donald Trump landslide outside of California and New York.

Even David Plouffe, who did not attend the conference and who was a key architect of Barack Obama's demographic strategy that drove his impressive numbers-driven Get Out the Vote (GOTV) ground-game strategy in 2009 and 2012, had to admit he got it all wrong when it came to strategizing for a Hillary Clinton win in 2016. In a *New York Times* mea culpa, Plouffe said that "presidential campaigns are driven in large part by personality, not party." He noted that Ronald Reagan, Barack Obama, and Donald Trump were all able to create electoral coalitions unique to each of them. Abandoning the "one model fits all candidates" approach to conducting demographic analysis for Democratic Party candidates, Plouffe acknowledged his assumption that Clinton would be a repeat of Obama was wrong.[84] In the final analysis, Hillary Clinton lost a second time in 2016 precisely because she was Hillary Clinton—a two-time loser presidential candidate with low approval ratings on character and trustworthiness, who was unable to shake a personal political history littered with scandals piled upon scandals and lies followed up with lies.

Although they will try, what Hillary Clinton and her team of lawyers will never be able to cover up is the damage she did to the Democratic Party brand in a campaign pock-marked by rigging the election against Bernie Sanders, her elitist sense of entitlement, and the release of thousands of emails that showed the disdain she and the far-left elite currently running the Democratic Party have for the American working-class voter in "fly-over" Middle America—Nixon's Silent Majority—the precise group Democrats still need to win elections.

The Harvard discussions were chaotic, at least in part because the Trump team's fractured leadership was overrepresented in many of the panels.

Corey Lewandowski, for example, was included in both the primary-election panel and, inexplicably, the general-election panel. He seemed to play a bigger role at the conference than he had on the campaign trail. Incredibly, Lewandowski would tell the Harvard conference that he had written Trump's announcement speech, which was ludicrous given that Trump spoke without notes and there was no prepared text to memorize.

The Clinton team expectedly responded to questions with emotion and venom. Jennifer Palmieri actually broke down during part of the public session. Throughout the conference, there were a variety of panels on the election media coverage, the primary campaign, whether or not Trump has a mandate to lead, possible Russian hacking, and many other topics were discussed.

On the media, Lewandowski said:

> This is the problem with the media: You guys took everything that Donald Trump said so literally. The American people didn't. They understood it. They understood that sometimes—when you have a conversation with people, whether it's around the dinner table or at a bar—you're going to say things, and sometimes you don't have all the facts to back it up.

Of this, Chris Cillizza of the *Washington Post* said:

> As silly as Lewandowski's media critique is, he is totally right when he says that some Trump supporters did not take the billionaire literally. The *Post*'s Jenna Johnson interviewed a bunch of such supporters in June, around the time when a Fox News poll showed only two-

thirds of Trump backers believed he would actually build a wall on the border with Mexico. The rest just liked his attitude—and didn't care when journalists pointed out the challenges Trump would have to overcome to make the wall a reality.

More from the *Post* on Lewandowski's comments:

> The strangest criticism of the media, however, was by Trump's former campaign manager, Corey Lewandowski. His complaint: journalists accurately reported what Trump said.

Lewandowski threw Trump under the bus on the Judge Curiel issue:

> LEWANDOWSKI: I had the privilege of being in that San Diego event when Mr. Trump called out Judge Curiel and we had talked about it on the way to the venue, and you know I made the strategic recommendation as did others not to do that.
>
> DAN BALZ: You give him advice. When you say don't do that, does he just simply clam up? Does he say, 'Corey, I know what I'm doing now.' Was anyone telling him to do this with Judge Curiel?
>
> LEWANDOWSKI: Donald Trump is a person who takes input from a lot of people and listens to every side of an argument before he makes his decision.
>
> BALZ: But, was there anybody telling him to do this with Judge Curiel?
>
> LEWANDOWSKI: Uhh, no. (Laughter) Look, again you have a person who has achieved remarkable business success relying on their own gut . . . And his instincts of what the American electorate has wanted and what it has been looking for have been so spot on. And he has been so successful in the business world that candidly—look it's very difficult I think for any one person to give him advice on something where he has his mind set and change that opinion. And this narrative gets developed on the Judge Curiel thing. It is always the team that comes in after this has been done that tries to talk him into understanding either the severity of it or that it's time to change a narrative. And what we know about Donald Trump is he has the ability to change a narrative with 140 characters.

This was similar to the session on the primary campaign, when Lewandowski also bailed on Trump, when asked about the McCain incident.

> QUESTIONER: Speaking of early outrages, one of the seminal moments early on in the campaign was Donald Trump's remark about John McCain. I guess I'll go back to you, Corey. Was that another one of these instances where it was not realized in the moment, and the firestorm came after and where do you think that came from?
>
> LEWANDOWSKI: No that was realized immediately—that one I knew. (Laughter.) I've said this you know and I'll say it again. I was in Iowa when Mr. Trump made those remarks. As soon as he was done speaking at that particular event, I said to him 'Hey Mr. Trump can I speak to you for a second in the green room.' And he said, 'That was great, wasn't it?' And I said, 'I'd like to talk to you for a second.' I closed the door and I said, 'You know, sir, I think we have a problem.' And, you know, because I'm a campaign guy, my advice was, 'Look, probably we need to go apologize to John McCain for making a remark,' and Donald Trump said, no, we're going to do a press conference— and if you remember, it was a 28-minute long press conference in the basement of a building in Iowa, where he fielded a series of questions and pushed back on the notion that he was going to apologize to John McCain, by saying he believed that the veterans haven't been served to the fullest capacity, and that the veterans' scandal in Arizona is something that should have been fixed and solved. Lewandowski recalled that many people had phoned, particularly that day—"and we flew back to New Jersey and had a series of phone calls, and wondered what to do." Finally, Donald Trump did what he always does. "He doubled down. The media outcry was fierce . . . I actually called my wife and said 'Look I think the campaign is over, I'm coming home.'" Donald's instincts are so different, and he is so willing to fight and run with what he feels in his gut. "We didn't poll-test things, we didn't go out and focus-group things like other campaigns did. We just did it." Because we were such a small team and because Donald Trump was so insistent on just doing what he feels, we relied on his ability to read the American people and fight through that like we did so many other things to ultimately be successful."

A key exchange that came between Palmieri, pollster Joel Benenson, and Kellyanne Conway is worth noting:

> JOEL BENENSON, CLINTON CHIEF STRATEGIST: Don't act as if you have some popular mandate for your message. The fact of the matter is that more Americans voted for Hillary Clinton than Donald Trump.
>
> CONWAY: And there was nothing that said the road [to the White House is measured by] popular vote anywhere.
>
> BENENSON: Kellyanne, I'm not—
>
> CONWAY: It's the road to 270. That's where we all competed.
>
> BENENSON: I premised my statement by saying that.
>
> CONWAY: Hey, guys, we won. You don't have to respond.
>
> PALMIERI: OK, there you go.
>
> CONWAY: I mean, seriously?
>
> BENENSON: No.
>
> CONWAY: Hold on. Why is there no mandate? You've lost 60 congressional seats since President Obama got there. You lost more than a dozen senators, a dozen governors. 1,000 state legislature. You just reelected a guy who represents liberal New York and a woman who represents San Francisco as your leader. You've learned nothing from this election.

And between Conway and Clinton manager Robby Mook:

> ROBBY MOOK, FORMER CLINTON CAMPAIGN MANAGER: I think there's a lot of things we need to examine coming out of this. And you just named a lot of them. Congress has got to investigate what happened with Russia. We cannot have foreign aggressors I would argue intervening in our elections. And we know that the Russians were promulgating fake news to Facebook and other outlets.
>
> KELLYANNE CONWAY, DONALD TRUMP'S ADVISER: I think the biggest piece of fake news in this election was that Donald Trump couldn't win.

And again:

KELLYANNE CONWAY, TRUMP SENIOR ADVISER: You think
this woman who has nothing in common with anybody . . .
(CROSSTALK)
JENNIFER PALMIERI, DEMOCRATIC STRATEGIST: I'm not
saying why, but you won, that's the kind of campaign that was run.
CONWAY: He flipped over 200 counties that President Obama won
. . . you think that's because of what you just said or because people
aren't ready for a woman president, really? How about it's Hillary
Clinton? She doesn't connect with people? How about they have
nothing in common with her?

Some felt the real fight came before the main Harvard roundtables, with
what became an interrogation of CNN chief Jeff Zucker.

The issue—his favoring of Trump with massive coverage, and his hiring
of ousted Trump manager Lewandowski as a CNN contributor. The various campaign managers for the losing Republican primary candidates came
at Zucker like a gang of chum-hungry sharks. These campaign managers
shouted Zucker down with increasing anger as he defended how much airtime the network gave Trump during the primary season. They contended
that it was both out of whack and out of balance. Zucker's self-defense essentially amounted to asserting that when CNN reached out to the various
candidates, Trump was most often the only one who answered the call.

Several of the campaign managers assembled told Zucker that they'd
not received these alleged calls. Others joked about how CNN was willing to give their candidates only a brief amount of time or air segments
at off-hours. As anyone who actually witnessed the primary campaign
can attest, none of the other candidates' events got the lavish, fulsome
coverage that Trump's got. And that includes coverage of Trump events
during times when Trump wasn't even in range of the camera lens. As
one audience member shouted, "You showed empty podiums!" (Which
was technically accurate, as there were podiums at these events.)

Zucker was unable to explain sufficiently to the assembled campaign
managers how it came to pass that CNN offered so many hours of coverage to Trump's many empty stages and unoccupied lecterns. With the
limited exception of Corey, the Trump strategists peppered throughout
the room didn't stand up to defend Zucker. Even Corey, however, snuck
out of the room for a while.

In the afternoon Lewandowski, the erstwhile CNN contributor, was in more of a fighting mood, getting confrontational once the conversation turned to Zucker's decision to hire Lewandowski in the first place: Lewandowski seized the microphone from the questioner who broached the topic in a bid to defend himself, allowing the student to finish asking it, but insisting he was adding value to the CNN airwaves. Zucker said Lewandowski was a "good investment and decision," as Lewandowski clapped and the rest of the room remained silent.

Politico reported that Lewandowski eventually turned his attention to the *New York Times* over their Trump coverage. We had one of the top people at the *New York Times* say, "I'm willing to go to jail to get a copy of Donald Trump's taxes so I can publish them." Dean Baquet came here and offered to go to jail—you're telling me, he's willing to commit a felony on a private citizen to post Trump's taxes, and there isn't enough scrutiny on the Trump campaign and his business dealings and his taxes? It's egregious. He should be in jail."

Lewandowski said this in reference to the *Times* report on fragments of Trump's tax returns from 1995. Not only did the documents suggest that Trump lost nearly $1 billion in a single year, but the *Times* also noted that Trump might have used it to avoid paying income taxes for almost two decades. The deduction, in fact, was perfectly legal and allowable under IRS rules.

The Trump Presidency

Donald Trump has the opportunity to be a truly great president. He comes to office beholden to no one but the American people. His campaign was eschewed by financial and political elites and he triumphed despite being vastly outspent in both the primaries and the general election. This freedom gives him wide latitude for reform.

While campaigning for the Republican nomination, Trump unveiled the most dynamic and pro-growth tax reform plan in US history. It would drop corporate tax rates below those of Mexico and China, bring at least $2 trillion into the country through fair taxation in inversion and enact an across the board tax cut like those of presidents John F. Kennedy and Ronald Reagan. One only wishes CNBC analyst and apostle for economic growth Larry Kudlow and supply-side economist Steve Moore, the architects of this plan, were on the inside working with the president on this rather than someone from the Goldman Sachs team. It is the way forward for the Donald and America.

The danger for President Trump is if he fails to recognize the machinations of the establishment-types who didn't support his candidacy but now kiss his ass while they seek appointments and other favors. They are not committed to a reform agenda and will do their best to derail his. President Trump must not be seduced by the very people whose policies have run the country into a ditch, remembering that his election was a rejection of these very same people.

The thing to remember about Donald Trump is that he is very, very tough. Beneath a generally genial nature lies a fierce competitor who leaves little on the table. He is indeed a master negotiator and a pragmatist. Although his election is compared to Ronald Reagan's sweeping 1980 victory, Trump is more like Nixon than Reagan—a pragmatist who speaks for the Silent Majority.

Like Nixon, Trump is no ideologue. He is essentially a populist with conservative instincts. On the biggest issues facing the country in 2017—the economy, terrorism, and immigration—Trump takes the populist/right position. At the same time, on the issues of trade and war, Trump's views are closer to Bernie Sanders than they are to Hillary Clinton or say, George W. Bush. Indeed, Trump had to win three out of ten Sanders voters in order to win—a goal he achieved.

Trump must revitalize the economy, secure our borders, revamp our immigration laws, rebuild our infrastructure, and renegotiate our trade deals. This is a tall order but Trump is capable of doing it all if he is not seduced by the courtiers and Washington insiders who belittled his candidacy and financed his opponents.

Donald, as he told me to call him in 1979 when we first met, is surrounded with some enormously capable people. Eldest daughter Ivanka Trump is a wonder woman, balancing a marriage, motherhood, her own businesses, and her father's business, all the while remaining physically fit and remarkably well-dressed. Poised and approachable, she is her father's best ambassador. Ivanka's husband Jared Kushner is highly intelligent, appropriately discreet, effective, and trusted by his father-in-law. Donald Jr. and his brother Eric were incredible surrogates for their father, working talk radio like demons in the swing states, as well as appearing at rallies and events to galvanize their father's supporters.

With the leading candidate for the chairmanship of the Democratic National Committee being a radical Islamic who blames the Jews for the Holocaust, the choice of a wealthy white woman named Ronna Romney, Mitt Romney's niece, as the national chairwoman of the Republican National Committee is puzzling. It appears that Reince Priebus was allowed to call this shot. I suspect the president will paper her over with a "General Chairman" with greater outreach appeal to working-class Democrats.

The antics of the Democrats in harping on the popular vote victory of Hillary Clinton, demanding and getting a $3.5 million recount in Wisconsin, which actually resulted in a net gain of 131 votes for Donald Trump, failing in a random recount in a cross section of Michigan counties and a last-ditch effort to persuade electors to reconsider voting for Trump, which in the end garnered exactly one vote, demonstrate the resolve of the globalists not to release the reigns of power that they have held through the Presidencies of Bush, Clinton, Bush, and Obama. The "Russian's hacked the election" meme grows tiresome and is still unproven, but it's not going away.

President Trump needs to remember who his supporters are, and remember that they are the "forgotten Americans" who are choking on high taxes, leery of Wall Street, allergic to Goldman Sachs, tired of the lack of job opportunities, and convinced that the entire system is rigged against them (which it is).

These voters will sustain him if he will remain true to his reform agenda.

Even if Trump had not won the general election, the nation would still owe him a debt of gratitude for keeping Jeb Bush out of the White House. That he would take on the vaunted Clinton machine with a guerilla-oriented campaign, built largely around his communication skills, and win, is nothing short of a miracle. The media tried to count him out of the race at least three times but, in truth, his polling numbers had remarkable resilience and consistency where short term gaffes cost him little and his support remained steady. Trump voters were far more intense and passionate about their support for their candidate, an enthusiasm gap that Hillary was never able to bridge. As I look back at it now, Hillary's awkward attempt to dance on the *Ellen DeGeneres Show* probably doomed her candidacy.

How sweet is the irony that Hillary's special gal-pal Huma Abedin, who jealously guarded access to Hillary, and was measuring the drapes for her White House office, would bring her candidate down on 650,000 emails the New York City Police Department found on her husband's laptop. The announcement of FBI Director Comey that there was nothing improper in these emails was false, with the NYPD pressured not to contradict the Bureau, lest the Department of Justice indict several officers in the Eric Garner affair. Indeed, NYPD officials who have read these email files confirm that they show proof of corruption, treason, self-dealing, and sexual exploitation of minors. While President Trump has announced he does not favor the prosecution of the Clintons over Clinton Foundation corruption, Trump has said nothing of the new crimes that these 650,000 emails could reveal. The NYPD retained a copy of the files before forwarding the originals to the FBI. Congress directed the Department of Justice to preserve all files for future examination. In other words, the Clintons and their daughter, having lined their pockets through a level of greed and avariciousness never before seen in any post-presidency, may yet be brought down. Paying for Chelsea's $5 million wedding with Clinton Foundation funds? Really?

Looking to the future, will Hillary Clinton's most radical supporters on the far-left ever really support "The Donald," or will they descend into the frenzied, intolerant rage that typifies the worst of their "feminist superiority complex?" Will the Democratic Party devolve into a self-righteous, name-calling fringe party dominated by the educated white elite on both coasts? More importantly, will minorities living in America's aging metropolitan areas wake up to the reality that the media elite in Hollywood and New York City care little about their true econmoic plight, as along as continued welfare dependency and a sense of victimized entitlement keep them voting Democratic?

Donald Trump spared America from the return of Bill Clinton to power. Clinton chuckled to a longtime New York Democratic consultant that, if Hillary retook the White House, "he would be running things again." Unlike Trump whose issue agenda was very specific, Hillary essentially ran without ideas or proposals, merely vowing to do Obama one better in every regard. Their time had passed.

"Conspiracy theorist" is what they call you when you refuse to accept the conventional or media-backed narrative of any particular event. Politics is a game of smoke and mirrors where the reality of most things is far more complex than what the rubes are being told on the TV networks.

That this election marked the tipping point at which the so-called mainstream media lost its monopoly on truth, on the dissemination of information, as more and more voters started receiving their political news on their handheld device from outlets more diverse and in many cases more accurate. What is remarkable is the sheer magnitude of the CNN assault on Trump and the fact that it seemingly had no effect on

Trump's support or election whatsoever. The voters are clearly wise to the establishment media and the fact that they are parroting the narrative of the ruling elite who have all but run the country into the ground.

Trump's victory was as improbable as it was spectacular. He himself would tell you that, for all of his skill and foresight, luck has always smiled upon him. That's why he is a "winner."

Donald Trump loves winning and he hates losing. He is determined, stubborn, and incredibly smart, and his masterful use of social media has transformed American politics. Trump has figured out that he can speak directly to voters without the filter of the old media. Perhaps he is our last best hope to return to being a nation of winners.

Appendix A

Clinton Rape Tee Timeline

1999—Juanita Broaddrick accused the former president of raping her during his 1978 campaign for Arkansas governor.

July 19, 2016—Alex Jones of InfoWars tweeted a photo of the Bill Clinton rape t-shirt calling it "Sneak Preview of the Next Big Fashion Statement." https://twitter.com/RealAlexJones/status/755548655847936008

July 20, 2016—The Guardian calls the Bill Clinton rape t-shirt "symbolic—not just of the tone of the Republican national convention but of the presidential election as a whole." The Guardian also credited Stone with being behind the t-shirt and noted that "the T-shirt is representative of some of the most important issues at play in this year's election." https://www.theguardian.com/us-news/2016/jul/20/bill-clinton-rape-shirt-republican-convention-hillary-merch

July 21, 2016—*Time* magazine features Roger Stone wearing a Bill Clinton 'RAPE' T-Shirt at the RNC convention in Cleveland.

July 21, 2016—Bloomberg Politics reporter Jennifer Jacobs tweets a photo of Roger Stone wearing the Bill Clinton rape t-shirt at the RNC. @JenniferJJacobs: "Trump ally Roger Stone unfurls anti-Bill Clinton posters outside the GOP convention." https://twitter.com/JenniferJJacobs/status/756225925260476416

July 21,2016—The Guardian highlights attendees lining up to buy Clinton rape t-shirts at the GOP convention. Headline: "Bill Clinton 'rape' T-shirt goes on sale at Republican national convention." https://

www.theguardian.com/us-news/2016/jul/21/bill-clinton-rape-t-shirt-republican-national-convention

August 9, 2016—Child rape victim Kathy Shelton came forward in an interview with the *Daily Mail* after forty years to take on Hillary Clinton who defended her rapist. The victim revealed how the champion of women rights was a vicious defense lawyer who smeared the victim, blocked evidence and laughed knowing her client was guilty.

August 13, 2016—Twitter @ClintonRapeTee account goes live.

August 13, 2016—Hashtag #RapeShirt begins spreading across social media.

August 13, 2016—Video of man wearing the Clinton rape shirt gets told at the UN building he must turn the shirt inside out and gets kicked out. https://youtu.be/yvLrss1H4G8

August 15, 2016—The Clinton campaign removes from the campaign website the pledge that all victims of sexual assault "have a right to be believed."

August 17, 2016—Over 1200 tees have been sold.

August 19, 2016—Clinton sexual assault accusers Paula Jones and Kathleen Willey defended Clinton rape accuser Juanita Broaddrick from NBC News anchor Andrea Mitchell who had falsely claimed Broaddrick's claims had been "discredited."

August 19, 2016—@ClintonRapeTee sends birthday wishes to the former president: "@billclinton happy birthday y'old RAPIST. #RAPE-SHIRT"

August 27, 2016—@ClintonRapeTee encourages social media to follow Juanita Broaddrick's Twitter account @atensnut.

August 31, 2016—Christian Josi spoke to Kathleen Willey and wrote about it on Facebook and Twitter. Immediately following talking to Willey, his accounts were hacked.

September 1, 2016—@RogerStoneJr was hacked.

September 2, 2016—Social media activism spreads. The Twitter account encourages people to "wear it somewhere that will kicked" and to "Send the video. Respect."

September 8, 2016—More supporters of the Clinton Rape Tee come out to show off their shirts at events. https://twitter.com/RogerJStoneJr/status/774073968114343941

September 9, 2016—Stacy, mother of three, shows off her t-shirt on her social media account.

September 13, 2016—Milo Yiannopoulos, the anti-PC movement commentator and Breitbart writer, joined the t-shirt movement by sporting it on social media.

September 17, 2016—Roger Stone passionately expresses on Vine how the women assaulted by Clinton deserve to be believed. "Can't wait to see Hillary's face when Juanita sits front & center at the debates," he writes on Twitter.

September 25, 2016—Juanita Broaddrick expresses interest in being at the first presidential debate. "Remember me? I'm the one your husband raped and you threatened. I'm still here telling the truth and you are a liar," she told American Mirror.

October 1, 2016—Stone begins offering cash money for protesters to out Bill Clinton as a rapist at events. This sparked a series of protesters popping up on television and Clinton rallies.

October 1, 2016—A man with a Clinton Rape t-shirt photobombs the set of *Fox and Friends* and caused a stir with the anchors.

October 5, 2016—Bill Clinton's speech gets interrupted in Canton, Ohio by a woman holding up a sign calling Clinton "A Rapist." The former president tried to dodge responding to her sign and heckling as she was being escorted out of the event. He claimed that she didn't "want to have a conversation."

October 6, 2016—At a Senator Tim Kaine rally in Las Vegas, a protester interrupts the event by shouting "Bill Clinton is a rapist!"

October 8, 2016—Juanita Broaddrick calls out Hillary Clinton for her attacks on Donald Trump. "Hillary calls Trump's remarks 'horrific' while she lives with and protects a 'Rapist'. Her actions are horrific," she tweeted.

October 9, 2016—Another protester appeared on live television yelling, "Bill Clinton is a rapist!"

October 9, 2016—At a Bill Clinton rally, his speech is interrupted by a protester yelling "Bill Clinton is a rapist!" Clinton responds, "That's what is a matter with politics. When other people try to pour poison down your throat, don't drink it. . . . Give him a hand. Tell him bye! We wish him well."

October 9, 2016—A man interrupts a Senatory Kaine rally with his Clinton rapist t-shirt.

October 9, 2016—In an exclusive *Breitbart* interview with the victims of Bill Clinton's alleged sexual assault—Juanita Broaddrick, Kathleen Willey, and Paula Jones—spoke about how their experiences forever traumatized their lives.

October 9, 2016—Kathy Shelton, the rape victim who Hillary Clinton attempted to discredit to help her client win, wrote on Twitter, "If I'd had justice vs my rapist, maybe I could have healed. But Hillary Clinton made sure I suffered loss of justice, then laughed it off."

October 9, 2016—Juanita Broaddrick, Paula Jones, Kathleen Willey, and Kathy Shelton held a press conference with Donald Trump before Trump's second debate with Hillary Clinton at Washington University. The women sat in the audience at the debate.

October 10, 2016—News media attempted to claim Clinton's accusers received money from the Trump campaign. Kathy Shelton quickly disputed these claims on Twitter, "No one from the Trump campaign paid me a dime! More dishonesty & lies from the media!"

October 10, 2016—African American protester disrupts a Hillary Clinton rally in Detroit with a Clinton rape t-shirt. As he was being removed by security, she told supporters that, "I do hope somebody follows that gentleman out and stages an intervention."

October 10, 2016—California television station KCOY reports on a high school student being told to change his Clinton rape t-shirt. The student had to get ACLU involved in fighting the school's decision.

October 12, 2016—A protester with a Clinton rape sign is tackled at a Hillary Clinton rally in Las Vegas.

October 12, 2016—Drudge Report headline: "Clintons Fed Up With Rape Protesters. Fear Voter Disgust."

October 12, 2016—Bill Clinton gets interrupted by several protestors in Waterloo, Iowa, shouting, "You're a rapist!"

October 14, 2016 - ClintonRapeWhistle.com rolls out a rape whistle for Clinton rallies.

October 14, 2016—At a Cleveland, Ohio rally, President Obama spars with a protester yelling, "Bill Clinton is a rapist!" Obama tried to distract the crowd by beginning the chant of "Hillary! Hillary! Hillary!" Then he remarked, "I noticed this has been happening everywhere."

October 20, 2016—The Clinton rape whistle was heard during pre-presidential debate telvision shows.

October 21, 2016—At a rally in Jacksonville, Florida, Bill Clinton gets called a rapist by a protestor and interrupts Clinton in mid-sentence.

November 1, 2016—Hillary Clinton loses it at a rally in Fort Lauderdale, Florida after a heckler shouted "Bill Clinton is a rapist!" Her voice grew shrill and pointed out the protester as what's wrong with this election. "I am sick and tired of the negative, dark, divisive, dangerous vision and behavior of people who support Donald Trump," she yelled. The *New York Post* noted that the protesters seemed to be wearing on her. "It's not uncommon for "rapist" protesters to show up at Clinton rallies, but the Democratic nominee offered a rare reaction," the *Post* wrote.

November 2, 2016—Clinton rape t-shirt wearing protesters from the Fort Lauderdale rally did an online video celebrating Hillary Clinton losing it at the rally.

November 6, 2016—Protesters came out in force to President Obama's Kissimmee, Florida rally. They are seen with signs, Clinton rape shirts, blowing rape whistles and yelling, "Bill Clinton is a rapist!"

November 6, 2016—While President Obama's motorcade passed by a crowd of protesters leaving Kissimmee, the crowd used rape whistles and used a megaphone yelling, "Bill Clinton is a rapist!"

Appendix B

Danney Williams, a case study of political communication through the new media

Bill Clinton's Black Son BANISHED—The Story of Danney Williams (36 million viewers on 24 different platforms

(950K Views Added) Bill Clinton's Son—Danney Williams

(480K Views Added) Arkansas State Trooper CONFIRMS delivering Xmas presents to Danney Williams

Danny Williams Page—https://www.facebook.com/Danneywilliam/
10.9 Million Total Reached
1.49 Million Post Engagement
Over 7.5 Million Views

Banished 1,484,068 views

Black Guy Calls Out Hillary—78,341 views

Arkansas State Police Deliver Christmas Gifts. . .—671,071 views

Bill Clinton's Son—Danney Williams appeals to. . .—1,016,616 views

Black Lives Matter—1,189,814 views

All publicity good publicity, so thanks Trevor Noah. . .—50,780 views

Bill Clinton Son—471,433 views

Bill Clinton "Son"—Danney Williams Banished By. . .—620,264 views

#BlackLivesMatter guest Laire on CNN brings my. . .—37,596 views

CNN Chief Jeff Zucker issued a black out, so. . .—43,475 views

Hillary Clinton Banishes Danney Williams—45,152 views

I thank one of my supports for changing, "Justice for. . .—109,250 views

Danny Williams is the son of Bill Clinton—332,997 views

I thank one of my supporters for asking. . .—188,998 views

Instagram:
  Final 3:
  Reach: 995,000
  Views: 675,000
  Previous efforts after funding netted. . .
  Reach: 376,000
  Views: 167,000
The people viewing these videos were not already fans of the page and
  centered in highly populated African American cities across the US
  and interests of our key DEMO (Rappers, Black Culture, ETC).

Attachments area
Preview: YouTube video Bill Clinton's Black Son BANISHED—The
  Story of Danney Williams
Preview YouTube video Bill Clinton's Son Danney Williams
Preview YouTube video Arkansas State Trooper CONFIRMS delivering
  Xmas presents to Danney Williams

Endnotes

Preface

1. "Transcript: Donald Trump announces plan to form presidential exploratory committee," CNN, "Larry King Live," October 8, 1999, http://www.cnn.com/ALLPOLITICS/stories/1999/10/08/trump.transcript/.

2. Donald Trump with Dave Shiflett, *The America We Deserve*. (Los Angeles, CA: Renaissance Books, distributed by St. Martin's Press, 2002).

3. Adam Nagourney, "President? Why Not? Says a Man at the Top," *New York Times*, September 25, 1999, http://www.nytimes.com/1999/09/25/nyregion/president-why-not-says-a-man-at-the-top.html.

4. "Transcript: Donald Trump announces plan to form presidential exploratory committee," CNN, op.cit.

5. Pat Buchanan, *A Republic, Not an Empire: Reclaiming America's Destiny* (Washington, DC: Regnery, 1999).

6. "Pat Buchanan insists controversial book not pro-Hitler," CNN, September 26, 1999, http://www.cnn.com/ALLPOLITICS/stories/1999/09/26/buchanan.GOP/.

7. Francis X. Clines, "Trump Quits Grand Old Party for New," *New York Times*, October 25, 1999, http://www.nytimes.com/1999/10/25/us/trump-quits-grand-old-party-for-new.html.

8. Stacey Singer, "Trump: I've Got What It Takes to Be President," *Sun-Sentinel*, Florida, November 16, 1999, http://articles.sun-sentinel.com/1999-11-16/news/9911150656_1_reform-party-robin-hood-donald-trump.

9. Adam Nagourney, "A Question Trails Trump: Is He Really a Candidate?" *New York Times*, December 10, 1999, http://www.nytimes.com/1999/12/10/us/a-question-trails-trump-is-he-really-a-candidate.html.

10. Joel Siegel and Corky Siemaszko, "Trump Will Run . . . AWAY. Donald's ready to call it quits in presidential race," *New York Daily News*, February 14, 2000, http://www.nydailynews.com/archives/news/trump-run-donald-ready-call-quits-presidential-race-article-1.868809.

11. Parker, Ashley, and Steve Eder. "Inside the Six Weeks Donald Trump Was a Nonstop 'Birther'." *New York Times*, July 2, 2016. Web. <http://www.nytimes.com/2016/07/03/us/politics/donald-trump-Birther-obama.html?_r>.

12. Ibid.

13. Ellison, Sarah. "Exclusive: Is Donald Trump's Endgame the Launch of Trump News?" *The Hive*. Vanity Fair, June 16, 2016. Web. <http://www.vanityfair.com/news/2016/06/donald-trump-tv-network>.

14. Michael Sainato, "WikiLeaks Reveals DNC Elevated Trump to Help Clinton," Observer.com, October 10, 2016, http://observer.com/2016/10/wikileaks-reveals-dnc-elevated-trump-to-help-clinton/. See also: Tyler O'Neil, "WikiLeaks Bombshell: Clinton Relied on Trump Primary Win, GOP Obliged," *PJ Media*, October 10, 2016, https://pjmedia.com/trending/2016/10/10/wikileaks-bombshell-clinton-relied-on-trump-primary-win-gop-obliged/.

15. Phillip Rucker, "On eve of book tour, Hillary Clinton rejects blame for Benghazi and vows to fight back," *Washington Post*, June 9, 2014, https://www.washingtonpost.com/

politics/on-eve-of-book-tour-hillary-clinton-causes-flap-by-saying-she-struggled-with-money/2014/06/09/0a21bcce-efe7-11e3-9ebc-2ee6f81ed217_story.html?utm_term=.8a54eb7c4b93. Hillary Clinton, "President Barack Obama endorses Hillary Clinton for President," posted on YouTube, June 9, 2016, https://www.youtube.com/watch?v=S9WoF2mz1jc&spfreload=10.

16. David French, "Hillary Clinton Greatest 'Accomplishments,'" *National Review*, July 16, 2016, http://www.nationalreview.com/article/437949/hillary-clinton-accomplishments-not-much.

17. Jonathan Chait, "Republicans Say Hillary Clinton Is Running for Obama's Third Term. Yes, Please," *New York Magazine*, September 13, 2016, http://nymag.com/daily/intelligencer/2016/09/clinton-is-running-for-obamas-third-term-yes-please.html.

18. Terence P. Jeffrey, "Obama May Become First President Since Hoover Not to See 3% GDP Growth," CNSNews.com, July 29, 2016, http://www.cnsnews.com/blog/terence-p-jeffrey/obama-may-be-first-president-hoover-not-see-3-gdp-growth.

19. Louis Woodhill, "Barack Obama's Sad Record on Economic Growth," *Real Clear Politics*, February 1, 2016, http://www.realclearmarkets.com/articles/2016/02/01/barack_obamas_sad_record_on_economic_growth_101987.html.

20. Susan Jones, "Record Number Employed: 152,085,000; But Record 95,055,000 Not in Labor Force," CNSNews.com, December 2, 2016, http://www.cnsnews.com/news/article/susan-jones/record-number-employed-152085000-record-95055000-americans-not-labor.

21. Tyler Durden, "Multiple Jobholders Hits 21st Century High, As Full-Time Jobs Tumble," ZeroHedge.com, November 4, 2016, http://www.zerohedge.com/news/2016-11-04/multiple-jobholders-hit-new-all-time-high-full-time-jobs-tumble.

22. Kelly Riddell, "No, Obama, you presided over a loss of manufacturing jobs and failed to deliver on exports," *Washington Times*, November 30, 3016, http://www.washingtontimes.com/news/2016/nov/30/no-obama-you-presided-over-loss-manufacturing-jobs/.

23. Rick Baum, "During Obama's Presidency Wealth Inequality Has Increased and Poverty Levels Are Higher," *Counterpunch*, February 28, 2016, http://www.counterpunch.org/2016/02/26/during-obamas-presidency-wealth-inequality-has-increased-and-poverty-levels-are-higher/.

24. Nadia Pfaum, "Trump: 43 million Americans on food stamps—True," Politifact.com, July 21, 2016, http://www.politifact.com/truth-o-meter/statements/2016/jul/21/donald-trump/trump-43-million-americans-food-stamps/. See also: Ryan McMaken, "Thanks, Bush and Obama: 1 in 7 Americans Were on Food Stamps," Mises Wire, Mises Institute, March 8, 2016, https://mises.org/blog/thanks-bush-and-obama-1-7-americans-were-food-stamps-2015.

25. "Full List of Obama Tax Hikes," Americans for Tax Reform, no date, http://www.atr.org/full-list-ACA-tax-hikes-a6996.

26. James L. Gattuso and Diane Katz, "Red Tape Rising 2016: Obama Regs Top $100 Billion Annually," Heritage Foundation, May 23, 2016, http://www.heritage.org/research/reports/2016/05/red-tape-rising-2016-obama-regs-top-100-billion-annually.

27. Dave Boyer, "$20 trillion man: National debt nearly doubles during Obama presidency," *Washington Times*, November 1, 2015, http://www.washingtontimes.com/news/2015/nov/1/obama-presidency-to-end-with-20-trillion-national-/.

28. Paul Sperry, "America has suffered a terror attack every year under Obama," *New York Post*, June 16, 2016, http://nypost.com/2016/06/16/america-has-suffered-a-terror-attack-every-year-under-obama/.

29. Megan Christie, Rhonda Schwartz, Josh Margolin, and Brian Ross, "Christmas Party May Have Triggered San Bernardino Terror Attack: Police," ABC News, December 1, 2016, http://abcnews.go.com/US/christmas-party-triggered-san-bernardino-terror-attack-police/story?id=43884973.

30. Ashley Fantz, Faith Karimi, and Elliott C. McLaughlin, "Orlando shooting: 49 killed, shooter pledged ISIS allegiance," CNN, June 13, 2016, http://www.cnn.com/2016/06/12/us/orlando-nightclub-shooting/.

31. Paul Bedard, "99 percent Muslim, 43,000 Somali refugees settled in U.S. under Obama," *Washington Examiner*, November 28, 2016, http://www.washingtonexaminer.com/99-muslim-43000-somali-refugees-settled-in-us-under-obama/article/2608316.

32. Stephen Dinan, "Obama administration to go beyond 10,000 Syrian refugees," *Washington Times*, August 5, 2015, http://www.washingtontimes.com/news/2016/aug/5/obama-admin-go-beyond-10000-syrian-refugees/.

33. David A. Fahrenthold, Tom Hamburger, and Rosalind S. Helderman, "The inside story of how the Clintons built a $2 billion global empire," *Washington Post*, June 2, 2015, https://www.washingtonpost.com/politics/the-inside-story-of-how-the-clintons-built-a-2-billion-global-empire/2015/06/02/b6eab638-0957-11e5-a7ad-b430fc1d3f5c_story.html.

34. Gallup Poll

35. Massimo Calabresi, "Remembering 1980: Are the Polls Missing Something?" *Time*, October 31, 2012, http://swampland.time.com/2012/10/31/remembering-1980-are-the-polls-missing-something/.
36. For the comparison of the 2016 presidential election to 2008, see: Jerome R. Corsi, "Will This Election Day Be Repeat of 1980?" WND.com, October 19, 2016, http://www.wnd.com/2016/10/will-this-election-day-be-repeat-of-1980/.

Part 1

1. Theodore H. White, *The Making of the President 1960* (New York: Atheneum Publishers, 1961), p. 79.
2. Editorial, "Ben Carson for President," *Wall Street Journal*, February 8, 2013, http://www.wsj.com/articles/SB10001424127887323452204578292302358207828.

Chapter 1

1. Quoted in Daniel Schulman, "Donald Trump Can't Stop Trash Talking Jeb Bush," *Mother Jones*, February 8, 2016, http://www.motherjones.com/politics/2016/02/donald-trump-cant-stop-trash-talking-jeb-bush.
2. Theodore Schleifer, "Bush takes on immigration—but at heckler's request," CNN Politics, updated June 16, 2015, http://www.cnn.com/2015/06/15/politics/jeb-bush-immigration-protestors-miami/.
3. United We Dream, @UnitedWeDream, Twitter.com, posted June 15, 2015, at 4:26 pm ET, https://twitter.com/UNITEDWEDREAM/status/610559137752215553. The tweet was linked to the group's press release, "Breaking: Immigrant Youth Interrupt Jeb Bush Presidential Announcement," also dated June 15, 2015, http://unitedwedream.org/press-releases/breaking-immigrant-youth-interrupt-jeb-bush-presidential-announcement/.
4. Phyllis Schlafly, *A Choice, Not an Echo* (Alton, IL: Pere Marquette, 1964).
5. "Full text of Jeb Bush's presidential announcement," *Politico*, June 15, 2015, http://www.politico.com/story/2015/06/jeb-bush-2016-announcement-full-text-119023.
6. "Jeb Bush Announces White House Bid, Saying 'America Deserves Better," *New York Times*, June 15, 2015, http://www.nytimes.com/2015/06/16/us/politics/jeb-bush-presidential-campaign.html.
7. Time Magazine Staff, "Here's Donald Trump's Presidential Announcement Speech," Time.com, June 16, 2015, http://time.com/3923128/donald-trump-announcement-speech/.
8. Alexander Burns, "Donald Trump, Pushing Someone Rich, Offers Himself," *New York Times*, June 16, 2015, http://www.nytimes.com/2015/06/17/us/politics/donald-trump-runs-for-president-this-time-for-real-he-says.html.
9. Jose A. DelReal, "Donald Trump announces presidential bid," *Washington Post*, June 6, 2015, https://www.washingtonpost.com/news/post-politics/wp/2015/06/16/donald-trump-to-announce-his-presidential-plans-today/.
10. Ben Terris, "Donald Trump begins 2016 bid, citing his outsider status," *Washington Post*, June 16, 2015, https://www.washingtonpost.com/politics/donald-trump-is-now-a-candidate-for-president-of-the-united-states/2015/06/16/5e6d738e-1441-11e5-9ddc-e3353542100c_story.html.
11. Jonathan Lemire, Associated Press, "Donald Trump says he has no regrets about '16 kickoff speech," Press Release, June 17, 2015.
12. David Bauder, Associated Press Television Writer, "Trump announcement a boon to late-night comics," June 17, 2015, Press Release.
13. Jerome Hudson, "22 Times Obama Admin Declared Climate Change a Greater Threat than Terrorism," Breitbart.com, November 14, 2015, http://www.breitbart.com/big-government/2015/11/14/22-times-obama-admin-declared-climate-change-greater-threat-terrorism/.
14. Video, "Donald Trump: John McCain is not a war hero," *Guardian*, July 19, 2015, https://www.theguardian.com/us-news/video/2015/jul/19/donald-trump-john-mccain-not-a-war-hero-video,
15. Eugene Scott, Mark Preston, and Eric Bradner, "Defiant Trump refuses to apologize to McCain," CNN Politics, July 20, 2015, http://www.cnn.com/2015/07/18/politics/donald-trump-john-mccain-war-hero/.
16. Nick Gass, "Donald Trump half-apologizes to John McCain," *Politico*, July 21, 2015, http://www.politico.com/story/2015/07/donald-trump-john-mccain-half-apology-120397.
17. "'I love Latinos,' says Trump at U.S.-Mexico border," Agence France Press—English, July 23, 2015.
18. Colin Campbell, "Donald Trump threatens to make Republicans' worst nightmare come true," *Business Insider*, July 23, 2015, http://www.businessinsider.com/donald-trump-third-party-run-2015-7.
19. Kevin Cirilli and Bob Cusack, "Exclusive: Trump threatens third-party run," *The Hill*, July 23, 2015, http://thehill.com/homenews/campaign/248910-exclusive-trump-threatens-third-party-run.
20. Sarah Caspari, "What if Donald Trump runs as an independent?" *Christian Science Monitor*, July 23, 2015.

21. Michael Barbaro, Maggie Haberman, and Jonathan Martin, "Can't Fire Him: Republican Party Frets Over What to Do With Donald Trump," *New York Times* July 9, 2015, http://www.nytimes.com/2015/07/10/us/politics/donald-trump-republican-party-debate.html?_r=0.

22. "Vladimir Putin's approval rating at record levels," *Guardian*, July 23, 2015, https://www.theguardian.com/world/datablog/2015/jul/23/vladimir-putins-approval-rating-at-record-levels.

23. Andrew Rafferty, "Trump Says He Would 'Get Along Very Well' with Putin," NBC News, July 30, 2015, http://www.nbcnews.com/politics/2016-election/trump-says-he-would-get-along-very-well-putin-n401051.

24. Ashley Parker and David E. Sanger, "Donald Trump Calls on Russia to Find Hillary Clinton's Missing Emails," *New York Times*, July 27, 2016, http://www.nytimes.com/2016/07/28/us/politics/donald-trump-russia-clinton-emails.html.

25. Tyler Durden, "How Matt Drudge Won the 2016 Election," ZeroHedge.com, November 17, 2016, http://www.zerohedge.com/news/2016-11-17/how-matt-drudge-won-2016-election. Original piece submitted by Ethan Harfenist with Tal Reznik, Vocativ.com, November 16, 2016, http://www.vocativ.com/376550/drudge-won-2016-election/.

26. Miguel Roig-Franzia, "How Alex Jones, conspiracy theorist extraordinaire, got Donald Trump's ear," *Washington Post*, November 17, 2016, https://www.washingtonpost.com/lifestyle/style/how-alex-jones-conspiracy-theorist-extraordinaire-got-donald-trumps-ear/2016/11/17/583dc190-ab3e-11e6-8b45-f8e493f06fcd_story.html?utm_term=.d2d8f61bd9ad.

27. Roger Stone with Mike Colapietro, *The Man Who Killed Kennedy: The Case Against LBJ*. (New York: Skyhorse Publishing, 2013).

28. Miguel Roig-Franzia, "How Alex Jones, conspiracy theorist extraordinaire, got Donald Trump's ear," *Washington Post*, loc.cit.

29. Ibid.

30. Kit Daniels, "Hillary Clinton Directly Attacks Alex Jones," Infowars.com, August 25, 2016, http://www.infowars.com/hillary-clinton-directly-attacks-alex-jones/.

31. Harper Neidig, "Clinton video ties Trump to conspiracy theorist Alex Jones," *The Hill*, October 16, 2016, http://thehill.com/blogs/ballot-box/presidential-races/301266-clinton-campaign-releases-ad-tying-trump-to-conspiracy.

32. Liam Stack, "He Calls Hillary Clinton a 'Demon.' Who is Alex Jones," *New York Times*, October 13, 2016, http://www.nytimes.com/2016/10/14/us/politics/alex-jones.html.

33. Maggie Haberman, "Alex Jones, Host and Conspiracy Theorist, Says Donald Trump Called to Thank Him," *New York Times*, November 16, 2016, http://www.nytimes.com/2016/11/17/us/politics/alex-jones-trump-call.html?_r=0.

Chapter 2

1. Donald J. Trump, posted on Twitter, August 7, 2015, https://twitter.com/realDonaldTrump/status/629553442944602112?ref_src=twsrc%5Etfw.

2. Sarah Dutton, Jennifer DePinto, Anthony Salvanto, and Fred Backus, "CBS News poll: Donald Trump leads GOP field in 2016 presidential race," CBS News, August 4, 2015, http://www.cbsnews.com/news/cbs-news-poll-donald-trump-leads-gop-field-in-2016-presidential-race/.

3. Transcript, "Read the Full Text of the Primetime Republican Debate," Time.com, August 11, 2015, http://time.com/3988276/republican-debate-primetime-transcript-full-text/.

4. Holly Yan, "Donald Trump's 'blood' comment about Megyn Kelly draws outrage," CNN Politics, August 8, 2015, http://www.cnn.com/2015/08/08/politics/donald-trump-cnn-megyn-kelly-comment/.

5. Ben Jacob, "Donald Trump banned from RedState over menstruation jibe at Megyn Kelly," *Guardian*, August 8, 2015, https://www.theguardian.com/us-news/2015/aug/08/donald-trump-black-balled-by-conservatives-over-menstruation-comment.

6. "232 Photos, 131 Quotes, 43 Numbers that tell the story of America's craziest election," *Politico*, November/December 2016, http://www.politico.com/magazine/2016-campaign-in-photos.

7. M.J. Lee and Chris Moody, "Donald Trump signs RNC loyalty pledge," CNN, September 3, 2015, http://www.cnn.com/2015/09/03/politics/donald-trump-2016-rnc-pledge-meeting/.

8. Robert Costa, "Trump's party loyalty pledge ends one GOP problem, brings others," *Washington Post*, September 3, 2015, https://www.washingtonpost.com/politics/trump-to-sign-gop-pledge-commit-to-back-party-nominee/2015/09/03/c5d9ea7c-5242-11e5-9812-92d5948a40f8_story.html.

9. Ryan Teague Beckwith, "Transcript: Read the Full Text of the Second Republican Debate," Time.com, September 16, 2015, http://time.com/4037239/second-republican-debate-transcript-cnn/.

10. Steve Peoples, Associated Press, "Analysis: Trump underwhelms, Fiorina shines in GOP debate," Press Release, September 17, 2015.

11. Paul Solotaroff, "Trump Seriously: On the Trail with the GOP's Tough Guy," *Rolling Stone*, September 9, 2015, http://www.rollingstone.com/politics/news/trump-seriously-20150909.

12. Leah Libresco, "Who Spoke the Most?" FiveThirtyEight.com, in an analysis entitled "What Went Down in the Second GOP Debate," on Nate Silver's website, September 16, 2015, http://fivethirtyeight.com/live-blog/2016-election-second-republican-presidential-debate/.

13. Harry Enten, "Was the Second Debate the Beginning of the End for Donald Trump?" FiveThirtyEight.com, September 24, 2015, http://fivethirtyeight.com/datalab/was-the-second-republican-debate-the-beginning-of-the-end-for-donald-trump/.

14. CNN Rush Transcript, "Trump, Bush Speaking at Campaign Events Tonight; Trump Takes Questions at Town Hall; Trump and Fiorina Attack Business Records," CNN television broadcast September 17, 2015, http://transcripts.cnn.com/TRANSCRIPTS/1509/17/ebo.01.html.

15. Joy Y. Wang, "Donald Trump fails to correct man who calls Obama Muslim," MSNBC.com, September 18, 2015, http://www.msnbc.com/msnbc/donald-trump-fails-correct-man-who-calls-obama-muslim.

16. Jill Colvin, Associated Press, "Trump condemned for not correcting statement that Obama is Muslim," September 19, 2015.

17. Michelle Toh, "Obama a Muslim 'problem'? Trump says: 'I'm not morally obligated to defend the president,'" *Christian Science Monitor*, September 19, 2015.

18. CNN Political Unit, "Trump takes credit for Obama birth certificate," April 27, 2011, http://politicalticker.blogs.cnn.com/2011/04/27/trump-takes-credit-for-obama-birth-certificate/.

19. Charles C. W. Cooke, "Donald Trump's Birther Moment Tells Us about Donald Trump, and Not Much Else," *National Review*, September 18, 2015, http://www.nationalreview.com/article/424271/donald-trumps-Birther-moment-tells-us-about-donald-trump-and-not-much-else-charles-c.1

20. Khorri Atkinson and Joy Y. Wang, "Donald Trump fires back on anti-Muslim controversy," MSNBC.com, September 19, 2015, http://www.msnbc.com/msnbc/donald-trump-fires-back-anti-muslim-controversy.

21. Jill Colvin, "10 moments from Trump's Iowa speech," Associated Press, November 13, 2015.

22. Tim Hains, "Trump's Updated ISIS Plan: 'Bomb the S. . . Out of Them,' Send in Exxon to Rebuild," RealClearPolitics.com, November 13, 2015.

23. David Sherfinski, "Trump targets 'single problem' in world—and it's 'not global warming,'" *Washington Times*, April 28, 2016, http://www.washingtontimes.com/news/2016/apr/28/donald-trump-wont-rule-out-using-nuclear-weapons-a/.

24. Jill Colvin, "Trump says he saw people celebrating 9/11 in Jersey City," Associated Press, November 22, 2015.

25. Lauren Carroll, "Fact-checking Trump's claim that thousands in New Jersey cheered when World Trade Center tumbled," Politifact.com, November 22, 2015, http://www.politifact.com/truth-o-meter/statements/2015/nov/22/donald-trump/fact-checking-trumps-claim-thousands-new-jersey-ch/.

26. Press Release, "Donald J. Trump Statement on Preventing Muslim Immigration," DonaldJTrump.com, December 7, 2015, https://www.donaldjtrump.com/press-releases/donald-j.-trump-statement-on-preventing-muslim-immigration.

27. Press Release, "Poll of U.S. Muslims Reveals Ominous Levels of Support for Islamic Supremacists' Doctrine of Shariah, Jihad," Center for Security Policy, June 23, 2015, http://www.centerforsecuritypolicy.org/2015/06/23/nationwide-poll-of-us-muslims-shows-thousands-support-shariah-jihad/.

28. Edith M. Lederer, "U.N. rights chief: Trump call for Muslim ban 'irresponsible,'" Associated Press, December 8, 2015, https://www.nexis.com/results/enhdocview.do?docLinkInd=true&ersKey=23_T25139946242&format=GNBFI&startDocNo=0&resultsUrlKey=0_T25139946248&backKey=20_T25139946249&csi=304478&docNo=15.

29. Collins, Gail. "Trump Deals the Woman Card." *New York Times*, April 27, 2016. Web. <http://www.nytimes.com/2016/04/28/opinion/trump-deals-the-woman-card.html>.

30. Alastair Jamieson, "Donald Trump: Bill Clinton Has 'Terrible Record of Women Abuse,'" NBC News, December 28, 2015, http://www.nbcnews.com/politics/2016-election/donald-trump-bill-clinton-has-terrible-record-women-abuse-n486671.

31. Veronica Stracquarlursi, "Donald Trump Turns Up Attacks on Bill and Hillary Clinton," ABC News, December 28, 2015, http://abcnews.go.com/Politics/donald-trump-turns-attacks-bill-hillary-clinton/story?id=35975280.

32. Steven Ginsberg and Robert Costa, "I. Will. Never. Leave. This. Race," *Washington Post*, December 9, 2015, https://www.washingtonpost.com/politics/i-will-never-leave-this-race/2015/12/08/af1b1d46-9ad2-11e5-8917-653b65c809eb_story.html.

33. Nick Gass, "Trump proclaims he will 'never' leave the race," Politico, December 9, 2015, http://www.politico.com/story/2015/12/trump-not-leaving-2016-race-216585.

34. Jeremy Diamond, "Trump: I could 'shoot somebody and I wouldn't lose voters,'" CNN Politics, January 24, 2016, http://www.cnn.com/2016/01/23/politics/donald-trump-shoot-somebody-support/.

35. "Beware of Unauthorized Trump PAC's, Ed Rollins and Teneo," BeforeItsNews.com, May 29, 2016, http://beforeitsnews.com/tea-party/2016/05/beware-of-unauthorized-trump-pacs-ed-rollins-and-teneo-2572846.html.

36. Nick Gass, "Trump super PAC chair predicts he would 'lose badly today,'" *Politico*, August 24, 2016, http://www.politico.com/story/2016/08/ed-rollins-trump-lose-227363.

Chapter 3

1. Steve Holland and Valerie Volcovici, "Eyeing an Indiana victory, Trump says 'It's over,'" Reuters, May 2, 2016, http://www.reuters.com/article/us-usa-election-trump-idUSKCN0XS1AE.

2. Tierney Sneed, "Ted Cruz: I Would 'Absolutely Not' Bail Out the Big Banks Again," TPM.com, November 10, 2015, http://talkingpointsmemo.com/livewire/ted-cruz-banks-fail.

3. Mike McIntire, "Ted Cruz Didn't Report Goldman Sachs Loan in a Senate Race," *New York Times*, January 13, 2016, http://www.nytimes.com/2016/01/14/us/politics/ted-cruz-wall-street-loan-senate-bid-2012.html.

4. Jerome R. Corsi, "Ted Cruz Battles 'Globalist' Charge Against Wife," WND.com, March 31, 2015, http://www.wnd.com/2015/03/ted-cruz-again-battles-globalist-charge-against-wife/,

5. Theodore Schleifer, "Meet Ted Cruz's top fundraiser: his wife," CNN, August 21, 2015, http://www.cnn.com/2015/08/21/politics/ted-cruz-2016-heidi-cruz-fundraiser/.

6. Stephen Labaton, "F.D.I.C. Sues Neil Bush and Others at Silverado," *New York Times*, September 22, 1990, http://www.nytimes.com/1990/09/22/business/fdic-sues-neil-bush-and-others-at-silverado.html.

7. "Trump campaign says Donald won't participate in Fox News/Google debate," Fox News, January 27, 2016, http://www.foxnews.com/politics/2016/01/27/trump-campaign-says-candidate-won-t-participate-in-fox-newsgoogle-debate.html.

8. John Whitsides, Ginger Gibon, and Steve Holland, "Trump overshadows Republican debate even as he sits it out," Reuters, January 29, 2016, http://www.reuters.com/article/us-usa-election-idUSKCN0V619Q.

9. David Bauder, Associated Press, "GOP suspends partnership with NBC News for February debate," published at PBS.org, October 30, 2015, http://www.pbs.org/newshour/rundown/gop-will-allow-nbc-co-host-february-debate/.

10. Julie Bykowicz, Associated Press, "Marco Rubio's strong third-place finish in Iowa could sound like a starting gun to the Republican Party's top donors," published by US News.com, February 3, 2016, http://www.usnews.com/news/politics/articles/2016-02-03/rubio-could-see-campaign-fortunes-rise-from-iowa-finish.

11. Bill Barrow and Emily Swanson, "In Iowa, late deciders and evangelicals sided against Trump," February 3, 2016.

12. Mark Hensch, "Carson slams GOP rivals' 'dirty tricks' in Iowa," *The Hill*, February 2, 2016, http://thehill.com/blogs/ballot-box/presidential-races/267849-carson-slams-gop-rivals-dirty-tricks-in-iowa.

13. Ibid.

14. Mark Hensch, "Rep. Steve King: I had 'obligation' to tell Iowa voters about Carson," *The Hill*, February 3, 2016, http://thehill.com/blogs/ballot-box/presidential-races/268051-steve-king-i-had-obligation-to-tell-iowa-voters-about.

15. Jose A. DelReal, "Donald Trump accuses Ted Cruz of fraud in Iowa caucuses, calls for results to be invalidated," *Washington Post*, February 3, 2016, https://www.washingtonpost.com/news/post-politics/wp/2016/02/03/donald-trump-accuses-ted-cruz-of-fraud-in-iowa-caucuses-calls-for-results-to-be-invalidated/?utm_term=.6abe441ebdba.

16. Eliza Collins, "Trump calls Cruz a liar," *Politico*, February 2, 2016, http://www.politico.com/story/2016/02/trump-ted-cruz-liar-219190.

17. Michelle Ye Hee Lee, "Ted Cruz's claim that he has 'ever supported legislation' of undocumented immigrants," *Washington Post*, December 18, 2015, https://www.washingtonpost.com/news/fact-checker/wp/2015/12/18/ted-cruzs-claim-that-he-has-never-supported-legalization-of-undocumented-immigrants/?utm_term=.8a1f71bf3eb8.

18. William Saletan, "The Real Ted Cruz," Slate.com, January 10, 2016, http://www.slate.com/articles/news_and_politics/cover_story/2016/01/ted_cruz_may_be_the_most_gifted_liar_ever_to_run_for_president.html. See also: "Cruz: Obama, Hillary, Dems out of touch with American people," Fox News, December 18, 2015, http://video.foxnews.com/v/4667702262001/?#sp=show-clips.

19. Eugene Kiely, "Cruz Loans Not 'Transparent,'" FactCheck.org, January 15, 2016, http://www.factcheck.org/2016/01/cruz-loans-not-transparent/.

20. Ibid.

21. Robert Farley, "Cruz's Record Before the Supreme Court," FactCheck.org, March 3, 2015, https://www.factcheck.org/2016/03/cruzs-record-before-the-supreme-court/.

22. Deroy Murdock, "Cruz Campaign Tactics Can't be TrusTED," *Natonal Review*, February 20, 2016, http://www.nationalreview.com/article/431661/ted-cruzs-dirty-campaign-tactics.

23. Liza Mundy, "The New Power Wives of Capital Hill," *Politico*, July/August 2014, http://www.politico.com/magazine/story/2014/06/the-new-power-wives-of-capitol-hill-108012_Page5.html#.WGbr_neZM9y. See also: Ana Marie Cox, "The Truth Behind Ted Cruz's Lies," *Daily Beast*, March 22, 2015, http://www.thedailybeast.com/articles/2015/03/22/the-truth-behind-ted-cruz-s-lies.html.

24. Paul LeBon, "Liar Liar Cruz on Fire: Exposing the Biggest Fraud in U.S. Political History—Stunning Revelations About Pastor Rafael and Ted Cruz," Kindle Edition, Amazon Digital Services LLC, July 23, 2015, https://www.amazon.com/Liar-Cruz-Fire-political-Revelations-ebook/dp/B012GPF6PU.

25. Jill Colvin, "Trump campaign shows a different side after Iowa loss," Associated Press, February 5, 2016, https://www.nexis.com/results/enhdocview.do?docLinkInd=true&ersKey=23_T25140849888&format=GNBFI&startDocNo=26&resultsUrlKey=0_T25140857822&backKey=20_T25140857823&csi=304478&docNo=39.

26. Ben Jacobs and Sabrina Siddiqui, "Marco Rubio's broken record blunder costs him the New Hampshire debate," *Guardian*, February 7, 2016, https://www.theguardian.com/us-news/2016/feb/07/republican-debate-new-hampshire-marco-rubio-chris-christie-donald-trump-ted-cruz.

27. "Transcript of the New Hampshire GOP debate, annotated," *Washington Post*, February 6, 2016, https://www.washingtonpost.com/news/the-fix/wp/2016/02/06/transcript-of-the-feb-6-gop-debate-annotated/.

28. Steve Peoples and Julie Bykowicz, "Debate Takeaways: Rubio shaken, Trump not stirred," Associated Press, February 7, 2016.

29. Katie Reilly, "14 Times Donald Trump and Ted Cruz Insulted Each Other," Time.com, September 23, 2016, http://time.com/4506350/donald-trump-ted-cruz-insults/

30. Katrina Lamansky, "What makes Super Tuesday so 'super' for the primary?" ABC, Channel 8 WQAD, Davenport, Iowa.

31. Glenn Kessler, "Donald Trump and David Duke: For the record," *Washington Post*, March 1, 2016, https://www.washingtonpost.com/news/fact-checker/wp/2016/03/01/donald-trump-and-david-duke-for-the-record/?utm_term=.669a1e5fb390.

32. Eric Bradner, "Donald Trump stumbles on David Duke, KKK," CNN Politics, February 29, 2016, http://www.cnn.com/2016/02/28/politics/donald-trump-white-supremacists/.

33. Patrick O'Connor, "Mitt Romney Attacks Donald Trump, Pushes for Contested Convention," *Wall Street Journal*, March 3, 3016, http://www.wsj.com/articles/mitt-romney-to-attack-donald-trump-as-a-fraud-1457021229.

34. Transcript of Mitt Romney's Speech on Donald Trump, *New York Times*, March 3, 2016, http://www.nytimes.com/2016/03/04/us/politics/mitt-romney-speech.html?_r=0.

35. Tom LoBianco, "Donald Trump: Mitt Romney 'would have dropped to his knees' for my endorsement," CNN Politics, March 3, 2016, http://www.cnn.com/2016/03/03/politics/donald-trump-mitt-romney-would-have-dropped-to-his-knees-for-my-endorsement/index.html.

36. Jim Dalrymple II, "Romney Says He Won't Support Trump, Warns of 'Trickle-Down Racism,'" *BuzzFeed*, June 20, 2016, https://www.buzzfeed.com/jimdalrympleii/romney-says-he-wont-support-trump-warns-of-trickle-down-raci?utm_term=.yu66Xv6wlX#.ecBomvoXQm.

37. Alex Altman, Zeke J. Miller, and Philip Elliot, "Why a Contested GOP Convention Just Got More Likely," Time.com, March 16, 2016, http://time.com/4260668/republican-convention-contested-super-tuesday-donald-trump-delegates/.

38. "Trump builds momentum with big night, narrowing field," Fox News, March 16, 2016, http://www.foxnews.com/politics/2016/03/16/trump-builds-momentum-with-big-night-narrowing-field.html.

39. Maggie Haberman, "For His Unconventional Campaign, Donald Trump looks to an Unorthodox Manager," *New York Times*, September 3, 2015, http://www.nytimes.com/2015/09/04/us/politics/donald-trump-corey-lewandowski-campaign-manager.html?mtrref=www.google.com&gwh=F88DEBE20D33845E7C970BC8D3712286&gwt=pay.

40. Michael Sebastian, "14 Things to Know About Hope Hicks, Donald Trump's 27-Year Old Former Model Press Secretary," *Cosmopolitan*, June 20, 3016, http://www.cosmopolitan.com/politics/news/a56404/who-is-hope-hicks-trump-press-secretary/.

41. Kenneth P. Vogel, Ben Schreckinger, and Hadas Gold, "Trump campaign manager's behavior prompts staff concerns," *Politico*, March 15, 2016, http://www.politico.com/story/2016/03/donald-trump-corey-lewandowski-220742.

42. Michelle Fields, "Michelle Fields: In Her Own Words," Breitbart.com, March 10, 2016, http://www.breitbart.com/big-journalism/2016/03/10/3276486/.

43. Ben Terris, "Inside Trump's inner circle, his staffers are willing to fight for him. Literally," *Washington Post*, March 10, 2016, https://www.washingtonpost.com/lifestyle/style/inside-trumps-inner-circle-his-staffers-are-willing-to-fight-for-him-literally/2016/03/10/4b2b18e8-e660-11e5-a6f3-21ccdbc5f74e_story.html?utm_term=.92f9bf8c0a13.

44. Alex Pappas, "Reporter Posts Photo of Bruise After Saying Trump Campaign Manager 'Yanked Me Down,'" *Daily Caller*, March 10, 2016, http://dailycaller.com/2016/03/10/reporter-posts-photo-of-bruise-after-saying-trump-campaign-manager-yanked-me-down/.

45. Rebecca Savransky, "Trump campaign denied altercation with reporter," *The Hill*, March 10, 2016, http://thehill.com/blogs/ballot-box/presidential-races/272565-trump-campaign-goes-after-reporter.

46. Jerome R. Corsi, "Trump Camp Spotlights Fields' History of Becoming News," WND.com, March 31, 2016, http://www.wnd.com/2016/03/trump-camp-spotlights-fields-history-of-becoming-news/.

47. Dylan Byers, Tal Kopan, and Tom LoBianco, "State will not prosecute Donald Trump's campaign manager," CNN Politics, April 14, 2016, http://www.cnn.com/2016/04/13/politics/corey-lewandowski-donald-trump-charges-dropped/.

48. Dylan Byers, "Donald Trump says reporter made up story about being grabbed by his campaign manager," CNN Politics, March 11, 2016, http://www.cnn.com/2016/03/11/politics/donald-trump-breitbart-reporter-michelle-fields-corey-lewandowski/.

49. Alexander Burns and Maggie Haberman, "Donald Trump Hires Paul Manafort to Lead Delegate Effort," *New York Times*, March 28, 2016, http://www.nytimes.com/politics/first-draft/2016/03/28/donald-trump-hires-paul-manafort-to-lead-delegate-effort/?_r=0.

50. Chris Enloe, "Report: Trump Campaign Manager Corey Lewandowski Demoted, Replaced by the Campaign's Delegate Strategist," *The Blaze*, April 19, 2016, http://www.theblaze.com/stories/2016/04/19/report-trump-campaign-manager-corey-lewandowski-demoted-replaced-by-the-campaigns-delegate-strategist/.

51. Andrew Prokop, "Donald Trump's amazing incompetence at delegate selection, explained," Vox.com, April 14, 2016, http://www.vox.com/2016/4/14/11406062/donald-trump-delegates-convention.

52. Nick Gass, "Trump blasts delegate fight as 'crooked deal,'" *Politico*, April 11, 2016, http://www.politico.com/story/2016/04/trump-delegate-fight-crooked-221789.

53. Lauren Fox, "How Can Ted Cruz Pretend He Deserves the Republican Nomination Now?" TalkingPointsMemo.com, TPM, April 21, 2016, http://talkingpointsmemo.com/dc/ted-cruz-isgoing-to-have-a-hard-time-convincing-voters-he-deserves-the-nomination.

54. Kyle Cheney and Darren Samuelsohn, "Cruz campaign hunts for 'Trojan Horse delegates," *Politico*, April 19, 2016, http://www.politico.com/story/2016/04/cruz-campaign-hunting-for-delegate-deserters-222176#ixzz46Ou2a9cE.

55. Ashley Killough and Eugene Scott, "Trump on Cruz: 'He's bribing people, essentially' for delegates," CNN Politics, April 25, 2016, http://www.cnn.com/2016/04/24/politics/donald-trump-jr-ted-cruz-bribery/.

56. Jacob Engels, "Ted Cruz: Closet Pentecostal," *East Orlando Post*, March 10, 2016, http://eastorlandopost.com/ted-cruz-closet-pentecostal.

57. Sarah Pulliam Bailey, "Ted Cruz's logo: A burning flag, Al Jazeera's logo or a Pentecostal church logo?" *Washington Post*, March 25, 2015, https://www.washingtonpost.com/news/acts-of-faith/wp/2015/03/25/ted-cruzs-logo-a-burning-flag-al-jazeeras-logo-or-a-pentecostal-church-logo/?utm_term=.b7a771ff4816.

58. National Enquirer Staff, "SHOCKING CLAIMS: Pervy Ted Cruz Caught Cheating—With 5 Secret Mistresses!" *National Enquirer*, March 23, 2016, http://www.nationalenquirer.com/celebrity/ted-cruz-sex-scandal-mistresses-cheating-claims/.

59. 166 Dick Siegal, National Enquirer Online Editor, "How the Enquirer Broke the John Edwards Love Child Scandal," *National Enquirer*, June 19, 2014, http://www.nationalenquirer.com/photos/how-enquirer-broke-john-edwards-love-child-scandal/.

60. Tim Hains, "Ted Cruz Denies Affair Allegations: 'Sleazy Donald' Trump Is 'Inventing a Tabloid Smear," *Real Clear Politics*, March 25, 2016, http://www.realclearpolitics.com/video/2016/03/25/ted_cruz_denies_affair_allegations_sleazy_donald_trump_inventing_a_tabloid_smear.html.

61. Jessica Earnshaw, "Racy naked pic of Donald Trump's wife Melania used in political campaign against him," *Express*, published in the U.K., March 25, 2016, http://www.express.co.uk/celebrity-news/655230/Donald-Trump-wife-Melania-naked-photo-Ted-Cruz-Twitter-row.

62. Jesse Byrnes, "Trump revs up Heidi Cruz attacks," *The Hill*, March 24, 2016, http://thehill.com/blogs/ballot-box/274159-trump-doubles-down-on-heidi-cruz-attacks.

63. Jesse Byrnes, "Cruz on Trump threat to wife: 'That should be beneath Donald,'" *The Hill*, March 23, 2016, http://thehill.com/blogs/ballot-box/presidential-races/274007-cruz-on-trump-threatening-wife-that-should-be-beneath.

64. Michelle Moons, "Donald Trump: 'Ted Cruz's Problem with the *National Enquirer* is His and His Alone,'" Breitbart.com, March 25, 2016, http://www.breitbart.com/big-government/2016/03/25/donald-trump-ted-cruzs-problem-with-the-national-enquirer-is-his-and-his-alone/.

65. Wayne Madsen, "Special Report. Mysterious 'Mr. X' in photo with Oswald—FBI couldn't Identify Him," *Wayne Madsen Report*, April 15, 2016, http://www.waynemadsenreport.com/articles/20160415_2.

66. J.R.Taylor, "Ted Cruz's Father—Caught with JFK Assassin," *National Enquirer*, April 20, 2016, http://www.nationalenquirer.com/celebrity/ted-cruz-scandal-father-jfk-assassination/.

67. Maria Recio, "Trump links Cruz's father to JFK assassin, channeling *National Enquirer*," *Miami Herald*, April 22, 2016, http://www.miamiherald.com/news/politics-government/article73449297.html.

68. Jerome R. Corsi, "Source of Trump's JFK Claim Also Accused Rubio," WND.com, May 3, 2016, http://www.wnd.com/2016/05/source-of-trumps-jfk-claim-also-accused-rubio/.

69. Chris Cillizza, "Ted Cruz just threw a Hail Mary named 'Carly Fiorina,'" *Washington Post*, April 27, 2016, https://www.washingtonpost.com/news/the-fix/wp/2016/04/27/ted-cruz-picks-carly-fiorina-as-his-vice-presidential-nominee-but-why/?utm_term=.ffd4d6ab425c.

70. Eric Bradner, John Berman, and Phil Mattingly, "Mike Pence endorses Ted Cruz," CNN Politics, April 29, 2016, http://www.cnn.com/2016/04/29/politics/mike-pence-to-endorse-ted-cruz-friday/.

71. Fox News Insider, "WATCH: Trump Connects Cruz's Father to Lee Harvey Oswald," FoxNews.com, May 3, 2016, http://insider.foxnews.com/2016/05/03/watch-trump-calls-out-cruzs-father-old-photo-lee-harvey-oswald.

72. Evertt Rosenfeld, "Ted Cruz suspends presidential campaign," CNBC, May 3, 2016, http://www.cnbc.com/2016/05/03/ted-cruz-suspends-campaign.html.

73. Matt Flegenheimer, "Ted Cruz Suspends His Campaign for President," *New York Times*, May 3, 2016, http://www.nytimes.com/2016/05/04/us/politics/ted-cruz.html.

74. Matthew Nussbaum, "RNC chairman: Trump is our nominee," *Politico*, May 3, 2016, http://www.politico.com/blogs/2016-gop-primary-live-updates-and-results/2016/05/reince-priebus-donald-trump-is-nominee-222767.

75. Thomas Kaplan, "John Kasich Suspends Campaign for President," *New York Times*, May 4, 2016, http://www.nytimes.com/2016/05/05/us/politics/john-kasich.html.

76. Ed O'Keefe, "Jeb Bush drops out of 2016 presidential campaign," *Washington Post*, February 20, 2016, https://www.washingtonpost.com/politics/jeb-bush-suspends-2016-campaign/2016/02/20/d3a7315a-d721-11e5-be55-2cc3c1e4b76b_story.html.

Part 2

1. Saul D. Alinsky, *Rules for Radicals: A Pragmatic Primer for Realistic Radicals* (New York: Vintage Books, 1971).

2. Hillary D. Rodham, Political Science, "THERE IS ONLY THE FIGHT . . . An Analysis of the Alinsky Model," a thesis submitted in partial fulfillment of the requirements for the Bachelor of Arts degree under the Special Honors Program, Wellesley College, Wellesley, Massachusetts, 1969, http://www.hillaryclintonquarterly.com/documents/HillaryClintonThesis.pdf.

3. Dolly Kyle, *Hillary: The Other Woman* (Washington, DC: WND Books, 2016), p. 32.

Chapter 4

1. Donald J. Trump, posted on Twitter, May 11, 2016, https://twitter.com/realDonaldTrump/status/730343346204508160?ref_src=twsrc%5Etfw.

2. Amy Chozick, "Hillary Clinton Announces 2016 Presidential Bid," *New York Times*, April 12, 2015, http://www.nytimes.com/2015/04/13/us/politics/hillary-clinton-2016-presidential-campaign.html?_r=0.

3. "Transcript: Hillary Clinton Announces Run for President. What she said in her highly anticipated video," *Bloomberg Politics*, April 13, 2015, http://www.bloomberg.com/politics/articles/2015-04-13/transcript-hillary-clinton-announces-run-for-president.

4. Amy Chozick, "Hillary Clinton, in Roosevelt Island Speech, Pledges to Close Income Gap," *New York Times*, June 13, 2016, http://www.nytimes.com/2015/06/14/us/hillary-clinton-attacks-republican-economic-policies-in-roosevelt-island-speech.html.

5. Sam Frizell, "Transcript: Read the Full Text of Hillary Clinton's Campaign Launch Speech," Time.com, June 13, 2015, http://time.com/3920332/transcript-full-text-hillary-clinton-campaign-launch/.

6. Jane Kasperkevic, "Hillary Clinton 2016 campaign rally on Roosevelt Island—as it happened," *Guardian*, June 13, 2015, https://www.theguardian.com/us-news/live/2015/jun/13/hillary-clinton-campaign-rally-new-york.

7. Anne Gearan, "How Hillary Clinton launched her campaign's latest phase," *Washington Post*, June 13, 2015, https://www.washingtonpost.com/news/post-politics/wp/2015/06/13/after-staying-small-hillary-clinton-goes-big-with-splashy-kick-off-rally-in-new-york/?utm_term=.91aa5fd8cea1.
8. Edwin J. Feulner, Ph.D., "Assessing the 'Great Society,'" Heritage Institute, June 30, 2014, http://www.heritage.org/research/commentary/2014/6/assessing-the-great-society.
9. Bill Chappel, "U.S. Students Slide in Global Rankings on Math, Reading, Science," NPR—New Jersey Public Radio, December 3, 2013, http://www.npr.org/sections/thetwo-way/2013/12/03/248329823/u-s-high-school-students-slide-in-math-reading-science.
10. Tim Mak, "Bernie's Past with the Far Far Far Left," *Daily Beast*, January 30, 2016, http://www.thedailybeast.com/articles/2016/01/30/bernie-s-past-with-the-far-far-far-left.html.
11. Katharine Q. Seelye, "As Mayor, Bernie Sanders Was More Pragmatist than Socialist," *New York Times*, November 25, 2015, http://www.nytimes.com/2015/11/26/us/politics/as-mayor-bernie-sanders-was-more-pragmatic-than-socialist.html.
12. Chris Cillizza, "Bernie Sanders isn't going to be president. That's not the point," *Washington Post*, April 29, 2015, https://www.washingtonpost.com/news/the-fix/wp/2015/04/29/bernie-sanders-isnt-going-to-be-president-but-he-matters-anyway/?utm_term=.9676d40fec8c.
13. Ben Terris, "Bernie Sanders: 'Now is not the time for thinking small,'" *Washington Post*, May 26, 2015, https://www.washingtonpost.com/news/post-politics/wp/2015/05/26/bernie-sanders-speaks-to-thousands-at-first-big-campaign-rally-now-is-not-the-time-for-thinking-small/?utm_term=.bf0bbac31073.
14. Russell Berman, "Bernie Sanders Launches His Vermonster Campaign," *The Atlantic*, May 26, 2016, http://www.theatlantic.com/politics/archive/2015/05/bernie-sanders-launches-his-run-for-president-in-2016/394118/.
15. Terris, op.cit.
16. Ibid.
17. "Text of Bernie's Announcement," Burlington, Vermont, May 26, 2016, BernieSanders.com, https://berniesanders.com/bernies-announcement/.
18. Eric Levitz, "Entitled Millennial Workers of the World Unite!" *New York Magazine*, February 4, 2016, http://nymag.com/daily/intelligencer/2016/01/entitled-millennial-workers-of-the-world-unite.html.
19. John Wagner, "Why Millennials love Bernie Sanders, and why that may not be enough," *Washington Post*, October 27, 2015, https://www.washingtonpost.com/politics/in-bernie-sanders-anxious-millennials-find-a-candidate-who-speaks-to-them/2015/10/27/923d0b74-66cc-11e5-9223-70cb36460919_story.html?utm_term=.b9042cd42c3c.
20. Cenk Uygur, "Why Millennials Love Bernie Sanders," *Huffington Post*, May 4, 2016, http://www.huffingtonpost.com/cenk-uygur/why-millennials-love-bernie_b_9839450.html.
21. Tony Lee, "Ed Klein: Obama Urging Biden to Make WH Run, Rejecting Meetings with Hillary," Breitbart.com, October 19, 2015, http://www.breitbart.com/big-government/2015/10/19/ed-klein-obama-urging-biden-to-make-wh-run-rejecting-meetings-with-hillary/.
22. Alex Seitz-Wald, "Elizabeth Warren: 'I'm not running and I'm not going to run,'" MSNBC, April 9, 2015, http://www.msnbc.com/msnbc/elizabeth-warren-gives-strongest-denial-presidential-run-yet#51859.
23. Coleen McCain Nelson and Peter Nicholas, "Joe Biden Decides not to Enter Presidential Race," *Wall Street Journal*, October 21, 2015, http://www.wsj.com/articles/joe-biden-decides-not-to-enter-presidential-race-1445444657. See also: Carol E. Lee, Colleen McCain Nelson, and Peter Nicholas, "How Joe Biden Decided Not to Run for President," *Wall Street Journal*, October 21, 2015, http://www.wsj.com/articles/how-joe-biden-decided-not-to-run-for-president-1445460995.
24. Coleen McCain Nelson, "Beau Biden, Son of Vice President Joe Biden, Dies at 46," *Wall Street Journal*, May 30, 2015, http://www.wsj.com/articles/beau-biden-vice-president-joe-bidens-elder-son-dies-at-age-46-1433037918.
25. David Lightman, "Inside Democratic Party, growing concerns about Clinton," *McClatchy DC*, August 27, 2015, http://www.mcclatchydc.com/news/politics-government/election/article32561658.html. See also: Francesca Chambers, "Democrats worry that Hillary's not ready for 2016 as campaign clock ticks down and email-gate rages on," *Daily Mail*, March 12, 2015, http://www.dailymail.co.uk/news/article-2991933/Democrats-worry-Hillary-s-not-ready-2016-campaign-clock-ticks-email-gate-rages-on.html.
26. David Weigel, "Larry Lessig ends presidential campaign, citing unfair debate rules," *Washington Post*, November 2, 2015, https://www.washingtonpost.com/news/post-politics/wp/2015/11/02/larry-lessig-ends-presidential-campaign-citing-unfair-debate-rules/?utm_term=.bf9b856c3e5e.
27. Dan Merica, "Clinton to DNC: 'Party of Lincoln has become the party of Trump,'" CNN Politics, August 28, 2015, http://www.cnn.com/2015/08/28/politics/hillary-clinton-2016-dnc-meeting-minneapolis/.

Chapter 5

1. Tara Golshan, "Donald Trump actually read his victory speech from a teleprompter. Here's the transcript," Vox.com, June 7, 2016, http://www.vox.com/2016/6/7/11880448/donald-trump-victory-speech-transcript.

2. Hadas Gold, "CNN's Dem debate draws a record 15.3 million viewers," *Politico*, October 14, 2015, http://www.politico.com/blogs/on-media/2015/10/democrat-debate-a-ratings-record-214784.

3. Dominic Patten, "Fox News Channel Wins GOP Debate with Record-Smashing Ratings," Deadline.com, August 7, 2015, http://deadline.com/2015/08/gop-debate-ratings-fox-donald-trump-megyn-kelly-1201495153/.

4. Lisa de Moraes, "CNN GOP Debate Draws Nearly 23 Million Viewers," Deadline.com, September 17, 2015, http://deadline.com/2015/09/cnn-gop-debate-record-ratings-20-million-viewers-1201531579/.

5. Brian Stelter, "Fox's GOP debate had record 24 million viewers," CNN Money, August 7, 2015, http://money.cnn.com/2015/08/07/media/gop-debate-fox-news-ratings/.

6. Julie Pace and Lisa Lerer, "Clinton, Sanders clash on guns, economy, foreign policy," Associated Press, October 14, 2015.

7. Patrick Healy, "After Months of Difficulties, a Night That Turned Clinton's Way," *New York Times*, October 14, 2015.

8. Associated Press, "Democratic debate on CNN draws 5.6 million viewers," April 15, 2016, https://www.yahoo.com/tv/democratic-debate-cnn-draws-5-6-million-viewers-194924581.html.

9. Michael O'Connell, "TV Ratings: 12th GOP Debate Drops to 11.9 Million Viewers on CNN," *Hollywood Reporter*, March 11, 2016, http://www.hollywoodreporter.com/news/tv-ratings-12th-gop-debate-874461.

10. Manuela Tobias and Nolan D. McCaskill, "Bernie Sanders wins Michigan in stunning upset," *Politico*, March 8, 2016, http://www.politico.com/story/2016/03/politico-breaking-news-sanders-wins-michigan-220460.

11. Carl Bialik, "Why the Polls Missed Bernie Sanders' Michigan Upset," FiveThirtyEight.com, March 9, 2016, http://fivethirtyeight.com/features/why-the-polls-missed-bernie-sanders-michigan-upset/.

12. "Hillary wears glasses on campaign trail for first time at late-night event in Las Vegas—after coughing fit and the admission she worries about her health," *Daily Mail*, February 18, 2016, http://www.dailymail.co.uk/news/article-3452950/Hillary-wears-glasses-campaign-trail-time-late-night-event-Las-Vegas-coughing-fit-admission-worries-health.html.

13. "Hillary Clinton suffers from her THIRD public coughing fit while speaking about race relations in Harlem," *Daily Mail*, February 17, 2016, http://www.dailymail.co.uk/news/article-3450558/Hillary-Clinton-suffers-public-coughing-fit-two-years-speaking-race-relations-Harlem.html.

14. Tom Kertscher, "In Context: Hillary Clinton's 'What difference does it make' comment," *Politifact*, May 8, 2013, http://www.politifact.com/truth-o-meter/article/2013/may/08/context-hillary-clintons-what-difference-does-it-m/.

15. Amie Parnes, "Clinton breaks into coughing fit hours into Benghazi testimony," *The Hill*, October 22, 2015, http://thehill.com/blogs/blog-briefing-room/news/257843-clinton-breaks-into-coughing-fit-hours-into-benghazi-testimony.

16. Emily Smith, "Karl Rove: Hillary may have brain damage," *New York Post*, Page Six, May 12, 2014, http://pagesix.com/2014/05/12/karl-rove-hillary-clinton-may-have-brain-damage/.

17. Karen Tumulty, "Rove on Hillary Clinton: 'Of course she doesn't have brain damage,'" *Washington Post*, May 13, 2014, https://www.washingtonpost.com/news/post-politics/wp/2014/05/13/karl-rove-hillary-clinton-has-to-be-forthcoming-about-her-2012-health-episode/?utm_term=.abcaa4a87397.

18. "Hillary Clinton Hospitalized with Blood Clot," ABC News, December 30, 2012, http://abcnews.go.com/blogs/politics/2012/12/hillary-clinton-hospitalized-with-blood-clot/.

19. Press Release, "Judicial Watch: Email Reveals Top Aide Huma Abedin Warning State Department Staffer that Hillary Clinton Is "Often Confused," *Judicial Watch*, November 16, 2015, http://www.judicialwatch.org/press-room/press-releases/judicial-watch-email-reveals-top-aide-huma-abedin-warning-state-department-staffer-that-hillary-clinton-is-often-confused/.

20. Amy Chozick, "Finally, an Explanation for Hillary Clinton's Long Bathroom Break," *New York Times*, December 20, 2015, http://www.nytimes.com/politics/first-draft/2015/12/20/finally-an-explanation-for-hillary-clintons-long-bathroom-break/.

21. Alex Swoyer, "Law Enforcement Officials, Medical Professionals: There's Something Seriously Wrong with Hillary Clinton's Health," Breitbart.com, January 6, 2016, http://www.breitbart.com/big-government/2016/01/06/law-enforcement-officials-medical-professionals-theres-something-seriously-wrong-hillary-clintons-health/.

22. WikiLeaks Podesta email #11,562, Subject: "Fwd: Office," from Robby Mook to John Podesta, March 14, 2015, https://wikileaks.org/podesta-emails/emailid/11563. See also: Ezra Dulis, "WikiLeaks: Hillary Clinton Campaign Plans to Get Ahead of 'Hyper Sensitive' Health, Tax Issues," Breitbart.com,

October 16, 2016, http://www.breitbart.com/2016-presidential-race/2016/10/16/wikileaks-hillary-clinton-campaign-health-hyper-sensitive/.

23. WikiLeaks email #29,549, Subject: "Re: Jeb," from Huma Abedin to Joel Benenson, April 21, 2015, https://wikileaks.org/podesta-emails/emailid/29549. See also: Andrew Stiles, "WikiLeaks: Huma Warned: Hillary 'Still Not Perfect in Her Head,'" *Headstreet*, October 25, 2016, http://heatst.com/politics/wikileaks-huma-hillary-cracked-head/.

24. Lisa Bardack, MD, "Healthcare Statement, RE: Hillary Rodham Clinton, Date of birth: 10/26/47," letter dated July 28, 2015, https://m.hrc.onl/secretary/10-documents/01-health-financial-records/2015-07-28_Statement_of_Health_-_LBardack.pdf.

25. Heidi Evans, Daily News Staff Writer, "Hillary Clinton: My life at 60," *New York Daily News*, October 27, 2007, http://www.nydailynews.com/news/hillary-clinton-life-60-article-1.228020.

26. Jerome R. Corsi, "Hillary's Medications Could Explain Health Scares," WND.com, January 27, 2016, http://www.wnd.com/2016/01/hillarys-medication-could-explain-health-scares/.

27. Paul Joseph Watson, "WikiLeaks E-Mails: Hillary Looked Into Parkinson's Drug After Suffering 'Decision Fatigue,'" Invowars.com, August 23, 2016, http://www.infowars.com/wikileaks-e-mails-hillary-looked-into-parkinsons-drug-after-suffering-from-decision-fatigue/.

28. Jerome R. Corsi, "Doctor: Hillary's Mix of Old-Fashioned Meds Pose Risk," WND.com, February 2, 2016, http://www.wnd.com/2016/02/doctor-hillarys-mix-of-old-fashioned-meds-pose-risk/.

29. Becca Stanek, "Superdelegates explained," *The Week*, April 4, 2016, http://theweek.com/articles/615261/superdelegates-explained.

30. Rebecca Kaplan, "What is a superdelegate?" CBS News, February 25, 2016.

31. Alvin Chang, "What are Democratic superdelegates? A cartoon explainer," Vox.com, February 12, 2016, http://www.vox.com/2016/2/12/10978302/what-are-democratic-superdelegates.

32. Callum Borchers, "We need more questions like this one from Jake Tapper to Debbie Wasserman Schultz [video]," *Washington Post*, February 12, 2015, https://www.washingtonpost.com/news/the-fix/wp/2016/02/12/we-need-more-questions-like-this-one-from-jake-tapper-to-debbie-wasserman-schultz-video/?utm_term=.02fe04508f85.

33. Ben Norton, "Un-Democratic Party: DNC chair says superdelegates ensure elites don't have to run 'against grassroots activists,'" Salon.com, February 13, 2016, http://www.salon.com/2016/02/13/un_democratic_party_dnc_chair_says_superdelegates_ensure_elites_dont_have_to_run_against_grassroots_activists/.

34. Catherine Lucey and Lisa Lerer, Associated Press, "Eight years later, Clinton ready to break one glass ceiling," June 7, 2016.

35. Hope Yen, Associated Press, "Delegate math: Clinton wins, and how AP counts delegates," June 7, 2016.

36. "Text of Clinton's 2008 concession speech," *Guardian*, June 7, 2008, https://www.theguardian.com/commentisfree/2008/jun/07/hillaryclinton.uselections2008I.

37. "Full Transcript of Hillary Clinton June 7 Victory Speech," *Blue Nation Review*, June 8, 2016, http://bluenationreview.com/full-transcript-of-hillary-clintons-june-7-victory-speech/.

38. Erica Werner and Josh Lederman, Associated Press, "Sanders under pressure to quit as Democrats look to unite," June 9, 2016.

39. Clare Foran, "Bernie Sanders Signals the End," *The Atlantic*, June 9, 2015, http://www.theatlantic.com/politics/archive/2016/06/bernie-sanders-president-obama-white-house-hillary-clinton/486416/.

40. Catherine Lucey, Associated Press, "Sanders to back Clinton. Will supporters follow?" July 12, 2016.

41. Stewart Ledbetter, "Sen. Bernie Sanders ends bid, endorses Hillary Clinton for president," NBC Channel 5, July 13, 2016, http://www.mynbc5.com/article/sen-bernie-sanders-ends-bid-endorses-hillary-clinton-for-president/3327708.

42. Ben Norton, "'This system is so rigged' Outrage as undemocratic superdelegate system gives Clinton unfair edge over Sanders," Salon.com, April 12, 2016, http://www.salon.com/2016/04/12/this_system_is_so_rigged_outrage_as_superdelegate_system_undermines_democracy_giving_clinton_unfair_edge_over_sanders/.

43. "Sanders takes aim at 'rigged system' of superdelegates," Reuters, May 2, 2016, http://www.reuters.com/video/2016/05/02/sanders-takes-aim-at-rigged-system-of-su?videoId=368334396.

44. Nick Gass, "Clinton press secretary: Superdelegates can help Clinton clinch nomination by early June," *Politico*, April 14, 2014, http://www.politico.com/blogs/2016-gop-primary-live-updates-and-results/2016/04/hillary-clinton-needs-superdelegates-221943.

45. Calvin Woodward, "AP News Guide: Trump sweeps 5 states, Clinton wins 4," Associated Press, April 27, 2016.

46. Tom Cahill, "DNC Committee Rejects Amendments to Eliminate Superdelegates After Locking Sanders Delegates Out of the Room," *US Uncut*, July 23, 2016, http://usuncut.com/politics/dnc-rules-committee-superdelegates/.

47. Jon Queally, Staff Writer, "Establishment Wins Again as DNC Rules Committee Rejects Proposal to Abolish Superdelegates," July 23, 2016, http://www.commondreams.org/news/2016/07/23/establishment-wins-again-dnc-rules-committee-rejects-proposal-abolish-superdelegates.

48. Stephen Braun, Associated Press, "Hacked emails show Democratic Party hostility to Sanders," July 23, 2016.

49. WikiLeaks, "The DNC Email Database," Wikileaks.org, July 22, 2016, https://wikileaks.org/dnc-emails/.

50. Email from Brad Marshall, entitled "No shit," dated May 5, 2016, Wikileaks.org, "The DNC Email Database," email #7643, https://wikileaks.org/dnc-emails/emailid/7643.

51. Kristen East, "Top staffer apologizes for email on Sanders' religion," *Politico*, July 23, 2016, http://www.politico.com/story/2016/07/top-dnc-staffer-apologizes-for-email-on-sanders-religion-226072.

52. Email from Mark Paustenbach to Luis Miranda, entitled "Bernie narrative," dated May 21, 2016, Wikileaks.org, "The DNC Email Database," Email #11,056, https://wikileaks.org/dnc-emails/emailid/11056.

53. Michael Sainato, "WikiLeaks Proves Primary Was Rigged: DNC Undermined Democracy," *Observer*, July 22, 2016, http://observer.com/2016/07/wikileaks-proves-primary-was-rigged-dnc-undermined-democracy/.

54. Guccifer 2.0, "New DNC Docs," Guccifer2.wordpress.com, July 14, 2016, https://guccifer2.wordpress.com/2016/07/14/new-dnc-docs/.

55. Ryan Koronowski, "Debbie Wasserman Schultz Resigns from DNC in Wake of WikiLeaks Email Dump," ThinkProgress.org, July 24, 2016, https://thinkprogress.org/debbie-wasserman-schultz-resigns-from-dnc-in-wake-of-wikileaks-email-dump-d294bbdffb16#.y7ua949lt.

Chapter 6

1. Jenna Johnson, "At Florida rally, Trump resumes attacking 'Crooked Hillary Clinton,'" *Washington Post*, September 27, 2016, https://www.washingtonpost.com/news/post-politics/wp/2016/09/27/at-florida-rally-trump-resumes-attacking-crooked-hillary-clinton/?utm_term=.b4655a999321.

2. Jennifer Steinhauer, "Elizabeth Warren Endorses Clinton and Goes Taunt-for-Taunt with Trump," *New York Times*, June 9, 2016, http://www.nytimes.com/2016/06/10/us/politics/elizabeth-warren-hillary-clinton-donald-trump.html?_r=0.

3. Josh Blackman, "Donald Trump's Dangerous Attack on U.S. District Judge Gonzalo Curiel and the 'Rigged' Federal Judiciary," *Josh Blackman's Blog*, May 27, 2016, http://joshblackman.com/blog/2016/05/27/donald-trumps-dangerous-attack-on-u-s-district-judge-gonzalo-curiel-and-the-rigged-federal-judiciary/,

4. Adam L. Silverman, "Senator Warren's Speech at the American Constitution Society," BalloonJuice.com, June 9, 2016, https://www.balloon-juice.com/2016/06/09/senator-warrens-speech-at-the-american-constitution-society/.

5. Jerome R. Corsi, "Attorneys Suing Trump U Paid $675,000 to Clintons for Speeches," WND.com, June 1, 2016, http://www.wnd.com/2016/06/attorneys-suing-trump-u-paid-675000-to-clintons-for-speeches/.

6. Rachel Stockman, "Guess Who Else Paid Out Big Bucks for Clinton Speeches? LawNewz.com, May 31, 2016, http://lawnewz.com/high-profile/guess-who-else-paid-out-big-bucks-for-clinton-speeches/.

7. Josh Gerstein, "Clintons made $25 million in speeches since 2014," *Politico*, May 15, 2015, http://www.politico.com/story/2015/05/bill-and-hillary-clinton-made-roughly-25-million-in-speeches-since-2014-118009.

8. Ibid.

9. Diana Hull, "La Raza-Chicano Activism in California," *The Social Contract Press*, Volume 9, Number 4 (Summer 1999), http://www.thesocialcontract.com/artman2/publish/tsc0904/article_766.shtml.

10. "National Council of La Raza (NCLR)," DiscoverTheNetworks.org, December 8, 2016, http://www.discoverthenetworks.org/printgroupProfile.asp?grpid=153.

11. Rosalind S. Helderman, "Trump agrees to $25 million settlement in Trump University fraud cases," *Washington Post*, November 18, 2016, https://www.washingtonpost.com/politics/source-trump-nearing-settlement-in-trump-university-fraud-cases/2016/11/18/8dc047c0-ada0-11e6-a31b-4b6397e625d0_story.html?utm_term=.64d1174f0f03.

12. Stone, Roger. "Trump U Is Nothing Compared To Laureate Education." *Daily Caller*. N.p., 2 June 2016. Web. <http://dailycaller.com/2016/06/02/trump-u-is-nothing-compared-to-laureate-education/>.

13. Peter Schweizer, "Bill Clinton Bagged $16 Million from Company that Received Millions from Hillary's State Department," Breitbart.com, August 5, 2015, http://www.breitbart.com/big-government/2015/08/05/bill-clinton-bagged-16-million-from-company-that-received-millions-from-hillarys-state-dept/.

14. Steven Salzberg, "For-Profit Colleges Encourage Huge Student Debt," *Forbes*, July 12, 2015, http://www.forbes.com/sites/stevensalzberg/2015/07/12/for-profit-colleges-encourage-huge-student-debt/#35f8f4db2a05.

15. Joanne P. Cavanaugh, "Sylvan's Fast Learners," *Johns Hopkins Magazine*, September 1998, http://pages.jh.edu/jhumag/0998web/sylvan.html.

16. Irvin Molotsky, "Encyclopedic Medical Card Shows the Worth of Young Ideas," *New York Times*, May 19, 1985, http://www.nytimes.com/1985/05/19/us/encyclopedic-medical-card-shows-the-worth-of-young-ideas.html.

17. Eric Owens, "Why are the Clintons hawking a seedy, Soros-backed for-profit college corporation?" *Daily Caller*, January 13, 2014, http://dailycaller.com/2014/01/13/why-are-the-clintons-hawking-a-seedy-soros-backed-for-profit-college-corporation/.

18. "Laureate International Universities Broadcasts Clinton Global Initiative's Annual Meeting," Laureate International Universities, Press Release, Sept, 24, 2013, http://www.laureate.net/NewsRoom/PressReleases/2013/09/Laureate-International-Universities-Broadcasts-Clinton-Global-Initiatives-Annual-Meeting.

19. "President Clinton Announces Program for the Fifth Annual Clinton Global Initiative University Meeting," Clinton Global Initiative, Press Release, March 8, 2012, http://press.clintonglobalinitiative.org/press_releases/president-clinton-announces-program-for-the-fifth-annual-clinton-global-initiative-university-meeting/.

20. Jennifer Epstein, "Bill Clinton Leaves For-Profit College Position," *Bloomberg Politics*, April 24, 2015, http://www.bloomberg.com/politics/articles/2015-04-24/bill-clinton-leaves-for-profit-college-position.

21. Jerome R. Corsi, "Clinton For-Profit Education Scandal Dwarfs Trump U," WND.com, June 3, 2016, http://www.wnd.com/2016/06/clinton-for-profit-education-scandal-dwarfs-trump-u/.

22. Kevin McDermott, "Trump jeers at rivals, protesters, media in raucous St. Lois appearance," *St. Louis Post-Dispatch*, March 11, 2016, http://www.stltoday.com/news/national/govt-and-politics/trump-jeers-at-rivals-protesters-media-in-raucous-st-louis/article_6d17d069-5996-58a4-9fa3-70a032b820ad.html.

23. Ibid.

24. Sam Reisman, "Trump Tells Crowd to 'Knock the Crap Out' of Protesters, Offers to Pay legal fees," *Mediate*, February 1, 2016, http://www.mediaite.com/online/trump-tells-crowd-to-knock-the-crap-out-of-protesters-offers-to-pay-legal-fees/.

25. Josh Feldman, "Trump on #BlackLivesMatter Protester at Rally: 'Maybe He Should Have Been Roughed Up,'" *Mediate*, November 22, 2015, http://www.mediaite.com/tv/trump-on-blacklivesmatter-protester-at-rally-maybe-he-should-have-been-roughed-up/.

26. Jerem Diamond and Theodore Schleifer, CNN, "Trump supporters, protesters clash after Chicago rally postponed," CNN, March 12, 2016, http://www.cnn.com/2016/03/11/politics/donald-trump-chicago-protests/.

27. Jonathan Chait, "Donald Trump Poses an Unprecedented Threat to American Democracy," *New York Magazine*, March 13, 2016, http://nymag.com/daily/intelligencer/2016/03/trump-poses-unprecedented-threat-to-democracy.html.

28. Joe Tacopino, "Violent protesters force Trump to climb over wall to get to event," *New York Post*, April 29, 2016, http://nypost.com/2016/04/29/hundreds-of-protesters-gather-outside-trump-speech-after-night-of-violence/.

29. Jill Colvin and Russell Contreras, "Protests turn violent outside Trump rally in New Mexico," Associated Press, May 25, 2016, http://www.pbs.org/newshour/rundown/protests-turn-violent-outside-trump-rally-in-new-mexico/.

30. Ibid.

31. "The Latest: 4 arrested amid protests at Trump rally," Associated Press, May 25, 2016.

32. John Santucci, Candice Smith, and David Caplan, "Violence Breaks Out at Trump Rally in San Jose, Protesters Hurl Eggs, Throw Punches, Intimidate Supporters," ABC News, June 3, 2016, http://abcnews.go.com/Politics/violence-breaks-trump-rally-san-jose-protesters-hurl/story?id=39576437.

33. Paul Elias and Martha Mendoza, "San Jose, California police under fire after Trump rally," Associated Press, June 3, 2016, https://www.nexis.com/results/enhdocview.do?docLinkInd=true&ersKey=23_T25187897380&format=GNBFI&startDocNo=51&resultsUrlKey=0_T25187897399&backKey=20_T25187911100&csi=304481&docNo=64.

34. Sergey Gladysh, "Anti-Trump protests are paid and staged, Craigslist reveals," November 12, 2016, http://theduran.com/anti-trump-protesters-paid-staged-craigslist-reveals/.

35. Tim Hains, "James O'Keefe: Clinton Campaign, DNC Coordinate with Organizations to Incite Violence at Trump Events," *Real Clear Politics*, October 17, 2016, http://www.realclearpolitics.com/video/2016/10/17/new_okeefe_video_clinton_campaign_dnc_coordinated_with_organizations_to_beat_up_trump_supporters.html.

36. Victoria Taft, "Dem Operatives Admit on Hot Mic They Started Chicago Riot that Shut Down Trump Rally & That's Not All," *Independent Journal Review*, October 2016, http://ijr.com/2016/10/715882-dem-operatives-admit-on-hot-mic-they-started-chicago-riot-that-shut-down-trump-rally-thats-not-all/. See also: Joe Burgess, "69-year-old woman punched at Trump rally," *Asheville (NC) Citizen-Times*, http://www.citizen-times.com/story/news/local/2016/09/13/69-year-old-woman-punched-asheville-trump-rally/90301468/.

37. Valerie Richardson, "Democratic heads roll after video shows agitators planted at Trump rallies," *Washington Times*, October 18, 2016, http://www.washingtontimes.com/news/2016/oct/18/undercover-video-shows-democrats-saying-they-hire-/.

38. "Trump campaign: Video shows Clinton coordinated with liberal group to incite crowds," Fox News, October 25, 2016, http://www.foxnews.com/politics/2016/10/25/trump-campaign-video-shows-clinton-coordinated-with-liberal-group-to-incite-crowds.html.

39. David Brock, *Blinded by the Right: The Conscience of an Ex-Conservative* (New York: Crown, 2002).

40. Michelle Goldbert, "How David Brock Built an Empire to Put Hillary in the White House," *The Nation*, December 15–22, 2004 Issue, https://www.thenation.com/article/how-david-brock-built-empire-put-hillary-white-house/.

41. Ibid.

42. David Brock, *The Real Anita Hill* (New York: Free Press, 1993).

43. "David Brock Interview," National Public Radio, July 2, 2001, http://www.npr.org/programs/atc/features/2001/jul/010702.brock.html.

44. David Brock, *The Seduction of Hillary Rodham* (New York: Free Press, 1996).

45. Ibid., p. ix.

46. Jacob Laskin, "David Brock: Media Liar," *Front Page Magazine*, September 21, 2005, http://archive.frontpagemag.com/readArticle.aspx?ARTID=7186.

47. David Brock, "Confessions of a Right-Wing Hit Man," *Esquire*, July 1997, http://classic.esquire.com/confessions-of-a-right-wing-hit-man/.

48. Edward Helmore, "Once the scourge of Democrats, former Republican plays tough for Hillary Clinton," *Guardian*, November 2, 2014, https://www.theguardian.com/world/2014/nov/29/david-brock-former-republican-hitman-hillary-clinton.

49. Jonathan Turley, "Podesta Warned: 'I Hope Hillary Truly Understands Now How Batshit Crazy David Brock Is," JonathanTurley.org, November 4, 2016, https://jonathanturley.org/2016/11/04/podesta-warned-i-hope-hillary-truly-understands-now-how-batshit-crazy-david-brock-is/. See also: WikiLeaks Podesta Email #43904, email from Neera Tanden to John Podesta, dated February 11, 2015, https://wikileaks.org/podesta-emails/emailid/43904.

50. WikiLeaks Podesta Email #35061, email from John Podesta to Neera Tanden, Subject: "Re: Why?" May 13, 2015, https://wikileaks.org/podesta-emails/emailid/35061.

51. Maggie Haberman, "Hillary Clinton-Aligned Group Gets Closer to Her Campaign," *New York Times*, May 12, 2015, http://www.nytimes.com/politics/first-draft/2015/05/12/hillary-clinton-aligned-group-gets-closer-to-her-campaign/?ref=politics. See also: Matea Gold, "How a super PAC plans to coordinate directly with Hillary Clinton's campaign," *Washington Post*, May 12, 2016, https://www.washingtonpost.com/news/post-politics/wp/2015/05/12/how-a-super-pac-plans-to-coordinate-directly-with-hillary-clintons-campaign/?utm_term=.5a5186355f7b.

52. Amy Chozick, "As Trump and Clinton Clash, 2 Operatives Duke It Out in Their Shadows," *New York Times*, May 23, 2016, http://www.nytimes.com/2016/05/24/us/politics/roger-stone-david-brock-trump-clinton.html.

53. Roger Stone and Robert Morrow, *The Clintons' War on Women* (New York: Skyhorse Publishing, 2016).

54. "FBI's Comey: Clinton 'extremely careless' about emails, but bureau will not advise criminal charges," Fox News, July 5, 2016, http://www.foxnews.com/politics/2016/07/05/fbi-recommends-no-charges-to-be-filed-against-clinton.html.

55. Edward Klein, "Bill Clinton's airport run-in with Loretta Lynch was no accident," *New York Post*, October 3, 2016, http://nypost.com/2016/10/03/book-details-how-team-obama-schemed-to-let-hillary-skate/.

56. Kevin Johnson, "Loretta Lynch, Bill Clinton meeting raises eyebrow," *USA Today*, June 30, 2016, http://www.usatoday.com/story/news/politics/elections/2016/06/30/loretta-lynch-bill-clinton-meeting/86555274/.

57. Ken Thomas and Eric Tucker, "Lynch meeting latest episode to strain Clinton trust," Associated Press, July 2, 2016.

58. Dan Balz, Chief Correspondent, "How everyone looks bad because Bill Clinton met with Loretta Lynch," *Washington Post*, July 2, 2016, https://www.washingtonpost.com/politics/how-everyone-looks-bad-because-bill-clinton-met-with-loretta-lynch/2016/07/02/a7807adc-3ff4-11e6-a66f-aa6c1883b6b1_story.html?utm_term=.3b02a44b3a3e.

59. Mike Gallagher, "Republican Presidential nominee @RealDonaldTrump is on today's Mike Gallagher Show," June 30, 2016, http://www.mikeonline.com/republican-presidential-nominee-realdonaldtrump-is-on-todays-mike-gallagher-show-mikeonline/.

60. Maggie Haberman, "Bill Clinton's Meeting with Loretta Lynch Causes Stir in Both Parties," *New York Times*, July 1, 2016, http://www.nytimes.com/2016/07/02/us/politics/bill-clinton-loretta-lynch.html.

61. "Hacker Targets Clinton Confidant in New Attack," *The Smoking Gun*, March 15, 2013, http://www.thesmokinggun.com/documents/sidney-blumenthal-email-hack-687341.

62. Matei Rosca, "EXCLUSIVE: Jailed hacker Guccifer boasts, 'I used to read [Clinton's] memos . . . and then do the gardening,'" Pando.com, March 20, 2015, https://pando.com/2015/03/20/exclusive-interview-jailed-hacker-guccifer-boasts-i-used-to-read-hillarys-memos-for-six-seven-hours-and-then-do-the-gardening/.

63. "Hacker Begins Distributing Confidential Memos Sent to Hillary Clinton on Libya, Benghazi Attack," *The Smoking Gun*, March 18, 2013, http://www.thesmokinggun.com/buster/sidney-blumenthal/hacker-distributes-memos-784091.

64. Pierre Thomas, Mike Levine, Jack Cloherty, and Jack Date, "Former CIA Head David Petraeus to Plead Guilty," ABC News, March 3, 2015, http://abcnews.go.com/Politics/cia-head-david-petraeus-plead-guilty/story?id=29340487.

65. Zeke J. Miller, "Transcript: Everything Hillary Clinton Said on the Email Controversy," Time.com, March 10, 2015, http://time.com/3739541/transcript-hillary-clinton-email-press-conference/.

66. FBI National Press Office, Washington, DC, "FBI Releases Documents in Hillary Clinton E-Mail Investigation," Press Release, September 2, 2016, https://www.fbi.gov/news/pressrel/press-releases/fbi-releases-documents-in-hillary-clinton-e-mail-investigation.

67. Jessie Hellmann, "FBI identifies 13 mobile devices Clinton potentially used to send emails," *The Hill*, September 2, 2016, http://thehill.com/blogs/ballot-box/presidential-races/294319-fbi-report-clinton-possibly-used-13-mobile-devices-to.

68. Lauren Carroll, "FBI findings tear holes in Hillary Clinton's email defense," Politifact.com, July 6, 2016, http://www.politifact.com/truth-o-meter/statements/2016/jul/06/hillary-clinton/fbi-findings-tear-holes-hillary-clintons-email-def/.

69. Michelle Lee, "Fact check: Trump's claim Clinton destroyed emails after getting a subpoena from Congress," *Washington Post*, October 19, 2016, https://www.washingtonpost.com/politics/2016/live-updates/general-election/real-time-fact-checking-and-analysis-of-the-final-2016-presidential-debate/fact-check-trumps-claim-clinton-destroyed-emails-after-getting-a-subpoena-from-congress/?utm_term=.c0e0a15cf861.

70. Spencer S. Hsu, " FBI uncovers 14,900 more documents in Clinton email probe," *Washington Post*, August 22, 2016, https://www.washingtonpost.com/local/public-safety/fbi-uncovered-at-least-14900-more-documents-in-clinton-email-investigation/2016/08/22/36745578-6643-11e6-be4e-23fc4d4d12b4_story.html?postshare=3331471876111787&tid=ss_tw&utm_term=.c760c10246bb.

71. Press Release, "Judicial Watch Forced Out Email Showing Clinton Blamed Benghazi on 'Al Qaeda-like group' on Night of Attack," *Judicial Watch*, November 13, 2015, http://www.judicialwatch.org/press-room/press-releases/judicial-watch-litigation-forced-production-of-key-email-showing-hillary-clinton-blamed-benghazi-assault-on-al-qaeda-like-group-in-email-sent-to-daughter-on-night-of-september-11-att/.

72. David Horsey, "'GM is alive, Osama is dead' is Obama's answer to Republicans," *Los Angeles Times*, September 5, 2012, http://articles.latimes.com/2012/sep/05/nation/la-na-tt-obamas-answer-20120905.

73. Richard Benedetto, "Obama Got Pass on Benghazi, Thanks to Romney," *Real Clear Politics*, May 11, 2013, http://www.realclearpolitics.com/articles/2013/05/11/obama_got_pass_on_benghazi_thanks_to_romney_118361.html. See also: Deroy Murdock, "Hillary Clinton and Obama's Lies on Benghazi—Too Many to Count, but Let's Try," *National Review*, October 29, 2015, http://www.nationalreview.com/article/426289/hillary-clinton-and-obamas-lies-benghazi-too-many-count-lets-try-deroy-murdock.

74. Peter Schweizer, *Clinton Cash: The Untold Story of How and Why Foreign Governments and Businesses Helped Make Bill and Hillary Rich* (New York: HarperCollins Books, 2015).

75. "'Clinton Cash' Author: WikiLeaks Emails Confirm Clinton Foundation Pay-to-Play Allegations," Fox News, October 17, 2016, http://insider.foxnews.com/2016/10/17/clinton-cash-author-wikileaks-emails-confirm-clinton-foundation-pay-play-scam.

76. Jerome R. Corsi, *Partners in Crime: The Clinton's Scheme to Monetize the White House for Personal Profit* (Washington, DC: WND Books, 2016).

77. Rosalind S. Helderman, Tom Hamburger, and Steven Rich, "Clintons' foundation has raised nearly $2 billion—and some key questions," *Washington Post*, February 18, 2015, https://www.washingtonpost.com/politics/clintons-raised-nearly-2-billion-for-foundation-since-2001/2015/02/18/b8425d88-a7cd-11e4-a7c2-03d37af98440_story.html?utm_term=.3401e44107cb.

78. Jerome R. Corsi, "Clinton Foundation Auditor Also in Global Crossing Scandal," WND.com, October 27, 2016, http://www.wnd.com/2016/10/clinton-foundation-auditor-also-in-global-crossing-scandal/.

79. Chuck Ross, "WIKILEAKS Emails: Chelsea Clinton Acted Like a 'Spoiled Brat Kid,'" *Daily Caller*, October 10, 2016, http://dailycaller.com/2016/10/10/wikileaks-emails-chelsea-clinton-acted-like-a-spoiled-brat-kid/.

80. Email from Doug Band to John Podesta, dated November 16, 2016, Wikileaks.org, "Podesta Email File," Email #32,240, https://www.wikileaks.org/podesta-emails/emailid/32240#searchresult.

81. Kenneth P. Vogel, "Eric Braverman Tried to Change the Clinton Foundation. Then He Quit," *Politico*, March 1, 2015, http://www.politico.com/magazine/story/2015/03/clinton-foundation-eric-braverman-115598.

82. Isabel Vincent and Melissa Klein, "Clinton confidant cuts ties with the formidable family," *New York Post*, June 21, 2015, http://nypost.com/2015/06/21/clinton-confidant-cuts-ties-with-the-formidable-family/.

83. Email from Doug Band to John Podesta, dated November 17, 2016, Wikileaks.org, "Podesta Email File," Email #21,978, https://wikileaks.org/podesta-emails/emailid/21978#efmAALABKAD5AGdAGfAHV.

84. Paul H. Jossey, "Clinton Foundation memo reveals Bill and Hilary as partners in crime," *The Hill*, October 31, 2016, http://thehill.com/blogs/pundits-blog/presidential-campaign/303663-bill-and-hillary-partners-in-crime-literally.

85. Roger Stone, "Roger Stone: It's Time America Got Some Answers About Huma Abedin," Breitbart.com, June 13, 2016, http://www.breitbart.com/national-security/2016/06/13/roger-stone-its-time-america-got-some-answers-about-huma-abedin/.

86. "Huma Abedin," DiscoverTheNetworks.org, no date, http://www.discoverthenetworks.org/individualProfile.asp?indid=2556.

87. Ibid.

88. Andrew C. McCarthy, "The Huma Unmentionables," *National Review*, July 24, 2013, http://www.nationalreview.com/corner/354351/huma-unmentionables-andrew-c-mccarthy.

89. Andrew C. McCarthy, "Huma Abedin and the Muslim Brotherhood: Closely Connected," *PJ Media*, July 24, 2012, https://pjmedia.com/andrewmccarthy/2012/07/24/huma-abedin-and-the-muslim-brotherhood-closely-connected/?singlepage=true.

90. "Naseef optimistic about Rabita trust reactivation," *Arab News*, March 23, 2014, http://www.arabnews.com/news/544526.

91. Jorgen S. Nielsen, "Contemporary Discussions on Religious Minorities in Islam," *BYU Law Review*, Volume 2002, Issue 2, http://digitalcommons.law.byu.edu/cgi/viewcontent.cgi?article=2116&context=lawreview.

92. "Comprehensive List of Terrorists and Groups Identified Under Executive Order 13224," The Office of the Coordinator for Counterterrorism, U.S. Department of State, December 31, 2001, https://2001-2009.state.gov/s/ct/rls/fs/2001/6531.htm.

93. US District Court for the Southern District of New York: "In Re: Terrorist Attacks on September 11, 2001 (September 21, 2005), in "Developments in international law, prepared by the Editorial Staff of International Legal Materials, October 31, 2005," American Society of International Law, published in *International Law in Brief,* http://web.archive.org/web/20130906194225/http://www.asil.org/ilib051031.cfm.

94. "Treasury Department Statement on the Designation of Wa'el Hamza Julidan," Office of public Affairs, U.S. Department of the Treasury, September 6, 2002, https://www.treasury.gov/press-center/press-releases/Pages/po3397.aspx.

95. "Founders meet and form al-Qaeda," GlobalSecurity.org, no date, http://www.globalsecurity.org/security/profiles/founders_meet_and_form_al-qaeda.htm.

96. "Advisory editorial board," *Journal of Muslim Minority Affairs*, Volume 18, Issue 1, 1998, http://www.tandfonline.com/doi/abs/10.1080/13602009808716388.

97. Spencer Morgan, "Hillary's Mystery Woman: Who Is Huma?" Observer.com, April 2, 2007, http://observer.com/2007/04/hillarys-mystery-woman-who-is-huma/.

98. "Property Detail, District of Columbia, Owner Huma Abedin," purchase price listed as $649,000, found on Photobucket.com, sale date of September 18, 2006, http://s242.photobucket.com/user/kayeyedoubledee/media/District_of_Columbia_Property_Detai.jpg.html.

99. Raymond Hernandez, "Questions on the Dual Role of a Clinton Aide Persist," *New York Times*, August 18, 2013, http://www.nytimes.com/2013/08/19/nyregion/questions-on-the-dual-role-of-a-clinton-aide-persist.html?ref=politics&_r=0.

100. John Solomon, "Hillary Clinton personally signed deal that let top aide collect two salaries," *Washington Times*, September 24, 2015, http://www.washingtontimes.com/news/2015/sep/24/hillary-clinton-signed-deal-let-huma-abedin-double/.

101. Chris Frates, "New company established 11 days before Huma Abedin left State Department," CNN Politics, August 19, 2015, http://www.cnn.com/2015/08/19/politics/hillary-clinton-huma-abedin-zain-endeavors-llc/.

102. Benjamin Siegel, "Hillary Clinton's Top Aide Huma Abedin Questioned About Benghazi Attacks," ABC News, October 16, 2015, http://abcnews.go.com/Politics/hillary-clintons-top-aide-huma-abedin-grilled-benghazi/story?id=34508529.

103. Nina Burleigh, "Meet Huma Abedin, Mysterious Clinton Aide Whose Emails Might Change History," *Newsweek*, April 28, 2016, http://www.newsweek.com/2016/05/06/huma-abedin-hillary-clinton-anthony-weiner-453204.html.

104. Lee Stranahan, "The Truth About Huma Abedin that Media Matters Doesn't Want America to See," Breitbart.com, January 18, 2016, http://www.breitbart.com/big-government/2016/01/18/the-truth-about-huma-abedin-that-media-matters-doesnt-want-america-to-see/.

105. Katie McHugh, "Donald Trump Repeatedly Warned Anthony Weiner Was a Security Risk," Breitbart.com, October 29, 2016, http://www.breitbart.com/2016-presidential-race/2016/10/29/donald-trump-repeatedly-warned-anthony-weiner-was-a-national-security-risk/.

106. Alex Swoyer, "Trump on Huma Abedin, Anthony Weiner: 'Just Another Example of Hillary Clinton's Bad Judgment," Breitbart.com, August 29, 2016, http://www.breitbart.com/2016-presidential-race/2016/08/29/trump-on-huma-abedin-anthony-weiner-just-another-example-of-hillary-clintons-bad-judgment/.

107. Jessica Chasmar, "Trump ally Roger Stone: Clinton aide Huma Abedin could be 'terrorist agent,'" *Washington Times*, June 13, 2016, http://www.washingtontimes.com/news/2016/jun/13/roger-stone-huma-abedin-top-clinton-aide-could-be-/.

108. "If not Hillary Clinton, who? 20 women who could shatter the glass ceiling," CBS News, no date, http://www.cbsnews.com/pictures/hillary-clinton-president-20-women-who-could-shatter-the-glass-ceiling/7/.

Part 3

1. Alonzo L. Hamby, "1948 Democratic Convention: The South Secedes Again," *Smithsonian Magazine*, August 2008, http://www.smithsonianmag.com/history/1948-democratic-convention-878284/.

2. Museum of Broadcast Communications, "Presidential Nominating Conventions and Television," no date, http://www.museum.tv/eotv/presidential.htm.

3. David Gergen quoted in the following book: John Anthony Maltese, *Spin Control: The White House Office of Communications and the Management of Presidential News* (Chapel Hill, NC: The University of Northe Carolina Press, Second Edition, 1994), p. 96.

4. "Bill Corruthers, TV director-producer," *Variety*, Obituary, March 7, 2003, http://variety.com/2003/scene/people-news/bill-carruthers-1117881918/.

5. Bill Carruthers quoted in the following book: John Anthony Maltese, *Spin Control*, loc.cit.

6. Zachary Karabell, "The Rise and Fall of the Televised Political Convention," Discussion Paper D-33, published by the Joan Shorenstein Center for Press, Politics, and Public Policy, at the John F. Kennedy School of Government, Harvard University, October 1998, https://www.hks.harvard.edu/presspol/publications/papers/discussion_papers/d33_karabell.pdf.

7. Callum Borchers, "How political conventions became sanitized, made-for-TV infomercials," *Washington Post*, July 21, 2016, https://www.washingtonpost.com/news/the-fix/wp/2016/07/21/how-political-conventions-became-sanitized-made-for-tv-infomercials/?utm_term=.438ba81fd27e.

8. Stephen Battaglio, "TV viewership for Hillary Clinton speech is smaller than for Donald Trump," *Los Angeles Times*, July 29, 2016, http://www.latimes.com/entertainment/envelope/cotown/la-et-ct-dnc-ratings-20160729-snap-story.html.

9. Brian Stelter, "Debate breaks record as most-watched in U.S. history," CNN Money, September 27, 2016, http://money.cnn.com/2016/09/27/media/debate-ratings-record-viewership/.

10. Jill Serjeant and Lisa Richwine, "TV audience sharply down for second Trump-Clinton debate, despite tape furor," Reuters, October 10, 2016, http://www.reuters.com/article/us-usa-election-debate-ratings-idUSKCN12A1LF.

11. Cynthia Littleton and Oriana Schwindt, "Final Ratings for Third Donald Trump-Hillary Clinton Debate: 71.6 Million," *Variety*, October 20, 2016, http://variety.com/2016/tv/news/tv-ratings-donald-trump-hillary-clinton-final-debate-1201895174/.

Chapter 7

1. Jesse Byrnes, "Trump chooses Pence for VP," *The Hill*, July 15, 2016, http://thehill.com/blogs/ballot-box/presidential-races/287892-trump-officially-chooses-pence-for-vp.

2. Stephen Collinson, "Trump, Pence step into the spotlight together," CNN Politics, July 16, 2016, http://www.cnn.com/2016/07/16/politics/donald-trump-mike-pence-campaign-trail/.

3. Amber Phillips, "Who is Mike Pence?" *Washington Post*, October 4, 2015, https://www.washington-post.com/news/the-fix/wp/2016/07/14/10-things-you-should-know-about-mike-pence-who-may-join-donald-trump-on-the-gop-ticket/?utm_term=.5375b4439e10.

4. Gretchen Frazee and Daniel Bush, "What you need to know about Trump's VP pick, Mike Pence," PBS News Hour, July 15, 2016, http://www.pbs.org/newshour/updates/need-know-trumps-vp-pick-mike-pence/.

5. Jessica Taylor, "Dumpster Fires, Fishing and Travel: These Republicans Are Sitting Out the RNC," National Public Radio, July 18, 2016, http://www.npr.org/2016/07/18/486398726/dumpster-fires-fishing-and-travel-these-republicans-are-sitting-out-the-rnc.

6. Shane Goldmacher, Ben Schreckinger, and Katie Glueck, "Trump's disastrous Day One," *Politico*, July 18, 2016, http://www.politico.com/story/2016/07/rnc-2016-convention-clashes-donald-trump-225761.

7. "Melania Trump's RNC speech is strikingly similar to Michelle Obama's 2008 convention speech," Reuters, published in the *Las Vegas Review-Journal*, July 18, 2016.

8. Andrew Kirell and Justin Miller, "Melania Trump Plagiarized Michelle Obama, a Woman Republicans Said Hated America," *Daily Beast*, July 19, 2016, http://www.thedailybeast.com/articles/2016/07/19/melania-trump-plagiarized-michelle-obama-a-woman-republicans-said-hated-america.html.

9. Evan Thomas, "Michelle Obama's 'Proud' Remarks," *Newsweek*, March 12, 2008, http://www.newsweek.com/michelle-obamas-proud-remarks-83559.

10. Kayla Ruble, "Trump campaign admits Melania's speech plagiarized Michelle Obama," *Vice News*, July 20, 2016, https://news.vice.com/article/donald-trump-campaign-admits-melania-trump-speech-plagiarized-michelle-obama.

11. Bill Rehkoph, "FULL SPEECH: Ted Cruz addresses Republican convention delegates," *The Hill*, July 20, 2016, http://thehill.com/blogs/pundits-blog/presidential-campaign/288611-transcript-ted-cruz-addresses-republican-convention.

12. Todd J. Gillman and Robert T. Garrett, "Update: Cruz says he's no 'servile puppy' as Texas delegates bemoan his refusal to back Trump," *Dallas News*, July 21, 2016, http://www.dallasnews.com/news/republican-national-convention/2016/07/21/cruz-defiant-refusal-endorse-trump.

13. Jerome R. Corsi, "Texas Delegation Consensus: Cruz Hurt Himself at RNC," WND.com, July 22, 2016, http://www.wnd.com/2016/07/texas-delegation-consensus-cruz-hurt-himself-at-rnc/.

14. Nicholas Confessore, "G.O.P. Convention Day 4 Takeaways: It's Donald Trump's Party," *New York Times*, July 21, 2016, http://www.nytimes.com/2016/07/21/us/politics/republican-national-convention.html.

15. "Trump claims GOP nomination, tells struggling Americans 'I am your voice,'" Fox News, July 22, 2016, http://www.foxnews.com/politics/2016/07/22/trump-claims-gop-nomination-tells-struggling-americans-am-your-voice.html.

16. Patrick Healy and Jonathan Martin, "His Tone Dark, Donald Trump takes G.O.P. Mantle," *New York Times*, July 21, 2016, http://www.nytimes.com/2016/07/22/us/politics/donald-trump-rnc-speech.html.

17. "American Nazi organization rally at Madison Square Garden, 1939," Real Historical Photographs, no date, http://rarehistoricalphotos.com/american-nazi-organization-rally-madison-square-garden-1939/.

18. Joan Walsh, "Donald Trump's Angry, Dark Speech Caps Off a Disastrous RNC," *The Nation*, July 22, 2016, https://www.thenation.com/article/donald-trumps-angry-dark-speech-caps-off-a-disaster-rnc/.

19. Reena Flores, "Donald Trump offers dark vision of America in GOP convention speech," CBS News, July 22, 2016, http://www.cbsnews.com/news/donald-trump-gop-convention-speech/.

20. Jeff Zeleny Ryan Nobles, and M.J. Lee, "Hillary Clinton selects Tim Kaine as running mate," CNN Politics, July 23, 2016, http://www.cnn.com/2016/07/22/politics/hillary-clinton-vp-pick/.

21. Ken Blackwell, "Tim Kaine's radical roots," *The Hill*, September 9, 2016, http://thehill.com/blogs/pundits-blog/presidential-campaign/295229-tim-kaines-radical-roots.

22. Betsy Woodruff, "Catholic Leaders Smite Tim Kaine's Gay Marriage Hope," *Daily Beast*, September 18, 2016, http://www.thedailybeast.com/articles/2016/09/18/catholic-leaders-smite-tim-kaine-s-gay-marriage-hope.html.

23. Editorial Board, "Hillary Clinton picks a strong running mate in Tim Kaine," *Washington Post*, July 22, 2016, https://www.washingtonpost.com/opinions/hillary-clinton-picks-a-strong-running-mate-in-tim-kaine/2016/07/22/fd9c5978-4f6b-11e6-a7d8-13d06b37f256_story.html?utm_term=.0a5fca74718a.

24. Christina Lorey, "Kaine shows off not-so-secret talent in first joint appearance with Clinton since running mate announcement," ABC News, July 23, 2016.

25. Evan Popp, "What You Need to Know About Tim Kaine, Hillary Clinton's Vice President Pick," *Think Progress*, July 22, 2016, https://thinkprogress.org/what-you-need-to-know-about-tim-kaine-hillary-clintons-vice-president-pick-832de5b910a0#.1f66smzb9.

26. Amy Chozick, Alan Rappeport, and Jonathan Martin, "Hillary Clinton Selects Tim Kaine, a Popular Senator from a Swing State, as Running Mate," *New York Times*, July 22, 2016, http://www.nytimes.com/2016/07/23/us/politics/tim-kaine-hillary-clinton-vice-president.html.

27. Gabriel Samuels, "Michelle Obama's DNC 2016 speech: Read the transcript in full," *Independent*, July 25, 2016, http://www.independent.co.uk/news/world/americas/michelle-obama-speech-in-full-dnc-2016-barack-hillary-clinton-democratic-party-us-election-a7156031.html.

28. Geoff Mulvhill and Megan Trimble, "Thousands Hit Philadelphia's Steamy Streets to Protest DNC," NBC Channel 10, Philadelphia, http://www.nbcphiladelphia.com/news/local/DNC-Protest-Philly-Police-March-Sunday-388063632.html.

29. *Washington Post* Staff, "Transcript: Bernie Sanders's full speech at the 2016 DNC," *Washington Post*, July 26, 2016, https://www.washingtonpost.com/news/post-politics/wp/2016/07/26/transcript-bernie-sanderss-full-speech-at-the-2016-dnc/?utm_term=.05cad3a30132.

30. Alexander Burns, "Democratic Convention Day 1 Takeaways: Michelle Obama Steals the Show," *New York Times*, July 25, 2016, http://www.nytimes.com/2016/07/25/us/politics/democratic-national-convention.html.

31. James King, "The Father of a Muslim War Hero Has This to Say to Donald Trump," Vocativ.com, December 8, 2015, http://www.vocativ.com/259159/the-father-of-a-muslim-war-hero-has-this-to-say-to-donald-trump/.

32. ABC News, "FULL TEXT: Khizr Khan's Speech to the 2016 Democratic National Convention, " ABC News, August 1, 2016, http://abcnews.go.com/Politics/full-text-khizr-khans-speech-2016-demo-cratic-national/story?id=41043609.

33. Richard A. Oppel, Jr., "In Tribute to Son, Khizr Khan Offered Citizenship Lesson at Convention," *New York Times*, July 29, 2016, http://www.nytimes.com/2016/07/29/us/elections/khizr-humayun-khan-speech.html.

34. Kate Scanlon, "Bill Clinton Details His Love Story with Hillary Clinton, Leaves Out a Key Part," *The Blaze*, July 26, 2016, http://www.theblaze.com/stories/2016/07/26/bill-clinton-details-his-love-story-with-hillary-clinton-momentarily-i-was-speechless/.

35. Nick Allen and Ruth Sherlock, "Barack Obama admits 'Donald Trump could win' as Hillary Clinton prepares to make history," *Telegraph*, July 27, 2016, http://www.telegraph.co.uk/news/2016/07/27/barack-obama-admits-donald-trump-could-win-as-hillary-clinton-pr/.

36. "Watch Obama Refer to Himself 119 Times During Hillary Nominating Speech," *Grabien News*, July 28, 2016, https://news.grabien.com/story.php?id=414.

37. Colleen Kratofil, "Hillary Clinton's DNC Pantsuit Is Her Most Powerful Yet: Here's Why," *People*, July 29, 2016, http://people.com/style/hillary-clintons-dnc-pantsuit-is-her-most-powerful-yet-heres-why/.

38. Steve Turnham, "Donald Trump to Father of Fallen Soldier, 'I've Made a Lot of Sacrifices,'" ABC News, July 30, 2016, http://abcnews.go.com/Politics/donald-trump-father-fallen-soldier-ive-made-lot/story?id=41015051.

39. Maggie Haberman and Richard A. Oppel, Jr., "Donald Trump Criticizes Muslim Family of Slain U.S. Soldier, Drawing Ire," *New York Times*, July 30, 2016, http://www.nytimes.com/2016/07/31/us/politics/donald-trump-khizr-khan-wife-ghazala.html?_r=0.

40. Ibid.

41. Alexander Burns, "Ignoring Advice, Donald Trump Presses Attack on Khan Family and G.O.P. Leaders," *New York Times*, August 2, 2016, http://www.nytimes.com/2016/08/03/us/politics/donald-trump-gop.html.

42. Philip Rucker, "Trump refuses to endorse Paul Ryan in GOP primary: 'I'm just not quite there yet,'" *Washington Post*, August 2, 2016, https://www.washingtonpost.com/politics/trump-refu-ses-to-endorse-paul-ryan-in-gop-primary-im-just-not-quite-there-yet/2016/08/02/1449f028-58e9-11e6-831d-0324760ca856_story.html?hpid=hp_hp-top-table-main_trump-440pm%3Ahomepage%2Fstory&utm_term=.2e3f3db2f7f5. See also: Sean Sullivan, "Broad array of military luminaries condemn Trump over attacks on Khan family," *Washington Post*, August 1, 2016, https://www.washingtonpost.com/politics/mccain-adds-latest-salvo-in-gop-dismay-over-trump-clash-with-khan-family/2016/08/01/10ca7e10-57e8-11e6-831d-0324760ca856_story.html?tid=a_inl&utm_term=.d8f91b2b8159.

43. Matthew Boyle, "Clinton Cash: Khizr Khan's Deep Legal, Financial Connections to Saudi Arabia, Hillary's Clinton Foundation Tie Terror, Immigration, Email Scandals Together," Breitbart.com, August 1, 2016, http://www.breitbart.com/2016-presidential-race/2016/08/01/clinton-cash-khizr-khans-deep-legal-finan-cial-connections-saudi-arabia-hillarys-clinton-foundation-connect-terror-immigration-email-scandals/.

44. Investment Watch Blog, "Khan was paid $25,000 & speech written by staffers; Constitution bought 2 hours before DNC speech," *Investment Watch*, August 4, 2016, http://investmentwatchblog.com/khan-was-paid-25000-constitution-bought-2-hours-before-dnc-speech/.

45. See, for instance: Jeff Zarronandia, "Khizr Khan's 'Deep Legal and Financial Connections' to Hillary Clinton," Snopes.com, August 4, 2016, http://investmentwatchblog.com/khan-was-paid-25000-con-stitution-bought-2-hours-before-dnc-speech/.

46. Thomas E. Patterson, Bradlee Professor of Government and the Press, "News Coverage of the 2016 National Conventions: Negative News, Lacking Content," Harvard University, Kennedy School of Government, Shorenstein Center on Media, Politics, and Public Policy, September 21, 2016, http://shorensteincenter.org/news-coverage-2016-national-conventions/.

47. Josh Silverstein, "Hillary Clinton crushes Donald Trump in another national poll as Khan controversy disgusts voters," *New York Daily News*, August 7, 2016, http://www.nydailynews.com/news/politics/khan-controversy-hits-trump-new-poll-clinton-pulls-article-1.2741813.

Chapter 8

1. Donald J. Trump, posted on Twitter, October 4, 2016, https://twitter.com/realDonaldTrump/status/783494014276218884?ref_src=twsrc%5Etfw.

2. Andrew E. Kramer, Mike McIntire, and Barry Meier, "Secret Ledger in Ukraine Lists Cash for Donald Trump's Campaign Chief," *New York Times*, August 14, 2016, http://www.nytimes.com/2016/08/15/us/politics/paul-manafort-ukraine-donald-trump.html.

3. Maggie Haberman and Jonathan Martin, "Paul Manafort Quits Donald Trump's Campaign After a Tumultuous Run," *New York Times*, August 19, 2016, http://www.nytimes.com/2016/08/20/us/politics/paul-manafort-resigns-donald-trump.html.

4. Tom Hamburger and Andrew Roth, "Trump campaign chief Paul Manafort named in Ukraine anti-corruption probe," *Washington Post*, August 15, 2016, https://www.washingtonpost.com/politics/trump-campaign-chief-paul-manafort-named-in-ukraine-anti-corruption-probe/2016/08/15/fa180f20-6327-11e6-be4e-23fc4d4d12b4_story.html?utm_term=.3fafbb92d1bb.

5. Ekaterina Bilnova, "Clinton's Charity Ties with Oligarchs Behind Ukranian Coup Revealed," *Global Research*, March 23, 2015, http://www.globalresearch.ca/clintons-charity-ties-with-oligarchs-behind-ukrainian-coup-revealed/5475866.

6. Jerome R. Corsi, "Hillary Campaign Chief Linked to Money-Laundering in Russia," WND.com, October 13, 2016, http://www.wnd.com/2016/10/hillary-campaign-chief-linked-to-money-laundering-in-russia/.

7. Jerome R. Corsi, "How Hillary's Campaign Chief Hid Money From Russia," WND.com, October 17, 2016, http://www.wnd.com/2016/10/how-hillarys-campaign-chief-hid-money-from-russia/.

8. Government Accountability Institute, "From Russia with Money: Hillary Clinton, the Russian Reset, and Cronyism," August 2016, http://www.g-a-i.org/u/2016/08/Report-Skolkvovo-08012016.pdf.

9. Benjy Sarlin, "Analysis: Breitbart's Steve Bannon Leads the 'Alt Right' to the White House," NBC News, November 14, 2016, http://www.nbcnews.com/politics/white-house/analysis-breitbart-s-steve-bannon-leads-alt-right-white-house-n683316.

10. Amy Chozick, "Hilary Clinton Calls Many Trump Backers 'Deplorables and G.O.P. Pounces," *New York Times*, September 10, 2016, http://www.nytimes.com/2016/09/11/us/politics/hillary-clinton-basket-of-deplorables.html.

11. Donald Trump, "Wow, Hillary Clinton was SO INSULTING to my supporters, millions of amazing, hard working people. I think it will cost her at the polls!" post on Twitter.com, September 10, 2016, 7:47 am, https://twitter.com/realDonaldTrump/status/774590070355529728.

12. "The Latest: Streisand sings of Trump, 'sad, vulgar clown,'" Associated Press, September 10, 2016.

13. Jonathan Easley and Amie Parnes, "Hillary Clinton faces dilemma following 'deplorables' remark," *The Hill*, September 15, 2016, http://thehill.com/homenews/campaign/296031-hillary-clinton-faces-dilemma-following-deplorables-remark.

14. Todd Beamon, "Trump: Hillary's 'Deplorables' Comment 'Far Worse' than Mitt Romney's '47 percent,'" *Newsmax*, September 13, 2016, http://www.newsmax.com/Politics/Donald-Trump-deplorables-47-percent-Mitt-Romney/2016/09/13/id/748140/.

15. Aaron Blake, "Voters strongly reject Hillary Clinton's 'basket of deplorables' approach," *Washington Post*, September 26, 2016, https://www.washingtonpost.com/news/the-fix/wp/2016/09/26/voters-strongly-reject-hillary-clintons-basket-of-deplorables-approach/?utm_term=.19f9f350ec90.

16. Leo Hohmann, "'Epic': Hillary Suffers 2 Violent Coughing Fits," WND.com, September 5, 2016, http://www.wnd.com/2016/09/hillary-suffers-epic-coughing-fit-on-labor-day/.

17. Christina Lorey, "Trump, Clinton pause campaigns to honor 9/11 victims at Ground Zero," ABC-8 WQAD, Davenport, Iowa, September 11, 2016.

18. Emma Stefansky, "Did Hillary Clinton Faint at This Year's 9/11 Ceremony?" *Vanity Fair*, September 11, 2016, http://www.vanityfair.com/news/2016/09/hillary-clinton-faints-911.

19. "Clinton has health 'episode' at 9/11 memorial, doctor says she has pneumonia," Fox News, September 11, 2016, http://www.foxnews.com/politics/2016/09/11/hillary-clinton-has-medical-episode-at-911-ceremony-source-says.html.

20. Monica Alba, Kristen Welker, Ali Vitali, and Hasani Gittens, "Hillary Clinton Leaves 9/11 Memorial Early After Feeling 'Overheated,' Having Pneumonia," NBC News, September 11, 2016, http://www.

foxnews.com/politics/2016/09/11/hillary-clinton-has-medical-episode-at-911-ceremony-source-says.
html.

21. TMZ Staff, "Hillary Clinton 'Medical Episode' During 9/11 Ceremony," TMZ.com, September 11,
2016, http://www.tmz.com/2016/09/11/hillary-clinton-faint-9-11-memorial-medical/.

22. Russ Vaughn, "The Democrats have one very sick candidate," *American Thinker*, September 13, 2016,
http://www.americanthinker.com/blog/2016/09/the_democrats_have_one_very_sick_candidate.html.

23. Joseph Farah, "Hillary Health 'Conspiracy' Goes 'Mainstream,'" WND.com, September 11, 2016,
http://www.wnd.com/2016/09/hillary-health-conspiracy-goes-mainstream/.

24. Chris Cillizza, "Can we just stop talking about Hillary Clinton's health now?" in "The Fix," *Washington Post*, September 6, 2016, https://www.washingtonpost.com/news/the-fix/wp/2016/09/06/the-
questions-about-hillary-clintons-health-are-absurd/?utm_term=.6741e73130fe.

25. Chris Cillizza, "Hillary Clinton's health just became a real issue in the presidential campaign," in
"The Fix," *Washington Post*, September 11, 2016, https://www.washingtonpost.com/news/the-fix/
wp/2016/09/11/hillary-clintons-health-just-became-a-real-issue-in-the-presidential-campaign/?utm_
term=.edd e5e7193f0.

26. Jerome R. Corsi, "Doctors: Hillary Suffering Serious Neurological Disease," WND.com, September
19, 2016, http://www.wnd.com/2016/09/doctors-hillary-suffering-serious-neurological-disease/.

27. Dr. Ted Noel, "Hillary Clinton's Illness Revealed," YouTube.com, postd August 29, 2016, https://
www.youtube.com/watch?v=Zr1IDQ2VIeM. See also: Dr. Ted Noel, "A Quick Roundup of Hillary's
Parkinson's Signs—by Request," Vidzette.com, http://www.vidzette.com/index.php/2016/10/17/a-
quick-roundup-of-hillarys-parkinsons-signs-by-request/.

28. Joe Concha, "ABC reporter asks Clinton if she needs neurological tests," *The Hill*, September 22, 2016,
http://thehill.com/media/297189-abc-reporter-asks-clinton-if-she-needs-neurological-tests.

29. Alex Burns and Matt Flegenheimer, "Did You Miss the Presidential Debate? Here Are the Highlights," *New York Times*, September 26, 2016, http://www.nytimes.com/2016/09/26/us/politics/presidential-debate.html.

30. "MRC's Brent Bozell Slams NBC's Lester Holt's 'Failed' Performance as Debate Moderator," NewsBusters.org, September 26, 2016, http://www.newsbusters.org/blogs/nb/nb-staff/2016/09/26/mrcs-
brent-bozell-slams-nbcs-lester-holts-failed-performance-debate.

31. Patricia Garcia, "Who is Alicia Machado? The Beauty Queen That Trump Once Fat-Shamed," *Vogue*,
September 27, 2016, http://www.vogue.com/13484080/alicia-machado-beauty-queen-trump/.

32. Kristine Solomon, "Trump Doesn't Regret Calling Beauty Queen Alicia Machado 'Miss Piggy,'"
Yahoo.com, September 27, 2016, https://www.yahoo.com/beauty/this-is-alicia-machado-the-beauty-
queen-who-was-the-kicker-in-the-presidential-debate-105901358.html.

33. Scott Detrow, "In Post-Debate Interview, Trump Again Criticizes Pageant-Winner's Weight," NPR.
org, September 27, 2016, http://www.npr.org/2016/09/27/495611105/in-post-debate-interview-trump-
again-criticizes-pageant-winners-weight.

34. Michael Barbaro and Megan Twohey, "Shamed and Angry: Alicia Machado, a Miss Universe Mocked
by Donald Trump," *New York Times*, September 27, 2016, http://www.nytimes.com/2016/09/28/us/
politics/alicia-machado-donald-trump.html.

35. Michael Barbaro and Megan Twohey, "Crossing the Line: How Donald Trump Behaved with Women
in Private," *New York Times*, May 14, 2016, http://www.nytimes.com/2016/05/15/us/politics/donald-
trump-women.html.

36. "Venezuelan Beauty Queen Accused," Associated Press, January 23, 2998. Cited in: Steve Sailer,
"The Hilarious Life of Alicia Machado, Hillary's Tragic Latina Victim of Trump's Sexism," The Unz
Review: An Alternative Media Selection," unz.com, September 27, 2016, http://www.unz.com/isteve/
the-hilarious-story-of-alicia-machados-hillarys-victimized-woman/.

37. Steve Gutkin, "Ex-Ms. Universe Accused of Threat," Associated Press, February 5, 1998, cited in Steve
Sailer, "The Hilarious Life of Alicia Machado, Hillary's Tragic Latina Victim of Trump's Sexism,"
op.cit.

38. David Martosko, U.S. Political Editor, "Miss Universe 'fat-shamed' by Donald Trump was accused
of threatening to kill a judge and being an accomplice to a MURDER bid in her native Venezuela," *Daily Mail*, September 27, 2016, updated September 28, 2016, http://www.dailymail.co.uk/news/
article-3810484/Miss-Universe-fat-shamed-Donald-Trump-accused-threatening-kill-judge-accom-
plice-MURDER-native-Venezuela.html.

39. "'El Indio' tuvo hija con Alicia Machado," *El Economista*, April 22, 2010, http://eleconomista.com.mx/
seguridad-publica/2010/04/22/indio-tuvo-hija-alicia-machado, cited in Steve Sailer, "The Hilarious
Life of Alicia Machado, Hillary's Tragic Latina Victim of Trump's Sexism," op.cit.

40. David Barstow, Susanne Craig, Russ Buettner, and Megan Twohey, "Donald Trump Tax Records
Show He Could Have Avoided Taxes for Nearly Two Decades, The Times Found," *New York Times*,
October 1, 2016, http://www.nytimes.com/2016/10/02/us/politics/donald-trump-taxes.html.

41. "Donald Trump's Letter," *New York Times*, October 1, 2016, http://www.nytimes.com/interactive/2016/10/01/us/politics/donald-trump-letter.html.

42. Martin Pengelly and Joanna Walters, "Trump a 'genius' over federal income tax after $916 million loss, say allies," *Guardian*, October 2, 2016, https://www.theguardian.com/us-news/2016/oct/02/donald-trump-federal-income-tax-new-york-times.

43. David Barstow, Mike McIntire, Patricia Cohen, Susanne Craig, and Russ Buettner, "Donald Trump Used Legally Dubious Method to Avoid Paying Taxes," *New York Times*, October 31, 2016, http://www.nytimes.com/2016/11/01/us/politics/donald-trump-tax.html.

44. Betsy McCaughey, "How Mike Pence won the debate," Fox News Opinion, October 5, 2016, http://www.foxnews.com/opinion/2016/10/05/how-mike-pence-won-debate.html. See also: Pamela Engel, "Tim Kaine couldn't stop interrupting Mike Pence during the vice presidential debate," *Business Insider*, October 5, 2016, http://www.businessinsider.com/tim-kaine-interruptions-vp-debate-2016-10.

45. "VP debate scorecard: Our judges unanimously give the debate to Pence, but the decision was close," *Los Angeles Times*, October 4, 2016, http://www.latimes.com/nation/politics/trailguide/la-na-vice-presidential-debate-live-updates-trailguide-10042016-htmlstory.html.

46. Nicholas Confessore and Matt Flegenheimer, "Vice-Presidential Debate: What You Missed," *New York Times*, October 4, 2016, http://www.nytimes.com/2016/10/04/us/politics/vice-presidential-debate.html.

47. Daniel White, "Read a Transcript of the Vice Presidential Debate," Time.com, October 5, 2016, http://time.com/4517096/vice-presidential-debate-kaine-pence-transcript/.

48. Peter Schroeder, "RNC: Kaine interrupted over 70 times," *The Hill*, October 4, 2016, http://thehill.com/blogs/ballot-box/presidential-races/299338-rnc-kaine-interrupted-debate-over-70-times.

49. Danielle Paquette, "Why the most part of Donald Trump's 'hot mic' comments isn't the vulgar language," in "Wonkblog," *Washington Post*, October 7, 2016, https://www.washingtonpost.com/news/wonk/wp/2016/10/07/the-real-issue-with-donald-trump-saying-a-man-can-do-anything-to-a-woman/?utm_term=.f810e6607f63. See also: David A. Fahrenthold, "Trump recorded having extremely lewd conversation about women in 2005," *Washington Post*, October 8, 2016, https://www.washingtonpost.com/politics/trump-recorded-having-extremely-lewd-conversation-about-women-in-2005/2016/10/07/3b9ce776-8cb4-11e6-bf8a-3d26847eeed4_story.html?postshare=3561475870579757&tid=ss_tw&utm_term=.3c9b54a632d2.

50. Erin Gloria Ryan, "Donald Trump Brags About Nonconsensually Groping Women in Newly Uncovered Recording," *Daily Beast*, October 7, 2016, http://www.thedailybeast.com/articles/2016/10/07/donald-trump-brags-about-nonconsensually-groping-women-in-newly-uncovered-recording.html.

51. Paige Lavender, "These Might Be Donald Trump's Most Disgusting Comments Yet About Women," *Huffington Post*, October 7, 2016, http://www.huffingtonpost.com/entry/donald-trump-women-comments_us_57f8016de4b0e655eab4148d.

52. Garance Burke, "Associated Press: 'Apprentice' cast and crew say Trump was lewd and sexist," Associated Press, BigStory.AP.org, October 3, 2016, http://bigstory.ap.org/article/2778a6ab72ea49558445337865289508/ap-how-trumps-apprentice-moved-capitalism-sexism.

53. Peter Baker, "Clinton Settles Paula Jones Lawsuit for $850,000," *Washington Post*, November 14, 1998, http://www.upi.com/Top_News/2002/03/06/Final-Lewinsky-report-No-one-above-law/49691015442173/.

54. Kathleen Willey, *Target: Caught in the Crosshairs of Bill and Hillary Clinton* (Los Angeles: World Ahead Publishing, 2007).

55. Aaron Klein, "Exclusive—Video Interview: Bill Clinton Accuser Juanita Broaddrick Relives Brutal Rapes," Breitbart.com, October 9, 2016, http://www.breitbart.com/2016-presidential-race/2016/10/09/breitbart-news-exclusive-video-interview-bill-clinton-accuser-juanita-broaddrick-breaks-describing-brutal-rapes/.

56. Jerome R. Corsi, "Bill's Sex-Assault Victim Lashes Out Over Hillary Terrorizing," WND.com, May 13, 2016, http://www.wnd.com/2016/05/bills-sex-assault-victim-lashes-out-over-hillarys-terrorizing/.

57. Dolly Kyle, *Hillary: The Other Woman* (Washington, DC: WND Books, 2016).

58. Ibid.

59. Katie McHugh, "Media Scramble to Claim Hillary Never Laughed About Kathy Shelton's Rape as a Child—Despite Video Evidence," Breitbat.com, October 14, 2016, http://www.breitbart.com/2016-presidential-race/2016/10/14/media-scramble-to-claim-hillary-clinton-never-laughed-about-kathy-sheltons-rape-as-a-child-despite-video-evidence/.

60. Katie McHugh, "Fact-Check: Yes, Hillary Clinton Did Laugh After Successfully Defending a Child Rapist," Breitbart.com, October 9, 2016, http://www.breitbart.com/live/second-presidential-debate-fact-check-livewire/fact-check-yes-hillary-clinton-laugh-successfully-defending-child-rapist/.

61. "Trump holds pre-debate press conference with Bill Clinton accusers," Fox News, October 9, 2016, http://www.foxnews.com/politics/2016/10/09/trump-holds-press-conference-with-women-whove-accused-bill-clinton-sex-assault-rape.html?refresh=true.

62. Frank Camp, "Check Out the Bill Clinton Face at the Second Debate that Has the Internet Abuzz," *Daily Wire*, October 10, 2016, http://www.dailywire.com/news/9832/check-out-bill-clinton-face-second-debate-has-frank-camp.

63. "Transcript of the Second Debate," *New York Times*, October 10, 2016, http://www.nytimes.com/2016/10/10/us/politics/transcript-second-debate.html.

64. Hugh A. Mulligan, Associated Press, "War's End Made Non-Person of Eisenhower's Devoted 'Shadow,'" *Los Angeles Times*, May 28, 1995, http://articles.latimes.com/1995-05-28/news/mn-6970_1_germans-gen-dwight-d-eisenhower-official-photo.

65. Brian Vitagliano, Holly Yan, and Kristina Sgueglia, "Bill Cosby to stand trial for assault charges, judge rules," CNN, May 25, 2016, http://www.cnn.com/2016/05/24/us/bill-cosby-hearing/.

66. Alex Burns and Matt Flegenheimer, "Presidential Debate: Here's What You Missed," *New York Times*, October 9, 2016, http://www.nytimes.com/2016/10/09/us/politics/presidential-debate.html.

67. Catherine Pearson, Alanna Vagianos, and Emma Gray, "A Running List of the Women Who've Accused Trump of Sexual Assault," *Huffington Post*, October 28, 2016, http://www.huffingtonpost.com/entry/a-running-list-of-all-the-women-whove-accused-donald-trump-of-sexual-assault_us_57ffae1fe4b0162c043a7212.

68. "PROOF—Woman Paid $500k to Accuse Trump of Sexual Assault," Political Insider, November 4, 2016, http://www.thepoliticalinsider.com/trump-sexual-assault-woman-paid-500k-accuse/. See also: Jim Hoft, "List of Debunked Groper allegations by Corrupt Media Against Donald Trump," TheGatewayPundit.com, October 15, 2016, http://www.thegatewaypundit.com/2016/10/list-debunked-groper-allegations-corrupt-media-donald-trump/.

69. Alex Daugherty, "Trump says sexual assault accusers are lying," *McClatchy DC*, October 14, 2016, http://www.mcclatchydc.com/news/politics-government/election/voters-guide/article108154827.html. See also: Patricia Mazzei and Amy Sherman, "Seething Trump says female accusers lying," *Miami Herald*, October 13, 2016, http://www.miamiherald.com/news/politics-government/election/donald-trump/article107992952.html.

70. WikiLeaks, Tweet posted October 7, 2016, "Release: The Podesta Emails #HillaryClinton #Podesta "imWithHer Wikileaks.org/Podesta-emails/" https://twitter.com/wikileaks/status/784491543868665856. See also: "The Podesta Emails; Part One," Wikileaks.org, October 7, 2016, https://wikileaks.org/podesta-emails/press-release.

71. Tyler Durden, "Here Are Hillary Clinton's Three Speeches to Goldman Sachs for Which She Was Paid $67,000," ZeroHedge.com, October 15, 2016, http://www.zerohedge.com/news/2016-10-15/here-are-hillary-clintons-three-speeches-goldman-sachs-which-she-was-paid-675000.

72. Jeff Stein, "What 20,000 pages of hacked emails teach us about Hillary Clinton," Vox.com, October 20, 2016, http://www.vox.com/policy-and-politics/2016/10/20/13308108/wikileaks-podesta-hillary-clinton.

73. Jack Shafer, "WikiLeaks and the Oily Washington Press," *Politico*, October 18, 2016, http://www.politico.com/magazine/story/2016/10/john-podesta-emails-wikileaks-press-214367.

74. Ezra Dulis, "WikiLeaks: Journalists Dined at Top Clinton Staffers' Homes Before Hillary Clinton's Campaign Launch," Breitbart.com, October 17, 2016, http://www.breitbart.com/big-journalism/2016/10/17/wikileaks-journalists-clinton-staff-homes-before-hillarys-campaign-launch/.

75. Jim Hoft, "The WikiLeaks List: At Least 65 MSM Reporters Were Meeting with and/or Coordinating Offline with Top Hillary Advisors," TheGatewayPundit.com, October 24, 2016, http://www.thegatewaypundit.com/2016/10/wikileaks-list-least-65-msm-reporters-meeting-andor-coordinating-offline-top-hillary-advisors/. See also: Jim Hoft, "WikiLeaks Exposes Corrupt Media: This List of Reporters Were Taking Marching Orders from Hillary," TheGatewayPundit.com, October 9, 2016, http://www.thegatewaypundit.com/2016/10/wikileaks-outs-corrupt-media-list-reporters-taking-marching-orders-hillary/.

76. Dave Boyer, "Leaked emails detail cozy relationship between Clinton, media, campaign," *Washington Times*, October 13, 2016, http://www.washingtontimes.com/news/2016/oct/13/emails-show-cozy-relationship-between-media-and-cl/.

77. Kelly Riddell, "Donna Brazile out at CNN after WikiLeaks reveals she leaked more debate questions to Clinton," *Washington Post*, October 31, 2016, http://www.washingtontimes.com/news/2016/oct/31/donna-brazile-leaked-2nd-debate-question-wikileaks/.

78. Gabrielle Levy, "DNC's Donna Brazile Denies Giving Hillary Clinton Earl Access to Town Hall Question," *U.S. News*, October 11, 2016, http://www.usnews.com/news/articles/2016-10-11/dncs-donna-brazile-denies-giving-hillary-clinton-early-access-to-town-hall-question.

79. Michael M. Grybaum, "CNN Parts Ways with Donna Brazile, a Hillary Clinton Supporter," *New York Times*, October 31, 2016, http://www.nytimes.com/2016/11/01/us/politics/donna-brazile-wikileaks-cnn.html.

80. Nicholas Confessore, "Corey Lewandowski Continues to be Paid by Donald Trump's Campaign," *New York Times*, September 21, 2016, http://www.nytimes.com/2016/09/22/us/politics/corey-lewandowski-donald-trump-payroll.html.

81. Jerome R. Corsi, "'Clinton's Black Son' Demands DNA Sample," WND.com, October 19, 2016, http://www.wnd.com/2016/10/clintons-black-son-demands-dna-sample/.

82. Kit Daniels, "Banished: Bill Clinton's 'Son' Speaks Out, Asks for DNA Test," Infowars.com, October 11, 2016, http://www.infowars.com/banished-the-untold-story-of-danney-williams-search-for-his-father/. See also: Neil W. McCabe, "Exclusive—Danney Williams: President Clinton Knows the Truth, I Am His Son; Arkansas Man Demands Paternity Test," Breitbart.com, October 20, 2016, http://www.breitbart.com/2016-presidential-race/2016/10/20/exclusive-danney-williams-president-bill-clinton-knows-the-truth-i-am-his-son-arkansas-man-demands-paternity-test/. See also: Jerome R. Corsi, "'Bill Clinton Son' Makes Video Plea to 'Father, Stepmother,'" WND.com, October 11, 2016, http://www.wnd.com/2016/10/bill-clinton-son-issues-plea-to-father-stepmother/.

83. Filmmaker Joel Gilbert, "Bill Clinton's Black Son BANISHED—The Story of Danney Williams," YouTube, published October 11, 2016, https://www.youtube.com/watch?v=rLOp2yBhuTE.

84. David Emery, "Paternity Jest," Snopes.com, October 3, 2016, http://www.snopes.com/bill-clinton-illegitimate-son/.

85. Alex Pfeiffer. "Danney Williams Campaign Is Targeting Black Users Online." Daily Caller. 8 November 2016. Web. <http://dailycaller.com/2016/11/08/danney-williams-campaign-is-targeting-black-users-online/>.

86. Blake Neff. "Trump Did BETTER Than Romney Among Hispanics, And Blacks." Daily Caller. November 9, 2016. Web. <http://dailycaller.com/2016/11/09/trump-did-better-than-romney-among-hispanics-and-blacks/>.

87. Amy Walter and David Wasserman. "African American Voters: The Overlooked Key To 2016." Cook Political Report, 10 July 2015. Web. <http://cookpolitical.com/story/8666>.

88. Jeremy W. Peters, Richard Fausset, and Michael Wines. "Black Turnout Soft in Early Voting, Boding Ill for Hillary Clinton." New York Time, November 1, 2016. Web. <http://www.nytimes.com/2016/11/02/us/politics/black-turnout-falls-in-early-voting-boding-ill-for-hillary-clinton.html>.

89. Ledyard King. "Black Turnout Could Be Issue for Democrats." Florida Today, November 6, 2016. Web. <http://www.floridatoday.com/story/news/politics/elections/2016/11/05/black-turnout-issue-democrats/93382474/>.

90. Charles Ellison. "Black Voter Turnout: A Look at the Numbers." Philadelphia Tribune, November 12, 2016. Web. <http://www.phillytrib.com/news/black-voter-turnout-a-look-at-the-numbers/article_49d1aed9-76be-550e-b063-15ad7639dc97.html>.

91. Albert Hunt. "Clinton Lost Pennsylvania More Than Trump Won It." Bloomberg.com. Bloomberg, November 16, 2016. Web. <https://www.bloomberg.com/view/articles/2016-11-16/clinton-lost-pennsylvania-more-than-trump-won-it>.

92. Sabrina Tavernise. "Many in Milwaukee Neighborhood Didn't Vote—and Don't Regret It." New York Times, November 20, 2016. Web. <http://www.nytimes.com/2016/11/21/us/many-in-milwaukee-neighborhood-didnt-vote-and-dont-regret-it.html?_r=0>.

93. Jesse Singal. "Why Black Voters in Milwaukee Weren't Enthused by Hillary Clinton." New York Magazine, November 22, 2016. Web. <http://nymag.com/daily/intelligencer/2016/11/why-black-voters-in-milwaukee-werent-enthused-by-clinton.html>.

94. Ron Fonger. "Weaker Democratic Support in Detroit, Flint Made Trump Stronger in Michigan." MLive.com, November 9, 2016. Web. <http://www.mlive.com/news/index.ssf/2016/11/detroit_flint_voting_muscle_we.html>.

95. Eric Bradner, "Clinton leads Trump, two new polls show," CNN, October 16, 2016, http://www.cnn.com/2016/10/16/politics/hillary-clinton-donald-trump-presidential-polls/.

96. Andrew Restuccia, Sarah Wheaton, and Nancy Cook, "Clinton's transition team hits the gas pedal," CNN, October 21, 2016, http://www.politico.com/story/2016/10/hillary-clinton-transition-team-hiring-staff-230157.

97. Aaron Blake, "The final Trump-Clinton debate transcript, annotated," Washington Post, October 19, 2016, https://www.washingtonpost.com/news/the-fix/wp/2016/10/19/the-final-trump-clinton-debate-transcript-annotated/?utm_term=.b9149b74767f.

98. Stephen Collinson, "Donald Trump refuses to say whether he'll accept election results," CNN, updated October 20, 2016, http://www.cnn.com/2016/10/19/politics/presidential-debate-highlights/.

99. Jeremy Diamond, "Donald Trump: 'I will totally accept' election results 'if I win,'" CNN, updated October 20, 2016, http://www.cnn.com/2016/10/19/politics/presidential-debate-highlights/.

Chapter 9

1. Ian Schwartz, "Trump: Hillary Clinton is 'Low Energy,' Takes Naps; 'No Naps for Trump!'" Real Clear Politics, July 25, 2016, http://www.realclearpolitics.com/video/2016/07/25/trump_hillary_clinton_is_low_energy_takes_naps_no_naps_for_trump.html.

2. James Comey, FBI Director, letter to Congressional leaders, October 28, 2016, http://media.washtimes.com.s3.amazonaws.com/media/misc/2016/10/28/Comey_Letter-Oct28.pdf.

3. Stephen Dinan, "FBI reopens Clinton email investigation," *Washington Times*, October 28, 2016, http://www.washingtontimes.com/news/2016/oct/28/james-comey-fbi-director-reopens-clinton-email-inv/.

4. "Hillary Clinton Holds Press Conference After FBI Reopen Investigation," YouTube, October 28 2016, https://www.youtube.com/watch?v=WnNv16IJHqU.

5. Evan Perez and Pamela Brown, "Comey notified Congress of email probe despite DOJ concerns," CNN Politics, October 30, 2016, http://www.cnn.com/2016/10/28/politics/fbi-reviewing-new-emails-in-clinton-probe-director-tells-senate-judiciary-committee/.

6. Adam Goldman and Alan Rappeport, "Emails in Anthony Weiner Inquiry Jolt Hillary Clinton's Campaign," *New York Times*, October 28, 2016, http://www.nytimes.com/2016/10/29/us/politics/fbi-hillary-clinton-email.html.

7. "FBI reopens Clinton probe after new emails found in Anthony Weiner case," Fox News, October 28, 2016. http://www.foxnews.com/politics/2016/10/28/fbi-reopens-investigation-into-clinton-email-use.html.

8. "New Abedin Emails Reveal Hillary Clinton State Department Gave Special Access to Top Clinton Foundation Donors," Press Release, *Judicial Watch*, August 22, 2016, http://www.judicialwatch.org/press-room/press-releases/new-abedin-emails-reveal-hillary-clinton-state-department-gave-special-access-top-clinton-foundation-donors/. See also: "Huma Production 10" in Judicial Watch Document Archive, August 17, 2016, http://www.judicialwatch.org/document-archive/tag/huma-production-10/.

9. Jerome R. Corsi, *Partners in Crime: The Clintons' Scheme to Monetize the White House for Personal Profit* (Washington, DC: WND Books, 2016). The description of the Clinton Foundation as a "vast criminal conspiracy" was developed originally by Wall Street analyst Charles Ortel and was first published by Corsi in the following WND.com article: Jerome R. Corsi, "Wall Street Expert: Clinton Foundation a 'Vast Criminal Conspiracy," WND.com, September 19, 2015, http://www.wnd.com/2015/09/wall-street-expert-clinton-foundation-a-vast-criminal-conspiracy/.

10. Jerome R. Corsi, "1/3 of Abedin Emails 100% Redacted," WND.com, August 25, 2016, http://www.wnd.com/2016/08/13-of-abedin-emails-100-redacted/.

11. Jerome R. Corsi, "Huma Abedin Forwarded Sensitive Material to Personal Email," WND.com, August 29, 2016, http://www.wnd.com/2016/08/huma-abedin-forwarded-sensitive-material-to-personal-email/.

12. Brendan Bordelon, "New Huma Abedin E-mail address discovered ahead of Benghazi Committee Appearance," *National Review*, October 15, 2015, http://www.nationalreview.com/article/425641/new-huma-abedin-e-mail-address-discovered-ahead-benghazi-committee-appearance-brendan.

13. Stephan Dinan, "State Dept. confirms Clinton aides had other unreported email accounts," *Washington Times*, August 14, 2015, http://www.washingtontimes.com/news/2015/aug/14/clinton-aides-had-unreported-email-accounts-state/.

14. Acknowledged in the following: Tyler Durden, New Clinton Emails Emerged as Part of FBI Probe into Anthony Weiner," ZeroHedge.com, October 28, 2016, http://www.zerohedge.com/news/2016-10-28/new-clinton-emails-emerged-part-probe-anthony-weiners-electronic-devices-nyt.

15. Jerome R. Corsi, "Security Vet: 'Smoking Gun' Email Should Put Hillary in Prison," WND.com, September 8, 2016, http://www.wnd.com/2016/09/security-vet-smoking-gun-email-should-put-hillary-in-prison/.

16. CNN staff, "Anthony Weiner scandal: A timeline," CNN Politics, updated August 30, 2016, http://www.cnn.com/2016/08/30/politics/weiner-scandal-timeline/.

17. Delvin Barrett, "FBI in Internal Feud Over Hillary Clinton Probe," *Wall Street Journal*, October 30, 3016, http://www.wsj.com/articles/laptop-may-include-thousands-of-emails-linked-to-hillary-clintons-private-server-1477854957/.

18. "Flip-flopping Dems, once big Comey fans, now piling on," Fox News, October 31, 2016, http://www.foxnews.com/politics/2016/10/31/flip-flopping-dems-once-big-comey-fans-now-piling-on.html.

19. Matt Apuzzo, Michael S. Schmidt, and Adam Goldman, "Emails Warrant No New Action Against Hillary Clinton, F.B.I. Director Says," *New York Times*, November 6, 2016, http://www.nytimes.com/2016/11/07/us/politics/hilary-clinton-male-voters-donald-trump.html.

20. James Comey, FBI Director, letter to Congressional leaders, November 6, 2016, http://www.nytimes.com/interactive/2016/11/06/us/politics/fbi-letter-emails.html.

21. Adam Goldman and Matt Apuzzo, "How the F.B.I. Reviewed Thousands of Emails in One Week," *New York Times*, November 7, 2016, http://www.nytimes.com/2016/11/08/us/politics/hillary-clinton-donald-trump-fbi-emails.html.

22. Jerome R. Corsi, "What Next for Hillary Investigation?" WND.com, November 16, 2016, http://www.wnd.com/2016/11/what-next-for-hillary-investigation/.

23. Zachary Karabell, *The Last Campaign: How Harry Truman Won the 1948 Election* (New York: A Borzoi Book published by Alfred A. Knopf, 2000), p. 133.

24. David McCullough, *Truman* (New York: Simon & Schuster, 1992), p. 655.

25. Ibid., p. 209.

26. Ibid.

27. Phyllis Schlafly, *A Choice, Not an Echo* (Alton, IL: Pere Marquette, 1964).

28. David Weigel and Jose A. DelReal, "Phyllis Schlafly endorses Trump in St. Louis," *Washington Post*, March 11, 2016, https://www.washingtonpost.com/news/post-politics/wp/2016/03/11/phyllis-schlafly-endorses-trump-in-st-louis/?utm_term=.8c1c4ced9d15.

29. Phyllis Schlafly, with Ed Martin and Brett M. Decker, *The Conservative Case for Trump* (Washington, DC: Regnery Publishing, 2016), "Introduction," pp. ix-xix.

30. Ibid.

31. Glenn Thrush, "10 Crucial Decisions That Reshaped America," *Politico*, December 9, 2016, http://www.politico.com/magazine/story/2016/12/2016-presidential-election-10-moments-trump-clinton-214508.

32. Zachary Karabell, "The Last Campaign," op.cit., p. 212.

33. Ibid., p. 213.

34. Ibid., p. 242.

35. Sopan Deb, "'Stay on point, Donald,' Trump tells himself in Pensacola," CBS News, November 2, 2016, http://www.cbsnews.com/news/stay-on-point-donald-trump-said-at-his-last-rally-of-the-day/.

36. Jim Hoft, "Exhausted Hillary Is Taking Off Weekends—And Media is Covering It Up," *Gateway Pundit*, August 15, 2015, http://www.thegatewaypundit.com/2016/08/hillarys-taking-weekends-off/.

37. Ibid.

38. Jim Hoft, "Stunning Numbers: Trump Leads Hillary in Rally Attendance by Half a Million People Since August," *Gateway Pundit*, October 23, 2016, http://www.thegatewaypundit.com/2016/10/no-joke-hillary-rarely-has-more-than-1000-at-her-events/.

39. Jim Hoft, "Enthusiasm Matters: Trump Spoke to Nearly a Million Supporters Since August—Clinton Spoke to 110,000," *Gateway Pundit*, November 13, 2016, http://www.thegatewaypundit.com/2016/11/hard-work-and-excitement-win-elections-trump-with-nearly-1m-at-rallies-since-august-1st-to-clintons-110k/.

40. Ford Springer, "Trump's Plane is Big League Compared to Clinton's," *Daily Caller*, October 20, 2016, http://dailycaller.com/2016/10/20/trumps-plane-is-big-league-compared-to-clintons-photos/.

41. "Top 10 Facts about Donald Trump's Boeing 757," AviationCV.com, May 10, 2016, https://www.aviationcv.com/aviation-blog/2016/top-10-facts-about-donald-trumps-boeing.

42. Jennifer Palmieri, email to John Podesta, Subject: "Re: Topper for New Hampshire," April 4, 2015, WikiLeaks "Podesta Email File," Email #4433, https://wikileaks.org/podesta-emails/emailid/4433.

43. Kaitlan Collins, "Leaked Emails Reveal That Hillary Clinton Had To Be Told When To Smile During Speeches," *Daily Caller*, October 11, 2016, http://dailycaller.com/2016/10/11/leaked-emails-reveal-that-hillary-clinton-had-to-be-told-when-to-smile-during-speeches/. See also: "WikiLeaks: Hillary Told When to SMILE During Interviews," *Right Wing News*, October 11, 2016, http://rightwingnews.com/top-news/wikileaks-hillary-told-smile-interviews/.

44. Brent Budowski, email to John Podesta, Subject: "Bernie, Elizabeth, and deBlasio," March 13, 2016, WikiLeaks "Podesta Email File," Email #3990, https://wikileaks.org/podesta-emails/emailid/3990, See also: Kerry Picket, "WikiLeaks: Left Wing Journo Tells Podesta Hillary Lies 'Candidly,'" *Daily Caller*, October 11, 2016, http://dailycaller.com/2016/10/11/wikileaks-left-wing-journo-tells-podesta-hillary-lies-candidly/.

45. John Podesta, email chain with Neera Tanden, Subject: "Re: Emails—my thoughts," August 22, 2015, WikiLeaks "Podesta Email File," Email #11,136, https://wikileaks.org/podesta-emails/emailid/11136#efmACoAGw.

46. John Podesta, email chain with Robby Mook and Cheryl Mills, Subject: "Re: From the *Washington Post*: The Fix: How Hillary Clinton can correct the biggest mistake she made in 2008," March 22, 2014, WikiLeaks "Podesta Email File," Email #2528, https://wikileaks.org/podesta-emails/emailid/2528.

47. Ben Wolfgang, "Clinton campaign mocks Catholics, Southerners, 'needy Latinos' in emails," *Washington Times*, October 12, 2016, http://www.washingtontimes.com/news/2016/oct/12/hillary-clinton-campaigns-wikileaks-emails-reveal-/.

Conclusion

1. "Transcript: Donald Trump's Victory Speech," *New York Times*, November 9, 2016, http://www.nytimes.com/2016/11/10/us/politics/trump-speech-transcript.html.

2. Theodore H. White, quoted in Eric Pace, "Theodore White, Chronicler of U.S. Politics, is Dead at 71," *New York Times*, May 16, 1986, http://www.nytimes.com/1986/05/16/obituaries/theodore-white-chronicler-of-us-politics-is-dead-at-71.html?pagewanted=all.

3. Larry Celona, Richard Johnson, and Bruce Golding, "Hillary already planning her giant victory celebration," *New York Post*, October 31, 2016, http://nypost.com/2016/10/31/hillary-planning-election-night-fireworks-show-on-hudson-river/?utm_campaign=SocialFlow&utm_source=NYPTwitter&utm_medium=SocialFlow&sr_share=twitter.

4. "Hillary Clinton Pulls Plug on Election Night Fireworks," TMZ.com, November 17, 2016, http://www.tmz.com/2016/11/07/hillary-clinton-cancels-fireworks-election-night/.

5. Ciara McCarthy and Claire Phipps, "Election results timeline: How the night unfolded," *Guardian*, November 9, 2016, https://www.theguardian.com/us-news/2016/nov/08/presidential-election-updates-trump-clinton-news.

6. "Reports: Clinton Had a Violent Meltdown on Election Night," *Political Insider*, http://www.thepoliticalinsider.com/hillary-drunk-violent-meltdown-election-night/.

7. Kay Meyer, "Hillary Clinton Declines to Appear at Election Night Rally; Podesta Tells Crowd to Go Home," Mediate.com, November 9, 2016, http://www.mediaite.com/tv/hillary-clinton-declines-to-appear-at-election-night-rally-podesta-tells-crowd-to-go-home/. See also: Kaitlan Collins, "Hillary refuses to address election night party—sends Podesta to give speech!" *Daily Caller*, November 9, 2016, http://dailycaller.com/2016/11/09/hillary-refuses-to-concede-sends-podesta-to-give-speech/.

8. "Leaked Video Shows Hillary Celebrating Election Night!" Live Leak, http://www.liveleak.com/view?i=458_1479715541, published on YouTube, https://www.youtube.com/watch?v=NKhGEeZSQso.

9. R. Emmett Tyrrell, Jr., "Where was Hillary? Losing it on a losing night," *American Spectator*, November 14, 2016, https://spectator.org/where-was-hillary/.

10. Daniel J. Flynn, "Hillary Clinton Screaming Obscenities and Throwing Objects in Election Night Meltdown," Breitbart.com, November 15, 2016, http://www.breitbart.com/big-government/2016/11/15/hillary-clinton-screaming-obscenities-and-throwing-objects-in-election-night-meltdown/.

11. Eun Kyung Kim, "Donald Trump's campaign Chief: Calls from Obama and Clinton were 'warm' and 'thorough,'" Today.com, November 9, 2009, http://www.today.com/news/donald-trump-s-campaign-chief-calls-obama-clinton-were-warm-t104826.

12. CNN Staff, "Here's the full text of Donald Trump's victory speech," CNN, November 9, 2016, http://www.cnn.com/2016/11/09/politics/donald-trump-victory-speech/.

13. CNN Staff, "Here's the full text of Donald Trump's victory speech," CNN.com, November 9, 2016, http://www.cnn.com/2016/11/09/politics/donald-trump-victory-speech/.

14. Israel Shenker, "2 Critics Here Focus on Films as Language Conference Opens," December 28, 1972. See also: James Wolcott, "The Fraudulent Factoid That Refuses to Die," *Vanity Fair*, October 23, 2012, http://www.vanityfair.com/culture/2012/10/The-Fraudulent-Factoid-That-Refuses-to-Die.

15. Kristina Rodulfo, "Why It's Important that Hillary Clinton Wore Purple Today," *Elle*, November 9, 2016, http://www.elle.com/fashion/news/a40669/hillary-clinton-purple-suit-concession-speech/.

16. Kenzie Bryant, "The Symbolism of Hillary Clinton Wearing Purple During Her Concession Speech," *Vanity Fair*, November 9, 2016, http://www.vanityfair.com/style/2016/11/hillary-clinton-purple-concession-speech.

17. "Hillary Clinton's concession speech (full text)," CNN Politics, November 9, 2016, http://www.cnn.com/2016/11/09/politics/hillary-clinton-concession-speech/.

18. Paulina Firozi, "Quote from Clinton concession speech the most retreated of the election," *The Hill*, November 17, 2016, http://thehill.com/homenews/campaign/306699-quote-from-clinton-concession-speech-the-most-retweeted-tweet-of-the.

19. Clare Malone, "Clinton Couldn't Win Over White Women," FiveThirtyEight.com, November 9, 2016, http://fivethirtyeight.com/features/clinton-couldnt-win-over-white-women/.

20. Jack Brewer, "Why Hillary Clinton couldn't rally the black vote," CNBC, November 11, 2016, http://www.cnbc.com/2016/11/11/why-hillary-clinton-couldnt-rally-the-black-vote-commentary.html.

21. USAID, "Assessing and Verifying Election Results," April 2015, https://yali.state.gov/wp-content/uploads/sites/4/2016/01/Assessing-and-Verifying-Election-Results-Summary-Document.pdf.

22. Donald J. Trump, Posting on Twitter, November 10, 2016, 9:19 pm, https://twitter.com/realDonaldTrump/status/796900183955095552.

23. Donald J. Trump, Posting on Twitter, November 11, 2016, 6:14 am, https://twitter.com/realDonaldTrump/status/797034721075228672.

24. Terrence Petty and Robert Jablon, "Oregon is epicenter as Trump protests surge across nation," Associated Press, November 11, 2016.

25. Ibid.

26. Leah Sottile, Samantha Schmidt, and Brian Murphy, "Anti-Trump protestors take to the streets in many cities for a third night, *Washington Post*, November 12, 2016, https://www.washingtonpost.com/news/morning-mix/wp/2016/11/11/violence-erupts-in-portland-riot-as-anti-trump-protests-continue-in-cities-across-the-nation/?tid=a_inl&utm_term=.76ddf45f5e71.

27. Kyle Iboshi, "Most of arrested Portland protestors are from Oregon," KGW.com, November 15, 2016, http://www.kgw.com/news/local/more-than-half-of-arrested-anti-trump-protesters-didnt-vote/351964445.

28. Aimee Green, "At least third of arrested anti-Trump protestors didn't vote," *The Oregonian*, November 15, 2016, http://www.oregonlive.com/portland/index.ssf/2016/11/nearly_13_of_arrested_anti-tru.html.

29. Jim Hoft, "Here's Proof that Soros Money Is Funding the Anti-Trump Leftist Protest-Riots," *Gateway Pundit*, November 14, 2016, http://www.thegatewaypundit.com/2016/11/heres-proof-soros-money-funding-anti-trump-leftist-protest-riots/.

30. Lisa Lerer, "Clinton blames FBI director for presidential loss," Associated Press, November 12, 2016.

31. Amy Chozick, "Hillary Clinton Blames F.B.I. Director for Election Loss," *New York Times*, November 12, 2016, http://www.nytimes.com/2016/11/13/us/politics/hillary-clinton-james-comey.html.

32. Ibid.

33. Lisa Lerer, "Clinton says Putin's 'personal beef' prompted election hacks," Associated Press, December 16, 2016.

34. Amy Chozick, "Clinton Says 'Personal Beef' by Putin Led to Hacking Attacks," *New York Times*, December 16, 2016, http://www.nytimes.com/2016/12/16/us/politics/hillary-clinton-russia-fbi-comey.html.

35. "Full Podesta: 'Investigate What Actually Happened' with Russia hacking," NBC News, "Meet the Press with Chuck Todd," Sunday, December 18, 2016, http://www.nbcnews.com/meet-the-press/video/podesta-investigate-what-actually-happened-with-russia-836030531626. See also: "Transcript: 'Meet the Press' 12/28/2016, NBC News, http://www.nbcnews.com/meet-the-press/meet-press-12-18-2016-n697546.

36. Alex Johnson, "WikiLeaks' Julian Assange: 'No Proof' Hacked DNC Emails Came From Russia," NBC News, July 25, 2016, http://www.nbcnews.com/news/us-news/wikileaks-julian-assange-no-proof-hacked-dnc-emails-came-russia-n616541.

37. "WikiLeaks founder Assange on hacked Podesta, DNC emails: 'Our source is not the Russian government,'" Fox News, December 16, 2016, http://www.foxnews.com/politics/2016/12/16/wikileaks-founder-assange-on-hacked-podesta-dnc-emails-our-source-is-not-russian-government.html.

38. Ibid.

39. Bradford Richardson, "Peter King: CIA doing 'hit job' against Donald Trump; 'no evidence' Russia behind Podesta hack," *Washington Times*, December 18, 2016, http://www.washingtontimes.com/news/2016/dec/18/peter-king-cia-doing-hit-job-against-donald-trump-/?.

40. Tal Kopan, "Polygraph panic: CIA director fretted his vote for communist," CNN, September 15, 2016, http://www.cnn.com/2016/09/15/politics/john-brennan-cia-communist-vote/.

41. Drew Zahn, "Shock Claim: Obama Picks Muslim for CIA Chief," WND.com, February 10, 2013, http://www.wnd.com/2013/02/shock-claim-obama-picks-muslim-for-cia-chief/.

42. Clare Kim, "What, no Bible? Conservatives angered that Brennan took oath on Constitution," MSNBC, March 11, 2013, http://www.msnbc.com/the-last-word/what-no-bible.

43. EmptyWheel, "John Brennan Sworn in as CIA Director Using Constitution Lacking Bill of Rights," March 8, 2013, http://www.emptywheel.net/2013/03/08/john-brennan-sworn-in-as-cia-director-using-constitution-lacking-bill-of-rights/?utm_source=rss&utm_medium=rss&utm_campaign=john-brennan-sworn-in-as-cia-director-using-constitution-lacking-bill-of-rights.

44. Jerome R. Corsi, "Brennan: Don't Use 'Jihad' to Describe Terrorists," WND.com, January 9, 2013, http://www.wnd.com/2013/01/brennan-dont-use-jihad-to-describe-terrorists/. See also: The White House, "John Brennan Speaks on National Security at NYU," YouTube, posted February 13, 2010, https://www.youtube.com/watch?v=mKUpmFb4h_U&NR=1.

45. Associated Press, "Here's What Jill Stein Is Doing with the Leftover Money She Raised for Election Recounts," December 13, 2016, as reported in Fortune, http://fortune.com/2016/12/13/jill-stein-recounts-money/.

46. Gabriel Sherman, "Experts Urge Clinton Campaign to Challenge Election Results in 3 Swing States," *New York Magazine*, November 22, 2016, http://nymag.com/daily/intelligencer/2016/11/activists-urge-hillary-clinton-to-challenge-election-results.html.

47. Zach Montellaro, "Jill Stein files for recount in Wisconsin," *Politico*, November 25, 2016, http://www.politico.com/story/2016/11/jill-stein-recount-effort-231829.

48. J. Alex Halderman, "Want to Know if the Election was Hacked? Look at the Ballots," Medium.com, November 23, 2016, https://medium.com/@jhalderm/want-to-know-if-the-election-was-hacked-look-at-the-ballots-c61a6113b0ba#.647sp9b04.

49. Shane Harris, "Sorry, Hillary Clinton Fans. There's 'Zero Evidence' of Election Hacking," *Daily Beast*, November 23, 2016, http://www.thedailybeast.com/articles/2016/11/23/sorry-hillary-theres-zero-evidence-of-election-hacking.html.

50. Jerome R. Corsi, "Green Party's Stein Files for Wisconsin Vote Recount," WND.com, November 25, 2016, http://www.wnd.com/2016/11/operation-steal-seeks-recount-to-declare-hillary-president/.

51. Eugene Scott, "Clinton to join recount that Trump calls a 'scam'" CNN Politics, November 28, 2016, http://www.cnn.com/2016/11/26/politics/clinton-campaign-recount/.

52. Kyle Cheney and Gabriel Debenedetti, "Rogue electors brief Clinton camp on anti-Trump plan," *Politico*, December 5, 2016, http://www.politico.com/story/2016/12/electoral-college-rogues-trump-clinton-232195.

53. Ibid.

54. Joel Kurth and Jonathan Oosting, "Records: Too many votes in 37 percent of Detroit's precincts," *Detroit News*, December 13, 2016, http://www.detroitnews.com/story/news/politics/2016/12/12/records-many-votes-detroits-precincts/95363314/.

55. Matthew DeFour, "Completed Wisconsin recount widens Donald Trump lead by 131 votes," *Wisconsin State Journal*, December 13, 2016, http://host.madison.com/wsj/news/local/govt-and-politics/completed-wisconsin-recount-widens-donald-trump-s-lead-by-votes/article_3f61c6ac-5b18-5c27-bf38-e537146bbcdd.html.

56. Byron Tau, "Jill Stein Supporters Drop Pennsylvania Recount Suit." *Wall Street Journal*, December 4, 2016, http://www.wsj.com/articles/jill-stein-supporters-drop-pennsylvania-recount-suit-1480810987.

57. "Roger Stone and John Haggerty Discuss Why the Stein Clinton Recount Was . . .," InRealTime. blogspot.com, December 22, 2016, https://inrealtyme.blogspot.com/2016/12/roger-stone-and-john-haggerty-discuss.html.

58. Add endnote: Roger Stone, "Can the 2016 election be rigged? You bet," *The Hill*, August 16, 2016, http://thehill.com/blogs/pundits-blog/presidential-campaign/291534-can-the-2016-election-be-rigged-you-bet.

59. Add endnote: Ben Wofford, "How to Hack an Election in 7 Minutes," *Politico*, August 5, 2016, http://www.politico.com/magazine/story/2016/08/2016-elections-russia-hack-how-to-hack-an-election-in-seven-minutes-214144.

60. HamiltonElectors.com, "About," no date, http://www.hamiltonelectors.com/about.

61. Lilly O'Donnell, "Meet the 'Hamilton Electors' Hoping for an Electoral College Revolt," *The Atlantic*, November 21, 2016, http://www.theatlantic.com/politics/archive/2016/11/meet-the-hamilton-electors-hoping-for-an-electoral-college-revolt/508433/.

62. Alexander Hamilton, "The Mode of Electing the President," Federalist Papers Number 68, March 14, 1788, http://avalon.law.yale.edu/18th_century/fed68.asp.

63. Daniel Brezenoff, "Electoral College: Make Hillary Clinton President," Change.org, no date, https://www.change.org/p/electoral-college-make-hillary-clinton-president-on-december-19-4a78160a-023c-4ff0-9069-53cee2a095a8. Petition website accessed at https://electoralcollegepetition.com/#gs.UbnDh14.

64. John Merline, commentary, "It's Official: Clinton's Popular Vote Win Came Entirely from California," Investors.com, December 16, 2016, http://www.investors.com/politics/commentary/its-official-clintons-popular-vote-win-came-entirely-from-california/.

65. Valerie Richardson, "Electoral College members harassed, threatened in last-ditch attempt to block Trump," *Washington Times*, November 22, 2016, http://www.washingtontimes.com/news/2016/nov/22/gop-electors-harassed-threatened-foes-maneuver-blo/.

66. Mark Moore, "Electors are being harassed, threatened in bid to stop Trump," *New York Post*, December 14, 2016, http://nypost.com/2016/12/14/electors-are-being-harassed-threatened-in-bid-to-stop-trump/.

67. Eric M. Johnson and Jon Herskovitz, "Trump wins Electoral College vote; a few electors break ranks," Reuters, December 20, 2016, http://www.reuters.com/article/us-usa-election-electoralcollege-idUSKBN1480FQ.

68. Associated Press, "Four Washington state electors defect from Clinton; one chooses Faith Spotted Eagle instead," December 19, 2016, reported in the *Los Angeles Times*, http://www.latimes.com/nation/politics/trailguide/la-na-trailguide-updates-four-members-of-washington-state-1482181899-html-story.html.

69. Scott Detrow, "Donald Trump Secures Electoral College Win, with Few surprises," National Public Radio, December 19, 2016, http://www.npr.org/2016/12/19/506188169/donald-trump-poised-to-secure-electoral-college-win-with-few-surprises.

70. "Donald Trump Completes Final Lap, Electoral College, to White House," *New York Times*, December 19, 2016, http://www.nytimes.com/2016/12/19/us/politics/electoral-college-vote.html.

71. Jerome R. Corsi, "Did CIA Pick Sanitize Obama's Passport Records?" WND.com, January 8, 2013, http://www.wnd.com/2013/01/did-cia-pick-sanitize-obamas-passport-records/.

72. Darren Samuelson, "Stone 'happy to cooperate' with FBI on WikiLeaks, Russian hacking probes," *Politico*, October 14, 2016, http://www.politico.com/story/2016/10/roger-stone-fbi-wikileaks-russia-229821.

73. Alana Goodman, "Exclusive: Ex-British ambassador who is not a WikiLeaks operative claims Russia did NOT provide Clinton emails—they were handed over to him at a D.C. park by an intermediary for 'disgusted' Democratic whistleblowers," *Daily Mail*, December 14, 2016, http://www.dailymail.

co.uk/news/article-4034038/Ex-British-ambassador-WikiLeaks-operative-claims-Russia-did-NOT-provide-Clinton-emails-handed-D-C-park-intermediary-disgusted-Democratic-insiders.html.

74. Pamela Engel, "Former CIA Director accuses Trump allies of working on behalf of the Russians," *Business Insider*, October 14, 2016, http://finance.yahoo.com/news/former-cia-director-accuses-trump-171136453.html.

75. Jerome R. Corsi, "Hillary Campaign Chief Linked to Money-Laundering in Russia," WND.com, October 13, 2016, http://www.wnd.com/2016/10/hillary-campaign-chief-linked-to-money-laundering-in-russia/.

76. Roger Stone, "Russian Mafia money laundering, the Clinton Foundation, and John Podesta," Stone-ColdTruth.com, October 13, 2016, http://stonecoldtruth.com/blog/2016/10/13/russian-mafia-money-laundering-the-clinton-foundation-and-john-podesta/.

77. Edwin Mora, "Security Contractor, DIA Docs Debunk Michael Morell's Benghazi Narrative," Breitbart.com, May 19, 2015, http://www.breitbart.com/national-security/2015/05/19/sources-military-intel-documents-debunk-michael-morells-benghazi-attack-account/.

78. Jim Hoft, "Surprise! Former CIA Director Who Altered Benghazi Talking Points to Benefit Obama Endorses Hillary," *Gateway Pundit*, August 5, 2016, http://www.thegatewaypundit.com/2016/08/news-former-cia-director-altered-benghazi-talking-points-benefit-obama-endorses-hillary/.

79. Patrick Poole, "Former CIA Deputy Director Mike Morell Can't Keep His Stories Straight," *PJ Media*, August 9, 2016, https://pjmedia.com/homeland-security/2016/08/09/clinton-defender-former-cia-deputy-director-mike-morell-cant-get-his-story-straight-on-syrias-assad-and-putin/.

80. David Leonhardt, "The Democrats' Real Turnout Problem," *New York Times*, November 17, 2016, http://www.nytimes.com/2016/11/20/opinion/sunday/the-democrats-real-turnout-problem.html.

81. Amanda Sakuma, "Trump Did Better with Blacks, Hispanics than Romney in '12: Exit Polls," NBC News, November 9, 2016, http://www.nbcnews.com/storyline/2016-election-day/trump-did-better-blacks-hispanics-romney-12-exit-polls-n681386.

82. Karen Tumulty and Phillip Rucker, "Shouting match erupts between Clinton and Trump aides," *Washington Post*, December 1, 2016, https://www.washingtonpost.com/politics/shouting-match-erupts-between-clinton-and-trump-aides/2016/12/01/7ac4398e-b7ea-11e6-b8df-600bd9d38a02_story.html?hpid=hp_hp-top-table-main_election750p%3Ahomepage%2Fstory&tid=a_inl&utm_term=.79785b00c5c9.

83. Kevin Drum, "The 3 Big Reasons Hillary Clinton Lost," *Mother Jones*, November 21, 2016, http://www.motherjones.com/kevin-drum/2016/11/why-clinton-lost-bitter-bernie-crooked-comey-and-wounded-working-class.

84. David Plouffe, "David Plouffe: What I Got Wrong About the Election," *New York Times*, November 11, 2016, http://www.nytimes.com/2016/11/11/opinion/what-i-got-wrong-about-the-election.html?_r=0.